78-1116

R.

DIALECTICAL
ECONOMICS

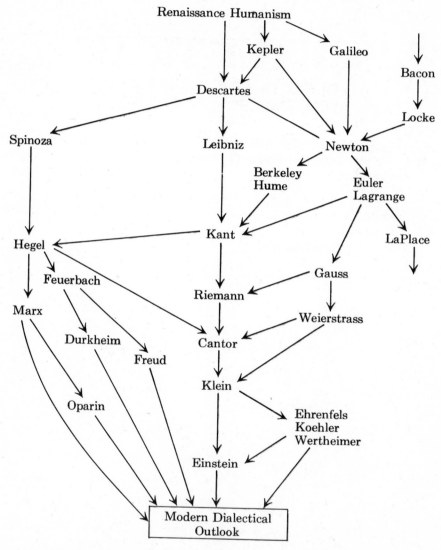

A "Genealogical" Diagram of Principal Currents of Modern Epistemology

DIALECTICAL ECONOMICS

An Introduction to
Marxist Political Economy

Lyn Marcus

D. C. HEATH AND COMPANY
Lexington, Massachusetts   Toronto   London

To my opponents, who made this
book necessary

AUTHOR'S FOREWORD

This text is the outcome of a one-semester course which the author has conducted at various locations since 1966. Like the course, it is principally designed to provide a working mastery of Marx's method and major economic-theoretical ideas for graduate students or advanced undergraduates in such specialized fields as political science, anthropology, and philosophy. For other readers, it introduces the actual Karl Marx, whose method and conceptions were fundamentally different than those offered in his name by contemporary "official Communists," "Trotskyists," and most other interpreters.

To minimize the book's polemical burdens, Chapter 1 states the general arguments against the positions of the author's better-known critics, and outlines points which may be of special usefulness to the instructor using this work as a main or supplementary classroom text.

This book demands that the instructor assume responsibility for a larger mass and variety of references than is customary for an elective course of this type and duration. This is a circumstance for which there is no remedy. To study any aspect of Marx's work, one must know the special dialectical method which permeates all his efforts; without it no proper sense can be made of a single one of his specialized terms, nor is it possible to competently follow the very special procedures of argument and proof on which he relies.

This necessity obliges authors and lecturers in this field to master an unusually broad range of source materials; we identify the most essential writings below. It also frequently compels the instructor to employ a style of exposition, for certain topics, which tends to offend prevailing academic tastes. Objections incurred on this account are not evidence of any actual defect in such passages. For reasons we shall identify here, it is impossible to competently elaborate any of the essential notions of Marxian political economy employing ordinarily preferred forms of literary usage. However, unless the possible objection on this account is anticipated, as we do here, there is a danger that the student will mistake essential but apparently egregious features of formulations for mere stylistic aberrations. If he discounts those as aberrations, he will understand nothing of importance in this field. The following paragraphs, therefore, are included as warning against such misassessments.

It is useful to emphasize, before identifying the specific problems, that our defense of a dialectical style is neither hypothetical nor a rationalization for continuing usages which are customary in the literature. In fact, to a considerable extent, it is the exceptional efficiency of this dialectical mode that has enabled the author and his former students to become, alternatively, influential or bitterly vilified among most leading governmental and labor circles in North America and Europe today. The significant question is, therefore: what is the underlying reason for such egregious success?

It would be conceded and even emphasized by scholars that, for the most part, we are obliged to conform to terminologies and special forms of literary construction established during a century and a half of English editions of Kant, Hegel, Feuerbach, and Marx. For that reason, a detailed glossary of the most important specialized terms and usages has been appended to this text. Yet, the importance of terminology acknowledged, we must go still further.

It is even more essential for the student to understand that prevailing usages of exposition include intellectually diseased habits of speech and writing whose widespread acceptance is no evidence against such a diagnosis. Specifically, we contend that the capacity of language to communicate important and profound conceptions has been undermined by acceptance of pathological norms of rhetoric that are accommodations to the empiricist's philosophical world-outlook. Such norms are accepted, not only by persons who regard themselves as informed by that outlook, but also by the broader masses who practice empiricism (as "horse sense") without being aware of it. Since a systematic critique of empiricism is provided in the text, we shall limit our attention here to a few most relevant features. We shall identify the systematic flaw which absolutely precludes literary forms agreeable to that outlook from representing either dialectical conceptions or the empirical reality to which those conceptions correspond. We shall situate that point, with an historical basis for its occurrence, in the development of certain modern European languages and philosophical outlooks.

In the informed epistemological outlook, occurrences in nature are represented for human knowledge in two distinct forms: universals and phenomena. Rigorous philosophy and fundamental specialist scientific inquiry have always considered the essential and only real knowledge of existence to be that view in which occurrences are comprehended as a determined outcome of necessity, or lawful occurrence. This depended upon the notion of universal laws whose primary basis was considered to be nothing less than the universe as a coherent totality. Kepler's approach to establishing the basis for a comprehensive physics is an example of this. At the same time, man had knowledge of particular occurrences whose actual causes were usually unknown or imperfectly known. This inferior and less reliable form of knowledge identified the domain of *phenomena*. In mathematics, such inferior knowledge is associated with the analysis of phenomena treated as self-evidently discrete events. In modern terms, we may distinguish these two aspects of reality as the respective postulational viewpoints of *continuity* and *discreteness*.

From its beginnings during the Renaissance, the general development of modern philosophy and the particular sciences was characterized by preoccupation with certain fundamental paradoxes of human knowledge in general. These were, specifically, the seemingly insoluble and yet inescapable difficulties of reconciling totalities (universals) with particular experience (phenomena).[1] As a consequence and correlative of this concern, at some point in their respective evolutions the languages associated with the Renaissance and Enlightenment acquired the capacity to express the rigorous distinctions this holistic outlook subsumed. But with the rise of empiricism in England, especially during the present century, the language faculties so developed became attenuated, even among the educated strata. The empiricist view, implicit in the works of Francis Bacon and elaborated by Hume, rejected fundamental scientific inquiry and limited knowledge to the *interpretation* of *phenomena*. (This is the view denounced by Kant as "indifferentism.") Thus, with the hegemony of the empiricist view, the educated man's comprehension of the world was banalized. Norms of literary usage were vulgarized to conform to the degradation of his mental powers so that habitual forms of speech and writing lost much of their former capacity for communicating rigorous conceptions.

By contrast, the German critical outlook—typified successively by Kant, Hegel, and Marx—represented a resumption of the earlier outlook of a Ficino, Kepler, Descartes, and Spinoza. It, also, of course, made some advances beyond that world-view. These differing philosophical developments make rendering the ideas of Hegel or Marx in certain modern languages extremely difficult; to do so requires the employment of certain older features of the tongues that empiricist usages have either muddled or entirely discarded. For the world-outlook in which the distinction between reality and mere phenomena is the primary scientific concern demands appropriate forms of usage, including generous employment of transitive forms and varied connotations for the verb "to be." The conditional and subjunctive tenses have special, rigorous importance in dealing with notions of causation, and so forth and so on. Eliminate the notion of the real, eliminate the effort to explore and solve the paradoxes of coherence of continuity and discreteness, and all the forms of speech that are required for such distinctions become disused or banalized to describe a flat world of interpretation of phenomena. Fortunately, the possibility of resurrecting and developing disused capacities persisted in the heritage of language's development, except where squads of grammarians and glossers have gained power to legislate formalism and thus effectively outlaw exercise of a language's former potentialities.

The foregoing observations partly reflect recent work by teams of the author's associates. The coordinated publication of journals in English, German, Italian, Spanish, French, Greek, and Swedish, translating items origi-

---

[1] This same problem was later attacked in mathematics by G. Riemann, G. Cantor, and others. The development of new concepts of mathematics by these outstanding scientists of the mid-nineteenth century made possible the Einsteinian revolution of the twentieth.

nally written in one language into several others, confronted us with exactly the kind of problem we are considering here. The texts of articles, usually employing a generous number of dialectical formulations, presented us with more profound difficulties than translators ordinarily experience. Under the circumstances, it became urgent to standardize approaches to recurring problems. A few examples are sufficient for the point at hand.

It was demonstrated that dialectical conceptions readily expressed in German or English could not be efficiently translated into standard kinds of French, Spanish, or Greek. In many instances, a single English or German sentence required several, in, for example, French. Even then, the meaning of the original statement was partly lost in translation. This could not be attributed to any special shortcomings of our teams' work, since these included individuals of exceptional qualifications in education, multiple fluencies and effective comprehension of the subject matter. Comparison of our efforts with standard French and Spanish translations of major works of Hegel, Marx, and Luxemburg demonstrated that our practice was in fact better informed than most of those. We suspected and demonstrated that the important difficulties originated in inadequacies of the language itself. For example, in the standard French translation of Hegel's *Phenomenology of Mind,* there is a long footnote on the impossibility of directly rendering *Selbstbewusstsein* (Hegel's *self-consciousness*) in modern French. It is not immaterial to the general problems of both French and Spanish that this and other dialectical conceptions cannot be rendered in those tongues within the scope of accepted usages. Working backward from the present literature, we studied leading models of French from various periods to find suitable precedents for such expressions. It was not until the case of Rabelais that a remedy was found. By applying a modern vocabulary and spelling to Rabelaisian literary French's freedom of usages we found the basis for the needed richer language. *Self-consciousness* then could be neatly rendered as *soi-conscience* and cognate forms of Spanish and Italian adopted as standardized translations.

Investigation showed that there was nothing accidental—or specifically, "genetically" French, Spanish, etc.—in the difficulty. We would not go so far as to blame modern French for the qualities of Louis Althusser's *Pour Marx,* but it *is* clear that the usages certified by the Immortals of the French Academy preclude the precise expression of profound scientific conceptions. As empiricism represented a driving force for vulgarization of educated use of English, formalism was the mode of stultification of French from Richelieu onward.

There is nothing outrageous in the assertion that today Rabelais (and, in Spanish, Cervantes) is a viable source for the enrichment of the expressive powers of contemporary languages. The Renaissance in Spain, Italy, France, the Low Countries, and England was distinguished by a revolutionary advance in the development of written languages. The most influential writers of those revolutions received considerable assistance from ancient Latin and Greek *theological-philosophical and philosophical* writings. Despite the first impression gained from a study of Erasmus, this emulation was practiced not as affectation, but in an effort to enrich in a definite way the conceptual powers of existing languages. What caused certain ancient writers to be most influential was the Renaissance thinkers' intent to render the tongue capable of communicating efficiently Augustinian and Neo-Platonic qualities of thought. It is assumed here that the impetus to this activity was the energizing effects of Renaissance society and the appropriate basis provided by social developments in that period—a point for which we account within this text. The argument to be made here is that the remarkable conceptual power of the best Renaissance and early Enlightenment literary models is the successful result of a largely deliberate effort to make languages capable of communicating the most profound concepts.

The later banalization of educated usages is also provocative and fruitful for consideration, because the degeneration occurred as a correlative of a massive advance in the quality of human life and institutions. The key to this irony is illustrated by certain uses of the transitive forms of the verb "to be." The Renaissance and Enlightenment were justly preoccupied with concepts of "becoming"; an excellent insight into this need is implicit in a comparison of Ficino and Descartes on the ontological paradox of perfection. (The Cartesian argument is developed in the text.) Descartes implicitly solves the paradox by making the "becoming" that connects successive advances in human knowledge the primary form of real existence. That is, rather than defining perfection and infinity as a succession of fixed occurrences, rather than conceiving of these as a succession of discrete events which apocalyptically, asymptotically converge upon a predetermined maximal value, the infinite must be seen as the immediate aspect of current development that expresses an energizing, determining principle of self-development. Although the problem of rigorously conceptualizing self-reflexive conceptions of this kind was not actually solved until Marx (and implicitly by Riemann and Cantor), Descartes and Spinoza succeeded in specifying some of the conditions such conceptions must satisfy. In contrast to the rigorous epistemological current from Fincino through Marx, Hume's approach degrades the verb "to be" to the banality of a simple equal sign and the limits of knowledge to the vulgarity of a mere interpretation of phenomena. In other words, the establishment of the basic notion of capitalist forms of heteronomic social equilibrium—as typified by Locke for England and Rousseau's solidarist utopianism for France—corresponded to the discarding of the problem of fundamental social evolution in favor of virtually exclusive emphasis upon the realization and development of social phenomena in their capitalist form.

It is not necessary to recapitulate here the explanation for the development of German critical philosophy made classic by Hegel, Heine, Marx, and Engels. It is sufficient for our present concern to note that Hegel, Feuerbach, and Marx successively developed the notion of rigorously defined self-reflexive processes. Marx's notions of *labor power*, of *capital in general*, and of *value* are specifically self-reflexive. The most rudimentary conceptions of Marxian economics cannot be elaborated or assimilated without mastering the notion of the self-reflexive. It is the elaboration of such qualities of concepts in this text (as in the writings of Hegel and Marx) that prompts occasional passages which the reader may at first regard as egregiously convoluted and intrinsically unclear. The problem, he will discover with patience, is not a matter of style but of the unavoidable obligations of language in the specification of the most advanced qualities of conceptions.

The sole remaining, last-ditch argument against the necessity of a style appropriate to self-reflexive conceptions would be of the form: Marx is obviously wrong as self-reflexive conceptions are merely chimeras. So impressive a figure as Bertrand Russell has insisted that such forms do not exist. Yet, as the text demonstrates, the recurrence of capitalist depressions is in itself sufficient evidence that self-reflexive conceptions are fundamental to the processes underlying experience. After mastering such notions, the student's objections to style will vanish, and he will be qualified to judge for himself how banal are the arguments of Russell and others on this point.

The study of Marx's economics can eliminate no part of the four volumes of *Capital,* and must include the *Critique of Political Economy* and sections of the earlier *Grundrisse.* While Marx's distinctive method is uniquely defined by *Capital* as a whole, and especially by Volume III, in no part of that work does he explicitly set forth his method—an omission which has caused no end of difficulties. Even Marx's so-called early writings develop that method more or less exclusively in marginal commentaries on Hegel and Feuerbach, and Kant is alluded to less explicitly but nonetheless significantly throughout. Without the background in Kant, Hegel, and Feuerbach which Marx took for granted in his choice of style, one cannot know exactly how he diverges from his German philosophical predecessors, and must thus approach the interpretation of any section of *Capital* with, at best, considerable uncertainty about one's own judgment.

No assumptions are made about exactly how much of the reference material should be required reading. The following references may be regarded as most essential. From Marx's philosophical predecessors: Kant's *Critique of Practical Reason* (for its treatment of the fundamental antinomy); the preface, introduction, and opening chapters through the "Organic" of Hegel's *The Phenomenology of Mind;* the opening chapter of Feuerbach's *The Essence of Christianity* and his *Principles of the Philosophy of the Future.* From the "early" writings of Marx: "Contribution to a Critique of Hegel's 'Philosophy of Right' "; the concluding chapter of the *1844 Manuscripts;* the first section, "Feuerbach," of *The German Ideology;* and "Theses on Feuerbach." From Marx's *Grundrisse,* the *Pre-Capitalist Economic Formations,* edited by Eric Hobsbawm, is most useful. The preface and appendix to the *Critique of Political Economy* are also essential.

From *Capital* itself, the following sections should be emphasized. From Volume I: Chapter I, emphasizing the polemic against the "reductionist" interpretations of value and use-value embedded in the "Fetishism of Commodities" section. From Volume III: the opening chapter, emphasizing Marx's limitations of scope and conclusiveness for the two preceding volumes; the chapter on "Internal Contradictions," and all of Section VII. From the Moscow edition of *Theories of Surplus Value:* all of Part I, and Chapters XV, XVI, and XVII from Part II. Other brief sections of these volumes should be assigned as deemed useful to document and cross-reference points made in the classroom or in this text.

Marx's "Critique of the Gotha Programme" should be held in readiness for assignment whenever the instructor meets or anticipates the currently popular anarchosyndicalist or "Third Camp" fads, which Marx anticipated in that essay.

Major sections of Luxemburg's *Accumulation of Capital* and *Anti-Kritik* and sections of Preobrazhensky's *New Economics* are also eminently useful assigned readings.

For assigned study of an opposing view, Sweezy's *Theory of Capitalist Development* remains the most literate and is possessed of sufficient integrity of approach to merit consideration. For a course in which the number of opposing views considered must be limited, one can regard the blunders of Lenin, Hilferding, Bauer, and others as sufficiently documented by Luxemburg.

The portions of the course requiring the most intensive treatment and review will probably be as follows. The instructor must concentrate on clarifying the essential features of Kant's fundamental antinomy, without a grasp of which the student cannot successfully move an inch forward. The distinctions between Hegel and Kant must, of course, also be made clear. Contrasting Marx's *hylozoic monism* with Hegel's "idealism" is recommended as the most efficient means of identifying the mediating contributions of Feuerbach. Marx's early writings on this point should be read in conjunction with Section VII of Volume III of *Capital*, with special emphasis on the much-cited "Freedom/Necessity" passage from the "Trinitarian Formula" chapter. Because this subject necessitates cruel confrontation with the naive reductionist prejudices of "sense-certainty" the student brings into the classroom, formal analysis and classroom experience warn us that it elicits the greatest difficulties in student comprehension of the entire course, no matter how rigorous and clear the presentation.

Such epistemological difficulties invariably arise in connection with the distinction between productive and nonproductive labor. The student tends to fall back on naive prejudice to insist that anything "useful" or desired must represent use-value, and that the creation of such "utilities" is necessarily productive. He will undoubtedly entrench his objections at certain isolated passages of *Capital*, emphasizing only Marx's acknowledgment of what represents use-value for capitalists, and virtually refusing to acknowledge Marx's rigorous qualifications to the opposite effect in other superceding locations.

The same epistemological blockage may reappear in connection with both the idea of "primitive accumulation" and the fundamental contradictions of capitalist accumulation. The notion that consumption determines qualities of productive labor power is always a cause of difficulty. With respect to *fundamental contradictions*, the student may attempt to evade the equivalence of that term to *fundamental antinomy*, and therefore tend to join most "orthodox" Marxian economists in minimizing such contradictions as mere contingent "tradeoffs."

The instructor may experience special objections from adherents of the "zero growth" fads of the late 1960s and early 1970s. Since all of Marx's method is premised, to the most extreme degree, on the interconnected principles of Humanism ("Freedom") and the Necessity of Progress as the task of Freedom—notions which have become unpopular recently—it is impossible even to understand Marx if one entertains a favorable view of zero growth. Some students may demonstrate extreme resistance to acknowledging that Marx, the epitome of "radicalism," located the essence of man in his potential creative powers to effect large-scale technological progress. Such prejudices will prevent some students from assimilating enough knowledge "about the topic" to pass the course, even by the most generous grading criteria. Since capitalist accumulation depends upon growth, and since the entirety of Marx's critique of capitalism is addressed principally to the braking of necessary further rates of growth by capitalist crises, it is indispensable to demolish zero-growth prejudices.

The author must acknowledge here certain features of the text in which he radically departs from the pedagogical method of *Capital*, or introduces concepts significantly beyond any explicitly advanced by Marx.

It is unfortunate that Marx was unfamiliar with the work of leading mathematicians among his contemporaries, such as Weierstrass, Riemann, and Cantor. This is most lamentable—and should have been obvious for decades—in connection with the wretched condition and disputes respecting the fragmentary concluding chapter of Volume II of *Capital*. Engels' remarks on Marx's distraction by mathematical studies, and other evidence, indicate the degree to which Marx's work suffers from his failure to locate the actual nature of certain problems of formal mathematics. Although he clearly defines the fundamental contradiction of capitalist accumulation, especially in *Theories of Surplus Value* and parts of Volume III of *Capital*, he was manifestly unable to locate the representation of this same contradiction in terms of a transition from heuristic models of simple reproduction to expanded reproduction. Much would have been gained had Marx understood that phenomena of this sort admit of no formal algebraic representation.

The reader will note that this problem is emphasized in the text, and would be correct in assuming that the radical variance of this text from Marx's organization of the curriculum is partly attributable to recognition of the cited mathematical problem and its implications. As for the admittedly limited and preliminary treatment of that problem provided here, a few of the author's former students and present colleagues have been engaged for several years in preparing suitable presentations on the subject, which will appear relatively soon as oral presentations and professional papers.

The other major divergence from Marx in the scope and organization of subject matter is our emphasis on explicit development of the dialectical method—the feature of this text which has determined its title. The reasons for its inclusion are obvious. As to the propriety of attributing certain developed notions to Marxian method, our authority is the evidence linking the writings of the "early" Marx to, in particular, the last section of Volume III of *Capital*. Furthermore, Marx himself projected such an undertaking as urgent work to follow the completion of *Capital*.

Purists will undoubtedly object that our exposition of evolutionary social reproduction goes beyond anything explicitly stated by Marx himself. This is notably true of the material summarized in Chapter 6, "The Labor Process." To such an objection we respond that this work indeed represents an enlargement on Marx's own treatment, but that no other enlargement would be consistent with his explicitly developed views.

Some readers will protest our insistence that the fundamental, vicious fallacy of most population models is their attempt to define population growth in terms of simple numbers of individuals. "That's ridiculous," a leading zero-growth advocate at one university protested, "I can count them: one, two, three, . . ." Even so, we insist that such reductionist practices are epistemologically absurd even for models of plant and lower animal populations, and lead to devastating blunders when applied to human populations. The quantum to be measured in human population studies is individuals of definite *reproductive power*, a notion related to Marx's concept of labor-power, which involves "extrauterine gestation" and other considerations.

Two kinds of objections will undoubtedly be raised to a subordinate feature of our concept of evolutionary social reproduction: our usage of the term "negative entropy." As to whether this usage is consistent with Marx's, we refer to such sources as the previously cited "Freedom/Necessity" topic. It is conceded that we use this term in a somewhat different sense than might be tolerated by specialists at first glance. We shall only say here that our sense of the term will be shown in due course to be correct, and that in the meantime it is the only admissible interpretation of "negative entropy" as it occurs in human development.

Among professed Marxologists, critics will be most exercised by the obvious connection between the author's and Luxemburg's appreciation of Marx. To minimize unnecessary speculation by such critics, two points must be settled here.

First, the author's appreciation of Marxian economics arrived at its present form during the period 1955–1960, in connection with two major professional studies. The first of these was an analysis of long-term capital growth perspectives for the capitalist sector, out of which emerged the forecast analysis of the 1960s for which the author is now best known.

The second study, which arose out of the problem of applying the first study to the large-scale "second-generation" computers then in the offing, defined the theoretical limits of feasibility for computer applications of "comprehensive models" in terms of the absolute impossibility of simulating "artificial intelligence" in any possible future digital-computer system. Although the author was then more than ordinarily literate in Kant, Hegel, and Marx, the implications of the second study were no less than devastating, gelling his entire theoretical outlook in the form it has maintained ever since.

The author was unacquainted with Luxemburg's *Accumulation of Capital* and *Anti-Kritik* until late 1965, a failure remedied on the prompting of the British Marxist, Tom Kemp. Until that time the author had accepted the prevailing "official Marxist" deprecation of Luxemburg's economic-theoretical competence. However, once he discovered the similarity between his own and Luxemburg's differences with "orthodox Marxism," the author felt obliged to defend her on such points, even to the extent of minimizing his own secondary differences with her economic writings.

Secondly, the reader will note one major difference between the author and Luxemburg with respect to her systematic development of the notion of realization crises. Although explicit treatment of this issue is reserved for a magazine article,[2] it is sufficient to note that the margin of unrealized surplus value in Luxemburg's work is synonymous with the margin of "fictitious capital" in the present text. The fascinating feature of her error on this point is that it does not lead to any blunders in her principal conclusions—insofar as *Accumulation of Capital*, *Anti-Kritik*, and *Einführung in die Nationalökonomie* offer conclusions. This "good luck" of hers is less remarkable once the origin and nature of the error are more closely examined.

Luxemburg's contribution to possible confusion in economic theory is the outcome of her effort to maintain consistency with what she obviously regards as the historically specific objectivity of the way capitalist accumulation *normally* expresses a Law of Value. Consequently—although she repeatedly emphasizes the central feature of her factional differences with Lenin, Hilferding, Kautsky, Bauer, and others on Marxian economics, the contradiction between historic (capitalist) and real-reproductive valuations—she declines to take the next mandatory step of acknowledging a more-or-less definite magnitude of "fictitious capital" in current capitalist accumulation. Consequently, since the margin of fictitious capital in current accumulation appears within apparent surplus value (relative surplus value), Luxemburg's analysis of the problem of realization of surplus value is wanting; it must be assumed that her readers will attempt to interpret it from the standpoint of "closed models" of reproduction and circulation.

In this text such difficulties are avoided by stating the general problem of accumulation as an antinomy between "exchange-value" and "use-value" systems of valuation. This is no mere pedagogical device; it is

[2] Lyn Marcus, "In Defense of Rosa Luxemburg," *Campaigner* 6, no. 2 (Spring 1973).

absolutely indispensable for dealing with problems such as those represented by the Bretton Woods system. The defects in Luxemburg's analytical apparatus are most readily shown to be potential errors if one attempts to apply her approach to such modern issues. Only a small part of our contributions in this area are entirely new. If the reader were to consult the major "middle" portion of Volume III of *Capital*, he would find not only that Marx said most of what we have been charged with introducing to this field, but also that those topics on which we have been taxed with a "monetarist bias" are the subjects of fragmentary chapters in the "credit and money" section of Volume III. Considering also that this section of *Capital* was projected by Marx as the location for an extended treatment of Sismondi, we cannot regard much of our effort as original—relative to what Marx said or intended to say. Only where our elaboration focuses on problems of "actual infinity" bearing upon Marx's ignorance of the problems of theoretical mathematics do we probably advance significantly beyond what Marx stated or intended in the "middle," credit-monetary sections of Volume III.

In any case, it is necessary only to note the existence of such a problem in Luxemburg's work. As we have said, this shortcoming has no direct bearing on any of her principal disputed conclusions as such; furthermore, her fundamental methodological and theoretical views relative to "orthodox Marxism" are precisely those which the student must assimilate before proceeding to the more advanced matters to which her shortcomings pertain.

Lyn Marcus
New York City

CONTENTS

ILLUSTRATIONS

THE CRISIS
IN MARXIAN SCHOLARSHIP

1

THE CRISIS IN MARXIAN SCHOLARSHIP 1

Today, approximately a century after Marx drafted the bulk of the four volumes of *Capital*, "Marxist economics" is nominally professed by governments ruling a major portion of the world's population. In the capitalist sector, Marx's economic theories have a similar nominal status among the widest assortment of socialist groups, some representing millions of supporters. Few universities in the United States do not offer appreciation —or deprecation—of Marx, in their curricula, and there is no liberal-arts specialty which does not have a professedly "Marxist" faction. The quantity of books and articles published on this subject is stunning. Yet—for these very reasons, rather than despite them—there exists no significant body of Marxian scholarship which could strictly be termed competent.

Some will angrily protest such an assessment as outrageous. Others will maintain that it represents merely one person's opinion. But if Marx's economics is a science, as Marx proclaimed it to be, divergent assessments of competence cannot be indefinitely tolerated as a privilege of private opinion—scholarly or otherwise. Theories must be subjected to tests of appropriateness, formal coherence, and empirical demonstration. Opinion, however massive its accumulation, cannot be privileged in a science; this is particularly true with regard to fundamental principles on which Marx is in extreme methodological and theoretical opposition to most professed specialists in his works.

Even a cursory examination of certain outstanding features of the history of the socialist movement is sufficient to demonstrate the correctness of this assessment. Marx's devastating *Critique of the Gotha Programme*[1] shows that the founders of the Social Democracy constructed their economic, social, and political "Marxism" with a cheerful disregard for the highly incompatible contents of Marx's writings. The association of Marx's name with the ideas which became dominant in the socialist movement is chiefly the result of his personal hegemony in the First International.[2] For institutional reasons, each of the two dominant factions in the German socialist movement of the late 1860s and early 1870s considered it expedient to use the image of Marx's personal authority as a weapon against the other.[3] The relative dominance of the German Social Democracy in the world movement of 1875–1914 magnified the significance of the term "Marxist" as a factional self-designation.

At the outset of this process, as the *Gotha Programme* attests, "Marxian economics" meant the ideas that Wilhelm Liebknecht and August Bebel chose to attribute to Marx; they refused to tolerate Marx's own violent objections to the mish-mash thus concocted.[4] In subsequent decades, especially after Marx was no longer alive to object to misinterpretations of his writings, his phraseology was increasingly introduced into the Social Democratic platform, leading to an accumulation of exegeses and glosses on exegeses.[5] Despite certain aspects of Karl Kautsky's contributions,[6] the more important efforts of Rosa Luxemburg to reintroduce the actual Karl Marx,[7] and some lesser efforts of that sort, the net result has been that the impact of *Capital* and Marx's other writings on official socialist theory has been chiefly peripheral. The body of theory, economic and noneconomic, which has been attributed to Marx by leading socialist parties and governments has been developed and selected to rationalize their immediate interests and policies.

The impact of this development upon academic Marxology is illustrated by the remarkable frequency with which university courses in Marxian economics or "comparative economic systems" attribute to Marx the Lassallean "Iron Law of Wages."[8] Even those academics who represent themselves as adducing Marx's views directly from *Capital* and other original writings have been notably deferential to the massive body of tendentious secondary and tertiary sources. The net result is that the young specialist wishing to be accredited follows the prudent course of "taking into account" a mass of secondary literature which ought to be treated in the fashion of the little boy looking at the emperor's new clothes. Despite respected academic traditions, the student entering this field ought properly to regard the bulk of the secondary literature as of only clinical interest.

To substantiate this position, it will be sufficient to summarize and evaluate the cases against three of the most commonplace follies of accredited specialists.

CASE #1: THE FINAL CHAPTER OF "CAPITAL," VOLUME II

The first two cases to be considered oblige us to provide here a simplified exposition of material more adequately developed later in the text.

In Marx's Law of Value, one obtains the first approximation of the value of current production by subdividing the total productive labor of an economy into its principal constituents.[9] We shall ignore the agricultural population, in order to simplify our illustration, and divide the remaining nonagricultural population into two main categories. The principal category is the members of the total population whose households normatively produce the productive labor of society—in the sense of effecting useful *material* alterations of nature.[10] The residual category includes, in capitalist society, capitalists themselves, bureaucrats of all sorts, police forces, military forces, clerks, professionals, and "service workers." The current productive labor force, derived from the working-class population, is treated as "input" to the productive process. "Output" (still arbitrarily excluding agriculture) is divided into the following categories.

A certain portion of the total output is consumed in maintenance of the productive equipotential of nature (including materials, machinery, and other man-altered aspects of nature). This portion determines the category of *Constant Capital* (constant, that is, from the standpoint of the productive process itself). Another portion of the total output is consumed by the *entire* working-class population (not merely by employed labor or the families of employed labor). The magnitude of this portion is determined by the quality of consumption and leisure (e.g., education) necessary to reproduce the entire labor force at the technological-cultural "level" necessary for today's and tomorrow's production. (By "tomorrow," we signify here the visible horizon of advances in technological development affecting the employment of present and developing generations of workers.) This portion of the output determines *Variable Capital* (again from the standpoint of the productive forces). These two components of total output correspond to the current directs costs of simply perpetuating the whole of total current production *for present conditions.*

The residue of the output is therefore relatively "free energy" from the standpoint of simple reproduction of existing productive processes. This portion determines the category of *Surplus Value.* However, not all of this category of output is available for development. It is from this portion of total output that the economy obtains the consumption of not only capitalists themselves, but bureaucrats, military personnel, police forces, clerks, professionals, "service workers," and the like. *Capitalists' Consumption* includes not only personal consumption, but also the "capital goods" consumption associated with the activities of these persons (such as military equipment, office equipment, office buildings, and the like).

Since these portions of productive output correspond to portions of the labor-force input, we can derive the formula $S/(C + V)$ as a general expression for the "free energy" ratio of the society or, in other words, for the rate of potential expansion of the society with respect to both quality and sheer magnitude. Note that this ratio is not a ratio of products, but of the labor force. It expresses a population's power to reproduce itself in terms of the proportions of that part of the population's activity which represents its productive labor. The ratio $S/(C + V)$ thus expresses man's relationship to nature, his social-reproductive powers, or his productivity *in the sense of social-reproductive powers, not* the conventional definition of productivity.

Once that expression for *expanded social reproduction,* $S/(C + V)$, has been adduced, we discard the notion of simple reproduction. This rigor is absolutely decisive for human ecology generally, and for capitalist and socialist economy in particular. It is also decisive for solving the major formal problem of *Capital,* the fragmentary and confused condition of the concluding chapter of Volume II.

To bring that point to bear most firmly, the following amplification is needed.

Although the expression $S/(C + V)$ is specific in somewhat different senses to capitalist and socialist economies, similar expressions are necessarily characteristic of all societies. Naive contemporary opinion falsely imagines that nature itself has certain distinguishing features which are intrinsically resources. Contrary to such prejudices, a *resource* is so defined by the quality of the technology and associated culture of a society at some definite point of progress of human evolution generally. What each society defines as its resources are by definition *relatively* finite in extent. The inevitable result is that for every society, the more successfully it expands or even simply continues on the same scale, on the basis of a specific technology and associated culture, the more successfully it depletes the basis for continued human existence in such a specific mode. Consequently, the distinguishing feature of human existence as a whole is the increase in ecological population potential represented by successful supercession of one form of society by another, an accomplishment which depends upon both the existence of "social surplus" and its realization in the form of qualitative advances in the mode of existence (new technologies, new cultures).[11]

With the emergence of capitalist society—and notably since England of the mid-sixteenth century—this creative aspect of human existence, innovations in technology and specific social forms, has become the immediate, determining feature of the dominant forms of human existence in general.

The general result of such progress has been that despite both the rising costs of labor in *absolute material* terms and correlated increases in the *absolute material* measure of per-capita employed-worker Constant Capital costs, the general secular tendency has been toward a rise in the value of the expression $S/(C + V)$, *when that expression is determined by the proportions of employed productive labor as a whole.*

Even if we assume the ultrasimplified case, a direct correspondence between the prices of capitalist property titles and the value of production, it should be clear that all efforts to analyze capitalist development by means of historic accounting methods can lead only to hopeless follies. For, in a period of generally rising social productivity, despite rising absolute wage-content and rising absolute Constant Capital costs, the *value* of commodities is continually being cheapened, such that the per capita value of labor power and Constant Capital is decreasing as a proportion of the average working day! The result of rising productivity, itself a necessary condition of continued capitalist economy, must be the contradictory *net value-depreciation* of commodities held over from earlier periods of production. Therefore, any effort to examine the expanded reproduction of the economy in terms of constant prices can lead only to absurd conclusions.

The same problem occurs in a different way if we assume the case of no technological advance. In this hypothetical situation, the convergence of consumption of the resources upon the extent of those available in the required form results in a resort to marginal resources, and secularly rising costs, with the most devastating implications for constant prices.

Marx himself had no doubts about this.[12] Yet, in the notorious concluding chapter of Volume II of *Capital*, he appears to indulge in the assumption that constant prices can be employed to effect a comparative study of the models of simple reproduction and expanded reproduction. A variety of students, of whom Sweezy[13] and Luxemburg[14] are notable here, have occupied themselves with this uncompleted chapter.

There are actually two sources of internal difficulty in that chapter, at least as it exists. The first is the explicit problem we are treating here. The second is still more important for methodology, but is usually overlooked in the disputed treatments of the topic. We merely note the existence of the second difficulty now, relegating its more extensive treatment to later sections of this chapter and other chapters. We mention it here to point out that it accounts in large part for the fruitlessness of Marx's effort to complete the chapter.

The problem of establishing a correspondence between capitalist accumulation (in terms of prices of capitalist property titles) and expanded reproduction of the productive forces themselves actually *admits of no formal algebraic representation!* Marx was probably unaware of this fact, and in any case lost much time from the writing of the second and third volumes studying calculus, probably in a hopeless quest for a means to represent the problem he intended to state systematically in the chapter in question. That this was the nature of his difficulty in that connection is confirmed most forcefully by the fact that Marx elsewhere states the solution to the problem with absolute precision, but in nonmathematical terms![15]

As Luxemburg demonstrates, the effort to solve the problem of formal representation of expanded reproduction in accounting terms reduces to absurdity.[16] Despite one important flaw in her treatment of the problem,[17] Luxemburg's analysis of the error in the concluding chapter is not only correct in the main, but also provided her with the foundations necessary to reach the only empirically validated analysis of imperialist economy.[18] By contrast, each of her contemporary critics who offered a different appreciation of the problem produced an analysis of imperialism's development subsequently proved absurd by the past half-century's history.[19]

Sweezy, one of Luxemburg's more intransigent critics, resorts to the unsupportable allegation that her analysis of the problem is limited to the naive standpoint of "simple reproduction."[20] Apart from the fact that this allegation makes no sense to any literate person who has read beyond the first page of her *Accumulation of Capital*, it is Sweezy himself whose approach to the problem depends upon a banal interpretation of expanded reproduction in terms of crude amplifications of models of simple reproduction. He succeeds in wrestling with the chapter to the point of recognizing that the model represented must contain devastating contradictions.[21] However, his remedy is inevitably worse than the disease, and he is largely to blame for the notorious "theory of underconsumption" associated with his name.

If, as is the case, imperialist development is distinguished from simple colonialism by the system of international loans, and not by the mechanistic interpretation of a process of exporting capital, Luxemburg's evaluation is correct, and that of all her critics is wrong. If World War One initiated a general breakdown crisis, as it did (1919–1933), and if capitalism emerged from that crisis through the institution of statist forms of "military economy," as it did (Germany, 1933–1945; United States, 1933 to present), Luxemburg's systematic appreciation of the problem is correct and that of her critics is wrong. Yet the overwhelmingly prevalent view among professed Marxologists is that her critics are correct. Such is contemporary Marxology's regard for scientific treatment of evidence.

CASE #2: THE FALLING RATE OF PROFIT

The second major demonstration of the widespread incompetence among professed Marxian scholars involves their flagrant misinterpretation of the "Internal Contradictions" chapter of *Capital*'s Volume III.

Marx develops a notion termed *the organic composition of capital*. Taking capitalist economy as a whole, this phenomenon occurs as the ratio of Circulating to Fixed Capitals (current costs to dead costs), and may also be interpreted as the ratio of production of means of human consumption to production of means of production (materials, semifinished parts, machinery, and the like). Following the convention of designating the real part of this ratio as the denominator, as we attempt to discover the form of this same notion in respect to particular capitalist firms, it is implied by the ratio C/V.

It happens that increase in the organic composition of capitals correlates in a very special way with a phenomenon conventionally termed "the tendency for the rate of profit to fall." This term can be dangerously misleading in the hands of the amateur economist, since it may suggest a secular tendency toward declining profit rates in the annual accounting reports of particular firms, and the like. For this difficulty, one should blame Ricardo, not Marx.[22] The error committed by virtually all Marxologists, in defiance of the explicit language of Marx's writing, is that the rising organic composition of capitals directly ("algebraically") causes the phenomena properly associated with the falling rate tendency.[23]

What is immediately involved is the effect of rising general social productivity on the depreciation of dead capitals. By "dead capital" one can assume, at this preliminary stage of the text, the undepreciated, leftover balance of machinery, equipment, and the like at the beginning of a new cycle of production. More exactly, one might think of a secular rise in social productivity occurring while the inventory of left-over "dead capital" is being continually depleted, but while the mass of such "dead capital" nonetheless appears to be increasing. In general, we might say that a five per cent general increase in social productivity effects an approximately five per cent depreciation of the current valuation of dead capital outstanding.

Therefore, at the point at which the mass of Fixed Capital to Circulating Capital reaches 1/1, a five per cent increase in profit, through a net rise of five per cent in the ratio $S/(C + V)$, is more or less exactly offset by a corresponding book loss to capitalists on account of depreciation of the mass of Fixed Capital. If the ratio continues to rise, every further gain in social productivity will tend to be more than offset by depreciation losses on account of Fixed Capital balances. Thus, there is a tendency for the rate of profit to decline—*in capitalists' terms, not current values*—as the organic composition of capitals increases. Yet, it is obviously not the rising organic composition of capitals *in value-terms* which causes this tendency, since the charges for such productivity-caused depreciation of Fixed Capital do not involve actual value, but only *fictitious* (over-)valuations of Fixed Capital. Yet, virtually every Marxologist faithfully claims that Marx regarded the rising organic composition of capitals *in value-terms* as the direct "algebraic" cause of a tendency of the rate of profit to fall.

This particular bit of commonplace folly is compounded by the spectacle of professed Marxian economists investigating whether there is a secular decline occurring in the rate of profit of capitalist firms. Indeed, such Pantagruelian inquiries are the most popular topics for dissertations among matriculating novices in this field. The massive blunder of such studies will be clear to the reader later in this text.

Marx devotes major portions of his writings to the problem of "overproduction of commodities."[24] What might appear to the naive observer as a periodic excess of products is usually a reflection of a massive shortage of products (relative to human need by prevailing standards) but under conditions of such extreme overpricing of available products that even such a shortage appears to be an excess of commodities in monetary terms.

Naive readings of *Capital* to the contrary, this tendency for overproduction of commodities does not lead immediately to depression. Through rediscounting processes always closely connected to the debt of governments, the centralized financial markets of the capitalist system generate credit. In the healthy aspect of the capitalist system, this *capitalized* credit enables sellers to dispose of surplus value to *capitalist* buyers; these buyers, *as capitalists,* use the surplus value (as wage-commodities and means of production) to expand the scale of production of wealth, the expanded production so generated secures the value of the capitalized credit issued to set it in motion. However, the same rediscounting by central banks, or a market of financiers acting in lieu of a central bank, temporarily permits the capitalist market generally to circulate almost any amount of not only real surplus values, but also the margin of overpricing of commodities, or even the purely fictitious values of sheer speculation.

To offset the falling rate tendency, the capitalist system need only add the margin of discount of Fixed Capital to the aggregate selling-price of commodity production. Thus it would seem that, as long as credit-expansion is maintained in this fashion, the monetary system provides any number of built-in stabilizers capable of postponing a crisis of "overproduction" indefinitely.

That, however, is by no means the end of the matter. The result of what appear to be short-term monetary solutions is a long-term general tendency for inflation. Ignoring sheer speculation and related matters for the moment, let us assume that the fictitious values added to circulation were limited to the amounts needed to maintain a constant rate of profit under conditions of rising productivity and high rates of organic composition. Let us call this magnitude of fictitious capitals "X". It should be obvious that, taking the economy as a whole, X corresponds to a net excess of prices over values produced, a margin which has, in value terms, no corresponding product, wage-commodities, or added means of production. Thus, although monetary expansion can readily circulate this added mass of price, no expansion of the production of wealth results from the investment of X through such circulation. The result must be, in this simplified case, that the capitalized debt created for this margin of monetary expansion could never be liquidated—that is, it could never correspond to value. It follows that the capitalized margin of debt, X, must be a self-expanding mass of potential illiquidity in the monetary system, constantly being enlarged by new production's overvaluation while the formerly created debt also multiplies through its own demands for debt-service augmentation.

Moving from this hypothetical case to one more closely resembling actual capitalist accumulation, one must acknowledge that X is not limited to the magnitude we assumed in the preceding example, but includes sheer speculative gain and all other sorts of fictitious accumulation external to productive relations.

Credit-expansion thus accomplishes the capitalization of fictitious values, so that continuation as a short-term solution to "overproduction" results in a growing potential illiquidity in the monetary system and in debt-equity relationships generally. Long-term capitalist credit-expansion of this sort leads inevitably to what procapitalist economists generally describe as an accelerating shift in the "Phillips Curve,"[25] a point at which further credit-expansion to maintain "full production" must result in tendencies for rates of general inflation to spiral. At such a point, a capitalist economy faces the alternatives of proceeding through "full-production" credit-expansion to an inflationary explosion of Latin-American dimensions or accepting the depression.

All of this is not only explicitly developed in *Capital*, but also corresponds to the gross empirical phenomena of the past century's business cycles. Yet "Marxist economists" continue to search for simple declines in immediate profit rates.[26]

CASE #3: "DIALECTICAL MATERIALISM"

Even if one could constrict Marx's economics to the narrow perimeters of conventional "economic facts," it would be impossible to arrive at a defensible gloss on any of the most essential conceptions without first mastering the dialectical method.

As we shall demonstrate in later chapters, a capitalist economy represents a special kind of interdependence between two otherwise distinct processes. As we examine capitalist development, in one of its aspects, in terms of expanded rates of production of means of production and consumption, we discover what first appear to be special physical laws governing the material consequences of actions taken by capitalist man on that aspect of nature. Yet on the other hand, the sequence of events governing the actual development of the production of wealth is linked at every point by investment and related voluntary decisions.

The underlying "physical laws" do assert determining control in the final analysis. These rational principles assert themselves as dominant features only over such long spans as the period of major business cycles or the still longer term of development-breakdown cycles for entire phases of capitalist history as a whole. In the short run, the relatively voluntary processes of capitalist "market" behavior seem to be, and immediately are, the objectively determining aspect.

The reader familiar with German critical philosophy should have recognized more than a similarity between the problem stated above and Kant's exploration of the antinomy of Practical Reason.[27] In immediate perception and judgment, except during the crisis-phases of new depressions, the rules of successful capitalist forms of behavior seem to represent an invincible empirical *Understanding*[28] of the world-reality about one. But when we shift our point of view from the immediate "here" and "now"[29] of narrow, everyday capitalist experience to the approximate universality of cycles of depressions and breakdown crises, it becomes clear, and on the authority of the most overwhelming evidence, that reality has been ironically determined all along by rather different fundamental laws than ordinary Understanding could have imagined to have existed.

If one were to abandon the study of capitalist accumulation in that state, economic theory would stew forever in a Kantian predicament. On the one hand, we would have empirical vindication of the false laws which, despite their incontestable falseness, seem to perform as objective laws under most circumstances of the "here" and "now." At the same time, by the most rigorous reflection on the perplexing antinomies of discreteness and universality, we could demonstrate—both theoretically and empirically—that such objective knowledge, on which we seem usually to exclusively depend, is fundamentally false. This is precisely the fundamental, Kantian problem of human knowledge.[30] Even the very best non-Marxian economic theory, such as Ricardo's, can never progress beyond this predicament.

Despite such overwhelming evidence, it has become conventional wisdom among even accredited Marxologists that Marx's economic-theoretical writings are developed in an ordinary way from the work of such predecessors in classical political economy as Adam Smith and David Ricardo. If those critics concede that the dialectical method is reflected in *Capital,* they treat such features as merely contingent or even outright excesses. It is a conventional, "indifferentist" pretense that the essential features of *Capital* can be mastered, communicated, and criticized without considering the dialectical method at all.

Marx's fundamental critique of Ricardo, which has sweeping implications for all the main conclusions of *Capital,* refutes the notion that he is Ricardo's (or any other economist's) successor. The internal, epistemological content of Marx's exacting identification of Ricardo's crucial blunder makes this abundantly clear:

> . . . The rate of profit is the compelling power of capitalist production, and only such things are produced as yield a profit. Hence the fright of the English economists over the decline of the rate of profit. That the bare possibility of such a thing should worry Ricardo, shows his profound understanding of the conditions of capitalist production. The reproach moved against him, that he has an eye only to the development of the productive forces regardless of 'human beings,' regardless of the sacrifices in human beings and capital *values* incurred, strikes precisely his strong point. The development of the productive forces of social labor is the historical task and privilege of capital. It is precisely in this way that it unconsciously creates the material requirements of a higher mode of production. What worries Ricardo is the fact that the rate of profit—the stimulating principle of capitalist production, the fundamental premise and driving force of accumulation—should be endangered by the development of production itself. And the quantitative proportion means everything here. There is indeed something deeper than this hidden at this point, which he vaguely feels. It is here demonstrated in a purely economic way, that is from a bourgeois point of view, *within the confines of capitalist understanding,* from the standpoint of capitalist production itself, that it has a barrier, that it is relative, that it is not an absolute, but only an historical mode of production corresponding to a definite and limited epoch in the development of the material conditions of production"[31] (emphasis added).

The gulf separating Ricardo from Marx—"the confines of capitalist understanding"—is plumbed at length elsewhere, especially in *Theories of Surplus Value.*[32] The entirety of *Capital,* most notably its adducing of a *fundamental antinomy* in capitalist accumulation and the underlying universality of productive relations, depends upon this sharply defined break with Ricardo *et al.* in defining the content of each of Marx's economic-theoretical categories.

To attempt to study *Capital*—especially considering the fragmentary state of Volume III—without a grounding in critical philosophy is comparable to taking up the profession of nuclear physics innocent of such excesses as theoretical mathematics. All the methodological apparatus by which the facts of economic processes are conceptualized as facts-for-Marx is rooted in the successive efforts of Hegel, Feuerbach, and Marx to solve Kant's antinomy of Practical Reason.[33]

We do not exaggerate the monstrosity of the blunders on which various versions of "official Marxist" "dialectical materialism" are premised. To indicate the serious, practical character of such chimerical constructions, it is convenient, useful, and admissible to summarize the relationship of critical philosophy to certain fundamentals of theoretical physics. We request that the doors to the classroom be bolted until we have completed *all* of our remarks on this topic; there are already too many students—and others—rushing about in the euphoria of "a little learning," imagining themselves experts in physics who will revolutionize everything by properly juggling a few phrases. We have little enough to say here on physics per se, and little enough on the epistemological side beyond that which has already been well noted by leading specialists during much of the past century. It is only those engineers and other mass-produced professionals, victimized by "factory" science departments, whose bowdlerized education leaves them ignorant of such elementary rigor. (Later we shall redevelop part of the following material, to the limited extent that bears more or less directly on our undertaking. The following summary is presented not as an integral feature of the development of our subject, but as a means for situating some urgent points.)

Insofar as Kant and Hegel situated their investigations in respect to the corpus of theoretical physics, they addressed their criticisms to the world-outlook offered by the eighteenth-century mathematician Joseph Louis Lagrange, treating his work as epitomizing the related accomplishments of Kepler, Descartes, Leibniz, Newton, Euler, and others.[34] The problem confronted was this: if the fundamental laws of the universe were susceptible of comprehensive representation in the sort of mathematical physics typified by Lagrange, the human Mind did not exist as a subject of any interest to itself. For, presuming a sufficiently large and high-speed supercomputer situated handily "just outside the universe," with all the requisite equations and facts tucked into it, that computer could predict every future state of the universe—including, therefore, human actions and judgments—without additional data-input.[35] The substitution of "micro-indeterminacy" for simple cause-and-effect would annoy the computer's programmers considerably, but would not alter the underlying epistemological implications in any essential way.

The problem can be posed thus: if human beings, choosing their actions by Free Will, are able to put those judgments into effect, the consequent state of the universe could not possibly be comprehensively understood in terms of the kinds of laws appropriate to theoretical mathematics, even as we generally understand that to the present day.

Such a statement may seem egregious only to the layman, or perhaps also to the para-professional whose text-book, bowdlerized learning of his field has left him unacquainted with the original work of the outstanding figures. It is so obvious that the qualified specialist would not trouble himself to argue the point outside the classroom, that the development of what we call "physical science" has been restricted to those limited aspects of material phenomena generally which were susceptible of investigation by the limited analytical apparatus available[36]—in other words, to those special subject matters in which the axiomatic, hereditary fallacies of formal logic did not result in a hopeless lack of correspondence between calculated and actual experimental results.[37] Only amateurs or cranks would not reject out of hand the notion that existing analytical procedures might be effectively applied directly to the phenomena of life, or to such subsumed fields of inquiry as literature, music, psychology, anthropology, and a comprehensive political-economic theory.

Kant's special accomplishment on this point, for which he was rightly recognized by Hegel[38] as a pioneer, was to proceed beyond such preliminary identifications of the problem. He put the statement of the fundamental issue on a rigorous basis, thus establishing, despite his included errors, the indispensable preconditions for its solution. The practical problem is that the necessary Understanding of the world adduced from narrow ranges of immediate experience is not only fundamentally contradictory, but also necessarily false from the standpoint of those corresponding totalities identified as universals.

The rudimentary illustration of this type of difficulty is that of the relationship between a line and the set of points which can be located upon it. It is impossible to complete a line by filling in all the points which can be located upon it. Naive opinion may acknowledge the existence of some difficulty here but mistakenly attribute it exclusively to time, in the belief that the line could be completed in an "infinite time," and that one may therefore regard the process of filling in many such points as asymptotically "approaching" completion. This "asymptotic" fiction is a pathetic delusion. The difficulty is that *there could exist no specifiable procedure* by which the line could be completed in even an infinite period.

As long as one limits one's practice to crude short-term concerns, one does not seem to encounter this theoretical crisis as a difficulty of ordinary practice. From the standpoint of everyday Understanding, one believes one could survive—quite nicely, thank you—by resorting to such fantastic devices as the "asymptotic principle." We encounter the physical realities that correspond to the delusory character of such fictions only in certain special circumstances—a point most commonly and justly illustrated by reference to the case of relativity. There are unique aspects or areas of experimental work, pervasive in the study of social processes, in which the grey extremes of the Understanding constantly become practical problems, sometimes forcing us to overthrow entire previous conceptions of the fundamental laws of the universe.

Except under conditions of widespread crises in society or in the special disciplines so affected, laymen and the general run of professionals are ordinarily able to overlook the conclusive evidence to that point. This is the case principally because the solutions to such special problems are put into broad circulation as *results* of the creative methods by which they were solved *by others*. Dealing only with such results, and not with the internal life of creative work by which they were achieved, the ordinary professional is protected from what would be for him a paralyzing encounter with such empirical evidence as would upset the most favored philistine delusions of his Understanding.

One of Hegel's major achievements was to advance beyond Kant on this point, anticipating in passing the kernel of the major subsequent contributions of Riemann, Cantor, Klein, and others[39]—or, in short, those discoveries which represent the theoretical foundations of modern knowledge with respect to the principled barriers to fundamental progress toward more comprehensive insight into our universe. What is essentially demonstrated on this point by Hegel, and in part by the subsequent explorations leading from Riemann, Cantor, *et al.*, is that the fundamental fallacy of ordinary Understanding is the delusion that the universe is in the final analysis reducible to simple substance, or—the more Hume-like view—that the content of human knowledge in itself is limited to simple-substance-like, self-evident sense perceptions. This discredited outlook—whether it takes the naive classical mechanistic outlook, or the more-or-less equivalent mechanistic outlook of empiricism—is inclusively termed *reductionism*.

All varieties of reductionism are formally premised on the fallacious assumption of any formal logic, that the universe can be represented as consisting of discrete parts interconnected by formal relations. The intrinsic fallacy of all formal logic is readily identified by comparing such constructs generally to those involved in the attempt to complete a line by asymptotically filling in points. In short, all reductionism demands *the fallacy of formal induction*.

Ordinarily, it is more-or-less sufficient to debate reductionist views by attacking only the intrinsic formal fallacy. However, a complete treatment of the problem demands further probing of the pathology, to uncover the deeper, *ontological* assumptions of which the formal fallacies are symptomatic and hereditary. The ontological blunder of reductionism is the assumption of *simple substance*, that the universe is reducible to discrete elements—"elementary particles" or "sense perceptions"—each of which has a unique quality extended as simple magnitude.

To eliminate such fallacies, it is essential to reorder the approach to knowledge entirely, proceeding not from the simple event to totality but from totality to particular phenomenon. The result, to summarize, is that what seemed "simple quantity" to the reductionist point of view is shown to be *determinate*, complex. There is nothing obscure or mystical in this, once one is acquainted with a handful of essential principles.

The holistic approach would indeed be as mystical as is sometimes charged by reductionists if we meant by "totality" a naive inversion of simple discretenesses—that is, simple undifferentiated totality, or what Hegel ridiculed as a "night in which all cows are black."[40] A totality is not a simple whole, but something developing. By defining one's notion of a totality in terms of *the principle of its self-development*, we have located what we term *invariance*, that *invariant* which remains characteristic of the entire process through all the successive transformations occurring in every other respect. The fashion in which Christian Ehrenfels and his students applied this notion to the occurrence of *Gestalts* in cognition is a subject on which to premise useful reflections.[41]

In Chapter Six, on the labor process, we shall state the case for comprehensive models of evolutionary social reproduction, in which this notion must be directly applied.[42] We demonstrate that the invariant for evolutionary social reproduction as a whole is typified by a tendency for exponential increase in the value of the expression $S/(C + V)$, where the magnitudes of the terms are, in first approximation, proportions of total productive labor. However, we also show that the derived value of $S/(C + V)$ is determined not by the simple magnitude of total productive labor, but by the *labor power* of that labor, which quality is expressed as the effect of actualized labor power on the value of the function of $S/(C + V)$ for the whole! The formal difficulties created by this conundrum would preclude comprehensive mathematical schemas of development even for a socialist economy, such that we are able to use certain mathematical procedures only to approximate comprehensive models for the short term, through introduction of permissible short-run assumptions about the valuation of either labor power or the rate of reproduction generally. At least, this is the predicament for the present state of the art.

The distinction between simple labor and labor power exactly parallels Hegel's distinction between *Being-in-itself* and *Being-in-and-for-itself*. Otherwise, there is a central flaw in Hegel's ontology, from which all his other errors (relative to Marx!) derive. Hegel assumed the dualism he professedly took over from Heraclitus, of a physical universe already completed in the development of a pseudo-invariance, a *relatively* fixed invariance. The physical universe was assumed to have finished laws, coexisting with a human development which was still laboring to attain a similar state of perfection.[43] Hence, the only actual invariant quality of human behavior for Hegel is the self-development of *practical cognition*. This assumption prescribes that all the subsumed particularities have for him the ontological invariant quality of the self-development of abstract thought, the *Logos*.

Marx's fundamental accomplishment, relative to critical philosophy, is summarized in the opening section, "Feuerbach," of *The German Ideology*. The totality for Marx is the entire process of evolutionary social reproduction, whose basis he locates in man's alteration of nature by successive revolutions in the qualities of labor: technology and culture (culture is defined as organization of the social-productive forces). Marx is thus the first true *hylozoic monist*,[44] in that he sees the highest form of life, Man, emergent from the process of development of the universe generally, both expressing the highest forms of the laws of the universe in the invariant quality of his own development and further advancing the development of the universe through his own progress. As Marx's notion of Constant Capital illustrates, it is this process of self-development of human social reproduction, to which nature is both integral and subject, which shifts the notion of invariance from the Logos to Marx's dynamic modification of Feuerbach's "self-subsisting positive."[45]

Such matters are elaborated in the following chapters. This outline suffices to indicate the kind of problems and solutions represented by the dialectical method. Hence, it provides an adequate basis for summary criticism of the way in which all "official Communist," "Trotskyist," "Maoist," and most other varieties of Marxology reduce the dialectical method to a banal empty construct.

In the preface to the second edition of *Capital*, Volume I, Marx acknowledged his debt to Hegel by reporting that he had turned Hegel over and made him a materialist. Thus Marx chose to signify the hylozoic monist shift in his definition of invariance. "Official Marxists" have constructed a chimerical "dialectical materialism" largely from a crude gloss on that passage from the preface.

The "official Marxist" scholar extracts some diluted Hegel from a pony on comparative philosophy, props this clone on its head, and extracts the Logos. He spends a bit more time scraping out the cavity he has created, until he is satisfied that he has thus purified the clone of "idealism," and then begins stuffing the cavity with what he imagines to be the "good, solid, materialist essence"—of naive reductionism. Closing the cavity, he packs this mewling *Golem* into his briefcase and begins his lecture tour to reveal the latest achievements of the scientific laboratory to the credulous. There we have it: "dialectical materialism"!

What have these wretched Marxologists done but parallel the reductionist follies of a Sweezy? What but such bogus "dialectical materialism" do we encounter in the banal "individual material greed" theory of "historical materialism"? Or—again—in the representation of expanded reproduction as the addition of increments to models of simple reproduction?[46]

The result of the method employed by Sweezy, Hilferding, and virtually every other Marxologist taking up the topic, is to "demonstrate" the nonexistence of the depreciation of historic valuations as the consequence of expanded reproduction, the nonexistence, in other words, of the phenomenon which Marx identifies as the fundamental contradiction—the invariant!—of capitalist accumulation. Every leading school of official Marxism, in mounting attacks on Rosa Luxemburg or, in recent years, on the author, has rejected the fundamental arguments and conclusions of

Capital in exactly this fashion. They differ only with respect to the proprietary nuances applied to what is otherwise the same product under various labels. One school limits the "contradictions of capitalist accumulation" to "proportionalities"—that is, the imprudent consequences of clumsy incrementing—denying the possibility of contradictions in the base of accumulation.[47] Another brand expresses the same thing in different language, making simple competition the "fundamental principle" of its nostrum, and thereby limiting the contradictions of accumulation to what conventional economists term "tradeoffs."[48]

While this is immediately a case of smug illiteracy, it reflects and arises from the same origins as the chimerical "dialectical materialism." This fallacy, a poor relative of the more sophisticated reductionism attacked by Hegel and Cantor in connection with "bad infinity,"[49] prevents its adherents from understanding any category of Capital and degrades them, at best, into modified Ricardians or even Malthusians.[50] The formal root of the blunder is the ontological assumption of *simple quantity*, consistently reflected in the conceit that amplified models of simple reproduction represent systematic solutions or proof germane to accumulation.

WHY?

Whenever we are confronted with such vicious discrepancies between text and glosses as are typified by Marxology generally, analysis of the problem inevitably fails to answer the crucial questions until it transcends the confines of so-called objective formal criticism to examine the psychological lives of those whose personal behavior is precisely at issue. The kind of selective ignorance of even the most explicit and central of Marx's statements represented by most "official Marxism" must be regarded as a variety of *hysteria*, in the clinical sense of the term. We must locate the deep, compelling, obsessive psychological needs that selectively baffle the otherwise demonstrable powers of comprehension of the typical Marxologist whenever he is confronted with a concept at odds with what he believes Marx to have said.

Fortunately, we lack neither the apparatus nor the appropriate clinical evidence to settle this question. However, it cannot be considered accidental —on the principle that discussion of the rope is outlawed in the house of the hanged—that the appropriate procedures have been ruled impermissible in socialist organizations generally. In those groups, which express the most generous public concern about the personal motives of factional opponents, there is nonetheless a strong tradition of "principled" opposition to "psychoanalytical methods." Such means are canonically denounced as efforts to "smuggle in alien idealism"—to check and discipline the methods by which character evaluations of opponents are (not less hastily) composed for publication.

The recurring minor eruptions of "Marxist-Leninist" fads favoring

Wilhelm Reich are only apparent exceptions; the internal evidence that Reich's metaphysics is wildly reductionist proves more completely the rule.[51] The abuse heaped upon the happier contributions of Erich Fromm[52] by "Marxist-Leninists" is more obviously consistent with prevailing policies.

Provided we exclude quackery and attempts to improvise instant "psychoanalytical studies" of particular individuals, methods deemed "psychoanalytical" by ordinary standards are not only admissible but necessary, to deal with the urgent practical problems posed by factional ferment within socialist groups and, most decisively, ebb and flow in the mass labor movement.

It is not speculation to state that official Marxism's policy against such methods represents an attempt to protect itself against confrontation with the truth about itself. It attempts to ignore and even suppress the ironic fact that the principal *general* accomplishments of psychoanalysis (as distinct from the particulars of therapeutic practice) were first developed and proven beyond doubt through the progress of critical philosophy. The psychodynamics of Ego and Id[53] were systematically explored in a manner more rigorous and comprehensive than Freud's in Kant's *Critique of Practical Reason*.[54] The internal dynamics of psychophysical parallelism, including those of perception, are a central, integral feature of Hegel's *Phenomenology of Mind*. The notion of psychophysical parallelism itself was first rigorously developed by Ludwig Feuerbach, introduced in his *Essence of Christianity*[55] and systematically developed in his *Principles of the Philosophy of the Future*.[56] As Fromm partially acknowledges, Marx developed Feuerbach's first approximation into a dynamic psychophysical parallelism as the sole premise of his entire theory of knowledge[57] and, by implication, of his method throughout his later works.[58] As for Freud's own major discoveries, it can be said that he redeveloped, *de novo*, a limited version of the prior achievements of critical philosophy on this subject.

Admittedly, from the standpoint of Marxian knowledge most of the efforts of psychoanalysis to extrapolate its findings to humanity in general have been disastrous. Nothing is gained but a pose of ineffable self-righteousness to leave matters at that; we know the methodological root of such failures: "bad infinity." In a happier vein, we also know that insofar as Freud limited his extrapolations to certain more immediate issues, respecting the significance of psychopathology for the population from which his patients were drawn, his judgments were perhaps as valid as the individual analyses on which they were premised. Freud himself was not entirely unaware of a kind of dialectical rigor on this point, as is most remarkably demonstrated in the concluding paragraphs of *The Future of an Illusion* and elsewhere.[59] Provided that appropriate rigor is exercised, including suitable self-development by the analyst, there is no reasonable basis for objecting to application of the "psychoanalytical" method *developed by Marx* and his predecessors to *such broader problems as admit of no effective alternate approach*, problems whose central feature is hysteria, obsessive belief.

Ego/Id

The central feature of human behavior under capitalism (in particular) is the apparent division of the *Self* into two selves, a phenomenon frequently associated with Freud's exposition of Ego/Id dynamics.[60] The resources of the clinic are not required to verify this statement; the most conclusive evidence is the extensive, permeating actuality of everyday experience. The best way to *begin* to systematically examine such phenomena is outlined in Kant's *Critique of Practical Reason*—in which, in any case, the most advanced contemporary understanding of every question begins.

The result of the "extrauterine gestation"[61] of the individual personality in an adult society itself alienated in a particular mode is a corresponding dichotomy of the individual personality so created. The "deeper" of the two regions—the location of the actual processes of cognition and perception—is usually considered to be the "unconscious" Self. This process is acknowledged by ordinary self-consciousness only as the misty vastness from which feelings, almost invincible impulses, and general "psychological needs" come erupting forth, sometimes overwhelming the resistance of conscious self-discipline. The lesser, taken as the "outer" region of the Self, is the domain of self-conscious identity, conscious reflection, "reason," and related processes.

It is no accident that the division between the two parts of the personality is commonly regarded as that of "inner" and "outer." The widely-used term "headshrinker" has its sources in the experience, scarcely limited to the consulting room and sometimes violent in form, of "resistance" to any intellectual exertion which criticizes, and thus threatens to make conscious (and *alterable*), a part of the character attributed to the "inner" Self—and thus to *shrink* the "inner" Self. Although the conscious Self is the locus of the individual's social identity—just as a suit of business clothing expresses the value one demands society place on the hidden flesh beneath, as make-up and foundation garments more cruelly express the same pathetic relationship of the "inner" Self to society—the conscious Self is only what one *outwardly* professes to be "my real self." We "feel" that the "real" Self, like the flesh under the socially distinguishing outer garments, lies beneath, in the unknown vastnesses which express themselves as "psychological needs." The feeling of outerness attributed to the conscious mind expresses its mediating function respecting the others—the "outer world"—whose favorable opinion (rights and privileges) its mediating role is intended to solicit, on behalf of the right to exist of the secret, inner Self.

Among the more immediately relevant illustrations of this phenomenon are varieties of reductionism: empiricism, or the more pathological state expressed by "agnostic" professions that "there might be something to astrology." (To say nothing of what is certified by overt profession of astrology!) Such neurotic disturbances of large populations all express a compulsion to defend the conceit of the self-evident existence of a secret, inner—and *unchangeable*—"real me," just as do psychological resistance and street-corner varieties of prejudice against intellectual activity.

For, if one regards the inner Self as self-evident and unchangeable, the possibility of its relationships to the "outer" world depends upon the existence of an outer world whose ontology and thus-implied formal relations are of the same invariant quality imputed to the "unchangeable," "self-evident," "discrete" Self. It is this reductionist disorder—its character and motivation properly located in its victim's most intimate notion of nothing less important to him than his own identity—which is the pathological root of the widespread acceptance of empiricism and related features of "orthodox Marxism."

In radical politics, this general pathological condition of *bourgeois character and ideology* is expressed most simply as anarchism, and in its most degraded form as the special sort of anarchist pathology, verging upon fascist ideology, associated with predominantly petit-bourgeois or lumpen social formations. The same general alienation is expressed more articulately by the otherwise irreconcilable prosocialist (e.g., Jean-Paul Sartre) and profascist (Camus, Heidigger) forms of existentialism. The same *heteronomic*[62] pathology is embedded in the axiomatic basis of such derivative ideologies as anarcho-syndicalism and so-called *structuralism*.

In the professedly Marxist socialist organizations, excepting the anarchist varieties of "Maoist" cults, heteronomic hysteria is classically represented by the approximation of anarcho-syndicalism, "build a party base in the existing trade-union organizations"; or, more broadly, by the varieties of socialist adaptations to pluralist forms of ferment (e.g., "constituency radicalism," the view of socialism as a confluence of the autonomous radicalisms of heteronomic groupings).

All such reductionist tendencies, mediated by alienation of Self from Self, depend upon assumptions which characterize all reality, including that respecting the Self, inside-out and upside-down. Ordinary opinion to the contrary, the "inner," "personal" Self is not a particularity determined to be such by individual biological distinctions, not an epiphenomenon of the particular biology. It is the general, a *concrete universal*, in contrast to the *determinate*, particular character of the "outer," conscious Self. *Except to the extent that this "general" is dysfunctionally developed—by alienation!—it represents the actual location of the cognition, i.e., creative mentation, through which our species has progressively altered its technology and social organization to the effect of increasing the ecological population potential—i.e., existence—of the species as a whole.*

The dysfunctional aspect of most "unconscious" selves is that they *are* unconscious, and thus suffer particularization by alienation and, as a result, virtual decortication of those aspects of cognition we associate with creative mentation. Hence, "feelings," "psychological needs," which erupt from that repressed Self ordinarily express not the healthy, higher aspect of the Self which functions of the "unconscious" phase ought to be, but are the effluvia of a deformed and diseased Self. In Hegelian language, what should be a *Being-in-and-for-itself* has been deformed into virtually a mere *Being-in-itself*. What in individuals of a healthy society would be the master—creative mental powers employable for society's advancement, the aspect of the Self most prized by society—has become an endungeoned slave, and expresses the irrational rage of the unjustly imprisoned, the tortured, the morally crippled.

It is with respect to the positive side of this repression of the Self that Freud tended to be most viciously misguided, and Kant, while wrong on his own account, closer to the truth.[63]

Marx's Solution

Marx situates this general difficulty as the alienation of *universal labor* from *cooperative labor*,[64] which he situates, in turn, in the notion of the invariant principle of Freedom/Necessity.[65] It is this alternative to the alienated world-outlook which most professed Marxists oppose and even denounce, which in the interests of that very alienated world-outlook (i.e., the "chains of illusion")[66] they thus represent and fight to preserve.

Universal labor may be roughly defined as creative mentation, typified by scientific discoveries which increase the social-reproductive powers of humanity in general—to the extent that those new technologies are *realized* as the practice of cooperative labor.

The effect of capitalist alienation is that the value attributed to an individual is ordinarily a function of his *learning of a fixed mode of behavior*, e.g., a particular skill or profession. Those leisure activities which involve creative mentation and require a prolonged, task-oriented attention span are merely the privileges (not the rights) of a few selected persons, and are in practice generally prohibited to the mass of the population. The mass of the population reflects the reification of this denial of its human potential as a pseudo-positive, self-degrading "anti-intellectualism," priding itself on its bestial, e.g., "practical," philistine habits of mentation. (The "chains of illusion"!) Although some individuals are able to win the privilege of creative leisure, even they do not obtain it *as a right*. The mode of alienated—brutalized—character development characteristic of the entire society, which is the mode of their own individual development, is general for all individuals of that society, including themselves.

The historic valuation which ought to be placed on *any* human being —as human—is properly defined in a way opposite to that of prevailing conceptions. An old cartoon by Abner Dean gets close to the heart of the matter. It portrays a crowded line of passage of a funeral procession in which all the figures are sad or weeping—but one. Inside the glass casket he reposes on his side, head propped on bent elbow, his expression bemused. The caption reads: "I wonder what that was all about?"

What could there be in one's life that would make one's death a loss to humanity? What except some ongoing power for contribution of universal labor, the power to contribute to the greater cumulative capacities of humanity to exist into coming generations? Obey all rules, live an orderly life above reproach? It all vanishes into dust; the passed life mourned only because it betokens the ultimate futility of the mourners' *own* orderly, uncreative existences. The only thing for which one deserves to be loved and remembered—deserves to have existed at all—is a contribution to realized universal labor, a contribution by the individual to the whole, the exercise of Freedom (creative mentation) to comprehend man's increasing mastery of Necessity. Without that, individual man is reduced to a beastlike state, a creature of fixed modes—like a lower beast, doing whatever the mere perpetuation of present, routine species-practice demands of him. Divorced from his right to be human, his potential for creative mentation, he finds his powers of cognition imprisoned and tortured within the Hell of his "unconscious" *Being-in-itself.*

If in uneasy and fragile moments of loving and being loved we experience a hint of real humanity, only thus is the hollow play-acting of ordinary life momentarily superceded by an instant of unmediated social identity of the "feeling," "under" Self. Only in such love does alienated man achieve any satisfaction in being human. For all but those rare few privileged to experience the empyreal excitements of creative life, it is chiefly the best moments of the relationship between man and woman that touch our potential humanity.

The struggle for socialism, for Marx, does not spring *originally* from a vulgar muckraker's concern for relieving the material oppression of "downtrodden workers," or creating rationalizations for irrational revolts against such conditions.[67] The origin of Marx's world-outlook, *expressed by the history of his emergence from critical philosophy,* is that of one who as a creative intellect, one of the privileged few, has thus tasted in more than an ordinary fashion the immanent possibility of humanity. He seeks to effect a new form of society in which the Self is no longer bestialized to be an "Id," but rather in which the locus of healthy, self-conscious social identity is the now-diseased, "unconscious" Self of alienated man. The immediate motive for his struggle is constantly impinging upon him, not merely in the "downtrodden" state of the oppressed, but also in the clangorous philistinism to which he is subjected in the company of his dearest friends and acquaintances. One who has tasted what it means to be human has no choice but to become human; this is the motive of struggle. To accomplish that transformation, it is essential to "educate the educator,"[68] to lay hands on the social processes of "extrauterine gestation" so that future generations may be gestated to become human beings.

We thus propose that the formal, objective dispute between Marx and "orthodox Marxism" is a reflection of the struggle between two irreconcilable world-outlooks. The differences—differences which govern the shaping of formal distinctions in argument—are not matters of formal learning, and therefore cannot be settled in the "objective" realm of formalities. Were either proponent totally ignorant of philosophy or economics, he would still approach those topics with the same axiomatic distinctions to his opponent that are voiced in palpably learned disputations. The location of philosophy is the notion of the nature of one's "inner" Self—a notion, whether conscious or not, which determines what formal philosophies one can digest and regurgitate. The problem represented by the hysterical reifications of "orthodox Marxism" is its adherent's alienation, psychopathology, and struggle to maintain his reductionist personal character.

Therefore, to locate the real—as distinct from formal and derived—errors of "orthodox Marxism," we must accept no account that does not trace reductionist formal error to the reductionist character structure, and to the consequent governing motives of hysterical beliefs arising from it.

The Socialist History of the Problem

In two senses, the key to the wretched state of Marxology is the history of the German Social Democracy we cited at the outset of this chapter, from its roots in the German political labor movement organizations of the 1860s through the "revisionism" debates of 1898–1899.

In the narrower of these two senses, the common quality of the 1875 Gotha and 1891 Erfurt programs of the SPD is an evolving body of pseudo-Marxism with pervasive implications for each of the proliferating doctrinal descendants, including "Marxism-Leninism." This pseudo-Marxism represents the key to the *formal* history of the doctrinal features of all traditional varieties of modern Marxology, whether pro- or anti-Marxian in profession.

In the broader and more fundamental of these two senses, we draw upon the preceding discussion of reductionism. The history of the SPD exemplifies prevailing, contextual, lawful social processes which determined a reductionist climate of receptivity to, and psychological need for, the kinds of pseudo-Marxism with which we are confronted.

The Erfurt program of 1891, with its division into "maximum" and "minimum" programs, ironically exemplifies most socialist professions, even to the most unstinting of present-day socialist critics. Its significant difference from the Gotha draft is the incorporation of a parody of the 1848 Communist Manifesto as literary flavoring for the operative part of the draft, the banal "minimum" program. This practice became traditional in the festivities of each SPD congress up to the war, and is still the characteristic posture of most socialist organizations on holiday occasions.

Between the two opposed aspects of replicated dualism in the programs of traditional socialist groups and their splinters, only a gulf of skepticism is possible. Skepticism first develops as a psychological phenomenon, a convenient, consoling intellectual fog veiling the irreconcilable discrepancy between two beliefs one holds more or less equally dear. Skepticism of this sort *respecting one's own inconsistencies* usually does not remain mere skepticism for long. For psychological reasons, it is soon reified by a pseudo-dialectic to appear to the credulous as a positive principle—an empty construct—giving the appearance of connection, and thus "consistency," to an entirety composed of absolutely irreconcilable parts. The result of this reification for the SPD center was what became "orthodox Marxism," which reached its apex in the prewar "constructivist" theses of Kautsky and the scholastical glosses on "positions" by which modern descendants of the SPD differentiate themselves from one another.

The central feature of Marx's own political theory and practice was the notion of the "class for itself," an expression paralleling Hegel's Being-in-and-for-itself. It is precisely his distinction between the class-conscious worker ("class for itself") and the brutalized worker who accepts bourgeois ideology and practice ("class in itself") which makes Marx's political theory a basis for dialectical practice. Despite various "official Marxist" efforts to find a contradiction in method and essential conception between the "young" and the "mature" Marx, this class-for-itself outlook permeates and dominates all his work from *The German Ideology* through the last section of Volume III of *Capital*.[69]

The practical realization of this monistic notion of Marx's is most widely experienced as the qualitative changes in consciousness which briefly appear among a significant plurality of workers drawn into mass upsurges of the sort Luxemburg terms "mass strike processes."[70] During such episodes, the ordinary parochial divisions which reinforce reductionist outlooks among workers—the separation of employed from unemployed, organized from unorganized—are temporarily submerged. Workers most affected by such upsurges briefly abandon their characteristic alienation, cease to conceive of self-interest in individualized or localized terms, and unite around the almost axiomatic acceptance of a classwide interest: the individual worker's interest must be only that which is simultaneously in the immediate interest of workers as a whole.

Our discussion of the prevailing psychological dichotomy should make clear what this phenomenon signifies: an approximation of true humanity, in which the individual discovers a larger, actual basis for his own existence in his conscious contributions to humanity generally. These developments do not signify what they seem to suggest to philistine onlookers —"self-sacrifice." The individual who has located the unique importance of his existence in the good for the whole does not "lose himself" or devalue his individual Self. On the contrary, his raised estimation of his social importance prompts him to demand as a right that which he, as an individual, requires to fulfill his social role, including his right to those qualities of material consumption and leisure necessary to the personal development and related capacities to fulfill socially urgent functions previously beyond his capacities. He is Being-in-and-for-itself.

This outlook represents no mere Kantian "categorical imperative," although that interpretation might be suggested by the fact that *we have thus solved the Kantian predicament*. This ennobled state of the worker's conscious Self is appropriate to the "natural" yearnings for real social identity of his "deeper" Self. What he may privately esteem as the importance of his acting existence for humanity generally is confirmed for him by his access as a participant to mass events, the very shaping of human history, the sweeping-away of old institutions and the construction of new institutions unprecedented in his experience. He is visibly building humanity's future; he is Promethean man![71] His power to love and be loved is magnified; his mental capacities are suddenly enormously expanded. The dichotomy of Ego/Id is undermined by the alteration of the normal social relationships in which that duality is created and perpetuated. The "educator" is being "educated."

Unfortunately, such developments draw largely upon the undamaged portion of the worker's "unconscious" potentialities. Undoubtedly, however, some small but permanent gain is made toward the desired development of the Self by even a brief experience of this sort; and there is evidence that the effects of even brief participation in mass upsurges may be visible, to positive effect, in an individual's children and grandchildren. Otherwise, unless there is prolonged self-development, the ebbing of such upsurges results in a general regression to philistine habits.[72] The worker's Ego/Id dualism and his reductionist world-outlook are reasserted.

Such ebbs and flows have a decisive role in the history of the socialist movement. It is the approximation of a Marxian world-outlook "spontaneously" generated among masses by such upsurges which gives nominally "Marxist" organizations their relative hegemony over other varieties of "left radicalism," and which sometimes results in mass-based "Marxist" socialist parties. The subsequent evaporation of this spontaneous outlook with the ebb induces a philistine, reductionist regression in those same parties during the ebb, and during longer terms of "normal" capitalist life. In August Bebel's almost counterrevolutionary hostility to the mass strikes by German workers which swept away Bismarck and the "antisocialist laws," we should recognize the sociology of centrism: a left-hegemonic socialist party so insulated against the Marxian world-outlook that it opposes even the degree of "spontaneous" Marxism expressed by workers' upsurges outside the organized political workers' movement! We see in Bebel's centrism, connected as it is to the pseudo-Marxism of Gotha and Erfurt, reductionism which has reached a state of case-hardened resistance to the Marxian outlook, a resistance far more extreme than that of the most politically uneducated worker!

The major clue, therefore, in the continuity of anti-Marxian "orthodox Marxism" through successive periods of upsurge, ebb, reaction, and so forth is the failure of most recruits to socialist organizations to develop the desired growth of their "deeper selves." Even if they recognize in some fashion the alienation of their selves, and seek a new form of society in response to proddings of conscience, they have not essentially altered the quality of the bourgeoisified "unconscious." Socialism is for them largely confined to the "outer" Self, the *persona*.[73] Through "socialist work" they seek to mediate gratification of the "unconscious" Self, a bourgeoisified Self, by means of the subsumed, characteristic "psychological needs" of a bourgeoisified Ego. They "need" short-term, mediated gratification in the form of an increase in approval of their activities by persons inside and outside the socialist organization; this is the determining feature of their "political judgments."

They react to ferment and the lack of it in the labor movement and other "potential constituencies" around the socialist organizations in an ordinary bourgeois way, to the effect that most socialist groups respond to circumstances very much as does the proverbial small businessman "struggling to get ahead." Groups whose leaderships display such bourgeoisified character structure are inevitably playgrounds of the most rampant reductionist dualism.

This predicament is not inevitable, though it is unavoidable that the majority of recruits to socialist organizations are dominated initially by their acquired bourgeois characters. The only remedy is leadership whose self-development enables it to act as a barrier against such influences, and to mediate the relationship of the membership to the "outer world" in such a way as to approximate the longer view, in which mass-strike upsurges are the connection of the socialist organization to the mass labor movement.

Otherwise, in their day-to-day pursuits, socialists afflicted with bourgeois ideology must wrestle with their desire for social acceptance in terms of the criteria implied by the alienated world-outlook of bourgeoisified militant workers and others from whom they seek short-term approval. What self-debasing antics the small centrist group will perform in its frantic efforts to propitiate some ideal militant-rank-and-file worker! Toadying, pandering, groveling . . . all the elements of philistine self-debasement, all the elements of Uriah Heep's wretched character! Consequently, their "socialist politics" is either an outrightly opportunistic adaptation to parochialist forms of militancy among organized workers and others, or, less commonly, a violently ascetic sectarian negation of such "guilty" opportunistic impulses. Their politics, in either the opportunistic or sectarian modes, is a kind of catechism of "do's and don't's" for reacting to *immediate* situations according to "correct positions"—the persona-politics of the "radicalized" but nonetheless bourgeoisified ego.

If there remains any doubt about the philosophical content of such groups' political postures, their essential world-outlook is uniquely demonstrated by their interpretations of Marxian economic theory, all of which share a reductionist approach to models of expanded reproduction, involving "bad-infinity" methods of adding increments to simple reproduction accounting models. If this is insufficient evidence of reductionism, only hysterical skepticism could fail to recognize it in the efforts of "Communist," "Trotskyist," and "Maoist" cults to locate a fundamental principle of "historical materialism" in "individual material greed." Such a theory, however ineffable in one sense, has enormous significance as a clinical reflection of the kind of Ego/Id dynamic governing both such groups' interpretation of the world and their social practice. It is this pathetic condition which such theories attempt to rationalize, to cloak in respectability. The outer garment reveals the form of the body it is fatally fitted to conceal.

It could be argued that there is another, simpler explanation for such groups' economic "theories" and adherence to "historical materialism." The outlook of simple reproduction corresponds to the world-outlook of either anarcho-syndicalism or simple "trade-union consciousness." It sees the division of surplus value only among the workers in a given plant, and acknowledges nothing positive in the realization of surplus value as wage-commodities and means of production for the productive employment of the unemployed. Expanded reproduction does not exist for the anarcho-syndicalist or trade-unionist mentality. And the "individual material greed" theory of history expresses the same anarcho-syndicalist or trade-unionist outlook, pure and simple. There is abundant evidence that these socialist groups' pandering to trade unionism serves to confine their economic "theory" to that which gives no affront to pure-and-simple trade-union chauvinist militancy. This is less an alternative explanation of the problem than a description of the social form in which the underlying problem and motives are mediated.

With one principal exception prior to the 1960s, all of the splits and splinters from the Second International and its descendants have attempted to maintain a continuity of "orthodox Marxism" of the reductionist varieties described above. They differentiate among themselves only on a specified number of "principled differences" respecting the interpretation and application of isolated features of an otherwise shared corpus of belief. The only unequivocal exception is Rosa Luxemburg, who rejected virtually the entirety of the old orthodoxy to premise a new theoretical approach and practice on the direct application of Marx's writings to the emerging developments of her time. The two points on which her remarkable achievements are most easily proven are her rejection of "pluralism"—whether the "nationalist" version or the strategy of "building a party base in existing trade-union organizations"—and her sweeping repudiation of reductionism, particularly with respect to the issues of capitalist accumulation itself.

Unfortunately, the leading Bolsheviks—notably Lenin and Trotsky—supported a wretched, criminal factional pogrom to rid the socialist movement of "the virus of Luxemburgism."[74] They even went so far as to attack her contributions to points on which Lenin, Trotsky and others tended to concur with her or were directly indebted to her.[75] Both Lenin and Trotsky —principally Lenin—were guilty of conniving to reassert the reductionist, anti-Marxian economic-theoretical orthodoxy of the SPD as the antidote to Luxemburg's alleged errors.

To the extent that there has been, until recently, any organized movement founded on the actual method and theoretical conceptions of Karl Marx, that momentary achievement was virtually liquidated by the combined resources for slander of the Social Democracy and the Communist International. To the extent that Marxologists depend upon established authorities to guide their interpretation of Marx's writings, the results have been largely tendentious, and often outrightly fraudulent, reductionism-motivated fallacy of composition in exegetical approaches to the texts. The corpus of traditional Marxology lawfully represents a gigantic hoax, principally adapted to the pursuit of bourgeois ego-gratification in the approval of bourgeoisified militants from trade unions and other "constituencies."

Our object in these pages is to initiate a body of competent scholarship in the field of Marxology.

WHAT IS
ECONOMICS?

2

WHAT IS ECONOMICS?[1] 2

The study of political economy, or "economics," is about 400 years old, its first discovery most efficiently dated as the Spanish bankruptcy of the sixteenth century.[2] Unlike Columbus' transatlantic voyages or Kepler's geometric interpretation of planetary motion, the discoveries of early economics did not deal with material which had existed for millions or billions of years. Political economy began to be discovered almost as soon as its subject matter came into being; actual political economies came into existence in Europe in the period from the fourteenth through the sixteenth centuries.

By contrast with the so-called physical sciences, economics has other distinguishing peculiarities. Like such physical science, economics deals with the relationship between cause and effect: between man's actions and their material consequences for human existence. However, economics, like all social sciences, also deals with an equally determining subjective process: how man's interpretation of nature results in consequent human action.

Every significant school of political economy bases itself on some form of recognition of this dualism. Each distinguishes between the price of capital and the intrinsic value of commodities: between price and "use value" or "utility." The important schools of political economy differ mainly in their expressed or implicit explanations of the relationship between the two notions of value thus associated with each commodity.

We may restate this point for a special purpose by saying that a capitalist economy is the resultant of two antagonistic "optimizing criteria,"[3] loosely identified as follows: the objective side is the maximization of real wealth produced; the subjective side is the maximization of the price of capitalist accumulation. Most political economists implicitly accept the fallacious postulate of von Neumann and Morgenstern[4] that the price and utility of commodities are in formal correspondence.[5] Marx's economics alone specifies that the two "criteria" are so qualitatively distinct that no comprehensive mathematical solution of their interconnection is possible.

Marx, who was an indifferent mathematician, does not put it quite that way but, as we shall see, he treats the distinction between capital (for the moment considered as subjective) and real value (in the general course of human history, the objective side) in such a way throughout *Capital*, and notably in certain sections of Volume III,[6] that von Neumann's statement concerning the limits of mathematical analysis would apply.[7] If one accepts Marx's analysis of capital and value, respectively, throughout *Capital*, political economy differs from so-called physical science in that its problems do not admit of systematic formal-mathematical interpretation.

This distinguishing feature of Marx's economics is simultaneously the key to all of his theories and a not accidental reflection of the way in which his economic theories evolved: not as developments within the context of political economy, as that field is defined by specialists among Marx's predecessors and contemporaries, but as an outgrowth of German critical philosophy. From its beginnings, critical philosophy occupied itself with the problem of providing a methodological solution to the devastating paradoxes of formal logical reasoning (classical rationalism), basing this effort mainly on the failure of classical materialism to explore competently the subjective-objective dualism of social phenomena. Marx, resolving the questions left unsolved by Feuerbach's revolution in philosophy, produced in the process both the necessary method of adducing what we have termed the objective side of political economy and a coherent approach to what we are momentarily regarding as its subjective processes.

The need for such an approach, based in philosophy rather than empirical political economy *per se*, will be demonstrated within this chapter. (Definitive proof is left to the text as a whole.) The organization of this presentation is ultimately modelled on that of *Capital*. By examining the empirical evidence historically, we identify the main contradictions to be resolved. Then, after turning to Marx's dialectical method to develop the required solutions and necessary economic categories, we return to the empirical domain to demonstrate that those are appropriate conceptions. In this chapter we present the two aspects of capitalist economy—which we have temporarily designated its subjective and objective sides—from an historical standpoint. Our object is to demonstrate why it is indispensable to examine the dialectical method, and thus assemble the necessary analytical apparatus, before attempting to unravel problems which could not otherwise be comprehended.

MERCANTILE CAPITALISM

Mercantile capitalism has been in existence, with ups and downs, since at least as early as the Hittite period.[8] The most conspicuous difference between mercantile capitalism and modern capitalism is that modern capitalist production is the principal means for producing both capitalists' new wealth and the basis in production of material means of continued existence of most of the capitalist world's population. Mercantile capitalism in earlier periods did include some small capitalist production (in the descriptive sense of capitalist employment of wage-labor for production of commodities) as a minor feature of its existence in those periods, but the principal source of capitalist accumulation of wealth was noncapitalist production. Furthermore, although mercantile capitalism played a highly important mediating role in bringing about the otherwise fated collapse of the Achaemenid and Roman empires,[9] it was not the dominant or characteristic form of those societies, but existed as a more-or-less parasitical or symbiotic growth within noncapitalist societies.

For these reasons, as we shall see, mercantile capitalism was not subject to a Law of Value, and was not immediately subject to the social-economic categories of capitalist accumulation. Mercantile capitalism *per se* is not capitalism.

Renaissance mercantile capitalism, by increasingly emphasizing the contingent feature of capitalist production, and accumulating new wealth through capitalist production (although not the bulk of *its* wealth), extended the scale of accumulation beyond the limits within which capitalist accumulation could continue without expanding the production of wealth in general in a capitalist way. This transformation is exemplified by the Spanish bankruptcy.

Spain appears to have, in effect, "lost money" on its looting of the New World. To conquer this new domain, Spain was compelled to finance ships and other material directly or indirectly through loans from the leading bankers of Europe. Risk, liquidity, and usury being what they were, and voyages taking as long as they did, the landing conquistadores behaved in the unchivalrous manner of common landlords, seizing from the native population every bit of loot which might be sold in Europe to pay off the loans. Without inquiring too closely into Spanish waste and the hard-bargaining practices of the buyers of New World loot, we can see that the net effect of the whole undertaking—involving less than a century— was that Spain perennially lacked the means to pay its current debt-service obligations on the growing mass of loans. The unpaid portion of current payment due was refinanced in the form of additional loans, pyramiding the debt and raising the level of current Spanish debt-service closer to the stratosphere.

It had to happen. The amount of loot in the New World suitable to be carried to Europe in small ships for quick sale at prevailing prices was obviously limited by the division of productive labor and associated development within the conquered regions, and by the limited technology of the conquerors, limiting the forms of "natural" wealth which could be exploited as wealth. Certainly, the rates of social surplus in the wealth-creation of the conquered population could hardly match the debt-service ratios of European bankers' loans. Inevitably, therefore, a point of intersection was reached at which the debt-service owed by the Spanish throne exceeded the rate of potential loot from the New World—a point, in fact, at which the debt-service exceeded Spain's national income!

At this juncture, His Most Catholic Majesty the King of Spain became sensible of the sins of his predecessors, and was embarrassed to discover that he too had been guilty of seducing his creditors into the mortally sinful practice of usury. His Most Contrite Majesty imposed upon himself the canonical penance of repudiating his sins (his debts), and the leading banking houses of Europe collapsed in the ensuing epidemic of Christian virtue.

In repeated, if less celebrated, episodes of this sort was born the branch of knowledge called political economy or "national economy," based on the pragmatic reflection that the amount of debt-service pledged by a monarch ought not to be greater than the national income. Conversely, it became apparent that capitalist accumulation would cease, and capitalists would be compelled to subsist by taking in one another's financial laundry, unless the scale of production of wealth was increased at approximately the same pace as the growth of paper values. Wherever emerging monarchs, Huguenots, and others inquired into the means for thus increasing the national wealth, the same duality—the price of capitalized debt and the amount of national revenue in commodity forms available to meet the debt-service—confronted them in the most persistent fashion.

We shall consider this period more fully in a subsequent chapter. The period from the thirteenth through the seventeenth centuries is only naively considered feudal. In fact, it was characterized by a form of society intermediate between feudalism and capitalism, a mercantile capitalist transformation of the decaying feudal process of expansion into a mercantile capitalist society based on *increasingly reified* former feudal modes of production. In English history, this phenomenon is traceable in changes in political forms from the thirteenth-century Edwardian reforms through the Tudors, and in the emergence of the emphasis on alienable product and alienable wage-labor. For our immediate purposes, it is sufficient to emphasize the fundamental contradiction between mercantile capitalist rates of accumulation and the lower rate of accumulation of real wealth possible with reified feudal forms. The collapse of this mercantile-capitalist development in the period from the midsixteenth through midseventeenth centuries reflects, as we shall see, the results of the effort to meet the debt-service and related military costs of mercantile capitalist accumulation by looting the material basis of existing production and social reproduction, such that—but for a few pockets of imminent capitalist progress—the general picture is exemplified by French Jacquerie and the Thirty Years' War. As the "new model" army of Wallenstein expresses the essence of the Thirty Years War, the looting of Europe brought about general decay in most parts of the old order, accompanied by depopulation of large regions and the relegation of large portions of the discarded populations into vagabondage and banditry, thus resembling the ebb phase of "oriental despotism's" cycles.

The Tudor Enlightenment, which reached a preliminary climax about 1589, reflected the appearance of a solution to this general collapse in the form of a progressive surge in those urban centers where an explosive ferment of realized new technological progress was demonstrating the fundamental principles of Humanism (man's creative capacities as the unique basis for human existence and the individual's value to society) and Progress (seen as the only alternative to extinction). Humanism and Progress then meant capitalist development—capitalist political freedom and the realization of the useful-to-capitalism aspect of that freedom, capitalist technological development.

Mercantile capitalism passed through the necessary process of a great bankruptcy, which wiped out bankers and associated political institutions of the old order. As the revival from this general breakdown crisis occurred in England, the Low Countries, and France, there emerged a revived mercantilism, which inevitably resorted to its old tricks wherever possible or permitted, but accepted as its general fate emerging capitalist forms of accumulation.

Thus, beginning with the rudimentary notions of national economy exemplified by the Tudors, the late seventeenth century saw the emergence of the germs of a systematic political economy, and the eighteenth century witnessed the explosive development of political economy in the Physiocrats, Adam Smith and Ricardo.

This historical approach to political economy, as contrasted with the autistic fantasizing exemplified by Robinson Crusoe models of "natural principles of capitalist exchange," demonstrates two principles. First—that is, more immediately—capitalism's emergence as the solution to the breakdown crisis of the preceding mercantilism demonstrates the nature of the problem to be solved: the ironic relationship of the accumulation of capital as a political form of property title to a material basis. The irony is located in the necessary correspondence between the rate of debt-service on capital which can be paid and the available surplus product portion of the material basis for payment in the production of social wealth. This approach eliminates the delusion that there is anything *natural* in the exchange values of capitalist production and circulation, locating the determination of exchange values as a process created at a definite point in the evolution of human society and further developed in a definite, historically specific fashion. Further, this lesson implies a point of even more profound importance. If we proceed to take an anthropological overview of all human existence along similar lines of inquiry, we are compelled to recognize elementary "physical laws" of human development in general. This point is summed up by Marx in the "Feuerbach" contribution to *The German Ideology* and, especially, in the concluding section of Volume III of *Capital*, where he observes that man's existence depends upon Freedom (creative innovations in technology and associated forms of social organization of the productive forces, and in culture) and Necessity (the expression of the laws of the universe in the form of both the conditions of the problem to be solved and the characteristics of a positive remedy for those problems). The *invariant* feature of this interconnection is Progress, which is expressed both as qualitative advances in the productive power of individuals in a more advanced society, and as an increasing rate of social surplus ("free energy") in the mode of production associated with that society. On the other hand, we are compelled to acknowledge that this evolution does not occur as a simple, single general mode of social evolution, but in distinct steps—distinct forms of society which are each characterized by a different set of specific laws of development. Although there is, of course, a single invariant principle underlying this process, the acting individuals and classes making up each specific society do not act according to identical underlying laws, but different laws. These laws of immediate behavior for entire societies and their constituent individuals necessarily represent a solution, in terms of the underlying invariant, to the failure of the preceding, superceded form. To that extent, they must be progressive, successful, and relatively positive for humanity. Yet, because they are not the underlying invariant principles, they must also be false, and accordingly represent a profound source of error which must ultimately express itself in the downfall of that society as a useful form of human existence.

Thus, to focus for a moment on this second notion, a society represents two invariant principles. Immediately, it represents its own characteristic principle; but this principle contradicts another, underlying invariance. The outcome of this contradiction is a new invariance *of the first order*, similarly related to the underlying invariance. The elaboration so defined is human history, anthropology-in-general.

CAPITAL AS A POLITICAL FICTION

We are confronted repeatedly with cranks representing themselves as political economists who attempt to prove that capitalist economy is an outgrowth of the natural economy, to which end they employ this or that "mathematical model," usually constructed from the starting-point of a "Robinson Crusoe economy" or an "n-person game." Those of the same political persuasion, caught on the beach of the old liberal arts when the recent storms of advanced algebra struck postwar academic economics, make the same general point with arguments to the effect that "statist intervention," often blamed on Franklin Roosevelt's "socialist bias," is an alien and corruptive intrusion into "competitive capitalism" or unadulterated "free enterprise." The truth of the matter is evident in the repressive political means such defenders of "freedom" customarily advocate for the purpose of achieving "freedom from the state." In vain might the wealthiest proponent of such political views explore the known and yet-unknown universe seeking a world in which such "free enterprise" existed. It could not exist in the universe of Kepler, Newton, Lagrange, or Einstein.

All forms of capitalism, including the mercantilist forms, come into existence in the mode of an agreement between a capitalist and a party of armed men to extract a mass of wealth from a third party naively termed "the victim," juridically known as "the debtor." Capitalists come into being as bandits, pirates, and mafiosi, whether in ancient Ionia and Tuscany or in the building of Great American Fortunes. To shed the larval form of capitalist—the employer of a band of thugs—and elevate the looted person to the dignity of "debtor," the hooligan must either establish a state, conquer a state, or enter into collusion with a state. With that step, thuggery becomes "law and order." It is only an Ayn Rand fantasy that capitalism is the "objective" consequence of value previously advanced by the prudent ants of society, the "savers." *Capital is always a political fiction*, mainly a patent or charter granted to certain persons (capitalists) by a state, licensing them to extract designated wealth from designated persons.

Such legal instruments naturally have cash value, proportional to a pre-vailing rate of profit and the estimated amount of looting the purchaser imagines the patent to be worth.

Two examples will suffice to demonstrate that modern capitalism is a reification of an embryonic political principle of Achaemenid tax-farmers: the case of the title to a multiple dwelling unit for rental in a large U.S. city and, secondly, the mercantilist aspect of the title to actual productive capacities.

A real-estate property title to a multiple dwelling unit is our closest link to fourteenth-century Northern Italy. It is an agreement between the owner and the capitalist state to loot a group of third parties, the tenants. The market value of the title ordinarily bears no relationship to the capital advanced to create the building (particularly in the resale market for such properties). The price of the property is generally a simple multiple of the amount of rent which can be extracted.

During the 1950s and 1960s in New York City, for example, the "rule of thumb" price for a multiple dwelling unit was between six and seven times the gross annual rental income. To grasp the point of this, one had but to look at the range of ages and conditions of properties which, by virtue of comparable annual rental incomes, commanded the same general market price! The "rule of thumb," which often seemed to defy the principles of risk and liquidity (relative to a general rate of profit), was a feasible arrangement, facilitating a fabulous market in these proper-ties, because of what was euphemistically termed a state rent control law. While occasionally seeming to impose "hardships" on some owners *rela-tive to other owners*, this law actually created a floor under the local real-estate market. This was the case until approximately 1967.

In field studies of the title history of a mixed group of "controlled" and "decontrolled" properties, involving real-estate speculators operating on a citywide basis, several of the author's students demonstrated that these speculators were making between 20 and 30 per cent annual return on their equity, with no significant correlation of the difference for the distinction of "controlled" versus "de-controlled" rental units.

In most of these cases, the original outlay and subsequent mainte-nance expenditures for the building had long since been totally depreciated, such that the value of the entire speculation was economically comparable to "ground rent," and the structures—from this standpoint—essentially represented a useful arrangement for stacking a large number of renters one above the other on the same plot. If one discounted the small amount of actual maintenance expenditures and the more significant amounts of real-estate taxation, the entire real-estate market in question could best be analyzed as pure speculation.

Such high yields (20 to 30 per cent on equity) for principal specula-tors tended in two ways to prevent the construction of new dwelling units. Directly, the yields were greater on old, speculative properties than on new construction. According to the author's limited studies of new residential construction—apart from speculative construction of "cardboard"-type "luxury" units—the best expected yield was approximately 10 to 15 per cent, as against 20 to 30 per cent in speculative old rubble. The second, related check on new construction arose out of the fact that what seemed to be the capitalization of structures was in effect the capitalization of ground rent. The costs of site acquisition for replacement housing construction were determined by the fabulous rates of speculative gain in rubble. If one used the rule of thumb that site acquisition must not exceed 20 per cent of the total price of a new construction, and took into account the costs per square foot of new rental units using various methods of medium- and high-rise construction, the speculative market in rubble—so long as legally established condemnation procedures persisted—created a boundary condition in which no new construction of "middle-income family housing" could occur. This situation reenforced the housing shortage, feeding the speculative market in old stones: *a self-aggravating problem*, within the legal terms of the existing housing market.

The process described above had another boundary, of a different sort. The entire market operated in the fashion of a "chain letter" in mortgages. The speculative gains of A were passed as capitalized debt to B, who passed them along, with capitalization of his own gains, to C. At the terminus of this process, particularly regarding properties collapsing from the weight of age as well as paper, was some unfortunate dupe, Ayn Rand's "saver," who took on the whole mass of debt, operating on the thinnest of margins, in the credulous expectation of becoming a "capitalist"—a successful "real-estate tycoon," no doubt.

This chain-letter market in mortgages not only aggravated the housing shortage, but also resulted in a catastrophic aggravation of the condition of old dwelling units in general. The margin of gains in properties was accelerated, in wide areas of speculative activity, by reducing maintenance, thus increasing relative yields directly and also by increasing the rate of occupancy turnover. The passing along of such buildings, already becoming slums, to the end-of-the-line owner operating on the thinnest of after-debt-service margins resulted in a proliferation of "substandard" dwelling units far in excess of the rate at which they would deteriorate with only normal levels of maintenance. (One could use European maintenance practices as a standard for comparison.)

Skew to this process, but extremely important to its success for real-estate operators, were federal, state, and local governments' public and semipublic housing programs. Government provided for some housing construction by either assimilating the intolerable margin of site-acquisition costs or making tax concessions which, in effect, passed the most oppressive burden of site acquisition onto state revenues. The state thus placed itself at the terminal end of the "chain letter" of mortgages or, more exactly, at the point at which the process was renewed—appropriately known as "urban renewal."

This delightful "monopoly game" was briefly threatened with interruption during and after 1967. The wave of recessions in Western Europe and Japan during the middle 1960s signalled a general ebbing of the Bretton Woods system, a development which took notice, in a sense, of the New York City real-estate proceedings.

The capitalization of real-estate gains obviously depended in large part on the "leveraging" of speculators' small margins of equity against savings-bank and other bank credit. A tightening of credit, combined with the limited market and the monstrous pyramiding of mortgage debt and interconnected values, threatened to bring the whole process of speculative aggregation to an end. Since the valuation of existing values was premised on the continuation of speculative gains—the chain letter game—an end to the speculative bubble's growth meant its threatened collapse, which would so affect financial markets as to make the Penn Central's demise seem a minor nuisance indeed.

Characteristically, the city government, with the support of Mayor John V. Lindsay, commissioned at least three major reports, whose purpose was virtually to eliminate rent control by means of new statutes directing a systematic, orderly forced rise in rental incomes—to provide, out of increased rentals, a renewed market for speculative real-estate gains. There was a report compiled by the RAND Corporation, based on an outrageous fallacy of composition which caused all but the report's conclusions to be shelved out of sight. There was a descriptive report by a leading local professor, and a major report by a genuinely qualified specialist, Sternlieb of Rutgers University; the latter, though presenting the facts in a somewhat slanted fashion, nonetheless outlined the general situation as we have described it above.

On the premise that the low rate of return on speculative real estate prevented "landlords" from investing in new housing construction (sic!), the city government under the leadership—nay, energetic proddings—of the mayor, passed a law subsidizing the speculators out of tenants' pockets. In keeping with the spirit of the whole enterprise, the specter of the Sternlieb report was widely noised about in order to drum up support for the proposals of the RAND report.

Capital: Private Enterprise or Political Fiction?

The key to the property title to productive capacities is the purchase of means of production not as means of production but as means of extracting payment from the economy. The capitalist employer does not pay for the purpose of creating the labor power of labor, nor for the produced product, but for the right to alienate part of the entire social product of production for profit.

The fundamental difference between the former and latter examples —speculation and production—is that in the latter case the result is progressive for human existence. In the case of useful capitalist production, the form of capital (as a political fiction) is the ideological form (i.e., a false consciousness of the actual result for man) of a useful act.

The important point to be adduced from a comparison of the two examples is that the same principles of capital as a political fiction are operative in both cases. It is impossible to have the latter without also incurring the former; it is impossible to separate the means by which capital produces healthy life (material means of human existence) from that by which it produces cancer (speculation). This observation, as we shall show, is the key to the historically specific character of capitalism— that it has a beginning (in England and the Low Countries during the sixteenth and seventeenth centuries) and an end, resembling the breakdown crisis out of which it emerged from the preceding form of society.

The following subsumed points ought simply to be noted for future reference, until we take them up afresh in different terms. First, all capitalists' capital, insofar as we refer to the price of debt instruments and property titles as income-bearing forms, is essentially speculative, having no possible intrinsic relationship to a price equivalent determined by the material relations of useful production. Second, a capitalist title—or capitalists' capital—is subject to speculation because it does not by its nature represent any value *in itself*, but only insofar as it appropriates something external to itself which does have value. In itself, it represents an agreement between its holder and the state (the body of respectable armed men) to extract wealth from a third party, the debtor. This is the relationship of capital to wage-labor; the laborer incurs the capitalist's commitment to pay him wages as a form of indebtedness, which he discharges by producing wealth. This is the definition of the term *wage-slavery*, which is appropriate only in the precise sense implied by this debtor relationship. Capitalists' capital is *in itself* a pure political fiction.

However, as we shall discover in due course, the distinction of capitalism is that capital does not exist simply *in itself* but, in a sense we shall examine later, *in-and-for-itself*. It is in this respect, as capitalism makes *capital-in-general* capital-in-and-for-itself, that the real value embodied in commodities determines to a large extent the price of commodities as a whole, thus imparting to *capital-in-general*—all forms of capital in an entire capitalist economy—a definite Law of Value.

REAL VALUE CONTRASTED

Marx develops his conception of a general law of value—in the sense of an invariant principle of all human existence, to which we have already alluded—in "Feuerbach," his major contribution to *The German Ideology*. Insofar as this principle determines the value of production for the furthering of human existence generally, it represents what we shall hereafter describe as *use value*, or real value from the standpoint of social reproduction.

Another way of stating the same point is to abstract from capitalist production with reference to socialist economy: from the standpoint of socialist economy, what is the value of capitalist production? This version is perhaps easier for the reader to follow at this point, postponing certain conceptual difficulties raised by the notion of *general* use value until a later chapter.

Our notion of use value differs absolutely from the definitions of intrinsic value encountered in conventional economists' writings (utility) or in those of most professed Marxist economists. To these latter authors, the intrinsic value of a commodity resides either in the produced commodity itself or in the localized relationship between that object and its consumer or purchaser. To the latter, utility is either an epiphenomenon of the object in itself or, in the Humean sense, of the relationship of the individual to the particular object. To maintain consistency within *Capital* on this matter, it is necessary to attribute to Marx the view that no particular object can have any real value in itself, and that no relationship between an individual commodity (or array of commodities) and an individual consumer or purchaser could be a means for determining intrinsic value.

To a considerable extent, Marx specifies exactly that. He absolutely rejects the epiphenomenal view, most notably by attributing the connection between *Capital* and a dialectical method in the preface to the second edition of Volume I of *Capital*, and by including the "Fetishism of Commodities" manuscript from *Theories of Surplus Value* in the first chapter of that volume. In numerous locations he explicitly rejects the second version as forcefully as he does the first. The principal difficulty for some students on this point is that Marx seems, in their view, to contradict such explicit statements in other sections of the same text by his seemingly equivocal definitions of "productive labor." However, he settles such apparent difficulties by specifying that none of the categories of capitalist economy can be competently interpreted except from the standpoint of the economy as a whole, and by his observations respecting the conditional validity of the contents of Volumes I and II at the outset of Volume III.

Merely to identify the nature of this problem of interpretation, let us interpolate some brief remarks at this point. In *Capital*, one encounters two apparently contradictory definitions of "productive labor." On the one hand, any wage-labor which represents a means by which a capitalist obtains surplus value is "productive" from the standpoint of capitalism. On the other hand, Marx is absolutely explicit in declaring that clerical and service labor are nonproductive! The origin of this apparent discrepancy is largely in the eye of the reader. From the standpoint of the capitalist, certain forms of wage-labor are use values for capitalists as wage-labor; whereas, when we consider the social-reproductive implications of the same wage-labor—its material activity—the opposite determination occurs. To the capitalist, a teacher for a profitable private school is "productive," no matter how incompetent; a brilliant pedagogue employed by a public institution is nonproductive. A farmer of the most magnificent skill and productivity who gives away all of his product he does not consume himself is nonproductive, whereas the less successful farmer working as an employee is productive!

We shall for the moment merely identify the solution to this conundrum, which we shall actually solve in due course. To the extent that capitalist accumulation is the objective basis for man's material existence under capitalism, whatever advances the process of capitalist accumulation is objectively useful. However, if we abstract from capitalism the social reproduction of wealth as wealth would be determined for general human interest, we have a different standard of objectivity, and only the material alteration of nature in certain ways is productive. The problem is that capitalist accumulation involves two irreconcilable "optimizing criteria," and the definitions of "productive" and "use value" vary according to which of the criteria is being abstracted. Thus, where Marx considers capital-in-general and the fundamental contradictions of capitalist accumulation—which is to say the effect of the underlying material-productive process on the capitalist superstructure—our strict definition of use value applies. Where he considers only the normal form of capitalist accumulation as an historically specific form of objectivity, the notion of use value "for the capitalist" is pertinent.

In any case, since Marx nowhere states the argument in as extended a fashion as we do, we must take responsibility for seeming to go beyond Marx here. That conceded, the fact remains that Marx explicitly rejects the epiphenomenalist and Humean interpretations of utility. As we have said, the notion we offer is the only one that is consistent with Marx's "Freedom/Necessity" invariant principle.

Intrinsic value resides only in the relationship between a whole society and the entirety of material conditions for its continued existence. The test of value is whether the consumption of a given aggregation of value enables the society to reproduce *improved* material conditions for its continued existence as a "species." The relative "intrinsic" value of the particular part of the whole exists empirically as value, as subtracting, adding, substituting particulars with respect to the entirety of such values alters the rate of reproduction for the entire society.

Without indulging in extended review of particular cases, let us consider the ways in which a pro-capitalist or typical professed Marxian economist would measure the rate of U.S. economic growth since the 1957–1958 recession. The procapitalist would accept the Gross or Net National Product data, adjusting them for inflation in a conventional fashion. Under certain circumstances, the Marxist would use the same data to arrive at a different result, as do Baran and Sweezy in *Monopoly Capital*. It is sometimes necessary or useful to debate capitalist points of view on their own terms—an undertaking otherwise known as good muckraking. One proves very little by such enterprises, except the pedagogical point of exposing the flaws of the entire method and the need to approach the question in a fundamentally different way.

What Sweezy and Baran did, for example, was to employ a distinction well-known to Marx's contemporaries and predecessors in political economy—including Malthus—such that no competent procapitalist economist could find fault on his own terms with their approach. This, of course, is the axiom of muckraking: confront one's opponent's *own conscience* with matters germane to himself. Malthus, in particular, was highly concerned that large categories of personal income do not belong to the classification of wages of productive labor, but to a category Marx terms Capitalists' Consumption. Military production, office buildings, governmental administrative expenditures of all types, and the like belong to the same nonproductive category. One of the best-known, professed modern followers of Malthus, J. M. Keynes, made a basic point of proposing to increase nonproductive Capitalists' Consumption as a way of absorbing and thus selling the unsold margin of surplus value in order to minimize the effects of depressions and recessions. Thus, although Baran and Sweezy have slightly amplified their understanding of the category of Capitalists' Consumption with the aid of Marx, their general approach to the matter is in keeping with standard procapitalist economics. Their muckraking approach was justified by their useful social criticism of the contradictory character of postwar capitalist prosperity. All quite acceptable.

Beyond such a point, however, the muckraker's approach becomes worse than useless. It is perhaps most important to relate this point to the significant proportion of professed radical economists who delude themselves that something positive can be contributed to the subject of political economy through mere refinement of the sort of effort undertaken by Baran and Sweezy, whose gross blunders ought to have warned them off such fruitless efforts.[10]

When the Marxist economist wishes to make a positive statement about a capitalist economy, he employs an approach altogether different from that of the procapitalist or socialist muckraker.

Reflection on the origins and development of capitalist economic theory ought to reveal the fundamental fallacy of the Gross National Product approach. The conceptions of political economy arose, in the fashion and circumstances we have summarized, out of the ironic relationship between national debt-service and national income. In other words, the original function of "national economy," even in the most rudimentary Tudor form of Gresham's precepts, was to measure the capacity of the state to sustain debt or to design policies favoring the capacity of the state to sustain such debt.

This inquiry had two interconnected lines of development. Of immediate concern was the relationship between the debt-service on total capitalized debt and the margin of gross national income which could be applied to debt-service without, so to speak, killing the chicken who laid the eggs of debt-service payment. As we shall see in a subsequent chapter, this interpretation of the problem was refined to a considerable degree as early as the eighteenth century by the Physiocrats, who already distinguished between *absolute* and *relative* profit; that is, between the absolute amount of chicken which could be culled for society's consumption without lowering the level of tomorrow's chicken diet (absolute), and the individual retail chicken-merchant's view of the matter (relative). Since the existence of this profit (in the forms of profit, debt-service *per se*, and rent) had a definite relationship to the total mass of wealth (the total national chicken flock) in circulation, and since the entire mass of such wealth had to be turned over to actually extract its profit complement, the notion of national wealth developed out of an initial concern with only the net revenue, or surplus value. Application of these criteria evolved into the attempt to measure total wealth as the sum of the particular wealth of local capitalists and others.

This is all very well, up to a point, if our concern is limited to payments of profit, debt-service, and rent against historic valuations of capitalized property titles. It collapses entirely if we discard the notion of capital as the yardstick for measuring wealth. As technological advances occur, the absolute amount of per-capita consumption required to maintain an employable productive labor force increases, not only in simple magnitude but also in types and proportions of categories of consumption. The absolute amount and types of means of production required per capita of the productively employed labor force similarly varies. If our criteria are those pertaining to social reproduction, the notion of a simple aggregation in terms of historic valuations becomes worse than absurd, indeed, even viciously wrong.

What the Marxist economist does, in counterposing his judgments against those of the procapitalist economist, may be described as follows.

The Marxist divides all national output into the following four general categories: Variable Capital, Constant Capital, Capitalists' Consumption, and Net Surplus Value. The first, Variable Capital, represents the level of income required by the entire working-class population to reproduce a productive labor force at the level of culture applied modern technology requires. As a first approximation, one may overlook the determination of how much Variable Capital ought to be and simply substitute the amount of payments actually made for this category of consumption. The second category, Constant Capital, represents the portion of expenditures for machinery, plant, equipment, raw materials, semifinished materials, and supplies required to maintain the material preconditions for modern production on at least the present scale (capacity). By determining the rate of such new investment and maintenance required to keep the stock of such capital in a certain condition of magnitude, level of quality, and average age, we can neatly estimate what this category amounts to. (The age of Fixed Capital stocks is a rough, indicative sensing of relative obsolescence. If the mass of capital expenditures is associated with an increase in the average age of Fixed Capital stocks, that level of expenditure is not sufficient to maintain the preconditions of production.) Capitalists' Consumption, as we have said, represents the income and "capital" expenditures associated with capitalists' own consumption, that of bureaucrats, military personnel and establishments, police, professionals, "service workers," including office buildings, computers, yachts, etc. The residue is Net Surplus Value.

Representing these four categories with the letters V, C, d, and S' respectively, we have the ratio

$$\frac{S-d}{C+V} ; \frac{S'}{C+V}$$

which can be variously termed "Net Rate of Profit," "Rate of Actual Accumulation," or "free energy ratio." If we reduce this ratio to its corresponding labor-force terms—that is, equate the product of each category to a proportion of the entire productive labor force required to produce that category—the ratio becomes a measure of the internal ratios of the labor force. If we then acknowledge that the entire labor force represents that proportion of the entire population which is society's sole means of producing its material existence, material consumption, and material preconditions of continued production, the ratio is properly interpreted as a measure of the society's ability to reproduce itself.

We thus have a useful measure of economy. We can now compare the ratios for successive intervals, interpreting a rise in the value of the ratio as progress, a constant value as stagnation, and a decline as decay or retrogression.

This is not a perfect measure, since it fails to specify the expenditure for the material consumption and leisure of the entire working-class population (in particular) necessary to insure a labor force adequate to tomorrow's productive technology. It is merely a useful, quick, preliminary statement with which we can proceed to work out necessary refinements.

Our first refinement is not statistical but conceptual. The simple ratio does not express what we want to determine. If we acknowledge that stagnation means decay—due to exhaustion of the relatively finite resources of present technology—we must posit a rising ratio as the condition of equipotentiality for continued human existence. Since advancing technology means rises in per capita values of V and C, relative to current prices or the current labor costs of producing such values, a net gain in the ratio after these added costs must require an *exponential tendency* for increase in the value of the ratio in terms of present per capita valuations of V and C!

The latter qualification of the ratio provides us with an *invariant*— that is, a yardstick which remains constant despite changes of every other sort in the social-productive relations of the economy. We have not, of course, defined this invariant precisely; it has subsumed characteristics we have not yet considered. Nonetheless, the general point should be clear enough. It should also be clear that we can approximate such notions even in terms of the wretched official statistics provided by governmental and private sources.

Yet an obvious objection arises. "What about the magnitude of wealth produced?" Proof of our contention with respect to this problem is beyond our state of progress at this juncture. Indeed, a discussion of the approach the typical student might wish us to take to develop such proof is beyond the capacity of this text. Later we shall argue the point in terms which will permit the student to conceptualize the notion in such a manner that he can empirically demonstrate the case to his own satisfaction. For the moment, we shall merely supply a summary description of the response to this objection.

Social reproduction is usually thought of in terms of an increase in absolute numbers of simple individuals. Indeed, as Marx himself states in the "Feuerbach" section of *The German Ideology*, a simple increase in population is the "first approximation" of successful social reproduction. We qualify this statement by saying that it is *only* a first approximation. Granting nothing to the Zero Population Growth program, which is now directed against the population below the Tropic of Cancer, we nonetheless emphasize that an absolute increase in the number of simple individuals is not the measure of successful social reproduction. If we consider an individual in capitalist society from the standpoint of the invariant, as we have thus far defined it, his significance to society as a whole is determined as the effect of his activity upon the tendency of the ratio to rise or fall. This notion of the value of an individual's activity is termed *determination* by Hegel and Marx. Instead of treating entireties as aggregates of simple events, we determine the value and content of simple events from the standpoint of the invariant principle of self-development of the entire process of which the simple event is a part. Thus, the value of the individual is not "one," but the implied *power* he represents to increase the value of the tendency ratio. In Marx, for example, this approach produces the concept of *labor power* as the measure of labor. In studies of reproduction in general, it is the increase in the individual's productive powers, directly or indirectly, in much the same sense which determines the proper measure of the individual.

For example, where Marx in *Capital* repeatedly notes that the *value* of commodities (the value *embodied* in them) is determined by the quantity of necessary labor power socially required for their production, he is assuming that the value of labor power has been measured, so to speak, in exactly the way we have just described it. At any instant, the price of labor power represents, *approximately*, a scalar measure in a certain kind of correspondence to a set of "nonlinear" magnitudes (determinate magnitudes) of labor power. This scalar is not, however, the content or absolute measure of labor power.

We must note that this labor power does not simply exist. Variations in labor power are determined by consumption—in the broadest sense of the term. An increase in the conceptual (cognitive) power of individuals, which is the basis for increases in their productive potential for advancing technology, requires increases in the absolute level of consumption and the amount of leisure. Such consumption and leisure represent a definite proportion of existing production, in the sense of the total available productive labor time of all labor power. Thus, the input-determination of the increases in power of labor power is measurable, in this sense, in terms of definite proportions of the output of total labor power!

This exposition suffices to demonstrate at least that increases in the value of the tendency ratio, since they are mediated through individual labor power and since increases in the power of such labor are mediated through increases in the relative magnitude of consumption, subsume—and determine—corresponding increases in magnitude. In other words, to note a rise in the value of the tendency ratio is to imply, uniquely and sufficiently, any necessary mediating changes in magnitude.

The extension of this argument to Constant as well as Variable Capital should be partially obvious. What needs to be further elucidated is that the possibility of realizing potential increases in labor power depends upon the existence of corresponding material preconditions of production. Computer programmers, to offer a very crude illustration, are quite useless without computers. The significance of this point is that the task of increasing the value of the tendency ratio cannot be accomplished by simply increasing to the limit the proportion of output devoted to material consumption and increased leisure. A balance must be achieved between the expansion of labor power's quality and the development of the means of production. There is a similar apparent paradox between material consumption and leisure. If we increase leisure indefinitely, the result is obvious. If we indefinitely increase material consumption at the expense of increased leisure, the potential benefits of a higher material level of consumption will tend to be lost for lack of the associated increases in realized cognitive powers achieved through leisure. (Education can be used as a crude epitome of leisure in this context.)

In general, these "countervailing" considerations, together with the need for rising values of the tendency ratio, represent a general necessity; increased material consumption and greater cognitive (creative) powers through increased consumption and leisure, represent freedom. Labor power or, more generally, social-reproductive power, together with our notion of invariance represents for Marx—and for all Marx's economics—the notion of true Freedom; that is, Freedom comprehending Necessity through practice.[11]

This preliminary outline of the situation should make it clear that our concept of the invariant completely subsumes all notions of *determined* magnitude of the entirety. As to whether this means an absolute increase in the number of simple individuals, two points will complete our exposition. The notion of the magnitude of the human population is primarily a qualitative consideration; that is, the primary consideration for any society is the tendency ratio, which expresses the social-reproductive powers of individuals and of the entire society for that specific mode of human existence. The secondary consideration is the quantity of individuals of that power, which corresponds to the power of the society as a whole. Hegel summarizes such notions in the motto: quality *determines* quantity. Although this axiom suggests that there is no urgency for indefinitely increasing the simple number of individuals in the population, and although the question of "standing room only" troubles those who have not made the necessary elementary population-density calculations for the existing world population, we have the strongest doubts—by no means on the basis of mere personal inclination—that the human race would rationally desire at any time in the future to restrict its population-expansion rates in the sense of zero population growth.

First, the value of an individual human being ultimately resides in his creative powers. Such powers signify the capacity for inventions which become the increased powers of virtually every other existing individual. Less obviously, but also fundamental, the capacity of human beings generally to assimilate, and thus *realize*, new inventions depends upon increased creative powers (cognitive advances). Let us confine our attention to the first aspect of this formulation for the present. If we define the human race as a mass of "inventors," it is apparent that the more persons who exist the greater is the society's rate of advance. (This is, of course, the ultimate principle of Humanism: to value every human being for his human quality, for that quality which distinguishes him from the lower beasts, his capacity for creative mentation.) The ecological crisis is actually a reflection of *a lack of* realized technological progress. On such premises alone, every Marxist finds himself in uneasy alliance with the Pope on the subject of zero growth.[12] *The more creative human beings exist, the better for each and all.*

Second, it is the wildest presumption imaginable to calculate the space and resources available for human existence solely in terms of the earth. Since there is no possibility that human existence will continue beyond this century without the massive conversion of our technology on the basis of thermonuclear fusion, and since that realization means the most explosive scientific advances in the history of mankind, it is the wildest delusion, a literally pathetic delusion in every respect, to doubt that man will soon be populating the moon and Mars. Entering solar space on the rocket of thermonuclear revolutions in technology, man will—as no responsible specialist doubts—instantly begin to bring the massive energy output of the sun under his control. What lies beyond that may be relative speculation for the moment, but it would be the wildest speculation to imagine that anything less than the most explosive and titanic advances in man's mastery of the universe are not unfolding for our species once we have safely negotiated the difficulties just ahead.

There is really only one significant objection to our procedure for determining "national wealth." All other sorts of objections are, as we have just indicated, attributable to pathology of approach. The sole ponderable objection is that the actual determination of what happens—what is produced, what consumption and leisure are enjoyed, what rates of growth actually occur, and the like—is determined by capitalist investment and related market decisions. Absurd as the GNP and related capitalist criteria for national wealth may be, they are, as reflected in the quasi-theoretical practice of conventional political economy, the basis on which actual decisions are made. Consequently, as a voluntary element in human material existence, these false criteria actually determine the course of development of the material conditions we attempt to measure from the real standpoint we have outlined. Considerations of real value have no immediate effect on the day-to-day course of events under capitalism, and therefore do not seem to represent in ordinary empirical investigations any actual, adducible laws. It is only during capitalist crises, which represent breakdowns of all the laws of capitalist accumulation *per se*, that the cumulative effect of the real underlying determinations breaks through the surface of day-to-day reality and we have a unique, gross expression of the fundamental laws to which we, as Marxists, subscribe.

For related reasons, Engels,[13] Luxemburg,[14] and perhaps Marx himself regarded his treatment of "a general rate of profit" in Volume III of *Capital*[15] as his greatest accomplishment in the domain of political economy as such. Marx demonstrates there that capitalist accumulation as a whole is characterized by a general rate of profit *in capitalist terms*. This general rate of profit is the shadow—grossly distorted—of the rises in the value of $(S - d)/(C + V)$ we have associated with the invariant aspect of social reproduction for capitalist (and socialist) industrial development. The value of every particular event, object, and person in capitalist society is *determined*, in the dialectical sense of the term, by this general rate of profit, much as our invariant determines the real value of labor power and the like. The value of labor power *for the capitalist* is immediately expressable as S/V, *in terms of capitalist prices*. This is the capitalist determination of the "productivity" of labor, its "profitability." The wage-rates a capitalist pays are ultimately determined by the price for V which yields the ratio, S/V, he requires in terms of existing commodity prices. However, his required rate of S/V is determined by the price of production as a whole, such that different industries, with different price-of-production structures, require different ratios of S/V. And so forth.

We shall demonstrate in later chapters why the dialectical character of capitalist accumulation makes it subject to a Law of Value, a Law of Value which is a shadow of the underlying social-reproductive relations created by capitalist accumulation. That is, there is a contradictory interdependency between the capitalists' general rate of profit for the total capitalist economy and its social-reproductive rates.

Thus it should be obvious that nothing important can be understood about a capitalist economy without investigating underlying real relations. The development of capitalism, as we shall show, is characterized by a succession of crises, each determined by the persisting discrepancy between exchange value and use value; and the possible capitalist solution to each crisis is delimited by the contradictory interdependence of exchange value and use value. *Exchange value* represents the dialectical determination of the particular value of a commodity (or person) from the standpoint of a general capitalists' rate of profit; *use value* represents the real determination of the social value of the same objects and persons from the standpoint of the invariant.

There is one nasty qualification to this argument—referred to from a different angle earlier in this chapter—which has severely perplexed the small number of serious readers of *Capital:* Since the voluntary aspect of the twofold process, capitalist accumulation, determines the actions of capitalist man to further the underlying real social-reproductive process, any event which prompts the capitalist system to act as to further the underlying process represents a use value, though it would not have that status in a society in which decisions were made immediately on the basis of use-value relationships alone. In particular, any event which furthers the capitalist development of the productive forces, by furthering successful capitalist accumulation through development of those forces, is a use value *for as long as capitalist accumulation persists!* We referred to this phenomenon earlier with respect to the apparent ambiguities in Marx's conflicting—and often unequivocally conflicting—definitions of productive labor.

Thus, in summary, the analysis of capitalist accumulation demands parallel determination of both exchange value and use value as expressions of two contradictory but interconnected processes. Furthermore, both processes are dialectical in form, and their resolution (elaboration) cannot be comprehended except in dialectical mode. That is the essence of Marxist economics.

The "intrinsic value" of a commodity is not locatable in the commodity itself, nor in the simple relationship between a commodity and its consumer or purchaser. Nor, for exactly this reason, do "constant dollar" measures of "national wealth" as a whole have much analytical significance except for muckraking purposes, even when analysis is restricted as closely as possible to that portion of output which represents useful products. The value of an object depends on the way in which it is *realized,* the effects of its consumption, and, ultimately, the effects of realization in terms of invariant features of the social-reproductive process as a whole.

This notion, which is conceptualized with the greatest difficulty by the layman, is the core of our entire subject matter; without it, nothing more can be competently understood. For reasons to be considered more fully in due course, the layman considers the consumption of a commodity as its final annulment, and thus regards the value attributable to it in terms of the isolated act of consumption as the only intrinsic value it could possess. The example of military production readily illustrates his predicament. In military production we are confronted, up to the act of production itself, with nothing but useful realization. The labor power employed in military production was created by useful consumption. The raw materials, machinery, and the like, all represent the mediating expression of a long series of antecedent useful realizations, ultimately traceable to the Pleistocene Age. But the production of military hardware brings all this invaluable antecedent realization to an end. It has no useful connection to social reproduction in the future. A whole segment of human history, reaching back to man's earliest appearance as man, has been obliterated. The blood, toil, and aspirations of all those men and women whose existence is partly embodied in the series of antecedent productive acts are destroyed—one can almost hear their moans as this cruel annulment of the meaning of their brief lives occurs in the military plant. Such contemplations demonstrate the fallacy of thinking in terms of a simple chain of particular events. What survives such catastrophes to the chain of productive acts? What is the alternative to this pathetic judgment of reductionism upon itself? There is only the horizon, on which one foresees the consequences of today's consumption for tomorrow's existence. How can we comprehend this idea except as a shadowy speculative conviction that what we do will be meaningful then? We are compelled to cringe before the awfulness of our self-doubts, unless we can locate in the present process some meaningful, comprehensible measure of the value of our own active existence. It is not necessary to ride a "time machine" to the horizon of today's tomorrows. The answer lies at hand: are we increasing the rate of social productivity for the immediate future of the economy and the society? If so, that increase will be the basis for a further advance during the next epoch. Thus, we free ourselves from the "asymptotic" "bad infinity" of the reductionist's simple, isolated chain of events stretching into the future. The concept of *realization*, which first suggests that we must trace the consequence of today's consumption to *its* consequence, and so on, is resolved in terms of "actual infinity"; it is that of increasing the current value of social reproductive *powers* in respect to what we have defined as invariance.

PRICE AND CRISIS

Despite the overwhelming evidence against the existence of a formal mathematical correlation between prices and intrinsic values, there has been a proliferation of professed economists who axiomatically or indifferently assume such correlations. This conceit has assumed the quality of polite thuggery in academic circles since the discovery of "mathematical economics" in the wake of the Second World War.

Functionally, "mathematical economics" can be divided into two branches, a dichotomy which certified itself in a brief factional flurry just over a decade ago. The healthy faction is that associated with Wassily

Leontief.[16] The opposing faction is a group of admittedly clever fellows whose impressive potential is fatally marred by the affliction known as radical positivism; we might characterize this group as "pure econometricians."[17] Outside the capitalist factions, there is the Soviet school of mathematical economics associated with L. V. Kantorovich, V. V. Novozhilov, and V. S. Nemchinov, whose pioneering work more closely resembles the approach of Leontief, despite Soviet priority on developing sophisticated mathematical procedures later independently replicated by leading U.S. econometricians. The healthy faction acknowledges, to varying degrees, that mathematics *per se* contributes absolutely nothing to political-economic theory in terms of concept, categories, or solutions to fundamental theoretical problems: but recognizes that economic applications, like applications in most fields of inquiry, encounter regions of practice in which mathematical procedures become useful—even indispensable—extensions of theory itself. The pure econometricians by contrast, replicate all the worst flaws of the *Principia Mathematica*[18] while avoiding the burden of its accomplishments. Sitting in their ivory towers[19] abstracted from all reality, they spin geometries like Arachne, "optimizing" the hypersurface to hypervolume ratios of an arbitrary "n-person game." To give them the credit due them, the econometricians have managed to produce, amid all the epistemological nonsense, a number of procedures which are by no means to be despised.

The problem, as we have indicated, is that one cannot simply dismiss the entirety of mathematical economics, even the positivist ravings of the pure econometricians, as pure hogwash. It may be principally hogwash, but therefore useful for washing hogs.[20] In order to dismiss this field's claims to authority respecting political economy as such, we are obliged to specify exactly where its limitations lie.

Mathematical economics is justified for certain tasks of corporate planning and certain applications to a national economy, an approach best exemplified by the pioneering work of Kantorovich. These procedures succeed in special tasks within fairly well-defined limitations. For relatively short periods, the pattern of consumption of kinds of commodities by persons and firms, in certain general tendencies of proportionality, does remain approximately constant. The only significant problem at any given moment is the relatively minimal fluctuation of quantities and prices around a set of central tendencies.

The layman, inundated with the standard nonsense about the freedom of the marketplace, is inclined to underestimate the validity of computerized projections for such ends. We will address this matter in a later chapter which explores the determination of consumption; the following preliminary insight into the matter will suffice for the moment.

All competent capitalist administration employs three principal instruments, termed respectively the *bill of consumption, process sheet,* and *bill of materials.* The bill of consumption analyzes the total household income of types of families and individuals into proportions representing general categories (e.g., food, clothing, housing) and details subcategories of requirements, sometimes down to specific commodities. The process sheet analyzes production into a network of operations, and associates with each "node" of that network a specific kind of labor and equipment. For a given quantity of a specific product, the process sheet identifies the proportion of available capacities required. The bill of materials, properly filled out, identifies the necessary quantity of raw materials, semifinished material, and supplies, as well as the vendors, purchase-delivery lead-times, and the like, for each of these items.

Using these instruments, a firm's departmental and divisional specialists and executives—in marketing, production planning, purchasing, and the like—collaborate months in advance of the beginning of a new cycle of production to plan the programming of a new "seasonal" slug of production. Equipment must be ordered according to advance lead-times, product design must be finished in pilot form, and so forth. In effect, the major portion of what the consumers will buy is thus predetermined months, and sometimes years, before they have the opportunity to exercise their sacred freedom of the marketplace at the store counter. Most consumers would be horrified, perhaps enraged, to know the degree to which their "preferences" can be predetermined by qualified management teams!

In any case, the most that management can do, with all this programming effort, with all its administration of production, sales, etc., is merely to effect a slight fluctuation from results which would otherwise be more or less predetermined. A five per cent overall fluctuation in total sales, occurring principally in the "reorder" segment of production and sales, can be enormously successful or disastrous for the typical program. Even drastic developments in one section of the economy have relatively minimal overall effects.

Consequently, in the relatively short term it is feasible, and indeed imperative, to introduce assumptions pertaining to "demand," "price," and related phenomena which would be epistemologically absurd from the standpoint of a comprehensive political economic theory for a longer period of development.

Within these relatively stable parameters of short-term programming of production and marketing, variations in profit and related problems of performance are immediately determined by the quality of administrative judgment and performance respecting what can be called "optimal allocations." A few quick examples will suffice. In some industries, the firm must deliver a broad selection of products, in well-defined minimal or larger lots, to a wide variety of customers within a very short period of delivery-time. The mass so distributed may or may not be larger than the rate of output capacity of the firm's productive facilities. Even if the output capacity is sufficient to produce within a given period an absolute output equal to the mass to be delivered in that period, economical production must be performed in minimum lot-quantities in most cases; thus few such firms could produce all the products they must deliver in the period during which delivery has to be made. Thus, with the emergence of

U.S. marketing practices, a premium has been placed on the development of an inventory of finished stock to serve as a buffer between production and delivery. The magnitude of inventory required to ensure rapid delivery on customer's orders is often so great that the necessary capital investment in inventory would either enormously reduce the profitability of the firm or cause actual illiquidity. So a lower inventory level must be established, resulting in inevitable lost sales from "stock outs." By calculating "marginal" losses and gains respecting fluctuations in inventory for effects on production, sales revenues, financial resources, and other phenomena, a reasonable policy for inventory-stocking can be reached. A similar problem occurs in production itself where an increase in the number of kinds of items produced often causes all sorts of horrible developments, most quite costly in one mode or another. A corporation is a mass of such fascinating little problems, most of which lend themselves to considerable overall profit improvement through the application of econometric procedures.

The nature of the difficulty ought to suggest the conclusion. Econometrics is not an aspect of political-economic theory at all, but a "spinoff" of ordinary industrial engineering. An econometrician, at his very best, is a skilled industrial engineer accompanied by two computer programmers and a portfolio of advanced algebra textbooks. A "pure econometrician" is like a pianist with enormous keyboard dexterity and no knowledge of music. There is nothing strained about the simile. A competent industrial engineer (as distinguished from the special case of the stopwatch-toting efficiency expert) is not a graduate student freshly stuffed with the latest array of procedures. All the important judgments he must make are *qualitative*. The analyst begins his real work, after a brief review of the overall data on hand, by "sniffing about," "getting his hands dirty," provoking personnel at various levels with embarrassing questions, and so forth, until he turns up a qualitative discovery of the sort the jargon of the trade usually describes as "getting a handle on the situation."

For example, with reference to the problem cited above involving inventory policies, the analyst who merrily proceeds, using company statistics, to calculate an optimal inventory policy is a reckless incompetent. If his recommendation succeeds, he is simply lucky. If he had "gone out into the field," he might have discovered an obvious tactic—for initial placement of stocks, say—to give the firm a powerful competitive advantage by taking up customers' shelf space (and capital) at the beginning of a selling season, with multiple effects on the reorder cycle. If he had examined some other aspect of the operations, he might have discovered the product-mix to be fundamentally unsound from the standpoint of raw materials and productive balance, on grounds not reflected in the "facts" given to him. Only after such qualitative judgments have been made does a competent specialist permit calculations to begin. Mathematical procedures are extremely useful at that point, but even in so philistine a domain as corporate administration, quality properly determines quantity.

There is no doubt a tendency for autistic character defects to impel students into mathematics—or to incline them toward behaviorist factions in other fields. One plugs oneself into a field, and is programmed as a professional, storing procedures in one's memory. One introduces computers to the composition of what appeals to one as "musical composition." The ivory-tower approach to the mathematicization of any field strongly suggests the influence of some such bias. Whatever the deeper motives for "pure econometrics," there is certainly something pathetic at the root of so obvious a blunder.

In any case, having acknowledged the conditional usefulness of such procedures within the proper context of qualitative judgment, it should be clear that the source of the error of extrapolating from such limited success to a pseudotheory of economics is nothing but an elementary fallacy of composition. The procedures work in a limited framework because microeconomics has the advantage of such limitations. To base a "macrotheory" on the poorly understood partial successes of "microeconomics" is an obvious fallacy of the sort identified.

Empirical economics—we shall momentarily indulge in the cant term "macroeconomics"—escapes such a fallacy of composition only when it refuses to select a domain of investigation narrower than a business cycle. In the crisis which inevitably follows a "boom," the reality of the developments of the boom period is finally revealed in clear, factual terms. Any investigation which omits such data is by definition fraudulent. The empirical domain from which meaningful judgments are adduced can be no smaller than the totality of the economy for an entire business cycle.

It is not accidental, therefore, that the revived self-confidence of procapitalist political economy, the toleration of "pure econometrics," and related developments of the postwar period depend absolutely on the fallacy of composition just described. By restricting the evidence under consideration to the data of "prosperity," the investigator arbitrarily excludes what is most essential. His argument is that the future occurrence of a "depression" for the present prosperity cycle is only conjectural, not "fact." Neither is Niagara Falls a fact for the canoeist upstream from it. Theoretical economics becomes science only when it competently undertakes the essential business of any science: to predict the consequences which, as topics, are integral features of the subject of its investigations. It tends to be characteristic of incompetent economists to argue against predictions, thus predicting the probable extended prosperity of contemporary capitalism on the premise that a depression could not be predicted![21]

Another feature of mathematical economics would lead it to wrong judgments in any case. Leibniz, in his letters to Samuel Clarke, implies his understanding of the problem by asserting that in Newton's universe it is periodically necessary for God to wind the whole thing up. The axiomatic, reductionist assumptions of ordinary mathematics generate two derivative assumptions about the dynamics of the universe which prohibit it from comprehending any phenomena incompatible with these assumptions. One is the assumption of "entropy"—Newton's problem, according to Leibniz. The other is the complementary notion of "homeostasis" or—a more restricted version of the same fallacy—the tendency to limit the definition of processes and universal laws to "mechanical equilibrium."

Such assumptions to the contrary, the characteristic feature of human existence is *metastasis*, the progressive development of the human species to higher states of "negative entropy" in terms of the invariant. This feature of human existence, associated with expanding powers of cognition, stands in direct conflict with the axiomatic assumptions of formal logic by virtue of the impossibility of logical induction of the creation of categories of thought, which is not only the characteristic feature of human behavior but also that upon which the development of mankind as a whole is immediately dependent. Since, in a capitalist or socialist economy, this capacity is expressed most forcefully in technological advance, and since the characteristic problems of capitalist economy arise in connection with the resulting rising general productivity of labor, any effort to adduce "natural principles" of economy from formal mathematical speculations must be nonsense.

APPROPRIATENESS OF ECONOMY

Despite the overwhelming empirical and epistemological evidence against any formal consistency between price and use value, the same evidence demonstrates that the two interconnected systems have some kind of *coherent* relationship. At this point, let us borrow from Sigmund Freud the useful concept of "appropriateness," which Freud employs in a circumstance not unrelated to what we are confronting here. The passage is self-explanatory:

> . . . an attempt has been made to discredit radically scientific endeavour on the ground that, bound as it is to the conditions of our own organization, it can yield nothing but subjective results, while the real nature of things outside us remains inaccessible to it. But this is to disregard several factors of decisive importance for the understanding of scientific work. Firstly, our organization, i.e., our mental apparatus, has been developed actually in the attempt to explore the outer world, and therefore it must have realized in its structure a certain measure of *appropriateness;* secondly, it itself is a constituent part of that world which we are to investigate, and readily admits of such investigation; thirdly, the task of science is fully circumscribed if we confine it to showing how the world must appear to us in consequence of the particular character of our organization; fourthly, the ultimate findings of science, just because of the way in which they are attained, are conditioned not only by our organization but also by that which has affected this organization; and, finally, the problem of the nature of the world irrespective of our perceptive mental apparatus is an empty abstraction without practical interest.[22] (emphasis added)

Compare Marx's famous summation of the same point:

> The question whether objective truth can be attributed to human thinking is not a question of theory but is a *practical* question. In practice man must prove the truth, that is, the reality and power, the this-sidedness of his thinking. The dispute over the reality or non-reality of thinking which is isolated from practice is a purely *scholastic* question.[23]

If we situate the problem within the overview provided by our notion of invariants, we quickly discover that all knowledge characteristic of large populations, and especially of entire societies, must necessarily possess a certain degree of *relative* truth, if by truth one means the power of successful adaptation to a certain social setting. It is merely necessary to situate the notion of cognition-in-general within the individual in respect to the fact that the characteristic invariant of the society appears to different sections and individuals within that society not necessarily directly, but in the form of some special "law"—determined by the characteristic principle of the entire society—for some aspect of the process as a whole.

For example, take the case of capitalist ideology. Most militant trade-unionists and black nationalists are more or less thoroughly committed to capitalist ideology. The principal source of difficulty in assimilating this observation is usually the prevailing insipid view of ideology as a collection of learned prejudices dinned into the individual by parents, teachers, and the media; no explanation of the phenomenon could be more fatuous.

It might appear outrageous to describe a militant trade-unionist actively leading the rank-and-file during a bitter strike as a victim of capitalist ideology. Yet, in general, he is just that, which is easily demonstrated by testing his attitude toward "outsiders" during the strike. In the extreme case, when his leaders are being jailed, his fellow-workers battered, imprisoned, and occasionally shot down—when the tactical weakness of his union's isolation is most apparent—a militant trade-unionist will characteristically react with hostility to the suggestion that he enlarge his forces by means of united fronts with the unemployed, certain previously unorganized workers, and groups engaged in organizing these forces into a coalition. The source of capitalist ideology is this case ought to be obvious enough: *pluralism.* The craft-unionist, in particular, regards his struggles with his employer as a private battle over the gross profit of the local industry or trade. He will ordinarily support his employers to "protect" the revenues of the trade or industry as a whole, especially from the depredations of greedy "outsiders."

The same phenomenon is characteristic of most black nationalists, who promote the pluralist approach to reality even more vigorously than do most trade-union members.

In each such case, the observer who absolutely insists on being shallow-minded can undoubtedly compile a long list of specific prejudices, apparently demonstrating the entire problem to be a result of mere learning

—from parents, teachers, specific experiences, and the media. This is a fallacy of composition. Slogans, formulas for argument, and other specific responses are merely determinate. The individual who exhibits such behaviors has acquired them because they conform to his characteristic world-outlook. And that outlook is pluralistic. There is massive, decisive evidence to this effect, which the usual observer cannot regard as evidence because pluralism is not for him a distinguishing world-outlook: he cannot regard his own characteristic world-outlook as a symptom of pathology or as characteristic of any view in particular. Pluralism is for most observers simply the natural and universal world-outlook.

This is no doubt why most writing on ideology and alienation, especially that of most "radical" groups and academics, is so banal. They are usually capable of distinguishing the effluvia, the contingent features of a problem. Yet, as the "remedy" widely advanced for "alienation"—the *pluralist* remedy of "local control"—attests, such observers have been incapable of conceptualizing or recognizing those empirical materials which bear directly and uniquely on the characteristic problem underlying the contingencies.

Yet, once we have adduced the characteristic features of capitalist ideology by an approach such as we have indicated, we are compelled to acknowledge that, in the ordinary course of successful capitalist accumulation, pluralism and all that it implies generally represents a successful practice for most members of capitalist society—including workers and black nationalists. Often enough, as in the rapid mobilization of workers for "protection" of their employers' industries and the susceptibility of most black nationalists to some version of "black capitalism," this point is most frankly articulated by the victim himself. This phenomenon suggests the *appropriateness* of bourgeois ideology to members of capitalist society.

In order to account for specific subordinate ideologies within the general one, we need only recognize that the invariant of capitalist accumulation is not directly expressed to each group in the same way. The invariant generates a variety of special sub-characteristics, more or less in the same way that postulates determine theorems, causing occupants of different regions of functional capitalist space to see the whole in terms of pseudo-invariants, or "special laws." Yet, while the immediate characteristics of consciousness may differ among social strata, the "hereditary" feature of the general principle, embedded in the "special laws," is adducible from individuals' conscious and "unconscious" behavior.

While we can correctly regard capitalist ideology as false from the standpoint of the underlying invariant—and, more important, from the standpoint of the feasibility of socialist organization of people and productive forces—we must at the same time recognize a larger truth. Relative to all preceding forms of society, capitalist ideology is truth. In its subsumed features, such as the practice of physical science, on which capitalist perpetuation of the conditions of the population's material existence depends, it also represents a comprehension of the universe superior in every respect to that of every preceding society. There is thus a coherence between the ideological determination of social behavior *per se* and the coherent ideology embedded within what we term theoretical scientific knowledge.

This is demonstrable by examining the ontological and derived formal notions of relationship characteristic of so-called theoretical physical science as projections of the axiomatic assumptions embedded in ordinary street-corner ideology.[24] The fundamental assumptions of reductionism are precisely identical with both pluralism and the dichotomy of individual psychology.

Retreating from close observation of capitalist culture to a vantage-point from which to survey the emergence of modern man from the Pleistocene, we grasp the problem more comprehensively. Once man begins to *produce* his means of existence, and employs what we understand as a technology, a qualitative advance occurs in the species. In every such culture, one could identify an equivalent of physical science, and could use that construct to more readily sort out the productive and related practice of that culture.[25] This technology, together with the characteristic mode of organization of the social-productive forces—in other words, "culture"—subsumes certain aspects of nature as *resources*. Because the resources so defined by a particular technology must be relatively finite for that population, the more successfully a society perpetuates itself in a given mode, the more successfully it is exhausting its potential for continued human existence in that mode. The only solution to this predicament is *noesis*, the development of a new technology which expands and otherwise alters the definition of resources for social-reproductive practice. This development occurs as a result of creative mentation—cognition in the strict sense of the term—inventing an hypothesis which is then tested in the struggle for human existence itself. Thus, the world-line of evolution of successively reproductive societies represents a world-line of creative mentation in experimental correspondence to all those laws of the universe which have been successfully tested by evolving human practice. In principle, the term *knowledge* is properly restricted to a concept which arises from systematic reflection on human evolution in that fashion, the concept which represents a special kind of reflection on the world-line of creative mentation embedded in that history and prehistory of our species. The movement of a point—human knowledge of advancing societies—along that world-line represents increasing *appropriateness* of scientific knowledge to the extent that scientific knowledge is adduced from reflection upon the progressive movement of that point.

The necessary coherence between the technology-in-general of a mode of existence and the organization of the social-productive forces to realize that technology suggests that in the laws of human conduct and thought peculiar to a given culture the principle of technology-in-general is embedded as "hereditary" content.

From this standpoint, there are no abstractly good or bad societies. There can be no such thing as a utopia, distinct from an existing society, which serves as an abstract standard against which the existing society can be measured and subjected to absolute moral judgment. Reality is the world-line. The only absolute which actually exists is the rate of progress of the point along that line. The only morality by which an existing society can be judged is that of the society represented by the point.[26]

> The so-called conditions of distribution, then, correspond to and arise from historically defined and specifically social forms of the process of production and of conditions, into which human beings enter in the process by which they reproduce their lives. The historical character of these conditions of distribution is the same as that of the conditions of production, one side of which they express. Capitalist distribution differs from those forms of distribution which arise from other modes of production, and every mode of distribution disappears with the peculiar mode of production from which it arose and to which it belongs.

> The conception, which regards only the conditions of distribution historically, but not the conditions of production, is, on the one hand, merely an idea begotten by the incipient, but still handicapped, critique of bourgeois economy. On the other hand, it rests upon a misconception, an identification of the process of social reproduction with the *simple* labor process, such as might be performed by an abnormally situated human being without any social assistance. To the extent that the labor process is [such a] simple process between man and nature, its simple elements remain the same in all social forms of development. But every definite historical form of this process develops more and more its material foundations and social forms. Whenever a certain maturity is reached, one definite social form is discarded and displaced by a higher one. The time for the coming of such a crisis is announced by the depth and breadth of the contradictions and antagonisms, which separate the conditions of distribution, and with them the definite historical form of corresponding conditions of production, from the productive forces, the productivity, and development of their agencies. A conflict then arises between the material development of production and its social form.[27] (emphasis added)

Thus, Marx posits the appropriateness of any economy, capitalist included, to a definite condition of progress in movement of the point of human development—and knowledge—along the world-line, the invariant of human existence.

Political economy, as we said at the outset of this chapter, was discovered almost as soon as it came into being. No economy existed before the emergence of capitalism, since no previous form of society or mode of production was based immediately on subsumed technological advances as the day-to-day basis for the continuation of productive development. The ironies of mercantile capitalism—that it posed the insoluble contradiction of a rate of accumulation (bounded by existing rates of risk) greater than the rate of social product, and also made existing society dependent on the continuation of the germs of a new mode of production (the cooperative labor process)—encountered the problem of obtaining a basis for its own continued existence in the expansion of national wealth at rates equal to the required rates of accumulation. It demanded a rate of self-expansion of national wealth corresponding to the rates of self-expansion of capitalist accumulation. Thus, although with massive false consciousness of the concept with which they were grappling, the emerging leaders of the new birth, like Tudor monarchs and their counterparts, focussed on the development of national wealth as the necessary basis for the power of the state, and the expansion of national wealth as the means by which the state could incur increased capitalized debts upon which the generalized exertion of monarchical power could be premised. To convert the will of the monarch into the armies and navies, by which that will could be realized against resisting forces, national economy had to exist.

The notion of static wealth was no longer applicable. Political economy was never in practice, in real content, a notion of *simple reproduction*. In place of Domesday lists, which assumed fixed wealth, there appeared the concept of changing, increasing wealth. Because this change was bounded by population, under conditions of general depopulation of Europe, even the maintenance of existing scales of wealth required changes in technology. The notion of political economy, or national economy, is better expressed by Tudor practice than by Tudor thought. The maritime development of England was the axis of much of the subsequent ferment of invention and scientific discovery. By drastically lowering the cost of "inland freight," it created the preconditions as well as the impetus for the explosive spread of cooperative labor. Thus it is the *practical* notion of political economy, the practical content—the appropriateness—within whatever rationalizations men advanced to express that content.

We can see political economy for what it is and was only in the work of Marx. Marx first consciously comprehended the actual nature of the problem: it is the interconnection of two antagonistic "optimizing principles," two distinct invariants. Immediately, with respect to capitalist accumulation, the invariant is expressed by the general rate of profit of capitalist accumulation *per se*, an invariant which determines the value, for capitalist accumulation, of every person and object subjected to it. More profoundly, this accumulation brings more immediately to the surface of human practice, to a qualitative extent, that invariant characteristic of human existence since the Pleistocene emergence of toolmaking, the principle of "negative entropy" in evolutionary social reproduction.

Ironically, because of the heteronomic principle of capital as such— the alienation of part of an integrated process from the whole for separate determination—and because of the heteronomic form of social relations determined by this mode of material existence of members of the society, the notions of reality which characterize such a society are heteronomic. Especially since the rights of *universal labor* (determination of technology, realization of technology, and the like) are not only appropriated by the capitalists, but appropriated in an heteronomic form alien to the very character of universal labor, the essence of man—his creative powers—is literally brutalized by externalization of the determination of how his own behavior and that of others may be changed in a progressive way. Thus, that within himself which represents the power to comprehend the content of the emerging productive process is stultified almost to the point of extinction. Human cognitive powers are not merely reduced to an unchangeable, largely unconscious "inner" self of fixed "psychological needs," but this alienation of man is generally reified into a false positive, causing men and women suffering this alienation to regard the very essence of their existence as a residue within them of the *unchangeable "real me."* Out of this reification of brutalized cognitive powers arises *reductionism,* which turns the entire universe inside-out and upside down. The particular, whose real value and identity are determined by the invariant of a self-developing whole, is made to appear primary and self-evident, and the whole is misconceptualized as an aggregation of formal relations (i.e., as abstract expressions of alienated social relations among discrete selves). Thus, intrinsic value is assumed to be intuitively a self-evident quality of either the object in itself or the simple formal relations of object to consumer or purchaser. And the notions of physical science—formal logical constructs—appropriate to a heteronomic, alienated population of this sort seem to accord with this interpretation of the world.

Thus, political economy, while an existent subject, becomes permeated with metaphysics. Since the mind of alienated man refuses to recognize the distinguishing features of political economy, features which are precisely dialectical in form, it must impute the notion of political economy to every imaginable society, from Robinson Crusoe to abstract civilizations millions of years hence. Its motive is to see all human existence as a vindication of the "true religion" of its present ideology, and its way of interpreting the world provides it with no contrary indications, since that interpretation—reductionism, empiricism, and related outlooks—is entirely consistent with its religious convictions. Unable either to identify the actual (dialectical) content of political economy or to recognize it as something which came into being, reductionism sees in it only an abstract metaphysical essence which can be readily imparted to any object at any time or place, provided only that the true faith of bourgeois ideology is breathed upon it.

Thus, the contradictions of Ricardian political economics (in particular) reveal Ricardo's ideology[28] and beg thus, as obviously fundamental antinomies, the recognition that the problem thus represented is one of the fallacy of formal induction, especially as Hegel and Marx successively located that difficulty. Thus, in general, political economy is false consciousness of its subject matter, an ideological disguise for the actual practice of political economy. A science of political economy can come into being only when the subject is freed from reductionism. Since the notions of invariance appropriate to a general rate of profit and a general principle of social reproduction are dialectical, in terms both of each and of their interpenetration, only a dialectical method permits us scientific comprehension of this field.

THE PRODUCTION
OF CONSCIOUSNESS

3

The central formal problem of contemporary knowledge is that the *fact*, which naive opinion takes for the elementary or simple basis of human knowledge, proves upon critical examination to be a highly suspect authority. The concept of a "fact," we discover through reflection, is the result of a process of judgment and therefore by no means as simple or self-evident as naive opinion assumes. In the process of judgment the experiential continuum is apparently arbitrarily bounded to form a notion of particularity from what is actually a continuous process; upon that constructed, artificed particularity of objective reference a mental construct as such is imposed. It is that mere mental construct which represents the best of ordinary opinion's "hard facts."

Proceeding along those narrower lines of investigation of the relationship between experience and facts, as is notably the case with John Dewey's "pragmatism," among numerous other modern examples, we must be driven toward philosophical despair at the impossibility of establishing universal knowledge. The investigator rather inevitably concludes that there is no certainty of human knowledge to be obtained in such a pursuit, no matter how many experiments or thought-experiments were conducted for that purpose. Frightened by this specter of their own metaphysics, most philosophers and scientists have withdrawn from this den of *anomie*, and in the course of terrified retreat have, by the consolations of philosophical amnesia, barred themselves from ever returning. It is as though a plumber called in to repair a television set, looking from his tool kit to the innards of the device and back several times, shook his head, preserving his notion of the universal powers of plumbing by certifying: "It doesn't exist." No plumber, of course, would be guilty of so silly a form of hysteria. Not so with the terrified philosophers and scientists. Confronted with the problems of continuity—universality—and looking back and forth from the problem to their reductionist's tool-kit, they shake their heads sadly and announce: "It doesn't exist."

That is the key to the triviality of most contemporary philosophical inquiries, and to the commitment of so many gifted mathematicians to the axiomatic viewpoint of reductionism.

As we have already noted, the central methodological problems of modern philosophers (in their various disguises) are eminently psychological. The area of inquiry into which every consideration of the problem of fact must lead challenges our confidence in our powers of reason, as we understand those powers. Since reason is—as we shall demonstrate—the method by which we organize our speech and other socially situated actions for the principal ultimate purpose of propitiating society, and thus controlling nature for our benefit through social actions, to lose confidence in this fetishistic or magical power of reason[1] is to contemplate the loss of reason's protection against the extinction of our psychological (social) identity by an ogre we can only name chaos.

Imagine yourself returned to the neighborhood in which you were raised as a child. You see all your old friends walking in and out of their homes, chatting with one another, laughing—doing all the old, familiar things. You speak to one; he does not hear or see you. Another: the same. Enraged, you strike one of your friends; he shows no sign of feeling the blow. You howl, but no one hears. You are dead; you exist, but you are dead. The persona by which society recognizes you has been stripped away, and you have thus become invisible. The ugly truth imposes itself upon you: "No one ever loved me for my real self." Without your mask—the play-acting images you don, impelled by what you regard as conscious reason—you do not exist for society. Only in rare moments of love, when the feeling Self seems to be touched, when reason seems to be of no consequence—indeed, in love it is a point of pride to consider reason of no consequence!—does someone "recognize" you. The moment of love, so tenuous, so fragile, passes; you are a ghost again. And for this reason, those who are dead for us exist—in our guilty feelings and fears—as ghosts, howling unheard in their torment at our failure to "see" them. They are ghosts, whose perverse nature is of the quality we impute to our inner, irrational, feeling selves.

It is not our physical selves we struggle to perpetuate, except insofar as we regard our bodies as the vessels of our social identity, the mediators of our "real" existence—our "soul." As the empirical evidence of centuries of religious belief attests, the central concern of all human beings is our abstract person, our social identity, in whose service life itself must be willingly sacrificed if the maintenance of social identity provides no apparent alternative.

It is along this line of inquiry, probing into the deepest aspects of our concerns, that we discover the solution to the predicaments of formal knowledge. Indeed, how could it be otherwise? What we commonly mistake for reason—conscious images marching in well-ordered ranks according to the prescribed drill—is not reason at all, but only the shadow, the footprint, the artifact of processes "more deeply embedded." From the artifact we can adduce only the implied movements of the artificing hand. We can attribute to the hand itself only its capacities for action. As for the movements of the hand—the exertion of its capacities—we must probe one level deeper to discover the motives and the coherent principle which organizes those motives into a single conception. Our task is to locate these areas of ambiguity—the most shadowy, contradictory aspects of ordinary reason—and in that restricted domain to isolate those phenomena which have the same significance for understanding the mind as did the constant velocity of light for adducing the necessary organization of the universe.

The key we require we have already supplied. It is the alienated form of our social relations—such that we are conscious of our social identities in an alienated way—which compels us to regard reason,[2] the mere shadow of our deliberative powers, as if it were the substance of our actual Self. This alienated form of social relations compels us to mis-locate the "substance" of our Self in mere formal reasoning (rationalism), and the active aspect of the Self in the imagined power of reason to select those words, phrases, and rituals by which we elicit favorable opinion of our selves (the social rights and privileges upon which our existence de-pends) from those groups and particular institutions from whom we secure or aspire to secure such recognition. Whatever threatens our confidence in the perfectability of our powers of formal reasoning ("What's the story?" "What's the gimmick?"), however differently individuals define their notion of formal reason, imbues us with a terror like no other. It is from that psychological terror that men flee to the hysterical consolations of em-piricism. Having conceded that "facts" are mere judgments, they reify the discovery of such "falseness" into a special kind of false truth; for such hysterics, however specious naive, classical materialism may be demon-strated to be, naive sense-certainty—coinciding with their peculiar habits of reason—persists as fact.

The relationship of this outlook to skepticism is easily demonstrated; Humean skepticism is the model. Accordingly, we have thereby situated the relationship of the problem at Kant's location of the key to its ultimate solution.[3]

There can be no remedy to this problem until we have arrived at an alternative premise for our social identity. It suffices, at least ultimately, to reflect upon the order of actuality of the unique intent of the greatest poetic works—in which that which is not explicitly stated is unquestion-ably the subject—to locate the way and form in which such an alternative premise can be and has been found by certain extraordinary individuals. Yet this process cannot be fully understood until we turn to more modern developments than those of Marx's period, to mass upsurges in which there occurs a general qualitative uplifting of intellectual powers and a shift in world outlook among significant numbers of participants. Applying the empirical evidence of these mass phenomena to such cases as Marx, we understand that he was at the vortex of mass upsurges occurring even after his demise *while he was yet alive*. There is no metaphysics or mys-tery in this assertion. Our social identities are located in the consequences of our actions. Even Kant understood this to be the key to the remedy for Humean skepticism.[4] Kant also more-or-less correctly recognized the as-sumption that the consequence of action is located in the immediate event itself as a pathetic fallacy.[5] He progressed, as well, to the point of under-standing that sanity begins with the reorientation of activity to its univer-salizing consequences, although he was unable to locate universality as a concrete experience for immediate judgment. Our practical concern is to determine the solution to Kant's predicament on this point, and to realize that solution in two interconnected ways. The first is to replicate Marx's accomplishment by making this new sense of identity accessible to the rare individual who has already cultivated leisure and cognitive powers to the extent he is thus so privileged to situate his social identity *intellectually*, and to organize his immediate social behavior around such a new self-conception of his human powers. The *intelligentsia* represents, in the pattern of Marx himself, the indispensable germ of a new society, without whose crystallizing influence nothing exists for the species as a whole. However, if the germ is to be that, we must confront the more general, historic tasks of discovering how the empirical results of mass upsurge can be consolidated and extended as the basis for a corresponding general shift in man's location of his social identity. The *universalizing labor* of discovering the new world outlook is the initiating task of the intelligentsia; the realization of that initiative is the business of what is now *cooperative labor*.

The source of these discoveries is capitalist ideology itself! When, as in the Tudor Enlightenment, man discovered that creative mentation by individuals was the key to the general progress on which the existence of society must depend, the value of the individual was acknowledged for the first time in human history. The invention of one creative intellect extended to the practice of individuals throughout society. Thus, as we have emphasized, the more such individuals existed, the greater is the power of each individual in society. However, in order to realize such inventions it was also necessary to increase correspondingly the cognitive powers of society as a whole; otherwise new ideas, however powerful, could not be realized. These interrelated notions of Humanism and Progress were the cornerstones of the Enlightenment. Kepler's humanism posited the necessary comprehensibility to man of the universe as a whole. Descartes' concern was with the dialectic of self ("cogito ergo sum": the universal for the particulars is as real as the particulars) and *Perfection* (the progress of knowledge is as real as the particular knowledge in respect to which it stands as universal—a rudimentary notion of invariant—as ontological proof of the existence of the invariant). English skepticism and French rationalism generally: it is their ferment, their preoccupation with Humanism (creative mentation) and progress (the actualization of creative mentation), whose internal predicaments (reductionism) led to Kant's preliminary restatement of the whole problem, and Hegel's discovery of the principle of invariance: the notion of self-development (invariant) which not only makes the holistic overview comprehensible, but thus resolves all the predicaments of ordinary reason. It remained, then, only for Feuerbach and Marx successively to remove this discovery from the realm of speculation and find the basis for this dialectic in actual social practice. Yet, all of this was the product of *capitalist* culture. This demonstrates to us the feasibility of a solution to the problem as susceptible of emergence from capitalist culture. What we seek does not lie beyond our reach; it is unnecessary to imagine becoming human by leaping into some ready-made utopian paradise outside the existing social process. With what we are, with the people and productive forces already at hand, we can set forth to accomplish everything we might desire to become.

THE PROBLEM OF "METAPHYSIC"

Although we have already said everything necessary to defend the reality of what we have to argue in the next sections of this chapter, most readers will not immediately make such a necessary connection between the foregoing explications and their own intuitive objections. In any case, the very nature of our subject matter, which is bound together by coherence rather than crude formal consistency, demands the restatement of previously developed points in each new context introduced, so that in the end a more or less all-sided comprehension may be developed.

Because classical rationalism and its skeptical offspring, empiricism, regarded only the particular empirical datum as real, the notion of a whole could exist for adherents of these outlooks only as a construct, an abstraction. As rationalism progressed in its investigations, it encountered two varieties of such constructs. The first—which appeared to be more readily comprehensible—was the aggregation of particularities. From this standpoint, wholes were deemed substantial, real, and material precisely because their states were interpretable, in terms of the dispersion of material entities. What was specifically abstract in these aggregations, the notion of relationship, was usually represented heuristically or geometrically, relying upon the known but little-understood paradoxical difficulty of attempting to complete a line with points, to adequately comprehend the notion of "abstractness." In general, this abstractness intensified as rationalism turned its attention from static aggregations to problems of development and motion, reencountering the point-and-line problem in a more insistent form—indeed, the paradoxes of Zeno. Thus, a general picture emerged of the aspect of the world termed "material," in which the particular was hard, real, and practicable, and wholes appeared increasingly abstract as one progressed first to static aggregations, and then to the attempt to construct heuristic images of dynamic systems from the same reductionist standpoint.

The same general difficulty prevails in a decayed form today in vulgar street-corner "rationalism"; consider the typical philistine's remark, "That's merely a theory, not a fact!" (Otherwise known as hound-dog wisdom, a relative of another version of the brutalized mentality called "horse sense": "If you can't eat it or copulate with it, urinate on it"—"It's only a theory!")

The second order of difficulty arose in connection with such discoveries as Descartes' two famous theorems, "Cogito ergo sum" and "perfection." The problem which these concepts posed for rationalism involved the difficulty of comprehending the actuality of their demonstrations and the impossibility of denying such conclusions without abandoning reason itself.

The "cogito ergo sum" may be explicated as follows. Every fact I know occurs as a fact in the form "I think that . . ." Thus, the subject of all knowledge ("I think") must be, in completion by all its predicates ("that. . . .") of the same degree of ontological reality (actuality) as its predicates. Therefore, to the degree that the facts of knowledge are real, my consciousness is real: *"I think . . .," therefore "I" am*.

The same dialectic is employed by Descartes in proceeding to the next one higher order of conception. "In the perfection of knowledge I experience progress respecting my knowledge of A from 'I think that "a" ' to 'I think that "b" '." Since both states of knowledge, insofar as they represent demonstrable (practicable) knowledge, are real, the "movement" from "I think that 'a' " to "I think that 'b' " is real. This set of predicates (motions of progress in particular knowledges) forms a universality which is the increasing perfection of knowledge. Therefore, if the motion of knowledge is real, then Perfection is existent. (Perhaps slyly, Descartes adds that, since God = Perfection, and since no particular man can universally encompass this perfection, God exists and is unique. The fate of Giordano Bruno and Galileo was in the forefront of the minds of Kepler and Descartes, not without cause.)

This problem, implied by Descartes' efforts to unify algebra and geometry, was not understood respecting even formal mathematics until Weierstrass, Riemann, Cantor, and Klein, among others, began to explore the metaphysical fallacies introduced to the calculus (in particular) by grounding mathematics on reductionist assumptions. The practical implications for mathematical physics, although anticipated by Klein—as he correctly insisted after the fact—were not located even in part until Einstein's discovery of special relativity and Minkowski's astonishing explication of that accomplishment shortly afterward. The problem is not solved, of course, and by its nature could not be resolved so long as mathematical physics limits its power of comprehension by adherence to reductionist conceptions of analysis. (The problem is obvious from this standpoint; unfortunately, the solution is not.) At least, from a modern standpoint, we profit by enormously increased respect for the accomplishments of Kepler and, in particular, Descartes.

Though Descartes was thus, by implication, far ahead of his times and though the same predicaments surrounded similar investigations during the late sixteenth through eighteenth centuries, none of the serious thinkers of that period could so easily discard his theorems. This aspect of Descartes' work was most intensively developed by Spinoza, to the effect that the reception given Spinoza until the beginning of the nineteenth century best typifies the problem we have to consider. Or, to put the point another way, the persistence of Spinoza into his revival during the early nineteenth century demonstrates the impossibility of refuting such "metaphysics" from the standpoint of self-respecting rationalism.

Spinoza—correctly, as far as he proceeded—took Descartes' theorems literally. If these theorems demonstrated the existence of two orders of actuality above ordinary particular consciousness, Spinoza reasoned, then the incompleteness and absence of perfection in particularity, the relative lack of perfection in the conscious individual, indicated that the order of reality in the universe was exactly contrary to the prejudices of ordinary opinion. Truth must be universal perfection, defined not as a goal being approached but as *the existing content of the process of perfection*. The particular accomplishment of Spinoza, which is sometimes—with the wrong implication—credited to his powers as a theologian, was to apply this conception to the nature of the individual's relationship to the universal. The kernel of Spinozan ethics, which clearly contains "preconsciousness" of invariant characteristics, is that the individual must locate the positive aspect of the progress of human development, and situate himself to further that, to *make himself necessary* to the furtherance of that progress. This aspect of Spinoza's work was not fully comprehended until Feuerbach's *Essence of Christianity* initiated the new revolution in human understanding known as Karl Marx.[6] Spinoza implicitly situated the question of scientific knowledge as primarily a matter of *anthropology*, proceeding from study of the empirical evidence of man's concern with his identity (religious belief), to examination of the guiding principles by which man attempts to serve that identity's perpetuation through the lower order of actuality called acts of reason. The anthropological standpoint, immanent in the Enlightenment generally, becomes more pronounced in Kant and Hegel successively, until anthropology is self-consciously posited as the "queen of the sciences" in Feuerbach's 1839–1843 writings.[7]

The problem of rationalism prior to Marx was that, although self-respecting rationalists could not throw out Descartes' theorems without abandoning reason itself, the constructs otherwise achieved, however real (rational), stood above and apparently outside all experience, seeming to define a realm of *metaphysics*. In this sense, customary usage of the term "idealism" contains an unconscionable element of semantic noise and romantic overtone, features perhaps enhanced over the past century or more by the popularity of vulgar atheism and agnosticism, which ignores *the seriousness of religious belief*. A better term, which we shall employ in the remainder of this text, is *realism:* whatever reason compels us to adduce from empirical knowledge is real, even if those judgments do not immediately find material actualization from the standpoint of ordinary Understanding. Idealism, as in the cases of Kant and Hegel in particular, is a meaningless term unless both its denotations and connotations are restricted to just that. Marx employs the term "idealism" in the first of his "Theses On Feuerbach" to mean just that and nothing else; if one understands the term otherwise, one makes a total hash of everything else in Marx's work. If, as we shall discover, Marx rejects such realism, it is because he locates the basis for determining the reality empirically, practically, of any construct reached through dialectics—and, of course, for sifting out from such constructs those realisms which *by virtue of having no practical realization* are demonstrably paralogical. Thus Marx eliminates metaphysics and in that sense, together with Feuerbach's preliminary contributions toward the same end, brings philosophy as such to a conclusion.

The principal flaw in metaphysics is not that it is impractical, but that it represents the failure of man to discover how to make such knowledge practicable. *As metaphysics* it becomes the terminus of the process of reasoning, attained by a last, magnificent conceptual leap over an uncomprehended void separating the process of aggregating knowledge from its implied completion. Metaphysics cannot guide the philosopher back to reality. He can only leap back, finding himself left with the memory of his acrobatics, but without the power to impart any tools from the universal into the empirical realm. Such souvenirs evaporate in the philosopher's hand the instant he arrives back on the terrain of reductionism. He has acquired only the knowledge that he has discovered something, that it thus exists, and that he must now view the old-socks reality of empirical work from a new standpoint. Beyond that, he is at a loss to bring the universal deliberately to bear on the domain of ordinary consciousness, and is greeted on his return as Columbus must have been by the most vulgar philistines after his first voyage: "You merely imagined you made the voyage and landed on the other side."

However, esteem for metaphysics did not diminish in enlightened circles because of such shortcomings. Exactly the contrary; modern contempt for metaphysics emerged among the educated strata after the universal had finally been demonstrated not only to exist but also to represent a more solid reality than that of reductionist consciousness. Educated people were content to accept the existence of the realm represented by metaphysics as long as it did not practically interfere with the course of everyday life. Once the first substantial evidence of that realm's practical existence began to be submitted to ordinary Understanding as evidence of a potential higher order of civilization, the rulers of native intellectual life lowered the customs and immigration barriers as forcefully as the Japanese expelled the Spaniards.

This phenomenon is exemplified by such hegemonic currents in contemporary philosophy as the writings of W. V. O. Quine and A. J. Ayer, widespread acceptance of the pathology known as positivism, and the pathetic attempt of indifferentists to represent the two interconnected theorems of Kurt Gödel[8] as consistent with the argument that there is no problem, of the sort first demonstrated by Georg Cantor,[9] in attributing the possibility of "completeness" to formal logic. Evidence that it is reductionism itself which is metaphysical (in the pejorative sense)—evidence which first appears to such modern philosophers and logicians in the form of skepticism about their own most prized obsessions—is reified by the pathological energy of obsession in such a way that a fundamental antinomy is reduced to the more tolerable status of a "slight ambiguity." The next step, especially in the most hysterical cases (positivism), is that this category of ambiguity is institutionalized as a term of the system, is interpreted as something positive, and thus itself supplies the necessary "completeness" and consistency for the entire construct.[10] Cutting through the pathetic involutions of such positivists and others, we can justly reduce their argument to the following essentials: incompleteness exists; let us make a category of incompleteness in our system; let us use symbol "w" for incompleteness; now, nothing can occur within our system to impair its completeness and consistency.

The most widely accepted form of this pathological phenomenon is that associated directly or indirectly with John Dewey's influence, perhaps because of his authority, and perhaps because of the air of authority with which he seemed to dispense with the most important problems by trivializing them. Formally acquainted with the literature of critical philosophy, and seized by despair over the First World War[11]—and the Bolshevik Revolution!—Dewey occupied himself with so banalizing the issues of universality that the shallow reader could console himself the whole matter had been objectively settled from the vantage-point of that Great Universal, the Abstract Name of Science! The highest point in Dewey's pseudo-philosophy is his attempt to deal with "reflection." He borrows from Kant just enough conceptual apparatus to account for the synthesis of the judgment of Understanding of the isolated particularity (!) and then abandons the entire issue, using his failure—refusal—to consider any of the real issues as evidence that they do not exist. With that concession to the smallest aspect of critical philosophy, he otherwise embraces the most pathetic moral and systematical indifferentism of empiricism: *pragmatism*.

The reader innocent of such corrupting influences may nonetheless find himself seized by intuitive objections much like those he would raise if he were the most obsessive follower of Quine, Ayer, Carnap, or Dewey. Indeed, since all philosophy has its "organic" basis in the psychological needs of the uneducated, we are on more solid ground here than in considering the pandering constructs of contemporary philosophers and logicians. Indeed, Dewey gives the whole show away by frankly conceding that his approach to philosophical reconstruction is guided by an overwhelming personal prejudice![12]

The difficulty to be addressed is one that we have referred to before, encountered in a new aspect.

Let us review the context of the difficulty. To the extent that the individual in a capitalist culture is alienated, his creative powers of cognition are largely suppressed. Denied unmediated social identity—society's valuation of him for his capacity for universal labor—his "inner" Self becomes an object. By the nature of its mediated relationship to social identity (its rights and privileges to exist), it takes on the character of the mediation, as something fixed, which stands as a particular object with respect to self-consciousness. Thus, to challenge the apparently fixed qualities of the psychological needs and impulses we sometimes like to call our "instinctual distinctions," our "character," to suggest that these aspects of the "inner" Self are *changeable*, is to experience a threat to dissolve one's identity, to completely alienate one's self into the process of change determined by the outer world. One no longer has a self-evident self.

Now, turning our attention to the origins of consciousness, the origins of the notion of self-identity, the very nature of that inquiry establishes as its premise the notion that the self is determined by social relationships. Thus, by implication, the self has been declared *changeable*, vulnerable to "dissolution," and, worse, not really us at all. Perhaps, such an inquiry by itself implies, if we went deeply enough into our "unconscious" self we would find not a self but a mere "it," a *Golem* or Frankenstein's monster created by society, and alterable by society—a mere thing without a "self-evident soul." Of course, that is precisely what capitalist man experiences when hypnosis or deeper analysis succeeds in probing deeply enough.

That this problem represents a pathological state of the "unconscious" self in capitalist man, rather than a natural "metapsychological phenomenon," is readily demonstrated by dialectics. *Descartes was essentially on the proper track, as was Spinoza.* The reality of the self can only be securely located in *the process of development* which is man's capacity to progressively alter his "unconscious" self. It is in the "capacity for perfection" within man that his real social identity is properly located.

Why is that terrifying? It should only be so if change meant transition from one brutalized state to another . . . and then, perhaps, still another. The self would then dissolve into the persona, incapable of unmediated social identity (love). "Turn myself into a better person?"—that could only mean to become another *brutalized* person.

Does this not give us an insight into the seriousness of religious belief? The necessity of religious belief for alienated man? "What of atheists?" one might ask. Ah, but do they not profess the most obsessive varieties of religious belief imaginable: empiricism, positivism, pragmatism? Are these not obsessive by every standard?

In the following sections, we consolidate the successive efforts of Kant, Hegel, Feuerbach, and Marx to arrive at a method for unravelling the mystery of the origins and content of consciousness. In this respect, we not only build into the elementary dialectic employed by Descartes the notion of self-development as a comprehensible notion, but locate the empirical demonstration of our judgments, identifying more fully the kinds of evidence to be considered. Undoubtedly, intuitive objections to this procedure will initially represent themselves as difficulties of comprehension—e.g., skepticism—rather than objections as such.

Yet the reader must not deceive himself that he is being confronted with judgments so altogether new and insufficiently tested that they need not be assimilated as knowledge. Although, generally speaking, few of the investigators responsible for the best empirical proof of our arguments have gone as far as we do, the relevant evidence and judgments on that evidence are long since virtual "common knowledge" in the specialties to which we refer. We thus emphasize that initial difficulties of comprehension arise less from the evidence itself than from the same source as does the obsessive refusal of behaviorists and others to acknowledge the overwhelming experimental evidence developed in their own professions.

The case of Freud need only be mentioned. Emile Durkheim—despite his disciples, and to some degree despite himself—covered related ground and investigated the nature of the evidence for such judgments in *The Elementary Forms of the Religious Life*. The work of Ehrenfels, Wertheimer, Köhler, and others has already been noted. In modern psychoanalytical practice, Lawrence S. Kubie is outstanding for his studies of the phenomena of creative mentation.[13] In general, Freud and Durkheim replicate to a certain extent the accomplishments of Hegel, Feuerbach, and Marx in discovering the principle of "psychophysical parallelism." The Gestalt psychologists not only discredited the entirety of behaviorist psychology and sociology with the most damning experimental evidence, but also, through Ehrenfels' recognition of the means for demonstrating invariance in this new field of inquiry, were able to design experimental hypotheses which represented unique demonstrations of the existence of *creative mentation*. Kubie, correcting Freud's principal experimental folly—failure to note creative mentation as such in the experimental evidence—locates repression in the abortion of the creative powers of cognition, thus begging the bridge between the accomplishments of Gestalt psychology and psychoanalysis. In locating such unique evidence for both psychophysical parallelism and the creative content of cognitive processes themselves, psychology and contiguous research has implicitly fully accounted for man's emergence as man beyond the mental capacities for progress through mentation of the higher apes! Thus, the entire body of human history and prehistory intersects that experimental evidence, the former supporting the conclusion offered by the latter.

HEGEL'S EMPIRICAL APPROACH

Hegel felicitously illustrates the kind of empirical studies necessary to the dialectical method by asking his readers to consider the varying notions which can be had of the term "grammar." In the first instance, he considers the notion of grammar for the student who knows only his native language; in the second instance, for the student with a command of foreign languages. We add the case of the "seasoned philologist."

The first student considers his grammar "natural," except to the extent that its rules contradict the argot of his everyday usage. It is "grammar in itself," self-evident. Let him now learn one or several "foreign languages," becoming the second case, and ask him to advance a notion of grammar subsuming German, English, French, Russian, Quechua, Chinese, and so on. Now, let us insist that he study the history of the development of several of these languages, some related (say the evolution of German and French since the time of Charlemagne) and some different (say Chinese). Let us insist that he present a notion of the process of development of grammars! (In that way we shall help him to avoid the trap of "linguistics," a field premised on a pre-Kantian fallacy.)

Reducing this and similar cases to a common abstract form, we obtain the following result. Relative to any empirical knowledge, "A," we define empirical knowledge from the same category of experience but not A as "not-A," including especially that aspect of not-A associated with the history of the phenomena leading up to A. The example of grammar applies. We now have a special, meaningful sense of the term "false" applicable to knowledge based only on A, such as the falseness of a notion of "grammar in general" adduced from a single language.

The assumption on which this construct depends is not speculative. It is merely the assumption that any two events experienced by the same person must be *coherent*, but not necessarily *consistent*. The problem, in fact, becomes interesting and meaningful only with respect to those aspects of the same universe which do not admit of a consistent interpretation in the formal, analytical sense. If A acts on a man and the man acts on not-A, then A and not-A are coherent, but not therefore necessarily in consistent relationship to one another.

A case from the debate between Einstein and the Copenhagen school is useful here, because it is so relevant and yet so elementary. (We state it in our own terms, acknowledging the priority of others.) Imagine two parts of a universe which previously had a common point, but which have moved so far apart that the constant velocity of light precludes connection between them in respect to the internal relations of each being simultaneously examined in abstract. There is no possible proof of consistency, but the two systems are necessarily coherent. This example represents an abstract portrait of a circumstance which we confront commonly enough in far less astronomical terms. Human speech, for example, is absolutely not consistent with mathematics, yet the two are coherent. The characteristic of living organisms is not consistent with that of inorganic objects, yet they must be coherent, subject not merely to the same "external" laws but to the same "internal" laws as well, due to their evolution from the same origins and common "point of departure."

The whole matter of A and not-A becomes trivial and uninteresting to serious thinkers if it is restricted to static totality: a "night in which all cows are black." That famous epithet from the preface to Hegel's *Phenomenology of Mind* suffices to assure us that he was absolutely unconcerned with the trivial reading of the point. A and not-A become significant respecting the problems of coherence only when those problems are situated within the context of development. To a limited extent, Hegel lends himself—especially in certain passages of his *Encyclopedia*—to misinterpretation *by careless readers*. This problem is not entirely accidental. Hegel's dualism and his restriction of the domain of fundamental self-development to the Logos[14] have this effect: one is compelled to make unduly abstract what were otherwise readily explicated in empirical terms from Marx's standpoint on the same notions. Thus we have among the writings of professed Marxian "dialectical-materialist" savants nonsense-explications of "positive–negative," "up–down," "inside–out," contributions to "Marxism" of dictionary-nominalism.[15] The same tendency is manifest, in a less patently silly form, in the attempt to separate Marx's method into the two specializations of "historical materialism" and a "dialectic" conceived as a "logic" *per se*.[16] Only under certain special circumstances could such terms as "positive" and "up" be dialectical "opposites" to such terms as "negative" and "down."

The best illustration of Hegel's intention on this point uses the point/ line paradox once again. Cantor's demonstration of the fallacy of "completeness"—the same distinction between "actual" and "potential" infinities previously made by Hegel—offers us a rigorous notion of the significance of A versus not-A. The category of "incompleteness" (or "ambiguity") in the induction of a line as the completion of its points, or the paradoxes of the "power set," stands in relation to the process of induction as not-A to A. Such problems, which do not admit of a consistent solution to the obvious relationship between the two categories, can only be solved by what Cantor terms a "metaphysic," which is better described as the cognitive process by which the line is directly completed (by *cognition*). The most notable such problem, from the standpoint of our principal concern here, is the contradiction between prosperity and crisis in capitalist accumulation; the simple induction of the principles of prosperity leads necessarily to a region of "incompleteness"—crisis—in which the existence of the phenomena of fictitious capitals corresponds to the discrepancy between the process of induction of point-enumeration and the completion of the line. The completion directly cognized from this contradiction is the invariant in the relationship between the "actual infinity" of expanded social reproduction and capitalist accumulation.

In general, as for Köhler's chimpanzees, real cognition (dialectical reasoning) begins at the point where reason fails to comprehend, by its nature, by "logic," or by previous *learning*, a task which is susceptible of solution (or conceptualization) from the standpoint of the circumstantial evidence of necessary coherence. Deliberative creative mentation, a better name for dialectics in this context, is the self-discipline of immediately extending A to the limits of its development such that a paradox of that form occurs. Forcing one's cognitive powers to work on such a problem, from insistent marshalling of similar efforts to the same end, is the method by which *deliberative* powers of creative mentation are *deliberately* acquired. One thus forces oneself to discover what constitutes the meaningful not-A with respect to A *as a process of development*.

In the case of grammar, cited at the outset of this section, the crisis demanding exercise of creative mentation (cognition) is the impossibility of extending the notion of grammar simply from one language to another. When this problem is situated in the development of a language, and that development is situated in the evolution of social relations (in which the use of language is determined), genuine cognition (dialectics) occurs.

The following examples of political problems within the socialist movement are undoubtedly of considerable use here.

Nationalism.　The conceptions associated with nationalism are false with respect to humanity. This is evident in the integral interconnection of the productive forces on which the material conditions of individual life within any one nation depend. If the cheapest cost of such imported resources is desired, the most effective development of the productive forces of all other nations is imperative in one's own self-interest. The conceptualization of A (nationalism) and not-A (internationalist self-interests) does not nullify one's concern for one's own national group, but rather directs one to mobilize the social association of one's nation in accordance with its internationalist self-interest. *Being-in-itself* is thus transformed into *Being-in-and-for-itself.*

The Lenin-Luxemburg controversy.　Until the First World War, Lenin and his supporters adhered to the Austrian-Menshevik "national stages" theory of development. This concept was based on the pathetic notion that each nation must pass—almost hermetically—through exactly the same metagenesis ("stages"). On this misguided premise, Lenin shared the belief that Russia, as a feudal or semifeudal nation, must pass through the "capitalist stage" of development (although he differed sharply with the majority of Mensheviks on how this "stage" was to be approached by an independent political labor movement). As a natural consequence of this mistaken outlook, Lenin approached the question of nationalities from the standpoint of nonoppressive relationships among *capitalist* states, joining Plekhanov in supporting the Polish nationalist faction of Pilsudski (during the pre-1905 period) against the faction of Rosa Luxemburg and Leo Jogiches. After 1905, Lenin modified his views on nationalism (after Pilsudski openly opted for the bonapartist, antisocialist standpoint which Luxemburg had dialectically imputed to his faction). Lenin reflected Luxemburg's influence in attacking the nationalism of the Jewish Bund but, still adhering to the Menshevik "national stages" theory, maintained his factional differences with Luxemburg from an only slightly modified standpoint.

Lenin justified this position by invoking the character of the Russian Empire as an oppressor of many nationalities, but used this correct and defensible aspect of his views (on which he and Luxemburg were in agreement, in any case) as a specious, sleight-of-hand defense of his "national stages" view on the national question generally.

Even after Lenin's abandonment of the "national stages" view, reflected in his recognition of international capitalist development of the Russian capitalists in the "Aesopian" *Imperialism,* and explicit in his 1917 "April Theses," he retained his old outlook on the "national question." Despite his pathetic insistence that he had been correct and Luxemburg wrong on the "national question,"[17] actual Bolshevik policy on "national-ities" was a mish-mash of flip-flops. Not too much should be made of such flip-flops in and of themselves, since all Bolshevik decisions during that period were, like the Brest-Litovsk treaty, made under extraordinary pres-sures and frequently undertaken as concessions contrary to Bolshevik policy. The "norm" was sacrificed neither on principle nor simply as a matter of expediency, in the pejorative sense of that term. The very existence of the Soviet state usually depended upon such cruel concessions. The significant error which can be adduced from that tangle of circum-stances is the failure of Lenin and others to apply class principles respect-ing nations. The notion that the majority of a nation has a right to decide on "independence" demonstrates an astonishing ignorance of class principles; what the working class and its allies decide in such matters is absolutely different from what the "majority of the nationality" decides. This is to ignore, of course, the not-trivial issue of how a revolutionary approaches the solution to such contradictions between the will of the working class and that of a nonworking class majority. In sum, the miser-able quality of Lenin's understanding of *Capital* is paralleled by his poor comprehension of the dialectical method—not noncomprehension but poor comprehension, manifest also in his unfortunate, reductionism-permeated *Empirio-Criticism* and even his *Philosophical Notebooks*.[18]

Trade-Unionism. The central problem the labor movement poses for so-cialist work is the regression of the organized labor movement from the mass-strike qualities of its initial formation (and major subsequent ad-vances) to a "pure-and-simple trade-union movement." Except for the influence in the 1920s of the centrist Foster-Cannon faction of the CPUSA, which subordinated Communist activity to the AFL organization, this was the principal issue between the AFL and right-wing Socialist Party leader-ship on the one hand, and the left wing of the labor movement and SP on the other, through the middle 1930s. The particular complaint of the "Wob-blies," and of the left wing before and after them, has been that the craft unions and later industrial unions forsook the unemployed and unorgan-ized working people in favor of a "private deal" with the employers.

This issue came to the fore in the German labor movement in the factional struggle of Rosa Luxemburg against the centrist "proletarian kernel" of August Bebel and Friedrich Ebert and their apologist, Karl Kautsky. Luxemburg correctly insisted that the working class, including the organized workers, becomes class-conscious only under those circum-stances when the organized workers are in common formation with the un-employed, unorganized, and specially oppressed wage-laborers. She used the experience of the Russian and Polish 1905 revolutions—and her analysis of the developments preceding them—to argue for a mass-strike strategy for the German Social Democracy and Second International.

Luxemburg's argument, although original in form, was not original. Marx's attack on Proudhon in *The Misery of Philosophy*, his emphasis on the commonality of the organized class struggle in the *Communist Manifesto*, and his entire exposition of class consciousness and forms of class struggle from *The German Ideology* through Volume III of *Capital*, make exactly that same point: the class-in-itself (Being-in-itself) must be transformed into a class-for-itself (Being-in-and-for-itself). The importance of this point can be readily demonstrated from the standpoint of the most elementary features of Marx's economics. The development of productive forces occurs through the realization of the surplus product created by the production of employed labor as wage-commodities and means of production for the productive employment of unemployed labor. An infinity of trade-union struggles, or any struggles confined to employed labor and its immediate employers, leads not one inch toward class consciousness of the historic task of socialist expanded reproduction, but in *exactly the opposite direction: the standpoint of the struggle between employed labor and its immediate employers is entirely confined to the viewpoint of simple reproduction.* A/not-A: only when employed labor is compelled to recognize its common class interest with unemployed labor does there occur the unique cognition of that common class interest generally: expanded reproduction. By realizing its surplus product as the means of productive employment of unemployed labor, employed labor realizes in the only way possible the general development of productive forces on which its advanced material standard of consumption and greater leisure absolutely depends!

Consequently, the left wing and Luxemburg, insofar as they addressed this specific criticism to "trade-union" parochialism, were absolutely correct. Trade-unionism, to the extent that it opposes subordinating trade-union interests to common class interests, is politically reactionary and represents the next-to-chief counterrevolutionary expression of capitalist ideology in the working class itself. The chief counterrevolutionary tendency, ironically, is that which proposes to *break* trade-union organization in the interests of the lumpen and unemployed (as scabs)! The objective of Luxemburg's strategy was by no means to break the trade-union organizations, but to transform them from Being-in-itself to Being-in-and-for-itself: that is, to transform the consciousness and policies of the trade-union organizations so as to realize their potential as the strongest and most advanced (culturally and otherwise) section of the class, to transform them into the axis around which the entire class could be, uniquely, assembled as a unified force.

The "Black Nationalist" Issue. The positive significance of "black nationalism" during the very late 1950s and early 1960s is illustrated by the case of Malcolm X. The degradation of black men as a result of their general inability to provide for families according to the prevailing working-class standard of material culture in the United States—the major feature of an Uncle Tom "chains of illusion" psychology—prevented them from achieving the self-respect necessary to mobilize a sustained struggle for improvement of their conditions. It was essential that black men improvise some means to develop sufficient self-respect, as a precondition to accomplishing anything else. Malcolm X exemplified the positive thrust of this development in his own personal evolution; by achieving self-respect as a leader, he transcended the very black nationalism under whose auspices he had accomplished this development. Having attained the self-respect necessary to deal with white working people and others as equals (being more than the equal of most), he no longer needed black nationalism *in its hermetic sense.*[19]

However, if one extrapolates hermetic black nationalism beyond the point of self-development typified by Malcolm X in the last months of his life, it becomes increasingly regressive and reactionary. The self-isolation of a black nationalist movement leads it either to impotence, as a result of its inability to match its tactical resources to its enlarged aspirations, or to the acquisition of a material basis for existence as a scab-force under the direction of employers and government. It becomes something in the image of Immamu Baraka's NewArk organization, or collapses of its own manifest impotence.

Thus black nationalism must, as Malcolm X's development portended, become the lever of the unorganized, unemployed, and specially oppressed to pry the organized labor movement into mass-strike alliances; otherwise it either turns reactionary (lumpen, tending to fascist) or collapses of impotence.

The "Woman Question." The most intriguing of all the "radical" issues that have recently emerged in the United States and elsewhere is the feminist ferment, because the questions involved go most directly to the very nature of human existence. In its most positive features so far, the recent ferment is typified by the work of the National Organization of Women (NOW), which has at its best limited itself to a variety of *obvious reforms.* Ironically but not accidentally, reactionary developments have all arisen from the most "radical feminist" positions.

The radical feminist upsurge developed in 1969, in the aggravated ebb of the student upsurge of 1968. The immediate impetus for the formation of most such groups was ostensibly the wretched treatment of young women within the principal anarchist groups of the New Left: women's efforts to play active intellectual and political roles were suppressed by young male "honchos"; women in the anarchist groups were used as a sexual "free lunch counter," most notoriously but by no means exclusively by young honchos on tour, and usually in the name of "sexual liberation." The woman who expressed doubts about the quality of "liberation" she was experiencing was "put down" with knowing lectures on her "bourgeois hangups." A hideous spectacle! Without question there was more than just cause for a more widespread outpouring of revulsion among women than occurred.

However, the women who "spun off" from the young anarchist

groups to form feminist cults carried with them every other imaginable defect of those groups, and introduced innovations of their own implicitly more hideous than the abuses to which they were ostensibly responding.

The form in which the most radical feminist cults developed was a replication of the anarchist pluralism already rife among the anarchist New Left groups most of the women had broken away from: a virtual nation of women, or women's national liberation movement. Though not usually described in such terms, this was both its thrust and the aspect of the phenomenon which drew the most energetic support from the anarchist men *of the very groups which had driven these women to such ends.* In content, this movement was justified by arguments which either verged upon or explicitly insisted that women represented a suprahistoric *class!*

Much of the content of radical feminism was vicious—not toward men, as some men argued, but toward women. In keeping with its commitment to "cultural relativism" regarding "women's natural culture," radical feminism reified as a virtue the most reprehensible features of the degradation of women within the petit-bourgeois households of our urban centers. Every pathological trait associated with the objectification and relative dehumanization of such women was treated as a virtue in the setting of "consciousness-raising sessions" and incorporated into a war-cry.

The characteristic expression of the relative oppression of women by capitalist relations is their *banalization,* a phenomenon often correlated with the notion that intellectuality is a male quality, and that women are "more practical, more feeling." This phenomenon differs *in tendency* among working-class and petit-bourgeois women. The working-class woman, though she generally endures greater material pressures, has the compensation of being *needed.* The petit-bourgeois woman, provided she makes a successful marriage according to the standard of the conventional self-image inculcated chiefly by her most immediate oppressor, *her mother,* is destined to be as useless as possible apart from child-bearing and -rearing (which she is presumed to supervise, availing herself of pediatricians, maids, nursery schools, and whatever other resources money can buy). The honeymoon and child-rearing past, she is sent into constant motion seeking a purpose in life; and usually finds no purpose but to continue her migrations in search of the purpose. If this takes her from bed to extra-marital bed, hobby to hobby, fad to fad, it's all part of the game. Not accidentally, the radical feminist movement, through "consciousness-raising" managed to raise little more than the most undesirable petit-bourgeois female norms in their most pitiful slight transmogrification.

To the extent that women are debased into appendages of the petit-bourgeois male's need for unmediated social identity, they best fulfill that role *for him* by being living caricatures of his philistinism and banalization. In general appearance and dress, they represent an aspect of his persona, to be prized and regarded by him as a "reasonable bargain." It is permissible that they glitter slightly as "conversationalists," provided they exhibit no serious mental exertion; and they may even have professional college degrees, provided they have in the process acquired nothing more insidious than a bit of learning: status, but no substance. If a woman is guilty of creative mentation, the typical male is terrified by the prospect of an unmediated relationship to her. A woman who has a real intellectual life should defy categorization as a potential sexual object in the eyes of those around her. A facade of knowledge, in the sense of learning, is permissible, and in some circles even considered desirable, but actual *human* qualities in women force men to confront their own lack of humanity at the most vulnerable point of their brutalized "inner" selves, and pose as deadly a threat to other women. As evidence of the latter, witness only the intensified sadomasochistic relationships endemic—or perhaps epidemic— among women in professions.

If one attempts to evade this characterization of radical feminism by disputing each point, the whole argument is readily short-circuited by asking oneself what radical feminist groups are concerned with: women's issues! The liberation of women can occur only to the extent that women fight on the model of Rosa Luxemburg—not necessarily replicating Luxemburg's difficult personal life, but asserting as she did their right to be intellectual leaders, to exert their potential for creative leadership outside the kitchen, parlor, and bedroom. By confining its struggle to the predefined limits of women's banalization, "radical feminism" has been rendered transparent to anyone with eyes to see.[20]

THREE–PLUS MODELS OF CONSCIOUSNESS

Figures 1a, 1b, and 1c illustrate the three general ways in which consciousness and knowledge are defined by various schools. We have simplified the diversity of views on these subjects, but not in any essential features; in the final analysis, all schools belong to one of these three types. A partial exception relative to the case represented by 1c, shall be discussed in due course.

Figure 1a represents the most naive conception of consciousness as sense-perception of an object. It is assumed that the construct in the individual's consciousness is a faithful representation of the sensed object.

How? Is the sense-perception *the object*? According to this model, the individual is a Frankenstein manufactured by some supercomputer firm. In the factory where he was prepared for birth, his memory banks received a complete set of images corresponding to all possible objects in the external world. Each image so filed was given a storage number. Meanwhile, technicians were hustling throughout the universe, attaching clever little transponders to all objects. When the individual's parturition in the assembly-line and finishing rooms is completed, he is born. He journeys out into the world, radiating impulses and exciting the transponders wherever he passes. He receives the prepared coded impulses, each cor-

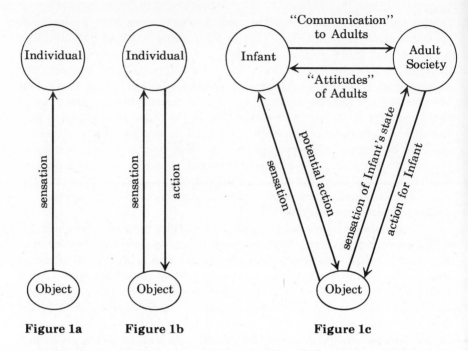

Figure 1a **Figure 1b** **Figure 1c**

responding to a datum in his storage banks. His memory is "excited"; on his cathode-ray display appears the appropriate image from storage.

Even without the computer technology that allows us to summarize the implications of the model so simply, philosophers saw through the obvious fallacies of model 1a and developed model 1b, which has certain Kantian components and has recently been rediscovered by specialists in "information theory."

The theorist of model 1b essentially discards the notion that the individual gains knowledge of objects from sense-perception as such. He receives sense-perceptions or, to put it more rigorously, the stimuli which form part of the essential basis for sense-perceptions. However, mental images do not arise directly from this source. The individual is simultaneously acting on the world around him such that an attempt to correlate the differences in his various sense-stimuli with the differences of his various actions upon the world creates the basis for a pattern—a pattern not of the external world, but of the correlation of differences for stimuli and action respectively. To accomplish such a correlation, the individual requires only *a priori* aesthetic and logical propensities, which give him self-programming capacities. The result, the image of reality, is a construct based on interpretation of the correlated differences, a construct achieved through the *a priori* criteria of aesthetic and logical powers.

This model appears quite satisfactory as long as one does not introduce anything corresponding to free will into it. As long as it remains a "learning device," a mere supercomputer of given specifications, nothing in its functioning can upset the reductionist notion of the universe. However, once we attribute to the device any creative powers, such that its actions are not determined by its perceptions, its cognition produces consequent innovations in the state of the universe which have the most devastating implications for ordinary reductionist conceptions.

If the individual is capable of cognition respecting his actions, the coherence of the universe which includes him is not subject to comprehensive interpretation by formal laws. Since the formal laws to which we refer as types are precisely the limits of his understanding, it follows that his knowledge of the universe and of events around him is appropriate but false. Outside him exist "things in themselves." Since they are really existent, and therefore subject to comprehensive laws beyond his Understanding, they are intrinsically unknowable to him. Yet since his actions do permit him to exist, his Understanding, however imperfect, is an appropriate knowledge of reality.

Somewhere in that condition of perfection represented by universality, time and space are resolved as distinctions, and all ultimate consequences are in immediate relationship to their causes. In this happy condition of "blah," Free Will becomes lawful and stands in immediate relationship to fundamental, comprehensive laws. Yet, since infinity is unknowable to individual man, such perfection is beyond his mind's reach. ("For this condition, count ten loops, signal error-condition 'paralogical,' and move to subroutine 21B, 'Dialectic of Practical Reason.' ")

But that which affects the universal must affect the immediate "thing in itself"; therefore, if the Understanding is to remain appropriate to the altered immediate laws of the universe thus effected, it must reflect this alteration. If the change is adverse, reality must act against the impulse of Free Will which caused this; the unsatisfactory impulses of the individual will must be *negated*. The individual, by setting the part of his will which is not so negated in opposition to the part that is (*negation of the negation*), thus makes positive in his will that which approaches agreement with what is good for the universe: "the categorical imperative."

"But," warns Hegel, "there are two fundamental errors here!" Your "truth" is not truth. You have simply made the exigencies of external authority the bonds of internal conviction; your state of perfection, your "bad infinity" is a mere chimera. To save the ontological assumption of the "thing in itself," the pathetic obsession of the Enlightenment, you have created a false positive and a "bad infinity." You have only put the ancient dialectic on a rigorous basis, without carrying out the implications of your own achievement.

You have failed, warns Hegel, to comprehend Spinoza, and your glib, credulous toleration of slanders against him has taken its revenge upon you. Granted, it is silly to regard Spinoza's *substance* as *simple* extended being, but you had only to look more closely at the germ of the notion of *development* in his *ethics*, and to recognize the heritage of Heraclitus, to have seen the solution to all your antinomies. Infinity is not located at the extremes of space and time; the concepts of infinite space and time, which you admit must be abandoned to arrive at true knowledge of actuality, are chimeras. Infinity, *actual* infinity, is *now;* it is, as Spinoza attempts to inform you, *progress.* Progress is a *self-subsisting positive* which must be directly comprehended as truth—not your pathetic "chains of illusion" categorical imperative!

In short, the universe which corresponds to model 1b does not exist. Let us move to model 1c.

The third case, 1c, is a general illustration of "psychophysical parallelism," and subsumes variously Feuerbach's, Freud's, and Marx's notions of consciousness (using the term *conscious* to subsume both conscious and unconscious states of knowledge).

The individual is at our first encounter with him a newborn infant. He has certain potentials for developing powers of cognition, but has neither judgment, strictly speaking, nor the perceptual powers which represent the simplest sort of judgment from the standpoint of ordinary opinion. Everything which will make him human we must give to him after his birth.

His potential humanity, at this point, exists for him in the "adult society" which acts for him on the "outer world." How does it act? It is burdened with attitudes which constitute for the infant certain rights and privileges of which he has no knowledge. In the first moments of life, he begins to experience those features of his social identity which come into existence outside him. If we likened him to the creature in model 1b, we would conclude that since he is not yet able to act deliberately on the outside world, he knows the world practically through both unjudged stimuli and the actions of the adult world upon him, actions which represent as a pattern his rights and privileges as an infant. He does not act on the outside world, as he begins from those first minutes and hours to give deliberate form to his actions. He acts deliberately *upon the adult world,* and it responds to his actions according to its notion of his rights and privileges. What the outer world does for him is done *by the adult world, his social relationships.* He does not know objects as objects, but as the activities of the adult world on his behalf, the embodiments of his rights and privileges. As he becomes increasingly deliberate, his deliberations thus take shape as actions upon the adult world, and upon his emergent perception of his rights and privileges. As he develops in this way, his knowledge of the external world is his knowledge of those rights and privileges as a Gestalt, as the idealized image of himself, as the embodiment of such rights and such *socialized powers.* His image of himself is a mirror-image of the rights the outer world gives to him and his powers over it, his *socialized powers.* Thus objects, as he comes to know them, exist for him not as objects qua objects, but as socialized objects, as objectifications of his socialized powers.

He knows himself as an object of his deliberations because he is the object of that on which he acts, society. His self-consciousness is thus not as self directly conscious of self, but as self-consciousness of that seen by others. What he sees in himself is what they see in him—not their conscious image of him, but that which is implicit in the socialized powers he is able to exert upon them.

There we have the essence of Feuerbach's notion. Since it is necessarily the powers of the entire society which are focused immediately in the powers the infant commands from the adults around him, he acquires species-consciousness as self-consciousness.[21]

Taking into account those qualifications we have already noted, we are immediately confronted with the general question of the role of biological development in determining the individual's behavior. The reader's immediate impression might be that we regard Freud as having overemphasized physiology, in too much emphasis on existent mental categories as rooted in the evolution of the cortex, and the like. Though this is in a certain descriptive sense true, it ignores the essential point at issue in the relationship between mentation and physiology.

The crucial issues can be attacked in the following way.

First, it is a massive assumption, the wildest conjecture, to assume that with the addition of new physiological functions previously existing functions merely acquire a modified function. It is similarly fallacious to assume that traumatically induced dysfunction of a region of the brain demonstrates that certain cognitive and similar categories of mental behavior lost as a result of that traumatization are therefore "seated" in what has been surgically damaged. It would be necessary to conclude, rather, that the evolution of new physiological powers transforms the characteristic functioning of the brain as a whole, creates a new invariant of mental functioning, such that every organ is reified as a mere phase in the functioning of the whole as an entirety, i.e., that all functions associated with mentation are functions of the entire physiological apparatus—at least in the sense that cognitive functions cannot be regarded as transactions among semiautonomous subfunctions of the physiology.

On what premise can such statements be offered? *On the premise that any judgment shown to depend upon reductionist assumptions is therefore pathological and false.* For reductionist characterizations of the relationship of brain to mentation to apply, it would be necessary that the brain belong to a different universe, characterized by different laws, than that in which we exist, and that it, moreover, have no effect upon our universe. There is no backdoor to reality through which reductionist assumptions can be competently ushered into our universe. *Nor are such matters subject to experimental verification.* Any hypothesis whose assumptions contradict the fundamental laws of our universe—such as astrology—is absolutely disproven without conducting a single experiment. Once we have demonstrated reductionist assumptions to be false in a single dimension of human knowledge, they have been sufficiently proven false in every dimension of that same universe. As Freud argued, if I take four persons down to the bank of the Thames, and hold their heads under water until they drown, it is not necessary to repeat that experiment in every river of the world.[22]

There remain, of course, large and important areas in which it would be speculative for us to propose to define the physiological correlatives of mentation. We cannot conjecture the results of such empirical investigations into being. However, by the nature of the problem, we know in what direction results will not be obtained, and we have preliminary indications of the area in which experimental inquiry would have to begin. This is as much as can be posited with respect to the physiology of mentation. We outline our views on this subject solely to give the reader a sense of the actual, necessary connection between Feuerbach's (and Marx's) views on psychophysical parallelism and experimental knowledge yet to be gained.

The demonstration of rudimentary powers of cognition in higher apes, against a background of studies of perception in other beasts, gives us a point of reference from which to identify questions to be subjected to experimental inquiry. The higher ape has powers of creative mentation. We need not consider dogs or other beasts; it is sufficient to know that our closest relatives, the higher apes, have such powers, keeping in mind that man evolved into man while apes did not *as a species* transcend their genetically acquired range of mentation, and that "culture" in apes is apparently limited to variations within generations, or at least that the cumulative advance in behavior from generation to generation is negligible by comparison with human history. The necessary experimental hypotheses must begin with the cognitive powers of the higher ape, and determine what distinctions are required of the hominid species to begin the process of evolution which produced human *history*, in the sense of a world-line of evolutionary social development.

The clue to the desired hypotheses is provided by human social evolution as a whole. The phylogenesis of societies, respecting the ranges of culture so determined, corresponds to the genetic evolution of higher orders of species from lower forms of life. This immediately suggests a hypothesis which, if not correct in itself, sufficiently satisfies certain necessary conditions to provide access to the general approach required: that the significance of creative mentation *as universal labor* is equivalent to genetic variations of a deliberative form, and thus that what we regard as intelligence must be akin to a general genetic alteration of the physiology of mentation after birth. This must be the case because the quality of intelligence differs from society to society despite the absence of a genetic variation and because individuals of different genetic hominid stocks are susceptible of equal intelligence. If it were established that cognition is a reification of genetic determination of tissue growth, then the answer to the hypothesis would lie in exactly that direction without need to explore other approaches.

If this were the case, the findings would readily correspond to strong evidence that memory is not located in storage of specific images, but rather each experience is recorded as a "genetic" alteration of the physiological processes of mentation with the effect of altering a Gestalt, such that these processes can reproduce such organs (e.g., images) in the same way that genetic determination produces the elaboration of organs. It would also locate creative mentation as a reification of genetic "evolution," which would be a happy discovery since individual creative judgments do alter mentation as a whole.

We leave further exploration of this subject, to avoid more speculation than is useful to illustrate the necessary direction of future investigations. The point to be emphasized here is that our knowledge of human development and behavior circumscribes the notion of the physiology of mentation, by excluding large areas of possibilities which could not possibly concur with the invariant features of the process whose physiological basis was being explored. Within such bounds, the rest is left to experimental investigation; it would be speculative, indeed, to encroach further upon that domain.

Nonetheless, from another vantage-point, certain further remarks can be made on the problem of physiological appropriateness. The faculties of mentation which our species possesses evolved from those of hominid ancestor-types whose life must have been similar to that of higher apes and baboons. The higher apes and baboons, in particular, are characterized by protosocial organization, and species-behavior appropriate to that form of organization has been developed. If the evolution of mentation's physiological basis were directed from such a state toward appropriateness to increasing socialization, defined in terms of the simplest sort of "tool culture," one would expect to find evidence of a succession of prehuman hominid species and varieties evolving in the direction of man. The point of such considerations here is that the newborn infant's physiological apparatus need not include any "instincts," in either the mechanistic or Freudian sense of the term. It is only necessary that his physiological potential be sufficiently evolved to a state of appropriateness for rapid development through extrauterine gestation, and probably that any "drives" he may possess at birth be rapidly reified by extrauterine gestation.

Where physiological and social determination overlap and diverge is a matter of indifference to us, insofar as the notion of psychophysical parallelism is our immediate concern. Whatever physiological basis for human behavior is inherent in the individual is sufficiently subsumed by extrauterine gestation. The phenomenon of self-consciousness and the social content of what we regard as "unconscious" traits are sufficient and conclusive evidence of the point. The invariant characteristic of human existence is uniquely consistent with the approximation provided by Feuerbach, once that notion of self-subsisting positive is situated within the notion of evolutionary social development given by Marx.

It is necessary merely to transcend the metaphysical dualism of reductionism to recognize that social and mental phenomena are in themselves material phenomena of the most primary sort. The anguished search for a "material basis" for consciousness is mere pathology on the part of the searcher if he means by that we must wait upon experimental verification of hypotheses about physiology or microphysics per se before we can understand the objective basis of mentation. We already know, from the most massive conceivable accumulation of empirical evidence—human history—what mentation is. Now that we have identified the essence of human history, its invariant, and recognized that socialized practice seen from that vantage-point comprehends every law of the universe knowable to man at the point along the world-line, the scientific basis for our judgment of mentation is of a qualitatively higher order than any which could be provided by a particular field of inquiry. Indeed, the authority of physiology and microphysics as science depends on the authority we are able to award it from that standpoint. The skeptic, like most skeptics respecting scientific knowledge, only fancies to himself that he recognizes weaknesses in our exposition; in fact, he acts on the obsessive, fallacious assumptions of his own pathetic ideology. To adopt such skepticism is to fall into the pitiable state of the angle trisector, the unhappy fellow bent under a load of eighteenth-century illusions, forever seeking a supermicroscope of magical resolving powers, that he might at last encounter those hard little balls of simple matter which are the ultimate "elementary particles" of his materialism.

Even those victims of the proverbial "little learning" who despise simple materialism will insist that there must be something amiss in our specifications. Typically, they impose the support of matriarchy on the great Gauss, and seem to overlook that that fellow made a few most hubristic anatomical alterations in his "Queen of the Sciences." It is commonly assumed that progress in science ought to develop in the manner in which pure mathematicians develop rigorous conceptions about the simplest relationships among the simplest conceivable abstract existences. Without doubt, it is occasionally necessary to clean house, to sort out the proliferation of books, notes, correspondence, sketches, and odd bits of mislaid tableware, pipes, and odd half-used packs of book matches which have drifted into the general accumulation. Some of the familiar homeliness is lost, in compensation for which one is able to work more efficiently—but scientific progress of a fundamental sort has never been brought about by spring cleaning. (Rather, some drastic cases of spring cleaning have been prompted, after the fact, by fundamental discoveries.)

Felix Klein makes the relevant point, in various forms and locations, that the great advances of nineteenth-century mathematical science, in particular, did not *originate* in pure mathematics, but in the gross huffing and puffing of the steam engine. The emergence of the need for thermodynamics—starting with steam, resurrecting the issue of light, and accelerated by the issues of magnetism and electrical phenomena—confronted mathematics with the most devastating problems involving discreteness and continuity, and compelled it to develop a new conception of function if it was to be of much practical account in the real world. This intrusion from the domain of general socialized practice had two results according to Klein. In one direction, the effort to isolate the internal antinomies of mathematics was brought to fruition by the work of Riemann, Cantor, and Klein himself, such that prevailing notions of geometry and number were absolutely revolutionized. Within a half-century, the practical outcome of this accomplishment was manifest in the work of Maxwell, Planck, and Einstein—the latter's most notable accomplishments being a direct reflection of Riemann's work. This phenomenon exemplifies the second development Klein noted: the proliferation of science's specific powers for general socialized practice.

What then is fundamental to scientific knowledge? Or, in other words, on what original premises are scientific revolutions founded, and to what authority does science appeal for vindication of its reply to such challenges? What but the confrontation of crisis in scientific comprehension of socialized practice? *Science is an abstraction of socialized practice*. It is socialized practice as a universal, universalizing basis which is the fundamental, the actually "pure" basis of real scientific progress.

(In contemporary academic life, the overwhelming mass of evidence to this effect is brushed aside by a cute sleight-of-hand trick. Wherever these fundamental epistemological issues are raised, the reductionist professional makes the specious debater's point of classifying such criticisms as "intuitionism." The tactic is understandable: faced with the prospect of climbing into the ring with Muhammed Ali, almost anyone would rather pick a fight with the ten-year-old kid down the block.)

In the matter under consideration here science in general is confronted not merely with another ordinary crisis in socialized practice, nor even with a challenge like that posed by the emergence of thermodynamics. In locating the world-line for human existence from Marx's discoveries, we have given socialized practice, and knowledge itself, an entirely new basis, implicitly overturning all previous assumptions in every field of knowledge. This itself represents the highest standpoint for scientific knowledge at this point on that world-line. The question is not whether our judgments find approval within ordinary reductionist scientific practice, but how we may most efficiently bring the development of those branches of knowledge up to the level of this fundamental breakthrough in the conception of socialized practice.

THE CONTENTS OF CONSCIOUSNESS

The first question we must confront respecting the contents of consciousness is that of determining the respective valuations to be assigned to each feature. We are obviously confronted with two valuations: a fundamental, world-line, valuation of the contribution of the individual's existence to movement of the point along that world-line—the fundamental valuation; and the immediate valuation of him reflected in the Gestalt of rights and privileges awarded him by his immediate society. Each must be interpreted as Being-in-and-for-itself, but twofoldly. We must determine the individual's value to humanity and also his contradictory value for his society's notion of itself.

Furthermore, the individual's self-consciousness, as a generalized, internalized Gestalt—in other words, his social identity—functions as a universal with respect to his particular acts and states of consciousness (and unconsciousness). We have three kinds of invariance, then, to consider: *the world-line, society's notion of itself,* and *the individual's internalized notion of himself.* Thus, there exists a threefold contradictory valuation of each act and each state of conscious (and unconscious) Being-in-itself.

How does one sort out this mess of contradictions?

Immediately, in general, a society's notion of itself operates on both the individual's particular states of consciousness and his generalized notion of himself in such a way that particular acts (transactions between the individual and society) mediate the relationship between his notion of himself (as a conditional universal) and the society's notion of itself. Immediately, this relationship seems identical to a circumstance Kant describes in his *Critique of Practical Reason.* Society seems to define an individual's identity—the positive value it places upon him—by negating those of his acts which are motivated by his own self-conception. Society implicitly negates corresponding tendencies of his generalized notion of himself. Because his persona as *a person for society* (a precondition to possession of the power to command socialized forces) is fundamental to his notion of social identity, what society does not prohibit is a positive act for society. The individual is, apart from prohibited tendencies, a being for society, one of its powers. What results is *negation of the negation.*

However, *for society* he must exist. He is an instrument of his society, and must protect it from the loss of him as one of its powers. Thus, his socialized tendencies for individual acts must constantly conflict with society—*the same society which determined these tendencies!*

This phenomenon becomes clearer when we examine capitalist society, in which it occurs. The dominant characteristic of capitalist society is *heteronomy.* On the one hand, the achievement of capitalism is universalization of production of the material means of human existence. Yet the very notion of capital, as subject to a large degree of voluntary determination by the owners of particular capitals, fragments the process on which human existence depends, alienating from society its power to exist. Similarly with the individual as wage-labor within capitalist society: his usefulness to society is generalized, but his notion of usefulness has been particularized, to make him a suitable subject for particular capital, he must be for heteronomic capital. He must not commit the crime of hubris, equating himself with universal labor, and deliberately determining his acts for society from the standpoint of what is universally required of him by his species.

Thus the individual's universalizing tendencies must be made *uncon-*

scious, and released for specific tasks only on a leash. The fundamental invariant, the world-line, must be suppressed. But his existence and society's depend upon those suppressed powers; even ordinary perception depends upon them—he could not serve as productive wage-labor without some cognitive powers, which are rooted in the suppressed functions. Thus, they cannot be destroyed, only suppressed. They exist, but are generally only unconscious. Such powers are not individual but socially determined powers; cognitive capacities are acquired during extrauterine gestation. If a society's social organization is to correspond to the organization of its productive forces, its universalizing technology, the aspect of the individual which is generally unconscious under capitalism *must be* conscious. The "metapsychology" ostensibly peculiar to the individual is in fact a peculiarity of capitalist society. The "negation of the negation" is a peculiarity of capitalist society!

Let us contrast socialist society. Is the individual in a socialist society in direct relationship to the world-line? First, we must briefly define socialist society.

A society in which the means of production are nationalized, without capital, and only workers (and selected allies) have the franchise, is not socialist but, at best, what Marx terms a "dictatorship of the proletariat." That is, the working class as a politically organized force has precisely preempted the position formerly occupied by the capitalist class; the term means nothing more or less. It is no more a "dictatorship" than France, the United States, and Britain in their most democratic phases have been dictatorships of the capitalist class. However, a "dictatorship of the proletariat" is not a socialist society.

A socialist society is, at least in Marx's and the author's vocabularies, what Marx signified in his earlier writings by the term "Communism." (The notion that there is a distinction between "socialist" and "communist" society is utter nonsense, a distinction between empty constructs.) That is, a socialist society is one in which universal and cooperative labor are one and the same. By contrast, a mere "dictatorship of the proletariat" may be analogous to the usual form of dictatorship of the capitalist class. In the latter, capitalists collectively do not formulate policy, and the like; instead, they collectively support various political and related institutions which function in their presumed collective interests. For example, a bonapartist dictatorship or fascist regime made up of petit-bourgeois and lumpen scalawags is a form of dictatorship of the capitalist class, although it may be that not a single capitalist participates directly in the regime or exerts direct control over the party in power. A surrogate—a group drawn from within the capitalist class or wholly or partially outside it—may conduct the dictatorship in the interests of a set of principles (such as capitalized debt) which serve to preserve the hegemony of capitalist property forms in accumulation. A similar phenomenon has invariably occurred in dictatorships of the proletariat: a substitute for the class as a whole formulates and administers the society in the name of the class, and actually in the relative interests of the working class vis-à-vis capitalist and feudal classes.

In a socialist or communist society—a society in which the collective class formulates accumulation policies (which we shall treat later)—the individual worker is in an apparently mediated relationship to the world-line mediated by the collective institutions of which he is a part. The distinction is not this mediated relationship in and of itself but the notion of his self which such institutions impart to the individual. It is essential that he have a mediated notion of himself as valuable from the standpoint of the world-line, as "world-historical man."[23] The value others place on him in his "interpersonal" relations thus corresponds to his actual positive relationship to the world-line.

In such a society the false-positive of Kant's (and, later, Hegel's) negation of the negation has been replaced by a self-subsisting positive. Society concerns itself with the individual's existence to discover how his powers may be developed for a contribution to advancing the point along the world-line, which coincides with his self-conception. The only solution to the ideal Necessity thus imposed on him is his capacity for task-oriented creative "problem-solving," respecting both his own inventions and his capacity to develop his conceptual powers to realize the inventions of others. Thus, too, his love of his fellow creature ceases to be a miracle, an act of "irrationality"; he loves and is loved, and knows why.

There is no *absolute* denial in capitalist alienation, because there is no absolute in a universe characterized by such a world-line except the world-line itself. There is only the movement of the point along the line, and that which corresponds to such movement. To determine what we lack we must determine what we can become; it is only what we are capable of becoming that we could be denied.

The other order of the contents of consciousness is that of the way in which the world is articulated for consciousness. Later, where we deal with the determination of consumption, we shall lay the basis for a more thorough consideration of this matter. For the moment, let us simply say that it follows from the foregoing discussion of model 1c that our notions of the external world are primarily notions about the socialized forces through which we uniquely exert upon the universe our power to exist. The social relationships which express that power, and our relationship to those relations in general, is necessarily the articulation of the external world for our consciousness.

Our earlier discussion of the connection between reductionist obsessions and the alienated form of the capitalist self bears directly here. The notion of the external world must necessarily appear to us in the form determined for our self-consciousness by the character of our social relations.

Such insights into the nature of the Self are supported in an extensive and highly significant fashion by religious belief. The distinction between the physical self and the "soul" represents an attempt to distinguish between the persona (persona = mask = flesh) and the "inner" Self, which seeks an unmediated relationship—oneness, atonement—with the Logos. To the extent that the "inner" Self is bound to the persona, it must be false to itself and thus heteronomic with respect to the universality (infinity) of the Holy Spirit. Yet the Holy Spirit is the *consensus gentium*. The secret is out: God is *within* the world, but as a universal; he is therefore *metaphysical* from the reductionist standpoint of the persona. (See Spinoza and Feuerbach.) "God the *Creator!*" The seriousness and importance of religious belief spring from the necessity of "inner conviction," the conviction that the "inner" Self exists. This Self must be human, and *seek* in religious belief the humanity *which is metaphysical for alienated man.* Religions, however, being of this world, use religious belief to rationalize the practice of the *consensus gentium of a given society.* Humanity thus runs full circle from alienation to the unmediated "feeling" of humanity, atonement and back to perpetuation of the alienation which the frightened religious individual imagined himself to be escaping. Religion thus becomes "the chains of illusion"; "the chains of illusion" are the general form of religion.

Because religious belief under capitalism was both the characteristic empirical expression of the aspirations of the "inner" Self and the medium in which a revolution in the *consensus gentium* was occurring, science began largely as reflection on religious belief (Spinoza, Feuerbach). With the advent of critical examination of religious belief came the beginnings of anthropology, the real "Queen of the Sciences." From an anthropological vantage-point, it became possible to understand the old philosophy as an imitation of religion, and vulgar atheism as only the obsessive worship of Mammon.

We still have much to learn on this account from observing the pulpit. As an institution keenly sensible of its own survival and a merchant of abstract love (unmediated self-identity), the pulpit survives to the extent that it appropriately addresses itself with the proper degree of disguise to the "psychological needs" of the population—the entire population, whose character is reflected in the segment of itself found in the pews and confessionals. Self-denial (negation of the negation) is posited as Ego! His desire for the self-subsisting positive (unmediated identity) is used to make the aspirant content with the real world; perpetuation of the bourgeois Ego (the negation-of-the-negation Ego) becomes the condition for atonement through self-denial. The clergyman may not be clever, but the commodity he offers, shaped by millions of hands and millions of individuals' psychological needs—especially their need for reconciliation with their persona-existence—embodies a remarkable amount of cleverness. Perhaps most clever of all is the mystery that God could not exist without Satan nor Satan without God—for in the same instant that God created Satan, the negation of the negation was created. By the Sixth Day, we may be certain, Satan existed—otherwise man himself could not have come into being. The truth of religious fables is within the teller and the believer, whose authority is not history, actual or fictional, but the correspondence of such objectifications with the polemical experience of his own anxiety, which must be objectified in the hope that by comprehending it objectively, it can thus be manipulated like other objects.

Indeed, on this point, religion is correct. The inner polemic must be made conscious. The practical question is: by what criteria? The world-line is the solution.

Finally, we must reconsider a question we approached from a different vantage-point earlier in this chapter: how is it conceivable, from the standpoint of Marx's correction of Feuerbach's determination of consciousness, that man, whose character is determined by capitalist culture, could free himself of the most inclusive—and thus, excluding—determinations of this alienated social form? How can an individual within capitalist society base his identity on a noncapitalist set of identity-criteria and world-outlook, and acquire knowledge beyond the bounds of capitalist epistemology?

The clue to the answer lies, as we have already stated, in the study of creative personalities. We have referred to poets and musicians not to exclude other creative media but to locate the discussion in terms of reference in which the author is qualified to speak. The need of capitalist society for creative mentation—to a limited, circumscribed extent—demands a social category of persons who acquire a special kind of leisure as a privilege (not, we have emphasized, as a *right*). Scientists, inventors, poets (who, with other artists, fulfill a special *religious* need within society), and other such individuals belong in this category. In rare cases, generally coincident with major upsurges in society, the heightened powers of comprehension of great artistic productions by a larger proportion of the audiences places a premium on creative activity for the creative artist himself. To the extent that he is "understood," he is realized, attaining thus a sense of unmediated social identity more compelling than that experienced in love, because it has an objective basis in the "inner" Self. This phenomenon results, in a few artists, in highly intense preoccupation with the creative faculties upon which this new relationship to the audience depends. Thus, creative activity acquires the quality of *substance*, and becomes a self-subsisting positive.[24] This is most apparent in the best works of Shelley, Beethoven, and Heine, in particular, works in which the subject of the composition is nowhere manifest in its sensuous or formal elements, or even in the ordinary forms of allusion. The subject is nonetheless clear (except to such unfortunate critics as class Heine a "romantic" poet, demonstrating that they understand nothing of Heine and little of poetry in general, an innocence exhibited by most modern "poets"). Shelley's "Ode to the West Wind" is an excellent example.

To clarify an important point, we add the otherwise irrelevant observation that in most great poets' most important works are their shorter works, almost of necessity. What poetry accomplishes is the communication of Gestalts which cannot be communicated by the established language. The poet communicates such discoveries by an ironical arrangement of predicates such that none of the intentional significances of any lesser parts of the composition could be the judgment adduced by a sensible reader. The reader must go entirely outside the explicit content, even the allusive topics of the composition, to find a concept or experience which makes the totality of the poem coherent for himself as reader. The problem of establishing such a unique "meaning" in the composition—a meaning which by its nature cannot be explicitly protected within the poem— imposes cruel economy on the poet. If he adds more, he opens the gates to something other than his intention. To sustain an idea in an epic or semiepic, he must attempt to protect his meaning with more explicit symbologies—as we do in ordinary prose—and thus must bring his subject matter within the scope of such first-order allusive devices. If he attempts to avoid such objectification, his poem will become a morass of alternative interpretations, even by his own reflection on it after the period of composition has passed. It will occur to him, that the composition does not say what he intended. Thus, in longer compositions, the need to protect his intention compels him to select such intentions as admit of the required devices. Relative to his shorter compositions, his epics and long poems are relatively trivial, necessarily didactic, almost prose in poetic form, enhanced prose using the discipline of poetic formulation for tighter expressions.

It is sufficient to note that in music, this problem is less severe.

We can only urge the student to approach the greatest short poems of the greatest early nineteenth century poets from this vantage-point. The most important works of Beethoven, especially his double-fugal composition, offer the same sort of empirical evidence of our point.

A lot of well-intentioned banal nonsense has been written about the correlation between the greatest art and great upsurges in humanity. It is often argued that poets, musicians, and other artists are inspired by revolutionary upsurges as such, and that the thematic aspects of their compositions contain the revolutionary hymns of their period—plausible nonsense that sometimes goes as far as "program music" commentaries to make its point. Such explications reveal utter ignorance of art and the essence of revolutionary upsurges alike. If they occasionally make a minimally valid point despite their general approach, it is usually with reference to an artist who was personally caught up in social ferment and applied his artistic talents to the "Jimmy Higgins" needs of a movement.

The essential point, which Shelley recognized in "In Defense of Poetry," is that periods of mass upsurge give rise to two interconnected developments which as indirect expressions of upsurge have the most direct effect on creative activity, even outside the realm of social ferment. First, as we have emphasized repeatedly, the approximation of an unmediated relationship between individuals in the vortex of the social ferment creates a qualitative advance in the cognitive powers of those most affected by this taste of a new humanity. This phenomenon is associated with the emergence of mass institutions which, by virtue of their social powers and inclinations to new undertakings, signify that all sorts of things formerly beyond human reach are now almost within grasp. This eruption in the quality of general intelligence and inclination to innovation affects the whole of society, creating, relative to ordinary circumstances, the most favorable conditions for the proliferation of art among those strata that have already developed their creative powers and have the means and determination to pursue the necessary leisure. It would be astonishing if a significant number of the best creative intellects did not participate significantly in the social ferment of such a period—but the urge to do so derives from their creative impulses, not the reverse.

Such periods of artistic ferment are not strictly coextensive with great social movements. The Bolshevik revolution produced virtually no great art; neither did the social ferment of the 1930s. The "proletarian" art of pre-Hitler Germany was degenerate, however amiable the political intentions of certain of the artists. The great flowerings of the Tudor period and the Civil War in England, and of the early nineteenth century in Western Europe as a whole, represented the resolution of the upsurge in Humanism. The battered Bolshevik revolution—enmired in mass starvation, as a result of prolonged civil war and invasions, and the post-1921 massive loss of morale in the workers' movements and related groups— was only a brief spark, dampened in the resurgence of anomie and philistinism which seized all intellectual and artistic life during the 1920s. The 1930s saw episodic flashes of revolutionary potential, but there existed no institution or mass movement with anything positive to say; such bittersweet *commedia* do not produce great upsurges in the quality of human consciousness, or great expectations respecting what lies within the reach of man.

Yet, in the minor occurrences of everyday life which pass unnoticed by history, the person disposed toward creative life repeatedly finds clues, fragile portents which he seizes as the basis for some future identity at odds with the social pressures prevailing about him. He lives like Schubert's Wanderer, in search of the land which speaks his language, the land of unmediated social identity whose substance is creative mentation.

In the early writings of Karl Marx, just this quality is outstanding. Although the formal contents of these works have importance enough in themselves, their most important element is total submission to creative activity as purpose and actual subject. Motivated by the working-class struggle? What rubbish! The working class begins to emerge in these writings as the mediation of the coming-into-being of the land which speaks the language of unmediated creative identity, the world of unmediated *Being-in-and-for-itself*. Marx here is Heine and Schumann, seeking the *Davidsbundler* to defeat the hordes of philistines. The working class exists for him not as the object of a muckraker's pity, but for what it does not see in itself: its historic essence, the invariant, the world-line which is in a certain relationship to that class, but of which relationship the class knows nothing, and towards which end the class is not directed rationally. Marx's working class is not the existing working class, but what it is capable of becoming. The notion of the class-for-itself as Being-in-and-for-itself is Marx's identity.

This is not utopianism, nor a set of prescriptions (or "positions") on the ideal society ("true communism"). It is acknowledgment of what working-class forces must become by the Necessity of their relationship to the world-line. To say that this is a perception of immanence is to imply the "bad infinity" of the old metaphysics. "Actual infinity"—the universality expressed in the contradictions between the form of capitalist accumulation and the contrary realization embodied in the same productive forces, embodied in the process of development of the productive forces—is the direct knowledge accessible to the individual who has located the activity of his identity in his deliberative creative activity. It is accessible but not inevitable, as the contrast between Marx and Heine or Marx and Feuerbach demonstrates. Whoever seizes access to it is, like Marx, a member of the revolutionary intelligentsia.

For the masses of people, such a transformation depends upon the pre-establishment of identification with their creative potentials as the basis for social identity. There is, however, no absolute distinction between a revolutionary intelligentsia and a mass as a mass. Throughout society there are various degrees of philistinism, as is true of the working class in particular. Different individuals thus have different "thresholds" of response to approximations of mass-strike ferment. Some respond to the modest influence of small aggregations, as disparate groups come together to further the common interests of the class they merely typify. In broader movements, there are still more. And so on, until we reach the hardier philistine who cannot be stirred from his parochialism by anything less than a general upheaval. And there are some lost souls who even then . . .

THE PRODUCTION
OF MAN 4

THE PRODUCTION OF MAN 4

Not lightly did Engels identify Marx's "Theses on Feuerbach" as "the germ of a new world-outlook."[1] The emphatic assertions of Soviet and "Trotsky-ist" writers to the contrary,[2] Marx was not an incompetent judge of his own "mature" works when he later referred to his 1845 writings as the premise for his economic theories.[3] Provided, as we have repeatedly stipu-lated, that the student has mastered the prerequisites from Kant, Hegel, and Feuerbach, all of Marx's theoretical discoveries are stated or implicit in two brief selections from that "early" year: the "Theses" themselves and six paragraphs from the "Feuerbach" section of *The German Ideology*.[4]

This assertion must not be construed to imply that Marx accom-plished nothing of significance in later works but elaboration of his earlier discoveries. It means that all those later discoveries—and they are num-erous—represent the application and elaboration of the "germ of a new world-outlook" established earlier.

It is utterly fatuous to suggest that Marx gave up philosophy in *Capital*, but this has been asserted often enough. Nor did he ever reduce the problem of historical development to "economic motives" in the sense of "individual greed" or any other conventional misinterpretation of the term "economic." One might resort to Engels' 1890–1893 letters on the "Paul Barth issue"[5] to defend our point of view on this subject; Engels' remarks are interesting, fruitful, and indubitably correct, but we would lack nothing essential if they had never been written. As we have already emphasized, a comparison of the contents of the "early writings" with the concluding volume of *Capital* is sufficient to make the case.

We have already provided the student with an overview of Marxian theory as a whole and its major implications, including a preliminary out-line of the essentials of Marx's economic theory. We must now situate that theory, while developing it in more detail, within the same general con-text as *Capital* itself. This chapter serves as a bridge to that undertaking, locating our point of departure. Our approach, as prescribed in Chapter 2, is to demonstrate that *Capital* provides the basis for establishing a co-herence between two interdependent processes otherwise as fundamentally inconsistent as subjective and objective processes. Our immediate concern in this chapter is to establish the origins of Marx's specific approach to such problems in the work he himself certifies as settling accounts with his past.

MARXIAN ANTHROPOLOGY

The six paragraphs from *The German Ideology*[6] cited above implicitly state Marx's "Law of Value," and explicitly define his notion of *use value*. The adducing of a Law of Value from this material is admissible only to the extent that we limit its applications to specifically capitalist society. The six paragraphs in question, and most of the material in the same section, are addressed to a larger purpose, and therefore achieve a more fundamental and broader result than the study of capitalist society alone might seem to require. What Marx establishes in the "Feuerbach" section of *The German Ideology* is that the *self-subsisting positive*, as he develops it, is *a law of evolutionary social reproduction* appropriate to all forms of human society, of which the Law of Value peculiar to capitalism is a single historically specific expression. It is correct, therefore, to insist that Marx, in defining such a law of evolutionary social reproduction, founded anthropology as a science—not only as the king and queen of all science, but also, in Feuerbach's sense, as immediately subsuming sociology, history, psychology, and political economy as facets of itself.

Before summarizing the six paragraphs and their immediate implications, we must specify our usage of the term *historical specificity*. We have stated the general basis of this concept in earlier chapters; we shall now offer a working definition for this part of the text.

The conditions of material existence are determined, on the one side, by the causal connection between human actions on man-altered nature and their consequent material results for human existence. Yet the connection between those results and further, consequent human actions on man-altered nature exists in what appears as a relatively subjective realm in which men interpret the consequences of their actions for further actions. Thus, to isolate either the apparently objective or subjective aspect of this process to investigate society would be nonsensical.

As we shall see in more depth later, it is not merely a question of societies governed by the same objective laws existing in differing, successive forms of subjective totalities. Although the invariant principle, the world-line, is an invariant, a general law of evolutionary social development, different point-intervals along the world-line correspond to different sets of special objective laws. This can be summarily illustrated by the following hypothetical (that is, impossible) example. Let us imagine that the people in Babylonian, Hellenic, European feudal, and capitalist society each act according to the objective laws, and that there is no discrepancy between the subjective determination of the universal consequences of actions and the actual consequences of those actions. In each society, the characteristic behavior of the people would be different. Indeed, as Marx himself insists, the subjective aspect of a society manifests appropriateness to the "development of its productive forces" in a particular way. It is not that the ideology characteristic of a society *is* a consistent expression of objective laws, but that the vicious discrepancy between the two interpenetrating sets of laws is an appropriate one.

Thus, the individual transferred from one society to another becomes a different kind of individual. Specific phenomena which may appear identical to empiricists in two societies are qualitatively different.

The coherent conceptualization of the interpenetration of the two sets of processes characterizing any society is unique to that society, as are the distinctions between animal species. For example, the exchange-value form of valuation peculiar to capitalist accumulation could not occur in any other kind of society. One could not abstract a value from capitalist accumulation and establish the slightest basis for valuing the same object similarly in any other society. Such distinctions are those of *historical specificity*.

Marx illustrates this principle by repeated references to the fundamental distinction between apparently identical modes of agricultural production *in itself* in the transition from feudalism to early capitalism.[7] The conversion of the feudal social surplus (essentially a surplus colonizing population) into alienable product as payment on capitalized debt represents a qualitative change from feudalism to capitalist production, even though no alteration has occurred in the immediate technology of estate production or the immediate relationship between lord and peasant on the estate. Of course, this changed "external" relationship rapidly reifies internal relations: intensification of production, alterations in modes of production, changes in balance of production to emphasize market income, and related phenomena. Though the *form* itself might seem the same, especially to a casual visitor dropping in from outer space on separate occasions, the *content* is absolutely different. In the feudal case, momentarily marginal shifts in the organization of internal life are undertaken to expand the feudal power of the nobleman, to whom peasants represent wealth. In the capitalist case, momentarily marginal shifts are undertaken to increase capacity to make payment on debt-service in a market economy. Peasants are becoming a cost for the nobleman; the more surplus product—e.g., the fewer peasants required to produce that surplus product—the greater his wealth. These slight differentiations in content are absolutely decisive for form. In both cases, the cow is pregnant; one shrugs. Pregnant by the prize bull or a passing bison? It will make a difference in form eventually: which is bringing the higher price, calves or cattaloes?

Abstracting from human history (e.g., Hegel's A/not-A), in which the interpenetration of such contrary (subjective/objective) processes determines a new specific form of society, one has the empirical basis for a notion of a law of evolutionary social development. Using as a criterion simple increases in population at comparable material levels of existence, one can empirically rank societies as more or less advanced than their predecessors. In the broader sweep from the Pleistocene, one adduces a general *though not merely unilinear* ordering of successful forms of two general types. The varieties which principally occupy our attention are those which represent predecessors of still more advanced forms. The second variety are those forms of society which seem to be dead ends, such as the commune-based forms of Oriental Despotism. The effects of conquests and the like, and of the voluntary element at certain critical junctures (e.g., the Gracchian reforms), introduce practical complexities but do not restrain us from making certain generalizations. The only generalization which is absolutely vindicated is the most general, the necessity of evolutionary progress as the alternative to decay and depopulation. At a lesser degree of generality, we can only undertake a limited articulation of a phylogenesis, and must ultimately resolve the connection between the general law and the particular case in specific terms.

Once we have discovered the specific laws of a mode of social reproduction, we do not merely discard the general law as having served its purpose. Plekhanov and other Mensheviks and Social Democrats tended toward just such a blunder (among other related follies) in marshalling arguments for the "national stages" strategy. First among the grosser empirical proofs against such hermetic specificity is the general phenomenon of "combined and uneven development" of societies, such that no society is a "pure type." We shall later demonstrate for both feudal and capitalist cases, a far more profound flaw in the hermetic approach, absolutely decisive in the long term, but sometimes less apparent in the short run than "combined and uneven development."

The key to analysis of the "internal relations" specific to a society lies outside it. In gross empirical terms, it is true of societies in general that they have a beginning and an end, that they develop into what they are out of what they were not, and that their progress toward the end of their existence is the most important aspect of their development, even in terms of internal relations. This is expressed in capitalist economy by crises, which are the summation, the revealed truth, of "successful" development in the preceding period. In the same vein are the facts that each boom period of capitalist development represents qualitative alterations in the specific forms of development, and that capitalist history as a whole is empirically a succession of long sweeps of development. The latter are typified by the transition, notably during the period of the Berlin conference, from a colonialist to an imperialist phase of capitalist development, and, during the Second World War, to the dollar empire of Bretton Woods. From the standpoint of political economy as a science—which is to say a body of knowledge useful for predicting the important consequences of present policies and developments—there could be no talk of "economic science" unless one adduced from each period and phase of capitalist development those development principles which seem, immediately, external to its intrinsic laws. Such principles must necessarily be the fundamental features of the process in terms of which everything is to be judged. The same thing is true, of course, for capitalist society as a whole, and in a different specific sense but the same general sense for all societies.

The development of a society must be understood in terms of that principle which determines simultaneously its most progressive features and, ultimately, its self-destruction. By "progressive features," we mean nothing arbitrary or dictionary-nominalist. Progress is increase in the social-reproductive powers of the society as a whole. Because that principle invariably employs a restricted definition of the term *mode*, the extent of potential development is restricted. The contradiction is defined by successful convergence upon the implicit limits of development defined by that mode. In certain societies, such as Mesopotamian riparian modes, this contradiction can be approximately defined in terms of the geographical extent of certain types of contiguous, potentially arable land *for that mode*, and of salination and related phenomena. A similar notion applies to a certain extent in the case of European feudalism. Such preliminary, gross considerations are merely that—preliminary. In every society there is discernible, necessarily, a tendency for development of the mode. In precapitalist society, for example, development seems merely relatively absent. In the case of feudalism, for example, the handful of rather fundamental agricultural and other "technological," as well as social-organizational, innovations on which the entire development of that culture depends are ridiculously marginal by contrast with a short period of capitalist development. This line of investigation, situated within a correspondingly adjusted definition of scale, provides us with the fundamental approach required. We must determine the intrinsic tendency for technological and related developments and locate the inherent boundaries placed upon the realization of such developments by a given mode of social organization.

The case of the transition from feudalism proper to mercantile capitalism is again a most useful illustration. Feudalism's emphasis on slight modifications in military technology, in particular, could be assimilated as long as such technological changes did not exceed a simple relationship between the estate and its internal capacities for creating such objects or the limited external resources of guild manufactures. The creation of permanent bodies of armed men, associated with significant, self-aggravating developments in realized military technology, enabled and demanded feudal employment of resources and means of production on a larger scale. To attempt to assimilate these developments meant the introduction of a qualitative change in feudal relations: the destruction of the characteristic feudal mode of reproduction (surplus, colonizing population) through the institutionalization of alienable debt-service payment. This germ of feudalism's self-destruction had to expand at a rate determined by general self-cannibalization and the advances in realized military technology—and enlarged bodies of armed men—which that cannibalization required. All of this occurred within the twofold bounding of feudalism: the Turks and Mongols, and the consumption of the remaining non- and semifeudal populations to be absorbed within Western Europe itself. Meanwhile, the rate of expansion of military technology outran the slower rate of improvements in agricultural technology, such that the existing scale of production could not be expanded much more *in effect* than feudalism could in geographic scale—and feudal relations themselves acted as a barrier against such developments!

As is illustrated by the case of feudalism, the form of a society's self-destruction is determined by the same principle on which the reproduction of the form itself depends. It may be, in one case, the creation of banditry as a result of depopulation of productive forces; or it may be the parasitical self-enlargement of certain social strata, such as an administrative caste, otherwise essential to the successful mode of reproduction. These objectified contradictions in the fundamental principle of self-development may assume either of two general forms, the distinction between which is of the utmost significance for our subject in general. As in the case of feudalism, the emergence of mercantile capitalism may lead to the development of the capitalist labor process, the basis for a more advanced form of society; or it may be a parasitical or regressive form, resulting in either cycles of rise and decay or a general regression.

Marx's law of evolutionary reproduction, to be adduced from the sources cited above, may be summarized in the following terms. First, we have the statement discussed above in relation to the notion of a self-subsisting positive. At the beginning of the section in question of *The German Ideology*, Marx stipulates that the sole premise for human knowledge is human existence. He qualifies this statement by explaining that he does not mean human existence *in itself*. The premise is not solipsistic; it is not that we, as individuals or aggregations of individuals, simply exist in an immediate sense. It is not a reductionist notion of existence. The premise is human existence *for itself*: man reproducing the material conditions of his own existence, both as nature provides them and as man before has altered nature. Man-for-himself is man evolving the productive forces, such that as any mode of technology and social organization exhausts the potential for maintaining human existence in that mode, new technologies and forms of social organization are developed. Whether or not particular forms of society succeed in creating their necessary successors is an important but nonetheless absolutely secondary matter. The fundamental premise of human knowledge is that man, having exhausted the potential of a whole array of modes, arrives at a generally ascending mode of existence in terms, by way of a first approximation, of an increased ecological population potential.

Examining these paragraphs from *The German Ideology* together with the "Theses On Feuerbach," the following argument immediately presents itself. It is unnecessary to know any "objective" *absolute* laws of the physical universe in advance. Such laws, in any case, exist only as pathetic chimeras in the minds of individuals "vulgarly squatting outside the universe." If man exists—and we have acknowledged the overwhelming empirical evidence of his evolutionary existence—his existence represents his successful mastery of whatever universal laws exist. By evolving in the process of producing his material means of existence, that is, deliberately altering nature, he has sufficiently demonstrated that the deliberative process by which he creates new species-behaviors for himself is in correspondence with whatever universal laws exist for him with respect to both the old and the new forms of social practice.

Therefore, the solution to this problem could have been discovered only through so-called idealism, which freed itself of all obligations to reductionism and explored the active side of the question of human deliberation subjectively. Feuerbach saw the flaw in limiting the statement of the problem to the subjective side *in itself* (Kant, Hegel) or, more exactly, to the subjective side *for itself* as a question of subjective development in itself. He regarded the theoretical aspect (the subjective development) as the only human quality of the process, as did Hegel. But in attempting to unify this realm of *development* (the subjective aspect) with the so-called physical universe, he conceived of the subject of creative mentation, the physical universe, in the strictly reductionist terms of its "dirty-judaical form of appearance" (appearance = sense-certainty). "Hence, he does not grasp the significance of 'revolutionary,' of 'practical-critical' reality." "The coincidence of the *changing* of circumstances and of human activity can be conceived and rationally understood only as *revolutionizing* practice." "Feuerbach, not satisfied with abstract thinking, appeals to *sensuous contemplation;* but does not conceive sensuousness as *practical,* human-sensuous activity."

With respect to the connection between the reductionist conception of the inner Self and reductionism generally, Marx emphasizes that ". . . the human essence is no abstraction inherent in each single individual." (So much for the Marxism of the individual-greed notion of historical materialism.) "In its reality it is the ensemble of social relations." (See Sections 32–33 in Feuerbach's *Principles of the Philosophy of the Future.*) "The highest point attained by *contemplative* materialism, that is, materialism which does not understand sensuousness as practical activity, is the contemplation of single individuals in 'civil society.'" Feuerbach frustrates himself by his inability to find the revolutionary expression of human practice in the content of the determinate object of his sensuous experience, and fails to transcend reductionism when he moves out of the subjective realm. He cannot locate his notion of a self-subsisting positive, which exists for him only abstractly in the subjective realm, in man's practical knowledge of the laws of the universe. Consequently, since he cannot demonstrate that creative mentation changes the material realm for man, he cannot see that man's knowledge, his creative mentation, itself evolves according to the changed material conditions created by evolving socialized practice. He could not possibly apply the notion he articulates in Section 33 of *Principles* to show that socialized practice—evolving socialized practice—hence determines the content of individual self-consciousness. He cannot see that, for just this reason, the notions of rights and privileges by which adult society determines the reflected self-consciousness of the individual do not represent notions of sensuous objects or of human relations to sensuous fixed objects, but that the objects of social relations are determinations of the category of perfection (e.g., Descartes' second theorem). He can determine neither the social content of the individual's reflected self-consciousness nor the dialectical content of the sensuous-object notions which, as consciousness within a particular form of society, are the images immediately mistaken for the contents of self-consciousness. Thus, despite the fact that he locates the social determination of reflected individual self-consciousness, that individualized determination is simply a terminus of a process repeated for each individual. Therefore, in place of the ordinary reductionist's self-evident individual, Feuerbach has progressed only to an abstract individual.

Furthermore, failing, despite his appreciation of Spinoza, to grasp either the implications of Descartes' second theorem or the deeper implications of Spinoza's attempt to comprehend perfection as substance, Feuerbach presents a notion of the contents of consciousness which ignores its noetic element; thus, the "dirty-judaical" character of his notion of sensuous objects takes revenge upon him. Denying the "perfection" in the object-as-an-object for the (evolutionary) existence of man, Feuerbach fixes the object in the reductionist's sense, and the essence which he rightly locates in the reflected self-consciousness of the individual is degraded to a mere *dumb* generality.

THE PROBLEM OF ENGELS

Although the worst features of "official dialectical materialism" are mainly attributable to Lenin's miserable *Empirio-Criticism* (when they are not sheer concoctions), a considerable effort has been made to give an aura of legitimacy to these constructions with selected references to Friedrich Engels' writings, especially *Dialectics of Nature*, *Anti-Dühring*, and, to a lesser extent, *Ludwig Feuerbach*. In the main, at least insofar as Engels offers a summary exposition of the development of the dialectical method, one could only wish that Engels' admirers had studied his writings more carefully. *Ludwig Feuerbach*, in particular, is chiefly remarkable for its competence in that it was written for publication in the German Social Democracy's *Neue Zeit* of 1886, and was thus constrained by the need to represent profound questions in a "popular" form.[8] Still, there are isolated passages in Engels' writings which lend themselves to a reasonable misapprehension of Marx's conception of the dialectical method. This difficulty is most acute with respect to those notions discussed in the preceding section. Therefore, it is necessary to deal with this problem immediately, aiming at a sharpening of the student's comprehension of the material just covered.

Typical of the problem is the conventional interpretation of a chapter in Engels' posthumously published manuscript, the *Dialectics of Nature*. The problems attending posthumously published works are hypothetical, at least, for Marx's "Theses on Feuerbach" and the "Feuerbach" section of *The German Ideology*, critical examination of which reveals that the internal agreement with the last writings of Marx is complete,[9] but that the exposition would have had to be recast for the work to stand on its own feet by Marx's standards.[10] Parts of Engels' *Dialectics of Nature* require much more caution in attempting to discern Engels' reflective intentions.

An example is one aspect of an otherwise most promising chapter, "The Part Played by Labour in the Transition from Ape to Man."[11]

Engels emphasizes the distinction between the tool-appropriate hand of the human and the more limited capability of the hand of the higher ape. This is a minor point, whose intent Engels' manuscript makes clear enough: the physiological appropriateness of man as a hominid to be human is a determinate. The vulgar Marxist makes of the point the "materialist" observation that the opposable thumb has the epiphenomenon of labor! One need examine this interpretation no further.

The admittedly fragmentary sections entitled "Dialectics" and "Mathematics" in the same book are muddled as a whole. At one moment, and throughout most of the text, Engels is brilliant; at another he is confused on a point about which he is clear elsewhere. This occurs even in sections ostensibly composed during the same period. He is insightful on entropy, borrowing directly and indirectly from Leibniz's "clock-winder" remark to Samuel Clarke,[12] but trivial on bad infinity itself.[13] It is clear that Engels never fully comprehended the significance of Hegel's distinction between actual and bad infinity generally, with respect to a number of not-unimportant aspects of the point. We are obviously at the limits here of Engels' comprehension of dialectical method relative to such matters. This flaw in Engels' development is significant, as we shall shortly demonstrate.

Ludwig Feuerbach includes the following astonishing passage:

> . . . having got so far, Feuerbach stops short. He cannot overcome the customary philosophical prejudice, prejudice not against the thing but against the name materialism. He says: 'To me materialism is the foundation of the edifice of human essence and knowledge; but to me it is not what it is to the physiologist, to the natural scientist in the narrower sense, for example, to Moleschott, and necessarily is from their standpoint and profession, namely the edifice itself. Backwards I fully agree with the materialists; but not forwards.'[14]

And earlier: ". . . Feuerbach broke through [the Hegelian] system and simply discarded it."[15]

This assessment is exactly contrary to Marx's judgment of Feuerbach in the concluding section of the *1844 Manuscripts*, the "Feuerbach" section of *The German Ideology*, and "Theses on Feuerbach." We discover, searching the literature for some explication of this difficulty, that this is not the first time Marx and Engels differed sharply on Feuerbach; Engels had written part of a manuscript for the "Feuerbach" section of *The German Ideology* in which quite a different view than Marx's at that period is presented.[16]

In Marx's view, as we have adduced and presented it, Feuerbach's principal defect was that he merely continued what Hegel accomplished, with a certain major improvement, with respect to the subjective side. Admittedly, insofar as the later Feuerbach trivialized his own premises, his later application of "species-consciousness" and the associated principle of "love" are pathetically banal efforts to accommodate his earlier revolutionary achievements to a kind of "ethical solidarist" mush. For that, Feuerbach richly deserves the contempt Engels heaps upon him. However, Engels has thrown out the baby with the bathwater. Section 33 of Feuerbach's *Principles of the Philosophy of the Future* alone represents a major revolution within the fullest accomplishments of Hegel's dialectic. Not only did Marx explicitly acknowledge this in the last section of the 1844 *Manuscripts*, but the entirety of Marx's notion of social-reproductive relations depends upon nothing but the two fundamental corrections of Hegel's dialectic which Marx himself credits to Feuerbach.

Is there some flaw in Engels' thought which immediately corresponds to his basic difference with Marx on this point? Absolutely. Engels' notion of the dialectic of human development, while generally correct in broad terms, is only a simplified parallel to Marx's own, and not on account of his attempt to "popularize" the report.[17] *Engels fails to grasp Feuerbach's Section 33.*

This is not a unique shortcoming of Engels' writings. If the reader has begun to adduce what the author means by the notion of an *ordering of conceptions*, it should be clear that Feuerbach's notion of the social determination of reflected self-consciousness involves an insight into Hegel's Being-in-and-for-itself which corresponds to the notion of invariants we have developed in preceding chapters. Feuerbach has eliminated the "negation of the negation" approach to determination and replaced it with a self-subsisting positive, which Marx not only explicitly insists Feuerbach to have done,[18] but—more significantly—accuses him of failing to extend far enough.[19] This involves the problem of actual versus potential infinities, insofar as Hegel himself progresses on that point. It is precisely this aspect of Hegel on which Engels is demonstrably most unclear, most apparently alternately informed and muddled. It is also this aspect of *Capital* with which Engels, as Marx's editor, had the greatest difficulties.[20]

We do not wish to suggest that Engels is otherwise in any way unreliable in his account of Marx's views on dialectical method. Insofar as Marx's method can be accurately represented from the standpoint of a direct revolution in Hegel's dialectic, Engels is precise and accurate. It is with respect to those aspects of Hegel on which Feuerbach made revolutionary contributions, and on which Marx is most explicitly indebted to Feuerbach, that Engels' comprehension fails him.

Let us restate the case summarily. Feuerbach's failure, as Marx most explicitly emphasizes in the "Theses on Feuerbach," is that he was able to extend Hegel's achievements only in the subjective side of the matter. Feuerbach adopted Hegel's failure to comprehend sensuous objects as sharing the same dialectical development otherwise expressed in the subjective side. This error introduced, in one respect, an apparent retrogression in Feuerbach relative to Hegel. To the extent that Feuerbach nailed the subjective development to the crumbling rocks of the old materialism—reductionism—the effect of his effort to give a material basis to development was to virtually abort development, limiting it to the determination of each new individual, although within that determination Feuerbach not only adopted but qualitatively advanced Hegel's achievements. This Marx perceives thoroughly; Engels does not. Engels can see only the result: the stagnation of social development resulting from the attempt to reconcile the dialectic with simple matter.

To a certain degree, Engels' inability to comprehend this feature of the problem contributes to his too-credulous attitude toward nineteenth-century materialism. This failure never causes him to justify blunders of the sort found in Plekhanov or in Lenin's *Empirio-Criticism*, nor does it license Lenin's foolish criticisms of Engels' hylozoic perception. Engels never becomes generally a reductionist or an epiphenomenalist. The chief effect of his shortcoming is to make his explication of certain points muddled, and his choice of language and illustrations occasionally imprudent. What has occurred is that reductionists have sniffed out such odd corners of Engels' exposition, with less perception than "instinct," and have attempted to build a positive epiphenomenalism on such ambiguities and lacunae.

THE BAR-DIAGRAMS USED IN THIS TEXT

In order for the simplest form of human society to exist, in terms of Marx's definition of humanity, its production must not only produce the material conditions of life and means of production necessary for continued existence, but must also produce a social surplus.[21] This social surplus provides the means for continuation of society within a specific mode, and in most instances immediately creates those social formations and institutions which play a decisive role in bringing that form of society to an end. The determination of the objectified contradictions to which we referred earlier in this chapter does not leap into being out of an abstraction; it usually develops as a materialized form through a realization of social surplus. This division between the labor required for simple reproduction and the labor corresponding to social surplus is the simplest and most fundamental division of social labor in every society.

To avoid lending ourselves to suprahistoricism, we shall not use the terms Surplus Value, Variable Capital, and Constant Capital in the general statement we are about to make. Instead, we shall use similar terms, in a way which initially seems to replicate our representation of capitalist reproduction. We shall qualify the necessary distinctions in due course.

We shall retain the symbol S for social surplus and employ d for consumption approximately analogous to capitalists' consumption. However, instead of V we shall use P, and instead of C, N. P represents the material consumption required to reproduce the general productive sector of the population; N represents the costs of maintaining nature (and man-altered nature). The principal distinctions to be borne in mind are as follows. In many societies neither P nor N exists as a social category, but only as an ecological category. The "peasant," for example, whether feudal or alienated bow-tenure, may not distinguish, in terms of social categories of labor, between work applied to maintaining the means of production and work applied to producing his material means of existence. What does exist in any society *with castes or classes*[22] is the social category of social surplus and the category of nonproductive consumption. In "more primitive" forms of society, the distinction $S/(P + N)$ exists only in the form of general social reproduction as such.

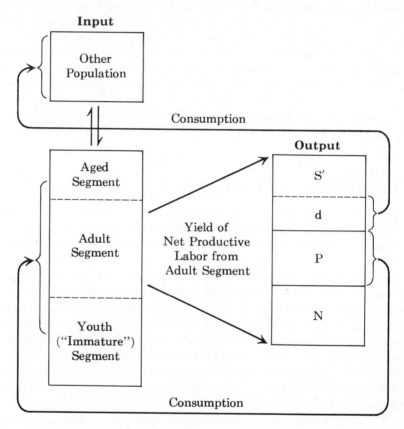

Figure 2 General Model of Social Reproduction

If we were concerned with treating the correspondence between the subjective and objective forms in specific societies, we would find numerous cases—indeed, most kinds of societies—in which the scheme illustrated in Figure 2 would not be the most appropriate. However, every society is ultimately in coherent relationship to the world-line, and despite the inappropriateness of such schema to the analysis of its specific internal relations, we can quite properly abstract from the specific relations a scheme of the form depicted. Provided the reader acknowledges that we are considering three notions of general invariants for each social form *as such*[23]— the subjective, the specific objective, and the world-line—the rigor of this schematic abstraction does not introduce any fallacies to our argument.

Note that Figure 2 contains three principal elements. On the left-hand side, a large bar represents the entire productive population; above it, a smaller bar represents the nonproductive population as a whole. To the right of the productive population, another bar represents the totality of the productive labor. Between these two bars, we have inserted arrows signifying the movement of persons and services: persons in both directions and services principally (in the simplified case) from the upper to the lower bar.

In general, the relative dimensions of the three bars have no significance. The height of each bar axiomatically represents 100% of the magnitude it identifies for each case, and has no necessary relationship to the magnitude portrayed for the other two. Only the relative proportions of subdivisions within each bar have any importance (although, for special purposes, it might occasionally be desirable to keep a population-magnitude scale for the two population bars). Our earlier references to the determination of magnitude will invariably apply.

The following conventions also apply. The left-hand side of each bar always represents input; the right-hand side always represents the principal quality of output. The lines connecting one segment of a bar to another bar always represent output-to-input connections.

In the illustrations throughout the remainder of this text, the size of the bars never changes, and any apparent differences in magnitudes have no significance. Only the relative magnitudes of the segments within each bar change. (In line with our parenthetical observation above, it might under certain circumstances be pedagogically useful to alter the proportional sizes of the two population bars relative to one another; however, we do not do so in this text.) Any alterations in magnitude are dialectically subsumed (determined) by changes in the relative size of segments of the same bars.

Throughout the text, we shall consider segments of both the productive population and the totality of productive labor. However, although we shall discuss the segments within the nonproductive population, we will not illustrate them diagrammatically.

The following description of the three bars is applicable to any such illustration.

Within the bar representing the productive population, we make three principal segmental distinctions.

First, every such population includes the social category "immaturity." Only to a limited extent does this category have a biological basis. As some lines of experimental psychology have indicated, the principle of extrauterine gestation can no doubt be meaningfully extended, although in a highly attenuated sense, even to the period between the fifth year and puberty. It may be the case—although this has been demonstrated only for certain capitalist populations—that some powers of mentation develop significantly only at certain points in biological maturation. Even if so, this means very little for our immediate purposes since, after approximately the fifth year of life, any biological potentialities of that sort are subsumed by social determinations.

It is sufficient, in defining this category, to note that every culture has a characteristic mode of maturation by which its new members are brought to adulthood, and that this mode determines a corresponding time span. The length of this period is not necessarily constant for all sections of the population, of course.

In the United States, the norm for maturation of young workers has shifted from approximately grammar-school age at the outset of this century, to 15 or 16 during and following the First World War, to about 19 or 20 today. Yet in parts of Western Europe, the standard of approximately 15 to 16 still prevails for a major social category of workers, the so-called apprentice strata. The variation is not simply a difference in customs; the majority of the *Lehrling* categories in the German Federal Republic, for example, represent qualities of skill which preassign all matriculants to a human scrapheap at any point in the near future. A similar problem, though not so acute, exists in Great Britain. Despite the contingencies of apparent "international competition," which are chiefly deceptive, the American worker is far more productive than his European or Japanese counterpart by virtue of his superior literacy, general culture, and the like. The *Volkschule* system in the BRD, for example, systematically deprives a major portion of young German workers of those human powers which are their right by the standards of contemporary capitalist technology.

(Not to leave the reader aghast at such a shocking rejection of commonplace truisms, we add the following summary of the paradox. To the extent that capitalism can sufficiently lower the cost of reproducing a working class, and compensate for the resulting lower social productivity by restricting technological development in the greatest number of kinds of employment, the apparent capitalist productivity of labor is increased. S/V is increased by lowering V. However, this short-term cleverness results in a population-brake on further technological development such as that the amount of cheap labor available becomes a mediating aspect of the development of crises.)

Thus, every mode of existence determines the mode and extent of normal maturation for each section of its subject population. In general, the farther culture advances along the world-line, the longer the term of maturation must tend to become, until something occurs to replace such an increase in leisure. Obviously, the term of maturation will not increase indefinitely; instead, it will tend to be fuzzily defined at its upper age limit, and a general increase in the proportion (and forms) of leisure available to all age groups in the population will become the principal focus of increased "maturation" of the entire population. However, before this occurs, the increase in the term of maturation is the most conspicuous empirical consequence of such a general principle.

This enhancement obviously demands a significant reduction in mortality rates. To increase the term of maturation is to reduce the available labor time per capita of the entire productive population and to increase the social cost of the death of each maturing individual. It also requires a higher standard of material culture and leisure for the adult population. We ordinarily see the rising cost to the household (and to public services per capita) of rearing a new individual as an "economic" incentive to reduce fertility rates in order to obtain a higher quality of new individuals. However, if we eliminated such "economic" boundary conditions by raising the material income of households to a very high level relative to present incomes, we would confront evidence that the immediate "economic" boundary in fact reflects something more fundamental, though in a highly distorted fashion. To raise the quality of new individuals requires an increased cultural expenditure by adult society. If the sheer increase per adult in the time required for cultural maturation of the young is not to become regressive, the leisure of the adult population must be increased. However, at the same time this entire notion subsumes a set of relative boundary conditions on the fertility rates per household. Increased leisure increases the potential number of new individuals of the same quality, but this leisure is in turn bounded in potential by the development of the productive forces, and puts a premium on improvement in the quality of new individuals.

These considerations suffice for the moment to justify the notion of youth as a determined social category or proportional segment of an entire population or class.

At another point on the spectrum we encounter persons modally beyond the age of productive labor. Again, this is emphatically more a social than a biological category. In capitalist society in particular, the category "old age" is viciously defined in general, according to norms of capitalist employment. There is no age at which a human being capable of functioning does not have the capacity—and need—to perform universal labor or the realization of universal labor. Different societies, obviously, deal with the category of elders in different, and sometimes opposing, fashions. It is sufficient for the moment to acknowledge this qualification and, more generally, to note the existence of this category.

The third segment has a specific significance with respect to the working-class population of capitalist society. In capitalist society, the upper and lower limits defined by the other two segments establish an adult age-interval from which the productive population is extracted, such that the productive labor force can be actuarily defined at any given moment and location as a percentage of the population within this age-interval. In studying the U.S. working-class population, one subdivides the adult population into narrower age-intervals and by sex. Within any such a narrow interval, a percentage of the male and female populations is identifiable as the active labor force. The total labor force has been contracting in range during the past quarter-century as a result of the rise in the age of maturation and the lowering of the modal and mean ages of retirement. Also, the expansion of higher education and the military forces has a significant effect on the definition of the net labor force at the lower end of this spectrum. On the other hand the proportion of women in the labor force has been rising since approximately 1949 (apart from the war-time and immediate postwar special cases), a phenomenon which becomes more noteworthy when we recast the data for wage-earning members of households![24]

It is necessary, in order to conceptualize the specific case of the U.S. productive labor force, to recognize that activities within households which are not productive are socially necessary to the existing mode of production and existence of the working-class population. Thus, the available labor force from these age-intervals must be regarded as *determined*. If we reduced the number and quality of intrahousehold services, the quality of the population would decline, such that the resulting increase in the labor force would be offset by a diminution in the quality of the entire labor force, in contrast to a numerically smaller labor force obtained from households in which such essential services were maintained.

This determination is characterized by certain ironies. Since the effects of reducing intrahousehold services become apparent, in capitalist terms, over the course of a generation, capitalism can in the short run violate the laws in question and seem to obtain greater labor productivity (by increasing the amount of labor per household for a modal family income). The emergence of the late 1960s' drug culture is a phenomenon of a similar type; the moral and cultural characteristics of the invincible suburbanite philistinism of the McCarthy period and its immediate aftermath have been cruelly reproduced in the post-war generation: hypocrisy, moral indifferentism, and parasitism have taken up residence in the pretty children into whom their germs were introduced.

Provided we recognize that the social categories we have defined are thus determinate in each case, and not necessarily empirically identical with their determinate values in other instances, we now have a generally correct notion of them for capitalist society and, implicitly, an insight into the means of adducing similar kinds of determination for different societies —not simply parallel determinations, but determinations adduced from empirical evidence by the same general method.

The lines connecting the adult segment of the productive population to the right-hand bar in Figure 2 represent the determination of the total productive activity of the society.

With respect to the right-hand bar, the strictest epistemological rigor will be observed throughout this text. *This bar never changes in magnitude for capitalist or socialist economy*, irrespective of changes in the magnitude of the labor force or other specifics. The only alterations occur in the relative proportions among the segments. *The numeric value of the left-hand height of the bar is always the absolute number 1.*[25]

This bar is divided into three principal segments, P, N, and S; S is then subdivided into d and S', yielding the ratio

$$\frac{S - d}{P + N}$$

such that a rise in the current value of this ratio is a measure not only of development but also of existence. Since P and N must increase relative to their values for preceding states, from the standpoint of such states the impulse which gives rise to development or existence is an exponential tendency for rise in the value of the given ratio. Thus, immediately, the invariant magnitude 1 is always in immediate correspondence to a specific exponential value of that form.

A strict hylozoic interpretation would demand that this notion be extended to all forms of life as the positive relationship of "genetic" determination to ecologies defined in cognate terms. The deliberative aspect of ecological progress would thus apparently shift from the species, *i.e.* humanity in particular, to the entire process outside any particular species, such that only an holistic ecological determination of genetic variations would be admissible. It would also be necessary, by implication, further to extend this notion from living forms to the material universe out of which living forms arise.[26]

If we increased segment P while reducing segments N,d, and S' we would approach an animal state of reproduction: N = 0, d barely greater than 0, and S' extremely small or 0. As we converge on human development, N increases "at the expense of" P, and S' increases. Then S' increases "at the expense of" both P and N, but N continues to increase relative to P, i.e., man produces the material preconditions for his productive existence.

Indeed, as Marx notes,[27] any convergence on "simple reproduction" bestializes man to the extent that it must be reflected in his outlook by the equation of his essence with that of animals and other objects of nature. Similarly, the most fanatical "ecology freaks," whose religion is not merely simple reproduction but regression, uplift of Nature to a position equal in value with human existence!

Taking into account our previous discussions of such matters, we conclude that ordered ranges of values for the ratio, examined with respect to the exponential impulse valuation of the expression, each correspond to a stage of development of society in general. The absolute ratio itself is not conclusive; what is conclusive is that ratio expressed in terms of a characteristic exponential tendency over the span of development represented by the emergence and collapse of that form of society as a specific mode of human existence. Thus it is proper to regard development as occurring in what appear to be discrete leaps. These are defined—determined—by the consideration we described in the feudal example above. Within limits, the changes effected by development are "absorbed" as "added energies" of the institutionalized forms peculiar to that society. These accumulations, however, reach a breaking-point, as the feudal example suggests. At that point, a qualitative change occurs. The range therefore corresponds to the limits of such a process of development, the lowest values corresponding to the minimal conditions of negative entropy under which the institutions can exist and be reproduced, and the upper limit corresponding to those conditions under which they become irremediably unstabilized.

In the jargon of the official Marxist, this interpretation of Hegel, Marx, Engels,[28] and Luxemburg[29] is bowdlerized in sloganeering versions of the motto "quantity becomes quality." It is not *simple* quantity, in the naive or reductionist sense of the term, that is involved in Hegel's, Marx's, Engels', and Luxemburg's notion of this point. That conclusion would require dismissal of the entire point of Marx's "Theses on Feuerbach," which Engels, for example, clearly understood despite his inability to comprehend certain of its deeper implications. Engels never understood quantity to signify material elementarity in what Marx terms the "dirty-judaical" sense. The quantum is not elementary, but determinate. The fact that discreteness exists does not make the quantum elementary, nor does it imply the obverse of the assumption of reductionist elementarity, "indeterminacy." Discreteness is a general reflection of the sort of "leaps" that are inherent in the notion of dialectical development in the general sense implied by the feudal example. This is exactly the sense in which Hegel developed this notion, and in which Marx and Engels understood it.

The determination of the breaking-point is usually associated with the emergence of new institutions as realizations of S. This can be generalized to include regression and degeneration if we extend the notion of S to apply to negative accumulation ($-S'$), signifying degeneration intrinsic to simple reproduction as the model for this notion. Realizing S' as new productive activities signifies not only an extension of the existing mode, but also necessarily the elaboration of the mode. Not only the increase of activity with respect to the relatively finite domain defined by a range of technology and the like, but also new kinds of activities and, in a more general and invariable fashion, the *simple extension of the scale of activity means new relationships characteristic of the entirety*. In capitalist development, in which the technological element is most immediate, realization tends to occur in terms of emergent technologies, which alter the division of labor as a whole, creating new categories of productive activities which tend to supplant or diminish the "weight" of the old while qualitatively altering the entire economy by virtue of their inclusion.

The case of the plumber illustrates the point. The skill of the plumber has not significantly advanced since at least the 1920s. Those particular skills he has gained are essentially nothing more than contingencies, and in this plumbing is analogous to the moribund textile, footwear, and garment manufacturing industries. Nevertheless, the plumber is more socially productive in the 1960s and 1970s than his counterpart was during the 1920s. And this is not attributable simply to the "speedup" that has occurred in this trade. Plumbing, especially its industrial and related applications, is an integral component of an entire effort which has advanced, and in which plumbing is a necessary activity. It is as part of the entire immediate division of labor, its essentiality to that immediate division of labor, that poor old plumbing acquires, despite itself, new productive powers. We shall develop this point more fully in subsequent chapters.

From the right-hand bar directional lines lead to the two population bars: specifically, the lines run from the output side of the production bar to the input sides of the population bars. This implies that the two sides of the bar, in each case, correspond to an intervening process. With respect to productive activity, the input side represents (for capitalist society) labor power. Its output is defined here as S', d, P, and N, which are materialized alterations of nature, including or analogous to products. The products are categorized among segments of the bar on the basis of their realization. They may represent a relationship to the material prerequisites of further productive activity (N), the material prerequisites of reproduction of the productive labor force as a whole (P), the material prerequisites of the existence and activities of the other population (d), or relatively "free energy," the realization of the extended existence of the society. Because we can thus apportion the output, we apportion the input correspondingly such that the ratio

$$\frac{S - d}{P + N}$$

is immediately a ratio of the *input* to itself by projection to its realization. Once we have projected that, as the directional lines from output of productive activity to populations and nature do in this example, we have an implied notion of *self-reflexive* projective relationships as a way of conceptualizing the notion of a law of social reproduction. To acknowledge the evolutionary aspect of this, as a law of evolutionary social reproduction, implies a modification of the initial heurism such that any specialist sufficiently familiar with such efforts will immediately recognize the sort of a "hairy beast" we are confronting from the standpoint of geometries. However, it is not necessary to work out such obvious implications to grasp the notion as we have outlined it.

THE CONTENTS OF CONSCIOUSNESS RECONSIDERED

Even in terms of the most limited discussion of the determination of segments within the population and the relationship of this process to the determination of segments of the productive process, it is feasible to enrich our previous treatment of the notion of the contents of consciousness. This result can be posed for fruitful reflection by considering again the allegation that Marx reduces all thought "in the final analysis" to the "economic side." One might thus assume the allegation to be true in a limited sense, and attempt to explain it by elaborating the sense in which it is appropriate.

First, of course, one's existence is subsumed by the law of evolutionary social reproduction, particularly as that law is reflected in the specific laws of development of one's own society: the entire organization of human behavior, notably the determination of productive activities, their relationship to all other forms of activity, and the notion of needs. One's relationship to the material conditions of existence of one's society (and, consequently, one's self) has what might be crudely described as a "structure"—the relationship within the productive forces and one's relationship to it. Similarly, the realization of any need has a structure of the sort implied by the model. Within the population, these primary existence relationships determine the segmental and subsumed conditions of maturation the society must impose upon itself. And these in turn represent the determined conditions in which the individual must locate his notions of rights and privileges.

From such a standpoint, it is obviously nonsensical to suggest that there is any aspect of individual human life which is not economic in the final analysis. Let us consider the case of the individual who claims that he "pays his own way" in society, that he is self-sufficient, and has some area of life which is rightly his "own business." We shall destroy his illusions.

Assume that this is a "rugged individual," a skilled worker who asserts that "my boss makes a good profit from my work," and that "I don't owe anyone anything." First of all, we have only to lower the price of his employer's commodities to cause that profit to vanish; lowering it a bit more will put this rugged individual on welfare. So, to the extent that society determines the prices of his employer's commodities and his own wage-labor, this rugged individual owes everything to society. And this observation is not limited to prices and wages. The materials he employs in his labor were produced by others; in fact, if we trace the antecedent process sheets and bills of materials for the materials, equipment, and tools he employs, we will find that a very large proportion of the human race is directly or indirectly engaged in making his production possible. If their contribution ends, his possibility of the "rugged individual" sort of productive activity vanishes. The same thing is true of the material consumption on which he depends. First, the prices at which he is empowered to buy these commodities are determined by others, on whose good will he is therefore dependent. Elaborating the network of process sheets and bills of materials for the constituents of his material existence—notably the glass of beer which so greatly assists him in expounding his views—we find most of the human race directly or indirectly involved in creating his existence.

"Quo vadis, Robinson Crusoe? Another bar, perhaps?"

The folly we have just disproven is commonplace among a certain variety of professed socialist, who asserts that the workers "at the local point of production" create wealth autonomously, and therefore that their employers' profits are a direct and simple exploitation of their production of wealth. This view was the basis for vicious racism and related forms of chauvinism among certain professed socialist supporters of AFL leader Samuel Gompers during the early decades of this century. If the wealth created in production is created autonomously by the workers employed in a given plant, then there exists no wealth which is the right of the unemployed. For the unemployed to become employed through the alienation of part of the wage-commodities and means of production (surplus value) created by employed labor thus amounts to exploitation!

The New Left of the 1960s indulged in a related bit of folly, asserting that the United States is approaching the ennobled state of a "post industrial society." Confronted with urban decay, poverty, and other evidence of a massive shortage of industrial production, representatives of the New Left shrugged their shoulders and retorted irritably, "Such material things have been overvalued; it is 'culture' and 'other values' that need to be stressed." The white suburban radical intellectual would then be struck by a thought. A manic gleam in his eye, he would gesture forcefully, raising his voice to add, "Like 'soul.'" This is a most instructive example of the problem to be considered.

First, to the extent that the radical intellectual acquired what he regarded as culture, and enjoyed such "other values," essentially because he had been reared as a member of a leisured suburbanite population, a point made abundantly clear by the academic settings in which this emphasis on "other values" was customarily voiced. Thus, he made the elementary blunder—if we do not label his beliefs for what they were, an obsession—of disregarding the material preconditions for leisure.

His fascination with black ghetto 'soul' was a form of unintentional viciousness. He was treating black people as "niggers." Preoccupation with "soul" arises among black people in the ghetto as a reification of their material deprivation. To accept material deprivation that determines cultural deprivation, to accept that reality under conditions in which expectations were almost non-existent, would be to accept, internalize, degradation. In order to maintain the self-respect necessary to endure such conditions, black people adopted the term "soul" to describe ghetto culture. Inevitably, this reified category of deprivation came to represent certain socializing forms of behavior by which black people manage to maintain their essential dignity and provide mutual assistance for material survival under degrading circumstances. "Soul" in this sense is what is sometimes termed a "survival culture" or "culture of poverty," which is positive only to the extent that one accepts the validity of the material and other circumstances to which this "culture" is adapted. The admiration of such a culture by a white suburbanite radical is quite a different matter than the acceptance of it by its victim. It is absolutely indistinguishable from the old southern white racist saw, "Niggers are happier that way." One has compassion for the means by which materially oppressed people manage to survive psychologically and socially; it is the most vicious, because the most insidious, form of racism to admire such things as "innate to black people."

Returning to the Third Camp political outlook we cited above—the belief that the workers in each plant autonomously produce wealth—we can see that the world-outlook of the capitalist is *relatively* progressive. By contrast to the Third Camper, the capitalist is, perhaps through no fault of his own, an absolute humanitarian. That is, to the extent that he develops the productive forces of society, the capitalist, in his characteristically capitalist way, not only gives the unemployed the rights the Third Camper would deny him, but makes possible improvements in the material conditions of life and potential for leisure of the employed worker—often against that worker's will.

The content of bourgeois ideology in the worker is thus seen as *conditionally* positive both for society generally and for himself. To the extent that the worker is heteronomic in outlook and that his alienated ideology is that of a subject of capitalism, he is opposed to the appropriation (socialization) of part of the product of the activities in which he is employed. The employer, by wresting this portion of the social product from such heteronomic individual workers and groups performs an indispensable service to society. He employs the unemployed productively, expands and develops the productive forces, and thus makes possible a rising social productivity, more advanced material culture, and both the forms and availability of increased leisure (cultural life) for employed workers. Thus the capitalist is necessary to the worker as a force which overcomes the fatal heteronomic (simple-reproductive) tendencies in particular employed wage-labor. Negation of the negation! The worker, however militant he becomes, as a pure-and-simple individual worker or trade-unionist negates his own anticapitalist impulses to be for the capitalist system's perpetuation.

Granted, such workers sometimes profess to be socialist, prosocialist, or simply anticapitalist. Such professions are entirely and literally religious in form and content. The aspiration which impels the worker to negate capitalism is expressed in a ceremonial belief; the content he gives to that belief, like religious self-denial, is revealed in his preoccupation with developing a prosocialist caucus more or less within the hermetic bounds of a particular union or organized group. His socialist practice could not be tolerated by the working class without the domination of society by capitalists. By his hermetic exclusion of the unorganized and unemployed, sectors of his own class from his interpretation of immediate socialist practice with respect to employed, unionized labor, he excludes the social relationships which could make possible the assumption of the positive social role otherwise performed by capitalists.

In these general illustrative observations we have indicated the proper approach to determination of the more explicit "objective" contents of consciousness. The notion of objects of practice and need exists only through the mediation of social relations. The heteronomic form of organization of the working class in capitalist society determines the form of relations among persons of different classes and sections of classes. These immediate elements are the particular features of consciousness whose interrelations, dialectically adduced, are the more general and abstract features of capitalist ideology. The same method applies to every society.

THE GENERAL FORM OF 5
SOCIAL REPRODUCTION

THE GENERAL FORM OF SOCIAL REPRODUCTION 5

If one were to follow the outlines of the Hegelian method, an economic theory of capitalism would be developed in the following fashion. One would begin with a critical examination of the simplest alienated conception from the domain of capitalist economy, negate it, and so on until he had thus arrived at a conception of the capitalist economic process as a whole. Then, having reached such a notion of capital-in-general, he would discard all the notions he had developed along the way as merely conditional, restating them in light of the notion of self-development of the whole as a whole. To a large extent, that is precisely the plan of organization of Marx's four-volume *Capital*.[1]

The internal structure of *Capital* is organized as follows. The first chapter of Volume I introduces the simplest alienated aspects of capitalist economy, the so-called "cell form" of the commodity in itself. The sense certainties of exchange value and use value are introduced in their sense-certainty, alienated forms. A preliminary dialectical operation is performed to negate the simple sense certainty of the cell form in these respects, and, to cap this point, the section on "The Fetishism of Commodities" from the *Theories of Surplus Value* manuscript is inserted here, to leave no doubt that Marx rejects absolutely the reductionist notions of determination of "exchange value" or "use value."

The lessons of the first chapters of *Theories of Surplus Value* are then applied to succeeding chapters to arrive at notions of first *relative* and then *absolute* exchange value. The discoveries elaborated in the middle portions of *Theories* involving the categories of capitalist production, are then introduced, and the volume proceeds to complete a preliminary view of capitalist economy, not as it actually exists but as its phenomena can be abstracted from the standpoint of capitalist production in itself. The categories of capitalist economy are treated as if capitalist production represented a closed model with respect to production itself.

In the second volume of *Capital*, as Rosa Luxemburg so aptly puts it, "The capitalist follows his commodities from his warehouse and from his office into the stock exchange, and in the second volume of *Capital* we follow the capitalist."[2] Marx here negates the view of capitalist economy from the restricted standpoint of production.

At the outset of the third volume, Marx declares his intention to upset the preliminary conclusions developed in the first two. This is no afterthought; consulting Theories of Surplus Value, which was virtually completed before undertaking even the first draft of the first volume of *Capital*, we are assured that this upset was Marx's intention all along. Marx describes the next step:

In the first volume we analyzed the phenomena presented by the *process of capitalist production,* considered by itself as a mere productive process without regard to any secondary influences of conditions outside of it. But this process of production, in the strict meaning of the term, does not exhaust the life circle of capital. It is supplemented in the actual world by the *process of circulation,* which was the object of our analysis in the second volume. We found . . . that the capitalist process of production, considered as a whole, is a combination of the processes of production and circulation. . . . We are . . . interested in locating the concrete forms growing out of the *movements of capitalist production as a whole* and setting them forth. In actual reality the capitals move and meet in such concrete forms that the form of the capital in the process of production and that of the capital in the process of circulation impress one only as special aspects of those concrete forms. The conformations of the capitals evolved in this third volume approach step by step that form which they assume on the surface of society, in their mutual interactions, in competition, and in the ordinary consciousness of the human agencies in this process."[3]

The first of these steps is the determination of a general rate of profit, not as it is actually determined but as it must exist from the standpoint of a closed model of both production and circulation. Marx proceeds to define the invariant quality of capitalist accumulation as such, its *self-movement,* thus embarking upon the notion of capital in general he stipulated at the outset of the volume. Here, he adduces systematically the contradiction between capitalist accumulation and the underlying basis, the contradiction between exchange value and use value as the form of movement of capitalist accumulation, a movement characterized by crises which represent the surfacing of the contradictions and which thus reflect the actual nature of the real movements occurring throughout the preceding period. The "internal contradictions"—the fundamental antinomy—thus defined, Marx turns to the actual form of movement of capitalist accumulation in a society which is by no means a closed economic model. He uncovers the means by which the capitalist credit and monetary processes—the actual forms of the process of capitalist circulation—reflect the internal contradictions in the form of an accumulation of *fictitious capital* such that all the contradictions of capital otherwise adduced actually occur not in the hypothetical forms of their formal necessity, but as contradictions associated with the accumulation of fictitious capitals in the monetary/credit facets of capitalist accumulation itself. Thus the internal contradictions of capitalist accumulation are manifest as monetary crises, crises of liquidity. That explained, Marx has completed the upward progress of his dialectical inquiry. He turns, then, to define capitalist accumulation as a specific form of human society, in terms of the fundamental relationship of man's productive labor to nature as man finds and alters it. This he situates within the empirical setting of the issue of rent. That settled, he sets out in Section VII, the incomplete concluding section of Volume III, to redefine everything from the standpoint of these accomplishments. We adduce the general law of evolutionary human reproduction first encountered in the "Feuerbach" section of *The German Ideology:* "Freedom/Necessity"[4] and, surrounding it, the treatment of the general notion of capitalist phenomena with respect to that general law. An entirely new view of capitalism begins to emerge, subsuming all the topics so laboriously considered "on the way up" in a fresh, comprehensive fashion. But, alas, after a few paragraphs on the issue of "Classes," the manuscript ends.

Only the internal features of capitalist development have thus been situated. To abstract capitalist development as a specific form—taken up in the last two sections of Volume III—we need a still more general approach, which not accidentally pervades Marx's entire approach to the question. Capitalist economy as a whole must be defined relative to what it is not, which means relative to European feudalism first and socialism second. It is capitalism as a movement from European feudalism to socialist world economy that is the positive comprehension of capitalist political economy.

We must, of course, qualify this statement; to so summarily define capitalist development must not mean to overlook the fact that in its world-ranging development capitalism has reproduced itself at the expense not only of the feudal and mercantilist economy out of which it arose in Europe, but of numerous forms of noncapitalist and nonfeudal societies as well. However small the mass of wealth absorbed by capitalism in its colonial and semicolonial depredations, its ravishment was decisive in various respects. An example is the development of slavery for colonialist plantations, which in turn depended upon and exacerbated a breakdown in African cultures.[5] Further examples are the importance of precious metals and, less celebrated but of explosive significance, of Aztec-Inca foods in revolutionizing European commerce and agriculture; the role of commercial development in colonialism; and the role of emigration in extending the scale of capitalism as a world system, thus forcing its qualitative development in the "home base." To know capitalism as a whole, one must take into account a major part of the development of other societies—"primitive" and "barbaric" as well as feudal.

This generalization reflects the content of Hegel's philosophy, of which Hegel himself was highly aware. As Heine's remarkable thesis partly states and further implies,[6] and as we have shown in this text, the issues of philosophy arose out of the post-Renaissance enlightenment, and the development of that philosophy not accidentally reflects its origins and the grounds of its continuation in leading through Hegel and Feuerbach to the notion of a self-subsisting positive, which is itself a reflection of both the world-historical implications of capitalism and the degree to which capitalist accumulation brought the noetic aspect of human existence to the foreground for the first time. Only a form of society whose dynamic impels it to reduce all human existence to an organic whole, as capitalism does by its creation of a worldwide division of labor, and which imbues that worldwide production of human existence with immediate comprehension of the creative aspect of mentation, could produce Hegel, Feuerbach, and Marx.

To study Hegel as a philosopher *per se*—that is, to study him relative to philosophy treated as an academic subject—is to comprehend absolutely nothing of philosophy in general or Hegel in particular. Hegel, even in his most passionately idealistic moments, would not have entertained the silly notion that his ideas can be explained in terms of the extant body of scholarly papers in that field. Indeed, the kernel of Hegel's philosophy on this point is that it was the creation of capitalist relations that made his philosophical reflections historically possible.

Yet, without Hegel, a scientific political economy would be impossible. Since the dynamic of capitalist development is located in its universalizing aspects, any attempt to understand it which fails to provide a solution to the problem of conceptualizing the universal in a practical fashion must be a failure of the type exemplified by Ricardo. Since the dynamic of capitalist development is premised on creative mentation as that which is realized through the universalizing character of capitalist development, it would be impossible without a dialectic of Hegel's type to understand even the simplest aspect of capitalist phenomena.

In Hegel, relative to actual political economy, there was only one—decisive—flaw. As Marx understood through Feuerbach as early as 1843,[7] the vicious fallacies of Hegel's *Phenomenology of Mind* and *Science of Logic* were revealed as soon as Hegel attempted to apply his pathetic misconception of productive labor to actual society in *The Philosophy of Right*. Hegel's dualism—his mistaken assumption, following Heraclitus' identical blunder, that the laws of nature were already perfected—was revealed when he attempted to locate the realization of creative mentation in the form of labor. For Hegel could not possibly comprehend labor as a process through which man is progressively changing the laws of his universe. Labor for him was only a matter of advantageous rearrangements of things and persons (social relationships); thus the administrative side of social development was inevitably in itself the location of what Hegel termed labor.

Granted, only recently has the deeper implication of the productive realization of universal labor begun to emerge, and even now it is generally sensed, so to speak, preconsciously. Once man begins to alter nature on a larger scale, to create new "elements" and introduce new processes into the universe around him, the laws of the universe, as we ordinarily understand such laws and as Hegel understood them, are being changed. The notion of an invariant—the world-line—as we have portrayed it represents a fundamental law of a different sort than one ordinarily imagines. It subsumes entire arrays of special laws of the universe as movement occurs along the world-line. This principle was implicit in man's first existence as man, that is, as he began to produce his material conditions of existence. It is only now on the verge of beginning to become grossly apparent.

Our knowledge on this point does not depend on gross observations of actual changes in such laws, nor is the point at all speculative. For the sort of reasons already given in several connections where the same variety of problem might seem to arise, when we examine the history (including the so-called prehistory) of man's existence, as we are able to do from the conceptual vantage point created by capitalist development, we discover the principle involved. So to speak, we show that the "measurement" of the "distance" along every "line" in social-evolutionary "space" places us in a universe of such characteristic features.

There are hints in Hegel's work that he considered such a notion and rejected it. At least, it was not something he simply failed to consider, but something he explicitly excluded. As one recognizes the specific cause of his difficulty on this point, one must appreciate Feuerbach's and Marx's successive "philosophical" achievements as absolutely essential, earth-shaking important steps beyond Hegel toward the possibility of a science of political economy. If the universe's elementary laws are not perfected, one must demonstrate a means by which the Logos itself can be externally changed to come into correspondence with the material universe. This brings up the most obvious and central vulnerability of both Kant and Hegel: the categories. Neither ever accounted for the categories. Kant merely plumps them down without explaining whence they came (as Hegel notes). Hegel in turn adjusts the same general set of categories, introducing only such qualifications and modifications as are required to make them coherent in terms of the rationalization his *Science of Logic* offers for them. If the universe is evolving in its laws, what happens to the categories? To preserve the perfection of the categories one must fix the laws of the universe as perfected. Otherwise, one must account not only for the coherent evolution of categories, but also for a means by which they are brought into correspondence with the evolution of universal laws.

Instantly, at least on principle, Feuerbach's true genius becomes apparent. The point is summarized, most compactly in the familiar Section 33 of his *Principles of the Philosophy of the Future*. If socialized practice, relative to the material conditions of human existence, determines consciousness, then consciousness, thus determined, reflects whatever universal laws prevail, and evolves as any evolution in universal laws evolves. That is the implication of Feuerbach's achievement, an importance of his discovery which he himself did not comprehend. It was left to Marx to grasp the point involved.

Feuerbach's failure, as we have noted in the preceding chapters, is that in advancing beyond Hegel on this point, he adopted Hegel's blunder with respect to the perfection of the laws of nature. Thus, as we have noted, Feuerbach nailed development to the Tarpeian Rock of perfected natural laws. His usual critics to the contrary, Feuerbach did not fall back into reductionism with respect to the individual Self,[8] but rather compacted the notion of development within the determination of self-consciousness. Within that compacted realm, Feuerbach's dialectic is more advanced, as a dialectic, than Hegel's, since he has transcended Hegel's false-positive negation of the negation to propose a self-subsisting positive. However, nailed to that rock, his dialectical figure is not capable of noteworthy amounts of movement. It is necessary to break the rock so that he may move once again.

Initially, Marx merely permits man to alter nature—or so it might seem. However, since Marx's man is a part of the universe he seems merely to alter, whatever laws he manifests for the universe in his capacity to deliberately alter it are also laws of the universe. The point is perhaps clearest from a pedagogical standpoint when contrasted with Hegel's reasons for refusing to consider even alteration, the most modest aspect of the point. Man's manifest ability to alter his comprehension of universal laws in practice demonstrates, if this power is itself a power within the universe, as power of the universe in respect to man. To this argument, Hegel says no. Yet simply extending the notion of development to the material universe as a whole, as Marx did, frees Feuerbach's man from the rock; Feuerbach has thus provided the key to the solution.

To mixed reaction from Ockham's freshly shaven ghost, we show that everything in the universe formerly considered fundamental is merely determinate, but for a single premise whose form is the world-line. The proof of this demonstration is human labor, the shapes into which the universe and man's own history fall under the working hand of man. However, consciousness and knowledge are also determinate forms of that history. Without the emergence of a form of society whose immediate impulse was to universalize self-development, the possibility of measuring displacements along the world-line could not have occurred to man, his consciousness of the possibility of such measurements could not have occurred. Thus, looking back upon our previous development, it is impossible for us not to color the past with the hues of the present. That is not such a defect as might be immediately supposed: it is impossible to understand the past from a less-developed standpoint than that premised in capitalist development. That we seem to impose capitalist *teleology* on the inner life of earlier forms of society is not such a fault as might initially be argued. Such societies could not possibly understand themselves, or be understood generally, except in respect to that movement within them which leads toward capitalist development. This tendency, which must be inevitable and unavoidable in any attempt to understand the past from the present, becomes an error only when capitalism is mistaken for completed perfection. This error would cause one to look at ancient societies, for example, for their specifically capitalist qualities. The only remedy for this error is to examine the past from the standpoint of the fundamental contradictions of capitalist development, and to locate in the invariant features of historical development thus adduced the principle which must be applied.

The historical specificity we require in empirical practice in understanding the past has two moments. On the one side, to the extent that our empirical knowledge of the past is necessarily limited in several respects, the primary requirement is to approach such studies with a profound sense of historical specificity. This means, immediately, less attention to the empirical evidence in its own right than reflection upon our own thought processes. The first task in all sane hypothesizing is to dismiss conjectures which represent demonstrably false assumptions. In general, this rigor may be identified by noting that the scientist rejects the method employed in writing so-called historical novels, that of treating the past as a costume closet and backdrop for the plots of present-day drama. The investigator adopts, as his fundamental rigor, a search for the specific ideologies of other societies in respect to the objective basis of such ideologies in the peculiarities of the sort of technology of social reproduction. To "get into the mind" of ancient man, he must first become ancient man for a moment, which he can accomplish in approximation by setting himself, his problems of existing as ancient man, within the "technology," the material mode of social reproduction, of ancient society. He must accept, for the moment, the limitations imposed upon the scope of man's problem-solving actions by that technology and by the social forms (e.g., "institutions") through which action is made feasible and permitted in those societies. Then, provided he has understood the nature of ideology in capitalist society, and thus the deeper structures of his own mentation, he is equipped to explore the history and literature of those societies, to gauge those people against his own mind relocated in that setting. No Robinson Crusoe games are allowed; he must gauge his own anguish in respect to what that society's characteristic ideology will not permit him to do—even to save his own life—in such circumstances.

The archeologist-anthropologist, after years of study, after digging on site after site, after completing much of his latest exploration, stands one evening in the midst of that site. The broken walls rise again in his imagination. People begin to move about the resurrected city. To the extent that he has been able to get inside the mind of man in that ancient city, he attempts to conceptualize what he elaborates from the mental outlook of that people. To this he adds one more essential thing. He is keenly aware of the contradictions, which he compares to the irony of the goldfish, liberated from his bowl, who continues to swim in circles. He sees the self-development of the ancient society in the contradictions of its characteristic mode, and sees the contradictions of that mode from the standpoint of its self-development. His concern is not with the solutions that might occur to the minds of Robinson Crusoe or Mark Twain's hero in King Arthur's court. He is preoccupied with the actual alternatives of supercession and decay confronting that culture. He sees the Semites harassing the Sumerians as he thinks of the daily life of the "black-headed people." He sees the "peoples of the sea" in the distance. He sees the Achaemenid tax-farmer making his cruel rounds, the wage-laborer and then the slave tilling tenures held in usury, and flinches at the obvious decline in the quality of maintenance of the basic productive mode. He collapses the construction of the Achaemenid palaces into a lapsed-time image, comparing the wages and workmanship of the successive generations of craftsmen and nodding sadly at the interconnected decline of both. He sees the recurring nightmare of the commune on the Asian subcontinent and shakes his head—because he is too sober a scholar to shriek aloud at the wretched destiny of so many human souls. He has a sense of historical specificity; he has learned what he must and must not transfer from the experience of capitalist society to his efforts to understand the dynamics of these cultures in their actual historical setting.

Even after one has acquired, through the intensive study of several societies, a working command of historical specificity, he is still hampered in actually elaborating the inner dynamics of those societies. Once one appreciates the kinds of understanding which were not possible for the greatest minds in earlier societies—for example, apropos the great issues of philosophy—he has a keener sense of what can and cannot be elaborated in the imagination. One cannot instantly derive theories of cultures from a handful of facts about history. Our limitations are only qualitatively less severe in exploring the past than in projecting the future. With respect to the past, all the laws and qualitative aspects of conceptualization are of an order inferior to those possible for us in capitalist society; with respect to the future, we do not have this advantage. We can discover the future only to the extent that it is immanent in the present. In the past, we are limited by lack of sufficient empirical knowledge. It is not that we lack a sufficient quantity of facts for statistical significance, but that the judgment guiding the collection of facts, whether by contemporaries of the period in question or by modern investigators, has ordinarily been hopelessly misguided, or nearly so. We do not have the right facts, properly adduced and conceptualized. Yet we cannot despise the research that has already been done; we must sift through it all, reflecting intensively as we proceed, in search of that peculiar evidence which has unique significance.

In the best work of anthropologists, historians, and ethologists—in particular—we encounter such a method, even when they do not profess a dialectical method. The case of anthropologist Louis Leakey comes to mind. What is his method? His method is evolution; each artifact is judged from the standpoint of human self-development, and such evidence is searched out according to the dictates of necessity: human development being coherent, the evidence must lie here. We are less concerned with the extent to which his constructs from his discoveries are exactly correct. Even if those conjectures and hypotheses are discredited one after the other, something more essential remains. Here lies the meager residue of Pleistocene man, or perhaps only his distant cousin: a bit of bone, a bit of rock, a few pieces located in such a way as to suggest a site. From such evidence the investigator must conjure up entire cultures and protocultures. How is that possible? It is possible because it is "not necessary to repeat the same experiment in every river of the world." When we deal with man and man's ancestors, it is the human question, respecting which we have the most abundant and conclusive evidence, which permits us to deduce whole architectures of reliable knowledge from a handful of simple facts. The essential question is evolution and those evidences which bear upon human cultural evolution. Wherever we locate even the most minimal bit of evidence bearing on the evolution of the physiology or practice of man, we can begin to reconstruct a culture. If the evidence is insufficient for conclusive insights, no matter; it tells us where to scratch next for the unique sort of similarly shard-like evidence that will enable us to reach conclusions.

Of course, the same principle applies in a modified fashion to all paleontology and related fields. Once we have situated the investigation in evolutionary development, we have defined necessity as *empirical* necessity, not the false necessity of conjecture as such. In the degree of articulation we give to evolutionary history in any of these domains, the completeness of the portrait of specificity we adduce is limited by the evidence. Yet we are nonetheless able to interpret the evidence we do have decisively. Such decisiveness involves, most importantly, a decisive judgment as to what we do not know, either respecting lack of a specific sort of evidence, or a specific feature or articulation of the sort of process under investigation. It is confidence in our powers of understanding, not doubt of them, that impels us fiercely to search for evidence, make experiments, and the like.

There is no difference between anthropological science examined from this standpoint and the scientific principles of investigation and judgment which underlie the mere appearance of so-called physical science. In both, the contradictory character of ideology and invariant processes is the focus of study—not ideology in the naive sense of ordinary error, but in the sense of the false understanding of reality necessarily embedded in our conception of science in particular. In general, ideology permits us to solve successfully numerous everyday problems involving work. Yet, we are repeatedly impelled—and this is real scientific work—to search out the grey areas in which ideology itself breaks down, and out of which a new elaboration of what we call physical science emerges. This is the nature of science in general, interpreted from the standpoint of historical specificity. And these are, in form, exactly the problems we confront in attempting to comprehend the specific laws of development of past societies, and in looking more than a few decades into the shape of the future.

In general, the method we have repeatedly described provides our fundamental guide. To understand any society, one must determine not only what kind of society it has emerged to supercede, but what contradictions in the previous mode of existence made the supercessor possible and necessary. We understand the internal laws of the supercessor only by adducing its downfall, by either supercession or degeneration. The most important phenomena are those that pertain to the emergence of the germs of the superceding form from the form of social reproduction characteristic of the existing society, or of such germs in the aborted form which, in so many instances, demands intervention by another outside society: combined and uneven development.

The emergence of mercantile capitalism and later capitalism from feudal decay provides the most accessible model. The Domesday book, Charlemagne's inventory, and other such documents define such societies' notion of wealth. The mode of reproduction is essentially fixed and changes occur as additions to the existing mode. There is no notion of productivity, except in the bestial sense. Feudal man has no notion of humanity except that provided by his religious beliefs. Whoever does not share his religion is therefore a mere beast, to be hunted down like a wild boar if that is his pleasure. Reproduction takes the form of colonization from particular estates or pseudouniversalities of combined estates represented by the vertical organization of feudal society. The number of knights and feudal peasants therefore constitutes wealth in the active sense, and the definition of social reproduction is increase in the number of knights with a supporting number of peasants attached to fertile plots. The notion of nature has two interconnected categories, arable unoccupied land and arable occupied land; the latter was much preferred for obvious reasons. The form of feudalism is therefore characterized by combined and uneven development, and by the use of the surplus population and population-time of the existing estates to subjugate contiguous occupied land. When the "natural" resources for such colonization converge on their approximate limits (as a relatively finite "natural" resource), feudal reproduction naturally expresses itself in cannibalization.

The law against usury, together with the presence of the Jew (e.g., Charlemagne's tame herd of Jews), provides the clue to the whole situation. Usury is antithetical to the feudal system because it represents the conversion of social surplus from its characteristic feudal form (surplus population and the material basis for surplus population) into a form of alienated product, by which serfs and nonfeudal populations can be realized in a nonfeudal way. Yet the Papacy, which gave the feudal system that universality every social system requires, instituted usury in the forms typified by Peter's Pence. Wherever magnates express universalizing tendencies for large aggregations of estates, such alienation occurs in various forms—endemically as the Jew.[9] Charlemagne's Jews were therefore milked, as a private herd should be, and returned to pasture to collect more milk for the next time the monarch became thirsty. The systematic persecution of Jewry, with the rise and spread of the plague of Lombards, thus expresses the denouement of feudalism as feudalism; the persecuted Jews either ceased to be Jews or migrated to those regions of Europe where feudalism still flourished. (Later, as feudalism collapsed entirely, the Jews became Christians in the guise of continuing to be Jews.)

Thus, in the feudal mode of reproduction—its intrinsic crusade against populated land wherever it was accessible for colonization—the need for alienation of the material means of existence of the crusader created a need for universalized wealth which could accompany the crusader on his social-reproductive rounds. The endemic expression of feudal social reproduction was the Jew—who therefore sometimes became a nobleman by alienating that function from the feudal lord who had not been sufficiently energetic or successful in prosecuting his universalizing conquests. When the papal treasury and its auxiliary, the Lombards, became the only source of alienation (credit) sufficient to meet the increased crusading spirit's demands (e.g., for cannibals' crusades), the Lombards took as incidental payment from their debtors the expulsion of the Jew.[10]

In the course of Marx's writings, *primitive accumulation* by emergent capitalism against the remnants of feudal forms of reproduction becomes the clue to understanding capitalism itself. The importance of this point from the standpoint of the fundamentals of scientific political economy is that in the reification of wealth from one social form to another, from one specific set of society's laws to another, we adduce that which is common and fundamental to both. Marx's views on this have recently become more accessible to the English-reading student with the 1971 publication of the Moscow edition of Part III of *Theories of Surplus Value;* most relevant is chapter XXI, "Opposition to the Economists," notably section 3, in which the ironies of the twofold nature of capital are developed. This point is also discussed significantly in the sixth section of Volume III of *Capital*,[11] and, in a different respect, in the concluding section of the same volume.[12]

Marx's approach, as defined in these and other locations, is the tactic we employ in this text. To enable ourselves to trace most directly the transition of a society from its predecessor to its supercessor, we must concentrate first on what we conditionally termed objective in Chapter 2. We must first locate the transformations in objective technology which most fundamentally distinguish one basic mode of production from its predecessor and supercessor.

Since this approach has been and will remain for some time hotly opposed, even by professed Marxists, we cite again a passage to which we have previously referred:

> The conception, which regards only the conditions of distribution historically, but not the conditions of production, is, on the one hand, merely an idea begotten by the incipient, but still handicapped, critique of bourgeois economy.[13] On the other hand it rests upon a misconception, an identification of the process of social reproduction with the *simple*[14] labor process, such as might be performed by any abnormally situated human being[15] without any social assistance. *To the extent that the labor process is a simple*[16] *process between man and nature, its simple elements remain the same in all social forms of development. But every definite historical form of this process develops more and more its material foundations and social forms.* Whenever a certain maturity is reached, one definite social form is discarded and displaced by a higher one. The time for the coming of such a crisis is announced by the breadth and depth of the contradictions and antagonisms, which separate the conditions of distribution, and with them

the definite historical form of the corresponding conditions of production, and the development of their agencies. A conflict then arises between the material development of production and its social form.[17]

Exactly. The principal task of Volume I was precisely to adduce the lawful form of the process of capitalist production—to the extent that could be inferred from the assumption that capitalism is a closed model with respect to production itself, and to the extent that the phenomena of capitalist development correspond to the underlying technology embedded in the principles of its productive process. This model contained the essential contradiction, even from the standpoint of equating the use values so determined with historic valuations of capital: in short, that the general rate of profit corresponds to the general rate of real development of the social-reproductive forces. It does not; and, assuming that the elaboration of this problem in *Theories of Surplus Value* was overlooked by the reader (as was the case universally until the end of the century), one had to wait for the third volume for the remedy to this flaw in the model.

The issue of mind and matter as it pertains to the general form of capitalist production is almost unmentioned in the first volume. Production appears, in the main, to be a matter of blind natural laws, insofar as the capitalist mode of production is treated as a closed system with respect to the specific mode of production it represents. Mind in the ancient mind/matter duality—the subjective side as we conditionally define it—is more directly represented in the processes of circulation, in which the process of capitalist accumulation reflects upon and interprets the consequences of its production and determines, through the interconnections of circulation, what next actions will occur, what wilful actions are next to become subject to the underlying objective laws of the specific productive process.

Yet that elucidation does not eliminate the fundamental flaw in the model, however more comprehensive and correct was the understanding achieved of the actual form of capitalist accumulation. For the consequences of the wilful actions taken by capitalists (investment, circulation) are not judged *by capitalists* according to the underlying objective laws. The results themselves are subjectively judged. Accordingly, as the outcome of the fragmentary chapter at the end of the second volume attests, no solution to the outcome of expanded reproduction could be secured as long as the results of that reproduction were judged from the characteristic *capitalist ideological standpoint* of historic valuations of previously accumulated capitals.

We take here only a more direct approach to the problem than that of *Capital* itself. The difference is essentially pedagogical, as the citation above from the conclusion of the third volume attests. We start with the real, underlying phenomena, constantly taking cognizance of the contradiction we must elaborate respecting the dualism of capitalist accumulation, and elaborate that contradiction as a Great Fugue at the end. Throughout the next four chapters, we emphasize the real approach, developing the essential underlying categories from the standpoint of the determination of use value. In the succeeding three chapters—9 through 11—we define and integrate the credit and monetary form of the process of circulation, elaborating the determination of exchange value, and in the final chapter we sum up their interconnection as a process to be comprehended as invariant with respect to these two interpenetrating processes of determination.

ENGELS' ERROR AGAIN

Apropos this approach, we now adduce the point on which Engels' disagreement with Marx about Feuerbach is reflected as a difference with Marx's approach to what is sometimes termed historical materialism. This issue is best exemplified by a passage from Engels' manuscript, *Dialectics of Nature:*

> The fact that our subjective thought and the objective world are subject to the same laws, and hence, too, that in the final analysis they cannot contradict each other in their results, but must coincide, governs absolutely our whole theoretical thought. It is the unconscious and unconditional premise for theoretical thought. Eighteenth-century materialism, owing to its essentially metaphysical character, investigated this premise only as regards content. It restricted itself to the proof that the content of all thought and knowledge must derive from sensuous experience, and revived the principle: *nihil est in intellectu, quod non fuerit in sensu.* It was idealistic, but at the same time dialectical, philosophy, and especially Hegel, which for the first time investigated it also as regards *form.* In spite of all the innumerable arbitrary constructions and fantasies we encounter here, in spite of the idealist, topsy-turvy form of its result–the unity of thought and being—it is undeniable that this philosophy proved the analogy of the processes of thought to those of nature and history and *vice versa,* and the validity of similar laws for all those processes, in numerous cases and in the most diverse fields.

So far so good, but Engels continues:

> On the other hand, modern natural science has extended the principle of the origin of all thought content from experience in a way that breaks down its old metaphysical limitation and formulation.

Not so! A grave error! But to continue:

> By recognizing the inheritance of acquired characters . . .

Aha! Lamarckianism, or at least a very strong bias toward attempting to fuse Lamarck and Darwin. He continues:

> . . . it extends the subject of our experience from the individual to the genus;

This point is correct; but what content does he give to it?

> the single individual that must have experienced is no longer necessary . . .

Again correct, but:

> its individual experience can be replaced to a certain extent by the results of the experiences of a number of its ancestors.

Engels, in part, understands exactly the thrust of Marx's criticism of Darwin. Indeed, he was a major contributor to Marx's development on precisely this point, at least if the priority of enunciation is indicative. Yet in rejecting the real solution to this problem, outlined in Feuerbach's Section 33 of the *Principles of the Philosophy of the Future*, Engels adopts a pseudosolution from the Lamarckian approach:

> If, for instance, among us the mathematical axioms seem self-evident . . .

This is not an incidental blunder; it correlates with an error which persists throughout Engels' writings.

> . . . to every eight-year-old child, and in no need of proof from experience, this is solely the result of 'accumulated inheritance.' It would be difficult to teach them by a proof to the bushman or Australian Negro.[18]

There we have it; not only outright Lamarckian metaphysics but a taint of something else, carefully contained in Engels, which would become reactionary if made the basis for social theory.

If a linguist found himself among some New Guinea highlanders who had never before encountered modern man, and, mastering their language, attempted to communicate to them the concept "ore," what would be the result? We have but to imagine the ridicule he would arouse, showing these people various bits of rock. Presuming that such people are more polite than we, they might nod appreciatively at the demonstration, but not an iota of the concept "ore" would enter their heads. However, once metal becomes an important aspect of their social practice, supplanting rocks as tools, their old discrimination among rocks (e.g., tool-making suitability, "Who can make such a tool from such a rock?" "What kind of social practice is such a rock useful for?") evaporates, and the significant aspect of rock-nature is shifted. Metal becomes a social relationship to the outside world, whose insidious technology has increased their powers over nature—their power to deplete nature from the standpoint of the old culture. Thus they come to depend upon the artifacts by which they can live in such a depleted nature. Rock may become to them that which is carried away by the outside culture. It becomes ore to the extent that the labor of extracting it is exchanged for metal artifacts. However, it is still perhaps not ore to them, as we understand the term, since the labor (servitude) of extracting ore is related to many other artifacts in addition to metallic ones. If they are put to work in smelters, for example, rocks of a certain type begin to become ore to them in our sense of the term.

More generally, "outside man," his practices, and the rights and privileges of the tribe and its individual members essentially depend upon this relationship of concept to practice. The new individual's relationship to his own rights and privileges becomes in part the relationships of the "outside world" as mediated through his immediate tribe. The emerging generation, without the slightest Lamarckian inheritance, may do brilliantly at Oxford and Cambridge.

Engels' solution to the problem is, in the main, pure rot—rot in the etiological sense of "infectious." This single error of Engels', reflected both in his Lamarckian bias and in his coherent blunders with respect to mathematics and nineteenth-century science generally, has been adopted by many alleged dialectical materialists as justification for chimeras that have no overall relationship to Engels' general views. What they have done is taken his error out of context and given it independent life, so to speak, as a legitimization of a general reductionist approach.

This point should be stressed, so that no error can arise from it. Because Engels refused to acknowledge the significance of Feuerbach's fundamental contribution to the interconnected notions of a self-subsisting positive and the social determination of the contents of consciousness, he was left with the effort to connect the dialectical world-outlook, which he otherwise represented, by this Lamarckian ruse. In Engels' writings, this difficulty occurs as an attempt to solve a conceptual problem within what is otherwise complete agreement with and comprehension of Marx's dialectical method. Engels, as passages from *Anti-Dühring* in particular show, was not a reductionist in his conception of matter. The same point can be readily demonstrated even in numerous sections of the *Dialectics of Nature* manuscript. The closest resemblance to Engels' ontology among physicists, for example, is that of the late Erwin Schrödinger involving the complementarity of wave and particle, to which Engels himself would add certain epistemological qualifications apropos the determination of such intervals (or discrete leaps in continuity) along the lines of Hegel's notion of Being-in-and-for-itself. To that extent only, Engels was guilty of simply turning Hegel over and making him a certain sort of materialist.

This error involving consciousness has "hereditary" implications for Engels' naive conception of mathematics itself, which includes a variety of fundamental epistemological errors reflected in his editing of *Capital*'s last two volumes. With respect to this hereditary aspect of Engels' bias, Marx himself was obviously credulous and uncertain—recognizing his own naive attitude toward mathematics, his credulousness was undoubtedly strengthened by his dependence upon Hegel's *Science of Logic*. For reasons we have already noted, it should be obvious to the specialist that Hegel's attempt to extend his rigor of actual infinity to his general treatment of the calculus certainly falls short of the self-conscious dialectical treatment of that problem by Georg Cantor, in particular.[19]

It is also permissible, from a special standpoint, to say that Engels lacked real insight into the ontology of a dialectic. However, although this is true and represents a further "hereditary" implication of his Lamarckian ingenuousness, there is virtually no aspect of his writings—apart from isolated fragments of manuscript—in which the implications of such a tendency—a *virtual* tendency—become practical problems. Discounting the single blunder cited, it is correct to state that Engels' comprehension of the dialectical method is essentially Marx's.

The difference between Engels and Marx shows up explicitly more in implication than otherwise, at least if one confines one's attention to Marx's later writings. It is impossible, for example, to reconcile Marx's views in the last section of *Capital*, where these matters are treated, with the hereditary implications of such Lamarckian prejudices in Engels.

Because this bears on Engels' authority regarding historical materialism, e.g., the general form of social reproduction, it is here—that is, where the determination of *new forms of consciousness* becomes a most decisive aspect of the investigations—that we must necessarily find Engels most wanting.

"The Origin of the Family," published in 1884, exemplifies the exact nature of the difficulties. Engels' general outline of man's historical (including prehistorical) development is in the main consistent with Marx's, an agreement which is happily reflected in numerous particular points. But wherever the issue in question involves the necessity for a category of consciousness, Engels is guilty of conciliation to a reductionist bias.

This work abounds with two types of errors. The first, a matter of factual error, is typified by the statement, "The transition to the human stage out of conditions such as those under which the anthropoid apes live today would be absolutely inexplicable." This blunder of Engels' largely represents outright misinformation on the internal relations of troops of gorillas, chimpanzees, and certain monkeys and baboons (although there is another sort of problem involved here, as we shall show). In the same paragraph, we encounter another variety of error, frequent allusions to the jealousy of the males. This type of error must be classed as vicious, as distinct from factual. That is, it represents a blunder which derives from a flaw in method.[20]

Provided the author has command of the dialectical method, factual errors of these sorts are not necessarily damaging to his hypothesis or theory. In dialectical method, as we have emphasized, one bases the case on unique qualities of empirical evidence. If the principal premises of the argument are valid, sufficient rigor suffices to ensure that the entire argument will be valid *as a whole*. In those instances in which a factual error of information is significant to the entire thesis, that error will tend to contradict the coherence of the entire thesis, and the dialectician will usually either discard it or, if it is a "fact" supported by considerable authority, criticize it on just a basis, showing why it appears suspect to him *in its given interpretation* as fact. This permits numerous particular errors of information to slip through, of course. On condition that a factual error merely illustrates or strengthens the thesis developed on other premises, there is little to prevent the author of the presentation from assuming it to be correct wherever sufficient authority is advanced for it.

This observation is not applicable to hypotheses constructed by the empiricist method, which does not merely rest on facts, but assumes that each class of correlated facts represents a *factor*; this factor is thus an epiphenomenon of the collection from which it is adduced. An hypothesis, in the empiricist and similar methods, is representative of an aggregation of such weighted epiphenomenal factors. By explicit or inverted methods of induction from the collection of factors as a collection, a thesis (an asymptotic thesis, if you please) is developed to fit all the factors of the aggregation. Thus, if one of the factors is fallaciously grounded or adduced with respect to actual or imagined facts, the entire hypothesis is correspondingly invalidated.

The source of error in the use of the dialectical method is of a different order. The problem of factual accuracy exists, but for the reasons given above it is limited to the quality and appropriateness of those kinds of empirical evidence that represent *uniquenesses*. One might suggest that even a dialectician could commit a gross oversight. So be it. That can occur, but it is not an interesting problem in this context. However, there is a kind of oversight, recurring oversight, that does interest us and belongs in the broader category of errors we have to consider. These are vicious errors: that is, the method employed by the theorist includes a characteristic blunder, of which selective oversight may be a symptomatic expression.

It is the latter sort of error that is typified by Engels' capitulation to reductionism in his astonishingly careless resort to the "method of factors" in his use of the term "jealousy." It is not only admissible but often necessary to employ such terms. Jealousy is a distinct social phenomenon, and within any society in which this psychological category is identified in a characteristic way, jealousy is a fact subject to empirical verification. It is quite another matter to use the term suprahistorically, and that is precisely what Engels is guilty of: crass suprahistoricism.

(In any case, Karl Marx would certainly not have regarded Engels as possessing any special innate qualifications of sensibility for speculating on relations between the sexes!)

We see immediately—or one hopes this is the case—that Engels' blunder with respect to the anthropoid apes is not exclusively a factual error. In the same paragraph he imputes human qualities (jealousy and the like) to a "primeval horde." What is a primeval human horde but "a night in which all cows are black"? In such a state of extended "Blah" precisely nothing can be determined dialectically. Engels, reaching for Hegel, has reached a bit too far back in the development of philosophy—to Joseph Schelling.

What is the epistemological issue here? It is that human qualities of consciousness (including unconscious states as aspects of consciousness-in-general) have to be determined by a *definite form* of social relations. Engels, unwilling to resort to the solution to this problem developed in rudimentary form by Feuerbach and adopted and corrected by Marx, arbitrarily introduces suprahistorical categories of mental life.

This error of his runs amok in "analysis" of tribal forms of organization. Engels proceeds from the axiomatic "material" basis of sexual behavior, an area in which Marx scarcely considered Engels gifted with innate powers to elaborate everything. He overlooks merely the social division of labor in "primitive" society. (On this point, Luxemburg's observations on Spencer and Gillen are dialectical precisely where Engels is not.) Engels holds so firmly to his "materialist," i.e., Lamarckian, hylozoism that he unconsciously discards Marx's materialist conception of history.

The primary consideration in "primitive" societies is the division of labor, which requires societies of a determined magnitude. The principal concern of a society must be to determine that magnitude both in terms of individual self-consciousness of that determination (of magnitude) and in the forms of determination of individual self-consciousness by social relations within that same determination. It is of primary importance to such a society that the dependency relationships (rights and privileges) of the child be defined in terms of the entire array of powers represented by a society of that determination, and in the specific form of mediated relationships which that society requires for its material reproduction. Only to the extent that sexual behavior must be regulated to that end does it have a *necessary* specific form for that society. The basis for sexual behavior, contrary to Engels' unwarranted imputation to Marx of his own rather philistine views on the subject, is what Feuerbach identified as "love": "species consciousness."[21] Marx attacked species consciousness only from the standpoint that Feuerbach reduced it to a mere "dumb generality," a suprahistoric category immediate for all societies. Marx's category of "class consciousness" is a dialectical—and, if you must, dialectical *materialist*, which is to say historically situated—expression of the same notion represented by Feuerbach's species consciousness and love. The basis for sexual behavior in human beings is the need for unmediated social identity, which must be sensuous but merely appears to be a matter of paired individuals, while it actually represents the most fundamentally social of all the acts that persons in most societies perform. Engels degrades human sexual behavior to an epiphenomenon: an act of reductionism. (One may consider this degradation not entirely accidental.) It is therefore inevitable that the form of sexual behavior is differently determined for different societies, that the criteria of sexual attractiveness be similarly various, and so on.

In the same fashion, Engels makes an even more obvious blunder. He confuses sexual behavior with what we, from a capitalist standpoint, tend to identify as family formation. The two forms of social life are scarcely the same in numerous societies. In societies in which there existed social categories of unchecked sexual intercourse between the sexes, there existed the most cruel prohibitions against family formation among persons who under other circumstances were quite free to copulate as they pleased. Except to the extent—and, of course, this is of extraordinary significance—that the momentary sense of unmediated social identity attained through the entire sexual act (including, essentially, foreplay and afterplay) is the quality of identity most useful for nurture of young children, there is no absolute reason why all societies should find a direct, simple correlation between sexual intercourse in general and family formation in particular. It is a specific historical question, which does not diminish the importance of the specific social form of determination of the correlation for the members of a specific society.

It must be acknowledged that Engels, perhaps half-sensible of the terrible inconsistency between such elementary assumptions and the dialectical method, attempts to extricate himself, and to locate the family as a determinate form of society. The result of his exertions is substantially plausible and undoubtedly bears some resemblance to a dialectical examination of the same topics, but the internal structure of his argument is absolutely not dialectical—and is not accidentally therefore substantially wrong on major issues. His entire essay becomes, in consequence, no better than an eminently enjoyable source of numerous brilliant insights, wherever the vicious flaw in his approach to the determination of consciousness is not being tested. Engels is specifically dialectical in his efforts to adduce principles of development from different branches of social evolution. However, he cannot account for the necessity of these otherwise useful adductions, and does not even pose the important questions to be considered.

THE CASE OF LENIN'S REDUCTIONISM

It is probably incontestable that the most significant consequence of Engel's vicious error is Lenin—because of both the importance of Lenin himself, and the extent to which official Soviet spokesmen and others have invoked the doctrinal authority of Lenin's writings on behalf of their own concoctions.

One cannot blame Engels for Lenin's wretched blundering in epistemology. Lenin manifestly saw only what he wished to in Engels' work, ignoring its main dialectical features. At least, this is the case with regard to the unconscionable *Materialism and Empirio-Criticism*, a miserable porridge on which Engels would have gagged—in the most public fashion!

However, to keep matters in perspective, there is another aspect to Lenin's unhappy tract. In the demoralization that affected the entire Russian movement following the ebb of the 1905 upsurge, a wave of neo-Kantian self-pity overtook a number of members of the Bolshevik leading committee, among others. On the basis of a letter from Lenin to Luxemburg about the tract in question, we know that Luxemburg, who was far more literate than Lenin in epistemological matters, suggested to him the need to attack this phenomenon as neo-Kantianism. On seeing the result of her suggestion to Lenin, she must have recalled Marx's experience with Proudhon.[22]

One is reminded of the long since abandoned practice of treating syphilis with malaria. We concede that Lenin's remedy, *Empirio-Criticism*, was directed against syphilis, but it is the malaria that occupies our attention here.

The characteristic feature of Lenin's thesis in this tract is as follows. In philosophy—he bowdlerizes everything—there are two factions: idealism and materialism. Although Hegelian idealism was necessary for a brief moment of history, materialism is the "good guy." The essence of materialism, for Lenin, is that the images in the brain are a direct reflection of the objects outside the brain. He states this thesis repeatedly, explicating it with arguments that leave no doubt he adheres to our good old ignorant conception of cognition, Figure 1a (see page 86). From Engels Lenin borrows only his vicious blunder apropos the determination of consciousness and his often exaggerated esteem for nineteenth-century mathematics and physical science. Appropriately, although Lenin sometimes manages to strike against the very worst side of epistemological tendencies in physical science, he supports the next-to-worst side, the reductionist tendencies, against ideas that are actually representative of a dialectical approach. It is no exaggeration to insist that this tract has done much damage to Soviet science and its reputation.

In the early part of the following decade, Lenin significantly improved his acquaintance with Hegel and other writers, to an extent reflected in the following note from that period:

> The identity of opposites (more accurately, perhaps, their 'unity' although the difference between the expressions 'identity' and 'unity' is not very essential here. In a certain sense both are correct.) is the recognition (discovery) of the *mutually exclusive* and opposed tendencies in all the phenomena and processes of nature (including spirit and society). The condition of the knowledge of all processes of the world as in 'self-movement,' is the knowledge of the unity of their opposites. Development is 'struggle' of opposites. Two fundamental (or is it the two possible? or is it two historically developed?) conceptions of development (evolution) are: development as decrease and increase, as repetition; development as a unity of opposites (the division of the One into mutually exclusive opposites and their reciprocal correlation).

The first conception is dead, poor and dry; the second is vital. It is only this second conception which offers the key to understanding the 'self-movement' of everything in existence . . ."[23]

Between this groping statement and the miserable passages of *Empirio-Criticism* there is a gulf. It is not difficult to demonstrate a significant corresponding advance in Lenin's powers of comprehension after the effects of his study of the dialectical method began to show, but that is not our concern here. More significant are the kinds of errors in his economic-theoretical and political judgments that correspond, as hereditary errors, to the reductionist pathology exhibited in *Empirio-Criticism*.

Luxemburg gets to the heart of Lenin's blunders in theoretical economics:

> Incidentally, the same author is responsible for the statement that enlarged reproduction begins only with capitalism. It quite escapes him that under conditions of simple reproduction, which he takes to be the rule for all pre-capitalist modes of production, we should probably never have advanced beyond the stage of the paleolithic scraper.[24]

Lenin, judging from the best available evidence in the English-language edition of his *Collected Works*, never comprehended the significance of the term "historical specificity." Luxemburg has put her finger on the proof of this assertion. Lenin's notion of capitalist economy's specificity is the specificity of his misconception of it. He proceeds from the standpoint of the most naive reading of the first volume of *Capital*, assuming that capitalism is a closed model with respect to the determination of use value and exchange value as (asymptotically) convergent. Therefore, as Luxemburg emphasizes, the phenomenon of expanded reproduction must be for him a specifically capitalist phenomenon—otherwise, the historical specificity of capitalist development would not apply. His closed model prevents him from conceptualizing capitalism as the interpenetration of two distinct processes not necessarily—and not in practice—coextensive in their immediate subject matters.

This blunder of Lenin's is consistent with his earlier rationalization of the national-stages strategy for the Russian Revolution, and its hereditary Menshevik feature, the nationalism question. The pathetic fallacy of Lenin's misconception of capitalist economy assisted in creating a deadly situation in the young Soviet economy, in which Lenin initially shrugged off Preobrazhensky's warning against the rapid development of a "scissors crisis" out of the NEP program. To a certain extent, Bukharin's attempt to ridicule the notion of a law of value for the Soviet economy, replacing it with his soon-doomed "administrative" chimera, was a faithful reading of Lenin's blunders. (The essential difference between the two was that Lenin corrected his blunders when confronted with disagreeable evidence.) This miserable heritage of disorientation is a source of aggravated blundering in the planning practices of Soviet and Eastern European states to this day—since "social surplus" as an economic-theoretical category "could not exist under socialism." This same aspect of Lenin has been gingerly filched by the Third Campers of the nominally Leninist varieties to justify their trade-union chauvinist economic theory.

The same blunder of Lenin's (among other Bolsheviks, etc., who shared such a profound delusion) was reflected in the pathetic features of the founding congress of the Communist International and in the even more pathetic "Twenty-One Points" pasted together from sundry improvisations to serve as "conditions" for entering the Third International. Here, Lenin's opposition to Luxemburg shifts from problems created by his lack of dialectical competence in economic and related matters to the issues of social process. At the outset—especially during the period of the first two congresses of the Communist International—most of the leaders of the Bolshevik party, Lenin included, had only the most fatuous notions of the manner in which a real international party could be constructed. Taking into account all the considerations beyond their control, its initial Bolshevik leadership fated the Communist International to collapse under the burden of its first two years of blundering. They failed—on exactly the premises that Engels failed but more completely, lacking Engels' dialectical comprehension of related matters—to grasp the essential principles of general laws of social reproduction. Luxemburg, and to a lesser extent, her epigone, Paul Levi, succeeded.[24]

Lenin and other leading Bolsheviks[25] proceeded essentially from an epiphenomenalist notion of class consciousness. It was they, in total contrast to Rosa Luxemburg, who were fatally afflicted with "spontaneism." They took no account of the fact that class consciousness among workers is a determined quality—a socially determined quality. The Bolsheviks, to the extent that they consulted Engels' writings on this subject at all,[26] took him at his worst, to assume *by their practice* a kind of Lamarckian determination of class consciousness in, notably, the German workers. Despite Lenin's much-cited strictures respecting disciplined party organization, it was the organizational question in its dialectical aspect that the Bolsheviks entirely overlooked, and that Luxemburg did not. The determination of consciousness occurs in relation to institutions and to those conscious articulations of the relationships that institutions regard as hegemonic for the organization of their collective practice. Without the preconditions for class consciousness specified in Luxemburg's *Mass Strike*, no German revolution was possible; no broadly based German working-class class consciousness was possible. Only after the wretched experience of the 1921 March Action and the contrasting achievements of Paul Levi's application of Luxemburg's Mass Strike/United Front strategy, did the leading Bolsheviks, notably Lenin and Trotsky, begin to comprehend and gingerly advance what Luxemburg had clearly understood from the outset —with respect to the key aspect of the social determination of consciousness in the general form of social reproduction.

THE "CLASS-FOR-ITSELF"

Not accidentally, the essence of Marx's notion of the historic potential of the working class, his notion of a labor theory of value, and his conception of the political forms of the labor movement are all projections of the kernel of Hegel's formal understanding of dialectical method. Marx transforms Hegel's Being-in-and-for-itself into the notion of the "class for itself," which he counterposes to "class in itself," the projective equivalent for him of Hegel's Being-in-itself.

This formulation occurs prominently in the conclusion to *Misery of Philosophy*, Marx's 1847 polemic against Proudhon's *Philosophy of Misery*; it expresses, not accidentally, the kernel of his differences with Proudhon then and with anarchism later. The working class under capitalism, he declares, is merely a class in itself. That is, its form of organized life is alienated and heteronomic, such that the worker in this state of being (Being-in-itself) not only lacks any awareness of classwide interest but has impulses opposed to those of classwide interest. For the working class to become a revolutionary class—consciously to assume responsibility for the worldwide universality of self-development (expanded reproduction) of the productive forces—the relationship of man to man within the class must first be fundamentally altered such that individual consciousness is socially determined in a fashion appropriate to this result. The fragmentation of the class into individuals and small, narrowly self-interested groups must be superceded by a new form of classwide organization, through which the working class in itself is transformed into a class for itself.

This point permeates the "Feuerbach" section of *The German Ideology*,[27] and surfaces next in the 1848 *Communist Manifesto*. In only one of numerous such passages, we find the statement: "The real fruit of their battles lies, not in the immediate result, but in the ever-expanding union of the workers . . . this contact . . . was needed to centralize the numerous local struggles . . . into one national struggle between classes."[28] And "the immediate aim . . . is . . . Formation of the proletariat into a class."[29]

This is the most fundamental point in Marx's conception of socialist strategy, and is not accidentally exemplary of the kernel of his historical materialism. It is absolutely decisive for analyzing and thus comprehending the characteristic subjective aspect of the behavior of the various classes under capitalism, in particular, and thus provides an indispensable key to the comprehension of political economy. It is by no means astonishing that Luxemburg, who grasped this notion, was the only noted Marxist economist of the century to comprehend *Capital*'s relevance to the historical actuality of her time.

The notion of identity, and thus of self-interest, is located in the reflection of rights and privileges as one's self-consciousness; thus, as should be obvious, one's immediate relationship to specific rights and privileges determines the general Gestalt of one's notion of identity and self-interest. To be a part of a class means to see the rights and privileges given to one as a member of that class *by that class* as one's immediate powers of existence. To be part of the working class, except in the sense of being *an object* (Being-in-itself, class-in-itself) *of capitalist accumulation*, demands that one have an immediate relationship to all aspects of one's class.

When, as we noted in Chapter Three, the immediacy of relations within the class includes both the employed and the unemployed worker, the notion of rights and privileges must necessarily be that of expanded reproduction. By contrast, to the extent that one locates one's identity in terms of one's wages-income, a positive relationship to other sections of the working class generally exists only as it is mediated through the expanded investment practices of capitalist employers. This view, as we have indicated, locates the material basis and conditional progressive feature of the typical procapitalist ideology of most alienated workers. The intensification of struggles along parochialized lines could never in itself produce an iota of class consciousness—to the point that super-militant trade-union consciousness and class consciousness are opposites, just as rank-and-file trade-union caucuses in themselves are politically reactionary from a socialist standpoint. The intensification of localized struggles can be positive, but that happy quality "lies, not in the immediate result, but in the ever-expanding union of the workers. . . ." (*Communist Manifesto*) Thus within the labor movement, according to Marx, the socialist is the person attempting to link, especially, the struggles of employed and unemployed, and the person who opposes this linkage is a procapitalist reactionary; it was on related premises that Marx denounced Proudhon and anarchism as a whole.

To apply the same principles of analysis to social reproduction more broadly, one need only emphasize that the social relationship that determines individual consciousness is not a passive one. Rights and privileges are not benefits dispensed by a candy machine; they involve an active and reciprocal relationship between the individual and the various institutions from whom he thus secures the various aspects of his human powers as a whole. Immediately these rights and privileges are locked to a value placed upon his activities, particular activities especially. He may increase his rights and powers by enhancing those activities in definite ways—within capitalist society, the notion of that which makes one more employable, more sexually attractive, and so on.

Thus every object of practice is an objectification of a specific right or privilege, or of its denial. Thinking of ourselves, being self-conscious in an ordinary form of consciousness, we do not think of ourselves as such, but of specific objects which stand for those rights and privileges which have become attached to those objects. Correspondingly, when we think of objects for consumption or other such purposes, we think inevitably of ourselves and of those institutions and persons whose relationship to us is characteristically mediated in terms of those objects. Fetishism? Exactly!

But . . . er, . . . isn't that normal?

The class-for-itself, which together with the evidence supplied by great art offers us the best empirical insight into such matters, does not depend upon the processes of bad infinity. It is necessary neither to buzz rapidly about the world, establishing an immediate relationship to every worker, nor to asymptotically approach such a gregarious state. In practice, the mental phenomena unique to the transformation from class-in-itself to class-for-itself are experienced in the breakdown of existing barriers of parochialism within the class, especially when the destruction of existing barriers takes in two special directions: a breakdown of the barriers between employed and unemployed, and between the dominant ethnic or cultural groupings and the most oppressed groupings within the same class —more or less as Luxemburg specifies in *Mass Strike*. It is the *motion* of transformation from class-in-itself *toward* class-for-itself that dissolves the reductionist self-consciousness of, for example, militant trade-union swinishness, thus representing a qualitative change in the state of consciousness. It is the shift from the relatively fixed state of self-consciousness to the location of one's identity in the self-movement of expanded class relationships that makes the class-for-itself state an *actual infinity*.

What becomes decisive at such points is identified by the problem of fixing the transformed individual's state of consciousness as one of self-movement. The empirical evidence of the spontaneous manifestation of class consciousness in upsurges is that the class-for-itself tendency tends to persist and even develop somewhat as long as the process of expansion of the social formations of the upsurge continues. Without that fueling from actual social motion, the spontaneous ferment ebbs in the mind, sometimes even more rapidly than it does in the organized movement. The problem, then, is to give the conscious self-movement a quality of actual self-movement, a degree of independence from the immediate ebb and flow of social ferment. To achieve this it is necessary to make this self-movement abstract in a certain sense, to base it upon events beyond the range of immediate developments. This is accomplished in the socialist movement by program—a program of expanded reproduction and conscious appropriation of the productive forces on a universal scale. (By the term "conscious appropriation" is meant a determination to act in ways that lead directly to the appropriation of such forces in *the act of expanded reproduction*.) A program that specifies the seizure of objects as objects is not a program; it does nothing to realize as self-consciousness the self-movement of the mass-strike ferment. It is necessary to match self-movement to self-movement; the only object appropriate to the class-for-itself state of consciousness is the self-movement of expanded reproduction as an object.

This notion of program, which appears in Marx's work as early as the "Feuerbach" section of *The German Ideology*, and also in a different, aphoristic fashion in the "Theses on Feuerbach," was immediately apparent to Marx in Feuerbach's notions of the interconnection between social determination of consciousness (species consciousness, love) and the notion of the self-subsisting positive. Once species consciousness is freed from its Tarpeian Rock and located in the actual capitalist world as class consciousness, the change effected within Feuerbach's discovery must be effected in the real world. It is the notion of revolutionizing social practice, self-movement of the form of evolutionary social reproduction, expanded reproduction, which is the necessary *content* of class consciousness.

Once the question of the general form of social reproduction is settled for this fundamental issue it is applicable to every other issue, respecting both the subjective determinations of capitalist accumulation and those of every preceding form of human society.

THE LABOR PROCESS 6

THE LABOR PROCESS 6

In this brief chapter we summarize certain of the most essential notions which must be absorbed in order to proceed to the analysis of actual political economy from its real, or use-value, aspect. The ground we cover here is chiefly a summary of the material developed in the first part of the Moscow edition of *Theories of Surplus Value* and the section on Malthus and Darwin in the second part.[1] Viewed formally, we are establishing thereby the conceptual premises upon which the theoretical superstructure of *Capital* as a whole rests.

It should be clear enough that no economic theory can begin to treat itself as a science until the very elementary definitions of wealth and of wealth-producing or *productive* activity have been settled with a reasonable degree of finality. In the first part of *Theories of Surplus Value*, Marx accordingly concentrates on defining wealth and productive activity, deriving his notions of both exchange value and use value in accordance with his earlier development of Feuerbach's self-subsisting positive. The connection to the notion of the self-subsisting positive is emphasized by Marx's use of the term "self-expanding value" for the determinate origins and content of both exchange value and use value.[2] The interpenetration of these two processes of determination is commonly situated in a unifying process known as the labor process. In this chapter we will show the relationship of that labor process to the determination of use value, one of the two forms of self-expanding value.

Since we are not immediately concerned with exchange value here, we will dispense with it for the present. Already, in the early portion of *Capital*, Marx acknowledges two contrasting notions of productive labor within the labor process. The definitions he provides for these two notions are superficially irreconcilable. Insofar as it corresponds to the self-expansion of exchange value (capitalist accumulation as a whole), productive labor has one definition. If we are concerned only with use value relative to the development of the productive forces themselves, it has a contrary definition. Here, we are considering only those definitions of productive labor which pertain to use value. We are also omitting consideration of those aspects of use value that pertain only to capitalist accumulation. We have noted such distinctions in earlier chapters; we adhere to them more strictly here.[3] It must also be emphasized, to dispense with further discussion of exchange value for the present, that neither exchange value nor use value are scalars in their content. Exchange value is not the price of an object, except in sense-certainty form: in content the price is determined by a general rate of profit, which determines the price, as a capitalist's purchase and/or sale, that satisfies the demand of the capitalists that self-expanding value be obtained through the purchase and/or sale of that object as a commodity. We shall return to this subject in Chapter 9 and subsequent chapters. Here we deal with the objects of production themselves as a mediation of self-expansion of the labor process, as self-expanding use value.

THE PHYSIOCRATS

Figure 3 represents the simplest abstract schema for discussing certain features of the labor process of capitalist society. It is identical in general respects with Figure 2, and is used with the same restrictions.[4] We introduce it again here to facilitate direct reference to Figure 4, in which we abstract certain features of the right-hand bar of Figure 3 to state the case for the Physiocrats' major contribution to political economy.

The reader will recall the following general conclusions adduced for figures of the form of Figure 3:

1. If P represents the population that produces productive labor, then V as the input to production of total labor is a function of P as

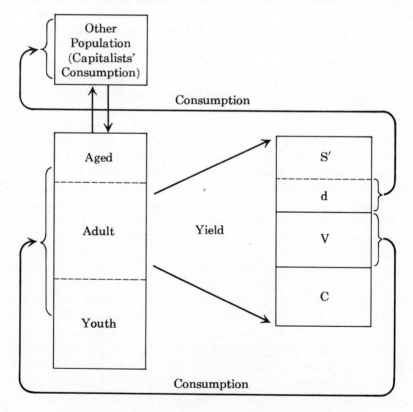

Figure 3 Nomenclature for Capitalist Reproduction

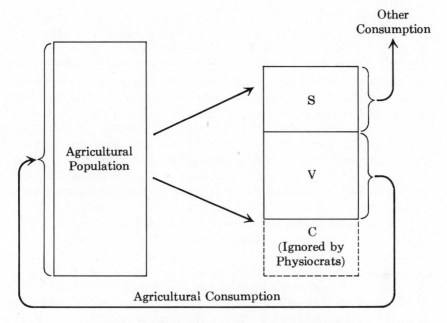

Figure 4 Physiocrat's View of Reproduction

we defined it. It represents, as a relationship, a determinate relationship, associated with a mode of existence and with the productivity of V.

2. The relationship $S'/(C + V)$, the form characteristic of capitalist society, and exponential expressions of this form define the necessary momentary impulses for continued existence of a capitalist economy as a whole.

3. Therefore, the realization of S' involves a determinate increase in the magnitude of P respecting quality/quantity, and rising values for current states of society in terms of $S'/(C + V)$. That is, the realization of exponential impulse-tendencies, relative to present current rates, is merely a higher current rate and an increased value of the exponential impulse-tendency for the next epoch.

The Physiocrats did not know constant capital in the form in which we recognize it from Marx's standpoint. The bar in Figure 4 thus corresponds, with that qualification, to the right-hand bar in Figure 3. The bar in Figure 4 is apportioned into V, the net agricultural output required to reproduce the cultivators of an agricultural population, and S', as rent or absolute profit. Constant capital of agriculture (in this simplified case) is treated as an internal feature of the existence of the cultivators and not a determined magnitude of wealth.

This provides us with the simplest imaginable illustration of a labor process (of a certain kind) and self-expanding value. The value of the input, agricultural labor, results in a product in excess of the magnitude required to reproduce agricultural labor. To the extent that one interprets this resulting absolute gain in the mass of existing social wealth to be the result of the productive activity of labor, we have just defined both a labor process and self-expanding value. The labor process represents, in such terms, a free-energy system, a system of greater than 100 per cent "thermal efficiency." The percentile in excess of 100 per cent represents the proportion of all products that could be alienated without, regressively, depleting the hen laying the eggs, and this amount is also the lawful limit of the amount of rent, or absolute profit, which can safely be exacted from this process.

If we assumed this negative-entropic labor process to hold only for agriculture and mining, for example, then all other activities in society (including manufacturing) would be subsisting from the rent obtained from agriculture. Their profits would then not add a penny's worth to the total absolute profit represented by rent, but would instead be relative profits. Similarly, if the revenues of activities other than agriculture were in part secured by taking some of V itself in the form of rent, this too would be relative profit, since what appeared to be an augmentation of absolute profit would actually be a diminution in the value of the labor process, and thus not a net gain (absolute profit) for society as a whole.

The second category of relative profit will hereafter be designated as primitive accumulation. The general definition of primitive accumulation, in the first approximation, is wealth alienated as income from the means of simple reproduction of existing productive forces. As we dispense with the notion of simple reproduction, we modify the definition, but without altering its essential intent.

From this we may adduce the following five preliminary definitions:

1. We have represented man's relationship to himself as mediated through his labor, and through the material changes in nature— products of or negation of labor—which in turn yield a population whose further useful material output is greater than that embodied in its own existence. Coquetting with Hegelian forms, we have what might be represented as a negation of the negation: labor as activity annuls (realizes) itself as the object of labor, which, annulled by consumption by labor, becomes increased labor . . . this is the simplest notion of *realization*.

2. We have a preliminary notion of the term "productive." Human labor which produces such material alterations in nature as to create the material existence of more labor than itself (through the production of material means of existence of labor) is productive labor.

3. We have a rigorous distinction between absolute and relative profit. Absolute profit is limited to that augmentation of wealth which represents a net increase in wealth for the entire society. Profit realized in other senses is only relative. Since local profit (that of particular firms, for example) cannot know whether it is in itself absolute or relative, the sum of the individual profits of an economy does not necessarily represent absolute profit, just as the sum of the net Value Added for an economy has no necessary relationship to the net wealth created by the economy.

4. Relative accumulation is accumulation at the expense of some real accumulation. Where relative accumulation occurs at the expense of the income of simple reproduction, it is *primitive accumulation*.

5. We have a conditionally rigorous definition of wealth itself. Once the criterion of negative entropy is applied to determine what is *productive*, those materialized values marginally essential as individual objects to maintaining or increasing the rate of negative entropy of the entire society's labor process are *self-expanding use values*.

The notions of use value we entertain here are not those of what Marx terms the "specific use value for capital."[5] In capitalist society the existence of a value for *concrete use value* is essentially immanent. For, by the very definition we have employed to approximate the notion in question, it is clear that the determination of the value of concrete use value could only be determined through some institution which actually determined the relationship of the particular to the entirety! Consequently, in capitalist society the determination of the use value of objects is generally the *specific* use value.

It is feasible today to identify within the capitalist economy the material resources (products and the like) required for a $1 billion annual program of development of thermonuclear power production and related technology by the United States. This task could be readily accomplished by appropriate teams of specialists. Since we have, in advance, certain preliminary indications of the savings in the social costs of power production which would be only one benefit of such a program, it would not be difficult to compare the national rates of social productivity under existing allocation policies with those which would result from such applications of resources. It is obvious, to take such calculations further, that if we make power cheap enough, not only is the cost of production correspondingly lowered for everything (the *social* cost!), but it also becomes economical to introduce large-scale modifications of technology rapidly into all aspects of the economy. It is safe beyond dispute to estimate that such secondary benefits would be far greater in impact than cheaper thermonuclear fusion power. Comparing the two sets of allocations, we can arrive at comparable rates of overall social productivity.

In this respect we can objectify the concrete products of labor as use values, in a meaningful fashion, in terms of the alternative programs of national production which the addition, subtraction, and substitution of such concrete use values makes possible. Or, to put it another way, the existence of such objects implies an adjustment in possible overall programs of production. If one were automatically calculating the optimal program of national production for each total array of concrete use values, the addition of even single concrete use value to that array would represent a determinate change in the rate of both $S'/(C + V)$ and the exponential impulse-tendency. It is in this sense that concrete use values have a determinate value.

The fact that an actual (social) determination of such values does not occur might seem to degrade this notion to one of mere immanence. Yet in the course of a capitalist cycle we have gross cumulative evidence of the determining implications of just such considerations. We find that beside significant advances in technology, set in the context of adequate means of production to realize that technology, we have not obtained the sort of programmatic gains such technological advances clearly indicate. If the value of a concrete use value therefore seems merely immanent, it is by no means an ineffable conjecture. Rather, since this socially undertermined value is shown to be decisive in such gross ways over longer spans of entire economies, the merely immanent notion becomes of the utmost importance to us. The failure of existing forms of social organization to measure this concrete value does not discredit its importance. Quite the contrary; the failure of existing institutions to take this determination into account discredits those institutions, demanding the creation of the specific sort of yet or existing institutions which will make the determination of such use value, and make it the focus of social determinations.

Marx treats this problem in Section 3a of Chapter XXI of *Theories of Surplus Value*, summing it up in mid-discussion as follows:

> One can only speak of the *productivity* of capital if one regards it as the embodiment of definite social relations of production. But if it is conceived in this way, then the historically transitory character of this relationship becomes at once evident, and the general recognition of this fact is incompatible with the continued existence of this relationship, which itself creates the means for its abolition.[6]

Luxemburg makes the same point in apparently different but ultimately identical terms:

> Ultimately, it was the limitation of their bourgeois mentalities which doomed both Smith and Ricardo to failure. A proper understanding of the fundamental categories of capitalist production, of value and surplus value as living dynamics of the social process, demands the understanding of this process in its historical development and of the categories themselves as historically conditioned forms of the general relations of labour. This

means that only a socialist can really solve the problem of the reproduction of capital . . .[7]

When, as we do here, we abstract the category of use value in such a fashion from the notion of the labor process as that process is developed by capitalism, critics rightly charge that this category of use value has no empirical determination within the day-to-day development of capitalist accumulation. Thus, they charge us with introducing *what is for them* a speculative element into political economy. As Marx repeatedly insists, once we have approached the understanding of capitalist accumulation in the historical specificity of primitive accumulation—that is, in the context of its emergence from a previous form of society, it becomes natural for us to adduce the underlying social relations of production as the content of the powers of capital itself. Once we have adopted that point of view, we have conceived of the capitalist form of development of the real productive forces without the capitalists, without capital. Production then becomes the self-production of the working class—the labor process: socialist society. From that standpoint, the only value is concretized use value, which the institutions of socialist society inherently "measure" just as definitely as capitalist accumulation determines exchange value.

More than merely the irreconcilable contrast between two world-views, two societies, is represented by the preference for concretized use value over exchange value. It is the inability of capitalist accumulation to take concretized use value *positively* into account that is the formal aspect of capitalist depressions and breakdown crises. It is the contradiction between exchange values and use values that determines the effective rates of real capitalist accumulation, crises, and all the other principal phenomena of political economy. Consequently, Luxemburg is necessarily correct. We agree that the notion of determinate use value is a chimera *for capitalist economists*, that is, exists only from the standpoint of socialist economy. Thus, since this knowledge, this standpoint is demonstrably indispensable for comprehending all the principal phenomena of capitalist political economy, "only a socialist can really solve the problem of the reproduction of capital."

It is most instructive to consider the way in which Marx uniquely demonstrated the solution to the problems discussed above in the context of the Physiocrats' theses. This exercise, which we amplify for the obvious further benefits to be obtained in that way, exemplifies his entire methodological approach to the evidence already known—but not comprehended —by the leading investigators before him.

The Physiocrats had a certain amount of ambiguity in their favor within the apparent evidence in reaching mistaken judgments. Firstly, it appeared to them that the existence of manufacturing labor was premised on part of the rent taken from the S in Figure 4. It is certainly the case that in the emergence of capitalism the appropriation of part of the alienated product of feudal agriculture was the material basis for appropriation of wage-labor by capitalists. To the feudal nobility the entire arrangement might well have seemed a pure swindle; the manufacturers, as capitalists, swindled part of the wealth from the rent of agriculture and used a portion of this wealth to support a nonproductive population of wage-labor, among other uses. As long as the productivity of society generally apparently remains static, the Physiocratic view might be considered as plausible as any other.

Secondly, a dominant tendency of the Physiocrats was to regard rent (S in Figure 4) as the bounty of nature. Why cannot nature just as well as agricultural labor be the source of the "free energy" of agricultural production? As long as social productivity remains fixed, what practical difference could it make which way we view the matter? The Physiocrats, in fact, seem to have the better of it as long as one concedes, as even Adam Smith did, the bulk of the Physiocrats' argument as to the principal source of wealth.[8]

Let us leap ahead a bit. According to the early census data, the rural population of the United States was once approximately 90 per cent. Today, the necessary proportion of agricultural labor represents about 5 per cent of the population (discounting this accomplishment for agricultural imports at substantially below their value). Has nature's bounty increased? Or has the productivity of agriculture increased? Meanwhile, out of the Physiocrats' category of rent has emerged a massive manufacturing population; is this population nonproductive, or has the development of industry something to do with the increased productivity of agriculture?

Were the Physiocrats, whose conceptions on these subjects have been totally refuted by unique evidence, simply wrong? On the contrary, above and beyond their recognition of the universal basis for distinguishing between relative and absolute profit—which is more than the GNP worshippers have been able to accomplish two centuries later—they situated the problem in the most useful terms of reference: man's relationship to nature as the locus of the problem of conceptualizing production.

What the Physiocrats mistook as the bounty of nature was not without a real significance. In place of a fixed quality of Nature, let us generalize their "nature" as the *material preconditions of a definite mode of production*, which is alterable by man in a positive direction. How altered? Not by whim but by labor, by the application of a definite proportion of total social labor. We need to extend this from agriculture and mining to production in general with the following restrictions: that the material preconditions of production are the restriction put upon this extension, and that the material conditions of human existence (material consumption) be the added form of wealth—in addition to improvements in the material preconditions of production.

By locating the problem of human existence in the input/output cycle of man's production of the material necessaries of human consumption, and by defining it as a free-energy relationship in those terms, the Physiocrats situated the problem of political economy.

There is a third fallacy in the notions of the Physiocrats. They shared with Lassalle a kind of "iron law of wages," distinguishing between "strict necessaries," or biological needs for human consumption, and "luxuries," in much the fashion caricatured by certain twentieth-century individuals less proximate to solid earth. Yet, again, the historical evidence is against them. The progress in social productivity manifest in 180 years of the U.S. census includes massive increases in the level of "absolute" material consumption with respect to both means of human existence and means (per capita of labor) of production! If we reduced the material means of production per capita to eighteenth-century rates, even the meanest sweat-shop-owner capitalist would protest that this is impossible. He might, of course, be more sanguine about the possibility of an eighteenth-century level of consumption for wage-labor, but even the most fanatical proponent of speedup in major corporations would rebuke him for the fool he is.

The empirical fact of the rising productivity of labor, and the changes in Constant and Variable Capital rates necessarily correlated with it, are the single premise, as an interconnected single notion, for all these extensive transformations of the Physiocrats' outlook. This exemplifies what we have identified as *unique* evidence.

Now, if we proceed from only this sort of empirical evidence, what are we compelled to identify as the content of capitalist accumulation? It cannot be static wealth, since yesterday's wealth is worth less today. It can only be the *movements in productivity* which express, and uniquely so, that which is necessary to distinguish production as the history of production distinguishes itself. If we are to measure the *outcome* of production, we cannot simply compare the numbers of input- and output-objects of the same qualities. The most essential feature of production, without which it must regress to a state of entropy, is negative entropy. The quality of self-expanding value is not a fixed ratio of input- to output-objects, but an increase, relative to such object-ratios, of the ratios themselves. The quality of self-expansion is thus empirically demonstrated to be necessarily *the self-expansion of self-expansion. The measure of the productive power of labor is an increase in the productive power of labor.* The immediate object-relationships only mediate that self-expansion.

This, just this, is Marx's discovery of a labor theory of value. We have merely enlarged the scope of his treatment of Steuart, Smith, and the Physiocrats (especially) and compacted his critiques of Sismondi, Malthus, and Ricardo,[9] so that the entire argument might be summarized in this fashion.

Marx locates a significant part of the Physiocrats' difficulties in their feudal outlook—or, to be more exact, their reified feudal outlook. Despite the reification accomplished by Colbert and others, leading features of their outlook correspond tidily to the feudal ideology: Generally, they attempt to define reality (the capitalist market for their alienated product) in terms of silly dreams of the past. They dream of the feudal period in which the feudal lord was productive by virtue of his "ownership" of the occupied land from which he took nature's bounty. (This sort of nonsense was also promulgated in England during the Restoration in distinguishing between productive and nonproductive persons.) Specifically, they regard man as a beast. Their brutalized definition of man ascribed to him, like a cow, a pig, or a wild animal to be hunted, *fixed* powers for gathering the bounty of nature.

Marx treats this problem most forcefully in connection with his critique of Malthus. He states the general setting of his argument as follows:

> To assert, as sentimental opponents of Ricardo's did, that production as such is not the object, is to forget that production for its own sake means nothing but the development of human productive forces, in other words the *development of the richness of human nature as an end in itself*. To oppose the welfare of the individual to this end, as Sismondi does, is to assert that the development of the species must be *arrested* in order to safeguard the welfare of the individual, so that, for instance, no war may be waged in which at all events some individuals perish (Sismondi is only right as against the economists who *conceal* or deny this contradiction). Apart from the barrenness of such edifying reflections, they reveal a failure to understand the fact that, although at first the development of the capacities of the *human* species takes place at the cost of the majority of human individuals, and even classes, in the end it breaks through this contradiction and coincides with the development of the individual; . . .[10]

Malthus' attack on the notion of the value of labor power is accomplished by attributing the price of that labor power to labor as its content, thus giving to humanity that sort of fixed qualiy. The Physiocrats generally made a similar error in confusing the quantum of objects for value, a general equivalence which is valid only to the extent that the power of man over objections is fixed and his requirement of them is similarly fixed. On the contrary, the value of labor power is its ability not only to produce increased amounts of the same quality of labor power, but also to increase this productive quality of labor power itself through the mediation of production. Unlike Malthus, whose concern for increasing the consumption of parasites like himself makes his entire effort transparent, the bestiality of the Physiocrats' assumptions situated the problem in such terms that the same demonstration which overthrows their other erroneous assumptions eliminates this one. The entire Physiocratic view of social reproduction was a bestial outlook, but one so consistently developed for mere beasts that with one touch of the empirical evidence of humanity each of their principal bestial assumptions is immediately corrected to the corresponding human one.

The most magnificent of the edifices the Physiocrats constructed on their bestial basis is the Quesnay *Tableau Economique*.[11] In form, it is identical to the network obtained by elaborating bills of consumption, process sheets, and bills of materials for an entire society.[12] This achievement correlates with the other principal feature of their construction which survives criticism more or less intact: the definition of absolute profit as that which increases the wealth of society as a whole. The tableau economique articulates the internal features of that universality as a universality. It is only essential, then, in order to give it life, to apply to this analysis the dialectical method's own comprehension of the problem of universality—actual infinity—to establish the essential conceptions of political economy. What we must introduce explicitly is the notion of self-expanding value and the notion of the simultaneity (as distinct from a mere sequence) of the division of productive labor represented by the network.

Once we have accomplished those transformations, all empirically premised on a single unique body of evidence, we have everything implicitly. For, in the effort to equate sequence and simultaneity under conditions of rising social productivity, there arises the fundamental contradiction between dead capital and current reproductive rates. It is necessary merely to locate that contradiction relative to the heteronomic form of capitalist accumulation and the twofold nature of value under capitalism (exchange value and use value) to have all the essential principles of political economy in finished form.

A MALTHUSIAN COUNTERVIEW

R. A. Fisher's *The Genetical Theory of Natural Selection* (1929) inevitably appears quaint in certain respects beside more recent representations of the Malthusian point of view. Nevertheless, the book is a classic modern exposition of that outlook and generally reflects all the underlying methodological bungling characteristic of Malthusian and related thought.

On the surface Fisher sometimes seems partially to refute himself, notably in the concluding chapter in which he comments at some length on the lower fertility of the upper classes and related matters. Evidence compels him to acknowledge that the lower growth rates of more prosperous classes are associated with social controls ostensibly aimed at maintaining the quality of new individuals born into the class. Perhaps unavoidably, he promulgates the charming view of the British upper classes characteristic of the British middle classes. If, as might be feared, the infertility of the aristocracy threatens Britain with the extinction of so noble an institution, then—in the interest of preserving such Merry Old Things for the edification and admiration of the next generation—a self-sacrificing (and upwardly mobile) middle-class observer might volunteer the remedy that the aristocracy open its bedchambers to the greater reproductive prowess of the nouveau riche.[13]

The essence of Fisher's argument occurs in the concluding paragraphs of his principal theoretical chapter, "The Fundamental Theorem of Natural Selection," where he insists: "As a means of progressive change . . .

Natural Selection can only explain these instincts insofar as they are individually beneficial, and leaves entirely open the question as to whether in the aggregate they are a benefit or an injury to the species."[14] Heteronomy! To which he adds:

> There would, however, be some warrant on historical grounds for saying that the term Natural Selection should include not only the selective survival of individuals of the same genus or family. The relative unimportance of this as an evolutionary factor would seem to follow decisively from the small *number* of closely related species which in fact do come into competition, as compared with the number of individuals in the same species; and from the vastly greater *duration* of the species compared to the individual . . .[15]

It might be argued, as it has been against Darwin, that such monstrous misconceptions of the evolutionary processes are speciously supported by the study of the variation of plants and animals under circumstances, such as those of selective breeding by farmers or the controlled conditions in the laboratory, in which the epistemological bias of the investigator usually introduces, however unconsciously, vicious bias into the design of experiment.

In general, in the empiricist method, the selection by the experiment's designer of the data taken into account introduces a vicious fallacy of composition, such that a vicious epistemological flaw in the conception will usually seem to be empirically validated by the experimental results. To obtain the right answer, one must ask the proper question. If one wishes to avoid certain answers, it usually suffices to avoid certain questions. The bulk of behaviorist experimentation exemplifies this fallacy. It is notorious, and is frankly admitted by B. F. Skinner, that his foray into what he calls psychology was preceded by an unsatisfactory literary career; this experience of his own lack of creative powers—by his own estimation—convinced him that creative mentation and mind itself do not exist. Since then, he has conducted a significant amount of experimental inquiry, all designed on the premise that mind does not exist; therefore no test was made to adduce what prejudice said could not be found—although Gestalt experiments had already demonstrated creative mentation even in higher apes! Consequently, the experimental evidence convinces the behaviorists that they did not find what they sedulously avoided encountering.

In the case of the work of Fisher and others, the same general vicious fallacy of composition is manifest. (We do not, however, wish to class the proponent of so excellent a rigor as the Null Hypothesis in the same category with a B. F. Skinner.) As Fisher himself well knew, it is necessary if one wishes to determine the absence or presence of a specific type of phenomenon experimentally to frame the investigation in a form which corresponds to the uniqueness of the notion (e.g., hypothesis) being explored. As early as 1929, he was not unaware of the so-called "holistic" or "developmental" currents in biology and ecology, whose conclusions could not be put aside without demonstrating that their strongly-premised assumptions were insignificant.

The case of the Physiocrats (and others) is exemplary here. In political economy, in particular, there are ample ways in which one can design one's investigations to insure that no significant reflection of the increase in social productivity occurs in the evidence one selects, provided that the period of study is sufficiently brief or that one constructs trend-lines of such data so as to "smooth" out exactly those indications that are of the most decisive significance.

Putting human population aside a moment longer, let us consider the problem represented by a particular species within an ecology. As long as we isolate the species' members, treating the background as fixed, or consider merely the interactions among a few members of the species, no fundamental finding relative to the interrelationship among different species can be made. Indeed, as long as one adheres to that procedure, the inconclusiveness arising from one's fallacy of composition will usually produce just the results Fisher advances.

To obtain competent insights into the evolution (or variation) of individual species, one must first establish certain things with respect to the ecology as a whole. Let us, for simplicity's sake, reduce the refinement of the investigation to the crudest notion of energy. Then we must develop a thermodynamic model of the entire ecology in terms of the various interconnected modes of energy transfer within the ecology treated as a negentropic system. Within this ecology one then situates the particular species with which one is concerned. First one locates the relationship between a characteristic activity (and reproduction rates) of the species and the changes in the negentropic rates and energy accumulation as a whole. Next one considers how alterations in these behaviors and rates affect the thermodynamic parameters of the ecology as a whole. A fascinating set of interrelations begins to emerge for consideration.

Immediately, except for certain classes of predators and special cases of ecological trauma, one discards all notions of competition as absolutely worthless features of experimental design. The reproduction of a species involves the throughput of free energy in terms of the adults' foodgathering, such that both the fertility rates and the quality of new individual are rather neatly determinable. The question posed is the effect of the species' activity on the ecology's thermodynamics, both as a whole and with respect to subsumed modes—ultimately, of course, those modes most directly affecting the species' foodgathering powers. High drama with a very large cast of characters emerges. In general, in all but the exceptional cases noted above, it is the ecology as a whole which determines the selection of variations by the effect on the thermodynamics of reproduction potential of the species, not by an after-the-fact "competitive" reduction of excess populations.

For example, one might inquire why certain types of predatory birds have smaller clutches. Competition? Nonsense. Even with all the ducks which might be provided, the admirable peregrine falcon could not have survived if it had four eggs in a clutch. If we consider the thermodynamics of the falcon's mode of existence, we see that even with the most abundant supply of ducks, an increase in the size of the egg clutch would eliminate the species (which DDT was required to accomplish). In the same vein, if one has observed a peregrine falcon in action, one is unable to find a basis for the wishful view that these falcons improve the stock of ducks by their role in "natural selection." No duck within the widest limits of duck-design could survive the aim of a falcon in its power dive. It is the business of consuming the blasted ruptured duck which puts a limit on the peregrine's activities for the day. Permit one to suggest that "competition" smacks a bit of quackery, or perhaps of projection of the negation of the negation of capitalist character-determination upon the domain of lower forms of life?

In general, the only approach to general evolution that survives these and other elementary epistemological rigors is that emergent from the tactic of A. I. Oparin.[16] The system of life fundamentally represents a world-line of increasing negentropy, not merely with respect to individual species nor always—as neotony warns us—in the most obvious fashion. What is primary is the negentropy of the ecology which, as this value advances through the participating development of species, creates the material (thermodynamic) basis for the advancement of species. Competition, like its cousin, the silly territorial imperative, is a fantasy in the mind of the beholder.

The fallacy of composition in Fisher's approach can be more exactly located by examining the point of reference on which he grounds more detailed examination of specific traits of individuals. He begins with an ordinary actuarial determination of the simple population, in terms of fertility and mortality rates. Not a hint of the sort of crude thermo-dynamic accounting of determination which must be adduced from the simplest model of ecology!

One knows why. If he took into account for a human population no more than the elementary historical data we applied to the Physiocratic model, the practice of counting in numbers of individuals would collapse. In first approximation, at any point in the process, it is feasible to give a thermodynamic interpretation to production, consumption, fertility, and morality. However, the next step—to take into account that self-expansion is realized as an increase in the rate of self-expansion, in which absolute energy levels are replaced by other modes—destroys this approach. The value of an individual under conditions of self-expansion is an "average" necessary portion of the entire productive span of his society, in which shifts occur along the path we have previously reviewed.[17]

In approaching populations of lower animals and plant life, the problem is simplified at first glance by the fact that the mode of activity within the species is fixed, to the effect that a thermodynamic model of the obvious sort would appear sufficient. Yet if it is the case that the ecosystems are generally self-expansive in negentropic terms, we cannot consider such problems as the variation of species within these ecosystems without treating such variations essentially as we must treat self-expansion for the capitalist economy.

That being the case, our notion of genetics is subject to considerable review with respect to the notion of genetic determination. Not only that, but our notion of so-called inorganic processes must be accommodated to the evidence that the laws of its universe are determined by the laws of all the processes which inhabit the same universe. These are, admittedly, large steps to be taken: since they have not been taken, no one need apologize for his lack of achievement on this point. Such ultimate implications of the problem do not, however, excuse crude reductionist blunders of the varieties typified by Fisher's approach.

ECOLOGY

The customary approach to a "scientific" notion of human existence assumes that the following order of progress is axiomatic. One must begin, it is argued, with a notion of those elementary particles on which all reality is premised, and define the "natural relations" among such particles. On this first stratum of inquiry, we have physics, chemistry, and related fields, in which we elaborate knowledge of "inorganic" nature. Next, it is proposed, one should study living processes generally, confining interpretation of those processes to fundamental physical laws and theorems adduced by the physical sciences. Next, it is permissible to study man as a biological being, confining oneself to the delimiting authority of those notions of law and theorem we have adduced for life generally. Next one is permitted to explore human social processes, mental life, and the like, provided one limits explanation of phenomena to the laws and theorems previously adduced for mere biological individuals.

What ought to be the obvious pathetic fallacy of such an approach is that the simplest experimental inquiry into any aspect of nature as a whole is a study of the consequences of human action upon the order of nature. Moreover, if the investigator defines and adjudges what he considers to be the results, this is also an entirely human activity. Thus, the most elementary truth of all experimental knowledge is that the "hierarchy of knowledge" is exactly the opposite of what has ordinarily been taken to be the case.

The only possible premise for genuine scientific knowledge is to examine the matter in a fashion exactly contrary to that of eighteenth- and nineteenth-century so-called physical science. The attempt to adduce firm conclusions about nature from so-called experimental approaches depends absolutely on two assumptions which could not conceivably be eliminated from the evidence: that human action is always the cause we introduce to the experiment whenever we attempt to demonstrate our power to reproduce certain effects, and that whether in experiment or mere "observation" the notion of effect is always determined in a twofold fashion by criteria external to the experimental domain. What we consider an effect, as distinct from those considerations attributed to externalities or otherwise overlooked, is determined by human consciousness; the way in which we evaluate what we designate as the effect is also determined by consciousness external to the internal relations of the experimental subject. To obtain scientific knowledge, we must exactly reverse this approach. We must focus first on the relationship, through deliberative mentation, between man's interpretation of nature and his consequent actions on nature.

This order of inquiry does not completely resolve the issue of scientific inquiry; it merely begins the investigation from the only effective point of departure. This is, of course, the point previously cited in connection with the first of Marx's "Theses On Feuerbach"[18]: the problem of knowledge could be attacked only by starting from the standpoint of critical idealism.

The fault in such realism is that it must assume that the connection between human action, as cause, and the succeeding interpretation of effect for consciousness is simply determined by the most thorough critical reflection on the internal dynamics of the processes of human deliberation. Once we have, first, settled accounts with the fundamental problems which could only be solved by critical idealism, we must examine the actual processes of nature within the context of fundamental laws of the universe reflected in the deliberate aspect of human knowledge.

The major contribution we make to knowledge by situating physics within the domain of critical idealism is the discovery of contradictions in extant forms of deliberative knowledge. In particular, we demonstrate that natural processes, themselves susceptible of comprehension from the standpoint of our fundamental laws, act in a way rather different from that attributed to them by any fixed body of consciousness of natural laws. In this way we discover that each progressive order of human social evolution, defined as progressive by the standard of increased social-reproductive powers, necessarily represents (implicitly or explicitly) a superior comprehension of the physical universe in practice—and, therefore, conscious reflections on that practice—superior to its predecessors. Relative to its predecessors, it is appropriate human knowledge of the order of nature generally. It is from this that the basis for fundamental antinomies in human knowledge practically arises. The practice of a society is appropriate to the social reproduction of that society, and from this standpoint represents true scientific knowledge. Yet the development of society in this way brings man into confrontation with new qualities of underlying processes—and even creates new qualities of underlying processes—for which the old body of deliberative practice is inadequate. Moreover, this antinomy involves old and new knowledge which are each absolutely comprehensible in respect to evolving human knowledge.

Therefore, if we abstract the successful order of human social development and the corresponding successful order of development of human deliberation, we have an empirical basis for conceptualizing Descartes' notion of perfection in the sense that Spinoza comprehended and developed it.[19] Once we have situated Hegel's dialectic in respect to the contradictions of the material social reproduction of man, the corrections thus introduced (radically) to his dialectic represent man's fundamental knowledge of his entire universe.

We have provided a useful location for that undertaking in our treatment of the Physiocrats. Once we locate the empirical basis for locating perfection in the process as the Physiocrats attempted to define that process, we overturn the entire internal system of the Physiocrats, arriving at a comprehensive notion of a labor process, of man's relationship to nature, and thus situating the notion of Spinoza's substance on its proper historically specific basis.

The distinction between a pathetic (bad infinity) and a scientific (actual infinity) comprehension of the empirical process so located is epitomized by the contrast between the reductionist, who locates the value of the output of labor in a collection of objects, and the dialectician, who locates the significance of such objects as a *mediation* of the increase in social-reproductive powers.

If the end product of increased productive powers were merely an increase in the quality of material consumption by society, each advance in productive development would be a self-completing process, a termination of advance with no necessary connection to any further consequent advances. That is, an attempt to situate such demonstrations within the empirical evidence of capitalist development would present us with a result exactly corresponding to Zeno's point/line paradox. The actual result corresponds more closely to the administrations of Gestalt experimental investigations of creative mentation. The array of expanded reproduction, situated in a task-oriented context, creates the material preconditions for a new act of cognition. Or, in other words, the results of expanded reproduction, under specified circumstances, create the condition determining new advances in cognition. These advances (universal labor), realized as increased productive powers of cooperative labor, are realized in turn as a new array of objects, which in turn are realized by the determination of new qualities of cognition-in-general (universal labor).

Thus, to the extent that we consolidate universal and cooperative labor as labor power-in-and-for-itself, the labor process is the process of self-expansion of labor power. What labor power creates, through the mediation of the objects of its production, is higher orders of labor power.

Dysfunctions in the labor process can therefore occur only to the extent that (a) universal labor is alienated from cooperative labor, and each is reduced to its corresponding phasal form of labor merely in itself, and that (b) labor power is alienated from itself by the alien appropriation of the mediating array of objects.

Otherwise, except for such alienation, the labor process is closed for the self-subsisting positive of labor power producing higher orders of labor power. Labor power as self-perfecting process (the labor process actually) is Spinoza's substance. This notion of self-perfecting labor power as an actual infinity (the labor process in self-development as a whole) is thus self-reflexive and actual, unique, infinite, and comprehensive. It is a self-subsisting positive basis.

The prevailing view of ecology is readily demonstrated to correspond intensionally to the notion of nature in the Physiocratic model. However, acknowledging this, it should immediately occur to us that the disproof of the Physiocratic notion of the relationship of man to nature by the evidence of the history of American capitalist development (1790–1970) suffices to overturn correspondingly all the notions of Physiocratic philosophy and its relatives and replications. Once we have demonstrated that the order of nature is susceptible of comprehension in practice through our self-subsisting positive (the labor process), and once we have noted the merely historically specific epitomization of a more general form of human existence in the labor process, the entropic notion of the order of nature put to the test by Physiocratic hypotheses is also entirely thrown over. The line of approach implied, leading from our observations through Oparin and others,[20] becomes mandatory.

We see at once the reductionist fallacies epitomized by Fisher's and related approaches. We are compelled not only to proceed to the notions of invariant we have introduced in this text, but also to consider the universe as a whole as subject to a similar form of invariant, such that it must ultimately be demonstrated to be subject to evolving sets of fundamental physical law, as we presently define fundamental physical law. However initially egregious or shocking this might appear, we know several things that bear decisively on the matter. We know, first, that the customary notion of scientific development from which contrary views are adduced is itself premised on a pathetic fallacy—which we have resummarized at the beginning of this section. We also know that the notion of entropy arises, by hereditary necessity, from assumptions which require a consistent physical science to insist that man does not exist; by such proofs of his own nonexistence the reductionist physical scientist succeeds in ceasing to occupy our attention. The only assumption consistent with the gross empirical evidence of human existence is that the universe as a whole is itself self-development, and that the seeming necessity of interpreting it from the standpoint of reductionist procedures of analysis arises from the paradoxes of "a night in which all cows are black." The task of empirical science is to discover the self-perfection of the universe as a whole, and to adduce necessary hypotheses and demonstrate those hypotheses. We have no explicit hypotheses to offer beyond what we have already stated. However, within the domain of our special competence, we have already satisfied the requirements of empirical scientific investigation in proving our hypotheses. Insofar as our competence compels us to venture slightly beyond that aspect of the matter, we do so on a competent basis—provided we do not go further than empirically demonstrated judgments within our field strictly compel us. If, at the same time, some fellow comes rushing into our domain of competence announcing that such and such in our elaboration is contrary to the evidence he has adduced from "mathematical science" as it now exists, we shall consider ourselves privileged to examine his epistemological credentials before considering his evidence.

CLASSES

From the advantageous vantage-point provided us by the preceding considerations, we are able to make rigorous distinctions among such distinct social formations as castes and classes. This supplies us with something of far greater importance than a strict, consistent set of definitions. The distinctions to be made are of the utmost scientific importance to our work.

The elementary definition of a class is equivalent to a rigorous definition of a species in the plant and animal kingdoms. Thus, Marx's definition of class consciousness is, contrary to Engels,[21] a definition of species consciousness. The difficulty which merely seems to arise is that a society composed of classes is a case of symbiotic species, while a classless society is a case of a society composed of a single class, such that it corresponds to a single human species.

A class is defined as a species by its unique mode of social reproduction. One defines a class society as a society, rather than a mere collection of species, by noting the unique fashion in which the modes of reproduction of the component classes are interdependent. The analysis of capitalist society as a class society is exemplary.

The working class is brought into being by a process of primitive accumulation. In general, the process is epitomized by the effect of debt-service in reifying feudal forms of reproduction. To alienate the surplus product, the feudal debtor must alienate means of development of the feudal population, which already implies an alienation of the corresponding magnitude of the feudal population. As the rates of debt-service increase to exceed the rate of feudal surplus production, the payment of debt-service becomes the means of primitive accumulation: the very basis for maintaining the magnitude and quality of feudal production is undermined through alienation. (Although other, auxiliary features of the process complement the debt-service relationship, the latter aspect of alienation is exemplary for our present considerations.)

The alienated product and population can be reunited (realized) only through the power of the person who commands (owns) the alienated product. The scale on which this actually occurs is, of course, originally far below the rate of creation of the proletarianized population.

This proletariat does not constitute the material basis of a labor process in itself. Nor does the uniting of a proletariat with means of production in itself suffice to define a labor process. It is the creation of labor power by the employment of alienated labor that sets the labor process into motion; the alienated proletariat as wage-labor represents only the precondition for the formation of that process. A labor process, as we have emphasized earlier in this chapter, must be closed with respect to the self-expansion of labor power. Labor power is not that which produces a product, but that which produces a product as the mediation of new increases in the quality of labor power.

This occurs under capitalism as capitalism itself begins to emerge from its mercantilist preconditions. When industrial production begins to become generalized even for urban centers, and to determine the growth of national wealth directly (and at first, more significantly, indirectly) such that the advancement of national wealth depends upon the existence of cooperative labor to realize universal labor (inventions), the labor process begins. It cannot be overemphasized that labor power is not a simple productivity of labor; labor power is a *momentary* simple productivity but also a capacity to assimilate and realize new productivities. Simple productivity of labor power is only the momentary aspect, in the here and now, of a process of self-perfection: it is the process, not its momentary aspect, that characterizes and thus defines labor power.

The indispensable complement of the emergence of labor power and the labor process from simple wage-labor is the development of industrial capital. In general, the two sides develop coincidentally. As the mercantile capitalist is superceded by the capitalist proper, the working class comes into being. As mercantile capital becomes subject to a metagenetical phase of life as industrial capital in its cycle for an economy as a whole, capitalism emerges from its material and social preconditions, and the working class, as distinct from a simple proletariat, comes into being.

Yet, as we have already underlined, labor power does not come into being as labor power-in-and-for-itself. It does not yet form the basis for a true labor process. First, its essential content as labor power is alienated to the extent that creative mentation respecting the productive forces' development is appropriated by an alien (capitalist) class. The second aspect of alienation—the alienation of its material power of mediating its own development, its product—also deprives the working class of the quality of self-reproduction, of embodying a true self-subsisting positive. These powers are appropriated by the alien class, the capitalist class.

Thus the two great classes of capitalist society reproduce themselves as classes (species), and yet neither possesses all the features necessary for social reproduction. The capitalist represents universal labor, both through the capitalists' deliberations respecting productive development and through control of scientists and science. This control of universal labor is expressed through appropriation of the mediating object connecting the successive moments of existence of cooperative labor. The working class represents the actualization of universal labor.

Outside these two great classes, especially at the outset of capitalist development, exists the agricultural population, composed of the residue of the nobility and the independent and semi-independent farmers. (Auxiliary to this class is the body of proletarianized agricultural labor, which assumes the form of wage-labor and evolves into labor power through the interconnections between the agricultural product and the capitalist market for that product.) The agricultural population forms a distinct class because it reproduces itself partially through its internal (or "natural") economy, and partially through its commodity-relations with the capitalist market. However, despite this distinction in the specific social mode of reproduction, the agricultural class does not exist outside capitalist society. It is capitalist agriculture, whose form of wealth is entirely capitalist, whatever fancy costumes inherited from its feudal ancestors it may affect.

Between the two great classes there is an intermediate class, the petit bourgeoisie. It is made up of small shop-keepers, professionals, clerks, house-servants, errand boys, and the professional military and police strata, and essentially represents house-servants of the capitalist class, subsisting on capitalists' consumption. The petit bourgeoisie is not a true class but a caste, dependent upon the species-mode of reproduction of other classes; it is a cuckoo-class.

The Mesopotamian priest-caste and the trade-union bureaucracy of modern capitalist society are examples of castes, as is the semipermanent social stratum of the Soviet bureaucracy. The Mesopotamian priest-caste did not alienate the product of labor—although it did alienate the Mesopotamian equivalent of universal labor. It therefore had no separate basis for existence as a social formation within the basic mode of social reproduction; it had no power to alienate the product of collective labor from collective labor in ways determined by its own distinct mode of social reproduction. The trade-union bureaucracy appropriates certain powers of the organized labor movement (and of unorganized labor as well), but it does not have a basis for reproduction as a separate species. The Soviet bureaucracy is in essence a distinct cuckoo social formation within nationalized productive property forms, but it has no basis for existence independent of the forms on which the reproduction of Soviet workers occurs. Such castes are distinguished as such by their privileged position as a social formation within another class (as distinct from a privileged position as individuals *qua* individuals).

The petit bourgeoisie of capitalist society is rightly termed a caste because it exists outside the existing classes. It is not a part of either of the two major classes; although it includes—in later capitalist development of independent capitalist farming practices—a section of the agricultural class, the petit bourgeoisie as a whole is not an extension of the agricultural class.

THE STRUCTURE OF CAPITALIST DEVELOPMENT

7

Capitalism, in the form in which it emerged in Western Europe during the period from the Tudors through the Restoration,[1] is, as Hegel and Marx insist, the first form of society to create the material basis for world-historical man and thus to establish the basis for conceiving of an actually human existence.[2] Hegel emphasizes that the new form of society made the existence of every individual immediately dependent upon the productive and associated activities of the entire society. Therefore, to the extent that the individual under capitalist development becomes self-conscious of the objective basis for his existence, his self-consciousness corresponds to a potential for an actually human society—socialist society—an advance not possible in any preceding stage of human development.

Unlike Hegel, who locates the vanguard of human self-consciousness in the monarch and bureaucracy of Prussia,[3] and unlike Feuerbach, who attempts to locate this potential in the mere "dumb generality" of static species consciousness, Marx locates the objective potential for the working class to become a universal class, a political class-for-itself. From 1843 on, thus correcting Feuerbach while building on his indispensable accomplishments,[4] Marx counterposes the only possible universal class for society as a whole to Hegel's monarch and bureaucracy, a surrogate in the form of the potentially self-conscious working class, a proletariat consciously comprehending its historical role for society's future evolutionary development.[5]

The legitimacy and even necessity of this approach to capitalist economy itself has already been stipulated.[6] The process of analyzing the miraculous transformation of feudal wealth (surplus, a colonizing population) into alienable commodity forms of wealth—the origin of capitalism—immediately demonstrates to us the actual content of capitalist accumulation. Its content is productive social relations. This standpoint, as we have emphasized in agreement with Marx and Luxemburg, immediately presents the world-outlook of socialist society. Moreover, as both Marx and Luxemburg emphasized, it is impossible to understand capitalist reproduction competently except from a socialist point of reference.

Therefore, in these immediate chapters we are examining the underlying basis for capitalist reproduction in exactly such terms: we are viewing it in terms of its material content, the labor process. Accordingly, forms of exchange value and specific use value (specific to capitalist accumulation) do not immediately exist for us, since we are not yet considering capitalist accumulation as such, but only notions of use value otherwise peculiar to socialist economy.

The two objections that might be advanced against this approach are that this is not consistent with the apparent procedure in Marx's revised organization of *Capital*[1] and that we are judging capitalist economy from the standpoint of a society which has not yet come into existence, rather than in terms of the actual phenomena of its emergence. With respect to these objections, we stipulate that the approach in question has already been used by Marx in *Capital* to reach all the principal conclusions we advance here apropos political economy as such and that "it is not necessary to repeat that experiment in every river of the world." Marx reached those conclusions by the same general method we employ here, afterward proving them in the formal terms of presentation the critic might require. Moreover, as we have just repeated our statement of the case above, we, following Marx and Luxemburg in the matter, have merely restated the argument already given for our procedure.

Our immediate tasks in this chapter are to develop the notion of actual underlying forms of capitalist expanded reproduction in terms of use-value relations, beginning with the analysis of the division of all capitalist production into two principal departments. As for the other required qualifications of our procedure, we next summarize the historical basis for the socialist outlook.

THE SOCIALIST STANDPOINT

Marx's judgment of the revolutionary potentiality of the working class has two interconnected aspects. In the first, lesser aspect, the proletariat as a whole has no objective interest in the perpetuation of capitalist forms. This negative feature merely fulfils the necessary precondition for wresting the working class from attachment to capitalist forms under certain circumstances, particularly those brought about by the fresh onset of recurring depressions. Only to the degree that the proletariat is alienated from its wholeness, and thus exists as a mere class-in-itself, does it have any positive relationship to the capitalist class and its institutions. When the working class is fragmented into such "competing" heteronomic forms as trade unions, ethnic groupings, employed-versus-unemployed, and the like, the notion of immediate self-interest limits the positive role of the working class to that mediated for it by the capitalists. Under conditions of crisis in which the subsistence of such parochialist institutions is undermined by the capitalists, the bonds of ideology to capitalist society are briefly broken, thus actualizing this negative aspect.

In the second, more decisive and positive, aspect of the two qualifications, the proletariat is the potentially universal class because it is the only class upon which the material existence of the entire society depends. It is the class whose activity, taken as a whole, uniquely and directly alters nature to produce new forms of physical means of reproductive potential as a whole. Indeed, the socially necessary but not productive activities of persons outside the working class may indirectly contribute to this negentropic process. Physicians, teachers, scientists, and the like perform services either directly or indirectly for the working class or its productive activities. These may be essential to production, and might be described as increased potential, as is the case for universal labor generally. The predicament of the teacher is typical of socially necessary nonproductive labor. The teacher contributes directly to increasing the potential labor power of workers, and is thus a socially necessary mediation of universal labor. But if the students are not productively employed, the teacher's "labor" dies. The services that persons outside the working class perform upon and for that class are embodied as increased potential, not as actual productive powers within the working class, and are realized as negentropic changes in nature accomplished by the activity of total productive labor as such.

Provided that the working class as a political formation assimilates teachers, scientists, and the like into its ranks in the process reunifying universal and cooperative labor, the political class-for-itself includes everything that is essential for a self-subsisting labor process. It is therefore merely necessary that the working class as a political entity counterpose itself to capitalism, organically assimilating its social allies as a political formation, to become self-conscious of itself for society as a whole.

Consciousness of itself as a class-for-itself is not the mere abstract, static attitude expressed by the slogan "workers' power." Self-consciousness means self-consciousness of labor power as a self-subsisting positive, self-consciousness actively expressed in terms of a program of socialist expanded reproduction. This consciousness, program, has inevitable social correlatives within the organization of the working class as a class-for-itself, a political class.

To be a class-for-itself, the working class must have some notion of itself as that quality of labor power which is defined by the increase in labor power as the measure of labor power. This increase occurs in a unified labor process through the mediation of the objects of production. This mediation has a definite social form, in which objects are reduced to their proper notion as objectifications of positive social relations and associated human powers.

The most obvious such definite social relationship is that between employed and unemployed labor. Without the realization of the surplus product of employed labor by unemployed labor there is no class consciousness, and no socialist program. Thus a self-conscious alliance between employed and unemployed labor on the basis of a single common interest in terms of such mediations is an absolute precondition and a fundamental feature of both internal organization and program. The second major division of labor within the class as a whole is between labor power employed in producing means of human existence and labor power employed in producing means of production. The third major feature of social relations within the political class-for-itself is the necessity of universal labor, a necessity whose social expression is the leading role played by the revolutionary intelligentsia within the political organizations of the class.

It must be acknowledged that numerous nominally socialist organizations define program otherwise. This diseased nominal socialism, which conceives only of the relationship of employed labor to employers, obviously reflects the bestialized outlook on man peculiar to capitalist ideology. It proceeds from heteronomic relations between employers and wage-labor, regarding the class as a whole as a mere aggregation, a bad infinity of such heteronomic relationships. It reaches its worst extreme in those nominally socialist and anarchosyndicalist groups that regard any alienation of surplus product from employed labor as exploitation. Such pathetic outlooks reveal themselves to be opposed to those forms of relationship within the class which are the active basis for development of labor power. By rejecting the social relations of development, these nominal socialists reveal their view of man to be limited to his present, seemingly fixed qualities of labor power—a bestial view of man. The same antihuman view is generally encountered in the disorder known as workerism, the anti-intellectual prejudice which reveals a similarly bestial outlook by rejecting the notion of the necessity of universal labor. Obviously, all such views make a virtue of the degradation of wage-labor under capitalism: they seek present-day society without "certain of its defects," ironically rejecting that which is most historically progressive for man under capitalism: expanded reproduction.

To understand capitalist economy, we must concentrate on locating those specific forms through which capitalism in its own specific way satisfies the three relations we have demanded for socialist organization and program: (1) the realization of surplus product of employed labor through the productive employment of unemployed labor; (2) the social relationship between production of means of production and production of means of human existence; (3) the realization of universal labor (science). The necessary tasks of socialist organization and program enable us to understand the tasks capitalist economy must subsume to the extent it is a positive form. Once we have located the capitalist forms of those tasks, we are able to adduce the conditions, the contradictions, that prevent capitalism from indefinitely performing those tasks satisfactorily. Then and only then do we understand capitalist political economy.

THE TWO DEPARTMENTS

The working class, as the content of the labor process, must not only materially reproduce itself and also the existence of other classes; it must also reproduce, extend, and qualitatively advance the order of nature for socialized (collectivized) production as a whole: production of the means of production. These two moments, or *departments*, of production as a whole thus actualize the fundamentals of the dialectical world-view with respect to industrial societies: nature as subsumed by definite, concrete (specific) forms of human self-reproductive activity.

It is a reflection of the fetishism within capitalist ideology, in particular, that we tend to think of the physical plant, machinery, materials, and similar components of production as a class of objects apart from nature. The Physiocrats were closer to the truth of human existence in insisting that the secret of production must be located in man's direct relationship to nature, that the means of production of wealth could be nothing but nature. Because of their bestial view of man, they placed the mythos of "natural nature" above all else, and therefore refused to consider man-altered nature as a matter of positive alterations in nature for man. Viewing laborers as mere beasts, they refused to extend a shrewd insight to the point of recognizing that physical plant and the like are as integral a part of nature as improved livestock breeds, cultivated land, and irrigation systems—increases in nature's fecundity for a specific mode of human practice.

We recommend that the student momentarily indulge in a harmless and fruitful exaggeration: to think of machinery and the like as belonging to the same category of improvements in nature for a specific human mode of existence as irrigation systems, cultivated land, and the like. A factory is not merely an object external to nature situated at a particular location. It is, together with movable materials or materials in transit, an integral part of nature.

The much-touted "ecology crisis" perversely vindicates Marx on this matter. Relative to pollution as such, each elementary facet of the crisis reflects a cumulative failure or outright refusal to meet a socially necessary cost of maintaining the equipotential of man-altered nature for life and productive activity. Electrostatic precipitators, treatment plants, and the like exemplify these costs. Indeed, deeper examination of this problem compels a consistent investigator to confront the evidence of the more deadly sort of pollution represented by the ecology movement itself.

The enormous proportion of aerial and related pollution attributable to the gasoline and diesel engine demonstrates the pathology of the "people pollute" obsession. It is qualitatively less costly in explicit costs, lapsed time, and other major considerations to move people by mass rail and related forms of transportation than in private automobiles. It is cheaper and more efficient to move long-haul freight by modern rail transport than by long-haul trailer-truck. Yet, due to the decay of urban mass-transit systems, the steeping of railroad systems in decay, mismanagement, obsolescent forms of equipment, ancient roadbeds, and the like, as well as massive subsidies of the trucking and private automotive "roadbed," it is often quicker and cheaper to move individuals by twos in private automobiles than by mass transit—if, indeed, comparable alternative mass transit exists at all. No invisible hand directing the economy as a whole has determined the preference for private automobiles and truck transport over modernized rails and roadbeds.

Meanwhile, since the principles of the laser began to be established, and the Atomic Energy Commission and other agencies began to recognize the possibility of a so-called "clean" hydrogen bomb, we have been able to foresee the possibility of developing cheap thermonuclear fusion power. Such power not only obviates further long-term need for petroleum-oriented power production, but is also qualitatively safer than ordinary unimode "boiling water reactor" fission plants (with their insoluble output of radioactive contamination) or the Russian roulette of breeder reactors. The magnitude and cheapness of fusion power not only eliminates the depletion and contamination aspects of existing power-production forms, but also provides ways of bypassing the inherently thermally-pollutant use of steam and gas turbines.

This is only the most obvious implication of the new technology. The massive increase in per capita cheap power also means the development of new uses of electrical power, including a massive electrification of industrial technology, reducing the necessary labor cost of each unit of output. Less immediately obvious but of more fundamental importance is the fact that fusion power represents cheap, abundant power for tens of millions of years at any presently imaginable rate of per capita power consumption or for any size of population; fusion power is only one predicate of an entire new technology, which in the most obvious ways erases every limit presently attributed to the earth's ecology for man.

It is obvious, however, that the outlook of the modern ecology-movement apologist is epistemologically that of the most banal eighteenth-century Physiocrat. More specifically, this banality of outlook is internally characterized by the same world-outlook that causes the ecology crisis: the heteronomic world-view. The expenditures required to prevent the pollution of a stream by a paper mill are not part of the mill owner's heteronomic investment, or costs of maintaining his investment; his investment, the paper mill, is in a deliberate entropic relationship to nature, as epitomized by the stream. Nature in this case is not "naturally entropic"; the entropy involved is the imposition of entropy upon nature by man's deliberative choice. Just as heteronomy in its abstract form (reductionist axiomatic architectures of logic and formal mathematics) posits an abstract world which God must periodically wind up, so in actuality, the heteronomic form of human practice on nature leads to entropy. Since the economic relationship, interpreted in terms of use value, involves depletion of the future basis of human existence for present income in that mode, the form of entropy in capitalist economy is shown to be primitive accumulation.

That such depletion of nature is not necessary—at least during more recent decades—is demonstrated by the fact that there have been innumerable practicable approaches to enormously minimizing the effects of pollution through existing scientific development. The only real barriers to the translation of science into applied science in this domain are cost and the heteronomic pathology of the mill-owner and the general population, which accepts the property-right notions of capitalist accumulation. Or, more profoundly, the notion of means of production and nature as distinct categories—the premise of the ecology-movement apologists—reflects the practice that has caused the ecology crisis in the first place. People pollute, in fact, only to the extent that they spread the filth of bourgeois ideology in the forms the ecology movement promulgates.

The other aspect of the same point arises in the examination of the cost of preventing pollution. The general conclusion arising from study of the costs of preventing and remedying pollution and depletion is that there would have been very little capitalist accumulation during the past half-century, in particular, without the looting of nature. From a human standpoint, considering the nature of labor power and scientific development as defined in preceding chapters, it was not inevitable that pollution costs should have risen to such a high proportion of current gross output. It was only necessary to accelerate development such that these constant-capital costs would have diminished proportionately after prophylactic expenditures had been included.

To argue that the ecology crisis is a consequence of "too much technology" is to propose to treat the remedy with the disease. It is a lack of realized technological development, reflected in obsolete industries and the like, that is the major direct cause of pollution and depletion of resources, and the chief cause of the costliness of attempting to remedy the problem today.

From the socialist standpoint, constant capital is not defined heteronomically, as it is for capitalism. From the standpoint of use value, constant capital is that expenditure required to maintain the equipotential of man-altered nature. This definition causes difficulty only if we associate it with simple reproduction. Since it would be silly to define equipotentiality as, for example, restoring to mines the same quality of ores we have extracted from them, constant capital cannot mean replacing what is being used up.

Applying even crude (engineering-school variety) thermodynamics, it is feasible to conceptualize the difficulty here. From the specific standpoint of capitalist development, we readily understand that the quality of natural resources, such as ores, is typified by the notion of the cost of (1) refining ore and (2) reducing it to its metallic form. As for the first step, refining the ore as a raw input to smelters and the like, we can use the parameter of costs per ton of gross aggregate for such processing, such that the costs for net aggregate rise in an obvious way as the richness of the raw extraction decreases. (Reaching the ore—accessibility—also reduces to a cost parameter.) As for the second step, the cost of the energy of reduction and the materials-handling aspects of the degree of richness of the smelter charge, and the like, are the essential factors to be noted.

Both these problems can be reduced to the general form of ratios of available throughput of energy per capita—even in the crude reductionist notion of energy as the ultima ratio of the process of "work." The first approximation of a notion of equipotentiality is thus seen to depend upon a *constant* rate of increase of per capita energy throughput. The notion is illustrated, following the outline of the example employed above to explain the difficulty, by considering the fact that if the constant rate of growth (as an exponential for absolute per capita consumption) is properly set, marginal resources become equal resources.

This can be more generally approached through the conception of the history of modern scientific development elaborated by Felix Klein and others. The work of Fourier—which implicitly poses the issue of the generality of light radiation, vibrating strings, and heat exchange as thermodynamics in the statement of his famous mathematical setting of the problem—expresses the way in which a quantitative increase in energy throughput produces the qualitative leaps which take man from marginal resource calculations to entirely new conceptions of resources. The array of objects in a task-oriented setting represented by quantitative increase in energy throughputs sets in motion the noetic process of mentation. To epitomize the latter we have Fourier posing the problem in a preliminary conceptual form, thus threatening the entire bowdlerized structure of existing calculus and demanding a new notion of function and fundamentally new conceptions of geometry and number as interconnected notions. The problem of function, fed into abstract mathematics by numerous channels (tributaries, so to speak, of Fourier analysis), leads into Riemann, Weierstrass, Cantor, Maxwell, Klein, and thence into Planck and Einstein.

To Hegel, Planck's wrestling with the discovery of the determinate quantum of action would have been just that—wrestling. To Hegel, Einstein would have appeared to be Kepler's revenge. Yet, contrary to Hegel, the geometric laws of the development of modern scientific knowledge—in its full first orbit from Kepler to Einstein—are not a matter of the internal elaboration of the Logos. Scientific activity must be conceptualized as an aspect of universal labor, which is realized and achieves its outcome as a further impetus to universal labor through cooperative labor. Break the chain, abort the realization of science, mire the economy in obsolescence, refuse to increase the number and enhance the education of mathematical physics Ph.D.'s, dump most of those matriculated into the sewer of military technology, limit oneself to the strictures of cost-benefit analysis—thus to prevent scientific applications from doing more than elaborating known discoveries—and the whole impetus to progress is aborted.

The notion of simple reproduction—replacement of what is used up—is absurd from this standpoint, and signifies etiologically the heteronomic conception of capital. The individual who deludes himself that constant capital is a matter of particular firms and particular capitalists, or of the relationship between particular employees and employers, is manifestly suffering the most pathetic sort of procapitalist delusions.

We have implicitly upset the conventional vulgar notion of work and the reductionist vulgar notions of energy. If ordinary notions of work imply entropic systems, and the ordinary street-corner notions of energy are hereditary derivations of such notions of work, we have thus located the underlying connection between the bestialization of labor in capitalist social relations and the origins of the intuitive impulses from which vulgar conceptions of work and energy arise. Energy, in the sense that such a notion is necessarily implicit in the thermodynamic overview of social reproduction, is determinate, an objectification of mediated social-reproductive powers in a universe of human labor power characterized by self-expansion as a whole. The notion of energy and quanta as aspects of a notion of fundamental particularities, self-evident particularities, or things-in-themselves, has no authority in itself or in its derived judgments for our definitions of the fundamental relations of social reproduction. Epistemological etiology enables us to identify precisely the social pathology of such reductionist axiomatic views: ". . . it is not necessary to repeat this experiment in every river of the world."

To understand constant capital dialectically, one must overcome the last remaining barrier to a correct notion of the use value seemingly embedded in the objects we regard as objectified use value. The experimental approach of the Gestalt psychologists, to which we have repeatedly referred, facilitates our settling of this issue.

It should be obvious, referring to Köhler's most famous demonstration, that the objects of a task-oriented setting for cognition are not merely for cognition, but are for cognition as the mediation of the new use of those objects as a materialized Gestalt of practice. Thus, the use value of the array for consciousness is an hypothetical use value in the ordinary sense of the term "hypothesis." The history of scientific progress may seem to obscure this fact only because the most celebrated aspects of scientific progress tend to de-emphasize the closing of the circle from the task-oriented posing of a problem for cognition back to the task. When we have properly closed that circle, the value for cognition (the hypothetical value) is a reflection of the actual value. But the actual value exists for practice only *through* cognition.

Therefore, the use value of the object is specific not to the object nor even to the entire array of objects. The use value attributed to the object is that of objectified social-reproductive powers, powers which essentially include the power of cognition. Granted, the objects reflect preceding social practice, and thus might seem independently to embody the practice that created them. Yet, on reflection, it becomes clear that such independent value could not exist, since it would plunge us directly into the paradoxes to which we have previously referred.

It becomes necessary to conclude that these objects are mediations of social-reproductive relations and that they have use value in no other sense. One objects, not without a certain amount of anguish, "But, these are real objects, which exist independently of their consumers!" Of course, but the universe in which they exist "independently" is a universe of hylozoic laws, such that the value determined for specific social-reproductive relations is the value for the universe. Admittedly, this merely aggravates the intuitive difficulties of the student, but it is therefore a solution to his difficulty, since it leaves him no alternative but to conceptualize the notion in question and thus to solve the problem for himself. At this juncture, the comprehension of Marxian economic theory becomes elementary in the true sense of the term. There are in every domain of inquiry certain notions that are elementary, in the sense that everything else is built upon them; everything else is theorem. What one ought properly to mean by "elementary" is not intuited axioms and their simplest applications, but rather those notions which subsume everything else, by exhaustive methods of determining what notions must necessarily be elementary from the standpoint of universalized human practice. Such notions and their hereditary implications for further practice and conceptualization of practice—implications embedded in the process by which the elementary notion itself is obtained—thus become elementary in a meaningful sense, determining every other judgment in the same fashion.

With respect to the student's difficulties, we acknowedge with considerable compassion that the problem posed by this notion is not of the type to which he has become accustomed. The conceptualization of the notion that solves the problem demands a quality of self-consciousness different from that associated with ordinary manipulation of images, or with the reductionist ways of thinking associated with adducing appropriate logical procedures for specific sciences from study of image-relationships in the experimental domain. To master the notion, he is compelled to encounter those powers of deliberative cognition we ordinarily sense as "preconscious" impulses for problem solving. He must rise above the reductionist world-view, for which such problem-solving impulses are intuitive, and directly cognize those powers of conceptualization. He must learn to call upon them at will in the same way that ordinary alienated forms of consciousness call upon the procedures of logical deduction.

This cannot be accomplished by learning. Such matters cannot be "explained," since explanation (e.g., edification) addresses itself to the authority of precisely what must be rejected. Just as the great poet or musician gradually becomes acquainted with his own creative processes as a subject, so creative mentation is made a subject of reflection through mediation. One must deliberately exercise one's creative powers, isolate the creative moment from the objectified activity and thus make it the subject of one's continued reflection.

Little more can be said on this point. The reader will have to assimilate the process we have described, to make it his own, in the development of his own creative powers through the exercise of his applied intelligence.

With respect to social-productive powers as a whole, the plenum of objects implying expanded reproduction represent the following moments: (1) They represent a mediated social relationship between existing labor power and the labor power mediated through the objects. (2) Relative to the potential labor power to which they are presented as means of production and existence, the plenum of objects represents an imputable optimal program of social reproduction in terms of objectified powers of *that form*; but, this is only conditional. (3) With respect to the limits such a plenum defines, and to the depletion of the continuation of that mode immediately embodied in such a program, the program imputed demands further development of social-reproductive powers; this expresses the necessity for creative mentation or science in general (universal labor). (4) The program that maximizes 2 and 3 together is the desired program, which fully expresses the value imputable to the plenum of objects as an entirety. (5) The value of the particular object is implicit by substitution, addition, elimination, or a related process, such that, first, its marginal contribution to the value of the exponential impulse-tendency of the function $S'/(C + V)$ is the first approximation of its use value. The basis for the replication of a determinate proportion of such objects in the next epoch defines the object as being-in-and-for-itself in form. Only in form, however; the content is the movement from the epoch in which the object is produced to the epoch for which it is realized, a moment of *progress* whose content is social-reproductive relations through the moment in which the use value is imputed for the object.

This is emphasized by the form of constant capital. As means of production, material preconditions of production, the objects of constant capital are one step removed from social reproduction per se. The irony of this is underlined by the tendency to increase in the ratio of constant to variable capital as an expression of the progressive development of the productive forces, man's increasing power over nature, and his increasing mastery of the development of the material preconditions of production. The notion of value involved is expressed in that this increase in the proportional development of the material preconditions of production is the basis for both an increase in leisure and an accelerated reduction in the proportion of total labor power required to materially produce a more advanced quality of labor power. In this expression of the invariant Freedom/Necessity, leisure is not freedom from labor, but a positive condition necessary to increase the cognitive powers of labor. Increased leisure is positive only as a facet of productive labor power as a whole, as an expression of its quality of universal labor.

These relations are elaborated as the relationships between employed and unemployed labor and between departments 1 and 2 of the production of employed labor. (Respectively, production of means of production, and production of means of consumption.) Leisure is universal labor as a social category and relationship. Positively, universal labor as leisure is scientific activity as a social category and its corresponding specific social relations. Passively, implicitly, the complementary facet of universal labor is the increased leisure of the working class (cooperative labor), a quality of leisure epitomized by education, which thus typifies the increased cognitive powers upon which the assimilation of new inventions by cooperative labor depends.

We emphasize again, since these are exactly the notions—so alien to ordinary opinion—upon which comprehension of political economy depends, that the qualities we abstract from analysis of the necessary distinctions of the labor process and its broader social setting are not merely abstract qualities peculiar to abstract reflection. They are concrete qualities of the labor process, concretely expressed in the elaboration of social relations within the labor process and its social setting. In addition to the division of labor in its most ordinary sense of "network," we have the qualitative distinction between constant and variable capital in the form of two major departments of production, and the motion of that network in terms of the productive employment of unemployed labor power as the active self-interest of employed and unemployed labor alike. The relationship of science and general education to this process typifies the completion of the immediate necessary social setting of a labor process-in-and-for-itself.

Having identified these principled considerations, we proceed from the standpoint of simple reproduction to describe the relationships between the departments.

Figure 5 summarizes the altered form in which we analyze the totality of productive activity in order to account for the two departments. In place of S',d,V,C, we have (in department 1) S'_1,d_1,V_1,C_1, and (in department 2) S'_2,d_2,V_2,C_2. Ignoring for the moment the problem of distinguishing precisely between the two departments, let us describe the form and content of each of the eight elements so denoted.

C_1 and V_2 are the same in form and content. C_1 is Constant Capital produced within department 1 and consumed by department 1 production. V_2 is means of consumption produced within department 2 and consumption by that proportion of the working-class population corresponding to all the labor employed in department 2. S'_1 and S'_2 involve no special treatment; they are, in form and content, respectively a net social surplus of means of production and means of consumption. The symbol d_1 represents means of production (in form) consumed as capitalists' consumption; (e.g., military equipment, office buildings, etc.). d_2 is means of consumption consumed as capitalists' consumption.

This leaves us with V_1 and C_2 to consider.

It might be assumed that C_2 and V_1 are equivalents, which can be neatly exchanged between departments. Then, the means of consumption which are the content of C_2 would be exchanged for V_1, means of production. Now, C_2 as V_1's new content is realizable as the means of consumption for that proportion of the entire working-class population corresponding to department 1's proportion of total labor power. V_1 as means of production for department 2 is suitably realized in the guise of substituted C_2 there. This would be the approximate social relationship between the two departments if socialist economy could be represented from the standpoint of simple reproduction—which it cannot be. This "solution" is only a pedagogical device useful for beginning to situate the problems involved.

In capitalist economy, in which the exchange occurs in the form of commodities, the effective reciprocal transfer of means of production within capitalist production as a whole is not necessarily, and is usually not, an

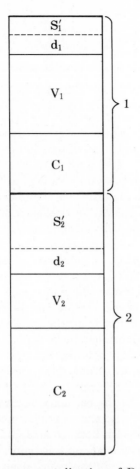

Figure 5   Departmentalization of Production

equivalent in terms of its mere labor power content. In socialist economy too, the use values of output do not correspond simply to the amount of labor power input, but for different reasons than in capitalist economy. However, neither of these problems can be resolved from the standpoint of simple reproduction, so we shall leave the matter in its unsatisfactory pedagogical form for the moment.

Using subscripts to denote the first and second epochs of production in successive cycles—e.g., V_{10} and V_{11} to designate the same category of V_1 in cycles 0 and 1—and substituting the values of cycle 0 in cycle 1 wherever the two are equal, the standpoint of simple reproduction gives us:

$$S'_{10} + S'_{20} + V_{10} + V_{20} + C_{10} + C_{20}$$
$$\leq S'_{11} + S'_{21} + S'_{10} + S'_{20} + V_{10} + V_{20} + C_{10} + C_{20}$$
$$= S'_{11} + S'_{21} + V_{11} + V_{21} + C_{11} + C_{21}.$$

but such that

$$\frac{S'_{10} + S'_{20}}{V_{10} + V_{20} + C_{10} + C_{20}}$$

$$= \frac{S'_{11} + S'_{21}}{V_{11} + V_{21} + C_{11} + C_{21}}$$

The symbol $\leqq$ in the first set of expressions signifies the condition in which $S = d$ which is the usual pedagogical definition of simple reproduction.

Our difficulty here is that we are presenting the problem of equivalents according to the philosophical world-outlook implicit in the notion of simple reproduction. This is the world-outlook of the poorest apprentice accountant. We have implicitly defined labor time as a simple magnitude, and reduced the notions of equivalents, wealth, and the like to aggregations of such magnitudes, in which input and output as a whole are related by simple multiples to $S'/(C + V)$ as a fixed ratio. This "logical" form of equivalents, introduced to construct such a pedagogical schema, is useful for that purpose, but it does not represent the way in which value is transferred through the process of realization from one facet of the productive process to another. Value must be actually transferred in the form of increased potential for the whole through the mediation of the particular.

In capitalist economy proper, the implications of the underlying labor process—the use-value relationships—are merely reflected, rather than directly embodied, in the exchange relationships. Despite the special distinctions between socialist and capitalist economies, one feature of the realization process obtains for both. In actuality, as we have emphasized in our references to the Physiocrats on this point, Constant Capital cannot be reproductive in itself; it cannot reproduce itself and surplus value. Objects are valued only as material preconditions for labor power's self-reproduction.

It makes no difference to particular labor whether useful means of production were produced by other labor, spontaneously generated from the soil, or dropped from a beneficent flying saucer. The notion of Constant Capital cost is not in itself a notion of value for particular labor power. It is not the cost of the object that determines its value, but its value that determines its permissible cost.

If we proceed, as we always must, from the totality of the productive forces (that is, the totality of labor power), this totality is to be treated simply as a unity, rather than a magnitude in the ordinary sense of an aggregation of particular magnitudes. The totality of labor power, however it might be measured by any other standard, is simply unity in all the successive transformations of reproduction. What distinguishes the successive transformations from one another is the relationship $S'/(C + V)$, in which $1 \geqq S' + C + V$. From this simple comparison of rising values of the ratio, we adduce a rate of increase. With respect to the social relationship between differing rates of social productivity in successive epochs of this process, we adduce the momentary impulse value of exponential increases in the value of the ratio. This momentary impulse value defines the notion of use value and "the state of the system." It represents labor power as a self-subsisting positive.

This point is elaborated by the following specific alterations, which we shall subsequently discuss in more detail.

If we equate the value of the labor force, 1, with a magnitude of population, we derive the following results as an elaboration of realization. The absolute per capita consumption of the working-class population increases relative to the preceding epoch, and there is an accompanying tendency (with special exceptions) for the amount of leisure of the population to increase. However, this increase tends to be less than the realized increase in social productivity. So, in such a "normal" case, virtual unemployment occurs in both departments. Since the costs of increased per capita consumption of means of existence and production have both been reduced, the same array of old products is produced in increased amounts with less than existing levels of employment: virtual unemployment. However, this virtual unemployment is absorbed by realization of S'_1 and S'_2. In which department? Generally, for obvious reasons, in department 1 at a greater rate than in department 2. The result is that $(C_1 + C_2)/(V_1 + V_2)$ will immediately tend to rise, and the ratio of department 1 to department 2 will rise. This rise is accompanied by a decline in the ratio $(V_1 + V_2)/(S + d + C)$. *However, S/V will rise more rapidly than C/V!* (Thus, a rising organic composition of capital, in these terms, cannot possibly cause a tendency for the falling rate of profit!)

Within such a framework, in first approximation, we have the following notions. Every alternative human productive activity represents a deduction from the unity for C or V, and as a deduction represents a tendency for a reduction in the ratio $S'/(C + V)$. Since the object of social reproduction is to increase the value of $S'/(C + V)$, the cost of means of production in this way negatively determines the value of all production. The notion of C/V as the "technological composition of capitals"[8] is not a true notion in itself, but is simply a way of expressing a certain empirical relationship between V and C for an otherwise determined specific value of $S'/(C + V)$. Similarly, S/V is not a true conception. The object expresses, as the potential subject of labor power, a certain potential of labor power to yield a resulting higher rate of surplus value (S/V), but relative to a definite prevailing value of $S'/(C + V)$. The question is whether incrementing C or V, or leisure, results in a greater increase in $S'/(C + V)$.

Yet, considering our earlier definition of C,[9] how is it possible to increase C above the "level of equipotential"? That, as we forewarned the reader, is one of the difficulties of employing the pedagogical standpoint of simple reproduction. In actual reproduction, there are obviously no distinctions in particular between C and S' or between V and S'. The distinction of absolute surplus value arises only as the Physiocrats appropriately defined absolute rent, if the economy is viewed as a whole. Whether the production of means of production by one capitalist represents C or S'_1 or d_1 is determined by what other capitalists do. If they produce more, his added means of production may be, relatively speaking, S'; if they produce less, it must be merely C. Only if one proceeded from a program of production as a whole could such distinctions be made in advance for particular productions; but even then, as each change in the plenum of objects alters the optimal program, we see how the problem is actually posed under even such desirable circumstances.

FIXED AND CIRCULATING CAPITALS: TECHNICAL COMPOSITION

The distinction between Fixed and Circulating Capitals arises from the phasal relationships inherent in the cyclical character of an extended network of the division of labor. It is sufficient to note here that the half-life of plant, machinery, and equipment may be on the order of seven to ten years (after which it may tend to become technologically obsolete in a modern economy), in contrast to the cycle of production from extraction of materials through final product, which may be no more than months or several years. Furthermore, what we commonly identify as Fixed Capital has a different relationship to production than do materials and the like. It is not embodied in the final product, but represents the material preconditions of production, like irrigation systems, and the like. It has value, which it appears to add to the value of the product—the necessary value of maintaining the equipotential of the conditions of production.[10]

Thus we already have a sense of the way in which Fixed and Circulating Capitals must be distinguished (apropos the material, use-value content of such commodity forms). Yet a further difficulty presents itself. Do we include the circulation of Fixed Capital in its final commodity form for sale in Circulating Capital? These are distinctions of such profound importance *for socialist economy* that we would not in that case include newly-formed Fixed Capital in Circulating Capital. Even in that case, if the category of machinery seems self-evident, the cases of bricks, structural steel, and numerous other products make the discrimination much less simple.

From the standpoint of socialist economy, it is advisable to segregate such "sunk costs" in the development of the fixed preconditions of production from those preconditions typified by materials. Again, it is not a simple matter. One must take into account distinctions in form and use (realization), and the problem looks different to us from the respective standpoints of production per se and circulation. The difficulty vanishes once we take into account the root of the distinction from the standpoint of the reproductive process: a phasal distinction.

In capitalist economy, that proportion of Constant Capital which appears to be the depreciation of Fixed Capital from the standpoint of production per se circulates not as replacement of depreciated capital, but as new capital, in the same form as materials and the like. In the value relations of capital, provided the term of accounting is sufficiently extended, fixed capital dissolves into the product as much as do materials and the like.

The significance of the distinction emerges only when we have located the distinctions determined for the entire economy from the standpoint of the time of circulation. If the rate of social productivity is rising at, for example, 7 per cent per year, in the short-term consumption of materials the depreciation of commodity values will have little effect on the cost accountant's estimation of replacement costs or values of raw materials inventories carried forward (provided such inventories are neither too large nor too aged). This is not the case for the undepreciated residue of Fixed Capital, which resembles in effect *oversized and overaged materials or finished goods inventory.*

This effect has two aspects. In one respect, we are confronted with that aspect of value which seems to pertain to cost apropos the *price of production.*[11] In another respect, we are concerned with technological obsolescence, exemplified in the extreme by an inventory of buggywhips. The form of the first sort of difficulty is peculiar to capitalist society, where historic (past-oriented) notions of exchange value predominate. The latter is the standpoint of socialist society, in which the effect on the future is the standard. Yet in both instances a kind of depreciation has occurred as a result of advancement of the general quality of labor power.

If we proceed from the standpoint of exchange value, the relationship of Fixed to Circulating Capital imputes an *organic composition of capitals,* which is determinate for particular productions in the form C/V. (We leave it to the reader to work out for himself why a given ratio of Fixed to Circulating Capitals should determine a relationship between departments 1 and 2 and, in turn, a ratio of C/V.) If we proceed from the standpoint of socialist economy, we regard the relationship as expressing a *technological composition of capitals.* The use of the term "capitals" in the latter case signifies that we are considering the problem in the form in which it arises, as a socialist overview of capitalist reproduction.

This problem will be treated more fully later, when we examine the fundamental contradiction of capitalist reproduction.

SIMPLE VERSUS EXTENDED REPRODUCTION

The notion of simple reproduction is introduced to political economy only as a pedagogical ruse, made necessary by the ideology of a society in which the naive standpoint of sense-certainty predominates. That is, pedagogy demands that certain basic phenomena be introduced in a way agreeable to reductionist prejudices, and that the dialectical view of the same phenomena be presented as a refutation of the reductionist interpretation of raw perceptions.

The transition from the false conventional notion of such phenomena as discrete magnitudes begins with the restatement of the initial datum as *potential*, as a cross-section of a continuous elaborated process in the here and now. But this is only an intermediate step, shown to be a crucial qualification by the abundant evidence of reductionist "dynamics," in which the usual representation of process as continuity is nothing but that of potential infinity, an asymptotic or bad infinity of individual potentials.

This discussion subsumes that of the concluding chapter of Volume II of *Capital*, in which Marx's text begins its movement from simple reproduction through bad infinity . . . and breaks off. We abruptly meet actual infinity in Volume III, and there exists no evidence of a systematic pedagogical development between the two volumes. Despite the fallacies that arise from the attempt to extrapolate from the fragmentary concluding chapter of Volume II, the difficulty involved in the transition is not what it might first appear. The transition from simple to potentially extended reproduction, the undertaking of the chapter in question, is susceptible to explication in conventional terms, as the chapter itself suggests. These terms are those of "logical" explanation, or—a term which Hegel rightly made one of devastating opprobrium—edification. There is no process of edification which could enable one to make the conceptual leap from potentially to actually expanded reproduction by logic.

We could return to our point/line example or to the cases developed by Cantor, which are more appropriate for illustrating the problem at hand. Historically, the conceptualization of actual infinities has occurred as a result of the extrapolation of potential-infinity notions to the point that an insoluble predicament (antinomy) is demonstrated. This in itself affords no solution until we attack the antinomy from the standpoint of an inclusive notion of self-development (that is, "a night in which all cows are black" does not permit us to conceptualize a cow). Consequently, all those creative personalities who have reflected upon their successes in such undertakings are compelled to describe the final step toward solution as either metaphysics or a term of the same epistemological significance. Not surprisingly, those who have either refused to make the leap or fallen into the abyss in the effort also use the term "metaphysics," with a different tone of voice and significance.

From the outside, the result does seem to be a metaphysical phenomenon in the same semireligious sense as is often ascribed to the notion of cognition in connection with such cases as Köhler's chimpanzees. From the inside, the process is viewed quite differently. The notion of reversing the conception of the problem-materials is quite as explicit from the latter standpoint as the conventional identification of a formal-logical procedure. One learns, from reflecting on solutions repeatedly obtained by such exertions, that the mental act of reversing the view is triggered by the actualization of a notion of self-development. No matter how faithfully one attempts to solve the problem by inversion, the mind refuses to perform the required procedure until it has been supplied with an appropriate notion of self-development for that field of contradictions. Once the notion has been supplied, the inversion occurs. It is not necessarily the solution, and is subject to judgment on this account in the same sense that the exercise of logical procedures is subject to judgment, formally (consistency) and empirically (experimentally). An unsatisfactory conception produced by such inversions requires a substitute notion of "self-development," just as a failed formal solution requires a modified logical procedure.

We have repeatedly referred to this empirical-psychological aspect of the dialectical method, emphasizing the empirical evidence of nonplastic art forms, in which such phenomena are best distilled for contemplation. It now becomes essential to clarify this matter further, since the whole point of the transition in progress here would otherwise be lost on the reader. The special difficulty in this undertaking is that it is unlikely that the reader will comprehend the method *as his own* in a straightforward section-by-section study of this text. We must therefore settle on a compromise here: we must present the relevant processes of judgment as phenomena subject to empirical demonstration, and relate the process by which we make the leap to such empirically verifiable procedures. Assuming that to correspond to the immediate limits of the reader's powers of comprehension, we have solved the formal problem of defending the results we obtain in further development of the subject matter. Of course, since the conclusions to be reached are subject to ordinary forms of empirical verification, provided the dangers of fallacy of composition are taken into account, the proof of those conclusions does not have to wait upon the reader's mastery of the internal features of the dialectical method. However, simply to describe the critical transitions would leave the empirical achievements ensuing from them in an aura of mystification. "They are absolutely correct, but I have no notion how such excellent results were produced," the reader would say to himself. To remedy this problem, a compromise is made with our desired result: we represent the dialectical method's internal features in the terms in which they are to be experienced as empirical psychological phenomena, thus eliminating the problem of mystification.

The possibility of such an approach is also subject to empirical verification. It is the same thing as learning a language. At the outset, a new language is a strange thing; it seems incredible that actual ideas could be communicated in such a way. One knows the language not when one has passed all the necessary examinations in translation of vocabulary, syntax, and the like, but when one is astonished to find that he can communicate ideas effectively in the new medium. One understands, in that specific sense, another speaker of the same language. It is the same with the dialectical method. One knows that one's own internal dialectical practice is not some egregious thing, but is identical in a broad sense to that of Descartes,

Spinoza, Kant, Hegel, Feuerbach, and Marx, as one recognizes a fellow-speaker of one's native language. The unique progression of ideas in which certain mediating devices are characteristic of getting from one point in connection to the next, is as distinct as a familiar face. The problem of interpretation of Kepler, Descartes, and other thinkers is not—as is too often and too confidently assumed—a matter of formal scholarship on externalities. It depends, rather, on "getting inside their heads" in a certain sense, on sufficient awareness of the necessary implications of externalities. One recognizes from one's own use of a certain mental language that some externalities exist only because that special mental language is being used. The entire external representation would be false, incoherent in its essential features, unless it had been produced by a distinct kind of mentation.

The most accessible demonstration of this point, relative to much of the literature by accredited—but badly misled—scholars of Descartes and Spinoza, is the banal representation of Descartes' theorems in the typical philosophy textbook. Comparing the textbook with the original source, one can immediately distinguish between the two irreconcilable kinds of mentation occurring in the minds of Descartes and his scholarly appreciator.

Other evidences include Hegel's effort to reduce creative mentation to a logic. Considering the fact that creative mentation bears no resemblance to a formal logic in any significant respect but one—a stipulation which must be made without immediate development—the mere fact of Hegel's effort to write *The Science of Logic* is a unique demonstration that he was self-conscious of creative mentation, or of what is ordinarily experienced as mere preconsciousness or deliberative powers. Section 33 of Feuerbach's *Principles of the Philosophy of the Future* is a magnificent example of a thought which could not be stated except by a person self-conscious of the deliberative nature of creative mentation. Most of Marx's early writings, especially those aspects we underlined in Chapter 4,[12] are another instance of such unique externalities. In each case, the very idea stated could not be articulated by a person who was merely creative; the ideas represented are unique to persons of self-conscious creativity, for whom creative powers are deliberative powers subject to deliberative reflection.

No individual who has experienced such mental life would tolerate the silly notion that degrees of intelligence are biologically or accidentally distributed in populations. It is absolutely certain, from the type of empirical evidence to which we are referring, that the quality of intelligence is and can be learned, though not in the ordinary sense of learning. Such intelligence is a distinct and an historically specific phenomenon. The name for it is the dialectical method, which is the quality of human intelligence made self-conscious.

In the subject matter at hand, political economy, there is a reciprocal relationship between such specific qualities of intelligence and comprehension of the subject under scrutiny. None of the concepts elementary to the subject can be mastered without the dialectical method, and yet, for this society, the study of political economy is uniquely the mediation, the empirical basis, for becoming self-conscious of one's creative mentation. The problems of political economy, set in the framework of investigation we have specified, offer that mediating activity of study which most directly allows for the conceptualization of the dialectical method as a task. By acquiring a preliminary comprehension of political economy in an external way, one confronts oneself with certain nagging problems of conceptualization which must be settled before one really comprehends the subject internally. The result of this reflection on one's study-exertions is the dialectical method, which, once grasped, leads to internal comprehension of the subject matter of political economy in a thorough way.

This is the kernel of this entire text, and the significance of the term "dialectical economics."

This argument may seem insufferably arrogant at first glance. Yet the contrary view is indefensible even from the most ordinary empirical standpoint. Political economy is the study of the process that determines one's material existence, and the culture intrinsic to that mode of existence. The person lacking such knowledge may be strongly convinced that he exists; however, he has no scientific proof of his right to exist, nor any knowledge of how to control his own existence. The real source of difficulty in comprehending political economy—the widespread profession of active disinterest in the subject matter—is nothing but skepticism, in the special sense in which we have used that term. Skepticism is a reification of the terror of directly confronting the evidence of one's alienated—apparently irremediably—state of being. Skepticism, incomprehension, and disinterest are what permit the man who is freezing to death to believe he is at last enjoying a comfortable doze.

We have stated the empirical psychological features of the dialectical method explicitly in order to advance beyond Hegel, Feuerbach, and Marx in articulating what was certainly empirically obvious to them from their own experience. By stating these things more explicitly, one hopes to make the result more accessible to the student.

In any case, it is at exactly this point, the attempt to leap systematically from simple to extended reproduction, that the issue of dialectical method is expressed within political economy in its most decisive and devastating form.

This aspect of *Capital* has, as we noted earlier, mystified most of its students. Rosa Luxemburg is unquestionably an exception, but we know of no other celebrated twentieth-century student who has not been baffled on this point. Though it should be emphasized that Luxemburg did not deal with the mathematical problems implied there, she finished the concluding chapter of Volume II essentially as Marx would have, at least if we can be certain that he would have relinquished his implied intent to introduce the application of advanced algebra to the problem. Luxemburg is entirely consistent with the evidence of *Capital* as a whole, and with the special evidence of Volumes III and IV, in accomplishing the leap to which we have referred in exactly the fashion Marx would have.[13]

Let us review the evidence supporting this evaluation of Luxemburg and her critics.

The problem was summarized to a certain extent in Chapter 6. The viewpoint of simple reproduction corresponds, in its bad-infinity potential dynamics form, to the mechanistic Darwinian notion of evolutionary development. In such a view, the evolution of the cell form (the individual member of the species) is assumed to be determined by crude utilitarian factors affecting the individual as such. The crude Lamarckian view is characterized by the same flaw. Darwin cannot comprehend the existence of actual ecology. He cannot comprehend processes in which the self-reproduction of the species-type is mediated through a negentropic contribution to the whole ecology. He cannot comprehend the view in which such contributions by an entire species reproduce the levels of articulated negentropy on which the existence of the particular species depends. Nor, of course, could he situate the individual member of the species as a necessary existence for his species in that way. This difference between Marx and Darwin[14] is not an incidental feature of Marxian economic theory. Theoretically, as we have emphasized, Marx's critique of Darwin on this point—the aspect of Darwin which seeks to coincide with Malthus—expresses the kernel of Marx's entire dialectical method; thus those passages of *Theories of Surplus Value* may be regarded as the capstone of the entire work. Here we locate Marx's agreement and fundamental differences with Hegel's notion of being-in-and-for-itself.

Correspondingly, as we have emphasized, the quality of living labor, labor power, is not the quality of a self-evident cell form. It is the determinate expression of an holistic process of changing particular quality of labor power. The definition of the content or essence of labor power is not, we have shown, a particular productivity, but the process expressing the rising self-productivity of labor power as a whole.

A discussion of certain apparent contradictions and difficulties in the application of these notions may help to correct a naive interpretation of them.

In the early development of capitalist industry, gains in the productivity of collective labor were attained during a period of relative decline in the quality of labor in particular—at least relative to most wage-labor. By dividing the productive process into its simplest individual phases for a division of labor, the manufacturing system permitted the employment of untrained wage-labor temporarily to supercede (outproduce) skilled (craft, guild) labor. This feature of capitalist development properly excited the attention of Sismondi. Sismondi correctly adduced the contradiction involving the decline in the quality of particular wage-labor, but did not comprehend the process of development occurring through such a brutally contradictory feature of progressive capitalist development. Relative to the fundamental contradiction in the Ricardian view, Sismondi advances the bare beginnings of the key to understanding everything, as Luxemburg demonstrates.[15] However, this contradiction is located in the bounding of capitalist development as a whole. Sismondi confused the merely potential form of the problem—its immediate particular reflection—with the actual form. Stepping back from the microscopic level to view capitalist development as a whole during the same period, we encounter a phenomenon entirely contradictory to Sismondi's microscopy: while the quality of life and skill of the modal wage-laborer is deteriorating, the social-reproductive powers of labor power as a whole are being rapidly increased. Sismondi committed a fallacy of composition. Moreover, as Marx emphasized, the outcome of this contradictory moment in the history of labor power was the subsequent advance of the quality of labor power even in its particular, abstracted sense. It is the species of labor power that concerns us, and within that determination the significance of particular labor power is to be judged.

Primitive manufacturing, which might usefully be termed the "neotonous" early form of evolutionary progress of wage-labor, reveals its quality of advance most clearly as one examines the connection between cooperative and universal labor during this period. The elaboration of such networks of divisions of cooperative undertaking by individually brutalized workers corresponds to an advance in universal labor, and expresses the basis for and realization of advances in universal labor. The philosophy of Bacon and Hobbes neatly expresses this point, as do the pronounced "antieconomist" tendencies among the social currents shading into the Levellers. The advancement of scientific knowledge, at those moments in which it was being most generally realized, was concerned with man's increased collective power over nature. The form in which this undertaking was conceptualized was classical materialism, in which the elementary object is reduced to its simplest form. But what is the content of the object? The object is the alienated notion of human social-reproductive powers. The simplification of the ultima ratio of classical reductionism is nothing but a disguise in which self-consoling reflection contemplates the brutalization of human practice (productive labor) in its simplest form! Yet this aspect of the problem, the focus of Sismondi's concern, is complemented by Newton. As Hegel correctly understands, the progress from Kepler to Newton is retrogressive in terms of world-outlook on man and of the notion of specific human qualities. Yet the irony of Newton's recognition of the negation of the negation, and similar astonishing overtones and undercurrents of his thought, point the way toward understanding in a manner superior to Hegel's. The essence of Newton's epistemology is the advance of society, of man's comprehension of nature through practice, by negation of the negation at the cost of the brutalization of man.

This development is not, however, entirely a brutalization. Whatever social criticism naive utopians and muckrakers may offer (at a safe distance from the event) on the way in which capitalist development dragged man so cruelly out of the muck of agrarian and village life, the most brutalized wage-laborer has greater humanity than the most cultured independent farmer. He is more human because he is socialized; he is a part of a labor process which imparts qualities of humanity to its meanest participant. He is qualitatively more human on this account than the *relatively* bestial independent farmer. (Those who sing the praises of rural life in opposition to urban existence either have not lived in rural communities or possess a petit-bourgeois world-outlook which makes the brutalization of the individualized farmer agreeable to their own doubly alienated natures.)

The proliferation of different qualities of productive technology and particularized skills—almost a dramatized enactment of the dialectical determination of the process of society's self-development—in turn alters the relationship of man to man in an altogether progressive way. The diversity of human productive and intellectual life and powers represents increased rights and privileges for each individual, at least with respect to his human qualities of existence as distinct from his mere individual existence in itself. This enrichment of his social relations means a corresponding enrichment of his intelligence. This may not be reflected in outward manifestations of learning, but is evident whenever we examine the superiority of the typical worker's and the typical farmer's cognitive powers under comparable circumstances of education. The notorious stubbornness of the peasant is simply a manifestation of his lower intellectual powers relative to those of the meanest urbanized worker. This difference is not biological, but is the determined outcome of the relative bestialization of agricultural and small-community life. The elaboration of the division of labor as a cooperative form of all labor as a whole for society is a qualitative leap forward for man from feudal and semifeudal forms. This is reflected in the seemingly innate differences in cognitive powers between predominantly rural and predominantly urban regions of the same nation. (Obviously, the lumpenization of a significant proportion of the urban population will have similarly brutalizing effects on cognitive powers.)

This point is necessarily overlooked or violently denied by those who view intelligence as exogenous to social processes. Consequently, they promulgate the notion that capitalist society, by significantly eliminating the inherited right to belong to the privileged strata, and thus preventing the aristocracy from perpetuating biological morons in ruling positions from generation to generation, has tended to insure that distinctions of power and privilege result in the eugenic determination of a biologically superior stock, such that each caste and class tends to occupy the position for which it is biologically best suited. This sort of thinking is today encountered most frequently and boldly in the realm of educational policy. The issue of educational policy is foolishly abstracted from the social process in which potential cognitive powers are determined. What is overlooked is that to educate children of farmers to the cognitive attainments of children of skilled urban workers it is essential to eliminate the basis for the difference between them—the relative idiocy of rural life. To educate children from ghettos, it is essential to attack the brutalizing effects of lumpenization. Teachers and schools cannot be miraculous brainwashing agencies which work their wonders without regard to the social circumstances in which cognitive powers are developed.

The seeming exceptions to such socially determined discrepancies in cognitive powers prove the rule. We need only compare the numbers of outstandingly creative individuals produced by large urban centers and small towns. Although fads in taste might seem to belie it, this rule applies as cruelly to art forms as to science. But occasionally we discover individuals from rural and lumpenized strata who show the most remarkable powers. In each case, if we dig deeply enough, this phenomenon is explicable. Leaders from the ranks of the civil rights and related movements during the past decade and a half offer the most revealing and inspiring evidence. Although it is sometimes extraordinarily difficult to locate the initial impetus that set the developmental process in motion for each such individual, their histories show increasing intellectual powers manifest in externalities as the socializing experience of the movement advances their cognitive development. In the relationship to a diversity of individuals and groups, these individuals who have justifiably become outstanding have accomplished what is less conspicious in the productive life of the more developed members of the working class. Such cases are not exceptions to be explained; they represent the most imperative sort of empirical knowledge. We understand intelligence only when we have begun to produce it at will. It is such individuals and special strata—apparent exceptions to a general rule—whose case histories reveal the processes by which the rule can be willfully overcome.

It is not the relationship to objects or to particular persons as such that represents such a socializing determination of intelligence. To ordinary self-consciousness, it does of course appear that particular objects and persons are the content of rights and privileges. These are, in that form of appearance, simply the mediating form in itself. To recognize those forms is the first step toward understanding intelligence, society, and the structure of political economy. However, the actuality is not a *structure* in that sense. Structuralism, a pathetic variety of epiphenomenalism based on the pseudodynamics of bad infinity, can be etiologically known from this standpoint. It is the actual dynamic linking these moments, the actuality in the sense of Descartes' notion of perfection or Spinoza's effort, which is the actual objective experience for consciousness. It is merely pedagogically necessary, as we have stipulated, to approach the cognition of the actual moment of experience through first approximation in terms of sense-certainty.

Once the actual cognition is attained, we immediately invert the notion of structure in the sense of unfolding manifolds, for which the process of unfolding becomes the actuality, the objective knowledge to be attained. Now the objects of sense-certainty, the simple structures with which we began investigations, are viewed in an opposite way as determinate. We have not lost the actuality of the objects of relationships; we have, instead, rejected the naive false notion of them in favor of their actual content.

The practical significance of this approach will become apparent when we examine the determination of need in the Bill of Consumption. There we shall employ this method to solve an empirical problem which every other approach to political economy inherently fails to solve. All reductionist political economy and all empiricist social science is inherently incapable of dealing with the Bill of Consumption. This is an absolutely devastating indictment, since the assumption of utility as determining is the foundation, explicitly or at least implicitly, of all their constructions. Consequently, lacking—rejecting—the dialectical approach, they can only pace about in circular tautologies which viciously assume something needs to be fixed, when the essence of their practical undertaking is to discover how need *changes!* This issue itself would suffice to demonstrate that the dialectical method is no abstract or mere academic issue apropos immediate forms of political-economic practice. Without the dialectical method it is impossible to make sense of the most urgent practical issue of simple capitalist marketing practices.

Using the approaches developed above, we will now work our way through several steps toward just that result.

We have already reviewed the general way in which the increase in the value of $S'/(C + V)$ determines the elaboration of the general structure of the division of labor. We have considered the point that since C must tend to rise in terms of its crude energy equivalent per capita, or relative to the values determined by the previous epoch of production, V must decline as a proportion of the total output of labor power. This results in a decrease of the proportion of department 2.

It is useful now to reconsider the example we applied to the Physiocratic hypotheses, the changed social composition of the United States population in the period 1790–1970. Approximately two centuries ago, nearly 90 per cent of the population was still mired in rural occupations. With development, the rural component is reduced to apparently a mere 5 per cent of the whole population. (We have noted that the United States is not and never has been an autarchy, and that prices of imports do not reflect the social significance of imports for the amount of agricultural production required. The indicated modifications would not change the general picture for our purposes.)

Despite the inhumane and sometimes retrogressive effects of capitalist primitive accumulation in the course of the more general development of this sort, the reduction of the rural component is capitalism's greatest single contribution to humanity in general. This is expressed, in one respect, by the fact that the social cost of diet has been drastically reduced. It is also clear, as we have indicated before, that the saving in agricultural cost is not something liberated for the expansion of industrial development, but is itself chiefly the consequence made possible for agriculture by industrial development. In certain respects the case for this point is obvious; we now require a more fine-grained examination of the relationships involved.

Until fairly recently, historians either overlooked or underestimated the exact way in which even the simplest inventions, when assimilated into general use, have qualitatively altered social-reproductive relations. A cruel demonstration of this principle is the effect of limited actions by the Hudson Bay Company on the Cree Indian, and similar phenomena in the Carolinas.

Pseudoanthropologists (e.g., "cultural relativists") have contributed to the credence given such outright quackery as the notion of an instinctual supraspecific "territorial imperative" by the extent to which they located "property right" in the most primitive forms of society. It is a magnificent irony that those very muddleheads who insist most vociferously on the autonomous values of each culture in itself should have implicated themselves in projecting a specific value of capitalist society—indeed, its most characteristic feature—upon not only every other human society, but every species of the animal and plant kingdoms as well. (No doubt we shall soon witness the territorial imperative advanced as the fundamental principle of astronomy.)

It is evident that primitive cultures like those represented by the Cree before Radisson do not have a notion of "property right." It is most instructive to note how and how quickly hunting territories become necessary after such a culture is impinged on with a few muskets and traps.

To illustrate this point, we can usefully resort to the crude thermodynamic models employed above. The introduction of muskets and traps increases the energy throughput per capita of the tribe by increasing the amount of "natural" energy placed at the tribe's disposal with the same amount of effort. The rate of social surplus is immediately increased in thermodynamic terms. But, since this increase is not accompanied by an advance in the mode of social reproduction of the society, its effect is to accelerate the depletion of its previous basis, even beyond the limits of its mode of existence. Continued existence now depends upon maintaining the higher level of throughput—that is, more muskets, powder, shot, traps, hatchets, knives, and the like. The means of existence of the tribe now depends upon a relationship to the Company, a relationship mediated by furs. The effect of the trading relationship is to impose debt-service upon the tribe, an actuality embodied in the capitalization of the Company. Since the payment of this debt-service (imputable debt-service) is located in a definite mode of hunting and trapping, the existence of the tribe becomes dependent upon the rate of gathering in a definite area.

Were the Cree *trading* during the first exchanges with Radisson and his companions? On the contrary; to the Indian, Radisson's trade was an exchange of gifts. Such exchanges are obviously necessary features of most primitive societies, and generally represent a means of realizing the equivalent of universal labor—although, in particular instances, they may have a different kind of significance respecting the change in the notion of social unit for an emerging innovation in social practice. In no case does a primitive society have a feature which permits it in itself to develop a notion of trade. Since Radisson, who was a trader, headed the party which recorded the exchange, recorded history documents the affair as one of trade. One is reminded of the movie *Rashomon*.

The problem assumes a different form in the terms we have applied here. The objects (muskets, traps, and so forth) have the significance of objectified social powers, which shift the negentropic parameters for social reproduction, with certain effects on the general relationship of man to nature and to the social relationships through which the new social practice is maintained. The developments significant here are those, such as the cited case, in which the shift is more or less irreversible. A culture has been changed in its thermodynamic characteristics. This unleashes a chain-reaction of alterations in the mode of reproduction and associated intracultural institutions, alterations which necessarily reflect the social relations through which the changes have been mediated or are being maintained.

The emergence of the category of manufacturing, as a growing proportion of productive human existence in the new United States, is a next suitable illustration of the point. Momentarily putting aside the important aspect of looting nature, the gains in social productivity of the new nation are customarily associated with the accumulation of an enlarged mass of social surplus, apparently from the rural sector. It was not so one-sided. Simple manufactures reduced the social cost of production. Manufacturing produced simple tools and other articles at a lower social cost than that at which they could be produced rurally. The development of highways, canals, and, later, railroads transformed the potential for efficient agriculture, making possible the systematic marketing of specialized agricultural output. Steel plows, simple household implements, and the like emphasize the reciprocal aspects of manufacturing's development of agriculture—and reflect the same underlying principles as the Cree experience. The emergence of manufacturing and the Industrial Revolution not only enlarge capitalist production at the expense of rural society; these developments make possible the productive improvements in agriculture which increase its efficiency—the thermodynamic content of the individual farmer—and set free wage-labor from the rural family for the expansion of the industrial and urban populations generally.

The anguished emphasis on inventions and the importation of skilled and semiskilled English (and, later, German) labor during the early period of U.S. development expresses the *actuality* of the development. The relationship between industry and agriculture was not a matter of objects, but of universal labor in its realized form. Relative to this, one can examine the shifts in U.S. capitalist policy toward independent political movements of labor before and after 1848–1850.[16] The shift from uneasy toleration to brutality corresponds to a temporarily decreasing emphasis on universal labor embodied in particular cooperative labor, in favor of the brutalized simple labor power of industrial expansion as such. There occurred a shift from solicitation of skilled and semiskilled English and German labor to importation of cattle-boat loads of poor cheap labor—largely proletarianized peasantry—from the 1850s onward. A related phenomenon is the toleration of the AFL—beside a brutal attitude toward industrial labor—during the period from the 1890s through the middle of the 1920s. The quality of labor power came to be emphasized as the United States achieved industrial and technological hegemony before the First World War, and was rapidly followed by concern for the quality of labor, such that the U.S. worker generally has reached 1970 levels of culture while the bulk of European labor is at First World War levels. More recently, with the move to reverse the liberal educational policies of the postwar period, and to emphasize vocational drill at the expense of cognitive development, we see, in circumstances of deepening depression, a new deemphasis on the quality of labor power and universal labor.

In general, the microprocess we are examining reflects the same general laws we have previously considered. The confrontation with a new, enlarged plenum of objects represents the objectified social preconditions for new cognitions. These cognitions, once realized, become altered productive powers. This alteration is obviously expressed in increased productive powers, which are the social preconditions for further cognitions. It is also an alteration respecting the objectified social preconditions of the change in mode. The objects on which the initiation and perpetuation of the new practice depend become necessary rights and privileges, and thus become the objectification of new needs for rights and privileges from definite other persons. The gift has become a need; by becoming a new power, it becomes a dependency upon the continued relationship through which that power is perpetuated.

This occurs as a need and a necessary right, as the effect of new powers on the domain of resources defined by that mode makes the alteration effectively irreversible for continued human existence in that mode. Thus, even in the microprocess so located, we find the immediate expression of a self-subsisting positive.

Somewhat as capitalist production, as a social category, emerges from agricultural advances under capitalism, so department 1 develops out of advances in department 2. Here, the immediacy of realization of universal labor is apparently everything. As we examine the microprocess aspect of this realization, we are immediately at the core of capitalist development—and collapse. The capital equipment, new technology embodied in superior materials, and so forth which represent more advanced technology from the standpoint of either simple productivity or means of more effectively meeting a need, seizes the capitalist possessor. If a single capitalist adopts such a new process, other capitalists in the same field must emulate him or go out of business. Then the increased power of the capitalist has become a savage power over him. New technology—yesterday's bonanza —has seized him and shackled him to its power. He can escape only by subjecting himself to a new technology, more powerful and more savage than the first. The relationship to department 1 becomes an increasing dependency for all of capitalist industry, just as the growth of capitalist industry seized agriculture. The proportion of all labor power directly consumed in the finishing of the final product, especially the final product for human consumption, dwindles—seemingly toward the vanishing point.

That is not the end. Constant Capital is not thus the final conqueror of all production. Constant Capital itself becomes enslaved to the source of its own power. The greater the rate of scientific progress in new technology, the more rapidly technology must develop to compensate for the increased rate of consumption of the newly expanded domain of newly defined resources. Science, as a category, begins to emerge and to hint at what it is yet to become. As increased productivities liberate larger sections of the population for leisure, that leisure must be increasingly consumed in the form of scientific activity. Development expands the appetite for development. There is no escape from this cycle; continued human existence depends upon it. Relative to the total population, it would seem, perhaps, that the production of means of human existence will become so fertile that the amount of labor required will be infinitesimal, and that the near-vanishing of department 1 will occur in the same fashion.

Is the dialectic of the labor process therefore headed for repeal or supercession? In one sense, that of capitalist and even socialist society, yes. Fundamentally? Never. Marx's summation of the matter in "Feuerbach" and in "Freedom/Necessity" in Volume III of *Capital* is a permanent law of human existence. Contrary to the pathetic delusions of the hippies and similar professed parasites, there is no slate of human existence that does not demand advance as the condition for continued human existence. These advances are always urgent tasks set before humanity for some form of productive labor. What has changed—the only thing that will ever change —is the form of human labor, the mode of reproduction. In the sense articulated in the preceding discussion of department 1 and 2 relationships, which is to say the unilinear aspect of progressive development, the new form of necessary activity comes into being in the realization of the social surplus of the preceding modes.

Speculation on this problem was afoot during the 1960s, focusing on the draft statement of the Triple Revolution Committee. Its entire argument is sheer quackery from the standpoint of science, but is of sufficient clinical interest to command our momentary attention. It was argued that a mysterious new agency, cybernation, had been introduced to the development of production, to the effect that the need for a labor process was evaporating at an estimated 7 per cent per year. This phenomenon, the Committee argued, underlies the growth of a disadvantaged lumpen-proletariat, squeezed out of a traditional productive role by the reduced need for productive labor. Taking certain other phenomena of the same period into account, also in a confused fashion, the Committee proposed in effect that the problem of the emerging "postindustrial society" was to effect more equitable procedures for distributing the largesse from the bulging warehouses of cybernated abundance.

Without diagnosing here the state of mind reflected in such absurd theses, it suffices to demonstrate in a few steps how patently nonsensical this whole proposition is. First, acknowledging the determination of culture by its necessary material basis in consumption, we can readily determine the estimated total consumption which would provide for worldwide enjoyment of the standard of living of a skilled U.S. worker today. One can, of course, introduce adjustments for our automotive pathology and other distortions better superceded by different forms of services and the like. Even so, the order of magnitude of consumption is not substantially changed. Second, once we have determined the level of annual output necessary for such levels of worldwide consumption, we can determine, at current ratios for modern plants and the like, the amount of productive capacity required to supply the output, public services facilities, and so on required. Third, one can determine the level of output of department 1 necessary to maintain department 2 at such a level of output. Applying such elementary calculations to our observation of urban decay and other situations, in the United States itself, we reach certain preliminary conclusions about "postindustrial society." The Triple Revolution Committee must be a group of primitive peoples seized by a "Cargo Cult."

More to the point is whether modern production is undergoing a development which represents even the germ of cybernation, in the sense in which the Committee employed that notion. By demonstrating summarily that no such tendency exists *in that sense*, we shall have negatively arrived at a useful point. We shall have developed a degree of insight into the question: under what conditions would labor power as we know it disappear?

Conveniently, there does exist a notion of what "complete automation" would represent. First, no means of production would need to be produced with the aid of productive labor. Reducing the ratio of productive labor is simply a perpetuation of the labor process, the self-expansion of labor power. For the Triple Revolution Committee to have encountered the fact that labor power is labor power in that sense merely reflects their ignorance of the profession into which they abruptly intruded themselves. For complete automation to occur, it would be necessary that the very nature of the productive process required absolutely no labor by anyone on a worldwide scale to accomplish the following: (1) The whole of production must become in effect a single worldwide machine which produces all human need-satisfactions. (2) The machine must be sufficiently variable to meet changing, expanding needs. (3) The machine must be entirely self-maintaining—that is, it must repair itself without a single maintenance worker. (3) The machine must constantly improve itself, constantly become more efficient, without intervention by human labor. There is no possible way in which "negative feedback loops" could satisfy those requirements. The introduction of computers to such loops could also not fulfill such requirements—by virtue of the intrinsic paradoxes of logic. In short, there presently exists no technology that even germinally portends cybernation in the sense employed by the Triple Revolution Committee.

However, if we approach the entire matter from a different direction, we encounter a line of necessary development which does lead toward the elimination of the labor process as we know it.

The tendency intrinsic to the historic thrust of capitalist development—the increasing interdependency of a worldwide division of labor—does portend the ultimate integration of the means of production into a single machine. This eventuality is presaged by the elaboration of the division of labor and the line of development implied by simple materials-handling processes in which several machines or plants can be integrated into a de facto single machine. However, capitalist forms of development negate this tendency by virtue of the alienation inherent in capitalist forms, not merely for the obvious juridical reasons but also by directing the developing of applied industrial technology into channels appropriate to heteronomic forms of production. Under socialist development, the tendency to integration will be more pronounced.

At present, with existing technology and science, it is not immediately practicable to consider those alterations in the form of products and productive processes which would result in a completely modular scheme of production. (Modularity in this sense signifies the principle of interchangeable parts carried to the proverbial "nth" degree.) Despite this difficulty, we do have preliminary indications—topological studies buttressed by very simple demonstrations—that the form of the problem of modularity does admit of solution in the course of the next general breakthrough in scientific development. The indications are sufficient that we must assume, and not as mere speculation, that this principled difficulty will begin to be overcome within a decade or so of socialist development.

Proceeding along the two lines of integration and necessary modifications in product and process design, the tendency toward the worldwide self-maintaining machine is undoubtedly the historic thrust of development of the productive forces under socialism on a world scale. Within that context, the evaporation of the labor process, the general result which the Triple Revolution Committee was mooting, does become significant.

It is the contrary implications of this development which are the main point for consideration here.

The first notion which must be introduced in considering the tendency toward the emergence of such a "super-Turing machine" is the fantastic ratios of energy per capita man will begin to consume even as such a development process begins. Right now, from the standpoint of present per capita rates of consumption of energy, the potentialities of thermonuclear fusion power seem downright fantastic—it appears that we have tens of millions of years at fabulous rates of consumption before us. But once we situate the required energy consumption rates within the context of the notion of invariant developed earlier, the backlog of fusion power is rather less impressive. There is no remedy for it; we shall have to soon conquer solar space in order to realize the potential of man on earth.

This rawest feature of the problem, and the mass of detailed human scientific and engineering effort required thus to develop the mode of production, make the earth appear underpopulated relative to the number of mathematical physics Ph.D.s, engineers, and other scientists who have to be trained.

Does the increasing productivity of labor as we know it signify that the need for human productive activity will vanish? Will humanity become a daisy-clad mass of strolling Lotus-eaters? Quite the contrary. At first glance—from the vantage-point of alienated culture—it might appear that we will have escaped one predicament to encounter one more awesome and demanding. To one who views the matter from that standpoint, we freely concede that man is increasingly to become a prisoner of the effort to meet his new needs for existence. However, from a human point of view, the significance of this fact is at precise odds with that attributed to it by the bestialized hippy of present-day advanced capitalist culture. What human being would wish to become a dog before the hearth? Only the view of oneself as a beast could inspire the hope of freedom from labor. There is no need to worry that man would persist long in the state of bestialization desired by the Manson Family. He would soon cease to exist. To be human is to locate one's identity for society in the activity of perfection; to rise to a condition in which that perfection is advancing at a more rapid rate, in which more human quality is demanded of one, in which one increasingly gains social identity because of one's human powers, is to fulfill everything that an actually human person could desire.

At this point we should recognize that we have struck upon evidence that socialist society is not the final, perfected form of human society. It is merely the beginning of a series of human societies distinct from the bestialized forms from which we now have the potential to emerge. The fact that material existence under socialist society must have a mediated form, even though that mediation is a classwide institution,[17] is a contradiction within that form. The relationship between universal and cooperative labor also involves a contradiction which is a different facet of the same difficulty. Under socialist society, man has not yet achieved the realization of universal labor-for-itself. We are therefore considering the process by which universal labor as a productive category—as the supercession of cooperative forms of the labor process today—emerges as universal labor-for-itself.

Science, the germ of an emergent category of universal labor-for-itself, was never an incoherent agglomeration of sly craftsmen's knacks. Even as the fragile germ of a future category, science can come into existence as self-conscious knowledge only to the extent that social relations themselves begin to generalize human practice, to give it a degree of universality. The general history of science or protoscience apparently begins at Sumer with the emergence of the priest-caste, which consciously generalized the practice by which that society as a whole existed. From this line of development, human knowledge took further strides forward toward science with the Ionian Greeks and the mercantilists, who reduced everything to a universal form by translating the relationships among entire existing societies into their mercantile commodity form. Then through the mercantile capitalists, in symbiosis with the universal church of the Renaissance, emerged the rudiments of a rebirth of protoscience.

Science is merely a universalized self-consciousness of human practice, which tends to come into being whenever society creates a social formation which self-consciously universalizes some aspect of the mode of reproduction. In the end, this formation will become a social-productive category in its own right, as universal labor-for-itself. How it will elaborate itself into further new forms is perhaps beyond our capacity to foresee. The point to be borne in mind is not so much that we are proceeding toward a society in which man fulfills himself as completely human, as entirely universal labor-for-itself, but that this moment is the active ingredient of all social phenomena in all societies; to adduce that moment is the unique way in which to determine the actual content of any aspect of social relations, no matter how microscopic.

We shall now summarize the representation of extended reproduction as such. After we have done so, we shall proceed to develop the elaboration of the Bill of Consumption according to these terms of reference.

Figure 6 includes two bars, a and b, intended to represent the total productive labor of a society in two successive epochs of expanded reproduction. Figure 6 summarizes this sequence for the main categories. Figure 7 depicts the same sequence for the more detailed features subsumed by division into two departments. We shall consider Figure 6 first.

If the labor forces and outputs of a and b were compared in a conventional way, the number of workers and the object-count (price of output) of b would be greater than that of a. However, the two bars are of the same height since, for any society, the height of the bar does not vary through successive transformations. The height, 1, signifies the totality of the labor power of a society as a self-defining magnitude, which is always 1 with respect to itself.

In the moment of transition from a to b we can identify the following contradictory tendencies. (1) Relative to the costs of reproducing the labor power and constant capital of a, these have been reduced in b. (2) However, to realize the higher qualities of labor power required for future states, labor power increases as a proportion of output. (3) The net result of 1 and 2 is that the ratio of V diminishes by an amount between those extremes in b. (4) But the qualities of Constant Capital required in b have

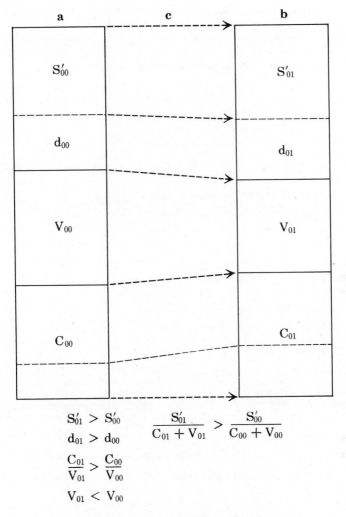

$$S'_{01} > S'_{00}$$
$$d_{01} > d_{00}$$
$$\frac{C_{01}}{V_{01}} > \frac{C_{00}}{V_{00}}$$
$$V_{01} < V_{00}$$

$$\frac{S'_{01}}{C_{01} + V_{01}} > \frac{S'_{00}}{C_{00} + V_{00}}$$

Figure 6 Expanded Reproduction

increased over a, so that C in bar b lies between the indicated extremes. (5) Capitalists' consumption increases, but such that the ratio $S'/(C + V)$ rises from a to b. This increase is necessary insofar as it subsumes universal labor. (6) C/V rises from a to b.

In Figure 7, the same general developments apply, with the added qualification that department 1 grows relative to department 2.

The dotted lines within segment C of Figure 6 introduced an added refinement. The segment below the dotted lines represents the portion of Constant Capital expenditures allocable to sunk costs. Assuming that the average life of fixed capital should not exceed ten years for the U.S. economy, and that Constant-Dollar measures of plant and equipment spending

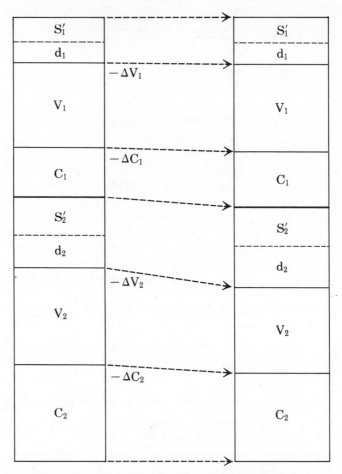

Figure 7   Expansion for Virtual Unemployment

correspond (as they do not) to value-equivalents, each growth in plant and equipment expenditures must add 10 per cent of itself to next year's Constant Capital requirement on the account of plant and equipment. Apply that consideration to the data on plant and equipment levels of spending during the postwar period in the United States. Compare the result with McGraw-Hill or other studies on obsolescence. Make a further adjustment. Discount Constant-dollar expenditures as a whole for rising productivity of labor power. This would mean including only *operatives* for manufacturing, mining, and the like as the baseline measure of productivity (ignoring clerks, service workers, and so on). Apply this as a further refinement to the data. Now compare the result of this adjustment with the pattern of obsolescence in basic industries.

This is only preliminary. Noting the key role of military spending in the postwar economy, and eliminating from the Gross National Product elements which do not represent production of consumer and producer commodities (tangible products), consider the proportion of total plant and equipment expenditure absorbed in expanding and maintaining military production capacity. Consider the residue of plant and equipment spending relative to the residue of the economy.

Next, consider the proportion of military spending that takes the form of capital-goods expenditure respecting capital-goods capacities used. Also estimate available unused capital-goods capacity. Add these two amounts to plant and equipment expenditure each year. Taking the average ratios for capital investment per operative employed in relatively advanced commodity-producing (tangible product) industries, determine the estimated number of added operatives employed as a result of the added Fixed Capital formation rates (adding in military production as useful).

For further investigations to similar effect, compare the growth of government and corporate administrative occupations with the number of operatives employed. Where growth is more rapid than that of Gross Profit from manufacturing, mining, forestry, and agriculture, trim off the excess as waste. Reduce the number of office buildings and the like constructed by the proportion of clerical positions eliminated (for a quick rule-of-thumb indication). Put this construction into useful production. Absorb the displaced administrative employees as operatives.

In short, take just a few of the more obvious steps to compare the actual U.S. economy of the past quarter-century with a rational development of the same sector of the world economy in terms of the models in Figures 5, 6, and 7.

A related investigation may be undertaken within the category of capitalists' consumption itself. Assume that the number of physics Ph.D.s and engineers employed must increase at least at the same rate as the growth of plant and equipment. Using estimates for what rational rates of growth of plant and equipment should be, estimate the total ideal growth in the number of Ph.D. physicists from 1953, and compare it with actual growth. Estimate the number of working physicists engaged in the development of military equipment (as distinct from basic research), and treat these as wasted. Increase the number of Ph.D. physicists graduated to compensate for that waste. Proceed similarly for engineers. What has been happening to the development of technology?

Another sort of large-scale indication employs any of the estimated required rates of growth of per capita power consumption by production and households. Use the average per capita consumption of any combination of industrialized regions of the United States (including metropolitan New York City) to establish a base rate of household and productive consumption of power relative to per capita industrial workers' families' income levels. Use this information to establish a baseline of power output requirements for the entire United States at a family income level (for four people) of $10,500 per year. Do the same for the rest of the world. Now apply the growth-rate recommendation you have selected to this base.

Next assume that the growth rate for power consumption corresponds to a 3–4 per cent annual rate of growth of the economy. Adjust it for a 10 per cent rate of annual economic growth.

A few special cases of grossly dysfunctional development of the U.S. economy during the past quarter-century (in particular) illustrate the significance of the sort of models implied by Figures 5, 6, and 7.

Employing the potentialities of existing computer technology, freight movements could be organized as follows. Most freight would move in pick-a-back mode. All long-haul movements would be by rail. (Long-haul is not purely a matter of mileage, but the movement of goods over 150 miles by truck is a net loss in total social cost to the economy.) Ordinary commodities would be shipped from consolidating warehouses which would receive bulk shipments from manufacturing and other facilities in a region, or from warehouses which would serve as breakpoints for localized distribution. The infrastructure for such low-cost, efficient freight movement should have been developed. Instead, rail systems have been in decay since the mid-1920s, when their peak was reached and passed. During the postwar period a fabulous redundancy has been built into transportation.

This problem intersects another dysfunctional development of the postwar period: the growth of suburbia. There is no rational reason for suburbia to exist. The cost of services per capita and per household is qualitatively higher than in urban concentrations. As for the so-called qualitative features of life in the cardboard slums of tomorrow, there is no essential amenity enjoyed in a suburb which could not be more rationally and better provided in an urban setting. Like the rail/highway nonsense, the pressures that drive people to surburbia are, first, urban decay and, second, a strategic policy of decentralization on the part of corporations to break the strength of unions. Urban speculation drives other firms and working-class strata into the suburbs, where suburban development speculators wait to greet them. Social costs soar, and the ecological cost is horrific.

Such basic industries as footwear, clothing, textiles, and construction are mired in technologies that are a half-century or more old. Peripheral gimmickry aside, this point is demonstrated by a stroll through any "modern" textile plant. The footwear industry, fixed in technological stagnation by monopoly, has since the mid-1960s moved backwards in shoe-making technology—as a glance at your feet should suffice to demonstrate. Clothing? Look at the clothes you are wearing. The fabrics are linearly cut, the seams are still fashioned by laying down one stitch after another. Your new house? Discounting a few gadgets, don't you wish it were as well built as a house erected during the 1920s?

As for the so-called computer age, the assumptions of the applications designers make a mockery of the very name of modern technology. Two observations will suffice here. The standardization of procedures for paper-processing would permit the general use of "man/machine language" documents suitable for the employment of what are called "optical page readers." This would permit a drastic reduction in the enormous flood of paper being shuffled and reshuffled throughout the economy today. It is not generally understood that a new technology demands a fundamentally different approach to a task.

Let us consider applications design itself. The basic daily problem of computer operations is garbage-in. If elaborate and costly preprocessing checks are used, the consequent delay in processing data itself produces garbage and creates opportunities for more to proliferate. As long as each computer application is designed to function as an independent procedure, there is no remedy for this situation. However, treating all applications as a simulation of the unified operations of the firm immediately provides cross-checking procedures which will automatically detect erroneous information of all the ordinary sorts. But no. The philistine plodders continue to grind out their unimaginative and inherently fallible applications and programs.

The U.S. economy, viewed with some knowledge of the ABCs of technology, is one horrendous mass of waste, redundancy, obsoles· ence, and managerial incompetence. Applying the criteria embedded in illustrations Figures 5, 6, and 7, any diligent student can spot numerous examples of obvious blunders and decay.

The only useful approach to the wretched state of the U.S. economy today is the scientific, rational approach to planned economy. Progress is not effected by bureaucrats tucked away in offices, spinning out models with the aid of data and computers. Rational progress begins with the sort of models we have indicated, which provide only the general criteria that must be satisfied in practice. The actual program of production which satisfies such criteria is designed by looking in the obvious places for potential savings and other improvements. (In general, one can assume that a $10 million saving cannot be achieved in an activity involving a $100 thousand expenditure.) The general laws and parameters we adduce from study of the process as a whole indicate not only the possible gains but also the principal steps to accomplishing them must be. We know, for example, that the leisure of the population must be increased, and that improved education is central to such leisure. Art, travel, and the like are complements to education. (We shall return to this subject later in this chapter.) We know also that the material standard of consumption must continually be raised. These are preconditions of rising social productivity. We also have a preliminary indication of the probable rate of improvement that can be realized as a base rate. We know more or less the extent to which categories of services must be developed, and we should have some notion of the order of magnitude of both basic scientific research and development needed, and some indications of how to apportion them into categories and major projects. We also recognize the major bottlenecks for development in the economy as a whole, and know that we must concentrate on eliminating or widening these as a precondition for other achievements. Within the scope of such broad knowledge, the specific steps must be uncovered—and, as we noted above, it is not difficult to select the locations in which to dig. The realization of a given rate of growth finally becomes an enormous aggregation of interconnected individual creative acts of mentation, all kept in a coherent task-oriented unity by the guiding overview. Socialist political economy as an applied science then becomes a concrete study of the shifting influence of certain kinds of development in effecting the critical aspects of the overall development. The finest "abstract" comprehension of the overall development depends upon the keenest empirical grasp of the particulars. Not empiricism. It is the plenum of concrete particulars that forces the conceptualization leading to a notion of what the basic thrust of development must be.

This approach might suggest the following scenario. The leadership of a U.S. sector of a socialist economy approximately six or seven years hence is confronted with the practical problem of winning the working class as a whole to the task of achieving an approximately 25 per cent annual rate of growth. How is this initiated and realized through a general discussion on the part of the working class as a whole?

It is obvious, at first glance, that such growth rates must always seem to be in conflict with the higher rates of immediate per capita consumption and leisure which could be programmed at, for example, a "more reasonable" 10 per cent growth rate (in terms of $S'/(C + V)$ as measure of the rate of growth). Certain nominal socialists would promptly declare, a certain manic glint in their eyes, "That's exactly the issue. This is nothing but the old problem of the capitalist 'exploiters,' who are always insisting on lower rates of growth of wages for the 'general good.'"

Let us compare the results of several years' production at the two rates, momentarily assuming for purely pedagogical reasons the existence of a U.S. autarchy. For the 25 per cent program let us specify that V is always a declining proportion of the total "output." For the 10 per cent program, V is whatever will permit one to maintain the 10 per cent rate. In some t-th year, we will reach the following condition. If, for that year, it were technologically feasible to increase V to the point that the rate of growth for that year were zero, the per capita value of V for that program would be less than the per capita value of V for the program elaborated from the starting-point of the 25 per cent program! Indeed, by that point, the rate of growth might well have increased to 30 per cent or more.

This is the problem to be mooted in discussions of programmatic policy within the working class as a whole. We shall examine that process in more detail after we have interpolated a few remarks on the use of the 25 per cent rate of growth in this example.

The specification of a 25 per cent rate of sectoral growth for North America within this decade is not arbitrary; it is the result of prolonged reflection by the author and others on the rate of potential growth implicit in the existing gross rate of waste. Even Baran and Sweezy's muckraking text strongly implies just this in its factual aspects. It is also a necessary rate of *sectoral* growth from the standpoint that the North American unit is only a sector of an international division of labor. The lowering of the cost of imports from the other sectors, especially the so-called underdeveloped sector—a precondition for maintaining high rates of growth within the advanced sector—depends upon rapidly advancing the productivity of the underdeveloped sector, which demands massive "capital imports" to that sector; this in turn demands massive capital formation within the advanced subsectors. At the same time, within the advanced sector, the inadequacy of the material conditions of life is attributable to inadequate development of the productive forces to the point of realizing modern forms of productive employment of the potential labor force. Unemployment, which according to the calculations of the author's collaborators reached 12–15 per cent by the beginning of 1973, combined with underemployment and other problems of backward industries, requires massive rates of capital formation in the U.S. subsector itself. Given the existing state of the productive forces and the concrete obligations before us at the present time, a 25 per cent rate of growth, materially quite feasible in conjunction with a substantial increase in the modal per capita real-income level, is not arbitrarily chosen. The issue of 25 per cent versus 10 per cent rates of growth is the best approximation of the actual form of the argument if a socialist economy existed in the U.S. sector at this instant.

Once the working class generally began to examine details of the growth rate, some most interesting considerations would come to the fore. We shall cite a few that have already been introduced.

Let us first consider one item of the Bill of Consumption. We shall treat certain elements of the Bill of Consumption as forming a category: housing and other elements of consumption and services provided by municipalities as a whole: education, transportation, medical services, and the like. How may we realize the most from this category within the constraints of limited capacities and resources? Obviously, if we extend suburbia we reduce the quality of life in several ways relative to any given mass of resources. We must totally reconstruct urban municipalities.

In response to an earlier presentation of the author's proposals on this topic, a student submitted materials he had accumulated while a student of Paolo Soleri: *Arcology*. A criticism of Soleri's approach locates more concretely the problem to be solved.

Soleri has intuitively comprehended one aspect of the problem: the need for urban developments in organic ways to solve the problems of ecology and the interrelatedness of life. To that extent, his work has the heuristic value of exciting the necessary criticisms. The glaring fallacy in his constructions is the misconception of man which permeates it, an anarchist conception of man as an abstract individual. What is wanted, in place of the abstract individual of fixed qualities in Soleri's schemas, is the notion of actual human beings in the process of developing new human qualities. If we attack from that correct starting-point the same problem Soleri attempts to confront, we shall have the required approach to planning.

Eliminating the obvious problems of cities which are in the wrong places, and the impossibility of salvaging anything for humanity from the present organizational context of Los Angeles' collection of villages, let us use the case of New York City's metropolitan region as a point of reference.

A city must be an aggregation of living-places for households and individuals, in which the following elementary criteria are satisfied. The physical organization of the individual living-place must meet current needs and be susceptible of economic change to conform to technological change and new kinds of need over a span of approximately fifty years. (We shall see later why the figure fifty years is introduced here.) Modularity is required to provide for the kinds of localized services immediately needed and to change the forms of localized services: nurseries, eating facilities, basic distribution of consumption goods, emergency medical facilities functioning as preventive medical service outlets, and what would today be mistakenly termed "community function" facilities. If this means backyards twenty stories up, so be it. Urban life must not be, and certainly need not be, a deprivation of any *sane* human need met by suburban life.

What of the individual dwelling-unit? Those of us who have any conception of man as human—that is, characterized by creative mentation —absolutely reject the trend in dwelling-unit design toward the "peek-a-boo" life in which various functional areas of the dwelling-place blend into one another. The increasing socialization of life does not mean this sort of pseudosocialization, the gregarious relations of cattle in a barn. The socialization of the individual means his or her fullest development as an individual for society. Social man demands the right to close the door, and behind a soundproof door and soundproof walls to pursue uninterrupted activities of a wide variety, to enjoy those external rights which are the externalities of creative activity and self-development. "Hey, whatcha doin'?" "Stop that racket, for God's sake!" and the whispering and growling in the next room are the commonplace characteristics of a deadened life. If there is creativity in some individuals from slums in which children are packed together in inadequate housing, subjected to the drill-and-grill of constant gregarious life or to the agony of revolt against the lack of opportunity to "work something out by myself," we should not—if we are human—use such exceptions to discount the importance of the necessary material conditions of life with such observations as: "Oh, they all could make it if they tried. Lok at the case of . . ." The creative person to whom philistines refer as the model exception is almost invariably a crippled person whose creativity is a mere micron of what it could have been; furthermore, he is a product of conditions which determine that only the tiniest percentile of the entire population living under those conditions attain even such a limited degree of creative achievement. The fuller realization of creative—that is, human—potential in the population demands the organization of the material conditions of life around the central needs determined to be the preconditions of the fullest creative development. "Let him (or her) go down to the music center if he (or she) . . ." is a philistine's cavilling; creative life demands the widest range of opportunities for its expression in whatever direction it rather unpredictably demands. The individual requires ready access to those external forms of activity that have been the characteristic mediations of his creative mentation, and the flexibility to incorporate new qualities of mediation as the progress of creative development demands.

We need, in short, to rid "arcology" of the principles of design appropriate to Jack Armstrong, to the philistine's image of red-blooded America. This does not mean that a creative life is a sedentary life of course.

To apply such principles to New York City would mean in practice, tearing entire sections of the city up by the roots, according to some planned checkerboard arrangement. Since one is planning flexibility for fifty years, this does not merely mean building in mass-transit and automatic goods-conveyer facilities, as well as ordinary sorts of services (heating, electrical, sewage, waste conveyance, water, and the like); it means providing for these in such a way as to facilitate ready conversion. This flexibility can be planned for such a span of time on the basis of the general "geometry" of centralized services. For a finite span the categories, if not the exact form, of services required are a group of enumerable types which will require definable space, access, and so forth, in the sense of building anything with anticipation of place to locate and means to "hookup" future improvements.

Our "fifty-year" forward planning span is already implicit. To make the result economical it must be durable both in the ordinary sense and from the standpoint of counterobsolescence.

The question of "how" thus becomes a concrete problem to be solved by scientists, architects, and others.

However, this specification itself immediately demands a twofold notion of growth rate. First, the very magnitude and technology of providing for human need on this count demands the development of productive facilities and the like. Without concrete growth in the involved industries and a certain rate of surplus value, such development of the municipal category of consumption on a national scale could not be realized. Second, the high initial cost, by present standards, of meeting such needs demands a rapid increase in social productivity to reduce these costs of meeting human needs. In sum, to meet any concrete need demands a corresponding rate of development of the productive forces. The cost of meeting such needs, as a cost which countervails the satisfaction of other needs, demands an increase in the rate of social productivity.

The general point being made here is that the issue of the "horizon" —the issue of immediate versus future rates of consumption—is not merely posed in the nature of such a contrast. The need for a rate of development is concretely posed in the satisfaction of concrete immediate needs. The very notion that this is merely playing off the future against the present signifies that a bad-infinity approach to "optimal" rates of growth has been employed. Or, to restate the same point in another way: once the working class has adopted, to scale, the standpoint of planning of the society as a whole, the problem of meeting of concrete local consumption needs itself immediately embodies the rate of progress otherwise abstractly represented as a horizon problem. As for Spinoza, Hegel, and Marx, the question of perfection (progress) is located concretely, actually, in the actualization of current revolutionizing practice.

The issue of categories of consumption, merely exemplified by the municipal category, extends directly to the development of the productive forces (capacities, technology) from each classification of products and services which is met more directly on a national and worldwide scale.

What socialist national planning means is that through the mediation of the "experts" on each category of human need, the working class as a whole acts as its own industrial engineer and marketing expert with respect to the productive forces which are the common property of the class as a whole. Using concrete professional skills to mediate its comprehension of technology and other phenomena, the working class becomes transformed from only cooperative labor into an holistic form of universal labor. The interchange within the class as a whole, which is the extended debate about economic program, becomes a kind of organic cerebration. The dialectic of counterpositions within the class apropos conflicting features of the program is neither a process of reaching a least common denominator nor a pluralistic democratic resolution, but is the completion of the circuit of synapses by which each individual progressively digests for himself an holistic view of what, in terms of the whole, is in his immediate interest.

The process of national planning is not, therefore, a matter of the workers passively voting for one of several proposed alternative programs; the initial programmatic proposals of a leadership serve to initiate a collective process of mentation, a process mediated by intensive examination of each concrete alternative.

The foregoing is, relatively speaking, merely descriptive. We have only been considering, reflection instructs us, the externalities of the process, however necessary that has been. What, we should inquire, are the concrete movements in the consciousness of the working class for which these objective externalities are only mediations? What are the contents of consciousness in this case?

The planning process we described above can be abstracted as a means by which the relationships among Bills of Consumption, Process Sheets, and Bills of Materials on a worldwide scale are introduced to individual consciousness in a definite way. The individual worker is not viewing the totality of productive forces in the fashion of the ordinary enlightened industrial engineer. The industrial-engineering view of input-output relations within such a network is only a useful pedagogical device. According to that pedagogical view of the matter, we are resorting to the dynamic view. We are representing the structure of relationships within the totality as a static structure; then we attempt to introduce movement to that structure by introducing universal labor as a momentary impulse. We then trace the new state of the static structure resulting from such a single moment. The generalization of such illustrations supplies us with the dynamic overview, but not the actual overview. The dynamic model is simply a useful approximation, pregnant with the fundamental epistemological blunder of reductionist approaches.

What planners in a socialist economy do is to proceed from such an abstraction. Undoubtedly we, in the immediate future, will use massive computerized procedures of the dynamic type. That is, by interlinking computerized administrative procedures and creating a network organized around a central computer complex, we shall effect a kind of real-time simulation of the actual economy. However, it will be more than a mere passive simulation.[18] It will be an administrative network which accomplishes much of the necessary paperwork of day-to-day production and distribution control. As a byproduct of such ongoing daily administration, the centralized facility will provide us with the capacity to abstract dynamic models for a variety of developmental parameters supplied by centralized economic administration. To such dynamic computer experiments the planners will supply their own powers of cognition to accomplish what the computer, by its nature, cannot. They will synthesize Gestalts of actual expanded reproduction. These syntheses will be re-entered into the computer system to produce dynamic elaborations corresponding to the estimated results of introducing the synthesized policies of development into actual production. A series of printouts, accompanied by a cognitive analysis of the various programs considered, represents the simulation of the planning process in the working class as a whole.

In the socialized planning process, each concrete cognition, of the sort illustrated by discussion of the municipal category of consumption, becomes a category of right and privilege for the consciousness (self-consciousness) of every section of the working class as a whole. These notions contain isolable cognitive elements in two complementary forms. The first form is "If this problem is solved." The second form is "This is the scientific solution to this previously isolated cognitive form of the problem of development." A cruder representation of this sort of element, in both variations, is "the implications of invention." Or the same point may be summarized as "the implications of universal labor within the planning process." Thus, the notions of right and privilege elaborated in categories of national planning become self-consciousness of right and privilege as located in universal labor. Self-consciousness becomes consciousness of one's reflected identity with respect to one's cognitive powers. It is this qualitative transformation in social relations, effected through the process of formulating the national economic plan, which uniquely brings about the qualitative transformation of the working class as a whole from a sort of pluralist collection of competing wills into an organic cognitive process. It is this that makes the process of centralized planning by the entire working-class population a true cognitive process.

In comparing this process with the dynamic models of expanded reproduction exemplified by the outer limits of computer application, we locate the qualitative distinction between a dictatorship of the proletariat and a socialist economy. The dictatorship of the proletariat, in which planning is accomplished by a surrogate for the class as a whole, has the limits of planning effectiveness, as absolute limits, implied by the computerization; it delimits the consciousness within the working class to the alienated form approximating pluralism. The reactionary tendency in a dictatorship of the proletariat (relative to socialist economy) becomes an actively reactionary principle, a source of qualitative alienation, in the emergence of such determinate policies as "to each according to his work."

The case of capitalist economy is shown, respecting the analogous limits of capitalist planning, when capitalist valuations are substituted for socialist real valuations, and the element of capitalist heteronomy (particular capitals) is also introduced into the socialist planning model.

Thus, the three forms of society—socialism, dictatorship of the proletariat, and capitalism—can be conceptualized from an epistemological overview of the forms of extended reproduction occurring in each.

ELABORATION OF STRUCTURE

The detailed structure of capitalist production and circulation, from a real rather than a capitalist-accumulation standpoint as such, is elaborated in the three forms we have already described: Bill of Consumption, Process Sheet, and Bill of Materials. We shall restate the case for the use of these forms in an ordinary way here.

A Process Sheet is a list of a set of interconnected sequences of productive operations for a particular productive facility. Each operation can be represented, for this purpose, as a "node." Each such node represents one or more qualities of productive labor. This grouping is determined by a definite "work center," usually identified by a particular machine or other piece of equipment. The exact number of such distinct qualities of productive labor is usually peculiar to the use of that machinery or equipment, but is specifically defined for the specific product with which each Process Sheet is concerned.

Certain processes may be regarded as special cases of this: the petroleum facility, or other chemical processing, in which a node may not involve specific labor peculiar to each node. In such cases, a node is defined as a qualitative stage in the sequence, and/or any point at which the network of processing branches in any way. Subtler distinctions are occasionally encountered in practice, but we need not consider those here.

The Process Sheet represents not only a network of production, but also other kinds of implicit connections to the whole economy. Each quality of productive labor is a link to a specific Bill of Consumption. Each machine or piece of equipment is a link to the Process Sheet for the creation of such capital goods.

The further qualifications to be noted on this topic are as follows. The Process Sheet, when properly developed, includes a specification of "Economic Lot Quantity" or cognate determination. In addition to "setup time"—the time required for a changeover from production of one product-type to another—every productive process has "learning time," even when the same type of production has been performed repeatedly in the recent past. In addition, every productive process requires a buildup of in-process inventory. The simplest illustration of this kind of problem is the observation that different products do not require the same proportion of time per unit or batch on different constituent productive capacities in the same network. Excluding consideration of the more complex problems of "balancing mix" which often occur for this reason, it is sufficient to consider the need to build up an inventory to buffer the linking of successive nodes in the network. Many further considerations enter into the proper calculations at this point, but the following summary will suffice. In production one attempts to minimize the cost of fixed factors of setup, learning, inventory lag, and the like, and also to minimize the bottlenecks in product-mix created by large lots of any one product. One must reckon this consideration against the capital costs of building finished goods and other inventories as a way of reducing production costs and maintaining a large product-mix. All these and related considerations determine increasing degrees of refinement of the determination of "economic lot quantity."[19]

The fact that a phase of the overall production of any product, as defined by a Process Sheet, requires finite numbers of productive labors by type, finite capacities, and the like determines the following fundamental point. For a given stage of development of productive technology, the amount of capacity an economy must "buy" to obtain even a token quantity of any kind of product is fixed at a lower limit of capacity. For example, a certain type of foundry production may not be economical at less than fifty tons of throughput per day. If the economy wants only ten tons per day of that kind of production, it must still invest in fifty tons of capacity. Every kind of production is associated with such minimal economical capacities at each stage of development. In general, although there are occasional exceptions, the smaller the capacity one buys, the more costly the individual product of that type. Even where this may may not be true, savings in minimal capacity in particular plants are more than offset by the increased requirement of capacities in facilities supplying raw and semifinished materials and capital equipment.

The more advanced an economy becomes, the greater the division of labor in number of kinds of production. Each of these kinds of production has a minimal capacity, usually increasing as technology advances. This is, for example, one of the major reasons that "socialism in one country" is absolutely impossible. Modern development of the productive forces, which is based on capitalist utilization of the potential for technological advancement of worldwide division of labor, demands a scale of productive labor and associated varieties of capital equipment such that no national economy could conceivably develop a modern economy on an autarchical or semiautarchical basis. In the case of the economy of the Soviet Union, for example, the more successfully that economy approaches technological parity in major categories with the advanced capitalist sector, the more autarchical Soviet development becomes a brake on possible further development of the economy. Thus, imperialist blockade of the Soviet Union, especially if that blockade is directed to critical categories of Soviet capital import requirements, effectively sabotages the development of the Soviet economy. In partial compensation for this, the Soviet economy is compelled to abort productive development outside the critical capital-goods sector, creating internal developmental brakes on the standard of living and rate of potential economic development.

The Bill of Materials lists the gross materials, semifinished products, supplies, and power associated with a specific Process Sheet, or, in certain instances, a particular balanced mix of Process Sheets. Properly extended, this Bill of Materials takes several other matters into account. Setting the first step of production of the Process Sheet equal to 00 00 00 in days, hours, and minutes, one properly determines the lead-time necessary for obtaining production materials. One then adds the necessary lead-time for placement of the purchase order for each specific material.

Such considerations are by no means trivial. In numerous tragicomic cases, one finds U.S. firms in particular attempting to sell products they could not possibly produce, an error made either in ignorance or in obsessive refusal to consider such "strictly theoretical" considerations. If the production cycle is four weeks, and the materials-order lead-time is six weeks (the typical parameters in several soft-goods industries), it is obviously impossible to sell products to be delivered in six to eight weeks unless the materials required are already in-house or currently due. Yet one sees firms pathetically, obsessively repeating such blunders season after season, delivering products weeks after the close of the delivery season; the various departments of the firm (sales, production, purchasing, and so on) curse one another liberally ("It's all your fault!") when the flood of returned merchandise and cancellations inundates the receiving and shipping floors.

The same general principle of managerial incompetence and hysteria applies to "depth of line." These blunders are not limited to small or medium-sized firms lacking "sophisticated scientific management." The author has repeatedly witnessed the following scenario in some of the largest financial houses. A given firm has excessive inventory. To any sufficiently simple-minded person, the solution is all too obvious: cut production to the level necessary to reduce inventory. Such "solutions" are the most ingenious method imaginable to cause major losses or even bankruptcies. Excessive inventories are inherently overaged inventories. In a sales line with a diversified product mix, the capacity to "bleed off" marginal product lines depends upon effective marketing of new product lines. If this is not possible, the only alternative is to write off the inventory until its value falls to an economical level. Since, from the viewpoint of accounting, the former remedy means raising inventory levels, and the latter means producing massive losses, one sees the "thinking" behind the production-cutting prescriptions of the financiers for their client firm. Either way, the valuation or turnover losses involved in inventory have already occurred. Refusal to face that fact results in a fallacy of the same type seen in the connection between Fixed Capital generally and the tendency for the rate of profit to fall. In this case, excessive or excessively valued inventory is demonstrating the phasal character of Fixed Capital as a category, since excessive inventory is acting economically, functionally, as Fixed Capital.

From the standpoint of current operations, the best way to deal with excessive inventory buildup is to ignore it once one has located and corrected the reasons for the buildup. Production and marketing must now be based on the profitable turnover of new production. In the intracorporate furor arising in discussion of inventory-cutting proposals, this point is often made by the more intelligent production and marketing executives . . . who sagely shut up when it becomes clear which side their future employment prospects are buttered on. If they are really astute, they quickly and discreetly seek employment elsewhere—or, in some cases, make plans to move into the chief executive position as soon as, but no sooner than, the disastrous consequences of the inventory-cutting program have put the incumbent chief executive on the street.

From the standpoint of finance, with the rare exceptions of a few financial executives, the burden of past values is primary. Thus, some of the otherwise most astute, shrewdest, and best-advised financiers become absolute cretins in such predicaments.

Between the outlook of the more intelligent production or marketing executive and the cretinism of the financial officers and financiers we are encountering the reflection in the microstructure of the fundamental contradictions of capitalist accumulation in the macrostructure. This is exactly Ricardo's problem, enacted as a contradiction in the polemic between two groups of capitalist administrators. The historically progressive thrust of capitalism, which Ricardo emphasized, is exemplified by the standpoint of the production and marketing executives, whose point of view is that of profitable production per se. They are oriented to current valuations, expanded reproduction in terms of Circulating Capital. The contradictory moment, whose very existence astonished Ricardo and others, is the standpoint of dead capital represented by the financial officers, the momentary expression of the tendency for the rate of profit to fall.

It is useful to consider the customary reason for such inventory accumulations in the same light. This example illustrates how the contradiction between production executives and financial executives comes into being out of their initial agreements.

The formal reason for excessive inventory accumulations is readily located in our outline of Process Sheets and Bills of Materials: excessive depth of product lines. In the effort to saturate every pore of the market with sales, and thus to realize the maximum turnover of the capital tied up in existing capacity, there is the strongest impetus to diversity. This tendency reached an extreme in the U.S. during the postwar period, accelerating to monstrous proportions from 1954 onwards. The notion of mass production formerly associated with the image of the model T reached such proportions that at one point during the 1960s, we estimated, from data in industry publications, that the total number of varieties of models of automobiles offered by Detroit exceeded the total number of units sold. To accomplish such diversification of product lines within finite capacities required large accumulations of inventory.

Worse: the total cycle of production is not that indicated by the elapsed unit-productive times of nodes of Process Sheets. The elapsed time of production is the combination of that represented by the lapsed unit-time per node and that required to pass in sequence through each inventory queue. Thus, in a manufacturing facility where the total production time is several hours, the actual time required for complete movement through both production and in-process inventories may be days. The author has frequently seen this cycle time build up to weeks on the basis of mere hours of production time. This buildup of total lapsed time for production of the complete line means a production cycle way in excess of the selling period. The amount of production that must be completed well before the first delivery date for the marketing season grows larger. Attempts to economize on inventory accumulation result in monstrous bungling in production administration. The proportion of late deliveries, cancelled orders due to late deliveries, necessary "washouts" of excessive inventories, and the like all accumulate. Yet, for competitive reasons, the process of diversification is aggravated to more monstrous proportions.

This process of diversification is directly linked to both general credit expansion and certain specific features of credit expansion of marketing. Enormous redundancy in marketing occurs. This situation, typified during the mid-1950s by the crisis in automotive distribution that resulted from the increase in consumer use of credit, was by no means limited to automotive distribution, but it is undoubtedly the best example. In fact, it was intensive study of this example that led the author to develop a now-confirmed prognosis for the course of development of the U.S. economy and world monetary system during the latter part of the 1950s.

In the effort to market competitively, automobile manufacturers began peddling franchises like pencils. Gas stations became dealerships overnight. As a result, despite the massive expansion in automotive retail sales, increasing numbers of dealerships became distressed. The growth of this market was immediately due to the loosening of restrictions on consumer credit terms following the Korean War and the apparent end of the postwar inflationary crisis. Typical terms of sale were successively expanded from twelve to eighteen months, and then to twenty-four, thirty, and thirty-six months. Finally, there was added the competitive sales gimmick of "thirty-six months with a 'balloon note' at the end." The latter development, which expressed the essence of the whole process, kept the monthly terms and down payment required on a new car sale well within the budget of the purchaser by making the last payment due the proverbial "real lulu." The purchaser of the new car was hooked into such an arrangement by the supposition that he would be trading in his used car within twenty-four to thirty months and that, therefore, the cost of possession of a new car would never rise above the budget represented by his low monthly payments on such financing terms.

Reality interceded. The point was reached, when the car was about twenty to twenty-four months old, at which the purchaser's outstanding obligations on it exceeded the purchase price of an identical make and model at his friendly neighborhood used-car lot. Here was the entire essence of a capitalist boom-bust cycle enacted in microcosm.

The dynamics of this system were concealed from the more credulous dealers by the fictions incorporated into the monthly accounting statements they were obliged to maintain by their franchise agreements with the automotive manufacturers. The dealer, according to these fantastic rules of accounting, was obliged to list the new-car sale on his statements at list price. Worse, in some cases the new-car sale was listed at what was known as a "packed price." In the effort to offer the retail purchaser an apparently better price, the new car sales manager, on behalf of the dealership, would rig the price of the new car one or more hundred dollars above its factory nominal list retail price and award this additional markup to the retail buyer in the form of a larger allowance on the used car he was trading in. Thus, we witnessed the phenomenon of the "packed new car price." In general, all the discounts given to the new-car purchaser (with a few exceptions for cash sales) took the form of overvaluations of the used-car trade-in allowance. The result was a massive overvaluation of the dealer's used-car inventory.

In the author's and others' numerous studies of these cases, it became apparent that the dealer was making an actual gross profit of two hundred dollars or less per unit on new car sales, instead of the fictional 25 per cent standard gross profit at list shown on his books. At these margins, considering dealers' out-of-pocket commissions, "new car make-ready," and other direct costs, the new-car dealer was usually operating at a direct loss. Although his mandatory franchise bookkeeping showed his used-car operations as a loss, he was usually making a significant profit on used-car sales, although insufficient to cover his losses on new-car sales. To survive, a dealership had to absorb from 70 to 90 per cent of its operating and fixed costs from gross profits on retail automotive service.

Two "solutions" to this problem were developed for dealerships during the mid-1950s, one by a shrewd leading dealership whose name we shall not mention, the other by the author.

The shrewd dealership developed a tactic which became known as the Wing-Ding. All of the salesmen's "closing booths" in the dealership were bugged, and the monitoring station was located in the sales manager's office. The salesman led the prospective buyer into the closing room, and began attempting to close the sale by using every possible ploy, including, of course, the packed-price tactic. Occasionally, and increasingly, the retail customer had done considerable shopping around, and the salesman in such cases often ran out of competitive offerings. At that point, the sales manager rang the salesman on the intercom and instructed him to proceed with the Wing Ding. (This instruction was based on the sales manager's estimation of the "psychology" of the prospective customer in question.)

"Mr. Customer," the salesman would now say, "I might be able to do a little better for you on your car. Do you have it handy?" There followed a personal reinspection by the service manager or his surrogate, after which the prospective customer learned that the dealership had a prospective customer for the used car if the sale were made immediately. On that basis, the dealership could allow him another hundred or so dollars on the used car. If the customer "bit," the Wing Ding was set in motion. He was now without an automobile, but expected delivery of his new car within days. Naturally, the delivery of that particular model became mysteriously delayed. Eventually, his patience worn thin by delays, he would accept a substitute new car, whose accessories and other features were manipulated to insure a profit to the dealership.

The author's scheme was aimed at a different victim: competing new-car dealerships. Because the profits of a new-car dealership were made in used-car sales, the principle was to maintain a large balanced inventory, based on the optimal ratio of new- to used-car sales. This inventory was obtained by purchasing selected better-quality used cars at wholesale prices from overstocked competing dealerships; these cars were then sold at competitive prices to retail customers. Since the competing dealership was attempting to make a profit on combined operations by selling used cars retail at inflated inventory valuation costs, it was selling fewer used cars (due to overpricing) than its normal tradedown ratio justified and required. (There is a standard "washout" ratio of new first-quality, second-quality, and third-quality used cars, based on trading patterns and customer traffic patterns.) Thus, the dealership in question would be using its competitors' own used-car trades and, indeed, part of their own capital to put them out of business.

These ploys, especially the latter, empirically verify the author's analysis of the nature of the marketing situation. (The second tactic was not feasible constantly throughout the period in question. There were, necessarily, occasional drops in the used-car market profits, reflecting periodic washouts of inventory accumulations by desperate new-car dealers. The tactic depended upon buying in during the prime periods of such cycles, and staying out during washout periods. Such exceptions merely prove the rule.) This pattern was most explicit in the retail automotive market, but was not limited to that market. It was almost impossible for dealerships in this and similarly affected fields to make a profit without swindling the customer or looting one's competitors' capital. The automobile dealership accounting system was eventually changed after the dealers belatedly became aware of the swindle, but its basic principles persisted in other forms throughout the economy.

What broke the market open was, as we have noted, the fact that at a certain period of maturity of the credit sale, the customer owed more on the clunker than its used-car replacement price. This, as we have noted, is the essence of a capitalist crisis. It is also an example of the determination of the particular event by the entire process, an empirical demonstration of the fallacy of bad-infinity methods of approach to political economy. The approach exemplified by the manufacturing inventory problem and the automotive marketing example are appropriate to case studies of the decay of railway systems over the past half-century, the pattern of obsolescence in textile manufacturing, the aggravated technological rot feeding on highly exploited labor in the garment industry, the decay of the footwear industry, and any number of comparable cases which add up to a very large sector of the economy. The crisis in air transport is another such case. A somewhat different approach, which nevertheless reflects the same principles, applies to construction and, indeed, to every aspect of the economy. If one applies the proper approach one finds cruelly reflected in every detail of the structure of capitalist economy, in an absolutely necessary way, all the components of a future breakdown crisis in the economy as a whole.

The Bill of Consumption for families and persons identifies for each income range, family size, type of occupation of head of household, and region the total consumption of various categories and types of commodities and other services necessary or modal for that section of the population. Again, the author adds extensive personal experience to the general evidence otherwise available.

Despite the insipid truisms frequently heard at Chamber of Commerce luncheons and similarly edifying gatherings, the most uplifting allusions to the "free decisionmaking of the marketplace" are claptrap from the most rudimentary standpoint of marketing practices. For reasons implicit in the nature of the Process Sheet and Bill of Materials, U.S. production could not have achieved even its current degree of semirationality unless product-line and product-mix planning decisions made six to eighteen or more months in advance of consumer purchase represented a statistically significant projection of public tastes for categories, product specifications within categories, etc., even down to such refinements as color preferences. If there is a deviation from the distribution planned months in advance, it is marginal, usually well within the 5–10 per cent range, and usually involves the replacement of obsolete items by new product specifications. With good marketing and "scientific management" within the firm's planning and operations, the usual sort of difficulty blamed on customer or consumer caprice would simply not occur. When most executives complain about the mysterious behavior of customers and consumers, the real culprit is the managerial incompetence that prevented them from taking into account knowledge properly within the grasp of any competent management.

There are two principal points to be considered here. The simpler of the two is that a customer cannot purchase what is not presented for purchase. The second observation involves a fundamental point involving the determination of consumer needs.

Let us look first at the first of these two points. The most credulous and robotic consumer cannot be regarded as exhibiting unpredictable free will if he declines to buy what is obviously junk or fails to purchase what the manufacturer and retailers have failed to place on the shelves. One of the most important determinants of the sales of a product line is what is termed "shelf position." Some of the gimmicks used by manufacturers to exploit this principle are most instructive.

In most retail sales, the guiding principle is gross profit per month per linear foot of shelf-space. For obvious reasons, the greater a proportion of total available shelf-space a product occupies, the greater its sales relative to comparable products with less shelf-space (provided the customers will tolerate the product). Generally, but not always, the product should be *apparently* competitive in price, and it must always sustain itself in terms of retailer's gross profit per linear foot. On the other hand, the retailer's gross traffic depends upon selection offered, up to a point, so that his total rate of turnover depends upon diversity—within limits. The interconnection between these two considerations makes it extremely difficult for one product to be sold by a single agency to individual retailers. The effective approach is that of the broker of categories who supplies a retailer with a mix of products for an entire category or categories of shelf-space, so that the manufacturer must either attempt to offer a more or less complete line for such a merchandising category or fight for favorable position with a reseller agency. Large retail chains, for example, are not a collection of stores; the stores are a vehicle for a merchandizing operation, which by its concentrated power can control a large share of total national shelf-space, and can use its control of retail distribution to exert back-pressure on manufacturers, contract growers, and the like. Once one has seen what is essential and what is determined in such facets of the economy, the capitalist determination of consumer purchases begins to become comprehensible. And its significance becomes clearer once we have the second point, which is even more fundamental.

There is nothing magical or psychologically intrinsic to consumers that facilitates such a determinable consistency. The systematic and detailed examination of popular life readily locates the operating necessity that determines the underlying determination of consumer tastes.

There are two general kinds of constraints upon the head of household and his family which compel him to order the proportionalities of his consumption in a definite way. These determinations may indeed seem to be determinations of his individual free will, but only because the constraints of social practice have determined the constituents of what appears to the observer as the individual will (not in the mechanistic Darwinian or Lamarckian notion of such determination, but with respect to the historical social process that created his consciousness during infancy and childhood and has coherently acted upon that consciousness, that thus-created material, thereafter.

The first constraint, which ought to be obvious to the investigator, is that the consumer's income is finite, and that its finiteness therefore predetermines the number and varieties of commodities he can "choose" to purchase. Since each purchased commodity represents a finite portion of his total income, leaving a determined residue for other purchases, once we have empirically established his need to purchase one commodity we have delimited his possible choice of purchases of other commodities.

Each commodity represents no mere possession in itself, but must primarily represent the fulfillment of the purchaser's need for the material means of his existence; otherwise the particular consumer would soon cease to occupy our attention in marketing studies. Since these essential purchases can initially be reduced to a primary group of obvious categories (food, housing, clothing, transportation, education, and the like) which represent the necessary material preconditions for reproducing modern labor power, and since the necessary magnitude of each of these categories is established as representing a certain price, the consumer's choice of purchases is already largely segmented before any consideration of choice can be introduced.

Before completing our analysis of the finiteness of the consumer's income, we must define and partially explore its complement, the finiteness of the activities that make up his living-time.

For the worker himself (taking the male head of household as a prototype) time is already divided into categories: so many hours for sleep, for work, for travel to and from work, for meals, and for the chores incidental to the living-day. For other members of his household, the order and proportions of the categorical elements of the living-day are similarly determined.

In general, commodities, as they are true commodities, are not consumed in the form of mere static possessions, but are used up. The effect, in general, is that the purchase and possession of a category of commodities corresponds to and interpenetrates the categorical activity of a determined segment of the living-day. Hence, the activity of consumption and the consumption of the commodity are inseparable as subjects and predicates of the same moment of existence.

Even to the extent that certain commodities and activities are initially of the form of "mere" psychological needs, these needs are not actually matters of "free" choice. Without fully exploring the details of this important aspect of human existence, it is sufficient to note that recreation and other leisure activities are not only determined in amount, but are necessary either in some natural way or because the individual lives a life that is determined by capitalist accumulation. Sports may, among their other benefits, correct for the onesideness of life outside of leisure activities. Education, in the broadest sense of cultural life, is necessary to the reproduction of labor power, its cognitive powers.

Particular exemplary consideration can be given to religious activities, which ordinarily occupy a certain portion of the individual income and living-time, and tend to order other features of the totality of life. If we acknowledge religious belief as a need within the alienated circumstances of capitalist life, we have thus located as strict needs what some might discount as irrational needs.

The proportionality of categories of personal activity-time (at this moment, the subject) and categories of commodity-consumption (at this moment, the predicate) is itself determined, of course, by the totality of the productive relationships for capitalist accumulation. The form, cost of production, and price of housing, food commodities, and other goods are determined by capitalist technology—by that technology's determination of the quality of employable labor power, and so forth. The form of personal activities interpenetrating consumption of commodities is determined by the length and intensity of the working-day, by the necessary quality of development of labor power for particular development of the productive forces, and by the existing form and rate of development of the productive forces. This is exemplified by shifting policies on education and related public services, or by shifting policies on unemployment and welfare practices. If the capitalist economy is expanding in technology and rates of employment, a premium is placed on education and on the cultural prerequisites in family life and other spheres for cultural and specifically educational activities; in periods of stagnation or depression, these policies are reversed. Welfare and other unemployment policies are also so determined.

This obvious aspect of reality determines the prevailing idea of proper activities and proper commodity-consumption, and is reflected through the phenomena of notions of personal social identity. The point is to order one's personal activities and consumption not only for one's material existence-in-itself as potential labor power, but also in the form that outwardly expresses one's membership in a corresponding stratum of society, such as one's class. Relationships in capitalist society are not direct relationships between human individuals, and knowledge of an individual (including, usually, self-knowledge) is not awareness of his or her human powers as such, or even of his or her productive powers. Relationships in capitalist society are mediated through objects and through the mask of self, the persona. This persona, which determines one's immediate social relations in capitalist society, is not only associated with power over objects as an expression of social powers, but is itself identified by the individual's power over (that is, possession of) corresponding objects. The individual, in the more immediate view, attempts to approximate universal knowledge of what he should be (through activity-consumption) by simply comparing his consumption and activities to those of a certain stratum of his class.

This rule is manifest in fads. In a given period one is fascinated by certain objects and certain leisure activities. These things become "old" and no longer attractive as a new fad arises. It is monstrous to suggest that these objects and activities are intrinsic to the individual's "natural" desires. He likes one thing and dislikes another because others seem to like or dislike them. To like such objects and activities is to exercise the rights and privileges of membership in a certain stratum; to dislike other objects, even those one seemed to admire passionately a few months earlier, is too. "Why do you buy that?" "I like it." "Nonsense. You like it because you wish to be seen liking it." A woman uses makeup to be liked "for herself." The advertiser says: become a member of such and such a stratum by being seen consuming Baltho. Or: don't be an ordinary stiff; become a member of the elite and share its social esteem by ordering your personal tastes and activities by the following eccentric criteria. These criteria do not represent personal idiosyncrasies. In capitalist society one's life usually depends upon one's persona; if one does not keep it in "marketable" up-to-date condition, one's real existence suffers. Indeed, the most passionate desires and needs are those associated with the needs of the persona. One resents the boredom of a secretarial job, but "loves" to expend the major portion of one's leisure and income maintaining the appropriate persona for that or equally boring employment.

The housewife, sensible of the limits of personal time and income, reflects her false consciousness of this determination by "working out a household budget," in which exercise of "free will" she only demonstrates her lack of freedom. She allots various proportions of the household's total disposable income to its categorical constituents, selecting particular commodities within each such category according to her estimation of determined needs. She buys "luxuries" by the same criteria. Her explication of her decisions may be shallow, but they reflect the materiality of determination acting through actuality upon her "will" to determine its constituents.

In general, the consumer does not make purchases by determining which product should be available at which price in the greater relative abundance. The consumer buys the products that exist—eats the food capitalist mother sets before him—in the approximate proportions and at the prices capitalism offers them to him. In no case could the degree of "freedom" in this consumer choice be greater than the alteration of useful commodity production as finally determined by capitalist accumulation in extended reproduction. In any case, the principal task assigned to the marketing analysts or advertising specialists is to sell a certain volume of particular kinds of products. The quality and quantity of these products represent merely a distinct form of existing or imminently existing productive capacities. The price at which each will be sold is determined by the gross profit ratios demanded by prevailing rates of accumulation of the manufacturer, wholesaler, and retailer. What, then, does the consumer choose? How much could he be brainwashed by the advertiser? Perhaps the marketing specialist and advertising man are essentially extensions of capitalists' *competition?*

In the final analysis, the Bill of Consumption is just as rigorously predetermined—if not in the same way—as the Process Sheet and Bill of Materials by the process of capitalism accumulation in general.

It is, again, these three elements of the industrial engineers' and marketing analysts' practice, applied to the general input-output structure of interfirm and production-consumption relations characterizing world trade and social reproduction which defines an elaborated worldwide network—capitalism accumulation as a whole. In turn, it is the entirety of that network which determines capitalist accumulation in particular, the evolving structure of capitalist economy down to the smallest detail.

If we trace a few of the simplest commodities of the working-class families' material existence through their various antecedent stages of production, we will shortly have outlined such a worldwide network in principle, to the extent, as we have noted, that the entirety of the world's population, through the mediation of its productive labor force, is intrinsic and necessary to the existence of every workers' family in the United States. Indeed, as we trace the production of any commodity back toward the original extraction of raw materials, we are confronted with Fixed and Constant Capitals which demand the tracing of an entire new network of successive productions.

Our dynamic model is based on the observation that the reduction of the socially necessary cost of production of any commodity in the entire network, provided that the others do not increase in such costs, results in an immediate tendency toward the reduction in cost of every other product. In this portrait of actuality, the ratio of materials in a Bill of Materials is immediately a ratio of the manufacturing facilities, mines, and the like that produce those materials. The Process Sheet, as it defines productive labor, is a ratio of Bills of Consumption. It is also, with respect to capital equipment, a ratio of the plants which produce that equipment. The existence of the simplest particular "cell form" of capitalist production and consumption is a necessary expression of the entirety of production on a world scale: extended reproduction from its appropriate "total capitalist" standpoint. But to locate production in extended reproduction is to locate reality not in a static totality, but in the changing technology accompanying extension. This fact demands cognition of our dynamic model as a dialectical one.

REVIEW: IMPLICATIONS OF DISTINCTION

It is most useful to explore more deeply the implications of Marx's point of view from the standpoint of the Kantian representation of the problems Marx thereby resolved. The student, of course, usually brings to this subject decidedly pre-Kantian prejudices, which are reflected in the current popularity of a regression to the standpoint of Hume—or to Hume's flaws without his virtues. The significance of Kant for the Humean is that Kant shares with the outlook of the French and English Enlightenment the fallacies of bad infinity and the thing-in-itself. Kant's usefulness for our present purposes is summarized in the fact that he recognized all the pathetic fallacies inherent in the Humean outlook insofar as they could be defined within the assumptions of bad infinity. Kant remains useful today for just that reason. He provides the means for reducing the naive, otherwise chaotic empiricist point of view to the form in which it can be systematically considered. Furthermore, unlike that wretched brand of neo-Kantian who attempts to circumvent the fundamental antinomy by attributing indeterminacy to the thing-in-itself, he demonstrates the insolubility of that antinomy except from a dialectical standpoint. In sum, he states the problem to be solved in such terms that we can re-examine the question whether or not we have actually solved that difficulty by applying our solution to the issues as Kant states them.

By implication, simple and extended reproduction correspond to two irreconcilable philosophical world-outlooks. The former, which naively imagines that it assumes no postulates external to the facts as such, necessarily regards the cell form of political economy (commodity, labor power, value, use value) as self-evident or simply derived from self-evident facts, and thereby imports into its investigations the whole bag of metaphysical mechanist's postulational assumptions about the nature of everything in the universe. Extended reproduction treats the same cell form merely as a phenomenon whose quality is to be determined from the standpoint of the process of change expressing the whole. This is the Marxian world-outlook—as distinguished from that of most professing Marxists—whose "imported" postulates are, unlike those of the empiricist, located in the primary, uniquely self-evident fact of human (historical) existence. Unlike the empiricist or classical materialist, who imports countless wild postulational assumptions to the real world from the fantasy world of common sense, the sole postulate of the Marxian world-outlook is, as we have shown, the distilled empirical "fact" of world-historical human existence as a whole.

Acknowledgement of this point does not solve all the student's difficulties. Just as the empiricist method has its assumed methods of proof—

its methods of distinguishing reasonable hypotheses from utter rubbish—so must the Marxian method. Yet that method cannot be the method of the empiricist, the method of formal logic. Not accidentally, this is a matter of some importance to us when we begin to proceed beyond the vaguest critical generalizations and yet, also not accidentally, this is the aspect of Marxian method that has been most inadequately discussed in most of the literature to date. Borrowing from the work of leading dialecticians—Hegel, Feuerbach, and Marx—we choose to give the required method the name "phenomenology," and to ignore the fact that there are persons who call themselves phenomenologists with whom we have no connection. We shall examine the general peculiarities of *Capital* from this standpoint, reviewing certain features we have already considered from this special vantage-point.

As Rosa Luxemburg has shown, throughout most of Volumes I and II of *Capital*, Marx's pedagogical ruse seems to be principally the standpoint of simple reproduction. Yet, when Marx was preparing Volume I for publication, he had already written out the main features of Volumes II, III, and IV.[20] During the same period he had added to the *Theories of Surplus Value* manuscript its sections XX–XXIII,[21] in which the notion of self-expanding value is systematically presented.[22] It follows that the notion of extended reproduction we have elaborated here was already more or less fully developed by Marx (self-subsisting positive = self-expanding value) before Volume I was written and the modifications in its second edition were made.[23] On the basis of such evidence, supporting the remarks at the outset of Volume III, it becomes certain that the simple-reproduction viewpoint of the first two volumes was not only deliberate, but a deliberate pedagogical ruse. As we have noted, Marx proceeds from the starting-point of sense-certainty to develop the view of capitalist production, and then to amplify that from the standpoint of the sense-certainties of circulation. In Volume III he negates this to arrive at the notion from which he had started Volumes I and II, the notion of capital-in-general. Luxemburg thus rightly makes *Theories of Surplus Value* and key sections of Volume III the principal basis for representing her *Accumulation of Capital* as a Marxian critique of problems occurring in Volume II.

It is therefore impermissible to deny, even from the standpoint of mere formalities of scholarship, that the notion of self-expanding value is the required historically specific form of the self-subsisting positive to which Marx refers as early as the *1844 Manuscripts*.[24] The evidence to this effect, demonstrating the continuity of Marx's approach from at least 1845 to his last writings, also demonstrates that it was Marx's intent throughout the composition of *Capital* to proceed in a definite way toward a definite result of the form we have already indicated. According to Marx, to determine value for a particular commodity or product, we must first consider the whole process of expanded reproduction of capitalism, in terms of functions of $S/(C + V)$, and thus determine the significance of the particular (value) for the increased valuation of the entire process in terms of

$S/(C + V)$. Thus Luxemburg, the only noted twentieth-century Marxian economist to acknowledge this fact, is the only actual Marxian among them. In order to determine competently the significance of the particular national sector, firm, commodity, labor power, or whatever, we must proceed from the total-capitalist standpoint—from the standpoint of the entire inclusive process of capitalist accumulation.

The procedure thus stipulated is in absolute opposition to that which takes the unit of self-evident labor-time, or labor-time at a certain wage-rate, as the qualitative starting-point for actual determination of value. Once such a mistaken metaphysical mechanist assumption is introduced, as it is by Ricardo, and modern Ricardians such as Mandel,[25] the attempt to establish the edifice of a labor theory of value is degraded into a useless chimera.

As we have noted, it is not strictly necessary to be familiar with Volumes III and IV of *Capital*; the distinction between the Marxian and Ricardian methods should be obvious to any literate reader of even Volume I. Although the outlook of simple reproduction generally predominates throughout the first two volumes, the text is nonetheless permeated with passages warning that this viewpoint is conditional, and indicating the imminence of a contrary viewpoint. The famous "Fetishism of Commodities" section of the first chapter of Volume I ought to suffice for that purpose. That section warns one against a reductionist interpretation even when the pedagogy might seem to suggest it for the moment. The lack of sufficient literacy to note these warnings cannot be accounted for except by obsession. The student has usually consoled himself with adducing Marx's viewpoint from passages which seem "more understandable" to the commonsense viewpoint; any passages which conflict with that viewpoint become relatively incomprehensible, and are set aside for future exploration, when it is assumed that they too will "make sense" from the standpoint of the reductionist world-outlook. The reader usually puts his own philosophical construction on those selected passages he "elects" to understand. (Forewarned, we have boobytrapped this text to avoid being subjected to the same kind of misinterpretation. If we therefore seem guilty of hubris vis-à-vis "institutionalized scholarship," that is proof that we have satisfied the first precondition for representing Marx's point of view.)

Why did Marx choose to present the material of *Capital* in a pedagogical order at odds with his development of the conclusions he thus represents? That organization was dictated by his notion of "phenomenology," an exploration of which should assist the student in two ways. Immediately, once the student has some notion of the problems represented by a "phenomenology of political economy," he should appreciate Marx's own problems in writing *Capital*. Exploring more deeply, he will discover the significance of this problem as a form of proof peculiar to the dialectical method.

Let us examine the first aspect of this problem. Consciousness of pedagogy is generally insufficiently developed even among the instructors who prepare curricular material according to partially prescribed and partially evolved procedures. The student, whose desire for a passing grade blinds him to the fact that the same subject could be argued in a completely different fashion, is generally unaware of peculiarities of classroom presentation and general course organization. He does not recognize that the organization of classroom materials biases his reception of those materials. Nor is he aware, generally speaking, that what passes for education is merely edification. In general, what is called education is a collection of assertions connected by plausible argument and a large portion of institutionalized authority. The student is aware of this only as he is troubled by the fact that he cannot see any internal necessity to the connection, a difficulty he usually pushes out of his mind in order to focus on habituating himself to connections he does not understand.

From the strictest standpoint of knowledge in any field, the customary procedures encountered in classroom and textbook are mere edification, from which the student could not conceivably develop any real cognitive powers with respect to the real subject matter. Worse, to the extent that the student brings his actual cognitive powers to bear on the subject, he obtains different answers than the prescribed curriculum demands. These answers may be wrong, but that is not the fault of the student's cognition. The fault lies in the edification; if it is taken as a representation of cognition, the student would often be unable to obtain anything but wrong answers with a cognitive approach. To succeed, to get a reasonable proportion of "right answers," he must therefore suppress his cognitive tendencies in favor of "learning" the material and procedures as presented. Such "drill and grill" is the pattern one sees in "cramming for examinations," which places a premium on drilled memory as opposed to knowledge by cognitive association.

Thus, most education is rightly described as stultifying; Lawrence Kubie has described the problem to a certain extent.[26] Institutionalized education has managed to evade this indictment to a certain extent, to conceal the fact that it destroys cognitive powers, by changing the usage of the term "cognitive" to mean the very opposite of creative mentation. By making "cognitive" signify the phenomena of curricular stultification, institutionalized education liberates itself from the nominal charge of stultification.

The most deadly aspect of most curricular practices is the presentation as truth of material the instructor knows to be absurd from a more advanced standpoint. If the same organization of material were used with the qualification that "this is merely the way it must appear to us until we know the subject more fully," the damage would be qualitatively less. The question of the relative truth of conditional knowledge will usually take one of the following forms: (1) this is the way the matter must tend to appear to us without more knowledge; (2) From the standpoint of our present progress in study, this represents something that happens but for which at our present level of understanding we can give no reasonable explanation; (3) this is the demonstration that this actually occurs, even though we cannot fully explain why; (4) this is why the two phenomena appear to be consistent; (5) these are the reasons, according to our presently limited knowledge, why these phenomena seem to share a common explanation; or, best, (6) given what we presently know, this must seem to be the subject of such various predicates of the common collection, if the collection is coherent. Once any of these admissible expressions of conditional knowledge is reified to present conditional knowledge as a logical certainty, stultification is introduced. Worse, the instructor or text-author is freed from the rigors of progress in conditional knowledge, to concoct some chimera in which knowledge in that field seems to emerge logically from axiomatic certainties.

The application of dialectical rigor to conditional knowledge *as conditional knowledge* is a phenomenology. It is a method for communicating conceptions developed in a certain way to students whose level of development does not yet permit them to think in that way. It is a way of advancing knowledge by developing powers of cognition in students whose cultural development compels them to begin from the standpoint of sense-certainty. It is a method of elevating them from sense-certainty by steps in which the contradictions of sense-certainty compel them to exercise cognitive processes to redefine their empirical knowledge conceptually.

Let us develop the point by considering a summary history of the matter.

One should begin by considering the point that, in intention, Heraclitus, Plato, Kant, Hegel, Feuerbach, and Marx were all hylozoic monists. That is, they shared the view that the processes of cognition must necessarily be in agreement with the fundamental laws of the material universe, on the condition that the empirical phenomena of cognition are considered as actual and primary empirical subject matters for human knowledge in general. To put it otherwise, man is incapable of knowledge except that realized through his processes of cognition. For each, in a different way, the problem of knowledge was that man's alienation caused a discrepancy between the apparent knowledge he acquired through his experience and knowledge of the universe as it actually was.

We shall not consider Heraclitus or Plato here except to recommend Hegel's *History of Philosophy*, which provides a sufficient and generally correct basis for relating them, through Hegel himself, to Feuerbach and Marx. We shall turn now to Kant.

Kant's notion of the need for a phenomenology can be summarized as follows.[27] Kant assumed that of necessity the mind, as the unactualized but active possibility of all judgments (conceptions), does indeed represent a coherent, true *potential* notion of universality. He also specified that in the formation of perceptual intuitions of existent objects, and in the formation of analytical judgments (conceptions), the active possibility of true judgments was the ultimately efficient determinant of those intuitions and judgments. Or, to employ the viewpoint of his *Critiques*,[28] pure mind represents (as potential) an implicit *a priori* synthetic knowledge of universality, a potentiality or efficient implication which is actualized or reflected in perceptual intuitions of existent objects (things-in-themselves) by abstraction from the moments of quality contained within perceptual intuition. However, because the mind could not directly attain a perceptual intuition of its own intrinsic activity as an existent thing-in-itself, mind could not create *a priori* synthetic intuitive or categorical knowledge of objective universality. Therefore, true knowledge of universality must be attained in an approximate, roundabout fashion. By abstracting qualities from perceptual intuitions of existent things-in-themselves, concepts are created, and thereafter new conceptions, creating a hierarchical structure of analytical judgments implicitly converging upon the same truth of universality implicit in the unknowable (directly) *a priori* synthetic notion of universality. This reflects the *perverse* form of the Kantian dialectic, and the notion of a phenomenology in general as the systematical progressive process of hierarchical analytical judgment—governed, of course, by a guiding method.

It suffices to say here that for Hegel, the problem of the unknowable Logos did not exist. The preface and introduction to *Phenomenology of Mind* and the introduction to *Science of Logic* sufficiently articulate Hegel's self-conscious relationship to Kant on this and related points.[29] A phenomenology nonetheless remained necessary for Hegel. Indeed, for Marx, the Hegel of *Phenomenology of Mind* is outstanding by contrast to the Hegel corrupted by quasi-Kantian formalism in *Science of Logic* and *Philosophy of Right*.[30] For Hegel, the mind does indeed from the start know itself directly as an extended universality, through the reflection of itself in its activity, but not as an actually developing process of extended universality—not solipsistically—except by proving, first, the singularity and actual existence of mind's determinations, and then exploring the actualized interpenetration of determinate particularity *of the whole* as the actualization of self-development, which is for Hegel mind as *being-in-and-for-itself*.

This does not signify the ingenuous practice of basing one's study on facts gathered like daisies—no doubt for statistical correlation by packaged computer program. (If it did mean that, as Hegel remarked, every forest animal could be a brilliant physicist.) It signifies reducing one's conceptualizations to the form of singularity, and then locating in empirical actuality the same conception, as the whole acting upon itself for self-development through particularities expressing that singularity. One's conceptions must be singularly demonstrated to exist as the process of development of whole processes within, of course, empirical actuality.

Hegel's notion of a phenomenology could not be Marx's. With Feuerbach and Marx, respectively and successively, the location of dialectical development is radically shifted away from the Hegelian Logos as such. For Hegel, the Logos is alienated from its ultimate basis in universal matter-motion. (Although, for him, it is the *form* of existence of universal matter-motion. Not ideas as such determining the existence of matter, but the form of Logos of universal matter-motion, a form expressing formally the real determinations of that universal substance: coherence.) Where Hegel sees the development of self-consciousness occurring in parallel to the actual (circular) development of matter—as Heraclitus too defines matter-motion and the Logos—Marx supercedes Feuerbach by locating self-consciousness in the continuing, positive, progressive evolution of universal matter-motion itself. That is, thought itself is for Marx a culmination of the evolution of inorganic into organic, organic species-evolution into man and social evolution, and so on, and self-consciousness is emergent as a qualitative transformation of social evolution. Marx is a total hylozoic monist, whereas Hegel alienates self-development of human consciousness from the relative circularity he attributes to the dialectical form of matter-motion itself.[31]

Taking Feuerbach and Marx together as a single moment of historical development of scientific knowledge, the basis is shifted from an abstracted (alienated in fact) Logos to the self-superseding (sublating) hylozoic-monist evolution of universal matter-motion itself. Consequently, Feuerbach's and Marx's respective notions of a phenomenology must reflect the degrees of such distinctions from Hegel and from one another.

Feuerbach's phenomenology is his *Essence of Christianity*, which may on this point be productively compared to *Capital*. Feuerbach correctly locates the determination of self-consciousness not in the relationship of the Logos (the abstract form of matter-motion) to itself, but in the practical relationship of man to man, a discovery formally summarized in Section 33 of *Principles of the Philosophy of the Future*. Ideology—false consciousness—must therefore be located in the alienation of man apropos his *practical* relationship to his species as a whole. Analysis of the historical aspect of the dominant ideology, Christianity, thus provides Feuerbach with the necessary phenomenology to supply the formal demonstration of the coherence and validity of his notion.

The notion of a phenomenology is that of the sort of formal proof appropriate to the dialectical method—the supercession of Euclid, Aristotle, and metaphysical modern ideologies respecting proof (formalism, empiricism, and so on). Its distinguishing feature is the systematic demonstration that the particular is not self-evident, but that its existence as particular is both determined by a universal process and that in this determination it necessarily exists (actively) for the self-development of that universality. The phenomenology not only shows this to be the relationship governing particular events, but demonstrates that the view of lesser universalities as the basis governing the particular is necessarily false.

The various specialized subject matters that might be examined in this way are not to be regarded as compartmentalized subjects (self-sufficient categories of inquiry or fact), but as a facet of a larger universality, all subsumed by that governing, unique, and comprehensive universality which immediately corresponds to philosophy. For Feuerbach and Marx, the universality corresponding to philosophy is anthropology. Physics is a determined subuniversality of a dialectical anthropology. This does not, of course, signify that mastery of anthropology is already an elaborated physics; it is merely the methodological basis properly governing what methods can be competently developed for physics treated as an aspect of human practice to advance the evolution of man.

We have already indicated the relationship between anthropology-in-general and political economy. Although the world-line overview of anthropology-in-general does determine the method required of political economy, the special dynamic of political economy is historically specific, and its contents (as subject matters), although they cannot be comprehended competently except from the standpoint of anthropology-in-general, cannot be decreed simply from the standpoint of that general knowledge. It is the same for physics or any other field.

In any field, whether political economy or physics, one begins with the simplest, most pervasive phenomena. To the extent that the interpretation of phenomena is not coherent with the overview of anthropology-in-general, we know we have not yet reached reliable judgments in the special field of inquiry. It is not, however, sufficient to know that these special judgments must be wrong; it is essential to situate the errors empirically in terms of the special inquiry itself. Epistemology (the formal aspect of anthropology-in-general) can tell us which notions developed in physics are absurd from the standpoint of necessity. It can aid us further; to the extent that one knows physics, epistemology can provide the needed sense of direction for development of necessary experimental hypotheses—but there the matter rests until we have submitted the hypothesis to empirical tests, and located the existence of the hypothesized condition or event as an actuality.

This is exactly the general procedure for a phenomenology. One begins with only the simplest, most obvious misconceived phenomena. Epistemology guides us in locating the nature of the immediate error in conception and in framing hypotheses. We must, as Marx does in *Capital*, next locate the empirical actuality corresponding to that hypothesis, criticize it epistemologically, form new hypotheses, locate the confirmation or rejection of the particular hypothesis in empirical actuality, and so forth. Guided by a method which has itself been adduced from understanding of human existence generally, we approach each field of inquiry, proceeding from the simplest phenomena until we have reached the point at which cognition is prepared to locate the field of inquiry as a universality within the setting of anthropology-in-general.

What centrally distinguishes a phenomenology from other modes of proof of systematical conceptions is the notion of freedom shared in a certain sense by Kant, Hegel, Feuerbach, and Marx (and, of course, Descartes and Spinoza). The fact of cognition as an efficient cause of subsequent states of the universe eliminates the possibility of comprehensive knowledge of any aspect of reality from the standpoint of formal logic or similar approaches. With Descartes, Spinoza, Hegel, and Marx, especially, this notion of freedom is located in a higher sense of necessity, rather than "freedom from" natural law. Not that freedom is simply an apparent, sophisticated feature of necessity in the vulgar sense of the term; the notion of necessity must be expanded from the vulgar to incorporate freedom as cognition (creative mentation) expresses it. *Necessity of Progress* is the general cognitive solution to that difficulty. Marx uniquely solved the problem by locating progress in the positive interconnection of human existence and the nature out of which human existence springs to comprehend its origins practically. Thus, the generalized notions implicit in the specific form, exponential impulse values for $S'/(C + V)$, become the characteristic standpoint for a Marxian phenomenology.

Let us review this point.

Admittedly, the notion of freedom occurs in Kant and Hegel, especially, partly in connection with ethical and related speculations, at least to the extent that the superficial student might mistakenly assume the term freedom to have the same significance for Kant and Hegel that it might have for Richard Nixon or Abbie Hoffmann. Both Kant and Hegel attempted to locate the basis for lawful freedom in the moral-political sense within the natural laws of the universe. It is in this sense that the term is developed and employed here.

In its naive, or commonsensical insipid interpretation, freedom signifies the right or privilege to be free of the explicit directives of natural and/or manmade laws. It is in this fatuous sense of the term that commonplace contemporary notions of alienation are adduced. This notion occurs in some Christian (and other neo-Platonic) theology as that of the privilege of the individual soul to escape the lawful end of total death and/or hell. To the common hysterical John Bircher or similar type, freedom is the right to abandon socially responsible conduct whenever some irrational impulse for asocial or antisocial individuality manifests itself within one. Freedom is presumed by such radical right-wingers to be essentially located in the right to hold property as individual property, and the consequent right to express freedom in the use of that property domain. Freedom is generally imagined to be the right to have one's neurotic impulses served by whatever representatives of society and nature (such as employees and members of one's family) lack the power to prevent such abuses. In certain circles, freedom is the liberating view of nature-in-general achieved through chemical aids to psychotic delusions; this outlook has, with or without the aid of LSD, taken the form of a mass neurosis among a large stratum of the "radical" children of habituated suburbanites. The latter is hardly accidental: in such families, the generally prevailing ideal of a large material income that "frees" one of the obligation to perform productive labor has laid the foundation for the children's hatred of work and natural law alike.

The more serious conception associated with the term "freedom" does indeed have a fundamental bearing on the morality of individuals with respect to society—and vice-versa. However, the essential notion is best grounded by considering the special definition of the term to which we have already referred: that is, the ironical implications of the term when it is posed as coherent with the proper notion of universal laws or, in other words, the phenomenology of physical laws as that study must proceed "upwards" once we recognize the need to incorporate the notion of progress into the self-evolution of physical laws. We cannot throw out physical law, the notion of necessity, merely because cognition demonstrates that physical law is not *fundamentally* of the form we impute to it in ordinary investigations. We have the most extensive vindications of physical law; indeed, our civilization rests upon that demonstration. If that notion of law did not represent a kernel of partial truth, we modern investigators would not exist to question it. It must be that the notion of physical law is true as far as it goes. What does cognition require? Only that the notion of "fixed" physical law be treated as a special case of a broader notion of evolving physical law. We are able to locate the significance of that notion of necessity with respect to the evolution of man's practice, which suffices to demonstrate that the notion of necessity is correct. If we have so far failed to locate the empirical demonstration of the discovery in the domain of physics *qua* physics, no one has attempted to accomplish that so far. However, despite the lack of a rounded realization of the point, the case has been empirically demonstrated—"It is not necessary to repeat the experiment in every river of the world"—and it provides us with the required notions of causality with respect to the consequences for society of actions by individuals and of actions on individuals by society. Spinoza was profoundly correct in recognizing such a systematical implication of the dialectical notion of necessity.

Marx certainly does not argue for freedom from natural laws. This would seem to be the case only to the individual who obsessively interprets the notion of natural law from the epistemological standpoint of religious belief in entropy. The notion of freedom is the notion of the universal necessity of evolution, the view of hylozoic monism from the standpoint of progressive evolution as its characteristic substance. It is freedom from the law of entropy—nothing more, nothing less.

The critical notion of freedom, as reflected in the domain of morality, is not a notion of the individual's prerogative to "do his own thing." Despite the moods and ideas inevitably characteristic of a society plunging in dionysiac frenzy toward total moral degeneration, every period of revolution and of progressive development of humanity rejects such moral imbecility. Hippies could not be a significant social phenomenon in a healthy society. The notion of freedom that emerged from the late eighteenth and early nineteenth century's philosophy, as the complement to the notions of progress and humanism, was that the creative powers of the individual (universal law) are the source of man's satisfaction of the necessity of progress. The individual was therefore obliged to develop and direct his creative powers toward the fulfillment of those forms of development of society which represented progress at that time. Even Kant, who deduced political anarchism of a certain sort from the unknowability of the thing-in-itself, could not regress even to the point of his student, Fichte, let alone the bestial imbecility of a Max Stirner. For Kant, the notion of quasi-anarchic freedom was the conception of an efficient means for realizing the universality of the categorical imperative, for realizing objective progress in the human condition. The advocacy of heteronomy, which becomes pathetic in Fichte and others and converges on an overtly fascistic philosophy in Stirner, was one issue on which Kant was cruelly frank. It is the anarchists of the middle-to-late nineteenth century and their descendants, the Italian, French, and German fascists of the twentieth century, who invert the Kantian notion into one of freedom for heteronomy. Where Kant saw political freedom as a means to realize social determination of individual nature, the anarchists and fascists represent degrees of motion in the opposite direction, toward the obliteration of social determination in favor of the irrational, the "triumph of the heteronomic will" over universal reason.

Both Kant and Hegel, in different ways, sought to realize freedom as political freedom for the actualization of what they regarded as objective progress. Hegel was guilty of degrading the germ of truth in his notion when he located the instrument of freedom in the Prussian monarch and state bureaucracy. With Hegel especially, the notion of progress is objectively determined, and *freedom exists to actualize the necessity of progress.* For Marx, the objective determinant of progress is this self-subsisting positive: the freedom of the potentially universal class-for-society, the freedom of the proletariat as a political class-for-itself. This class must be given freedom not to provide mere irrational (heteronomic) freedom for the proletariat-in-itself, but as the singular means for actualizing the existent potentiality of progress from capitalism to a society based on self-conscious humanity.

The notion of freedom, however it is necessarily reflected in the domains of morality, law, and the like, is essentially a *physical* notion: the requirement that all human practice be in conformity with natural law. Not freedom from natural law, but comprehension of the noetic character of actual universal natural law.

In this context, one sees more or less immediately that situating the notion of freedom within a universe of hylozoic monism immediately invalidates the methods of formal proof based on the assumptions of a mechanistic or empiricist philosophy. Since formalism demands that the existent is given and thus subject to more or less mechanical laws ("statistical correlations") for which the noetic sublating process does not exist, once we have rejected the notion that existence is a fixed quality of self-evident discrete phenomena as such, the entire structure of ordinary formal proof totally collapses. The phenomenology replaces the demolished edifices of formal proof as the means of replacing formal mechanistic *consistency* with dialectical *coherence.* The phenomenology locates the singularity of concepts for empirical actuality not in the persistence, but in the ordered change of quality, of the elements.

This signifies that the moment of freedom is mediately expressed in every determinate particularity of the process of social reproduction, provided that these particulars are studied from the standpoint of discovering the elaboration of such a universal evolutionary reproductive process. It is also properly adduced, ultimately, that the end of nonhuman matter (phenomena) for man (to use the scare-term: anthropocentric teleology) is not merely a subjective moment of man's attempted comprehension of nature, but ultimately the actual quality of universal matter-motion. This is so in the respect that human society is itself the highest known evolutionary development of the entire universe. This knowledge of matter is false anthropocentrism only if the definition of "for man" is itself narrowly or otherwise falsely situated. Provided that the universality of man for nature is the premise for stating the quality of man, the viewpoint of anthropocentric teleology is an *approximation*, a first groping toward the only correct, because uniquely coherent, view.

Fantastic? Pure conjecture? By no means. The present world ecological crisis compels us—on pain of extinction—practically to subsume nature *for* man within all of our comprehensions of either nature or socialized practice. Those who refuse to accept such a viewpoint, on grounds of bias against anthropocentric teleology, remove themselves from the argument and thus disprove their view by threatening to remove the existence of man to continue considering questions of knowledge from any philosophical standpoint. We are compelled to contemplate, for the development of science generally, the approaching task of ordering the entire earth for man, and human practice for the existence of earth as man-habitable. The ecology of the solar system is not that distant from the domain of earthly budgets—provided that society first survives the immediate ecological threat here on earth, as well as the developing capitalist crisis.

As for Kant, Hegel, and Feuerbach before him, it was essential for Marx to prove the empirical reality in terms accessible to his readers. He was obliged to prove the empirical reality of his economic (and other) theories by demonstrating the necessity of the principle of dialectical freedom (the self-subsisting positive) for the content of even the simplest particularity of the economic process under capitalism. It was necessary to establish the existence of such a universal outlook by starting from the simplest facts of experience, particular labor power and commodities. This could not be done by a Kantian phenomenology, nor by the method of analytical judgment from aprioristic intuitions. One had to prove repeatedly, at each successively higher level of the investigation, that the "ergodic" interpretation of the economic process not only failed to correspond to the empirical, but that it failed in a certain way. On this basis, new hypotheses about the higher-order solution were advanced, each tested for empirical actuality. Then, these new conceptions were again proven to defy the ergodic theorem. To accomplish this it was necessary to examine the empirical phenomena successively conceptualized for study in no lesser framework than the historical succession of development of capitalist society for entire periods of boom-bust for entire economies. Consistently, each of the cognitive moments experienced in progressing from one level to its supercessor depended upon the hypothesis $S'/(C + V)$. Finally, putting all the phases of capitalist reproduction together, and locating the emergence of capitalist forms from predecessor societies through the examination of rent, Marx demonstrates that the notion of $S'/(C + V)$ is the basis for the notion of capital-in-general.

Yet this is not exactly the way in which Marx himself discovered the notions he proves in this phenomenology! The core of the entire conception is already present in the 1845 writings to which we have referred. The organization of *Capital* itself is a reorganization of the material being elaborated in a different sequence. Marx presents his material in a different cognitive order than that in which he developed it. Comparing the pedagogical principles of *Capital* with the organization of Hegel's *Phenomenology*, and examining the concept of a phenomenology more generally, we discover immediately the significance of the arrangement. This is a method of proof.

EXTENDED REPRODUCTION 8

EXTENDED REPRODUCTION 8

Before turning in Chapter 9 to the notion of capitalists' accumulation as such, we shall review and summarize the ground we have covered with respect to use-value relations, interpolating certain considerations necessary to bring this phase of our exploration to completion.

On the grounds developed in Chapter 7, we shall now develop the notion of *socialist* "capital-in-general." Our general purpose, relative to the subject of political economy, is to establish our abstraction of the productive forces from capitalist accumulation, so that we may locate the peculiarities that arise for these productive forces under the objective determinations of capitalists' accumulation. We shall review, in particular, Marx's refutation of Ricardo's misconception that a rising organic composition of capitals causes a tendency for the rate of profit to decline.[1] That subtopic is properly regarded as an aspect of the supercession of capitalist by socialist accumulation, and thus it seems that we are backing into the notion of capitalist accumulation, historically and otherwise. Yet, as Marx, Luxemburg, and we have argued before, that is exactly the way—the only way—in which capitalist accumulation can be understood.

So that we may properly situate our present undertaking with respect to that from which we have abstracted our immediate subject, we shall recast some of the leading methodological points already made. In particular, since we have previously circumscribed the Hegelian and Kantian worldviews with the Marxian dialectic, we are now at liberty to point out certain of the enduring positive contributions of Kant's work without leading the reader into methodological blunders of the sort that can arise from Kant. Thus we are continuing an undertaking we began in Chapter 7. This retrospective view facilitates a synoptic historical perspective on the emergence of Marx's notion of extended reproduction within the evolutionary progress of German critical philosophy as a whole, founded and defined by Kant. While the fashion in which we are proceeding may seem almost a digression favoring the philosophical specialist, there is no digression of any sort involved. The notion of a Praxis, strictly developed by Kant in *Critique of Practical Reason*, persists in its most essential features throughout Hegel's work, epitomized in his notion of labor, and is retained in a revolutionary form as the foundation of the Marxian method itself. Properly construed, this notion of Praxis subsumes extended reproduction.

THE IDEA OF A PRAXIS

The empirical ordering of the facts of economic development might suggest to some that we ought to adduce laws in the guise of mathematical functions as the principles of a political economy. As we have noted several times, that is exactly the prevailing view among non-Marxian and many nominally Marxian economists. It might appear that the so-called objective domain of political-economic facts has its own "laws of movement" for particular objective phenomena, in the same sense that "laws" are defined in Newton's *Principia* or as this notion is stressed by Euler.

That sort of approach prevails among empiricists generally. Following Hume's formulation of empiricism—at least in a bowdlerizing fashion,[2] the equation of causality in human knowledge with mental habit—the vulgar economist assumes that a mathematical or statistically significant abstraction from objective facts per se can be treated in the fashion of a law of falling bodies, for bodies presumably existing independent of the human observer's actions. That this method more or less coincides with that of Hume, to the extent that contemporary nominal philosophers are increasingly compelled to return to Hume, has special significance for our immediate inquiry with respect to the relationship of Hume's failures to Kant's achievements.

The crudest reputable instance of such empiricism is the case of the short-lived "economic miracle" of the so-called Chicago School of Milton Friedman and others during the early months of the Nixon administration. Friedman, who is by no means useless as an economic historian of sorts, represents the most wretchedly naive school of thought in theoretical economics. He and his co-thinkers, guided by obsessive belief in the wisdom and efficiency of the invisible hand, rationalized their religious belief in such a deity by extracting from statistical studies a certain rate of growth of the money supply over the long pull of successful capitalist development. Certain refinements were made in this study, of course, but none which affected the banality of the approach. Friedman and his collaborators adduced, *post hoc ergo propter hoc*,[3] that governmental "interference" in the marketplace ought to be limited as strictly as possible to maintaining the indicated optimal rate of growth of the money supply. When the Nixon administration began its reign, Friedman was the chosen high priest, the chief voice from the Delphic shrine in Chicago speaking for administration policy. This was not accidental; radical right-wing faith in the invisible hand is more or less the characteristic tendency of the social strata which were the new administration's most immediate social base.

Then came May–June 1970, a period highlighted by the sudden bankruptcy of the Penn Central Corporation. The official reputation of Friedman and his collaborators was discreetly buried under the White House lawn on the first convenient moonless night. After a discreet interval of silent mourning, the Nixon administration announced its conversion to the spirit of John Maynard Keynes and launched a "New American Revolution," which came to its inevitable end during August 1971. The prophet was different, but the general empiricist method—and the outcome of its employment—was essentially the same. The post-summer 1970 fiscal-monetary jugglery, which was hailed as capable of realizing "full growth" through a "full employment budget," shortly experienced a new encounter with the precipice of world depression, following which it was officially conceded that even an almost unlimited expansion of money supply, abetted by startling rates of deficit spending, would fail to produce the modest gains in ficitious GNP growth Nixon had projected at the beginning of 1971.

The speeches prepared for Nixon on this subject were the most literal and basic Keynesian economic theory, and thus were among those rare occasions when the publicly stated intentions of government officials correspond to their real intentions. While the shift from tight to diarrhea-like monetary policies did indeed represent an abrupt turnabout in one respect, the basic method employed had not been altered. In the final analysis, Keynes committed the same type of methodological blunder as the cruder Friedmanites. Indeed, Friedman represents the *reductio ad absurdum* of Keynes. Keynes assumed a predetermined, inhering rate of potential growth for economies at each juncture, without ever considering—in print —how such contextual potentials were determined. His point of view was purely administrative, not theoretical-economic in any significant sense of the term. This is ironically in keeping with Keynes' point of view as a central banker alienated from the productive process whose wealth he appropriates. Keynes pretends to solve the problems of depressions by ignoring their causes. His remedies are of the type we have already described, monetary expansion based on the relationship between central banks and state treasury, undertaken to realize a rate of combined turnover of surplus value and fictitious capital sufficient to provide a level of employment and production corresponding to the potential exogenously determined respecting the subject matter of his economic theories. He eliminates depressions by assuming that they ought not to occur. At least that is the profession of the Keynesians, who have insisted that since "built-in stabilizers" can realize the potential growth of an economy to a high degree of approximation, and since capitalism has no intrinsic tendency for depressions, built-in stabilizers inherently prevent depressions. It all depends, as Keynes himself was sensible enough to recognize, on Malthus' silly assumptions.[4]

A word on built-in stabilizers. It should be clear to the reader from our earlier discussion of the problem that simple monetary expansion is analogous as a remedy for depressive tendencies to that of a simple martingale in betting systems. The amount of the stake very rapidly becomes so large relative to the game as a whole that the its size alters the odds in an unfavorable way. The general way simple monetary expansion very quickly produces disastrous consequences should also be clear: it creates a "takeoff" in speculative investment at the expense of circulation of real wealth. The built-in—stabilizer tactic attempts to provide a two-sided solution to these difficulties. First, one or more general equilibrating mechanisms dampen monetary expansion rates whenever employment reaches a certain level. Employment (unemployment) rates are thus being used as a more or less efficient parameter for the full circulation of goods produced. The second approach is the intervention of government to insure that the mediating vehicle for more drastic measures of employment expansion is employment, since employment is the mediation of consumption of goods and services, in contrast to simple speculative gains. A punitively high capital-gains tax, relative to profits on production, would be an obvious built-in stabilizer for drastic rates of monetary expansion under depressed circumstances, for the same reason.

What caused both the Friedman and Keynesian schemes to fail, with at least equally drastic consequences, was that built-in stabilizers of that sort cannot work any longer, for the reason we have already given in connection with the shifting values of the Philips Curve. When the ratio of growth of fictitious accumulation (potential illiquidity) to expansion of production is at a critical stage, any monetary policy—constipative depression, manic diarrhea, or the "safe, sane" in-between approach—must lead to disaster. Different monetary policies are merely different ways of speeding at various rates toward the same inevitable result.

What also fails in such periods as this is the method employed by all empiricist economists, whether anti-Marxian or nominally Marxian. The economic constructs they have adduced from periods of relative capitalist economic stability represent correlations which appear to persist as long as the fundamental epistemological flaw in the empiricist method is not reflected empirically in any of the facts selected for investigation. At the two extremes of the boom-bust cycle, its initial "takeoff" and its culminating entry into a region of metastability, it must seem to the empiricist that he has encountered a domain of discontinuity, at which point all the laws of the universe, as he understands them, have been momentarily suspended. What is actually demonstrated so forcefully during such critical phases is the problem of Praxis.

It is by now apparent to the reader that this methodological problem is subsumed by Kant's critiques.[5] Even in the introduction to the first edition of his *Critique of Pure Reason*, Kant refers to exactly the methodological blunder typified by Keynes, Friedman, and others: "indifferentism,"[6] a synonym for English-speaking empiricism. We refer to A. J. Ayer, W. V. O. Quine, and others, and to the essential agreement of Ayer and Quine on this methodological point with Carnap and others—despite the significant subsidiary disagreements among the various such schools. The cases cited thus represent pre-Kantian philosophy, an atavism, a retrogression to the mid-eighteenth century. The key to this error, which we explored in Chapter 3, is the refusal of the majority of twentieth-century philosophers, mathematicians, and other thinkers to acknowledge the existence of the fundamental problem they failed to comprehend. They proposed to free themselves of such embarrassing evidence of their incompetence simply by denying that the problem they had failed to solve existed. This is indifferentism exactly as Kant defines it. Thus, a sufficiently devastating refutation of Friedman, Keynes, Keynesian and semi-Keynesian "Marxists," can be obtained without disturbing the more advanced texts of Hegel, Feuerbach, and Marx; Kant would suffice.

We shall therefore situate our critique of classical and neoclassical political economy within the Kantian critique's accomplishments. Our object is not merely to accomplish a broader than Marxian refutation of classical and neoclassical economic theory, but to critically situate the notion of Praxis for positive notions of extended reproduction.

The empirical ordering of the facts of economic development can do nothing more, in practice, than locate the possibility (potentiality) of extended reproduction. Here, we are rightly impinging upon Kant's distinction between speculative and practical reason.[7]

First, the abstract notion of an economy, or that which might be adduced by an objective observer "vulgarly squatting outside the universe," is the practical-ideological image for idealism, just as the element of idealism in Plato, et al., is the location of the domain of the dialectic within the *fixed* material social-reproductive practice that determines the existence of the opinionator. Thus, Feuerbach is a "materialist" relative to Kant and Hegel, exactly as he locates the creation of God and religious opinion generally as the work of man-to-man practical relationships. This distinction is located within the implications of Feuerbach's determination of self-consciousness. Despite the fixed quality of Nature and "natural relations" in Feuerbach's view, since self-consciousness is determined to be creative mentation, as the mediation of other creative mentations through actions on nature, there is for him a "frozen moment" in which he contradicts himself by necessarily implying what he otherwise tends to deny: he necessarily implies that nature is not fixed, since the mediated relationship is subjected to creative mentation!

Second, the abstract or speculative adducing of facts which is empirical knowledge in itself cannot represent the truth of what is observed, except in the sense, as Kant expresses it, of problematic judgments. So, the abstract empirical ordering of mere facts pertinent to extended reproduction cannot in itself imply a definite, actualized tendency for extended reproduction. In Kantian terms, the notion of extended reproduction is the body of practical reason, which is in turn the predicate of the notion of freedom (i.e., negentropy). Since freedom cannot be located in the ordinary notions of causality pertaining to sense phenomena per se, no mathematically arranged array of economic facts could actually predetermine any specific rate of extended reproduction as a lawful quality of the empirical subject matter *in itself*. Or: Kant's fundamental antinomy.[8]

It is this notion of Praxis that is to be immediately elaborated, and then placed in its proper context within the Marxian philosophical world-outlook.

From the standpoint of empirical knowledge per se, the philosophical notion of causality is that associated with simple reproduction—simple mechanism. The "element of freedom" in nature is manifest for human knowledge only, as Kant insists, as the deliberative aspect of human practice when that practice is critically examined as a whole![9] This is the aspect of Kant's work that Hegel "turned upon its head"; it is the core of the Kantian dialectic (Kant's actual dialectic), and, as Kant himself insists, the key to everything else in his last two decades of literary productivity.[10]

This Kantian discovery of "pure practical reason" or Praxis (for its universal implications) constitutes the establishment of the notion of Praxis for critical philosophy as a whole, including the sense of that term as Hegel employed its notion in his conception of labor, and as the notion occurs in Marx's "Theses on Feuerbach." Marx fundamentally alters the holistic context within which he locates the term, but thus "merely" redefines the material content of Praxis as a phenomenon.[11]

Praxis signifies nothing less than an entirety (universality) of human practice. Kant properly insists that practical reason cannot be located in the notion of pleasure or desire associated with the actualization of a particular object or class of objects.[12] He thus adduces the a priori content for practical reason as "pure practical reason," since he locates substantiality in the thing-in-itself and the Understanding.[13] Where he dialectically demonstrates the existence of necessary principles governing particular objects, he necessarily attributes to those principles the efficient nature of pure reason (Logos) in the same broad sense as does Hegel (ergo realism = idealism). The difference between Kant and Hegel on this point is that Hegel demands the immediate equivalence of the extended Logos and the matter-motion process, regards the thing as determinate (and thus not unknowable), and shifts the dividing-line of the alienation of Logos from matter from Kant's thing-in-itself to the alienation (unintentionally, implicitly) of Logos-form from matter-motion as such.[14] In respect to practical reason or Praxis, the basis for Kant's view is systematically that of Hegel's dialectic on this point, as we shall demonstrate.

Kant articulates explicitly, and repeatedly, what amounts to the painstaking opposition of his notion of Praxis to the pragmatical-empiricist sophistries of Sidney Hook's bowdlerization of Korsch,[15] or the even more trivial dictionary nominalism of the "Praxisite" or "new working-class" cults of the late U.S. New Left.[16] Marx in turn retains Kant's essential notion on this point in his own use of the term. Marx locates Praxis in the bringing-into-being of a *universal* class as a class-for-itself (Being-in-and-for-itself); consequently the practice of bringing such a class-for-itself into being represents, for Marx, a universalizing practice.[17] The significance of Kant's notion becomes clearer, indeed, once we have Marx's solution to the problem located by Kant. In other words, Marx, by showing how an actually existent universal functions (through a worldwide interdependent division of labor), fully justifies Kant's sensibility of the need to locate practical reason uniquely in the universal. To use the term "Praxis" as a fancy synonym for "practice" in the cracker-barrel sense is an ignorant schoolboy's prank.

Let us now consider the dialectical notion within Kant's conception of Praxis.

Hegel locates the notions of "substance" and "mind" by the following types of pedagogical aphorisms. In *Science of Logic*, he compares the concept of a grammar held by a person who speaks only his own native language with that of a person who speaks several languages.[18] In the introduction to *Phenomenology*, rhythm is described as the self-movement "in between" and "among" successive "elements" of meter.[19] Reality is the substance which is the self-movement subsuming and determining the particularity of the object itself. This form of the dialectical (or polemical)[20] method was established in its essential features by Heraclitus, whose views Hegel incorporates in their entirety into his *Science of Logic*.[21] Indeed, all serious philosophers of the modern era[22] have made this "speculative" principle the kernel of their creative thought. Only in part is this empirical "social fact" of philosophy a reflection of their mere literacy in Plato, Aristotle, and such others.[23]

To situate the Kantian dialectic—to demonstrate that the notion of Praxis is dialectical—it is somewhat more than useful to consider the Heraclitan-Hegelian notion of dialectic in conjunction with formal logic. It is sufficient that we do not thereby attempt to degrade dialectical method into the mysticism of a logic.

At this point we must interpolate an important observation on the title and form of Hegel's *Science of Logic*. Various dull and plodding readers of this work have attempted to see in it a "new logic," correcting fallacies in the old, and so on. This was absolutely not Hegel's intent; however, it is not difficult to account for the common blunder, especially if one is acquainted with the authors of such "appreciations" of Hegel's "logic."

As we have said, creative mentation is not only susceptible to being made conscious, but is deliberative in the sense that the creative thinker experiences a definite succession of mental states in arriving at a creative judgment. From the external evidence provided by Descartes' meditations, critical features of Spinoza's writing, and Hegel's writings, it is evident that these individuals were creative not only in the ordinary sense of having synthesized conceptions which did not pre-exist; they attained deliberate control of their processes of creative mentation, and made them significantly conscious. There are certain kinds of externalities that can occur in the writings only of a person who has developed such conscious control of creative mentation. Feuerbach's self-consciousness thesis and Descartes' two cited theorems are compact examples of discoveries that could not be made by a person who had not previously made his creative processes substantially conscious. Hegel's *Phenomenology of Mind* is the most detailed exposition of a conscious view of those creative processes that are unconscious for most individuals. The preface and introduction to that work are sufficient evidence that this is the case.

Hegel's notion of a *Science of Logic* is the same notion that fiercely preoccupies the author. Once one has discovered that creative mentation is susceptible to being made conscious, and that its improvement can be *learned in a particular way*, several interconnected and obvious efforts ensue. Having realized that intelligence itself is not biologically determined (except with respect to the negative effects of physiological dysfunctions and traumas) but learned in a certain way, even if unwittingly, one must deal with this fact. The important task is to analyze the empirical moments of the creative process, both to discover what must be done to teach intelligence per se and to elaborate the laws adduced from this examination.

Once one notes the devastating implications of the fundamental flaw in Hegel, one must recognize that, apart from the effects of that flaw upon the elaboration, *Science of Logic* is nothing but a description of the ordered character of creative thought-processes made conscious. With the one qualification we have just noted, *Science of Logic* is a mediated representation of Hegel's conscious mind, a conscious mind that encompasses self-consciousness of its creative processes and a large degree of deliberate control over those processes. There is an element of the same thing, although less striking, in Kant's writings from the *Critique of Pure Reason* onward.

The flaw in Hegel we have already cited is also properly situated here, where its relevant implications for the point at hand may be considered. Hegel explicitly emphasizes the one discovery—a critical discovery—he rejected: the notion that the physical laws of the universe (as he applied Heraclitus to Lagrange and others) could be evolving. He prominently underlines this point in discussion of the "organic" and in his *Philosophy of Nature*.

Let us consider this point and one we have already made to locate the implications of Hegel's attitude toward it, and its implications for the notion of his *Science of Logic*.

The most useful means for examining this question within the terms of so-called physical science is the field of astronomy. Since much of the history of the stellar universe is laid out before us as current data, provided we have appropriately adduced data from observations, employed the proper instruments, and so forth, we should look for the following sort of difficulty. Considering regions of space corresponding to grossly different periods (perhaps a few billion years might be necessary—this is not for the author to determine), one would seek to discover evidence of a variation in the speed of light from that of our immediate section of relatively contemporary "space," or something equally fundamental, and an associated qualitative difference in other phenomena such that that different sections of space would seem to obey slightly different fundamental physical laws. However, having found several such different sets of fundamental physical laws operating in observed spaces, it would also be discovered that these different sets of laws were connected by an underlying coherence. See our case for social reproduction.

This illustrates the kind of discovery whose possibility Hegel rejected. (It is to be emphasized that the author is not specifying astronomy. This is merely an illustration of one way in which the necessary character of our universe as a whole might be shown to be subject to evolving law.)

The illustration should arouse in the student a certain amount of compassion for Hegel's rejection of the notion of changing fundamental physical laws. However deep and broad such compassion, however, Hegel's rejection of such a notion inevitably created a fundamental epistemological dualism in his whole view. If the ontological quality of creative mentation is that of changing fundamental laws, and if nature for man has perfected fundamental laws, then, using P for mind and N for nature, the sequence $P_1 \rightarrow N \rightarrow P_2$ is not epistemologically coherent. P and N must belong to different unique (mutually exclusive) universes. This is not the same difficulty as in the case of Kant's "thing-in-itself." Hegel's nature is a dialectical universe of determinate objects, in which objects correspond to the relatively "static" determinate moments of creative mentation. Thus, the object of nature now corresponds to something that seems almost to be mappable into the "space" of the lowest determinate order of mentation. But Hegel's effort to solve the problem of material causality is obviously a chimera, an obsessive blindness to the problem of epistemological coherence. What we have is a certain kind of administrative relationship between the Logos and determinate nature as its subject. If ones does not probe its epistemological flaws too exactly, it seems to work. However, thus locating Praxis or labor in this purely administrative relationship to nature, the elaboration of such a dualistic view in the *Science of Logic*, the germ of that blunder already located in the *Phenomenology*, we have already implied in *Science of Logic* the *Philosophy of Right*.

This means that Hegel's *Logic*, although subsumed by his self-consciousness of his own creative processes, represents those processes in a somewhat bowdlerized form, a flaw underlined most sharply in his treatment of the problem of the categories.

The only relationship between Hegel's *Science of Logic* and a formal logic is that Hegel's logic explains what the basis or origin of mere formal logics is. That is the point of the categories. Hegel is describing more or less accurately what Köhler, for example, was exploring. Hegel is describing cognition from the *inside;* Köhler is merely demonstrating the conditions for detecting and provoking it externally. Hegel is describing the process by which determinate images are created. Logic, in absolute contrast to Hegel's *Science of Logic*, is the attempt to develop plausible edifying descriptions of the apparent rules for relationships among such images. Logic is therefore a metaphysics in the bad sense of the term. Formal logic attempts to explain, synchronically, processes that have been determined historically.

For logic as such, the primary element is the reductionist's static discrete image. For Hegel's *Science of Logic*, the primary substance is the process of creative mentation. Thus, the attempt to represent Hegel as restructuring formal logic with "improved rules" is a pathetic sophomorism.

Let us return to the critique of formal logics as such. For this purpose, we shall interpret Kant's notion from the standpoint offered by Descartes, first stating the paradox to which Descartes' *cogito ergo sum* and notion of perfection (the two theorems) provide a solution.

Consider the demonstration that the common postulate, the so-called "law of identity," is a paralogism in the Kantian sense.[24] $A = A$ in the sense of a simple identity is indeed a vicious paralogism. Such a statement, $A = A$ is at best meaningless (an empty construct), and at worst viciously wrong. This is necessary and demonstrable from the standpoint of formal logic itself, as Cantor, Russell, and Gödel, among others, have variously shown. For $A = A$ to be a premise (as in the syllogism), A must be at the same time subject and predicate. But, A-subject = A-predicate can only be a paralogical identity, just as a man can be, only in formal logic, his own son.

Where statements of the form $A = A$ are competently employed, one must necessarily mean that there exist two nonidentical objects, one as subject and the other as predicate or both equivalent as predicates of the same common subject. These objects cannot be identical, or the statement is so trivial as to be an empty construct. The equivalence cannot be a simple ontological equivalence; it must signify a statement (such as father = son) expressing some necessary connection of subject and predicate in some ordered way. For example, the process of reproduction.

Employing one of Hegel's illustrations of this point, let A-subject be acorn and A-predicate be oak.[25] To dispel the problem that might seem to be implied, we must make it clear that the equivalence A-subject = acorn is not an identity in the formal-logical sense. It is a statement: "This *is* the *name* of the *thing*," or "This *is* (=) the *name* (A-subject) of the *thing* (A-predicate)." Thus, $A = A$: "Yesterday's acorn is today's oak." A-subject-in-itself and A-predicate-in-itself each now represent actualized existences, but false knowledge of the content of each such existence. The true statement $A = A$ must identify the existence of the process connecting the acorn and the oak, which is the reality of the existence of each—or, the essence or nature-outside-the-particular-in-itself, which is the reality of the existence of each. Or, as statements of identity in this true-notional form approach universality of all objects (e.g., the notion of perfection), one's use of the true-notional form of identity expresses the essence that determines the existence of each predicated particularity thus subsumed.

In the modern era, this notion of dialectical inference of real existence behind the appearance (phenomena) of existences-in-themselves was first systematically elaborated by Descartes in his second theorem, his ontological proof of a (therefore) non-Fideist God.[26] This is the moment of Descartes' work explored by Spinoza, in contrast to the pseudo-Descartes represented by Descartes' mechanistic epigonoi. Among the distinctions to be made respecting Descartes' proof, we must concede that a bowdlerized version of that proof is more or less standard in survey courses in philosophy.

Descartes, to summarize again, argued that the notion of Perfection was necessary certainty of the existence of a unique Being which was universal and comprehensive: the universal Being of Perfection. This arises in this second of the two great theorems as a consequence of the first. In the first (*cogito ergo sum*), we have "I think that x_1", for which the universality of x's determines the unique, perfected being of "I think" as primary with respect to the bad infinity of x_1. In the second, x_1 is replaced by x_{1j} (1, 2, 3, . . . j . . .), in which each successive condition, x_{1j}, x_{1j+1}, . . . represents improved knowledge of x_1. One can attempt to adduce a judgment from this by bad infinity, by logical induction, or by treating the movement from x_{1j} to x_{1j+1} as the first approximation of the primary existence. (Logical induction treats x_{1j} as a primary existence). Since such a movement is not complete, and since all movements for an individual are not complete, and so on, the primary empirical datum is the universal, which is unique and, by extension, comprehensive. This Being is self-perfection of knowledge; it is nothing but cognition or creative mentation in general: Hegel's Logos.

The difficulty of comprehending Descartes' theorems is that the empirical fact which is the subject matter of the second theorem, especially, is creative mentation. Hence, comprehension of the theorems demands that the student of the *Meditations* himself be conscious of his creative processes as deliberative. We can thus immediately understand why Descartes has been so widely banalized by persons stupefied by general alienation and the further stultification of the drill-and-grill method of secondary and higher education. One need only consider the usual procedure of preparing graduate students for their doctoral comprehensive oral and written examinations to locate the causes of the virtual imbecility of so many philosophy professors and others apropos the kernel of Descartes, Spinoza, Hegel, Kant, Feuerbach, and Marx.

We are also afforded by this standpoint a useful insight into important features of religious belief. Although it must be stressed that Descartes (like Kepler) took the Inquisition into account with respect to the doctrinal theological implications of his writings, it would be extravagant to conclude that Descartes did not see himself as a religious person in some sense. It would also be extravagant, barring the discovery of the most extraordinary evidence, to suggest on the basis of Descartes' extant writings that he saw himself as doing something other than eliminating the Fideist premise for religious belief with an altogether "rational" basis, provided that we stretch the definition of "rational" to signifiy "dialectical." We may also see in the same way the significance of Spinoza's and Feuerbach's efforts to situate treatment of creative mentation within the clinical domain of a criticism of theology.

Religious feeling has its root in the empirical form of creative mentation, as we have previously treated that phenomenon. As we have said, the association of the feeling of love with religious feeling is a content of the latter, the impulse for unmediated identity of the "inner Self." Religion is absolutely correct wherever it insists that human beings have souls, in contrast to the condition of the lower beasts, and locates the soul as the real Self in opposition to the external Self (persona). To make the processes of creative mentation conscious and deliberative is to understand immediately all the secrets of religious belief. It is therefore the most natural and most scientific approach imaginable to immediately represent one's discovery of creative mentation as such in the form of a critique of religious belief. The religious feeling is the reified moment of creative mentation, and the clinical form in which the most important facts of science are most widely reflected as more or less systematic social phenomena. Descartes' dialectical method, as developed in his *Meditations,* represents a transition from religious belief to actual dialectical knowledge, and it is therefore not inappropriately an analysis of the relationship of subordination of the individual soul (creative mentation *in* the person) to the necessary, unique, universal, comprehensive Being of self-perfection.

We can thus better understand why, up to this point in history, human beings had embraced religious belief in search of a place where their humanity would be acknowledged, and can see (rightly) in such practices a necessary celebration of their distinctions from mere beasts. Nor is the notion of God the Creator as silly as stupid atheists would make it.

It is consequently not accidental but only pitiable that so many of the textbooks and classroom lectures treating Descartes (and other dialecticians) should attribute to him the practice of pulling vague nominalist notions—good, pleasure, perfection, wisdom—from the contemporary air and thus should degrade Descartes to the level of the typical stupefied sophomore. By thus characterizing Descartes as a vulgar, cracker-barrel philosopher, and making him "intelligible" to the banalized intellects of most readers and students, such writers and instructors no doubt aim to secure for themselves reputations for lucidity![27] ("I understand what he writes so clearly, not like some of those others . . ." Naturally, they omit reporting anything that is beyond the most vulgar everyday comprehension, and what cannot immediately be seen as mere "common sense" they falsify to seem nothing but common sense.) Such philosophy instructors remind us, not inappropriately, of certain Marxist-Leninists, themselves innocent of anything but the most vulgar "commonsense" powers of mentation, who propose to communicate the most advanced, sophisticated notion in all knowledge, the dictatorship of the proletariat, by the mere shouting of the phrase,[28] or by the "dialectic" of discussing baseball and statistics in shops.

In one respect, as we have noted, Spinoza went beyond Descartes. At least, he went beyond Descartes' explicit development of the second theorem, and in this respect was far ahead of Kant and, in one respect, as

Feuerbach correctly notes, beyond Hegel. Spinoza was a true hylozoic monist insofar as he elaborated his notion. For Spinoza, as for Descartes, Hegel, Feuerbach, and Marx, the empirical moment of actuality, and the *form of substance* is not the existence in the form of the discrete object, but the movement (the self-evidence of the movement displaces the self-evidence of the discrete object or sense-phenomenon as such) connecting successive states of progress of knowledge of actuality.

Kant half-admits this fact by proposing to abandon aesthetic categories (and thus, implicitly, the thing-in-itself) at the extremes of space and time. In this respect, Kant is acknowledging, as he does with respect to heteronomy, the falseness of bad infinity, and is implicitly confessing that his thing-in-itself is merely an empty construct. This is a devastating internal contradiction in Kant's constructions, underlined by his fatuous attitude toward Spinoza.

This problem does not exist for Spinoza, which does not lessen the conditional efficacy of Kant in demolishing the various forms of empiricism, including positivism. Spinoza's notion of extended being, which is the first elaboration of the notion of extended reproduction, is based on noting the obvious fallacy of prevailing rationalist notions of infinity. Is infinity something we encounter only, so to speak, at the outer extremes of space and time, or is it located in the here and now? A critical examination of Descartes' second theorem shows that it must be in the here and now: where else did we discover the existence of necessary, unique, universal, and comprehensive being? *The empirical actuality of infinity is the moment of self-perfection.* This is the notion we developed for labor power.

Kant, like Hegel after him, rejected the implications of Spinoza's hylozoic monism with respect to substance, for the reasons stated above. One has only to put Kant's and Hegel's minds inside one's own to see their agony on this point. Kant's error, which we are privileged to make obvious, was not a fool's blunder. Kant's intellect touched again and again on precisely the points to which we give the greatest emphasis. His efforts to locate necessary coherence of perfection (practical reason) and understanding in the infinite, his critique of heteronomy, even his false-positive form of negation of the negation, are all reflections of a mind which has seen through its own creative activity to recognize the inevitability of the problem to which we have referred. In fact, it would have been impossible for him to have seen, as if at a glance, the fundamental blunder of Hume, or to have begun writing the *Critique of Pure Reason*, if he had not progressed to the point of critically viewing these very problems of infinity before writing a single line. Ecce! The preface to the first edition of that *Critique!* Neither Kant nor Hegel could muster the hubris to push aside Euler, Lagrange, Leibniz, et al. and say, "No! The fundamental laws of the universe as you define them *do change!*" So Kant in one way—the thing-in-itself—attempted to save the Understanding, as he assumed the authority of Euler, Lagrange on this point, while acknowledging its "impenetrable" falsehood. Hegel, confronted with the same kind of difficulty, was willing to tear mathematics apart up to a point, after which he too bowed before the "secular authority" of Euler and Lagrange—and consequently before the "labor" of the Prussian monarch.

It is only as Feuerbach solves the Cartesian-Spinozan notion, situating Kant and the Hegelian paradox in it, that the more advanced outlook of Spinoza begins to emerge in its proper realized form. By locating the existence of God in the immediate self-perfection (creative mentation) of man as a product of the material relations of man to man, the self-subsisting positive (creative mentation) becomes implicitly coherent with a natural self-subsisting positive: mind and substance are reunited in their essential nature, and God as mind alienated from substance disappears.[29] Unfortunately, Feuerbach, less gifted in reach of knowledge than Hegel, did not even explicitly consider the problem of mathematical physics as Kant and Hegel had; nonetheless, more naively, Feuerbach declined to extend the self-subsisting positive into nature a micron beyond the material social determination of creative mentation, as we have discussed that problem above.

Once these historical perspectives on the Cartesian notion are taken into account, the notion of perfection is necessarily the Kantian (and Hegelian) notion of freedom. This notion, arising uniquely from a dialectical overview of the implications of universality for the understanding (as Kant emphasizes), paradoxically counterposed to all immediate notions of understanding in its particular, nonuniversal moments, is the notion of freedom or, in contemporary language, negentropy as we have defined it. In the *Critique of Pure Reason*, this problem is situated as the fundamental antinomy of pure reason.[30] In form, this is Hegel's distinction between being-in-and-for-itself (truth is the whole)[31] and the false consciousness of mere being-in-itself. It is also, in form, Marx's counterposition of the universal (working) class-for-itself to the false consciousness (bourgeois ideology) of the members of the proletariat organized in the form of a mere class-in-itself.[32] Or, for Kant again, the particular (less-than-universal) analytical judgment is, dialectically, in fundamental opposition to the notion necessary for a universal analytical judgment. Also for Kant, as for Hegel, this overview expresses the necessary premises for the judgment that mathematical reasoning is inherently incapable of comprehending the notion of freedom (universal negentropy) except in a negative fashion. For Kant, the universal analytical judgment coheres uniquely, in opposition to all other analytical judgments, with the synthetic *a priori* universality of true possible (potential) knowledge. Praxis is for Kant the accessible instrument for proving the truth ("this-sidedness") of "speculative reason,"[33] and the only positive basis for locating the truth of freedom in opposition to the entropic notions arising from the necessarily false consciousness inhering in particular (heteronomic) analytical judgment.

One should recognize the ruse by which Kant and Hegel attempt to avoid the evidence of creative mentation's implications for matter-motion as such. In both Kant and Hegel the ruse is employed of assuming that the laws of the physical universe are perfected, and that man's knowledge is being brought into conformity with those perfected laws by creative mentation. Kant not only declines to consider the problem of determining the essence of such laws, but insists that all such exertions are inherently paralogical. Indeed, he would be correct if one limited one's inquiry to the premises on which he proceeds. Hegel declares Kant's notion of the unknowability of the essence of such laws of physics to be itself paralogical, an empty construct. The laws of physics are for Hegel (as for Engels) perfected dialectical laws, the expression of a dialectic which has reached a certain point and fallen exhausted on its labors. For Hegel the form of the dialectic for the Logos is the form by which the physical universe has perfected itself (note the sly concession to changing physical laws). It is as though the dialectic, having enervated itself in forming heavier substance, abandoned hard labor for the sedentary occupation of its powers and skills in fashioning lighter materials (of thought). The ruse employed by Kant and Hegel in different ways is to consider creative mentation as merely creating for thought and practice the progress of knowledge (and consequent human social practice) toward the completed perfection of underlying physical laws. In that sense, both Kant and Hegel are utopians. Kant recognizes creative mentation only as the element of freedom altering the daily routine of the Understanding. Hegel progresses qualitatively beyond Kant in making creative mentation the necessary constant basis for the immediate constituents of the Understanding, and making it the new form of consciousness to replace (supercede) Kantian Understanding. Yet these fundamental distinctions are bounded by the assumed limits of perfection of the physical laws of the universe.

With Feuerbach, the hylozoic principle is freed from Hegel's fixed universal laws and fixed categories, although in a stillborn guise. Even stillborn, however, this creation is a first attempt at real life, and possesses all the identifying features of real life (as Marx recognized and Engels did not). With Marx, for the first time, the hylozoic principle is born as a living, bawling infant of extraordinary durability.

Let us return to Kant. How is that which is contrary to all particular existence for perception to be objectively demonstrated? That is the problem of universalizing practice (Praxis). The proof has been restated for various notions of universality, not only by Kant, Hegel, Feuerbach, and Marx, but by Durkheim. Durkheim's major work, despite the solidarity with the philistine intellect that blights his great effort, is summed up in its *tour de force*, its Feuerbachian refutation of the Kantian aesthetic categories.[34] Freud's perception of psychophysical parallelism[35] is the same general sort of accomplishment, though of a lesser order than Durkheim's. Freud's notion coheres (even though it merely coheres) with the fundamental proof of hylozoic monism.

The solution is implied by restating the notion of perfection: "How is the objectivity (this-sidedness) of new knowledge expressing freedom from mathematical-type natural law to be objectively demonstrated?" The expression of freedom (the noetic process of creating knowledge) in the active form of the will—the will as the cause of occurrences—is a demonstration of the possibility of such freedom *in* nature, and consequently of the existence of the principle of freedom *within* natural law as it must be properly conceived.[36] If mathematics, by reason of its axiomatic, pathetic premises, cannot comprehend such forms of law, any representation of fundamental physical laws susceptible of direct comprehensive mathematical representation is false.

Kant expresses his idealism (realism) by distinguishing true natural law, which for him pertains to things-in-themselves, from natural law for the Understanding, which represents the conditional truth as it must appear to him from the mere phenomena of sensuous understanding. The student should compare Hegel on this issue of truth. He will see that the problem of truth does not exist for Hegel in the form of which it is represented by formalists and others, since self-consciousness of being-in-and-for itself is truth, which need not be distinguished from anything but false consciousness. Hegel, in short, destroys the Kantian form of the dualism of knowledge, although he himself fails to actualize the unity of Logos and matter-motion process.[37] On the stated grounds, Kant is properly emphatic in denouncing empiricism as both false knowledge and the basis for the self-degradation of man wherever, he warns, empiricism is employed to determine the proper lawful order of society.[38] (Those, notably nominal Marxists, who assert that Kant is the godfather of empiricism are therefore cheerful and sometimes manic frauds.) Positively, the world as it must necessarily appear to us from the standpoint of the will acting for freedom (a world thus necessarily determining the type of natural law which is possible for man) transforms the notion that free will = freedom from one of pure undetermined spontaneity into one of freedom as expressing the true lawful necessity of the universe. Or, in more modern language, the order of nature, as we have been compelled to adduce it from the power of active *new* knowledge to transform the world in practice, is simultaneously an expression and delimitation of the possible freedom of the sane mind and of the actual underlying laws of the material universe itself.

Thus, the history (including prehistory) of man's mode of existence as evolving from one culture to a higher culture, although it is not a unilinear history of society, does express a necessarily unilinear ordering of human development. When we locate the empirical actuality of human existence by this approach, locating self-perfection as the actual empirical phenomenon, we have adduced the empirical principle of freedom. If we shift our attention from specific technologies as such to the succession of technologies, according to the form of Descartes' second theorem, noting the succession—the movement of succession—as the empirical datum, the primary phenomenon, we are beginning to adduce the "boundedness" of freedom in the form in which this boundedness actually exists. The necessary form of the process of evolution of technology, for example—the process being the primary datum—expresses necessity. Then, freedom (as existent) and necessity (as its self-bounding) describe the fundamental law of the universe (by hylozoic implication).

Kant's *Critique of Practical Reason*, the concept of a universalizing Praxis, develops this notion, which is of permanent value for science. Freeing the notion from its Kantian and Hegelian deformations, it is as follows. In practice, knowledge is constantly distinguished into two moments which, taken in themselves, are irreconcilable notions of the order of nature. The first moment, which critical philosophy recognizes as mere Understanding, reflects the order of nature as adduced with the aid of existing concepts-in-themselves, representing in practice the notion of a fixed body of human knowledge. In the second moment, the noetic element of consciousness is producing new conceptions which, expressed contrary to existing concepts-in-themselves for practice on the order of nature, thus demonstrate the this-sidedness of such new conceptions. This must be true, since the resulting mastery of nature in new qualities expresses the appropriateness of such ideas for the deeper order of nature behind that for the preceding moment of fixed Understanding. The successive ordering of such moments demonstrates that the process of creating new such knowledge is appropriate to the underlying order of nature. It demonstrates that the underlying laws of nature indeed correspond to those processes of cognition by which new knowledge is being appropriately created, rather than to laws in the form prescribed for the fixed Understanding. It is therefore an absolute, pathetic paralogism to imagine that any form of natural law—natural law as it could occur for any fixed form of Understanding—could be actual natural law. (Yet, recognizing that implication, Kant and Hegel withdrew from its fuller implications, and assumed fixed forms of natural law.)

Kant himself is unquestionably sensible of the implicit hylozoic monism which he pursues up to a certain point. He distinguishes between the "instinctual knowledge of animals," which know nature only in an empiricist fashion, and the reason of man, in which the noetic, concept-creating process leads through the will (practical reason) as the cause of qualitative changes in the order of nature for the mere understanding.[39] (If this implies that empiricists are animals in a certain sense, we defend Kant's and our own right to suggest that.) Hegel, of course, made the same point about the knowledge of animals as distinct from man's. It is not necessary to be a rock to be a competent geologist, a cow to be a competent veterinarian, nor a psychotic to be a competent psychiatrist.

To review the changed implications of the notion of Praxis for Marx, the following will suffice here. Feuerbach, by locating the creation of God in the practical relationship of man-to-man, obviously transferred the issues of perfection, good, imperatives, and the like from the domain of speculative (alienated) reason into the realm of what Feuerbach terms species-practice. This was not absolutely out of keeping with Hegel, who verged in the same direction, but represents a counterposing of Hegel's best side and his regressive side. For Feuerbach, the practical, universal content of the categorical imperative is man's material basis for existence, and for "perfecting" man's capacity consciously to change the order of his existence in this way. This shift to the material basis and content of human existence frees dialectics from the negation of the negation and establishes the self-subsisting positive[40] in Spinoza's sense of extended being. It also replaces the categorical imperative with the Spinozan world-view, but on the more advanced basis made possible by Hegel's work following Kant.[41] The fallacy of Feuerbach's conception is efficiently located by Marx in the first of his "Theses on Feuerbach." Feuerbach, in retaining the implications of some of the attic rubbish of Kant's thing-in-itself —the discrete particle is a necessary assumption if one assumes the fixed understanding of matter-motion—could not realize a true hylozoic monism, even though that aim is immanent in his notion of the determination of self-consciousness. Only if the notion of freedom, as the self-subsisting–positive principle, were extended further than Feuerbach has the hubris to extend it, from the form of the evolutionary reproduction of self-consciousness into negentropy as the content (essence) of a universal matter-motion process, could the old Kantian rubbish be kept from invalidating the remainder of Feuerbach's seminal achievements.[42] Thus, conscious of the proper notion of Kant's discovery of Praxis, Marx directly counterposes this notion, within the context of hylozoic monism, as the explicit solution to the systematic error of Feuerbach.[43]

The immediate application of Praxis to political economy ought to proceed without too much more detailed exposition. Since political economy expresses the mode of man's deliberative determination of the material means of his existence (the active, causal will for man's productive and other actions upon nature), the question of extended reproduction as the objective realization and conceptualization of freedom (negentropy) is initially a question of human knowledge, the noetic element in the production of consciousness (universal labor as potential). In contrast, simple reproduction—the viewpoint expressing only existent objects and modes of production (the fallacy of induction)—thus represents the direct opposite of the reality which concerns us, and expresses the viewpoint of the alienated, fixed Understanding, false consciousness, and ideology. For this reason, the question of political economy must first be approached from its subjective side, from the standpoint of critical philosophy's uncompromising rejection of English philosophical imbecility (indifferentism, Humean skepticism, empiricism). Only then can we establish the premises to determine what is objective for actual nature.

This means that the notion of extended reproduction cannot be premised on conceptions of value associated with simple desires, adduced from heteronomous particular desires[44] such as notions of happiness, pleasure, and the like. It can be conceptualized only as an active determination of the human will, consciously altering the order of nature in a fashion contrary to that knowable from the standpoint of simple desires, and contrary to what ordinary workers believe are their self-interested objective goals, as long as they are subject to the class-in-itself determination of their consciousness and its desires by means of atomization into individual or small-group "self-interest" forms. (The idea of local workers' control is thus in fundamental opposition not only to Marx but to the entirety of critical philosophy. The philosophical and social origins of notions of socialist local control and anarchosyndicalism are formally British empiricism and its continental, North American, and other cousins. The notion of local control is thus a specific product of fundamentally anti-Marxian bourgeois ideology.) The existence of deliberate extended reproduction requires the existence of a universalizing class,[45] a being-in-and-for-itself, which proceeds from knowledge—that is, a corresponding economic program, a form of holistic development of the productive forces which corresponds to the dialectical self-perfection of labor power throughout the working class as a self-conscious, integrated whole. A false or approximate form of extended reproduction, more or less identical to the false truth of extended reproduction expressed by negation-of-the-negation determination of a categorical imperative, exists within capitalist accumulation. The capitalist class, through the general rate of profit of capitalist accumulations as a whole and through the growing worldwide division of labor as the basis for capitalist accumulation, becomes a universalizing class, whose knowledge and point of view indeed represent truth even in opposition to that of the small group of workers! Capitalist accumulation, through the generalized rate of profit, reduces all objects to a universalized form of false being-in-and-for-itself, the generalized commodity-form for capitalist accumulation in general. Thus, the rate of profit is a universalizing principle, although falsely positive, which actualizes extended reproduction, despite the contrary (heteronomic) moments of the individual capitalist or groups of capitalists. The universals are private property forms which reduce all objects of nature to their universal form for the mode of human existence (capitalist existence), labor to wage-labor (the false-positive form of labor power), and even new technology itself (universal labor) to a commodity form of this universalizing character and content.

It is necessary only to interpolate the basis for the historic correctness of the aspirations of anticapitalist labor to make this point quite clear. We have already emphasized that the development of labor power is necessary for extended reproduction, and that the contradictions of capitalism, which tend to abort both the development and realization of labor power through superexploitation and unemployment ("reserve army of misery"), thus create blocks to extended reproduction. Whenever the aspirations of workers for higher wages and leisure conditions are directed toward the appropriation of production or capital for extended reproduction to meet these needs, the working class is expressing its historic impulse. Thus, to the extent that workers propose to struggle for control of the "undiminished proceeds of labor" of the local plant, as craft unionists and extremely parochialist trade-unionists generally do, the workers are reactionary relative to their capitalist employer, who is realizing surplus product for extended reproduction. Whenever, as we have repeatedly noted, workers base their struggles against employers on alliances between the employed and unemployed, the historic thrust of the working class toward becoming a class-for-itself is expressed. (There is, of course, the intermediate condition in which localist trade-union struggles against unemployment—layoffs—and reduced wages and leisure, and the like, express the general interest of the class in extended reproduction, despite the false consciousness of the workers involved in these struggles.)

This point becomes the source of a major terminological difficulty for the usual reader of *Capital*. Marx seems to employ the term "objective" to describe phenomena that appear to the reader better termed "subjective"— for example, the capitalist form of social-productive relations. We have previously referred to this problem in a preliminary way, and must now settle the matter without having considered the special problems of the capitalist monetary system.

Objective value is determined in capitalist accumulation in general as the particularate (mediating) expression for the capitalists' rate of profit. Use value is similarly determined as *specific* use value, according to what material existence under capitalism determines at a given moment to be material needs. The objective reality, for capitalist society and its members, of productive and unproductive labor is determined not by the natural reality of the productive forces as such; nor is objective reality determined as if the actualization of the conditions of life were determined by rational comprehension of the underlying laws of the productive forces of extended reproduction. In place of the self-subsisting positive principle of socialist extended reproduction, capitalism supplies the universal principle of self-expanding capital as a whole. Since the rate of profit is the rate at which potential extended reproduction can occur relative to mere simple reproduction, capitalism thus approximates a "true universality." Since, furthermore, this unique material basis for human existence under capitalism determines what is and is not realized, capitalist accumulation is the objective determination of life. The only needs that exist under capitalism (barring the exceptions and contradictions noted) are those determined by and for capitalism. Thus, capitalist accumulation itself is objective, since the "subjective" movement in capitalism—capitalist accumulation—determines the causal sequence of events under capitalism. The subjective movement is thus objective in that it determines the objective form of life. It becomes subjective again only to the extent that contradictions of capitalist accumulation make it subjective—that is, not efficiently determining. Thus, the definition of productive, and nonproductive and the like, and notions of specific use value for capitalist accumulation are the objective forms under capitalism.

The "object"[46] is objective as an existence, not in itself. It is not an existence for that which is actually objective. In this respect, cracker-barrel philosophy blunders by limiting the usage of the term "objective" to the qualities of subjective perceptual intuition of the object-in-itself! It ascribes objectivity more or less exclusively to the empiricist form of particular analytical judgments, in which classes (concepts) can never be more than moments of an architectonic subject whose predicate is merely the qualities metaphysically attributed to the naive perception of objects-in-themselves! In short, the ordinary notion of objectivity is the clinical expression of imbecilic idealism.

While Marx, of course, adheres to the usage of attributing objectivity to the objective existence of empirical phenomena, the objective is located for him not in the objects-in-themselves, but in their existence. Their existence is not passive and fixed, as is the notion of them characteristic of the fixed, false-conscious understanding; but their objectivity, their existence, is the holistic determination of their existence. What exists is inseparable from that which determines its existence. The substance of the objective is not located in the object-in-itself, but in the reality of the process that determines the existence of the particular objects.

So, if Marx employs the term "objective content" for the "subjectively determined" will of *capitalist* society, he must mean—and therefore demonstrate—that the particular objects associated with this objectivity exist because the seemingly subjective will is the continuing cause for their existence. The object may exist, but its existence was brought about by capitalist accumulation, and its principal existence for capitalist accumulation and for the people of capitalist society is *as a commodity* in relationship to needs determined by capitalist society. It may be admitted, even emphasized, that an identical object would have a different significance for a socialist society. Unfortunately, it does not exist in a socialist society; it exists as a capitalist commodity, and its qualities, with respect to the actions taken upon it and the consequences of its continued existence or consumption, exist only for capitalist accumulation.

This point can be illustrated in the following way. Hegel rightly ridicules the bowdlerization of Aristotelean teleology which insists that cork oak trees exist to provide corks for bottles.[47] Hegel is correct in his contempt for the philosophy he attacks, but he is factually incorrect; cork oaks happen to exist for the purpose of corking bottles (and other commodity uses). Capitalist accumulation has governed the development of cork oak plantations. It was the use of cork that determined the cultivation of cork oaks! We might, in a moment of levity, even make a case for cork oaks as being-in-and-for-itself on this account. If the corks from cork oaks failed to perform their functions for bottles, imagine the effects on the wine-drinkers! With such regrettable effects on "corked wines," cork oaks would soon cease to exist. The solution to this weighty problem is that the purpose is located not in the cork oaks but in human society, which determines their existence. Yet, before man, the emergence of the cork oak's ancestor was dictated by analogous processes within whole ecologies.

We can resituate the notions of the ecology movement within this setting. Zero Population Growth's proposals may be reactionary nonsense, and the goal of zero growth may generally represent a proposal to treat the remedy with the disease, but there are phenomena in existence that correspond to those misinterpreted by the quacks and cranks of such movements. The fact is that capitalist accumulation, by virtue of the accelerating "energy throughput" of capitalist technology and the scale and depth of capitalist production, has qualitatively altered the entirety of the earth, both as a biosphere and inorganically. Thus, what the ZG faddists are reflecting, and refusing to admit, is that every object on earth exists for capitalist accumulation.[48]

Man determines nature thus: to the extent that the alteration of the order of nature becomes the process of creating the material basis for human existence, every object of nature—even the lawful processes of nature themselves—is (under capitalist accumulation) reduced to a commodity form for human existence. For this reason nature, even prehuman nature, (e.g., petroleum deposits, evolution to species-man, the emergence of species through "inorganic" hylozoic evolution, and related phenomena) also exists today for man. The development of so-called physical science—an aspect of perfection—has made the empirical laws of nature themselves the subject of capitalist accumulation. How science itself shall be developed (who shall be educated and what funded for scientific activity) and applied is determined by capitalist accumulation. How many scientists, engineers, and others shall be trained, and how they shall be employed—or unemployed—is determined strictly by capitalist accumulation. Capitalist accumulation is in this general fashion the essence, the objective existence of every object under capitalist rule, and the objective substance with respect to which particular objects are merely existences.

Capitalist accumulation, as we have already emphasized, can be seen as subjective only to the extent that we can counterpose a different universal objectivity (that is, socialist accumulation) to it.[49] If Marx appears to be egregious—no matter how justified by reason—in locating objectivity in the seemingly subjective, we must consider the tendency of most contemporary anthropologists, sociologists, economists, and other academies on this matter. They project idiosyncrasies (that is, subjective or capitalist notions of social fact) as the objective, suprahistorical essence of all men and all objects back to the "first man" (who is, of course, Robinson Crusoe). Thus, for such academics and professionals, all nature exists only in its capitalist form; all natural relations are capitalist relations and all capitalist relations are for them natural relations.[50] Because they decline to recognize historical determination of specific objectivity for successive societies, they see as a suprahistorical factualness that which capitalist culture takes for a fact. Marx's discrimination appears egregious only because readers and commentators have a naive conception of objectivity, falsely assuming that objectivity does not vary from society to society.

It is not so difficult for the creative intellect to recognize that the entirety of man's knowledge of nature is determined by the universality of human social practice. Nor it is difficult to grasp the notion of the social determinacy of knowledge relative to the subjective moments of human knowledge. It requires only a higher order of the same creative comprehension to see that this determination is also objective: that the existence of objects for men—their objective existence, so to speak, independent of the will of particular viewers—is also determined, as cork oaks exist to produce corks for bottles.

Limiting our material references for the moment to capitalist society, the order of existence of objects in production and circulation is not an order of nature existing independently of man, but an order of nature determined by the human will. The form and content of natural objects given to our senses is essentially that of capitalist accumulation; for the order of human will is the causal sequence of events that determines the practical (efficient) existence of each object relative to others. So, juridical notions of capitalist society are abstractions of what is objective reality *in the causal sense* for capitalist existence. The notion of individual property right, which is general only as a determination of the notion of individual right in the means of production, apparently subsumes the juridical notions of wage-labor and rate of profit, which are the mediating expressions of capitalist accumulation (individual property right in the means of production) as being-in-and-for-itself (self-expanding value). These juridical notions, the apparent subjective side, are the objective laws of the order of nature under capitalism, as they efficiently determine the order of nature with respect to material existence and the conditions of material existence.

As we have emphasized, it is possible and necessary to counterpose to capitalist accumulation other universalities. An example is the notion of a natural universality implicit in the idea of a physical science. However, as we have warned, this natural universality is not accessible to the senses in a simple, direct fashion. Man knows nature—that is, the order of nature— as a universal only to the extent that he has subjected the phenomenal order of nature to qualitative transformations for higher qualities of human existence. (Otherwise, every forest animal would be a physicist.) The fact that the scientist's knowledge, in the efficient causal form of his acting will, is accomplishing changes of this sort (rather than mere rearrangements) in the order of nature is man's demonstration of freedom in nature. This aspect of science, not the business of lawful rearrangements that might be learned by an animal, is man's unique means of adducing actual universal laws of the order of nature—however imperfect our conception of particular laws may be, or how wretchedly reified our understanding of what we have adduced.

It is a pathetic folly to argue that man's knowledge of the order of nature represents the aggregation of results of particular experiments. The secret of successful experiments (as the null hypothesis of experimental design ought to warn anyone in the field) is located in hypothesis, not in the experiment as such. One should focus one's attention on the process by which individual scientists or teams advance science experimentally, and chance wanderers into laboratories do not. In part, the point is obvious. The hypothesis for the successful or otherwise useful experiment—one learns as much from a well-aimed failure to demonstrate an hypothesis as from a success—obviously reflects the hypothesizer's assimilation of the cumulative knowledge of society. Thus, we have demanded that scientists be educated, but have exercised more wisdom in the demand than the execution. This state of affairs has some less obvious but more powerful implications. If we acknowledge that the principal content of scientific knowledge, even—especially—experimental knowledge, is hypothesis, then the evolution of human practice is what is reflected both in the education of the scientist and in his hypotheses based on such specific cognitive development. What, then, is the history of scientific practice but the successive development of scientific knowledge? Back to Descartes' second theorem! It is falsely assumed generally that it is the learning aspect of education that develops scientific skills. On the contrary, it is the limited, often unwitting, exercise of cognitive processes apropos the progress of science which occurs in the course of learning that molds the scientist's cognitive powers. That is the source of hypothesis and the actual content of the scientist's knowledge.

The point is sharpened by comparing the alternative view. The banal view, reflected in the ugly business of doctoral comprehensive examinations, is that scientific knowledge is a mass of learned procedures. Fortunately, scientific practice slyly circumvents this prescription; the doctoral student often develops actual cognitive powers despite the massive brain damage he suffers as a result of academic drill and grill, and sado-masochistic instructor-student relations. If scientific knowledge were a matter of learning or mathematical rigor, not a micron of scientific progress would have occurred in the past four centuries. The only value of mathematical formalism is that the requirement of consistency is a phase (the second phase of cognition) in the orderly assembly of materials for cognition. It is at this stage that the scientific worker eliminates obviously inconsistent features, and may also wilfully violate consistency in order to make creative advances. Mathematical formalism expresses the standpoint of the ordinary Understanding, which is the reified totality of formalized cognition up to that point. If we treat Understanding as the second stage in the approach to cognition, and thus as the slave of cognition, no problem is caused by the use of this indispensable tool. It is when the tool becomes the master that scientists become slaves of things and lose their creative powers.

Self-conscious scientific knowledge of the true universality of the order of nature depends upon man's prior comprehension of his evolutionary social existence as the primary universality. It is the negentropy of human social existence, with respect to successive qualities of society-for-itself, that demonstrates and determines the possibility of negentropy in knowledge. Since this practical demonstration involves altering the order of nature to produce the higher order of human existence through the material conditions of that existence, the demonstration of negentropy for knowledge in the universality of human practice upon nature is the sole possible basis for self-conscious scientific knowledge of the order of nature. Furthermore, the quality of human knowledge is necessarily the quality of the fundamental laws of the universe. A lesser corollary is the pathetic absurdity of the notion that science could prove knowledge of the order of nature experimentally contrary to this.

This is admittedly contrary to the consensus of academic opinion, but the predominant opinion depends upon assumptions which could be valid only if those who hold such opinions themselves did not exist. Or, to pursue Marx's argument to corollary effect, the holder of such opinions must be "vulgarly squatting outside our universe," and therefore must not exist in our universe. Otherwise, the argument for such opinion is itself a pathetic fallacy, a delusion.

In earlier chapters we developed the point that the subjectivity of capitalism can be known only from the standpoint of another social universality, for example, socialist accumulation. We adduced this notion from consideration of self-movement, and specifically from the notion of capitalism as the movement from feudalism to socialism. This examination, locating three distinct forms of society as predicates of social evolution, determines a subject: anthropology in general. At the same time, the necessary coherence of the three successive forms sufficiently identifies a principle of development (extended reproduction) which is peculiar to none of the the three societies but existent in all in the form of special laws. From this dialectical standpoint, each objective mode of existence (feudalism, capitalism, and socialism) is relatively (specifically) subjective only because the objective vantage-point of the underlying principles permits such a distinction. A similar effect occurs as we contrast the specific nature of one society with that of its successor. The objective is that which determines the material basis for the existence of the observer. This basis can only be the specific basis of the society of the observer or the underlying self-movement determining a succession of societies, including that of the observer. The subjective is the "objective-for-another" reduced to that which is grasped by *me* from a different basis.

This is in no sense relativism in knowledge. "Subjective" can mean nonmaterial only from the vantage-point of idealism of the worst sort, the kind of vulgar idealism that alienates self-development from its location as the substance of the objective world into an external principle of determination separate from the world on which it wilfully acts. To this effect, Kant was correct, after mistakenly dividing the noninfinite world into two parts, in recognizing that the intelligent form of Being (negentropy in knowledge) is the real Being, relative to which other Being is mere appearance leading toward false judgments of any universality. Subjectivity is that which distinguishes another mind from one's own or one's own from that of animals. Subjectivity is the determinate, particular form of universality peculiar to a moment of the hylozoic process. At the same time that it is subjective by reason of its particularity, it is objective for the extent of the moment in which its rule is determining.

Kant were properly corrected if his notion of autonomy of reason (true objectivity) is equated, as he occasionally demands, with being-in-and-for-itself, and if heteronomy, the false notion of self-interest peculiar to alienated individuals and "nationalities," is equated with the false consciousness of being-in-itself.[51] The same applies to the objectivity of the (subjective) political class-for-itself, in contrast to the subjectivity, false sense of self-interest, of the mere (objective) class-in-itself: racial groupings, national groupings, etc., within the *potential* political working class as a whole.

However, if socialist accumulation may be distinguished as subjective *from the standpoint of capitalist society*, the subjectivity of socialist accumulation is absolutely (objectively) distinguished in quality from that of capitalism, feudalism, Hellenism, oriental despotism, and so on. Capitalism does not represent a self-conscious universality, nor does feudalism; socialist accumulation (as distinct from forms of the dictatorship of the proletariat, such as the Soviet Union today) is and demands such a self-conscious universal knowledge of actual extended reproduction—of actualized negentropy through extension of the means of production. We shall return to this point shortly.

This distinction is implicit in the necessity of religious belief (whether theistic or logical-positivist) under capitalism. The need to postulate a perfect being is sufficient evidence that in capitalist society even the ruling class is not self-consciously (and, therefore, not objectively) a universal class: it does not know the historic principle of its existence as self-conscious Praxis. Capitalist accumulation, relative to the consciousness even of capitalists, is an anarchical form, which Kant would properly term a society based on heteronomic notions of self-interest.[52] It operates on the universal sensuous principle of private property in the means of production, which is its only notion of understanding. All other capitalist notions-in-particular are to it merely elaborations of that general notion of property—heteronomic property-interest as the location of objective self-interest. That is, greed.

Private property in the means of production is itself an absolute denial of the existence of the universal. It asserts that nature can be alienated from itself, such that each part is subject to a different intelligible order (heteronomic practical reason) than all others. It assumes that a coherent universe can be made up of autonomous but consistent parts, each acting under the direction of autonomously heteronomic wills! (God, as the invisible hand of the Chicago cathedral, leers at such conceits.) This point is exemplified by the chemical firm that pollutes a stream and does not account for this degradation of nature as a cost to the firm. Capitalism is intrinsically opposed to any scientific notion of universality. The universality of capitalist accumulation exists despite the will of the capitalists, contrary to their consciousness and their wills.

This irony is elaborated, and elaborates itself, in the following notable features. From the notion of private property in the means of production is derived the simple notion of private property. Not the reverse; private property in the means of production is not a special case of "each man's right to hold his own private property," but the reverse. In societies in which property in the means of production does not exist, there can be no property-form; there are only the individual's rights, as social rights, through his commune. Private property in the means of production means individual heteronomic possession, in opposition to the remainder of society, of some part of the causal chain of all production upon which all existence depends. Private property in the means of production requires that owners deny to nonowners the right to exist in a natural way. This reduces all objects, including one's right to occupy any part of nature (land), to private property, as it more generally reduces all objects necessary for human material existence to private property in the form of commodities. Capitalist ownership of the means of production reduces the right to existence itself to a commodity-form.

It also reduces productive labor to a commodity-form. If productive labor had access to means of production other than as the private property (wage-labor) of another (the capitalist), the notion of private property in the means of production would be an empty impractical fantasy. In this respect, the simple strike does not in itself violate the fundamental laws of capitalist property-forms; it is consistent with them, although the sit-in strike tends to violate the heteronomic prerogative of property-forms. The revolutionary strike is not a cessation of production, but the operation of the means of production for the class that strikes, thus nullifying the property-form and reducing it to an empty construct.

Into such fantastic capitalist arrangements intrudes a source of profound contradiction—the self-subsisting positive, reality. The fundamental, universalizing aspect of capitalism is not the juridical universality of private property, but the rate of profit. It is the rate of profit (that is, capitalist accumulation as distinct from capitalist property-in-itself) that is the positive, active expression of the capitalist social form of the human will. It is the rate of profit, even as a vulgar maxim spouted by the most boorish capitalist and his lackies, that expresses capitalist freedom, the capitalist form of negentropy, and thus the universal for capitalism. *It is the rate of profit that determines which property-forms shall exist and which expire.* The individual capitalist firm does not determine its rate of profit, since it cannot determine the price at which its production can be realized, nor the prices of wage-labor, materials, and the like. The individual capitalist is a beast whose existence is determined, who tends to survive if he behaves in a certain manner, but who is ignorant of the reasons why his actions succeed or fail. He is unconscious of extended reproduction in general; ergo, extended reproduction and its effects are for him a mysterious thing, an Invisible Hand. This irony makes the rate of profit the perverse expression of the universal (social) within the antihuman, bestial, anarchist contingencies of capitalist morality.[53] The rate of profit is the alienated disguise (false consciousness) of a universal, an economic program of extended reproduction within capitalist accumulation. It is only on this premise and in this way that capitalist accumulation (as distinct from capitalist notions of property-form) represents a universality of objective relations within capitalist existence.

This process can be heuristically summarized, as both Kant and Hegel demonstrate, as the positive achieved by negation of the negation. Kant argues that the universal negates the evil sensual falseness of individual notions of self-interest, and that the negation of this result, as opposition to falseness, becomes the positive notion of morality. Or, more rigorously, the universal, mediated through the actions of the many on the individual, negates particularities corresponding to the moments of the will (as judgments of self-interest) corresponding to negated actualizations. This negating process leaves a residue of moments of the will which society has not negated. By counterposing these non-negated moments to the negated moments, the negation of the negation thus effected approximates that which is positive for society. Thus, the positive notion of autonomy is achieved approximately to the extent to which the many, in cumulatively negating the individual's impulses, approximates the universal. Thus, the universal negates the falseness of heteronomy. It could be shown that this notion of Kant's is itself a determinate reification of actuality: capitalist ideology.[54] Hegel, who clearly sees through the ruse-likeness of Kant's negation, nonetheless falls into a negation of the negation on a different basis but to the same general effect, as both Feuerbach and Marx noted during the early 1840s. The *reductio ad absurdum* of negation of the negation is Darwinian notions of evolution, which locate the universal through the immediate utilitarian negation of evil (inappropriate) sensuous tendencies for the individual *qua* individual. Marx's rejection of Hegel's notion on this subject is therefore systematically developed as his refutation of Malthus in *Theories of Surplus Value.*[55]

The negation-of-the-negation fallacy[56] to the contrary, the rate of profit as a moral notion for practical capitalist reason arises not by negation but positively, as those capitalists who embody this notion in practice reproduce themselves and thus make production of commodities (the means of society's existence), through the practical reason of the rate of profit, the extended basis for the existence of society itself. The real root of the capitalist rate of profit is not the negation-of-the-negation determination of capitalist wills, but the positive outcome for the capitalist who realizes a certain minimal rate of profit. To become a capitalist, it is necessary to produce not sensuous objects but commodities. Capitalism is not the production of objects under juridical conditions of private property in the means of production, but the production of commodities. This is no mere terminological distinction. The term "commodity" implies the object existing for self-expanding value, as distinct from objects as such. This is the distinction between the cork oak grown to produce corks for bottles and the cork oak that grew before the use of corks. The two trees may be of the same species in themselves, but their existence is not of the same species. The one is produced to produce corks; the other is produced (e.g., by a gentleman farmer whose peculiar twitch demands that he have a cork oak to touch) as an object-in-itself.

Any capitalist who professed his determination to produce certain objects because they were "good objects" would quickly be handed over by his partners and family to the ministrations of a conservator. No capitalist court could be expected to deny a petition to that effect. Capitalist production, before it becomes capitalist production today, begins with a commodity as its premise—a commodity as a commodity, not an object which might become a commodity. Any person who denies this is either ignorant or, if a capitalist, legally irresponsible. (It is fortunate that certain academic economists are not capitalists; otherwise they would be the proper subjects of a rather different institution than a university. The proof of their sanity is that they do not practice what they teach.)

This determination of the form of objects is peculiar to for the consciousness of actual man within capitalist society. The reduction of necessary objects and activities (necessary for human existence under capitalism) to either commodities or coherent expressions of the commodity-form means that all those objects and activities that have practical significance for men in general exist for man in a specifically capitalist form. Their objective existence is an existence of and for capitalist accumulation (at least in the most general sense). Furthermore, the man-to-man relationships through which consciousness is produced in an individual, defining the individual in terms of his rights and privileges *in general* by defining his existence through others according to capitalist notions of right and privilege, make the general form of capitalist causality (the sense of practical reason) appear to him as the natural order of causation. When man then attempts to see natural objects as natural objects, he sees only their objectivity as existences of capitalist accumulation as a process—capitalist accumulation as an objective process. Hence, the very order of nature itself appears to him in a capitalist guise; he would, however, deny that this is the case, since he has defined the capitalist form as the objective form, and therefore could not distinguish it as peculiar to capitalist mental life. When the scientist fancies himself as examining nature independent of social-science issues or free of the influence of anthropocentrism, he merely deludes himself; his mental processes, formed under the influence of capitalist social relations, inevitably impose the capitalist order upon his cognition in every field, scientific inquiry included. This is demonstrated by the history of science during the past century, during which all the key evidence has militated against maintaining reductionist-formalist procedures and ontological assumptions; and yet those assumptions persist.

This subjectivity is not as catastrophic for human knowledge as it might first appear to be. The Praxis of capitalist accumulation, as the expression of negentropic knowledge, is a reflection (however reified) of the objective order of universal nature to the extent that capitalist accumulation as a process is positive for human existence as a whole. The relative achievements of so-called physical science under capitalism are not accidentally related to the circumstance that the advance of productive technology is the area in which capitalism most closely approaches the underlying reality of man's historic relationship to nature in a more general way. The overtones of falseness that accompany the use of the term "subjective" become actualities for knowledge under capitalism to the extent and in the fashion that capitalist notions of freedom are practically demonstrated to be antithetical to human existence as a whole. For example, to the extent that capitalism causes growing poverty and unemployment, or (ecologically) undermines the basis for production of the material conditions of the continued existence of a growing working-class population as a whole, the fallacies of capitalist accumulation become manifest; and, at the same time, those branches of knowledge that attempt to justify the relevant moments of capitalist behavior become the quackery and crankery of institutionalized knowledge.

This is not a simple matter. Sociology, because it occupies itself with the immediate forms of capitalist relations, is generally the most reactionary field of academic inquiry, and the most notorious nesting-place of semifascists and outright fascist apologists even in the United States. Yet anthropology, which has in actuality the same subject as sociology, to the extent that it occupies itself with noncapitalist society, has been generally progressive until the influence of sociology impinged upon it in such crankish guises as cultural relativism and behaviorism. Today, even the viable kernel of anthropology is withering, not—as some rationalize—because it has run out of peoples to classify, but because belief in progress has evaporated under conditions of general decay in the rate of actual extended reproduction, causing an ebb in the humanistic, evolutionary thrust which exerted its positive influence even upon antievolutionary figures in the field. Marx's critique of Ricardo vis-à-vis his antiscientific successors in capitalist political economy is another example. The way in which various branches of knowledge are affected by the contradictory features of capitalist development is not simple, but the broad principle is clear enough. The subjectivity of knowledge in capitalist society is not a cause for uncertainty about the authority for practice of various branches of inquiry. Through the First World War, the development of physical science corresponded to the progressive development of capitalist technology, and therefore produced a corpus of knowledge which, however reified by reductionist influences, had the highest relative degree of appropriateness to the realm of practice in which it was formed. In other fields, the degree of appropriateness broadly corresponds to the quality of capitalist practice for the domain each specialization regards as its subject matter. In general, all fields of inquiry are characterized by a general flaw permeating whatever other appropriateness may have been achieved. That flaw is reductionism, the pernicious effect of capitalist alienation of social relations upon the general form of consciousness in capitalist society. That flaw is distinguishable to the point that one can abstract from the field in question those aspects that remain valid (for socialist science, for example) after the reductionist flaw is discounted.

This comprehension of the matter can only arise as a positive notion from the study of human history as an evolutionary process in the sense we have represented it. When the particular manifestations of capitalist freedom's inappropriateness to the entirety of human existence are not only discovered but adduced from this historical vantage-point, it is possible, from such predicates, to adduce the necessity for socialist accumulation.

Socialist accumulation cannot be some abstract ideal form of society adduced from "human nature" in itself. Such human nature does not exist for scrutiny in capitalist or any predecessor form of society. The best approximation of a natural human nature is perhaps available only in study of baboon societies,[58] a fact reflected in the considerable body of literature demanding a variety of socialism best suited to baboons. Socialist accumulation can be no more than a fantasy unless it is predicated upon existent features of the productive forces of capitalist accumulation, and the consciousness of socialist man adduced as creatable under circumstances that actually exist under some moments of capitalist development.

Socialist accumulation would be a chimera unless it meant rescuing some positive feature of capitalist accumulation from capitalist accumulation—specifically, the capitalist rate of profit. Ironically, socialism is the revolutionary liberation of the rate of profit from the clutches of anarchism. Capitalism is historically progressive as long as it fully realizes extended reproduction through the accompanying development of the labor process. Under those circumstances, the conditions of wage-labor must improve secularly with respect to both material consumption and the quality and quantity of leisure. Under such conditions it would be impossible for any sane person to consider superseding capitalism. It is when capitalism aborts extended reproduction, fails to develop labor power *generally*, and so on, that there is something positive to be rescued from capitalism: extended reproduction.

This point is perversely demonstrated by the anarchists and Third Campers, who propose to throw out the baby to save the bathwater. For them, it is extended reproduction that is the villain. They are not really utopians, except in the conceit that they are socialists at all. They are capitalists, who seize upon the most reactionary aspect of capitalist society (heteronomy) and denounce the capitalist for his most progressive role, extended reproduction. This stance is promoted today by those anarchists who have become the most ardent advocates of zero growth. They propose to eliminate accumulation and technological advance—thereby consigning the human race to burial under its own refuse—while still-progressive capitalists oppose zero growth from the standpoint of the historic need for technological development and expanded reproduction.

As Marx and Engels absolutely distinguish themselves as a theoretical-political faction for humanity, their constant enemy within the socialist movement—the enemy of humanity within the socialist movement—is not procapitalist attitudes among workers but anarchism (and, not accidentally, anarchism's progeny, fascism). This is the burden of *The German Ideology, The Holy Family,* and *The Misery of Philosophy,* and is the basis for Marx's ruthless intolerance of such antihumanist tendencies as Bakunin's eclectic broth of Stirner and Proudhon (and his implicit fatherhood of Mussolini, Hitler, and their counterparts).[59] Anarchism, which seems "radically anticapitalist" to those who oppose capitalism in a reactionary way, is nothing but the distilled essence of that which makes capitalism itself reactionary: juridical heteronomy or pluralism. The petit-bourgeois or peasant notion of the rightful autonomy (actually, of course, heteronomy) of the small-group constituency (black nationalism, trade-union chauvinism, local control, etc.) in the actual or virtual form of a self-contained, self-determining "nation" is nothing but the essence of the notion of private property in the means of production, which must be realized (however initially radical anticapitalist it may seem to the shallow-minded) as nothing but proposals for black capitalism, trade-union cooperativism, women's capitalism, gay capitalism, and so on. In the real world, such heteronomous minestrone must have a bowl to hold its contents together; it requires a supraconstituency arbiter, a "man above the crowd"—a Mussolini, a Hitler. Anarchism can only be well-meaning posturing or it must become fascism.

The object of socialist transformation of the existing (capitalist) productive forces is to extirpate the last vestige of anarchism from both those productive forces and morality: to extirpate heteronomic distinctions and consciousness from all sections of the proletariat, to "reduce" every member of the proletariat to a member of the political class-for-itself, to locate his immediate material self-interest for his self-consciousness in the self-interest of the universal class-for-society. The object of socialism is to socialize positively the consciousness and material existence of every member of the political proletariat.[60] It was not necessary for Marx to write a treatise on ethics; Spinoza had already fulfilled that need.

Relative to capitalist accumulation, socialist accumulation appears both in form and initial actuality a subjective being. *In form* because socialist accumulation imposes upon the capitalist existence of the productive forces an arbitrary determination, at odds with that objective causal relationship to which those forces have been ostensibly and actually habituated. Relative to a fixed quality of the Understanding, the emergence of socialist accumulation must appear an arbitrary imposition of practical reason contrary to accepted (empiricist) notion of the order of nature (for example, the marketplace principle).

Socialist accumulation appears subjective in content because it is proposed within capitalist society as the practical reason for an agency which does not yet exist, the political class-for-itself. The political class-for-itself is both a certain kind of organic universality of self-organization of representative strata of organized, unorganized, and unemployed workers and their social allies, and a self-consciousness of organization around the purpose of socialist extended reproduction. We seem to find the question of content leading us back to the issue of form.

Socialist accumulation must first exist as knowledge of someone, since otherwise the working-class forces could not acquire knowledge of it. Thus it cannot emerge as the spontaneous creation of an assembly of class forces; someone must create the requisite consciousness before the working class becomes a class-for-itself. It exists first as a precondition of its actual embodiment (realization) within a class-for-itself, as a socialist program of expanded reproduction.[61] Consequently, according to the anarchist, socialist accumulation comes into being as the diabolical "theoretical arrogance" of an elite, which perniciously imposes its "external" will upon the purity of the working-class essence. It is, to the anarchist, an alien intrusion upon the natural (that is, capitalist) ideology of the worker and the natural heteronomic (capitalist) order of things. Socialist accumulation can originate only as the creation of a portion of the capitalist intelligentsia, because the necessary overview of world-historical reality and of universal labor exists under capitalism only within the ranks of the intelligentsia. Socialism is in this way the unification of universal and cooperative labor; it could not be otherwise. Since universal labor is alienated from cooperative labor, cooperative labor must become socialist as a result of fusion with something (universal labor) from "outside"; Marx himself typifies this process. Thus, the workerist has been, since Marx and Engels' first intrusions into the working-class movement, the most virulent enemy of socialism. The "socialist" who proposes to prevent a socialist intelligentsia from meddling in the affairs of workers is, in fact, a procapitalist reactionary.

This "elitist" form does not disappear with the advent of actualized socialist accumulation. Unlike capitalist accumulation, which operates through universal maxims within the individual heteronomous will, and thus adduces God (the Invisible Hand—the capitalists' only god) as the subject of such slogans,[62] socialist accumulation is and can be nothing but the self-conscious collective determination of the order of nature for man by the political class-for-itself as an entirety, directing its executive functions as a whole through centralized agencies of its creation. Socialist accumulation is fundamentally distinguished by its program of extended reproduction from capitalist accumulation's religious form of the capitalist practical reason.

That is Marx's notion of conscious revolutionary Praxis.[63] It is already, thus, the germinal notion of socialist extended reproduction and of socialist programs of extended reproduction.

PARTICULAR AND UNIVERSAL

We have already seen that even particular increases in social productivity must necessarily alter the potential and actual material existence of every individual.[64] By elaborating the self-determining relationship of the unity of the proletariat to itself, in terms of its smallest empirical constituents, through process sheets, bills of materials, and bills of consumption, and examining the interrelationships (interpenetration) of these particulars, we discover that the existence of every individual member of the proletariat is properly determined by the existence (practical existence) of every other member of the proletariat. To the extent that other classes (professionals, for example) perform services that are socially necessary either to the labor process apropos the reproduction of labor power or to the organization of the productive forces, these nonproletarians are properly subsumed into the dictatorship of the proletariat as a *political* class-for-itself.

This is the dynamic notion of the working class as a potentially universal class-for-society.[65] Only to the extent that the object of the individual will of the members of the proletariat (as a political class-for-itself) is a rising rate of profit $(S'/[C+V])$ for socialist accumulation does the working class become a true class (a class-for-itself). To speak of the class interests of individuals is to speak only of their freedom to act for the self-interest of this class; however, it is therefore also to stipulate for the interest of the entire class the advancing quality of existence (as reproducers of the entire class) of each individual member of the class.

This is no categorical imperative in the ordinary sense, no sentimental ethic demanding some unforeseeable utopian state of abstract perfection (in the vulgar sense of the term). It is an immanent, actualizable moment of capitalist production itself, expressed thus:

The general interest of society as a species (universal class) is the augmentation of the positive value for our heuristic notion of exponential functions of $S'/(C+V)$. This process depends not only upon increasing the negentropic potential imputable to nature for social reproduction, but also upon increasing the quality of labor power. The increasing quality of labor power demands acceleration in the quality of individual material existence (real income and leisure) as the precondition for the positive advancement of the potentiality of abstract labor. We have to optimize for two interpenetrating optimizing principles. The first is the function of $S'/(C+V)$, which demands reduction of C and V, to their minima. The second is the maximization of V (and implicitly, C). The successive moments of increasing value of $S'/(C+V)$, mediated through increase (relative to a preceding moment) of C and V, is the required notion of identity ($A = A$ as a notion of simple invariant; $A_1 = A_2 = A_3 = \ldots = 1$).

The apparent conceptual difficulties posed by this notion are nothing but the inherent fallacies of the capitalist form of the Understanding, which is presented to us as the empiricist world-outlook subsumed by notions of discrete elementarity in the elements of a function: simple reproduction. The seeming inconsistencies and paradoxes within our representation of extended reproduction are nothing but the paradoxical form of present reality. Such problems, such seeming paradoxes, can be resolved only through the sort of process outlined in Chapter 7. The seeming paradox represents the necessity of rising technology, which is freedom. Program expresses that freedom. (Thus, various anarchists, procapitalist and nominally anticapitalist to the contrary, socialist economy places an absolute premium on the actual freedom of the human mind, in opposition to the dictatorship and brutalization of the "free" marketplace.)

What we are demanding by citing such necessity is that the individual conceptualize the particular for the whole, and develop new conceptions appropriate to such an holistic overview. As a corollary, we are demanding that the individual, for the first time in the course of human existence, finally secure to himself the general right—for all members of his class—to consciously and practically locate himself and for himself and for his society in his historic importance to the evolutionary existence of the human species as a whole. Again, Spinoza's ethic.

This new outlook replaces the "chains of conviction" espoused through the idealistic formulation, the negation of the negation. For capitalist culture—which is to speak of the Kantian and Hegelian dialectics as its highest expressions—the positive notion of the Self is indeed attained by the negation of the negation. That which is prohibited to sensuous heteronomic self-interest by the universal (law, peer-group determination) defines for the individual, as what is not denied, what he may regard as positive. Thus, negation (superego in that sense), counterposing the particular (heteronomy) to its other (autonomy negatively determined from the whole), by negating itself, counterposing what has been left intact by negation to that which was denied and prohibited, is for capitalist society's morality, "respect for law,"[66] or positive morality. This process is, otherwise, the transformation of the first negation (the chains of authority) by its own negation into the chains of conviction. That is Kant's "pietism," Hegel's quasi-Lutheranism, and the Apollonian, anti-Promethean philistinism of both.[67]

Socialist morality rejects the negation of the negation not merely as empty formalism, but also as the abstract disguise for the chains of illusion, the "chains upon the heart."[68] Socialist morality, through consciously formulated economic programs of extended reproduction, eliminates idealism (and therefore the material basis in need for religious belief) by freeing man from the capitalist alienation—by freeing the individual from the anarchist delusion-in-practice of viewing the universal (autonomous) as the oppressor of the heteronomic individual Self. Socialist morality accomplishes this in a practical fashion, as conscious programs of socialist extended reproduction give individual man practical positive comprehension of the universality which is his new *right*, his true individual "essence" and self-interest.

This in no sense signifies the subordination of the individual to the mass in the vulgar sense of such a relationship. The individual's contribution to the mass depends upon the maximal appropriate development of his human powers—ultimately, the development of his powers of creative mentation, his freedom, and his social importance. To accomplish this for itself, society must expand his material powers over objects in such a way as to allow him the exercise of power over that which exemplifies the scope of its technological development. To realize the task-oriented creative mentation such materialized powers of consumption potentially represent, society must afford the individual not only leisure time, but also the quality of leisure he needs for the kind of mentation wanted from him. Hence, if the limitations of social development are constraints upon the exercise of his freedom (necessity), society's difficulty in providing him with the means for further advancement is the constraint upon it. His interest and society's interest are identical in the most immediate way.

This is the practical significance, which can be comprehended only through conscious economic programs, of socialist extended reproduction.

Only in this fashion does appropriation of surplus value, which seems oppressive and negative to the alienated individual (and to the small group's false notion of self-interest), become revealed as that which is most to be prized by the individual. The appropriation of the surplus value of individual labor (which fatuous pseudosocialists define as exploitation) is in truth the most essential premise for the continued existence of all individuals: extended reproduction.

The fatuous pseudosocialist, hesitating on his way out the classroom door, makes one last thrust: "Doesn't Marx himself denounce 'exploitation'?" they mewl. Yes! Of *class* by *class*. The exploitation in capitalism is located entirely in the fact that capitalism, which comes to stand in opposition to humanity itself by opposing "natural" or socialist extended reproduction, is taking the power to determine extended reproduction away from the productive class as a whole. The capitalist class, at the point where it aborts its own historic mission for humanity, refuses to relinquish the power to maintain the existence of humanity to the class qualified to do so. Individual exploitation has no meaning for scientific socialists except as a description of the particularized alienation of the proper powers of an as yet nonexisting class, the working class as a self-conscious class-for-itself.

However, superexploitation, quite another issue, is always a consideration. By "superexploitation" one must signify primitive accumulation against the labor process itself. The problem, with the special attendant definitional difficulties cited in Chapter 7, is that of paying labor below the level of consumption and leisure required to reproduce modern labor power. Acknowledging the special difficulties of drawing a precise distinction between exploitation and superexploitation (in fact, no accurate boundary can be drawn, since simple reproduction, the basis for such precise distinctions, is a chimera), it is evident that the notions of exploitation and superexploitation are related mainly in terminological respects, not in substance. The distinction between superexploitation and exploitation has significance from a socialist-accumulation standpoint, but very little significance in any particular case from a capitalist-accumulation standpoint. As Marx emphasizes in the *Communist Manifesto* and elsewhere, the significance of the struggle against employer exploitation is located in an associated tendency for such struggles to produce classwide organization, for the working class to appropriate the means of production for socialist expanded reproduction.

When this problem is considered from the anarchist standpoint, the capitalist class does seem to be the virtual savior of humanity. The capitalist performs, as we have noted, a revolutionary political service for humanity in frustrating the anarchists. The anarchists would prevent the appropriation of surplus value to provide productive employment for the unemployed, and thus would abolish the process by which the material conditions of life of all labor are advanced. The fundamentally reactionary qualities of capitalism, as we have also noted, all derive from its anarchist tendencies—from which source the anarchist obtains his own ideology and politics.

The practical, empirical distinction between the viewpoints of simple and extended reproduction can be restated for location within the notion of Praxis. Extended reproduction, rather than starting from the notion of a quantity of capital as such, proceeds from the totality of the population by class divisions, and the productive forces of society as a whole. As Marx and Luxemburg emphasize, "total capitalist" rigor—as the unique point of reference for comprehending the notions of value and extended reproduction—neither defines growth and similar phenomena in terms of current or constant dollars or other parameters of the same general epistemological character, nor proceeds from the capitalist-ideological standpoint of collections of competing capitalists or collections of objects *qua* objects, but takes the entirety as axiomatic ($A_1 = A_2 = A_3 = \ldots = 1$). This invariant entirety, examined as a reproductive process, converges through the analysis of the division of productive labors to the determination of the smallest particular.[69] The analytical procedure, as we have outlined it, is as follows. We begin with the proletariat as a whole, examining its reproduction as a whole, and the subsumed determination of total labor power as a unity. This unity we analyze in terms of the reproductive implications of categories of its output; we analyze in respect of principal departments, and of S', d, C, V, into subcategories, and so forth. We then elaborate the interpenetration of the universal and particular in the way Marx prescribes with respect to the interpretation of the tableau economique. We employ the equivalent of or actual process sheets, bills of materials, and bills of consumption to define the worldwide network through which the interpenetration of universal and cooperative labor defines world-historical man. This network, conceptualized for the self-movement of increased labor power rather than discrete object-relations, "closes the loop" for the reproductive labor process as a whole. From this holistic standpoint, we then determine the objective content, value, and use value for the particular element. That is the location of socialist Praxis. Simple reproduction, of course, employs the opposite procedure.

Only by such empirical rigors can we escape the essential fallacy of simple reproduction, the fallacy of regarding the particular object as, in effect, a thing-in-itself. Reduced to practical terms, this signifies that the quality of the particular object is constantly changing, such that all empiricist comparisons of such objects from one moment of the reproductive process to another are necessarily false, no matter what equations are employed. It is the simple-reproduction outlook, implicit in capitalist notions of historic valuations of dead capital, which manifests itself as devastating fallacies in the crises arising periodically from the falling-rate tendency.

THE TENDENCY QUESTION

Ricardo, as we have noted, was bemused to discover that increases in the simple-reproduction determination of the organic composition of capitals (C/V), which were energized by notions of rising rates of profit $(S/(C + V)$—practical reason)—should result in a tendency for the rate of profit, $S/(C + V)$, to fall. Marx criticizes Ricardo's mystification of this problem at length in both *Theories of Surplus Value* and Volume III of *Capital*.[70] In the latter, this examination properly follows a demonstration that the notion of a general rate of profit is determining, and the employment of that notion to show the tendency question to be merely a symptom of the fundamental contradiction of capitalist accumulation.

The systematic fallacy of capitalist accumulation, which is imposed upon its internal features[71] by the anarchist principle lodged in juridical notions of private property in the means of production, is that it cannot know itself practically as a totality. Nonetheless, it is a totality, and the ultimate value of its particular relations are determined for it as a totality. For example, the fact that capitalism immediately locates the capitalist will in competition does not mean that competition determines values in the final analysis. Competitive relations seem to do this up to a point, provided one makes certain assumptions about the God-given parameters within which the firm exists. In the final analysis, these God-given parameters seem suddenly to have fallen prey instead to Satan himself—and all hell breaks loose. Nothing from the standpoint of competitive models of capitalist accumulation in particular would ever give the slightest hint why this is the case. Consequently, any judgment based on the assumption of the primacy of competitive relationships is utterly incapable of detecting any of the important phenomena of the boom-bust cycle until some time after they have occurred, at approximately the same time that the farmer's cattle begin to sense that something has gone awry in the farmer's world.

Even after a depression has occurred, most capitalist economists and most pseudo-Marxian economists will continue to deny it is approaching. The problem is that the competitive model depends upon local determinations of "book values" of capitals, which, as each succeeding depression reveals, are contrary to the actual value relationships accumulating in the economy as a whole. The capitalist competitive model assumes the carryover of valuations attached to old capital as the general measure for values in the succeeding period (that is, constant-dollar valuations), or the standpoint of simple reduction.

That is the general case, although the actuality is not quite so clear-cut. The universalizing tendency of capitalist accumulation is actually expressed in a negative fashion through the existence of the general rate of profit in the monetary process. We shall turn to this subject in Chapter 9, although we have already referred to certain aspects of it. Let us summarize the most relevant point: (to the extent that) this moment of capitalist accumulation (the rate of profit) is universal for the internal features of capitalist accumulation as a whole, the discrepancies between local valuations and general valuations of individual capitalists' capitals must ultimately be reconciled. Indeed, they are reconciled, through the bust end of a boom or a general breakdown crisis, and in general monetary cancer. What we are about to state must be modified in this light in subsequent chapters. For the moment, it is sufficient to emphasize that what we say now is essentially correct as a description of a tendency, and will merely appear in a new light as an actuality when the monetary process is considered.

In general, either in an anarchist society (such as that implicit in the Soviet Union's "Libermanism" reforms or in Yugoslav decentralization) or in the special case of anarchist society which is capitalism proper, the value of capitals from moment to moment must be associated with their simple historic cost of acquisition, where cost is determined in the sense of simple reproduction. In any such society, profoundly disruptive functions of the economy inevitably arise from this heteronomic tendency.

External to the microuniverse of a particular firm, other firms are accomplishing increases in productivity, and alterations in technology which are changing the socially necessary costs of reproduction of the capital being consumed by that firm. These movements in the actual development of capitalism represent a secular tendency for continuously cheapening the socially necessary costs of reproductions of all capitals. Since the whole of capitalism is an interconnected network, and since any increase in social productivity's socially necessary costs in any part of the worldwide system is a reduction in socially necessary cost throughout the entire system, the lowering of socially necessary costs is continuous except in extraordinary circumstances of breakdown. It is continuous for all conditions of expanded reproduction—that is, all boom periods.

Insofar as costs of production involve only Circulating Capitals, no traumatic consequences would seem to ensue from the parochialist accounting of the simple cost of capital employed by the juridical anarchist, the entrepreneur. To the extent that current production involves a growing mass of accounting values in the form of Fixed Capital, the value depreciation of the dead capital is a source of potentially dead contradictions. As the ratio of the Departments increases throughout the economy, the ratio of Fixed Capital to Circulating Capital must rise, especially with respect to the Variable Capital constituent of Circulating Capital. Because the rate of productivity of labor power is rising rapidly, and the calculated life of Fixed Capital is increasing on the average, the rising organic compositions of capitals seem to cause a contradiction which the anarchist is less well-situated to explain than Ricardo himself. What we have, in consequence, is the usual academic response to any phenomena that cannot be competently explained—a plausible explanation, any plausible explanation (edification) that seems to coincide with appearances. It is argued in full bloom of fatuousness that the rising organic composition of capitals *causes* the rate of profit to tend to fall.

Historically, the discount of book valuations of dead capitals has tended to become large relative to Variable Capital. This discount may become larger than the increased rate of Surplus Value (S/V) realized through the increased productivity that caused the discounting—ergo, the tendency for the *calculated* rate of profit to fall!

If we designate the discounting of Fixed Capital for rising productivity as x, and the gains resulting from productivity rises as y, we have two obvious ways of absorbing the discount:

1. $(S' + y)/(F + x + C + V)$
   where F is the current value (at current socially necessary valuation) of Fixed Capital

2. $(S' + y - x)/(F + V + C)$
   where the real relationship is

3. $(S' + y)/(F + C + V)$
   In short, x is *fictitious*, but not for capitalist accumulation.

But F was advanced. Where does F go?!!!

In each expansion of the economy, part of S' is realized as means of production. Part of this is in the form of "sunk costs," which we shall label f, and which generates a small increment of Constant Capital, $\triangle C_f$, where $\triangle C_f < f$. The amount $f - \triangle C_f$ is lost or sunk. But not really; it is realized, generally, through rising rates of productivity. However, through rising productivity the cost of replicating f is always less than the outlay. From the standpoint of the reproductive process, the discount is fictitious, since the relationship $S'/(C + V)$ fully accounts for social reproductive costs.

The root of the fictitious element is anarchy. The uneven distribution of dead capital among particular capitals is the root of the maintenance of such fictions. If all capitalists had the same ratios of Fixed to Circulating

Capitals in an hypothetical capitalist economy which was closed for capitalist production as the only source of wealth, and if the valuation of wealth were determined by the socially necessary costs of social reproduction, this difficulty would not exist. However, in such an economy, capitalist accumulation would not be capitalist accumulation. Such a confusion between hypothetical and actual capitalist accumulation could arise if the pedagogical standpoint of Volume I of *Capital* were applied literally. Capitalist accumulation is not simply the accumulation of capital as determined by socially necessary labor power at value for a closed system. That model ignores both circulation—as we shall see in subsequent chapters—and the fact that capitalist accumulation is not, in any case, coextensive with capitalist production.

The fictitious element is entropy, which arises here in the general way entropy must arise in any system of corresponding design. It is sufficient to identify the point, it being unsuitable to develop it in the appropriate manner here.

For the real social-reproductive process, such developments for depreciation of dead capital must be a gain, since they measure negentropy! However, because of the "anarchy of capitalism" under whose terms the discountings are occurring at uneven rates relative to particular capitals, the maintenance of the rate of accounted profit on accounted valuations of particular capitalists' capitals, and the connection of this development to the general monetary-credit process, this process does produce a tendency for necessary ensuing crisis.

Through the monetary process, the apparent asymptotic tendency for the rate of profit to stagnate causes apparent overproduction. To maintain the price of commodities at levels that also maintain the rate of profit on apparent value of capitals, the gross price of all commodities must exceed the monetary equivalent of value for commodities actually put into circulation. So, in addition to the absolute surplus value earned by that epoch of the productive cycle, an additional relative surplus value has been charged to production, and has been capitalized as part of the enlarged mass of capitalists' capitals.

From this, two moments follow. The apparent overproduction tends to produce actual underproduction relative to the demand represented by the extended reproduction of the labor process. The rate of growth of capitals exceeds the rate of growth of the activity of producing surplus value, on account of the overcapitalization associated with relative surplus value and its capitalized form as fictitious capitals. The combined increase of underproduction and of fictitious capitals in this fashion exacerbates the tendency for the rate of profit to decline.

By contrast, if the value of capitals is maintained (through completely extended reproduction) at its strictly socially necessary cost of reproduction, the rising rate of productivity of labor power must produce *a secular tendency for a rising rate of profit*. To the extent that S' from one moment is capitalized as enlarged capital as a whole, this increment, S', must realize new surplus value (absolute surplus value) at a more efficient rate than old capitals, which must actuate further advances in technology. So the net surplus value (S′) must also rise.

The anarchist reification of this same process can be examined in two principal phases.

When fictitious capital is added to the mass of total capitals, this increment cannot possibly reproduce its own profits, its own surplus value. To produce surplus value—absolute surplus value—capital must correspond to added means of production and means of consumption. Where absolute surplus value is the basis for new capital, the enlargement of capital or the rising organic composition of capital cannot cause a problem, since:

1. $V_1 > V_2$

2. $C_1 < C_2$

3. $(C_1 + V_1) > (C_2 + V_2)$

4. $S/(C+V)_1 < S/C+V)_2$

and, for rising technology,

5. $S'_1 < S'_2$

even though

6. $d_1 > d_2$.

Under these conditions, rising organic composition represents no problem, since the tendency for rising productivity (even with extension in scale as such) virtually assures us that the rate of profit from real elements of the newly added capital will be greater than that generally obtained from previously advanced capitals. This principle applies not only to the added increment but to the replenishing constant capital as well. When the capital added to the total accumulation is fictitious, it can exist only as a parasite on the income (surplus value) of productive capitals.

To the extent that underproduction ensues from apparent overproduction, a shrinking rate of production of new value relative to existing self-expanding value as a whole will tend ultimately to occur. This may not occur as an absolute reduction, in the conventional sense of measure, but only as a relative reduction, which will appear as absolute for the condition $A_1 = A_2 = A_3 = \ldots = 1$. This rising tendency for underproduction exacerbates the tendency from which it arises, whether the fictitious capital is that originating in relative surplus value or capital gains of pure speculation.

In the latter moment of the tendency, the result must be that the rate of growth of capitals is accompanied by a tendency for a growing army of the impoverished, as unemployed and as lumpenproletarians proper, and other consequences of the shrinking of the scale of real extended reproduction relative to the proletariat as a whole.

This process can be reflected in our heurism in the following fashion. Include the entire labor force of the working-class population in the invariant $= 1$. Now, unemployment is charged to capitalists' consumption in the same sense as are clerks employed from working-class households. This reduces the value of $S'/(C + V)$. Now, reflect the lower quality of labor power on account of increasing proportions of enmiseried labor in labor power as a whole; this reduces both $S/(C + V)$ and $S'/(C + V)$.

This will signify a tendency to abort realization of capital in a productive form, since added capitals force a writeoff of dead capitals, which must either be absorbed as a loss or charged to the price of commodities. A general secular inflationary tendency will set in, in any case, but debt-equity ratios and other liquidity factors will demand higher rates of inflation than those prevailing to permit realization of new capitals productively. This results in an exacerbated market pressure against increased investment. The technological stagnation produced will impel replenishment of Circulating Capital toward the fringes of relative finiteness of associated resources, causing an absolute rise in C, and a rise in the organic composition of capitals without technological advance. The effect will be the same as that for technological reversal, but with a rising organic composition of capitals on this account!

The end result to be expected if this sort of decay reached an extreme would be noises announcing the advent of an ecological crisis and a general crisis of overpopulation. If the reader should encounter such empirical evidence at some point in the distant future of capitalism he will know that such hypothetical extremes have been reached.

Out of such tendencies emerge a deepening contradiction between the process of capitalist accumulation and the development of the productive forces. This, expressed through the monetary process of capitalist accumulation, is the cause of periodic cyclical busts during a period of general capitalist development, and general breakdown crises marking off whole periods of capitalist development, or the onset of general capitalist decay.[72]

This is merely the most elementary aspect of the problem. We shall explore it further in relation to the monetary system and statist war-economy as the last possible general phase of capitalist development.

These considerations demonstrate the false consciousness of capitalist morality. It is of the juridical-anarchist or capitalist-ideological form of practical reason for extended reproduction. The introduction of such anarchist notions to political economy, inherent in political economy, must result (as we shall see) in internal contradictions in the monetary process, and, more fundamentally, the growing failure of the economy to meet the existence-needs of the nature and population of that society as a whole. In the strictest view, the monetary crisis is not a mere contingency which unfortunately causes the further contingency of mass unemployment and related phenomena; it is the actualization of the growing discrepancy between capitalist morality (praxis) and human interest (praxis) which has been accruing during the preceding period of capitalist prosperity.

A matter for consideration within the scope of the monetary process is why so-called "built-in stabilizers" appear to offset the falling-rate tendency as a secular phenomenon during the period this tendency is accruing as self-expanding potential illiquidity within the monetary process of prosperous periods. It is sufficient to state here that to the extent that the credit-monetary process can capitalize fictitious values (such as relative surplus value) such that an accumulation of fictitious capital conceals the falling-rate tendency, up to the point that the credit mechanism cannot long endure this chore without becoming unhinged in an inflationary spiral.

We must locate the actual determination of capitalist phenomena for the vulgar Understanding, or the empiricist view, within the monetary form of capitalist accumulation. Just as crises otherwise determined in the underlying relations are only realized in the breakdown of the monetary process, so the objective phenomena of capitalist accumulation are necessarily determined (practical reason) in the capitalist form of the same monetary process.

CAPITAL 9

Throughout the preceding chapters we have emphasized the opposition of the subjective and objective aspects of the social-reproductive processes under capitalism. Now we must eliminate grounds for metaphysical misinterpretation of such distinctions by showing how the subjective and objective are interconnected as a single process. Our approach in this chapter will be that promised in Chapter 2: to locate the interconnection of capital and use value in the historical process by which they actually become interconnected to form capitalist society.

The immediate goal toward which we are working may be described as the establishment of the reader's qualifications to understand the concluding, summary section of the chapter entitled "Internal Contradictions" in Volume III of *Capital*. The thrust of this chapter's summary is highlighted by a brief selection:

> The stupendous productive power developing under the capitalist mode of production relatively to population, and the increase, though not in the same proportion, of capital values (not their material substance), which must grow much more rapidly than the population, contradict the basis, which, compared to the expanding wealth, is ever narrowing and for which this immense power works, and the conditions under which capital augments its value. This is the cause of crisis.[1]

Earlier, in one of numerous statements of the point leading to this conclusion, Marx notes:

> . . . the contradiction of this capitalist mode of production consists precisely in its tendency to an absolute development of productive forces, a development which comes continually in conflict with the specific conditions of production in which capital moves and alone can move.[2]

In sum, there is a contradiction between the capitalist side of the capitalist mode of expanded reproduction and the objective basis (use-value relationships) on which that mode of production depends.

Vulgar Marxism, which subsumes numerous so-called Marxist scholars,[3] simply declines to attempt to unravel this chapter of *Capital*, retreating into a kind of Ricardian theory of value in which value is determined by average concrete labor-times, and in which a rising organic composition of capital is assumed mysteriously to *cause* a tendency for the rate of profit to fall. Such absurd notions inevitably involve attempts to explain crises in terms of a closed economic model of the Ricardian form, and identify internal contradictions within such a mechanistic schema. The result of such enterprises, inevitably, is ingenuous metaphysics. Certain "principles" are simply asserted, as expedient edification, to apply to such a model. These principles are sheer parody of phrases in *Capital*. Yet the more poetically ingenious such parodies, the greater the exegesizer's difficulty in systematically demonstrating his assertions within his economic model.

The point to be particularly emphasized here is as follows. A capitalist economy can be made to appear as if it were, indeed, such a closed economic model of a mechanistic form—notably during those phases of boom periods in which the fluctuations in production, employment, and profit rates are at a minimum relative to the total labor force. Such actually subjectivist model-making is typified by the writings of Ernest Mandel, whom we have previously singled out as a clinical example of this sort of problem.[4] The false notion we must dispel is that capitalist crises are the outcome of some internal contradiction within such a mechanistic closed model. We do not argue that the kind of instabilities emphasized by Hilferding, Bukharin, and Mandel, do not occur; disproportions in the relationships between the two principal departments and among the mix of commodities is endemic. Although a lapse of time may be required to ease off such imbalances, the difficulties arising from proportionalities are of the form of mere tradeoffs and do not represent a fundamental problem for capitalism. There would be no intrinsic difficulty in enlarging the scope of built-in stabilizers to virtually eliminate such imbalances as sources of *significant* disturbances. By internal contradictions we signify, as Marx does, the kind of difficulty associated with a fundamental antinomy in Praxis for capitalist accumulation—the devastating, ultimately decisive contradiction which would periodically cause the economy to collapse despite the most perfect set of proportionalities imaginable. The internal contradiction involved is of exactly the form identified in the citations above: a fundamental antinomy between capitalist accumulation and the material basis (labor process) on which capitalist accumulation depends.

We shall resolve this contradiction by representing the reproduction of capitalists' capitals and the reproduction of self-expanding use value as, in first approximation, parallel processes. We shall momentarily examine the process of capitalist accumulation as a problem of knowledge, seeking to determine to what degree there could be a semblance of one-for-one correspondence between augmentations of capitalists' capitals in general and the augmentation of self-expanding use value in general. Or, in other words, to what degree can an increase in the absolute mass of capitalists' capitals be in precise correspondence with an increase in the absolute negentropy of the labor process? This comparison might usefully be regarded as an exploration of the cause of systematic discrepancies between the map (capitalist accumulation) and the actual terrain (self-expanded use value).

Once that conception has been explored, we shall examine the ways in which the demonstrated discrepancy's effects are reflected from the domain of self-expanding use value into the domain of capitalist accumulation. What happens to capitalist reproduction of capitals when the assumed value of those capitals outruns their objective basis? How is such a comparison possible? How does it occur? This investigation will present us with the essence of Marx's theory of capitalist development—that is, Marx's theory of capitalist crises. Capitalist development and capitalist crises are one and the same thing.

CAPITAL

Capital comes into being as a social fact[5] as the price of a license to loot. The Achaemenid tax-farmer is a useful prototype for pedagogical purposes. Assume that the Persian emperor is selling licenses to tax. Considering the amount that you, a merchant, might expect to squeeze from the farmers and other inhabitants of your tax district, how much will you bid for such a license?

The ratio of the expected gross yield to the price of the tax-farming permit determines a profit. The ratio of the profit to the price of the license crudely determines a rate of profit over the period of collection. To make a "management investment decision," compare alternative "investments" for rates of profits, and determine the price to be bid for the tax-farming license accordingly.

More generally, capital value is some multiple of the rate of looting made possible by possession of such a political patent, monopoly, or charter. This is to emphasize that the notion of the "face value" of capital does not intrinsically involve an obligation to values previously advanced. It is only in fables that capital is locked-up savings.

A crude but effective illustration of this point is as follows. Tax-farmer A buys a license for 10,000 shekels. He makes 20,000-shekel income after operating costs, and secures a bonus of 5,000 shekels in annual ursury from lands he seizes for nonpayment of taxes. But, in pricing his bid for the license at the prevailing rate of merchants' profits at equal risk, he expected to gain only 15,000 shekels. If the license is renewable, how much is it worth at the same rate of profit?

The gain represents pure speculative appreciation, but the license is not worth a shekel less for want of previous advances of "savings" against this gain.

This point is fundamental: the existence of any correspondence between the masses of self-expanding use value represented by capitals and the relative valuations of those capitals among themselves can only be the result of some process which limits the rate of return on capitals to a rate at least indirectly determined, in some countervailing fashion, by the rate of expansion of self-expanding use values as a result of capitalist investments. There is nothing in the nature of capital as capitalist's self-appreciating (income-bearing) property titles which determines any lawful connection betwen the valuations of capitals and production-determined valuations.

EQUAL RATES OF PROFIT

The notion of an "equal" general rate of profit by no means signifies an approximate prevailing mathematical equality among ratios of profit for capitals. An equal rate of profit subsumes wide variations in mathematical rates of realized profits for various capitals subject to an equal general rate. These variations can be principally attributed to notions of *risk* and *liquidity*. For these two conditions, which are the principal causes of actual variations within a constant general equal rate of profit, we may say that the rates of profit would be identical with the general rate or converge on the general rate if adjustments for risks and liquidity were taken into account. Conversely, we may say that divergences represent discountings for variations in risk and liquidity.

This sort of notion is commonplace, and no extended discussion should be required. In case of difficulties, any honest stockbroker can fill in the details—although it is sometimes necessary to discount the advice of even honest stockbrokers for moral risk and liquidity.

Risk can be reduced to its simplest conception by taking into account the mean effect on probable deviations from an expected "normal" income on capitals. The buyer must hedge or discount the purchase price of the title to income to compensate his future capital for the risk of such deviations. Such calculations have become standard business school classroom fare during the last decade.

Liquidity, no less important, is only slightly more sophisticated, as classroom and boardroom jargon has it. A few problems will help to bring the notion into focus. For example, a stock may have prime qualities of risk respecting payments of yields (dividends), but the market for this stock may be slow. One may expect to sell this security at par value or better, but may have to wait a week or more to find a buyer at that price. A low-risk bond will be redeemed at a prescribed maturity date but cannot be converted into cash on short notice (a variation on the preceding case). In general, we may say that a U.S. Treasury Bill of the shortest maturity is among the most liquid of securities because of low risk on yield and redemption price, relatively secure short-notice resale redemption, usefulness as security for credit, and early redemption. Normally, money itself is the most liquid, low-risk "security." Liquidity can be conceived of as resemblance to money, or degree of convertibility into money on short notice. Differences in liquidity are settleable by discounting.

Discounting for risk and liquidity are means of converting a general rate of profit into a particular rate of "equal profit" for particular instruments.

The rate of profit is obviously interconnected with a general rate of interest. Interest is the portion of total profit taken by the lender. The balance of income remaining after deducting interest from profit is a critical relationship. The following illustration suffices to identify the general form of the interconnection.

If the general rate of profit for a certain type of instrument is 15 per cent and the interest rate on loans to be used to purchase such an instrument is 7 per cent, does the borrower obtain less than the prevailing rate of profit by borrowing at 7 per cent on his investment?

Let us consider a hypothetical case in which he buys the 15 per cent-yield security (say $100,000 worth) with money borrowed at 7 per cent. What is his rate of profit? Infinite, of course. Obvious? You'd be surprised!

Let us consider a case in which he borrows half the amount at 7 per cent and buys the residue with his own savings. What is his rate of profit? Profit = $(0.15 \times \$50,000) + (0.08 \times \$50,000) = \$7,500 + \$4,000 = \$11,500$. This figure represents profit on $50,000 of his savings. What then is the simple relationship between rate of interest and rate of profit for such cases?

Consider the case of capital-gains income. What is the connection of this phenomenon to weird price-earning ratios on the stock market? Suppose a stock-buyer's yield is less than the interest on the money borrowed to supply part of the purchase-price of the stock, but a more than satisfactory capital-gains trend makes the purchase profitable. However, the capital-gains ratio is a result of the volume-price turnover in the market for that category of stock. If 40 per cent of the purchase payments in the turnover are from borrowed funds, what kinds of effects can result from a 1 per cent shift in the interest rate? Posit a few such cases, and have some fun.

The fantastical aspects of negotiable capital are such that the accounts of the Brothers Grimm seem the ultimate in sobriety by contrast. Don't be deceived by the financier's cultivated persona; he's as mad as the proverbial hatter. He has to be. Capital is a political power (e.g., to loot) magically awarded to the possessor of the patent. The relationship is comparable to that of Aladdin and his magic lamp, with emphasis on the stipulation that the genie can turn nasty. This power represents society's debt to the capitalists, but also—a discovery the Medici are assumed to have formalized[6]—creates an indebtedness on the part of the capitalist to his capital. The debt of the capitalist is what he must deliver to the purchaser when he sells the title. The same person, the capitalist, is liberated from that debt to the extent that his capital is looted by other capitals. Or his person may command another capital, and the second may loot the first. Scheherazade was a piker by comparison with the Mesopotamian who invented merchant's capital.

BILLS OF EXCHANGE

Fools still tell credulous children around the hearth or in the schoolroom that first there was barter; then there was gold; then there was paper money; then there was credit. On the contrary; first there was credit in the form of a bill of exchange. The universal bill of exchange—sometimes for gold, sometimes merely against the honest face of the government treasurer—is money. At the end of a day's trading in bills of exchange (money and other), imbalances in trading accounts are most amiably settled in gold.

By another hearth or blackboard, another informative old gentleman varies in the tale. First, he relates, there was Robinson Crusoe who married Wednesday. Nearby, Friday married Saturday—or perhaps it was Vulcan and Venus, or Uranus and Venus. Between these two original establishments there suddenly emerged the natural chemistry of "truck and barter." Capitalism was born when Robinson began saving and employed the less prudent Friday as his wage-labor for profitable trade with Monday and Tuesday. For a long time, capitalists tolerated all sorts of unsatisfactory governments, governments which invariably attempted to glove the Invisible Hand. Eventually, Robinson discovered anarchy and called it government, and capitalism prospered.

Such folk see the territorial imperative (capitalist property-forms) not only in societies where it does not exist, but even in one bull's fidgeting at the proximity of another bull. They discover protocapitalism in the form of barter wherever barter does not exist. Gullible students who hear such fairy-tales queue up at computers to calculate the imputed coupon-rates for Melanesia and, no doubt, Atlantis. In "potlatch" they find a House of Morgan with General Motors as well.

In the real universe, the existence of what might seem barter, or even of actual barter, does not establish the imminence of mercantilism. The reverse must generally be the case. Mercantilism finds in the possibility of instituting barter, or of regularizing the looting by armed merchant colonists, a fertile premise for its own proliferation. Barter is not the necessary precondition for the emergence of mercantilism; war, piracy, and banditry have served as suitable preconditions often enough.

The point to be adduced from a wide variety of evidence is aptly summed up, in principle, by the case of Pierre Radisson, and the Hudson's Bay adventure. What was barter in the eyes of Radisson and his colleagues was regarded as the exchange of gifts by the Indians—at first. Nor is there much reason to doubt that the more perceptive fur traders, particularly one like the picaresque Radisson, had any doubt about the ambiguity of the "exchange." It was the technology implanted in the Hudson's Bay Company's "gifts" that made such Aladdin's lamps a device for subjecting the Cree to an evil genie. The recipients became dependent upon capitalist means of shooting and trapping game. This dependency, the object assuming the mediating form of being-in-and-for-itself, created barter and the "trapping territory."[7] The kinds of barter that lead to mercantilism do not—and could not—spring from "innate," autochthonous developments of primitive societies. The problem here is that of generalizing the notion of combined and uneven development from the evidence available for a broad range of cases in which different societies interact, and for the inter-action of different social formations within the same societies in a more than casual way. The process to be examined is the special category of such combined and uneven development in which a need is imposed—by, for example, the establishment of colonists' armed mercantile factories or simple and official banditry and piracy, which compels a people to barter—or by taxation of one kind or another which fundamentally reorganizes the subject society.

Such conditions create the basis for the rudimentary forms of the bill of exchange, the "natural" form, the characteristic primary phe-nomenon, and the commodity form of mercantilism and mercantile capital-ism.

Before examining that form itself, let us return for a moment to a problem area we touched on in approaching the preceding point in our exploration. How and why must we distinguish between a general activity of exchange of objects and services among persons and groups within societies, on the one hand, and a specific activity like barter on the other? How and why must we distinguish between an exchange of gifts and barter?

Without exploring the subject sufficiently thoroughly to account for all the proverbial exceptions that prove the rule, we may say that it is a general tendency that societies on a certain scale are essential to each spe-cific form of human existence. From the vantage-point of capitalist society, the attribution of a "division of labor" to superficially scrutinized primitive societies may be more a matter of courtesy than of substance. Closer study of social relations may specify the location of the individual's exact place in the entire society so meticulously that, on encounter with the reported evidence, the ingenue anthropology student sometimes runs amok an-nouncing that "primitive peoples are just as advanced in complexity as we, just differently complex." It is sometimes difficult to decide which of the two extreme views is more pathetic. Perhaps, in the final analysis, the ingenue cultural relativist is in the worst fix, since his stupidity about primitive peoples has the quality of pathological ignorance rather than simple ignorance of a strange thing. In every human society is it essential that there be such "complexity." Because of the kinds of activities societies engage in, the fashion in which they are performed, and the relationships of these activities and their forms to the notion of the special identity of each individual, little more than simple arithmetic is necessary to demon-strate that the range of activities necessary to a culture's self-perpetuation requires a certain minimal population. It requires only more sophisticated "ecological analysis" of the same culture to see that the minimum is com-plemented by a maximum, and that in the relatively small grey area, the determination of the society's scale is bounded. It would seem to follow that the size of the society is a measure of its internal "complexity" of relations. The pitfalls of interpreting this point too simply are pointed up by the case of the Indian commune, for example. (The study of the history of Mesopotamia may be the most efficient approach to a general theorem; such a focal study could be used to order other evidence.)

What induces cultural relativism among half-educated anthropology undergraduates struggling through the internal mappings of a society is obvious enough. But the phenomenon ought to be briefly noted here, out of concern for similar difficulties affecting numerous of our readers. We have pointed out that alienation in capitalist society causes the most acutely estranged individuals, especially, of whom young university students are notoriously representative, to regard themselves as isolated, "natural," reductionist individuals in "natural relations" with objects and the like. To them, capitalist relations seem the natural form of relations of people to people and to things. This phenomenon is manifested most acutely in outbursts of "radicalism" among anthropology instructors and students, in particular, otherwise inclined to cultural relativist outlooks. Indeed, the dominant "radical caucus" among such persons is permeated with cultural relativism—a variety of radicalism that expresses the most reactionary world-outlook (epistemologically) in capitalist society. Some radicals! The point here is that they are not radicals at all in the literal sense of the term. They have assumed their own neurotic individual nature and world-outlook to be "natural," and employ it uncritically as the yardstick for all reality. Because they refuse to recognize that the sickness of this society is magnificently embodied in their "innate" world-outlook and value-judgments, or to question such implicit axiomatic assumptions, they must avoid examining capitalist culture by employing the tools they encounter in the undergraduate anthropology text's outline of the internal mapping of primitive tribes. They would never tolerate the mode of analysis implied by the starting-point of the process-sheet/bill-of-materials/bill-of-consumption network. They refuse to consider any evidence that would reveal how their own notions of self are determined. Yet such pathetic fools regard themselves as professionals.

In each culture, the socializing forces are the most important feature of social life. The division of food-rights, as well as duties, should warn us off any glib confusion of gift-exchange and barter. As we pointed out earlier, it is essential for a society that the mode of material reproduction of the population not be localized to groups smaller than the "whole tribe" —that is, smaller than the complete "unit" of necessary division of labor. A "division of labor" in this sense is the feature of life that makes a society a society. For example, careless observers (proceeding from their own profound problems *within this society*) often attribute "incest prohibitions" to "instinctual sexual" driver, morality, and the like, sometimes resorting to the fatuous presumption of "unconscious awareness of the genetical dangers of inbreeding," and other such rubbish. However—if we regard society as the unit of investigation, as we have noted before—society often could care not less about fornication practices among its youth at the same time that it ruthlessly enforces antiincestuous rules in the marriage relationship. Incest within marriage represents a deadly menace to society, since "inbreeding" in the acculturation of the society's members is a centrifugal tendency, whereas fornication patterns are significant only to the extent that they are relevant to the problems of acculturation.

The exchange of gifts, as we have noted, is not to be regarded simply as an exception to determinate relationships. Once we consider the implications of objects in light of the Hudson's Bay example, we realize that there are several ways in which gifts express something necessary. But we would not proceed intentionally from the pedagogical study to see in gifts the necessity of emergent barter. Barter need only arise when the gift is transformed into a need by shifting the "metastable equilibrium" in such a reversible or semi-irreversible fashion as to transform the gift not just into a need, but a need most effectively met through exchanges of a specific sort with a "tribe" other than one's own. In between, we have the problems of occasional need and a whole range of alternative needs for gifts, only special cases of which could lead to barter. From the limited standpoint that all societies are arrangements for socializing collective production, it would be sounder to call capitalism a communist society than to see barter in every manifestation of exchanges of gifts.[8] Because the organization of social-reproductive relationships within capitalism could be resolved and made coherent only through communism, in that sense the study of capitalist social-reproductive relations is a demonstration of the necessity of communism to that general model of social-reproductive relations. There is no such necessary implication in the general case of exchange of gifts.

A partly historic, partly heuristic definition of the evolution of the bill of exchange is as follows:

For the first approximation, let us take the semihypothetical case of three merchants living about the sixteenth century B.C. in the Near East. Merchant A is domiciled in upper Mesopotamia. Merchant B is domiciled in a Semite merchant ghetto in a Hittite city. Merchant C runs caravans between the two locations.

Merchant B trades the textiles, grains, and grain-laden pots to the second merchant. Oil and gold are consigned by B to A. C gets a cut of the trade both ways, and also does a bit of trading on his own account. The documents of the consignments, clay cuneiform tablets in clay cuneiform envelopes, become implicitly negotiable commodities in themselves. They are instruments bearing an expected profit, and thus implicitly represent capital. The trade of a variety of such bills of exchange of various "barter"-denominations will cause an imbalance in the community of merchants whose interconnected exchanges are the complete market. This imbalance is ideally, and to a certain extent actually, settled in gold.

Two notions are deduced from this arrangement. First, all of the exchanges are implicitly reduced to equivalents of gold. Second is the notion of the reserve ratio. It should be clear that the market for bills of exchange depends upon the circulation of sufficient gold to permit adjustments of the average level of balance of payments deficits occurring in a "day's" trading in such bills of exchange. The example of modern banking applies. Of the total current deposits of all kinds in banks, a certain maximum net outflow of cash may reasonably be expected each day as the net of new deposits less withdrawals of cash. To prevent bankruptcy, the bank must constantly have on hand sufficient cash to meet that contingency, or a consortium of banks must jointly maintain enough cash and share it (by buying and selling cash among themselves) to prevent the concentration of a day's withdrawals on any one bank from driving a member bank into bankruptcy—and perhaps thus triggering a chain-reaction collapse among all the banks. The ratio of such required cash to total deposits is a reserve ratio.[9]

In the same general way, there is a reserve ratio in any kind of capitalist economy as a whole. The amount of cash which must be on hand (in circulation) to insure the continuity of trade must be a certain percentage of the total transactions. If paper money is backed by gold, the same principle applies. It is not necessary to have a dollar of gold for each dollar of currency. It is required only that there be that proportion of gold "backing" equaling expected levels of gold withdrawals against the balance of withdrawals/deposits in paper money.

For example, let us now suggest that paper-money "gold certificates" are—as they are—bills of exchange for gold. If a 10 per cent reserve ratio obtains, a bank having $100 in gold may safely issue $1000 in currency. If there is also a 10 per cent ratio of net cash imbalance of average trading cleared by checking-account transactions through a bank, the bank's $100 secures $10,000 average deposits, or has the effect of circulating $10,000 in trading buying power throughout the economy.

The bill of exchange as a form of capital (merchant's capital) should be obvious enough. The debt to which the bill represents title is the mass of commodities specified in the terms and conditions of the bill. This bill *becomes* capital when it becomes "discountable"—when it ceases to be merely a barter instrument and becomes a source of profit-income to the purchaser, and thus a property title to self-expanding value. It then becomes a commodity itself; it becomes merchant's capital and a true bill of exchange.

This bill of exchange is not merely another disguise for capital in general. It is the form of capital that leads mercantile capitalism into capitalism proper through the development and outcome of the European Renaissance. It is the use of profitable (discountable) bills of exchange for trade in commodities *being produced for trade* that leads into mercantile capitalist production of commodities, which in turn establishes the germ of future capitalism within mercantile capitalist evolution.

CREDIT

It is an essential feature of capital in all forms that the existence of capital implies a separation of the acts of sale and purchase. Capital is determined as the rate and mass of self-expansion of income between two points in time, points which correspond to the time-lapse between purchase and sale, or vice-versa. Thus—to return to fundamentals—capital and credit are two aspects of the same social phenomenon.

It is not necessary to receive cash for the sale of goods; goods may be exchanged for a promissory note. What is a promissory note but a special kind of bill of exchange? It is an obligation to deliver "value" at some explicitly or implicitly stated future time. As this IOU becomes negotiable and discountable, it bears profit-income and thus becomes capital. It may be deposited or discounted with a bank, and new credit may be issued by that bank against such deposits to the extent that its reserve ratio permits.

This bears upon the most commonly posed pseudo-problem of capitalist economy, which we have reviewed before. The student inquires of the instructor, "Where does the money to buy the surplus production come from?" The question itself has only clinical, not scientific, interest. The mental state that attributes something magical to credit reflects nothing but a metaphysical fetishistic attitude toward the self-evident value of money in itself.

We already know that capital goods lent to a capitalist, to an employer, will, if they represent the material preconditions of self-expanding value, result in a future realization of more than the value consumed in their usage (annulment, realization). Thus this employer, as the borrower, will be able (willing or not) to pay back tomorrow more than he takes today. Not accidentally, every industrial borrower makes the same point to his prospective creditor; the creditor's willingness to make the loan depends upon his receipt of and belief in such an argument from the prospective borrower. An interest-bearing promissory note (or discountable bill of exchange in some form) is all that is required to accomplish the distribution of the surplus production. No "buy-back" problem really exists, unless the "surplus production" does not represent conditions of (potential) self-expanding value or is not productively employed.

An analytical catalogue of the architectonics of credit forms and relationships would require an encyclopedia. A full description of these constructs, and the machinations of the human intellect they represent, would make Balzac seem like a Candide. There is nothing quite so eerie as the feeling one experiences, after first mastering the art of credit, participating in negotiations among financiers and their clients, focussing one's attention on the workings of the minds behind the proposals and counterproposals. Behind the persona of the banker there is a feral little Levantine gnome, a manic little Rumpelstiltskin with a store of magical spells and incantations, a student and journeyman of black magic, a peculiar little

Faust. . . . Make no mistake: this fellow is capable of almost anything; he would destroy whole universes with his spells. The real world does not exist for him; he lives in a world of spells and incantations involving credit. But because his spells and incantations have power over the real world, it is necessary to understand his mentality. He is extremely dangerous.

To that end, let us use as an illustration the resale of credit. The industrialist sells (discounts) his debts with a financier; what does the financier do with such debts? He resells them, in large part, to obtain new credit with which he can buy more debts from industrialists. He, like the stock-buyer in our earlier illustration, may resell all his purchased debts at a favorable rate of interest. Alternatively, he may issue stock, debentures, or what-have-you against his financing company, or borrow "lump-sum" credit. The buyer of his debts is considering both the collectability (risk, liquidity) of the debts acquired by the financier reselling his holdings and the net liquidity of the financier's banking operations as whole. The purchaser of the resold (discounted) debts is considering both the quality of the paper he is buying (apropos the credit of the original debtor) and the liquidity of the banker discounting this paper directly or indirectly. The latter involves the notion of "recourse," one of the most fascinating aspects of financial chess-play.

There are two general ways in which a banker or financier may rediscount the debts of the industrialist: with explicit recourse or implicit recourse.

The first is simple. If the industrialist defaults on payment or certain other contingencies arise, the industrialist's immediate creditor of original record (who has rediscounted the industrialist's debts) must "buy back" the tarnished debt. There are innumerable variations on this theme in practice, and various formulas by which the matter of recourse is applied to the bulk of the sold debt rather than to item-by-item recourse. This process is much more interesting than the most ingenious mystery novel.

The highest drama, the most magnificent fantasies are evoked by implicit recourse, a term which refers, in general, to the sale of securities and the like by the banker. In a general sense, what the financier or banker is selling is the smell of the soup, the aromas of his financial statement. The buyer is often assuming that he is obtaining income at a lower rate of risk and higher quality of liquidity than would be appropriate for the discount price or yield. In other words, the financier or other purchaser of the stock or bonds of the financial house is assuming that the yield on the security is higher than would be necessary for instruments of comparable risk and liquidity.

Let us examine two illustrations.

Insurance is one of the most fascinating expressions of the operations of financial capital. The insurance company is buying a yield, net premium income, and playing that yield against the expectation of casualties and the like. The trick is to buy risk at a higher premium income than the prevailing actuarial ratios for that type of risk would prescribe. For example, if the type of insurance coverage provided to a certain general classification of insured persons is 1 per cent and the average claim is $100, the industry establishes what it considers is a permissible price for such coverage of the 100 per cent of the category. Now the gnomes go to work to attempt to beat the averages. The trick is to sell as much insurance as possible within this category and at the same time, by selectively weeding out insured persons, to reduce the average claim to less than $100 and the claim rate in that category of coverage to below 1 per cent.

Let us simply imagine that an unscrupulous insurance company decides to do the following. The insurance company executives, scrutinizing their payroll, note the number of high-priced actuaries and related personnel and consider ways to reduce this item of cost. "Isn't there some way we can break this down to use fewer skilled professionals and pass most of the work over to low-priced college graduates?" They muse for a while, until someone suggests: "Why don't we just arbitrarily cancel coverage of a certain percentage of policies in each category for any persons or areas or categories that smell like higher risk? By doing so, and selling new coverage, we would lower our claim rate in the turnover. We'd save on the cost of systematically evaluating policies. We could use ordinary college kids to screen policies and eliminate a certain percentage each month. We wouldn't need so many high-priced professionals. We'd really make more on the average than by going through policies in a professional way." Imagine an insurance company accepting such a proposal, and consider the result. Imagine the firm reducing experienced claims to 0.8 per cent and the average claim to $76, under circumstances in which the industry is calculating its profits on the basis of a 1 per cent ratio and $100 average claim.

The result of such an operation would be a capital gain in the value of the insurance company's holdings. What it "makes" is not merely what it saves in added marginal earnings. The value of the insurance company is increased by an amount determined by multiplying the added earnings by the price-earnings ratio for the firm.

Let us oversimplify the case (without affecting the basic principle) in order to illustrate the nature of the operation more exactly. The ratios of 1 per cent and $100 per claim represent $1.00 per policy sold. Let us eliminate the costs of operating, selling commissions, and the like, and note that a 10 per cent profit on sales would mean adding $1.10 to the costs of maintaining insurance per policy issued. However, at 0.8 per cent and $76, we have reduced the actual claim cost per policy to less than $0.61. We have saved $0.39, raising the income per policy to $0.49 from $0.10, and, if the price-earnings ratio for the firm is 10 and the volume of insurance has remained constant through turnover, we seem to have increased the capital value of the corresponding section of operations from $1.00 per policy to $4.90 per policy! In addition, the costs of administration have been reduced. Salaries per policy have been reduced by using cheap college graduates in place of professionals. The intake administrative activity has undoubtedly increased somewhat, since new policies received per month must be increased to maintain the same volume, but savings on processing claims probably compensate. Actual operations are not quite so simple, but the principle is as we have described.

The 1963–1964 case described in *The Great Salad Oil Swindle* by a former *Wall Street Journal* reporter, Norman C. Miller, is the other example we shall consider here. The book speaks for itself, in large part, and is recommended to the student as eminently useful background reading. The nature of the case, like that of the 1970 collapse of the Penn Central Corporation, involves implicit recourse, the sales of the aroma of a financial statement. In both cases the pattern is exactly the reverse of that of our insurance example. Here, it is the buyer of credit who is losing the leverage battle. He is buying debt at a higher risk and lower liquidity than is reflected in the yield of his purchase. What makes the salad-oil case and the Penn Central collapse so useful to us is the celebrity of the parties victimized, who were not generally ignorant bunglers who did not know their business. These cases illustrate a general vulnerability within the business-financial community. The author has had business dealings with some of the participants in both cases, and is convinced that some of the victims of the collapse were among the shrewdest operators, and others among the less competent, in such circles. The fact that both types were taken in illustrates the generality of the phenomena involved.

The case of the Penn Central is cited because the author was peripherally concerned with the inevitable collapse of both the Pennsylvania and New York Central railroads in the late 1950s. During this period he was briefed—which had the effect of confirming his own judgments—at the direction of one of the Pennsylvania's top executives. There was no doubt in 1958–1959 that unless the merger was immediately effected and a definite program of development and rationalization instituted, both railroads would go on welfare. This was clear to both top managements at the time—at least it was clear to the Pennsylvania management, who made the necessary points to the obdurate New York Central management. In this case, issues of short-term paper gain insured that the merger, when it ultimately occurred, would be much too late to do much good. Featherbedding and the other issues that were noisily discussed were absolutely not the problem. The issues of short-term gain, intrinsic to the heteronomic form of capital in a capitalist economy, prompted the management of the New York Central, especially, to pursue a course of action which meant undermining and continuing to undermine the very basis for existence of both railroads in a modern economy. However, this does not mean that the management of the New York Central acted imprudently by the ordinary capitalist standards applicable to its stewardship. Its heteronomic approach to the problem is the approved capitalist approach. If the Pennsylvania's management took a more enlightened, longer-term outlook, one wonders how much this is attributable to their knowledge of the circumstances, and how much to the fact that the proposed merger action then corresponded to their short-term situation.

The salad-oil case is exemplary, and all the more so because of the enormous injustice done to the alleged swindler, Anthony DeAngelis. A variety of critics, including Miller, probe the psychological origins of De-Angelis' conduct. Miller, like others, posits DeAngelis' background in marginal operations as a contributing factor in the situation. Nonsense! Miller, a superior reporter, typifies the inherent difficulty confronting capitalists and procapitalist analysts in attempting to account for peculiarities of this sort intrinsic to capitalist behavior. Once a catastrophe of this sort strikes, capturing the imagination, coveys of experts scurry back and forth attempting to demonstrate its abnormality. Miller gives all the facts necessary to the most compelling defense of DeAngelis. DeAngelis behaved with normal capitalist circumspection according to strict capitalist principles. It will require another depression and its muckraking revelations to convince more than a few people of this fact, but it is a fact nonetheless.

Miller goes off the track completely in his effort to locate the reason for DeAngelis' kiting of paper on nonexistent tanks of oil to the man's mental state, a "Napoleonic" complex or what-have-you. This is absolutely normal behavior for most capitalists facing illiquidity. Either they squat in self-pity, awaiting the inevitable disaster, or they fight with any imaginable weapon "to save the business." Kiting paper, or the equivalent, is the only resource available for this purpose; so every impending illiquidity results in one of only two general alternative behavior patterns. Either the capitalist behaves like the self-pitying wretch he is, confessing his bankruptcy to anyone who will listen, or he keeps his illiquidity strictly to himself, and digs in for a fight. In some cases, the result is what is called in the trade "a successful bankruptcy," in which capital is somehow bled from the imperilled firm to be squirrelled away in the name of wife, brother-in-law, cousin, or what-have-you, where it remains until it is resurrected to become the capital of a new firm. In general, the only alternative for the capitalist who has no remedy in the domain of real values is a temporary expedient in the realm of purely fictitious capital. The longer the crisis persists, the more tenuously fictitious the capital involved (created) becomes. The capitalist, like a member of any species, fights to save his species-existence. (That is the essential psychology of the matter, period.) His first "instinct" is to "save the business" on which his species-identity as a capitalist immediately depends; otherwise, his only alternative is a kind of metempsychosis, with capital from the old business serving as his ectoplasm.

In this magical realm of credit resides the germ of the solution to the problem posed by the cited passages from Volume III of *Capital*. Sweeping aside the various pseudo-representations of "natural capitalism" and pseudo-questions about the buy-back problem, the essential problem of capitalism in all forms is the risk that the gross income requirements of all capitals will exceed the absolute profit of the capitalist society, that the mass of profit obligations to capital in general will exceed the mass of commodities representing profit.

If that occurs, the balance-of-payments deficit in trade on the profit account must rise toward the point of exceeding the limits defined by existing reserve-ratio allowances. Through more complex intermediate processes, an apparent overproduction of commodities for sale leads to a run on gold and a depression or capitalist crisis. The inability of the borrower to realize sufficient increases in absolute profit by consumption of the "surplus commodities" prevents him from creating new credit in the economy. This causes a constriction in the scale of production, which causes a reduction in the absolute profit (in commodity values) available to capital as a whole. This increases the balance-of-trade deficits on the profit account, leading to a run on money, then to a run on gold, and so on to a bust.

The irony of this situation is that an increase in production of self-expanding use values and increased deliveries would result in an absolute increase in surplus values in real terms. The problem is that, at current price-earnings ratios for capitals, there is too much capital—in capitalist market terms. The only remedies are a general simultaneous devaluation of price-earnings ratios or a general devaluation of capitals—the same thing, in the final analysis. This is exactly what does occur in a capitalist fashion —through a depression. The spirally contraction ensuing from the starting conditions ultimately does wipe out masses of capitalists' capitals. Periodic depressions are the way in which the internal dynamics of capitalist accumulation attempt to maintain "equilibrium." To imagine an "equilibrium level" for capitalism exclusive of periodic depressions is a patent fallacy of composition.

EXTENDED REPRODUCTION

This sort of problem arises from a peculiarity of capitalist society proper, although—as we have indicated—genetically similar problems characterize mercantile capitalism. The significant aspect of profit is that portion which is accumulated as enlarged capital. Thus, we have the old capital demanding the same mass of new profit as it has just consumed; we also have the mass of newly accumulated capital (from previous profit-income) demanding its proportionate additional new profit-income to increase geometrically.

This assumes that the surplus production corresponding to profit in the capitalist economy consists of potential (as preconditional) self-expanding use value. To satisfy this qualification, not only must the use value of such commodities imply a potential profit yield resulting from their productive employment, but this productive employment must actually be realized. In the final analysis, *capitalist production is profitable only to the extent that it consists of such realized use value.*

If that condition is fulfilled, some additional assumptions must also be satisfied to prevent unavoidable depressions. First, the problem of rising productivity of labor must be assumed not to exist. Second, we must assume that capitalist production does not depend upon consumption of use values taken from outside the domain of capitalist production—that is, ravishing of natural resources. Third, we must assume that capitalists are not creating purely fictitious or speculative increases, in particular, in the mass of capital—that is, not creating obligations to capital outside the domain of usefully expanded production. It happens that capitalism never avoids precisely such violations of the preconditions for avoiding new depressions. All three problems are, in fact, inherent in the capitalist system, thus creating the fundamental contradictions between the expanded reproduction of capitalists' capitals in general and the development of the productive forces in general. This fundamental antinomy leads to new depressions or even general breakdowns in the economy.[10]

CAPITAL IN ITS "SUBJECTIVE" FORM

Let us now emphasize some points to be reconsidered in the succeeding chapters. Although the reproduction of self-expanding use value is the historical reality of production under capitalism, capitalist society is not conscious of self-expanding use value as such, but only of the self-expansion of capitalist valuations, which is at best in only partial conformity to the notion of a projective correspondence between values and use values. Furthermore, since the successive moments of the real economy (the historic process of social reproduction in use-value terms) are mediated through the social superstructure, the underlying laws of the social-reproductive process exist immediately for humanity under capitalism only to the extent that such laws are reflected through capitalist forms. This point, considered earlier, now impels us to recognize the need to systematically alter the notion of productive labor previously developed[11] to define productive labor now in the form of a social fact of capitalist accumulation. This compels us, on grounds considered in Chapter 6, to radically redefine the notions of wealth in a similar fashion. The capitalist notion of wealth cannot be the notion of wealth derived from a rigorous assimilation of the conception of self-expanding use value. Here again we find a key to the contradictions between capitalists' capital in general and the real social-reproductive basis.

The appropriateness of capitalist society to a certain phase of development of man's social-reproductive forces is mainly located in the "parallelism" of the processes of self-expanding use value, on the one hand, and enlarged capitalist reproduction of capitalist capital on the other. Capitalist economy behaves as if it assumes a one-to-one correspondence between these two process. The notion of productive labor must be altered, as we have said, from that stipulated for self-expanding use value to become defined as the production of capitalists' surplus value. Productive labor assumes the form of capital, whose price is defined as it is determined for capital, just as all capital is determined for capitalist accumulation in general. It is determined by a kind of price-earnings ratio, in which the price of labor is predicated upon its rate of surplus (capitalist) value, or upon the rate of capital accumulation derived from productive labor's employment, that labor's production of such surplus values.

Productive labor was previously defined as that which increases the ratio $S'/(C + V)$ in social terms for the entire society. Capitalist accumulation defines labor power in specifically capitalist terms of the expression $S' (F + C + V)$ or even $S' (d + F + C + V)$, but the value of these terms is that of capitalists' capitals, not their real social content. The definition of value is given for each term by the expression M into C into M', where M' is greater than M, and by M into C into M' into C' into M'', where C' is greater than C and M'' greater than M'. The specific measure of labor power is approximately given as S'/V, where the values of S' and V are determined by relations of the M–C–M form.

For related reasons, we have the following sort of ironical occurrences. Arms production in a government—nonprofit—arsenal is not productive, while production of the same arms in a private—profitable—arsenal is productive![12] In neither case is the production productive from the standpoint of $S'/(C + V)$ in use-value terms, and in the final analysis the more productive arms production a capitalist economy engages in, the more rapidly it is moving toward a breakdown crisis.

This does not mean that capitalism as a process does not approximately distinguish between use value and nonuse value. In the overall process, those varieties of commodities that are not a form of self-expanding value tend to destroy their consumers and thus eradicate the capital created as credit issued for the sale of such commodities. Destruction of the consumers means not physical extermination of the firm or individual but a reduction in the relative rate of increased power (profitability, productivity) of the firm or individual expending resources on useless rather than useful things. In the "organic" evolution of capitalism—the "organic" evolution of a general division of productive labors into a certain characteristic array of interconnected industries and specific forms of production of commodities—the reality of self-expanding value determines approximately what kinds of capitalist activities will be reproduced. These are merely general "organic" tendencies, which admit of the broadest exceptions over the longer term, as well as acute short-term deviations. Even in such a slovenly fashion, use value regulates the broad evolution of capitalist economy, and the effects of this process are reflected in the social facts of "superstructural practices," ruling ideas, and other alienated, "neurotic," and distorted representations of reality.

The principal immediate source of this latitude for the grossest deviations from reality is the anarchy of capitalism, such that capitalists, treating parochialized aspects of capital in general as virtually autonomous "economies" (heteronomy), cannot distinguish between absolute and relative surplus values in any immediate way.

The best illustration of this problem for the urban dweller in the United States is the cited case of the real-estate market in old buildings. Based on the price-earnings ratio for real estate, income properties (apartment buildings) are capitalized at a multiple of the profits exacted from rents. These capitalizations are discounted through first and second mortgages, milking the savings banks by leveraging capital from savings-bank depositors for the use of the major commercial banks and financiers. By reducing services in urban rental properties, for example, and by collusion with federal, state, and municipal governments to raise rents and reduce maintenance expenditures, the profits of the holdings are increased, multiplying the capitalization of the property titles through speculative resales, increasing the mass of capital-in-general intertwined with the cancerous mass of sheer speculation involved.

The cancerous enlargements of speculative or otherwise fictitious capitalists in these kinds of manipulations accomplish several things of devastating ultimate effect for the capitalist economy. First, the incomes on which these speculations are predicated come out of the real economy. What could otherwise be the basis for self-expanding value is thus destroyed, while the urban decay and accelerating costs imposed upon urban communities are spread by such decay. Second, this involves expanding capitalists' capitals in general by reducing the means for creating expanded future tangible wealth against the account of increased capitals.

A rational economy, by contrast, would restrict "profit" to absolute profit, and would distribute to the various parts of the economy portions of the absolute profit of the whole economy. In this way, the controlling factor governing investment would be the notion of those investments and capital formations which fulfill the conditions of realization of self-expanding value. The anarchy of capitalist economy (the system of autonomous property titles) precludes such systematical practical distinctions between absolute surplus value and fictitious relative surplus value. Under circumstances in which the rates of speculative gains tend to feed themselves, so that speculation, or the growth of fictitious relative surplus value, proceeds at an advantage relative to production of absolute surplus value, the anarchy of the capitalist organization of society leads inevitably and rather hastily toward a general monetary crisis of the sort described above.

Central to this process is the capitalist state. It is the police power of the state to enforce collection of profits for capital (in all capital's various forms) that is the fundamental political content of capitalists' capital. Consequently, the nature of capital could not be adduced by dissecting capitals in particular—by examination of the books of individual firms *ad infinitum*. Capital as an economic form is a determination of a political process. It is in the state that the essence and content of capital is situated.

This circumstance dictates that the postulates of capitalist society be those of anarchic (or heteronomic) capitalism. The individual wage, the form of the material existence of the wage-earner, is a form of capital (Variable Capital or Capitalists' Consumption). The mode of existence of society, which is actually an interdependent whole, is reduced to the form of capitalist anarchy, a mere aggregation of contending parochialist interest-group formations. The very notion of a liberal pluralistic society as an ideal is nothing but a poorly disguised epiphenomenon of capital. Capitalist heteronomic property right in self-expanding values is the nerve and fist of all capitalist law and is embedded in the determined "consensus" of the ruled.

As we shall see in Chapter 10, the distinctions between self-expanding use value and capital are such that the fundamental reproductive categories are defined quite differently in every respect for capitalism than we defined them for the social-reproductive labor process in earlier chapters. Not only are the notions of "productive" and "wealth" reduced almost to parodies of their reality, but the magnitudes of the categories of Constant Capital, Variable Capital, and Surplus Value are by no means in necessary asymptotic convergence upon monetary equivalents of the real (use) value. Worse, whole decisive categories of use value are viciously ignored, while purely fictitious valuations are "loaded" into the accounts of capital.

So we have the foundation for beginning to comprehend what Marx saw as the historic contradictions between capitalists' capitals *in general* and the real social-reproductive basis. We have a preliminary view into the "internal contradiction" between capitalist values and use values, the contradiction that is the inevitable cause of the recurrence of capitalist depressions and general breakdown crises.

FEUDAL TO CAPITALIST REPRODUCTION 10

FEUDAL TO CAPITALIST REPRODUCTION 10

In Chapter 9 we located the connection of "objective" social reproduction to capitalism in the imposition of those juridical notions of capital associated with simple mercantile capitalism. We must now consider the chemistry of this fusion, which produces capitalist economy as such.

In this undertaking we confront two problems. The first, the seemingly formal problem, is that of accounting for the actual, deliberate interconnections of two processes which cannot be comprehended as one in a mathematical fashion—maximization of the price of capitals and maximization of the use value of social reproduction. We have already indicated that the answer is implicit in Kant's notion of Praxis;[1] we shall indicate exactly how in due course. The second problem is that of synoptically describing the historical process by which mercantilism and social reproduction were fused to form capitalism.

FEUDAL VERSUS CAPITALIST REPRODUCTION

Survey-course descriptions of Marxism edify the student with this truism: Marxism asserts that socialism must emerge from capitalism, which emerged from feudalism. Indeed, we must conclude that some professed Marxists have catered to this nonsense, from either simple-mindedness or infection with their own rhetoric. However, it should already be obvious that none of the elements of capitalist society existed within feudal society —at least until feudalism had been radically transformed by mercantilism. But in European and North American capitalist countries, in particular, we find all the "objective" ingredients for socialist society: a working class, socialization of capitalist production and consumption on a world scale, development of the productive forces, and so on.

An accurate account of the evolution of capitalism is as follows: contradictions within feudal social reproduction prompted the emergence of mercantile capitalism, which transformed feudal society, creating the rudiments of capitalist classes and juridical forms as well as the rudiments of capitalist reproduction, which itself created the preconditions for the emergence of capitalism proper. This essential process of transition occupied the period of modern history from approximately the fourteenth century through the bankruptcies of the Spanish and Portuguese monarchies in the late sixteenth century. The latter point was followed by approximately a century of general collapse, and probably by the depopulation of Europe[2] as well, out of which collapse capitalist development proper emerged.

What do we mean by "feudalism"? To begin with, we do not mean a selected cross-sectional view of any particular section of feudal Europe at some point in time. Feudalism is properly defined as an abstraction of the process of social reproduction encountered in all the permutations of feudal social-juridical relations as the dominant mode of social existence. The objective nature of feudalism is no less real for appearing to us as an abstraction—for reasons already sufficiently developed. Moreover, we can readily identify concrete events which precisely expressed the universal essence of feudalism. That essence is the crusade—a concept which subsumes the Crusades proper, the Norman Conquest, the Albigenses, the petty rapacities of baronies, and the Teutonic Knights' easterly expeditions of conquest.

Essentially, the social surplus of feudalism existed in the form of an alienable population of surplus knights, serfs, and others. This surplus population, as an armed band, occupied new territories, sometimes exterminating the previous occupants and sometimes reducing them to the status of feudal serfs.

As this mode of reproduction encountered bounds of extent, it became cannibalistic. Or, always endemically cannibalistic, it became epidemically so. Out of the military system of social reproduction emerged the development of mercantile capitalism; out of the inward-turning of this military system came the looting of feudalism by emergent mercantile capitalism. This is the gist of the documented history of the House of Bardi, in the fourteenth century, when the marriage of poorly disguised usury with military expeditions became the history of Europe.

In order to obtain the necessary material and logistical support for wars and expeditions of conquest, the feudal potentate surrendered increasing proportions of his potential surplus. Thus, the juridical principle of alienable produced wealth began to displace feudal forms of social reproduction. The social forces commanded by mercantile wealth appropriated increasing portions of the proletarianized peasantry and professional soldiery. The mercantile process appropriated increasing proportions of the peasant population. As the feudal lord himself intensified exploitation of his serfs, thus depopulating his estates in order to pay his mercantilist suppliers and creditors, the rudiments of a proletariat were created. The putting-out mercantile system of cottage industry made further inroads into the feudal process of social reproduction.

Yet mercantile capitalism's involvement in emerging forms of capitalist production remained a modest part of its total capitalist accumulation, merely large enough to accomplish the systematic ruin of existing guild production. In this connection, one may consider the irony of the Medici as typical of the Italian bankers of that period. To the extent that the Medici extended the Italian system to northern Europe, where they fostered the development of mercantile capitalism and the manufacture of cheap woolens in England and the Low Countries, thus ruining the hegemony of the Italian broadcloth industry—and similarly creating a balance-of-trade deficit in the southern sector for the account of the northern, bringing about the collapse of the House of Medici and the shift of mercantile power to Augsburg and the Low Countries from the early through middle fifteenth century.

The essential character of mercantilism is made more apparent by examining the immediate causes of the collapse of the leading banking-houses during the period from the fourteenth through sixteenth centuries. The growing debt-service obligations represented by loans repeatedly outran the alienable income of the nation-debtors, bringing monarchies (and others) to the point of repudiating their debts and bankrupting the banking-houses involved—as in the general collapse which ended this period, the Spanish and Portuguese bankruptcies.

The lesson to be adduced from these prominent developments of the period is that the rate at which mercantilism caused an increase in national wealth was far slower than the rate of growth of debt-service obligations on account of the capital created to the account of the creditors. The objective content of this phenomenon is underlined by the thesis of Hobsbawm and others, to which we have several times referred: the century of collapse and even widespread depopulation of Europe that followed the Spanish and Portuguese bankruptcies. In the process of depopulation of the feudal estates through mercantilist primitive accumulation, the smallest proportion of the thus-determined "excess population" was absorbed in new forms of creation of real wealth—to the evident effect of a general decline in the scale of available wealth and, therefore, a contraction in the scale of loot available to support the mercantilist system.

Therefore, as we have indicated, the continued existence of mercantilism came to depend upon the success of mercantile capitalism in expanding the absolute scale of real social wealth—through capitalist forms of social reproduction. This thesis does not overlook the important role of mercantilist monopolies (that is, "gentlemen adventurers" chartered by monarchs in return for a "piece of the action"), or the continued general predominance of other forms of primitive accumulation in the period following the Thirty Years' War. However, this new wave of mercantilism would have led to nothing but a quick repetition and worsening of existing "depressed" conditions had not the scale of social wealth as a whole been on the increase because of the growing contributions of capitalist production.

It would be a digression from the purpose of this text to dwell on the elaborate reasons why a return to simple feudalism was impossible. It is sufficient to point out that both juridical forms and military technology precluded such a reversion. The survival of any part of Western Europe depended upon utilizing the most advanced technologies in terms of the juridical forms appropriate to such modes of production. The details of this process are a proper subject for dissertations by serious students.

The essential point is now situated; it has merely to be identified and developed. It is that the historically determined connection between mercantile capitalist price-earnings–ratio determination of the price of capital and an underlying, emerging mode of capitalist social reproduction is located uniquely in the contradictions of capitalist accumulation on (immediately) the scale of an entire capitalist society and, beyond that, in the connection between these two processes on a world scale—or what Luxemburg emphasizes as the "total capitalist" rigor of empirical investigations.

THE DIALECTIC OF CAPITALISM

The fallacy of mercantile capitalism is that it locates profit as capital in the buying of commodities for mere resale. Obviously, profits on resale can only represent mercantile looting of the wealth produced by society. Thus, to the extent that capital grows in aggregate as a result of mere buying and selling, usury, speculation, and other slick tricks, capital quickly outruns the material basis for continued payment on individual existing capitals as a whole. Capitalist accumulation obtains the material for its existence only as it appropriates real wealth not simply for resale but for social reproduction.

As emerging capitalist production joins together labor power and means of production (materials, machinery, plant) for the production of wealth, it brings into being the capitalist form of social reproduction of the working class as a whole while creating the working class itself. By thus creating and appropriating the social-reproductive process of labor power as a whole, capitalist production as a whole discovers, creates, and mulcts the basis in "negative-entropic" process for expanding social wealth as a whole. To this extent it creates the material basis for a successful expansion of capitalists' capitals as a whole.

Since, to reiterate, real wealth is limited to material objects which are either means of production or means of production of labor power, the mass of wealth corresponding to new capital corresponds to a mass of expanded social-reproductive forces (productive labor power and means of production). To the extent that this augmentation of real value content of new capital is "realized"—that is, employed as new production—the profit of new capital is ensured by the negative entropy of thus-expanded production as a whole.

In this way capitalists' capital as a whole acquires the content of self-expanding value. To the extent that all combined old and new capital represents newly created means of production (labor power, materials, machinery, plant), the investment of this capital (in the form of labor power and so on) as new production yields the rate of profit on *total* capital implicit in the currently prevailing rate of social reproduction (after, of course, deductions for capitalists' consumption).

However, as we noted in Chapters 6 and 7, the determination of social-reproductive negative entropy is not located in particular localized production. The relations of production (S, D, C, V, by departmental divisions) are uniquely located in the economy as a whole. Thus, there is no direct correspondence, in the causal or even strict probabalistic sense, between the mass of capitalists' capitals and a definite mass of use values (labor power, etc.) at any local point of production. The seeming correlation merely reflects the fact that the parallels between apportionments of capitalists' capitals and apportionments of social-reproductive categories have been historically determined by relations on the scale of the entire economy. (Again, Luxemburg's total capitalist rigor.)

Thus, we re-encounter with new understanding the meaning of the dialectical notions of the Value of Capitals and use value for social reproduction. In itself, as a mere object, capital of a certain price has no intrinsic value, even when it represents, as a property title, immediate title to a certain inventory of labor power, materials, machinery, plant, and the like. The value of capital is determined by its yield. Although idle capital may obtain an immediate yield by robbing other capitals or looting nature and wages, capital as a whole can have no yield except that determined by the rate of expanded reproduction in terms of the social-reproductive process as a whole. Thus, the content of capitalists' capital is located in such capital as a whole, and is identified as a definite rate of self-expansion in terms of titles to labor power and means of production which themselves represent the material basis for increasing the mass of social wealth at a profit. To realize such content, capital must command use values which represent self-expanding use value in terms of the social-reproductive process.

Thus, the imbecility of accounting for national output in terms of prices assigned to a mass of mere objects as such is apparent. The extent to which they represent wealth is not locatable in those objects as mere objects in inventory. They must be invested as productive forces, and the yield *which determines their value* is determined by the value of the exponential tendency associated with $S'/(C + V)$.

A MATHEMATICAL SOLUTION?

We shall shortly consider the twofold contradictions between capitalist accumulation and social reproduction. First, we should decide at this juncture whether the foregoing approximate model of capitalist accumulation actually describes an asymptotic process-relationship of the sort which would permit systematic, complete mathematical interpretation.

On the side of such hopes one could list the following factors. First, to the extent that either aspect of the process admits of mathematical interpretation, their mutual convergence would imply that the interpenetrating process as a whole would become increasingly susceptible to such treatment. Second, in defining the exponential representation of the law of social reproduction we have implied a variety of possible mathematical procedures either existing or suspected to be within reach. Indeed, to the extent that convergence exists between the empirical expressions for "self-expanding value" and "self-subsisting use value" respectively, mathematical descriptions of this sort are extremely useful and would play a large part in the computer support for national economic planning under socialism.

It is unfortunate that two problems preclude a complete mathematical analysis, in the sense of mathematical procedures amenable to formal-logical interpretation. To speak first of the broader, less sophisticated problem, the contradictions between capitalist accumulation and social-reproductive processes determine that the most significant features of capitalist development—the features bearing on prosperity and bust—are those involving a vicious want of convergence between value and social-reproductive values. Thus, the correspondence wanted exists only with respect to long periods of upward capitalist development of the sort that preceded the First World War. More profoundly, in the second instance, it should already be clear that the determination of the momentary tendency which determines the unity of successive empirical moments represents a quantity which is implicitly measurable after the fact. However, as the paralogism of the postulate of identity (A = A) indicates for all mathematical systems based on this postulate, the predetermination of this value is beyond mathematical schemes, and the complete description of the process of social reproduction, including this essential feature, is utterly beyond formal-logical comprehension.

What we can do with the aid of mathematical tools is to approximate a probable value for the *de facto* rate of social-reproductive negentropy, predicating such assumed values on certain current trends and the known effects of certain shifts in allocation of employment and means of production to various categories of production. Such assumptions do, indeed, provide the basis for planned economy over periods of three to seven years. These presumptions could not possibly predetermine the resulting rates of social reproduction; they merely serve as a guide in selecting a certain policy of productive development from among numerous alternatives.

Both the contradictions of capitalist economy and the inherent incompleteness of mathematical interpretation of socialist reproduction bring us to a consideration of notion of Praxis.

"FREEDOM" AND NATURAL LAW

Since this is by no means a textbook in mathematical physics, nor is the author a mathematical physicist, we address questions bearing on that specialized field with considerable irritation. As to the author's competence on this subject, two general points should be made. First, questions involving the limitations of mathematical procedure are elementary and do not properly involve even such elaborate around-the-barn approaches as were taken by Godel. Existing mathematical systems have a postulational structure, composed of a set of assumptions on which all the ensuing chess-play is premised. Second, the author's specific competence in mathematical economics is based generally on a uniquely successful outline of the entirety of the previous decade's economic history written in 1957–1958,[3] and on his efforts during the late 1950s and early 1960s to determine the necessary form of computer systems capable of simulating the entire operation of a firm—in the course of which, as a by-product, he was able to determine why computer simulation of human intelligence is impossible.[4] The practical urgency for considering this apparently specialized problem in this text is its bearing on both the competence of a "mathematical economics" generally and the more profound issue of proper social policies for a socialist economy. In this context, the fallacy of a mathematical economics is by no means a specialized question, but a practical question of immediate urgency to every future member of the human race.

Immanuel Kant was the first thinker to pose this problem in a systematic way. Kant divided knowledge into two major parts, continuing the paradoxical view of Descartes. On the one side, he posited the mere Understanding, containing pragmatically valid, mechanistic false knowledge of reality, which he deemed completely susceptible to mathematical interpretation. On the other side, he posited true, universal *a priori* knowledge beyond the direct knowledge of such imperfect beings as individual or collective man. In the *Critique of Practical Reason,* which we have previously considered, Kant developed his view of the distinction between these two kinds of knowledge and presented his notion of their actual practical interconnections for accessible human knowledge.

As we have noted, the element of knowledge which principally concerned Kant was the manifestation of "freedom" in human behavior of choice in action. This freedom represented, of course, an apparent freedom to violate predestination, in Euler's sense of universal determinism. In this Kant situated his greatest achievement: man, acting on his will, expresses this freedom in actuality, and thus introduces freedom to the realm of events comprehended by the mere Understanding. Kant concluded on such premises that real nature does not obey mathematical laws, and that the expression of freedom through the human will expressed itself as an efficient cause for nature outside man, thus making nature itself incompletely susceptible of mathematical interpretation.

Upon most English-speaking thinkers, who are professed fanatical philosophical imbeciles, this point of philosophy makes no impression. However, the most serious European creative mathematical intellects, who have been mainly responsible for fundamental scientific progress through the early decades of this century, have had a far more sensitive conscience on this matter. It is easily demonstrated from almost the entirety of the literature that, like Kepler, the founder of modern physical science, these thinkers have painstakingly considered problems of epistemology and, in most instances, developed their foremost innovations in scientific thought on the explicit basis of philosophical considerations. Most of the recent thinkers have been more or less closely associated with what is called the neo-Kantian point of view. (Even serious English-speaking scientists have obviously attended to these questions.)

In general, it must be recognized that the neo-Kantians have been less scrupulous than Kant himself—who condemned any effort to establish a logical positivism, on the grounds we have already cited. Instead, proceeding more from desperate faith than reason, those in the logical-positivist factions of the so-called neo-Kantian species have attempted to disprove Kant's fundamental point by locating the possibility of an immediate or ultimate possibility for mathematical completeness in the paradoxes occurring within their own investigations.

The literature of the past century, ironically, reflects a concern to eliminate the pernicious dualism of the Kantian system. It should be obvious that such an effort in itself is an attempt to do what Hegel accomplished in a preliminary fashion. If the dualism is false, Hegel is correct vis-à-vis Kant, since Hegel was the only thinker (excepting Feuerbach and Marx) who situated his solution to the Kantian dualism in the only location in which such a solution could possibly be located—in respect to the "Dialectic of Practical Reason." With few exceptions, mainly among those physicists who have explored the systematic problems of evolutionary biology, they have regressed to a narrow, one-sided view of the *Critique of Pure Reason*, and attempted to solve the Kantian paradox by ignoring the central feature of the Kantian system, the *Critique of Practical Reason*.

What all this signifies is precisely what we have been considering since Chapter 5. Once we consider the fundamental facts of historical human existence, even within the terms in which Kant posed the notion of universality of Praxis, the *a posteriori* fact of the consequences of the acting human will for freedom is the hylozoic-monist negative entropy of the underlying material universe. Since, as even the neo-Kantians recognized from the ancient Greek *tropes*,[5] there is no possible knowledge but human knowledge,[6] and no known universe except as it exists for human practice, Kant's revolutionary discovery of Praxis, the implicit solution to the old dualism problem, demonstrates that what we would today term the nonmathematical form of understanding of the universe is the only fundamental and the only possible complete understanding of the universe. Indeed, Hegel, Feuerbach, and Marx successively demonstrate just that.

Now let us assess the practical implication of this point for socialism generally and for the problem of understanding capitalist economy. The central practical question of human existence is precisely the noetic aspect of human collective mentation and resulting social practice on which rising values for the exponential function of $S'(C = V)$ entirely depend. The efficient determination of socioeconomic policy cannot, therefore, be a group of mathematical geniuses beneficently planning the economy from a vast computer complex. The implementation of economic planning and the posing of policy problems in economic planning may indeed require such experts, but the solution to the key problem can be provided by no other computer than the collective noetic mentation of the entire political class-for-itself.

This is by no means a denial of the indispensable role of the program which can only be developed by an initiating socialist vanguard. Hegel effectively deals with this special problem in the outset of his *Phenomenology.*[7] Without such programs, developed by an initiating elite, the political class-for-itself cannot be brought into being. However, the rational society can only be a society in which policy is noetically formulated by the collective Praxis of a class-for-itself as an entirety.

Apart from that important consideration, how does this notion of Praxis apply to the problem of analyzing the two-process interpenetration of capitalist economy? The description of the emergence of capitalism from the breakdown crisis of the sixteenth and seventeenth centuries should have made it clear that capitalist accumulation is nothing but a form of alienated Praxis. The capitalist takes actions based on the "freedom" of his will, such that he becomes the acting cause on behalf of his will in the domain of universal actuality. In this way the subjective aspect of capitalist society becomes objective for social reproduction.

However, since the capitalist does not represent the empirical reality of the social-reproductive class, his decision (his freedom) is not rational. There is no direct correspondence between his notion of freedom and the empirical universality (the reproduction of the social-reproductive class process) in which his "free" will is effective cause for the resulting condition of mankind. The capitalist knows the sequelae of his will as an efficient cause only at one remove from reality, in the fictitious form of the social-reproductive process represented by capitalist accumulation.

Here, the secret of Kant's negation of the negation and of the French Revolution itself are brilliantly illuminated. Kant posits that freedom expressed by individual egoistic will cannot directly know itself as true freedom for (as Hegel would put it, more correctly than Kant) the reproduction of the individual human being. That is, individual capitalist freedom, as Kant points out by using—appropriately—nothing but capitalist examples, cannot directly correspond to a categorical imperative. The universal must somehow act against the wrong freedom of the individual will to beat the individual will into conformity with the practical reality of a categorical imperative.

Thus, Kant demands that there exist some efficient means by which society collectively beats down (negates) the bad egoistical moments of freedom in the individual mind, to deprive the individual will of everything but those moments of freedom acceptable to society as a whole (the categorical imperative).

Does such a process of negation exist for the capitalist in capitalist society? In other words, is there some efficient reflection of the Law of Value in the fictitious realm of capitalist accumulation? Precisely, as we shall see: to the extent that disobedience to capitalist laws of the market tends to act in a countervailing way to destroy the identity of the misguided individual capitalist as a capitalist. The bankrupt capitalist ceases to be a capitalist, and thus his misguided freedom of will ceases to perturb the categorical imperative of capitalist "good order." If he reduces the rate at which he accumulates new capital (short of actual bankruptcy) his will, as an acting cause, is proportionately diminished relative to capitalist wills that behave more sensibly, and so on.

Indeed, what does this suggest but Rousseau's Social Contract? Anarchist individuals in capitalist society conspire to negate the adverse moments of freedom among their individual wills.

It is most productively ironic to compare Jung's and Freud's notions of the ego and id or social unconscious in this context. If we directly compare Freud's clumsy and perhaps unwitting use of the negation of the negation with its original representation in Kant's Critique of Practical Reason, a whole series of suggestive judgments follows.

Let us examine Freud's and Jung's views within the context of Kant's Practical Reason, which we view in turn from the standpoint of Hegel, Feuerbach, and Marx successively. First, Freud's notion of the ego and id are naive accounts of the peculiarities of mentation under capitalist society and do not directly bear upon the categories of the human mind more generally. Jung, who had a broader cultural competence than Freud, is correct in seeing the social unconscious as precisely that, as implicitly socially determined rather than biological-instinctual. This can by no means be considered a wild assertion respecting psychoanalysis, since the problem which Freud reports is nothing but a description of the necessary socially determined categories of human mental life under the peculiar conditions of capitalist alienations; his form of the negation of the negation has been rigorously demonstrated by Kant, Hegel, Feuerbach, and, especially, Marx to be a product of alienation of the type encountered in capitalist society.

Heine was in this respect a far better psychoanalyst than either Freud or Jung. Paralleling Hegel's brilliant insight into the Enlightenment, Heine, in his Religion and Philosophy in Germany, delineates the necessary connection between the anarchist outlook of the Enlightenment developing in Germany and the emergence of the most viciously reactionary forms of society.[8] Heine and Hegel were the first to recognize, in effect, that the anarchist point of view leads necessarily to something like fascism—as Mussolini, Hitler, and others have demonstrated in fact.

To the extent that the asocial consequences of the individual (anarchistic) capitalist will are reflected from the domain of reality (the social-reproductive labor process) into the fictitious realm of capitalist accumulation, the false-positive notion of "what is good for society" occurs precisely through the negation of the negation in the notions of individual "right practice" of individual "freedom" adopted by the capitalist.

While Kant and Hegel successively grasped this point brilliantly but in a one-sided way, their respective uses of the negation of the negation as the kernel of their antagonistic dialectical methods situate both of them inescapably within the bounds of capitalist culture. This is the systematic connection between the organization of Hegel's Logic around the negation of the negation and the reactionary notions of his Philosophy of Right.[9]

It is for this reason—as should now be more readily apparent—that Feuerbach's positing of the self-subsisting positive to replace the negation of the negation represented such an actually revolutionary breakthrough and led to Marx's discoveries.[10]

Freud's id is not a manifestation of the "animal" nature of man; it is the socially determined anarchist nature of man under capitalist social relations. No animal is capable of the degradation of a completely unhinged anarchist—Mussolini's Blackshirts and the SS have demonstrated the role of the id-rampant. The id is the socially determined degraded egoist capitalist society determines its individual members to be; and, having thus degraded man, capitalist society must supply checks on him by negation of the negation. In the final analysis, the degraded aspect of the id is nothing but the capitalist notion of private property in the means of production. (This is not to say that precapitalist forms of society are not characterized by comparable forms of mental horror. Alienation—the notion that other men or other tribes are competitors in the struggle for existence—is the essential vileness from which socialism must free future generations.)

IMPLICATIONS

However fictitious capitalist accumulation may be with respect to reality (the universality of the social-reproductive labor process), just because all individuals in capitalist society exist either as capitalists or as objects-for-capital, there is in general no immediate efficient cause for the connection between one event and another in capitalist society but capitalist Praxis.

It is precisely here that the mathematical economist must invariably fall into foolishness on the grossest premises. First, insofar as he adduces the systematic order of nature as nature presents itself, he is necessarily examining and correlating that sequence of events caused by capitalist Praxis. Since this Praxis is only a fictitious representation of reality, and therefore a viciously false account of the countervailing features supplied by underlying reality, such mathematical analysis can bear no correspondence to the determining processes of the underlying reality or to the systematic developments leading capitalist prosperity directly into new breakdown crises (monetary collapses and depressions).

Even so, for more or less the reasons discovered by Kant in connection with the *Critique of Practical Reason*, the emergence of a capitalist Praxis (the universality of capitalist accumulation, interpenetrating the universality of social reproduction) not only determines a certain kind of false knowledge of reality for the capitalists collectively (i.e., for capitalist Understanding), but also, as this body of false-conscious practice is a Praxis, gives to the thus-objective willful processes of capitalist accumulation a certain reflection of the content of the social-reproductive process.

Thus, the underlying laws of social reproduction (of the social-reproductive labor process) *must necessarily supply the immediate content, as a Law of Value, for the process of capitalist accumulation.* This is exactly what Marx intended by the terms "Law of Value" and "labor theory of value"—and nothing else.

USE VALUE REDEFINED

It is now necessary and possible to adjust our prior usage of the term "use value" to bring it into stricter conformity with *Capital*.

We have thus far employed the term to signify use value from the standpoint of socialist society. The "freedom" expressed in the collective will, as an efficient cause, is realized and measures itself in terms of the improved rates of social reproduction of the worldwide political working class.[11]

In a socialist society, therefore, use value and Value represent convergent notions. This does not merely mean that people under socialism gradually awaken to the idea that Value and use value *ought* to be the same; it signifies that the two converge in terms of evolving forms of society's universal Praxis.

This is not the case in the USSR, China, Cuba, or other nominally socialist nations. Nor could it be. Each of these nations is merely a relatively backward subsector of the international division of productive labor, and even under the best of internal regimes could not escape the consequences of capitalist-determined world-market price relations—capitalist Value penetrates deeply into production and circulation in each of these subsectors. The recent internal struggle in Yugoslavia is a most extreme example of this fact and of the powerful sociopolitical tendencies involved.

Socialist economy can exist in any country only when it first exists in the most advanced and powerful industrial nations. For, as long as any sector must "amortize" purchases of capital from more advanced sectors, the capitalization of Fixed Capital and the principle of tribute to "dead capital" are imposed on the sector with the weaker development. Socialism in the United States and Western Europe would begin to make socialist economy possible.

For just such reasons, mathematical economics of a certain sort becomes extremely useful, as advanced industrial engineering technology, in a socialist economy. Since mathematics (as it is presently defined) cannot comprehend "freedom" systematically, a completely mathematical economic theory is in the final analysis just as impossible in a socialist economy as in a capitalist. The effectiveness of mathematical analysis of the successive moments of economic development is vastly increased in socialist economy, due to the elimination of the error of calculating in terms of prices for capitalists' capitals. Or, to put it another way, the problem of completeness remains and gross error has been qualitatively narrowed.

It is no accident that mathematical economics developed first in the Soviet Union, and then in the United States only under wartime conditions. The development of mathematical economics by the late academician Kantorovich reflects a classical problem of planning and scheduling in a planned economy: the problem of allocating capital and input-output relationships on the principle that the most efficient capital investment is that which relieves the critical bottlenecks in the entire network.[12] In the United States, the impetus was supplied by the problems of planning a military economy during the Second World War; the resulting work was correlated with and benefited from pioneering work by the British. It is also relevant that when the most successful and gifted wartime mathematical economists and their collaborators attempted to extend their abstract industrial-engineering schemas and procedures into the domain of capitalist theoretical economics, the result was quackery. If we put aside the silly pursuit of mathematical completeness,[13] and restrict our inquiry to the usefulness of mathematical industrial-engineering procedures, the elimination of capitalist accumulation eliminates the elementary value-dualism of capitalist economy, permitting at least a systematic analysis of the mechanical order of use-value relationships in an industrial economy. The movement connecting these successive states can be recognized by mathematical procedures only in terms of their result; the noetic aspect of collective mentation, which determines the self-movement, remains beyond the mathematician's comprehension.

Some related points should be interpolated here. The horror stories of the late Oskar Lange and others[14] exemplify the state of the planning art under "genius" Stalin: it is idiotic to attempt to plan an economy down to the last bolt, and equally so to use simple parameters as regulators of local production performance.

The noetic aspect of productive development is stifled unless there is flexibility in the fine details of actual production schedules. Thus planning of specifics must be limited to the specification of a range of potential alternatives.

When this problem is approached foolishly, there occur spectacles of the sort reported by Lange. For example, if the parameter of local performance for a foundry is tonnage, the foundry managers will produce all the giant castings ordered and postpone manufacturing small castings. The same result would be elicited by a total–dollar-output parameter, with some variations.

If value added is used as the parameter, a somewhat better performance will tend to result; but, according to the pricing formulas used, criteria other than need for delivery by the entire economy will emerge to shift the actual output patterns away from those desired. For example, lot-size optimization for value added will produce a vile delivery pattern characterized by an array of half-completed projects awaiting next year's delivery of one or another components required this year.

Indeed, with respect to "economic reforms" (Libermanism) one must insist that the cure is more deadly than the disease. Certain problems will be solved in exchange for new problems that seem small at first but tend to produce the most destructive centrifugal tendencies and even tendencies to capitalize dead values to the point of introducing some form of falling-rate-of-profit sickness into overall production. There is no way to institute total responsibility for performance in terms of "objective criteria" applicable to local plants on a one-at-a-time basis.

The fundamental problem of industrial economy is the problem of realization in terms of the economy as a whole. This means that the key to socialist production is the class consciousness of the workers and managers. Guevara's "moral incentives" represented an unfortunately idealistic reification of this principle, but was nonetheless a step in the right direction. It is the individual worker's immediate identification with the well-being of the economy as a whole which is the only possible substance for real socialist planning.

"Comrades, we must get this lot out first because there is a priority project waiting for it." This principle applies to quality as well as quantity. Formally, outwardly, it is expressed as a matter of the individual worker's pride in his contribution to a project that functions in various distant parts of the economy. "That building has faucets we made; believe me, they'll last for years without trouble. Let me tell you—if you're interested—what we and our engineers did to give the builders something better than they had any right to expect." The individual's awareness of his positive role in the causal sequence of society's development on the broadest scale is quite unlike the mood which must justly afflict assembly-line workers in Detroit: "What crap they're putting through this month!"

The problems of the USSR on this point are essentially attributable to the bureaucracy. Bureaucracy creates a form of alienation which effectively atomizes local groups of workers, imposes plans on them without providing for discussion or comprehension on the part of the workers as a whole, and so forth. The central economic-planning problems afflicting and worrying the Soviet bureaucracy are actually nothing but the existence of the bureaucracy itself! That is why, until the bureaucracy proposes its own systematic liquidation, every bureaucratic solution to Soviet planning problems must tend to be as bad as the problems themselves.

Socialist planning is not difficult to understand if one combines mastery of the theoretical principles in question with recognition of the quality of enthusiasm among young skilled workers. (Older skilled workers, by negation of the negation, tend to lose enthusiasm and become case-hardened and cynical, limiting their subjective involvement in their work to mere craft-pride at best, and putting aside youthful dreams of accomplishment.) It is not so hard to visualize a society in which detailed national economic-planning programs are disseminated among all working people for thorough discussion; such proposals would form the basis for an organic political debate within the population. This simple procedure is the self-subsisting positive becoming real, each worker becoming directly and explicitly conscious of his positive relationship to the entire social-reproductive process.

Some concrete problems of planning in that way will be considered as aids in understanding the distinctions between use value and capitalist value.

Under capitalism, workers' consciousness generally reflects point-of-production chauvinism. This condition is expressed in the worst aspects of trade-unionism: hostility to "outsiders," and especially to the interests of unemployed workers. (Historically, united fronts whose programs united trade-unionists and unemployed workers have been political working-class movements and struggles, virtual revolutions in manifest potential and mood, if not in explicit goals and other such contingencies.) The same reactionary localist chauvinism is expressed in the worker's view of surplus value. He does not see surplus value as social, but as part of the private property of the plant in which he works. He fights to keep social surplus within his plant, to prevent its being taken away into the alien world.

National planning as a democratic process confronts every worker with the task of seeing surplus value as a collective creation, a positive existence whose realization in places other than the local plant is not only advantageous to him, but necessary to the enhancement of his own and his family's well-being. Consider, for example, the problem of a socialist United States' aid to Latin America, Africa, and Asia. Shall we convince workers to support this aid as a mere act of charity or redress for past wrongs? Or shall we demonstrate that certain results importantly beneficial to the U.S. sector can be obtained only by raising the level of productivity and material existence of millions of working people in those "foreign sectors"?

Democratic national planning compels every worker to confront the fact of a probably optimal balance in the apportionment of S', D, C, and V. If V is increased by a certain proportion, the rate of growth will suffer, as will his future material well-being. If V is too low, the productive potential of the working class will lag behind the skill demands of technology. There is a proportion among the elements which will produce—given three, five, or ten years—his optimum aggregate individual material level of existence. By placing the responsibility for that decision upon the individual worker (collectively), we shall create in him class consciousness and a developing socialist consciousness.

Socialism is a form of society whose Praxis corresponds to the notion of true use value. It is this notion which makes individual workers under socialism the first true human beings.

We have previously discussed the problem of considering "subjective" capitalist juridical relationships as objective relationships. Since the increasing ordering of nature for man is accomplished under capitalism only through the collective capitalist investment of surplus value in new production, the positive determination of reality occurs only through the mediation of capitalism's Praxis.

This applies to use value. To the extent that we can abstract a potential socialist economy from an existing capitalist economy, we can locate use value in many productive capacities, unemployed individuals, and the like where these same objects and people cannot become realized Value in the same moment of that society *qua* capitalist society. Thus, as we have previously stated, the notion of Value as objective Value is, for capitalist society, limited to that which is being realized as Value in terms of capitalist accumulation.

Marx defines the interconnection as follows. He limits the definition of true commodities to those objects that have both a price for capitalist accumulation and a use value. Or, in other words, true commodities are defined as objects and persons which belong simultaneously to two independent "sets": the set of all capitalists' capitals, and the set of all use values. However, the set of capitalists' capitals is by no means in correspondence with the set of all use values as defined for the potential socialist economy.

The most significant distinction for the analysis of capitalist economy is located in those instances in which the notion of use value is extended by capitalism to a category of profitable production of something other than true commodities. War production is perhaps the clearest illustration of this category. Let us approach this point by way of the following analogy.

A self-employed tailor who hires himself out to produce custom suits does not represent productive labor power in a capitalist economy; yet as a profit-producing employee he does so. The suit he produces has use value in either case—provided the wearer is a socially necessary person. However, only in the second case does the tailor himself represent use value as labor power, as a producer of capitalists' surplus value.

The union machinist employed in war production has the form of productive labor power and belongs to the working class' productive labor force. But in producing military hardware he is not producing use values. That is, the objects he produces do not represent useful means of consumption or means of production. They process no self-expanding use value. However, capitalist society assigns Value to this production and attributes use value to this labor power, since this worker expresses a tendency of the form of S/V.

If the same worker is employed in a government (nonprofit) arsenal he does not represent labor power, nor his production Value (unless it is sold).

Thus capitalist accumulation defines a body of Praxis which determines the objectivity of social-economic categories of use value and Value within capitalist society.

We may say that the subset of capitalists' capitals which does not also belong to the set of use values (from a socialist standpoint) represents what we shall hereafter define as *fictitious values* or fictitious capitals.

Ordinary empirical economics treats true commodity capital and fictitious capital in the same way, e.g., in computing Gross National Product. In large measure this accounts for the systematically vicious incompetence of conventional empirical economics. Since the ability of capital to reproduce itself as a whole depends upon that portion of real use values realized as self-expanding production of new values, the central question that ought to occupy serious economic theory is the ratio of fictitious capital to commodity capital.

Failure to recognize this, as we have indicated and shall soon discuss in fresh terms, is the cause of capitalist boom-bust cycles and breakdown crises like that of the 1930s. By failing to identify this discrepancy as the central feature of capitalist accumulation, ordinary empirical economic analysis is limited to examining the simple technical relations among undifferentiated capitalists' capitals.

Indeed, this is why leading procapitalist economists, and some socialists, have repeatedly pronounced Marx discredited and obsolete most vociferously just before a major new economic crisis, as during the most recent period. By assuming a more or less one-to-one correspondence between real value and capitalist prices for capitals, they have excluded the possibility of the very discrepancy that leads to new depressions. From their standpoint it is impossible to foresee a depression even when it has virtually begun. Thus they assert, "No new depression will occur; Marx, you see, was wrong."

CREDIT AND MONETARY PROCESSES 11

CREDIT AND MONETARY PROCESSES 11

We have previously pointed out that currency is not a surrogate for gold bullion; rather, the banknote is essentially a form of the commodity bill of exchange. Its relationship to gold, we pointed out, is of the following form. Gold, as a universal commodity, enters into the total exchange of bills of exchange and commodities as the means of settling the imbalance struck. Thus, the amount of gold required to provide backing for total bills of exchange and currency in circulation corresponds to the amount implied in a banker's reserve ratio. The amount of gold on hand must be equivalent to the expected withdrawals. Thus, dialectically, the value of bills of exchange is determined as an equivalent quantity of gold, and gold has provided the essential backing for the maintenance of world credit necessary to maintain world trade.

Thus, the simplest model of trade (circulation) sets a mass of bills of exchange (or their equivalent) on the one side and two masses of "other commodities" and gold on the other. In the exchange according to this simplest view, the bills of exchange vanish from circulation into dead accounting records after the exchanges of commodities and gold have occurred.

This could never occur in fact, since the period of exchanges overlaps extended periods, such that there is always a significant lag between purchase and sale of each commodity. This lag period represents credit to the account of either the purchaser or seller. Either, in the simple view, the purchaser has prepaid the amount prior to delivery or the seller receives payment after his initiation of shipment.

This credit, in turn, becomes subject to discount. A third party—for example, a merchant banker—buys the bill of exchange at some percentage less than 100 per cent of the bill's face value. Either this margin of income represents a loss to the seller or the seller previously negotiates credit charges on the bill which anticipate the discounting of the paper with the third party.

The discounting of credit instruments by a community of merchant bankers, or the establishment of a regular market in such paper, makes these discountable bills negotiable instruments, which may be used by bankers as banking for the printing and circulation of currency. It is merely necessary for the prudent banker to limit the amount of such money he circulates to some multiple of the necessary reserve in gold or its equivalent this currency circulation requires.

Various financial institutions proliferate in this way. Let us consider a not quite hypothetical insurance scheme. In the capitalization of an insurance firm, the firm itself must have on hand only the amount needed to pay current claims. Thus, if current claims ran approximately 10 per cent of the actual capitalization of the insurance firm in hard cash, and subordinate capital they had actively invested elsewhere would merely serve as a contingent liability to cover the remaining 90 per cent of their stockholding in the insurance firm. Thus, if the rate of profits after taxes for the insurance firm were 3 per cent per annum, the rate of growth of invested capital would be 30 per cent per annum. Not bad.

Meanwhile, liberal insurance regulations and understanding financial markets generally allow the stockholder of the insurance firm to find ways to use the face value of his insurance company holding as security for some further financial manipulations!

Let us reconsider a well-documented illustration of such arrangements: the New York City real estate example.

Let us assume, for the sake of illustration, that savings banks will write mortgages on the order of 60 per cent of the market price of a residential rental-income property in Manhattan. Let us assume that a buyer purchased such an apartment building for $500,000 in 1940, obtaining a $300,000 mortgage from a savings bank, taking on a $150,000 second-mortgage liability for five years at 10 per cent interest from the seller, and putting up $50,000 in hard cash. In 1960, the buyer has long since paid off the second mortgage and reduced the first mortgage. Now he sells the building to his brother-in-law for $1 million. His brother-in-law obtains a $600,000 mortgage from a savings bank, gives a $350,000 second mortgage to the seller, and puts up $50,000 borrowed from the seller. A short time later, he sells the building back to the seller.

Let us assume that the seller had paid off $150,000 of the old $300,000 first mortgage before selling. He received $600,000 from the savings bank on the new first mortgage, of which he paid $150,000 to retire the previous first mortgage and pocketed $450,000. On buying the building back, he tears up the short-lived second mortgage and receives the $50,000 back in cash (less the costs of buying and selling and a handout to the stooge, his brother-in-law). He now holds the building on the following terms. He paid originally $50,000; his tenants paid $300,000 on the first and second mortgages, plus interest charges. He now has the building and $450,000, leaving him a net pocket profit of $400,000; he owns the building without having put a nickel of his own money in it, and has acquired a $400,000 bonus. Under New York City's rent-control laws, he now applies for a hardship-case rental increase, on the grounds that he is not getting an 8 per cent return on the market price of the building![1]

Behind this charming and quite legal swindle lies the following fundamental logic of the capitalist monetary system. In the pre-1967 New York City rental-income real-estate market, a property generally had a rule-of-thumb market price of seven times the gross annual rental income. Under the "oppressive to landlords" rent-control law the landlord gained a 15 per cent rent increase plus options for various extras each time an apartment turned over tenancy within a statutory period. The city's high occupancy-turnover ratio, especially in slum neighborhoods, and various other loopholes in the law, allowed the general level of rental income to approximately double, and in some areas treble, during the postwar period. The price of the buildings, often deteriorating to a state of near-rubble, rose accordingly.

The basis for this spiralling market was not merely the rental-income rises themselves. Since the operators were selling in a rising market, they bought buildings in anticipation of major capital-gains profits as well as mere current-income profits. Thus, the prices of buildings went up faster than the rents.

After 1967, when the financial props for this process began to weaken, the landlords clamored about a disastrous shortage of profits, and there began a substantial abandonment of buildings by landlords. What had actually occurred?

With a shortage of credit to facilitate speculation, the capital-gains profits from building speculation declined, reducing the expected income on the property titles to something on the order of simple profits of ownership. Now, consider the quasi-hypothetical case of the landlord of record on a dilapidated slum building, with a small cash investment, perhaps a 20–30 per cent first mortgage, and a 60 per cent second mortgage. This miserable creature bought the building on those terms only because he expected to bail out through resale. With the resale market dropping off, the second mortgage hangs around his neck like an albatross. He "abandons" the building, inviting foreclosure proceedings by the mortgage-holders.

The reality is that the landlord of record is the "owner" only by courtesy of prevailing legal fictions. Real ownership lies with the major real-estate interests that are looting the second mortgages directly and indirectly.

The story is not complete without noting another point. Detailed studies of 1967–1968 building records for a run-down section of Manhattan including both rent-controlled and "decontrolled" apartment buildings demonstrated that the major real-estate operators "making a market" in that area were gaining a 20–30 per cent annual return on their equity investments. Since these firms were operating widely throughout New York City, it may safely be assumed that these rates of return were general. (Such returns did not prevent these owners from filing for "hardship" rental increases.)

At those rates of return, it was relatively unprofitable for real-estate interests to invest in new buildings, especially since site-acquisition costs were determined by the inflated prices of the properties occupying those sites. Thus, the high rate of profit in old real estate effectively prevented New York City real-estate interests from constructing anything but so-called luxury housing. Only a collapse of the real-estate market (and site values) in old buildings could create the conditions under which new housing would be constructed generally.

At this juncture, New York's Mayor Lindsay intervened. Approximately $1 million in city funds was expended on three studies. A RAND Corporation study reported what the city's real-estate interests wished to have reported and proposed, but was based on a decidedly questionable set of raw data. A more modest report offered no hard factual evidence but also said pretty much what the real-estate interests wished to hear. A third report, by a Rutgers professor specializing in the field, did delve rather substantially into the facts and, in effect, supported the findings of the 1967–1968 study cited above. The mayor waved around the latter report in order to motivate the RAND report's recommendations—successfully shepherding through the City Council a new "rent-control law" which re-established the speculative profitability of old run-down buildings. The mayor's "explanation," echoed by the capitalist press, was that these measures were imperative incentives for the construction of new housing by private interests.

A similar story could be told about suburban development, and the stock and bond markets operate on similar financial principles.

The point to be adduced from these illustrations is that a capitalist economy can create new masses of capitalists' capitals (stocks, bonds, and mortgages, and the like) on the basis of a narrow margin of actual income received. Furthermore, the rate of rise in this actual income, by the price-earnings multiple, creates fictitious gains in capital which are accounted as capital-gains profits, such that the combined profit-income and capital-gains profit become the figure used for multiplication. The discounting of such inflated paper by financial institutions, directly or indirectly, causes the issuance of paper money which inflates the means of current payment, providing the monetary basis for further speculative "multiplier" increases!

One of the most important sources of monetary inflation is state indebtedness. Against the guaranteed future revenues of the state, all sorts of valueless projects can be "financed." To the extent that the central banking system buys state debt or indirectly finances such purchases, this process represents pure printing-press coinage.

These sources and their various complements provide any capitalist economy with massive sources of monetary income and capital appreciation independent of the actual rate of growth of commodity production.

This process is not entirely unsound. In the transition period from capitalism, a socialist economy would create credit-money for the circulation of consumer commodities. An examination of this aspect of the matter is in order before considering pure speculations and fictitious capitalization in general.

THE BUY-BACK PROBLEM

Ignoramuses frequently insist that the basic cause of capitalist problems is "underconsumption." When this pseudo-solution is entertained by professed Marxists, it is presented in approximately the following terms.

It is argued that the money in circulation is limited to wages directly paid or paid on the account of constant-capital purchases. Thus, the money in circulation to "buy back" produced commodities would be equal to $C \pm V$, with a supplementary source of money in payments for capitalists' consumption (D). "How is S' sold?" they demand.

Their answer is usually of the same form as Reverend Malthus'[2] and the Triple Revolution Committee's: to distribute money to capitalists' consumption and increase welfarism.

They have simply ignored credit.

Let us assume the hypothetical case in which all produced values are realized. Let us restrict our attention, then, to S'. S' includes both new means of production and new consumer commodities, which, combined as consumption by workers and means of production used by those workers, produce not only new commodities of a value equal to their costs but also new profits at at least the same rate as previous production. So, a dated bill of exchange issued against S' to the capitalist employing the expanded labor-force segment is turned into its commodity equivalent plus profit.

The bills of exchange created on this account are discountable, and therefore can (and do) enter the banking system directly and indirectly to cause the printing and circulation of additional money. Thus, S', at each moment, tends to increase the mass of money in circulation proportional to the circulation of commodities required. It is merely required that sufficient proportions of new production go into gold mining to provide the reserve ratios of gold required for world trade.

This is simply classical bourgeois economics, which no serious Marxian economist should have trouble comprehending. Of course, as should be evident, this process has manifold permutations: little feral men all around the world are dreaming up new variations on this theme every day. The basic principles, however, remain unchanged.

A socialist economy would operate in a similar fashion. Exchanges for means of production would involve merely a central banking bookkeeping notation: no cash would be required. The cash put into circulation would be proportional to the consumer commodities put into circulation for sale. As the socialist economy proceeded, increasing proportions of consumer commodities and services would be added to a "free list": household water, electricity, telephone, public transportation, medical services, all education, room and board for college students, and so on. The growth of this free list would not occur for utopian reasons; it is simply cheaper to have bridges without tolls, free public transportation, cheaper to haul food to market without transport charges, and the like. Eliminating all the paperwork of sold distribution frees larger proportions of the work force for productive occupations. As class consciousness developed through the democratic formulation of national planning policies, all consumer services and commodities would be added to the free list—as the psychological origins of hoarding and grasping "because it's free" were extirpated. However, in the beginning, most consumer distribution would be accomplished by the issuance of money from a central banking system.

There is no buy-back problem in either a capitalist or socialist economy. The problem of "selling S' " is the chimera of the ignorant student.

MONETARY INFLATION

The willingness (nay, eagerness) of capitalists to accept payment in fictitious capitals, and the creation of money on the basis of discounting of a growing mass of fictitious capitals, frees the capitalist system from dependence upon immediate settlement of accounts in value terms. Thus, monetary statistics on capitalist accumulation bear no direct relationship to the development of processes leading to new depressions.

We need not repeat the explanation of the "falling-rate tendency" outlined in Chapter 9. It is sufficient to emphasize here that capitalist property titles to capitalist production are based, principally, on historic valuations so that rising productivity of labor power does invariably produce this tendency. The credit system, tied to monetization of fictitious capitals, now permits the capitalist system to circulate the margin of commodities representing "overproduction" to nonproductive income recipients, so that the occurrence of such *over-priced* production as overproduction does not produce any immediate manifestation of its occurrence within the market.

Indeed, as we have indicated, quite the opposite result usually ensues. The tendency for devaluation of existing capitals because of rising productivity manifests itself mainly in a tendency to reduce the productive working class as a proportion of the growing potential labor force. This liberates masses of capital from reinvestment in expanded production to be used in the more profitable domain of speculation, feeding speculation further and generating a monetary-fictitious capitalization spiral. The result may be a considerably increased demand for useful commodities, but generally at a slower rate than the rise of productivity. (It would be a good exercise for the reader to calculate the reason for this.)

Therefore, the surest sign of an oncoming depression has usually been a feverish apparent prosperity. The great stock-market or real-estate bubbles preceding collapses are legendary phenomena, from which we have certainly not been exempt in the post-1957 period.

However, as the ratio of formation of speculative (fictitious) to productive capital increases, the rate of inflation increases. If the inflationary expansion of the money supply attenuates, a shortage of payments against aggregate payments to profit, debt service, and rent must occur on the account of the vastly inflated capital: a depression. In the monetary spiral increases, interest rates must increase to offset the inflationary discounting of longer-term credit. Not only that, but lenders avoid the risks of long-term credit, such that the turnover of debt increases, increasing the short-term debt, the debt-service ratio, and the rate of demand for payments against debt service and rent as well as the profit account of debt-laden corporations. These countervailing tendencies in the monetary system are the contingencies that shape the formation of a monetary crisis or general depression.

PRIMITIVE ACCUMULATION

The inflationary spirals described above demand the looting of real wealth from somewhere. The two most recent forms of imperialism (1870–1913), (1945–1971) expressed this principle in one way; the Nazi war-economy (1936–1945) was another manifestation. Wage-price "guidelines" and "controls" are another extreme expression of the forms of looting to which capitalism resorts under conditions of threatened monetary collapse.

To be a commodity, it is not necessary that an object be produced through capitalist production. Simple looting of natural resources, the exploitation of slaves, and outright theft can yield objects that have the quality of self-expanding use value for capitalist production and circulation, and yet have not been paid for on account of capitalists' capitals.

On this account, such economists as Hobson, Hilferding, and Lenin were simple-minded in their failure to understand Volume III of *Capital* and *Theories of Surplus Value;* among all celebrated Marxian economists, only Rosa Luxemburg has heretofore understood the ABCs of Marx's theory of value. Imperialism is not intrinsically a process of exporting capital for the superexploitation of cheaper colonial labor. Lenin's blunder was, in significant part, his assumption that capitalists' capitals were necessarily priced according to the Law of Value.

The essential feature of the old imperialism was not the export of means of production to develop new industries, but the exportation of heavily prediscounted loans. The Suez Canal is, of course, the classic case. (The reader should consult Luxemburg's *The Accumulation of Capital* on this subject.[3] An excellent complementary reference is Herbert Feis's *Europe: The World's Banker, 1870–1914,*[4] which should be read as a follow-up to Luxemburg.) Although some means of production were exported on the account of these loans, the monetary value of the obligation incurred vastly exceeded the value delivered. It is in the discrepancy between these two amounts that the monetary side of imperialism is revealed.

The best-known symptom of the emergence of imperialism as imperialism is Disraeli's remarkable evolution from an antiimperialist to the founder of British imperialism. Close examination of this development should be sufficient to strongly suggest the central point to be made.

If one attempts to locate the origins of imperialism in the history of European–colonial relations, the date 1870 seems hardly precise. Those who have viewed the matter from such a "purely economic" standpoint overlook the fundamental principles of *political* economy and the nature—

the essence—of capital as a juridical, political form. Capital, as we stipulated at the beginning of this text, is the title to debt-service payment supported by the armed might of the state. What distinguished imperialism and made it possible as a distinct phase of capitalist development was the decision of capitalist governments systematically to develop and employ navies and overseas military forces to impose loans and the collection of debt service on existing semicolonial states, and to otherwise create new states for this purpose where the residents of lootable regions had neglected to construct such modern institutions. To undertake a vast program of international loans it was necessary to give these loans the attributes of low risk and high liquidity, qualities supplied by European heavy cruisers and bayonets.

Since the yield on production obtained through imported means of production did not meet the debt-service requirements on these loans, the local government (pre-existing or expediently artificed to become the person of the debtor) had to supply other wealth, at prices acceptable to the creditors, as the means of satisfying the "obligation." Vast natural resources were delivered to the creditors on this basis; hordes of natives were conscripted as virtual slave labor in the works and plantations of the colonial masters. The unpaid wealth thus delivered to the metropolitan countries as consumer commodities and means of production represented self-expanding use value to prop up the masses of fictitious capital.

With respect to existing European technology, the potential for looting in the known semicolonial and colonial world was distinctly finite—at least in terms of possible rates of extraction. Thus, by 1913, the available colonial world was exhausted relative to the requirements of the metropolitan countries—except for Latin America, which the Monroe Doctrine uneasily maintained against the eager depredations of the British and Germans as a private hunting preserve for U.S. imperialism's future exploitation.

Europe promptly set out to remedy this predicament by the conventional means of capitalist anarchy: to solve the shortage by reducing the number of feet in the trough; that is, to put some of the competitors out of business. An exercise in "free market competition" known as the First World War was lost not only by the Germans and Austro-Hungarians, but also lost to the United States by Great Britain and France.

The United States was the only advanced capitalist nation, with the marginal exception of Japan, to emerge victorious and prosperous from the First World War. On the home front, U.S. domestic economy continued to be propped up by the process of continuing the looting its independent farmers (until about 1926). A spurt of imperialist depredations in Latin America aided the process at about the same time, as did some bargain-basement investments in Europe, e.g., Germany in 1923–1928. But the United States itself was rotten underneath, a fact most sharply attested to by new policies restricting immigration; the basic means of production were no longer expanding at the old rate.

Germany was ruined and bled by French war reparations. Great Britain was in perpetual economic doldrums, and a state of near-insurrection prevailed for a time—a condition from which its home economy has never truly recovered. The pound sterling was propped up by imperial reserves and commercial-financial operations. France enjoyed a brief growth in reconstruction—a growth predicated upon acquisition of Alsace-Lorraine and the Saar and German war reparations. Italy was fundamentally sick.

Europe survived in a sick state due to U.S. credit and moratoria on war debts. France stagnated, contemplated par values of its internal debt. U.S. credit provided the critical margin for maintaining the pound's position as the basic reserve currency of world trade. The Great Vienna bank, the Kreditanstalt, a project based on U.S. ambitions and direct and indirect credit, kept Eastern Europe from total collapse. Germany enjoyed employment and an export boom propped up by U.S. credit until 1928–1929. Europe was too sick even to absorb the available loot from the colonial regions.

From approximately 1926 to 1929, the U.S. economy passed from a period of productive expansion to pure credit expansion; the collapse of the stock market in October 1929 did not cause the Depression, but it weakened the dollar to the point that the United States could not continue to satisfy Europe's need for increased credit. The Great Vienna Bank collapsed early in 1931. Germany, whose brief prosperity had been based on export production, had already plunged into a depression. In September 1931, the British government elected to cease buying and selling gold at a fixed price, after which the value of the pound plummeted by about 20 per cent, and the entire structure of world-trade credit collapsed. The Great Depression was on.

This total breakdown crisis vindicated Rosa Luxemburg entirely. Her thesis had been, in 1913, that the imperialist system was on the verge of a general breakdown crisis. If by some chance, she continued, socialist transformation did not occur during the period immediately following breakdown, capitalism would emerge in a new and final form—statist military economy. By 1931, the total breakdown had occurred at a rapid pace in Germany and at a slower pace in the United States (due to Roosevelt's NRA and ensuing New Deal schemes), leading, from 1936, inevitably toward the Second World War.

Considerable silly rubbish has been written attributing the cause of the Second World War to Hitler's psychological peculiarity. The history of the German economy during the First World War and from 1936 to 1945 demonstrates that Krupp's circle of smokestack barons and not some quirk of Adolf Hitler governed every hazardous diplomatic and military gamble made by the Third Reich. The principle of primitive accumulation was applied by colony-less Nazi Germany to the only accessible resource: Germany's neighbors.

The goal of the Nazi diplomacy and war drive was the looting of the existing plant, materials, and labor of all Europe. After the fascist-riddled

French officer corps had declined to destroy Hitler militarily over the issue of military deployment into the Rhineland after *Anschluss*-Czechoslovakia, the massive fictitious capital floated by Schacht's manipulations during 1933–1938 had been stabilized to the point of generating an even larger mass of fictitious capital which threatened to plunge the Nazi economy into bankruptcy. Physical plant, raw materials, food, and slave and semislave labor were appropriated with German thoroughness, down to the hair, gold fillings, and old clothing of Krupp-Hitler's butchered victims. Stolen use value, including the stored-up labor power in the blood and muscle of enslaved human beings, was looted to supply value for German fictitious capital.

Roosevelt accomplished the same economic result without resorting to fascist measures. From 1936 on, U.S. war aims were clear; by 1940, they were openly announced: to create an American century and a U.S. world empire out of the Second World War. At the end of the war, the United States imposed sharp devaluations on the currencies of its allies (France and Britain), and exploited the traditions of Nazi labor discipline among the conquered Germans to buy Europe and its colonies at rock-bottom prices.

Approximately on a par with the conventional wisdom about Hitler's psychology is the myth that cheap European currencies represent nasty competition with the U.S. dollar. Quite the contrary: if U.S. financiers can obtain use values from Europe at lower prices than in the United States, they are thereby enriched at the expense of the European populations . . . for as long as the United States can continue to export a gold-backed currency with which to buy Europe's constant capital and labor power at below-par prices. Those who chatter about European "economic miracles" have not examined the housing and other real-wage features of German working-class life, the secular decline in the real wages of British and French workers, and related phenomena.

Not to be overlooked, in the case of Germany, is the importation from East Germany (until the Wall went up) of approximately 10 million German-speaking persons representing cheap skilled or semiskilled labor, and the subsequent importation of 2 million *Gastarbeiter* working in Germany under the terms of the 1944 Nazi *Gastarbeiter* law.

Indeed, the postwar period represents a new form of imperialism—an imperialism based on a statist U.S. military economy which had reduced Europe and Japan essentially to economic satrapies. This arrangement had to continue until the inevitable new monetary crisis of the entire system redounded against that sector which had issued the great portion of the credit for the preceding period of general expansion—the United States. Recognizing the portents of such a denouement, foolish babblers speak of "competition" between the weakening United States and bumptious Europe and Japan—as if the instant the U.S. dollar slides world trade must slide, and those nations benefitting most from export production must for that very reason plunge most deeply into the abyss of general depression.

The fourth example of primitive accumulation is the wage-price austerity scheme. During the 1960's this was accomplished by creating a vast poverty population. That is, the cost of reproducing the entire working class was cut by U.S. capitalism by creating a vast army of unemployed, underemployed, and superexploited—an economy in the wage bill which contributed directly to capitalist profits. Europe began the period with post-war austerity. France was partially stabilized from 1958 by deGaulle's austerity program, which has been driving down French real wages in a spiral ever since. Britain is undertaking a vicious assault on real wages, which it hopes to accomplish more effectively by entering the Common Market. Wage-price controls in the United States—if U.S. workers tolerate them— will exacerbate the post-1966 general decline in real wages. This is a matter of reducing the portion of existing production devoted to wage-payments, in order to increase payments from real production on the account of profit, debt service, and rent: an historically temporary, "one-ride," but nonetheless a temporary stabilization of capitalist economy threatened with collapse.

THE NOTION OF PRIMITIVE ACCUMULATION

The editors of *Monthly Review* have presumed to instruct their readers that the author promulgates the concept of primitive accumulation only because he has not read Marx in German. The point of their jest is that Marx's term is better translated "original accumulation."[5] Two points should be made in rebuttal of such crude dictionary nominalism. First, on the semantics of the matter, one wonders naturally enough whether Sweezy attributes ignorance of the German language to Rosa Luxemburg, who offers exactly the same rationale for "primitive accumulation". Second, *Monthly Review*'s editors should consult (among other locations in Marx's writings) the preface to the *Critique of Political Economy*, where Marx discusses Proudhon's practice of attributing economic categories to their historical point of origin. Would Sweezy and his collaborators also argue that bills of exchange did not exist among the merchants of the 16th-century B.C. Hittite ghettoes? The question is whether the phenomenon of primitive accumulation exists. Since Luxemburg based her analysis of the breakdown crisis and statist military economy on such a systematic treatment of primitive accumulation, where all her critics invariably proceeded to ridiculous conclusions in fact, certain conclusions are to be drawn. In any case, since Sweezy has exerted himself for at least a decade to demonstrate that Marx's *Capital* is obsolete, how does he justify asserting that *Capital* has any systematic bearing on contemporary economic processes?

Apart from Sweezy, most professed "Marxian economists" have protested against the author's use of the category of primitive accumulation. However, Sweezy's cited resort to dictionary nominalism represents the only rebuttal which is not simply a bald unjustified assertion. So, in refuting his argument, we have refuted all those in view.

One of the principal legitimate difficulties facing the economic analyst attempting to measure primitive accumulation is that the magnitude to be ascertained nowhere appears in the financial accounts of either the looter or the looted. If semicolonial regions are looted of oil reserves at bargain prices, the genius of primitive accumulation is manifest in the fact that this oil is purchased at a price below its cost of true social reproduction. Nowhere is the discrepancy between true Constant Capital and actual Constant Capital outlays directly taken into account.

The same principle confronts us in accounting for the primitive accumulation reflected in pollution of air, water, destruction of marshlands, and the like. Obviously enough, the collective capitalist has enjoyed a substantial profit by avoiding the socially necessary costs of either preventing this depletion of nature or repairing nature to a state of equipotentiality to compensate for this depletion. This depletion plainly represents a major aspect of man's convergence upon conditions for decline in the material conditions of life and production; yet, through the period in which such depletion is occurring, no actual expenditure is occurring in such a way that the *incurred* market value of such costs could be measured. How does one measure a necessary but nonincurred cost of reproduction? The cost of primitive accumulation is only a virtual productive cost, the necessary cost of something that should be occurring but is not.

Thus, with respect to the capitalist looting of nature, one of the most decisive facts of political economy does not occur as a "tangible fact" of political economy until the accumulated ignored cost threatens society with a massive ecological crisis.

A somewhat different but related problem confronts us with respect to primitive accumulation at the expense of populations. Let us review various manifestations of this phenomenon in an arbitrary order and then summarize the universality of such predicates.

Let us consider, first, developments in the black ghetto during the past decade. Throughout this century, through 1953, there was a general tendency toward assimilation of black proletarians in the main bodies of the labor force. Many considerations might be reviewed in this connection, including the closing of the gates at Ellis Island in the early 1920s, but they all had the same general effect. As the case of Detroit epitomizes, the expansion of employment from the depths of the depression during the 1930s through the 1953 high-point of Korean War employment the condition of the black proletarian continued to improve with respect to the main bodies of the industrial labor forces.

From 1953–1954 to about 1957–1958, the wellbeing of the black proletarian strata virtually stagnated, so that there occurred (via southern emigrations to northern cities) an absolute growth of northern ghetto populations relative to an approximately fixed number of stably employed black proletarians. This situation was aggravated by a vigorous policy of importing Puerto Ricans and Chicanos, especially, to undercut the standards of living and employment of black urban and agricultural proletarians. From 1957–1958 on, the absolute conditions of black proletarians severely worsened because of the virtual halting of expansion of the productive labor force.

The use of super-cheap, terrified Puerto Rican labor in New York City sweatshops assisted the capitalists in lowering the standards of existence of the most-oppressed strata, which affected the relative standards of living of urban blacks most acutely. The condition of skilled and semiskilled black workers exposes the irony of the entire situation. The stagnation in productive employment insured that skilled and semiskilled blacks would be subject to part-time employment. This situation was highlighted in the construction crafts, where nepotism among journeymen, union bureaucrats, and racketeers insured that the new jobs made available by turnover generally did not go to blacks. This meant that a significant number of black proletarians was lumpenized even though partially employed. Part-time employment in their trades or low-grade employment outside their trades meant that these workers could not support growing families in the manner of most fully employed union workers. Thus developed a pattern of family abandonment and the rapid growth of welfarism, especially in the Aid to Dependent Children categories.

This lumpenization or semilumpenization of large portions of the black urban population had what should be obvious sequelae. In general it meant that a growing proportion of the population was deprived of the material-cultural conditions of life that are more or less imperative if today's generation is to become productive with tomorrow's or even today's technology. This deprivation was associated with a deepening deprivation in social perspective; the prospect of working-class productive employment was no longer a credible one for an increasing proportion of ghetto youth; thus, the ghetto "drug scene". Lumpenization—living by one's wits or strong-arm muscle: "hustling"—meant a self-aggravating demoralization and near-destruction of the urban black ghetto as a source of potentially productive labor. It meant that a growing proportion of the U.S. population was relegated to a human scrapheap.

More subtle is the effect of the process of primitive accumulation against the white labor force generally. By cheapening the quality of material-cultural existence of most of today's white labor force, this labor force is prevented from acquiring the productive potentialities demanded by modern forms of productive technology. Thus, for example, the "assembly line," a relic of the dark technological ages of the 1920s, becomes a sort of self-perpetuating evil, an obstacle in the path of productive development of the economy in real terms. That is, by refusing to provide the entire working class with the level of material-cultural existence needed for the most advanced technology of production, the capitalist state and employers create objective barriers to the general, efficient employment of new technology.

How does one measure that cost?

In the colonial and semicolonial world we encounter the modern forms of primitive accumulation, of the sort immediately visible in the United States or West Germany, combined with the methods of looting employed by mercantile capitalists (c. 1300–1600) and early British capitalism per se (1600–1848). The cost of producing the small productive labor force is paid not by the capitalist employers but by the "native economy" of the peasantry, whose emiseration is a direct subsidy to the imperialist employers. The creation of vast legions of lumpenized ex-peasants and proto-fascist strata for the armies, police, and "nationalist" movements is another social result of this process. In general, imperialism obtains wealth by primitive accumulation from the colonial and semicolonial sectors by destroying the entire population's potential to materially reproduce itself at the existing level. The loot thus gained from populations and natural resources is partially reflected in the form of payments of debt service on foreign public and private loans, but is also embodied in the unaccounted difference between the social-reproductive costs of primary commodities such as copper, oil, and the like, and the bargain prices at which these materials enter into the imperialist ledgers. There is no complete factual accounting for this very tangible loss to humanity on the account of capitalist primitive accumulation. Therefore, liars and fools calling themselves economists are able to console themselves that such facts do not exist— since the capitalists' accountants do not report their existence.

Nonetheless, these suppressed facts of primitive accumulation are tangibly manifest for any competent or simply honest observer to note. They are apparent in the form of an ecology crisis: one can demonstrate primitive accumulation's existence by counting one's coughs almost any day on a New York street, or by measuring the haze. One may demonstrate it by comparing the misery of Venezuelan and Arab peoples with the billions extracted from their countries by the United States-led oil monopolies. One may demonstrate it concretely in the existence of an urban ghetto, and in the extraction of rental payments against the account of mortgages on fully depreciated and dilapidated buildings. One may demonstrate it in proto-fascist rock-drug counterculture hooligans growing like a fungus out of the bedrooms of suburbia. One may demonstrate it in what fools and worse call "overpopulation," which is really underproduction and underfeeding. These qualitative phenomena are absolutely conclusive evidence that the self-reproductive costs of man's existence on earth are being grossly under-met by capitalism, and that therefore capitalist profits represent profits which could not exist for capitalism if the true social-reproductive costs (according to the underlying Law of Value) were being met. That is sufficient evidence of primitive accumulation.

"Statistics! Statistics!" one hears the nominalists crying. They do not know that quality determines quantity; it is not necessary to weigh an acquaintance before acknowledging that he exists. We shall measure such variables precisely once we have the power and the practical means to direct the processes of statistics-gathering according to scientific social-reproductive criteria.

VICIOUS DISCREPANCIES IN CAPITALIST STATISTICS

Once we have extracted approximate data for social-reproductive categories from capitalist statistical sources, the analysts must reckon with the vicious twofold error which permeates that data from a social-reproductive (Law of Value) standpoint. That is, with respect to C and V particularly, the existing data is grossly distorted on the account of both fictitious capital and primitive accumulation. A preliminary identification of those errors is in order here.

Variable Capital

On account of primitive accumulation, capitalist underemployment and superexploitation fail to meet the socially necessary costs of materially re-producing the entire proletariat at the rate demanded for tomorrow's pro-ductive technology. The most conspicuous empirical reflection of this primitive accumulation is the emergence of a vast lumpenproletariat and semilumpenized strata within the capitalist world economy. At the other end of the spectrum of social facts, it is reflected in the perennial shortage of sufficient employable labor force for realization of technologically feas-ible forms of new production; note, for example, the simultaneity of significant unemployment and a shortage of the necessary labor skills for new productive and administrative employment openings on the frontier of technological development.

On account of fictitious capital, Variable Capital is overpriced because of inflation of the costs of means of existence over their value and increas-ing wage-taxation imposed to provide profit and debt service on the ac-count of dead capital or fictitious capital per se—for example, military production, public porkbarrel-caused bonded indebtedness, and the like. The massive gouging of the housing component of the bill of consumption is by no means an insignificant factor. In urban rental housing, rents chiefly represent a means of providing debt-service payments against mortgage capitalization of properties whose dead-capital constituent itself has long since been depreciated to zero. In suburban owner-occupied housing, the debt service and taxation embodied in the gross housing cost of the bill of consumption also represent payments to the account of speculative fictitious capitals. If new apartments are constructed under public subsidy in U.S. urban centers, the land acquisitions cost is based on the "fair-market valua-tion" of the site, which is determined by the speculative valuation of the dilapidated structure previously occupying that site; this cost is transferred to the tenant and to the public debt where it is borne by the working-class population through taxation.

We shall consider, in the next major section of this chapter, the problem of properly valuing Variable Capital. For the moment, it is sufficient to have shown that these two cited contrary tendencies result in a gross undervaluation of the necessary real content of real wages (or their equivalents) because of primitive accumulation, while fictitious monetary valuations are assigned to the amounts actually paid.

Constant Capital

Constant Capital represents a more complex problem than Variable Capital because of the necessary distinctions to be made between its two principal constituents. Those constituents are, first, the Constant Capital on account as ordinary Circulating Capital (materials, supplies, semifinished parts, electricity, and the like), and, second, the element of total Constant Capital costs attributable to depreciation and obsolescence of Fixed Capital. We shall therefore consider each of these subsegments in turn before attempting to summarize the problem as a whole.

The undervaluation of the Circulating Capital component is caused first by primitive accumulation with respect to the unpaid looting of nature, and, second, by primitive accumulation against the account of the labor power which extracts raw materials. It is useful to consider the discrepancy between the prices paid for raw materials at the point of export from the semicolonial sector (for example) and the price (component) of these same materials embodied in finished consumer commodities in the United States. As in the case of Variable Capital, the real necessary costs have been grossly understated for primitive-accumulation reasons while the market valuation at the point of sale for consumption is grossly overstated due to fictitious capital charges added in.

Oil and plantation commodities are obvious illustrations, as are consumer commodities produced in Eastern Europe (e.g., Yugoslavia) for sale in the United States. The export price at which the Yugoslavs sell these commodities represents a net loss to the entire Yugoslav economy, a loss that economy is compelled to endure in order to obtain foreign capitalist money with which to pay debt-service obligations incurred by capitalist international loans to Yugoslavia. These products are ultimately sold in the United States at a small fractional discount below U.S. commodities of comparable quality, and the various merchant capitalists involved pocket the difference.

In the case of Fixed Capital, it should not be imagined that each firm operates in the market on the basis of the particular valuation of each plant and machine. Rather, the aggregate capital advanced for all capitals (Fixed, Circulating, and so on) appears as the capital valuation of the firm as a whole. In a finance-capital market, pricing of commodities must in each case reflect the necessary rate of marginal gross profit (surplus value) contribution required, on the basis of total capitalization by means of stocks, bonds, mortgages, and the like. If total capitalization is X, total Circulating Capital costs are Y, and the required rate of profit is given as Z/X, then W, net profits on sales, is expressed in ratio-terms as, $W:Y = Z:X$. The difference between gross and net profits for the individual commodities is calculated by various cost-accounting devices which distribute total overhead costs by a standard or marginal-contribution formula over the entire range of sold production.

The accounting methods employed to calculate depreciation of Fixed Capital by capitalist firms are essentially fictions with objective economic merits, except as they influence the judgments of financiers and plant managers. What actually determines the effective rate of depreciation is the rate at which the firm must buy new plant and equipment to keep even competitively. Studies by the Machinery and Allied Products Institute and the famous McGraw-Hill study published in the late 1950s represent only the more accessible evidence on this general problem.

Detailed studies of hundreds of individual firms, conducted by the author during the 1953–1967 period, indicate that virtually all firms that based their reinvestment policies on depreciation schedules have tended to go bankrupt. The accumulated effects of depleting accumulated Fixed Capital according to naive interpretation of simple accounting procedures bring the firm to the point that it is no longer competitive, and thus ripe for reorganization by clever "raiders." Numerous conglomerates created during the late 1950s and 1960s were nothing but clever manipulations of such pieces of individual corporate junk based on hot air and the credulity of the small-investor public. Close reading of prospectuses for some of the worthless corporations put on the investment market in the name of "synergistics" by clever (or unscrupulous) investment houses is most revealing.

We have referred to the use of the credit-monetary system to conceal temporarily the fact of a falling-rate tendency. Let us now examine the general manner in which this actually occurs.

Since the valuation of stocks, bonds, and mortgages of corporate capital is determined by a price-earnings ratio, holding back on reinvestment (distributing profits and debt service out of "depreciation funds") tends to increase or otherwise buoy up the value of capitalists' capitals—by the very means which ultimately lead to bankruptcy. Although chief corporate officers who have been apprenticed in the production or developmental aspects of business (especially) usually have a fair-to-middling grasp of the importance of "capital improvement programs" for the long haul, the schemes developed for this purpose during any given year tend to be tabled for future consideration when the problem of the current dividend is periodically raised at board meetings or, especially, in consultation with the firm's principal financial backers and creditors. "You're right," such a realistic corporate officer will usually confide (privately) to his frustrated production and engineering departments, "but we've got to be practical." "Practical" signifies: "If I don't distribute these funds as reported earnings, the financiers will have me out of here in short order."

Thus, very few chief corporate officers and economists ever actually calculate prices at overproduction levels to offset falling-rate tendencies caused by general rises in productivity. Rather, the appreciation of prices is built into the financial structure of the corporation as a whole. Earnings are reported at maximal accounting valuations in order to produce an appreciation of stock values and create the "justification" for increased bonded indebtedness. The enlarged capital obligations of the firm thus act to determine the required per-product gross profit in the general fashion we have already indicated.

So, except under the most exceptional circumstances, apart from depressions themselves, the effect of rising productivity is not a *manifest* devaluation of Fixed Capital in accounting or monetary terms. Instead, the actual underlying devaluation is expressed *after a significant delay* as a crisis of accumulated obsolescence. The firm often finds itself in the following situation. It is in danger of losing its market for reasons of technological inflexibility and underproductivity. Thus, there is a shortage of gross profit, at current competitive prices, which could only be remedied by massive modernization. This modernization requires a sudden, massive influx of new capital. However, the desperate need to inflate apparent earnings prevents such urgent outlays, and the structural features of the corporate labor force and organization would militate against immediate results even if the capital were allocated.

Not accidentally, new capital development requires from eighteen months to several years to plan and install, even before actual production begins. Such installations involve radical reorientations of applied productive skills and administrative positions. On the administrative side, which is a far greater obstacle to innovation than the skills-inertia of the labor force, technological reorientation involves major disruptions of the settled habits of bureaucratic life. Since the chief corporate officers must depend upon the vast administrative bureaucracy to develop the planning and implementation in details, the bureaucracy has the greatest resources for sabotaging such an undertaking. Every bureaucratic faction that foresees a diminution of its relative power in the new arrangements attempts to sabotage the project to that extent. For just such reasons there is, to the author's knowledge, no computer installation in which the proper approach to such technology has been competently implemented; indeed, computer manufacturers have prudently evolved a balance between, on the one hand, the subjective peculiarities of the corporate bureaucracy and, on the other, the technology manifested in the design of computer configurations and software. Few really intelligent corporate officers do not bitterly hate their bureaucracies for such reasons, but no prudent corporate officer will stick his neck out so far that the bureaucracy can effectively chop it off. Indeed, for related reasons, the fascist potential inherent in our vast legion of paper-shufflers is one of the more important sociological consequences of the post-1914 decay in general capitalist development. It is not accidental that a significant stratum of the campus New Left, the drug-rock counter-culture contingent, reflects the immanently fascist values of its parental households.

Thus, the falling-rate tendency hits the particular firm or middle-range corporation (especially) in the form of a bind. Just at the point when its survival obviously depends upon massive capital-investment injections it finds itself least qualified to consider such outlays. This is what occurs in a slightly different guise on the scale of the entire economy.

Thus, primitive accumulation in the domain of Fixed Corporate Capital is expressed as a general tendency to undervalue the necessary current mass of new investment necessary to stave off the cumulative, if momentarily marginal, consequences of accrued obsolescence. On this account the mass of depreciation of Fixed Capital account reported in National Product and Income statistics grossly understates the real requirement. At the same time, the current valuation of stocks, bonds, mortgages, and the like embodies an implicit but real gross overstatement (fictitious capitalization) of those same fixed assets.

If obsolescence is taken into account, the rate of depreciation (from a capitalist accounting standpoint) ought to be an exponentially declining proportion of the total outlay over the term of useful life of fixed assets. This would probably locate the life of fixed assets in the range of seven to ten years, which would mean that each $10 billion added to the stock of fixed investment would incur an average $1 billion or more each year to the total rate of investment required the following year (in constant-dollar terms), even using the crudest method of calculating depreciation. If we examine tables for annual investment in plant and equipment over the post-war period on this basis, we gain an immediate insight into the reasons for the stagnation of the size of the productive labor force after 1953. Since the ratio of Constant to Variable Capital must increase, and the constant-dollar valuation of Constant Capital must also increase, we must conclude that the development of the productive forces has been stagnating and declining in the United States during most of the past quarter-century.

Before protesting, remember that a constant-dollar figure for output signifies that a constant rate of output is, in fact, a declining rate of output relative to the effects of continued reproduction on marginal resources, and the like. Furthermore, since the value of total product is determined by the rate of social reproduction, a 6–7 percent annual rise in productivity in the *point-of-production* labor force ("equivalent of full-time operatives") means that constant-dollar values of output must be discounted by this amount to compare value of output between two successive moments of the economy!

That this is indeed a correct interpretation is attested to by the ecological crisis, the material decay of the cities, the collapse of the rail-transport and mass-transit systems, the growing shortage of housing, and related phenomena. In sum, the material conditions of production and of life itself, when considered relative even to the U.S. population, demonstrate exactly what is dictated by our proposed method of analysis: that the scale of production has fallen viciously behind the growth of the population and even behind the level of general productive development and consumption of a quarter-century ago (that is, if we take the population as a whole and the means of *useful* production as a whole).

Thus, despite the more complex features of the case for Constant Capital, the result is generally the same as it was for Variable Capital: a gross understatement of the real costs of Constant Capital (because of primitive accumulation) and a gross overvaluation of the acknowledged elements of cost (because of fictitious capitals).

Capitalists' Consumption

For every degree of development of a specific mode of productive development under capitalism, there does exist a required ratio of capitalists' consumption: capitalist managers necessary to the organization of production and circulation as a whole, scientists and engineers to maintain the progress of productive (in the general sense of the term) technology, teachers, physicians, clerks, and the like. In addition to the incomes represented by these socially necessary persons (and by police, firemen, military personnel, and the like), there is associated with those persons certain necessary capital consumption: office buildings and equipment, schools, and so on.

Earlier, we specified that to the extent that these elements of capitalists' consumption represent socially necessary forms and activities, they represent a transfer of potentially increased social productivity to the working class itself. It should and does follow that the costs incurred on the account of D must not more than absorb the increased social surplus created by the realization of the potential transferred to the working class. That is, $S'/(C + V)$ must rise.

First, we should dispense (again) with the component of military production, the most conspicuous element of capitalists' consumption in the postwar period. Approximately $50 billion or more of this outlay is directly attributable to a deduction from capacity for increased production of means of production. If this component of wasted departmental production had been usefully added to total plant equipment investment during the postwar period (whether it was $20 billion, $30 billion or $50 billion at each moment to be considered), we would already have generally accounted for much of the primitive accumulation manifest within the U.S. economy during the postwar period. Furthermore, if we recognize that the value of $S'/(C + V)$ tends to determine the potential rate of increased social reproduction, the "secondary" consequences of military waste vastly outweigh even the immediately obvious aspects. Indeed, this represents the basis for a potential 20–25 per cent annual growth in real output of the U.S. sector right now.

The growth of office buildings and bureaucratic employment has been largely associated with the growth of fictitious capitals, rather than productive development, so that most of this employment and plant and equipment expenditure is itself gross waste. As we have noted, the intelligent use of computer technology would vastly reduce even the currently necessary component of administrative bureaucracy, and elimination of the massive paperwork associated with the spread of "turnstile" practices would facilitate further reductions. The reduction and productive re-employment of the majority of present paper-shufflers would complement the redirection of present military and related aspects of Department 1 production to expanded reproduction.

Here we have not primitive accumulation, but its opposite. The real elements of capitalists' consumption have been vastly overstated. However, as in the other cases, this (overstated) real cost has been vastly inflated for fictitious capitals.

In even these elementary terms it is immediately clear that all capitalist monetary and related statistics for the past quarter-century are viciously misleading, and any statistical analyses predicated upon them must tend to lead to a judgment at odds with both momentary actuality and the course of economic development. Indeed, one should not be astonished that every procapitalist economist has been viciously wrong on all the major questions that have arisen during this period.

APPROPRIATE PROCEDURES

Let us now restate and amplify the procedures of analysis recommended in Chapters 5 and 7. The methods outlined are derived directly from Marx's *Critique of Political Economy* and *Capital*, and from those employed by the author in developing the theses on the next decade's social and economic perspectives in 1957–1958.

As a first approximation we may take a national economic sector, which will later be corrected for the world economy. That is, we initially assume that cost-prices of imports are of the same value content as cost-prices of domestic production.

We begin with the population as a whole, which we divide into constituent classes: capitalists, petit bourgeoisie, farmers, the working class. We then momentarily put the other classes aside and focus on the working class as a whole, which becomes the elementary unit for all our subsequent calculations. That is, we do not consider an increase in the numerical value of the working-class population as changing the value of the whole class as a unity.

We shall interpolate the following qualifying remarks to prevent undue restiveness in the mind of the reader on this point. Changes in population within the working class affect the unity's value in terms of the exponential functional value for $S'/(C + V)$, through the benefits of division of productive labor and economy of scale. The increased value of the whole is not treated as an increase in simple magnitude, but as an increase in negentropic value in terms of functions of $S'/(C + V)$.

This may seem strange, though we have directed the reader's attention to this point several times in preceding chapters. The significance of Hegel's "the truth is the whole"—a significance which has obviously escaped the practical comprehension of most professed Hegelians and Marxists alike—is that we shift the notion of elementary (simple self-evident quantity) from the smallest particular "fact" of sense-certainty to the whole as a whole. The number 1 now corresponds to "true infinity," and all quantitative valuations assigned to particular moments of the whole subsumed process are, relatively and loosely speaking, mere fractional parts of 1. (As most mathematicians will immediately recognize, the notion involved in such a relationship between the particular and the "infinite" has a more sophisticated aspect.)

Following Hegel, the primary determination of the unity is relationship. This is, of course, a productive (social-reproductive, negentropic) relationship to nature (as a universal) which is expressed as class relationships and as the determination of *qualities* within the whole (surplus value, capitalists' consumption, Variable Capital, Constant Capital). The relationships of these determined qualities then determine *quantity*, or "measure." Measure, as we have stipulated repeatedly, is of the form of exponential functions of $S'/(C + V)$ for the particular.

This differs from Hegel's notion on the premises advanced by Feuerbach and resolved by Marx. The whole is not a self-developing Logos or universal Idea, but collective human reproductive existence, e.g., real anthropology.

We analyze the working class as a whole in the following terms. First, we examine it for population-mode, noting those disqualified by youth (the preproductive years of maturation, including gestation) and advanced age from a "full day's work." This calculation determines the age-interval for the productive labor force, from which housewives and others are deducted to arrive at the total productive labor force itself.

We must then subdivide this proletarian labor force into employed, partially unemployed, and permanently unemployed categories. Then we must analyze the employed labor force for its categories of Variable Capital, Constant Capital, surplus value, and capitalists' consumption. Variable Capital is determined by analysis of a standard bill of consumption in terms of the proportion of all productively employed labor required to provide this mass of products and commodities. Constant Capital is estimated as that proportion of production of means of production required to maintain existing levels of output. The residue is surplus value, from which we deduct capitalists' consumption, or the reproduction of other classes (excepting farmers).

Farmers are accounted as wage-equivalents and users of agricultural means of production as an exchange with the working class for food production by that class.

Having thus examined the working class from the standpoint of existing relationships, we correct this view for the mode of *necessary* relationships. Necessary levels of working-class consumption are empirically estimated as the levels of consumption required by skilled and semiskilled workers being newly employed.

We now interpret the simple (simple quantity, or labor-content) value of all commodities in terms of these two criteria. That is, the value of all production is the proportion of the entire productively employed working class required to produce the population as a whole. For this we have two values; the first is the existing social (labor) cost of producing the working-class population as a whole; the second is the necessary cost, or the estimated level of material consumption required by the class for uninterrupted expanded reproduction.

Using the ratio $S/(C + V)$, thus determined we determine the value of each subcategory of commodity production according to its labor content. (The average "rate of profit" rigor.) This gives us the simple, quantitative first approximation of value.

If we then attribute to capitalists' consumption all surplus value not realized as expanded reproduction in the successive moments of our study, we have the two rates of reproduction we require. These are the (apparent) rate indicated by existing capitalist relationships, and the necessary rate of reproduction associated with the level of material existence of the working class for uninhibited expansion.

From such a twofold starting-point for analysis, we can compare the rate of capitalist accumulation with the rate of social reproduction: that is, the growth of all capitalist instruments, including stocks, public and private debt, and the like, with the growth of current value. Provided that we examine the tax-component of incomes by the same criteria as other empirical elements, we have the general portrait of the economy needed to begin analysis.

What must principally be examined are the following relationships and paradoxes: (1) changes in the ratio of existing to necessary relations in the labor process itself, and in the proportions of employed, semipauperized, and pauperized strata of the entire proletariat; (2) proportional shifts in the class-composition of the population; (3) changes in the ratio $S'/(C + V)$ for combined real and fictitious capitals in counterposition to changes in the respective existing and necessary values of $S'/(C + V)$; (4) relationships between gross profit, debt service, and rent requirement on existing total capitals with respect to total self-expanding value realized from surplus value; and (5) the correlation of these factors with technical changes within the monetary process.

These studies provide the analyst with everything essential that can be adduced by mathematical procedures.

What cannot be comprehended, by definition, is the causal relations associated with the role of noetic mentation. The effects of such noetic mentation, as a Praxis, can be adduced after the fact; certain empirical tendencies, involving the relationship of rises in $S'/(C + V)$ to increased innovation and the like, can also be adduced. From that point on, analysis depends entirely upon the creative insight of the analysts, whose task is not to produce plausible qualitative explanations of causal relations, but to create hypotheses that can be tested empirically.

It is remarkable but scarcely astonishing that such elementary analytical procedures have been overlooked by virtually all professing "Marxist economists."

CRISES

We shall now summarize the material we have covered so far with respect to the fundamental antinomy of capitalist accumulation. Thus we shall outline the processes which lead to periodic capitalist crises, either as depressions or as the general breakdown crises of longer periods of development.

The very notion of including Fixed Capital in the account of the extent of wealth in the same terms as C, V, and S implies a fundamental fallacy in capitalist accumulation, and points to the way in which that contradiction leads toward crises. We have shown that the value of objects, activities, and events in a society cannot be efficiently located except in terms of a notion of invariance. This notion of invariance evaluates the present in terms of its immanent consequences for the future. (The very notion of a nonpredictive "economic science" is a pathetic contradiction in terms.) The suggestion of controlling processes of reproduction according to the criteria implied by *past* valuations of any sort is thus, in itself, a contradiction.

Hence, in the hypothetical case of the entire capitalist system merged into a single supercorporation, in which all the capitalists are merely individual stockholders, the fundamental contradiction of capitalism must still operate with the same principled force and effect as in a capitalist economy composed of numerous competing firms. Similarly, a workers' economy (e.g., the Soviet Union, Yugoslavia, China) which foolishly succumbed to "historic accounting" criteria of a capitalist sort would suffer fundamental contradictions in the planning process emulating those of a capitalist economy. In the latter instance, the workers' economy would have regressed, in tendency, toward the restoration of capitalist forms.

(Indeed, such tendencies are inherent in the dynamics of a relatively underdeveloped workers' economy—such as the Soviet Union today—attempting to develop under circumstances in which the world market is dominated by a more advanced capitalism. Foreign trade relations, concessions, and the like transmit capitalist forms per se into the real capital formation process of Soviet development.)

This hypothetical model appears to be in violent opposition to the truism that Marx insisted that the "anarchy of capitalism" is central to the crisis-prone character of such economies. Luxemburg, following Marx on this point, includes the anarchy of capitalism within her emphasis, otherwise, on the total capitalist rigor.[5] Is there not, then, an important ambiguity, if not an outright inconsistency, between the notion that the anarchy of capitalism is the expression of a fundamental contradiction, and our present insistence that the fundamental contradiction of capitalist accumulation would also occur in a capitalism represented comprehensively by a single supercorporation?

The solution to such a merely apparent contradiction or ambiguity is that the notion of property right in the means of production is the content of the term "anarchy," rather than "competition" in and of itself. It is the alienation of a part of the process of social reproduction from the whole, in the sense of isolating it for separate investment appraisal and the like, which introduces the fallacy of reductionism (that is, anarchistic or heteronomic thinking and behavior). It is exactly the same fallacy that is introduced by measuring wealth in aggregate as either the sum of the wealth represented by the many individual holdings of a firm or the current value added from many such contributing sources.

The root of the apparent difficulty is uncovered once we focus attention on exactly what aspect of the whole cycle of reproduction is overlooked by even the unique supercorporation.

The fallacy of most so-called economics, including most "orthodox Marxian" versions, is that it devises a system which would seem equally appropriate to a society of men or of gifted baboons. No account is taken of that which not only distinguishes man from the lower beasts, but also makes the emergence of a capitalist economy itself possible. "Whence," one challenges the economists, "arises the remarkable quality of negentropy in expanded reproduction?" Obviously, the source of increasing powers of social reproduction is the noetic quality of human intelligence—the capacity, in particular, to synthesize inventions and to comprehend the inventions of others as means for one's own practice. "How," one further prods the economists, "does your 'economic model' provide for the determination of that increasing cognitive power on which the negentropic feature of expanded reproduction depends?"

There we have the nub of the problem, to which Marx supplies a summary answer in the concluding section of Volume III of *Capital*, "Freedom/Necessity."[6] The growth of man's cognitive powers demands a rising material standard of living and increasing leisure. Yet the result of the realization of such cognitive advances must be that the socially necessary cost per capita of an increased material standard of life must be declining as a per capita proportion of total labor power's output. This essential, underlying relationship demands not only the proper overall quantitative ratios, but also the forms of consumption and leisure suitable to the specific sorts of cognitive advance the society demands.

Therefore, to the extent that the notion of capital sets capital as a class interest in opposition to the advance of the necessary material conditions of life of labor power, the determinations of capital are heteronomic even when, hypothetically, capitalist accumulation might be perfected into the form of a unique supercorporation.

Marx, admittedly, does not take up the special problem of the hypothetical unique supercorporation from this standpoint. The apparent rationale for his oversight seems sound enough as we turn our attention to cases such as General Motors' automotive operations. There, as is more or less characteristic of oligopolies and supranational corporations generally, we find "competing divisions" within the firm. This tendency is not accidental, arising as it does from the corporate management's lack of other means for squeezing "maximum profitability" not only from its worker employees but also from its own bureaucracy. Because of the heteronomic relationship between capital and labor in the capitalist accumulation process, and because of a cohering heteronomic character structure in the individuals produced by capitalist social relationships, it is chiefly by playing one individual or group against another that capitalism administers every facet of the society it rules. Correspondingly, even though capitalism has a strong tendency toward the supercorporation, within such a juridical form the same capitalists who undertake supermergers simultaneously fragment the operating, administrative, and even financial aspects of the enlarged operations thus established.

The same sort of phenomenon is characteristic of the Bretton Woods system. By subjugating all parts of the advanced capitalist sector (former allies and enemies alike) to the dollar credit system at the end of the Second World War, the United States effectively established a single (dollar) superimperialism, superseding the "competing imperialisms" of earlier periods. Yet the political forms through which this was accomplished carried forward considerable nationalist baggage from earlier periods. This origin of this nationalism was not entirely the chauvinist sentimentalities of the ruled in each satrapy; the United States-based firms that appropriated large parts of the critical (world-market) sector of production in each subject satrapy wished to maintain certain regional distinctions—for essentially the same reason that General Motors maintains competing automotive divisions and the United States, under the "Fomento" program, maintained the special peculiarities of Puerto Rico.

Marx regarded the unique supercorporation as a merely hypothetical construct, and treated the theoretical questions implied by it from that standpoint. We have here conceded such an hypothetical case not to suggest that such a development is imminent, but to show that even such outrageous hypothetical circumstance does not upset the notion of the inherent fundamental contradictions of capitalist accumulation.

In this light, the notion that the fundamental contradiction of capitalism is "the struggle between capital and labor" has a much deeper significance than is ordinarily attributed to such a turn of phrase. Since reducing real wages is, in the final analysis, immediately advantageous to capitalist short-term profit rates, and since such superexploitation of the working class destroys the basis for the progressive material existence of capitalism itself, this form of the conflict between capital and labor is a devastating, decisive contradiction within capitalist accumulation itself. It is the heteronomic arrangement, by which the capitalist class determines the "good" even of the whole society in opposition to the most critical aspect of the holistic social-reproductive process, that would make even a society based on a unique supercorporation heteronomic or "anarchic."

The reason some pseudo-Marxians make such an hysterical fetish of competition per se is obvious once we consider the reductionist methods they employ to define such notions as a "labor theory of value" and their amplified simple-reproduction versions of expanded reproduction.[7] As we have emphasized, the only "contradictions" that could occur in such models would be those arising from disproportionate realization of net surplus-value increments; thus, they require the assumption of competition in order to claim that some intrinsic feature of capitalism causes such a major contradiction to occur. That precisely such reasoning underlies their use of the "principle of competition" is demonstrated beyond question by their diatribes against Luxemburg for her "total capitalist rigor." Since it was Marx himself who introduced "total capitalist" rigor, and since Luxemburg directly attributes her use of the notion to appropriate sections of *Capital*, for Mandel, Bukharin, and others to defend Marx against Luxemburg's "total capitalist" notion is a manifest case of hysteria.

The form of the contradiction of capitalist accumulation may be summarized as follows. The rising productivity of labor as a whole (cognitive advances realized as new technology according to the principle of Freedom/Necessity) devalues the balance of undepleted Fixed Capital, especially, such that the increase of the ratio

$$\frac{F}{(C + V + d + S')}$$

to a value greater than one signifies that the expression

$$\frac{S' - x}{F' + C + V}$$

must decline as the expression

$$\frac{S'}{C + V}$$

rises. Or, according to this model, there is a tendency for the rate of profit to fall.

However, we have also shown that this need not occur as a secular tendency, for the same reason that no buy-back problem could exist for capitalist accumulation. The magnitude of productivity depreciation of

Fixed Capital, x, can be added to the price of total commodity output, which is then more or less readily sold at such inflated prices through corresponding expansion of the monetary system.

The same principle applies to the corresponding forms of devaluation of other inventories of circulating commodities. In addition, all sorts of gains from pure speculation can also be included in the aggregate mass of commodities and pseudo-commodities sold through the same forms of expansion of the monetary system.

This is so because the transformation of *money into commodities into enlarged money holdings* (M_0 to C_1 to M_1 to C_2 to M_2 . . .), the hypothetical "normal form" of capitalist circulation, can be grossly modified for extended periods by forms such as M_0 to M_1 to M_2 to M_3 . . . . C_n.

The result of such monetary expansion must be to accumulate a mass of potentially illiquid capital holdings in the system in the form of the combined public and private (especially governmental and corporate) debt, D.

Since the M_0 . . . M_1 . . . form of monetary circulation per se can continue indefinitely to a point of crisis, it appears during a major portion of the business cycle that this accumulation of debt need never be reduced, and that old maturing debts can be exchanged for new prediscounted, larger debts, and so on.

However, in the expansion of credit (and the corresponding expansion of the debt basis for the money supply), the total debt service arising from fictitious valuations, such as x, and the expansion of the money supply to circulate S′ are not efficiently distinguished. So, if E represents the debt service on account of D, and d′ the incrementing of d (capitalists' consumption), the total expansion of the monetary system must be $S' + d' + E$, and we have the ratio $(E + d')/S'$ and the ratio $(E + d)/S'$.

Furthermore, the mass of D is self-expanding, since it represents capitalized debt which must expand at rates at least competitive with the expansion of capital held against the account of productive capacities and the like. Since the mass of D is also being augmented from new masses of x from current production and also from sheer speculations, D is growing more rapidly than the currently determined value for $(F' + C + V)$. If the ratio of Fixed to Circulating Capitals is greater than unity, then x is increasing more rapidly than S′; thus E is increasing at an accelerating rate relative to S′.

During part of the business cycle, the effect of this process may be dampened by the liquidity given to portions of D and, more immediately significant, E through primitive accumulation. Yet, since primitive accumulation rates tend to be constant in magnitude for a given quality of technology and level of productive capacities, this buffering of liquidity must be diminished in effect as the cycle develops.

So the rate of growth of the ratio $(E + d)/S'$ must signify that the rates of monetary expansion required to maintain "full employment" through circulation of S′ must begin to rise *at an accelerating rate* (shifts of the Phillips Curve), resulting in an inflationary spiral. This inflationary spiral now tends to discount the value of outstanding debt accumulation itself, which must be offset by increased prediscounting of new debt formations—where the tradeoff for accelerating inflation is depression (through automatic accelerations in basic interest rates).

Thus, we have the ratio $(E + d)/S'$ approaching a condition of "critical mass," at which point the alternatives are inflation of the sort exemplified by Latin America or Germany in 1923, or depression.

That, in brief, is the business cycle, or the form in which the crises arising from internal contradictions of capitalist accumulation are exploded afresh as an expression of the contradictions accumulated as potential illiquidity in the processes of circulation.

It need only be stipulated that the capitalist economy does not proceed to a new monetary crisis through operations based on the terms of calculation we have identified above. The actual form of the process is easily summarized.

At the point of the firm, the combined total corporate debt and equity, at prevailing price-earnings and debt ratios, predetermines a required combined profit and debt-service income above other costs and revenues. The predetermination of the required profits and debt-service payments is the first activity and concern of any competent capitalist management. It realizes this amount through the firm's operations. If it is a commodity-producing and -selling firm, it has a more or less limited (finite) capacity and marketing potential for the immediate period. Obviously, the profit and debt-service income required must be "loaded onto" the costs of production and sale, over the finite array of sold product. The firm that does not follow this procedure, at least in effect, secures a new management, is taken over in a raid, or goes bankrupt.

The response to this process at the level of banking and government is to maintain a sufficient supply of monetary expansion to prevent a shrinking of the capitalist economy as a whole. Thus, governmental and banking agencies respond to the aggregate effect of the corporate marketing and pricing "decisions" summarized above.

It should be obvious that all the finer distinctions we have taken into account in our analysis of this process are glossed over in the actual capitalist operations of the firm and the economy. Combined corporate equity and debt are a hash aggregately representing both real and fictitious accumulations; a fine indifference to distinctions is shown by the management and the financial market generally. Combined equities and debts simply provide the management with the base for predetermining profit and debt-service requirements. In turn, the "well-being of the aggregate firm"—each firm independently predetermining its profit requirement—regulates the decisions of government and bankers. However half-conscious or slovenly such operations may be, they work to the general effect we have described, resulting inevitably in a new crisis.

THE GREAT FUGUE 12

THE GREAT FUGUE 12

From the standpoint of phenomena viewed as facts, dualism is the essence of reality. The contradiction between capitalist accumulation and social-reproductive processes, the dualism of basis and superstructure, the dualism of natural science and nature, etc., all repeatedly confront us with an ostensibly insoluble discrepancy between a universality of appreciation and a contrary universality, an actuality underlying the phenomena of perception.

Yet these contradictory moments seem to represent a single form or theme simply accompanying itself, such that no account of the processes thus portrayed can sanely overlook the transformations of development occurring as a result of their counterposition. Each resulting new juncture is to be regarded as actuality for that place and moment. In each such juncture, it is thus demonstrated that neither of the contradictory moments is independently real in itself; the independence of the two disappears momentarily, supplanted by the single actuality that seems to destroy their identity within its own.

No sooner has this resolving chord been struck than the process takes up that actuality in turn as a renewed duality; the momentary actuality is counterposed to itself in new subjective/objective contradiction.

Apart from this initial approach it is impossible to reach a competent definition of capitalist society in general, or capitalist political economy in particular. We have distinguished the two principal contradictory moments of that society: its underlying objective basis, and the social superstructure that "selectively" actualizes the successive moments of that basis. The objective basis is the underlying social-reproductive process. The subjective moment is the process of capitalist accumulation, requiring that capital accumulation is comprehended in its broadest juridical-ideological implications. Neither moment of this process could exist as it actually does under capitalism without its contradictory companion; it is the constant resolution and dissolution of the successive actualities expressing the interconnection that is the basis for a competent notion of capitalist economy.

For our present systematic understanding of such processes, we have acknowledged our formal debt to Kant's rigorous initial examination of the contradictory moments. Kant founded the modern dialectical method by attempting to locate a practicable solution to the contradiction between a synthetic universality of apperception and objective reality, through the universalizing implications of even individualized social practice.

Kant's failure within his undertaking we have treated, abstractly, as his stubborn refusal to free himself completely of the crippling reductionist ontological assumptions respecting ultimate reality of the so-called Rationalist or "French Enlightenment" world-outlook. Less formally, to attribute formal interpretations of appearances to their real, social basis, Kant's system failed as a result of his attempt to find a practical solution within the anarchist assumptions characteristic of bourgeois social relations and ideology, the reductionist notion of the individual Self and object of practice, the thing-in-itself.

Hegel advanced our power to develop scientific knowledge by a two-fold principal advance over the Kantian dialectic. With respect to both man and nature, respecting both subjective and objective, Hegel replaced the empty construct of self-evident particularity with being-in-and-for-itself. Second, with respect to the subjective moment of the universal process, Hegel eliminated the Perfection of the fixed and "unconditioned" in favor of the necessary development of that whole process which is constantly "conditioned" by its own development.

Hegel's effort partially resolved the troublesome dualism of freedom and necessity by replacing the notion of mechanistic necessity with a notion of progress as necessity. This achievement is approximately illustrated today by assertion that the universal form of necessity is that which incorporates negative entropy as necessity. Not only is this alteration of the significance and conceptual content of negative entropy useful and admissable; this apparent mere heurism immediately illuminates the content and implications of Hegel's one vicious error, his inconsistent denial of the existence of such negentropic necessity in the domain of inorganic nature.

Once his vicious error is viewed in such terms, it ought to be immediately evident that Hegel's location of progress in the subjective realm alone alienated the subjective from the actual objective for his entire system. As a consequence of such a blunder, the objective world of material process could exist only as a grey reflection within the detached spirit-world of Hegel's "Lutheran" Absolute. As a corollary point, we have properly insisted that Hegel never successfully conceived a hylozoic monism.

Hegel preserved the consistency of his system by excluding further consideration of the problem of man's causal mediation of freedom (negative entropy) into the domain of inorganic nature. For this reason, Hegel could not distinguish competently between productive and nonproductive practice,[1] and could not situate the problem of determining what is and is not progress in the material-process basis of nature-in-general.

Feuerbach almost solved this major flaw in the Hegelian system. He correctly identified the location of the solution in a general, abstract fashion, by junking the Hegelian-Kantian negation of the negation in favor of the self-subsisting positive principle.[2] Contrary to those simple frauds who regard him as a mechanical materialist, Feuerbach was an holistic dialectician in the same sense as was Hegel before him. In making man the basis, Feuerbach made universal man, species-man, the basis, and defined individual man's self-consciousness as a social product.[3] He recognized the form of Hegel's mysticism, and sought to remedy it by transferring the question of progress from the domain of Spirit (abstract psychology) to the domain of the human species' existence through its collective (that is, universal) practice.

Feuerbach's systematic error in his *Preliminary Theses and Principles* is located in his retention of Hegel's viciously flawed notion of the "inorganic universality." Attempting to eliminate Hegel's alienation of self-consciousness from the universal domain of material practice but retaining much of Hegel's flawed "elliptical" conception of the latter domain, Feuerbach precluded distinguishing consistently between productive and nonproductive universalizing practice; thus he fell into the naive circular or elliptical conception of natural philosophy that had previously crippled Kant's and Hegel's successive treatments of inorganic nature. Feuerbach was by no means a reductionist, but he failed actually to solve the central problems otherwise explicitly posed by reductionism.

Marx's lack of formal training in mathematical physics, even relative to the achievements of his leading contemporaries in that field, compelled him to neglect representation of his conceptions in the literary forms that would have had the most immediate present-day impact for purposes of epistemological and ontological clarity. This omission significantly influenced the form of his exposition in the writings of 1843–1854 and after; much of his argument in *Capital* could be shortened considerably, much iterative development could be foreshortened, if the implications of our usage of negentropy are applied to such objectives.

Nonetheless, this fact has only collateral bearing on the efficiency of interpretation of his 1843–1845 and later writings, and not on their actual content. His conceptions are not only stated but heavily underlined, to the point that they can be interpreted in no other way than we have done.

So, with Marx's 1843–1845 writings, man first understands the fugue of social development—as a matter not of formal tonalities or harmonics, but of the potential new kinds of tonalities imparted to the whole by even a single noetic moment of counterpoint. This expression of freedom is not the imposition of anarchist "free-will" atonality upon a rigid formalism, but the necessary progress of music as a whole, the very core of life of that which it merely seems to negate and actually transforms.

DIFFICULTIES OF MASTERING THE FUGUE

The obvious source of difficulty in attempting to understand the contradictory movements of actual processes is the fact that the typical student of capitalist economy knows no standpoint but the capitalist ideological view. For him, the counterposed principal themes of superstructure and basis are simply elements which could never exist without each other; he is therefore persuaded that the underlying basis must always exist in nothing but its struggle for perfection of a divinely predetermined harmony within the capitalist superstructure. *He refuses to admit the notion that the same material basis might also be developed differently as the material basis for another composition, a noncapitalist society.*

The notion of value remains a merely speculative construct, a chimera, unless the determination of such a valuation has the content of an actual social practice, a practical form of realization. If a capitalist society is seen as a closed system—an eternal arrangement of human affairs—the valuation attributed to objects (for example, commodities) by the capitalist superstructure, the capitalist market, must appear as the only existing realization of value. The observer who regards the capitalist system as the only admissible social superstructure must regard whatever valuation the capitalist circulation process puts upon commodities as the only value of interest for the real, practical world.

The result is empiricism, including empiricist "economic theory."

The capitalist superstructure is ordinarily the determinant of the individual's existence. The rules by which the individual is bound to seek the rights and privileges of personal existence within the capitalist system are, to the ingenuous individual, apparently superior to nature itself. The mastery of nature, to the extent that social man has mastered it, is the *practical* aspect of nature for man. If the universal form of such mastery for an individual's existence is capitalist economy, the entire juridical hocus-pocus capitalism imposes upon the individual as the condition of rewards must seem to the naive citizen as a "logical" system equal to, if not altogether superior to, any laws of universal nature. In the worst instances of this, the mathematics of the stock exchange is assumed by such an unfortunate individual to represent the highest degree of "scientific knowledge."

Value becomes for the credulous whatever capitalism appears to value, in the fashion in which capitalism seems to value it. There is apparently no other reality; the superstructure and the basis represent a simple vertical harmony, in which schema there appear only occasionally imperfect performers and the need, therefore, for yet again more perfect—and dictatorial—regimes of instructions.

A different view of the process must either reflect or lead to the standpoint of an altogether different superstructural process, a different social superstructure which also forms a dialectical whole with the complementary objective social-reproductive process otherwise now characteristic of capitalism.

Contrary to simple-minded "radical theory," this new world-view cannot arise out of an intensification of the alienation peculiar to capitalist relations, since such alienation merely creates and intensifies the world-view appropriate to the capitalist superstructure. It must arise not from a negative, but from the positive transcendence of that alienation under capitalist relations.

Such a positive basis for overcoming alienation is implicit in the socialization of productive labor. Capitalism's human achievement to this effect is epitomized by its merciless destruction of "the idiocy of rural life," the distinctive inhumanity not only of feudal and early capitalist societies, but the deadend of the ancient commune as well:

> . . . we must not forget that these idyllic village communities, inoffensive though they may appear, have always been the solid foundation of Oriental despotism, that they restrained the human mind within the smallest possible compass, making it the unresisting tool of superstition, enslaving it beneath traditional rules, depriving it of all grandeur and historical energies. We must not forget the barbarian egotism which, concentrating on some miserable patch of land, had quietly witnessed the ruin of empires, the perpetration of unspeakable cruelties, the massacre of the population of large towns, with no other consideration bestowed upon them than on natural events, itself the helpless prey of an aggressor who had deigned to notice it at all. We must not forget that this undignified, stagnatory, and vegetative life, that this passive sort of existence evoked on the other part, in contradistinction, wild, aimless, unbounded forces of destruction and rendered murder itself a religious rite in Hindustan. We must not forget that these little communities were contaminated by distinctions of caste and by slavery, that they subjugated man to external circumstances instead of elevating man to be the sovereign of circumstances, that they transformed a self-developing social state into never changing natural destiny, and thus brought about a brutalizing worship of nature, exhibiting its degradation in the fact that man, the sovereign of nature, fell down on his knees in adoration of Hanuman, the monkey, and Sabbala, the cow.[4]

It is the genius of capitalism that it created the potential for man to become human for the first time in his history:

> Economic conditions had first transformed the mass of the people of the country into workers. The combination of capital has created for this mass a common situation, common interests. This mass is thus already a class as against capital, but not yet *for itself*. In the struggle, of which we have noted only a few phases, this mass becomes united, and constitutes itself as a class for itself. The interests it defends become class interests.[5] (emphasis added)

The potential idea of an alternative social-political superstructure is implicit in the very form of the class-for-itself. Since capitalist accumulation limits the workers' right to the material level of existence necessary for the reproduction of modern workers to the scale of capitalist employment, capitalism leaves increasing proportions of the working-class population as a whole out of account, abandoning literally billions (today) of surplus workers and potential workers either to the malnutrition widespread in the capitalist sector below the Tropic of Cancer (where caloric intakes frequently drop below the biological level necessary for individuals as mere animals),* or to the welfare and semiemployment human scrapheaps of the United States itself. Even a major portion of the regularly employed productive labor force in the advanced sector is condemned to obsolete modes of production (and income) which almost preclude them from future employability in jobs agreeable to modern technology. The very inclusive association of employed and unemployed workers and their families immediately represents a social, *material* notion of collective self-interest, which is the germ of an entire new social superstructure based on the productive forces capitalism itself has created.

This is necessarily the case for two interconnected reasons. As we have emphasized, the worldwide socialization of production by capitalist development has created the objective circumstances under which the material existence of every individual worker, or local group of workers, depends absolutely upon the productive activities of a majority of the entire world's population. No local group of workers has a real (that is, "national") self-interest independent of the world's working-class forces as a whole. Second, the strategic precondition for the victory of the organized employed workers and their families over the capitalist class is their unity with the larger mass of the unorganized, unemployed, and bitterly oppressed strata of their own class.

Such a unified force, if it acts collectively and reasons in unified self-interest, thus already represents an alternative social superstructure. It judges the value of the productive act and the particular product from the standpoint of the universal self-interest of the self-conscious world working class taking itself as a whole. It thus immediately counterposes the self-conscious interest of universal social reproduction of the productive class to the opposing interest of capitalist accumulation.

It is this implicit reality within the womb of capitalist economy that absolutely defines its duality. The same underlying basis, the same objective social-reproductive process, is now defined by two contending superstructures; the socialist's abstraction of the material basis from capitalist society follows rigorously, not speculatively.

The same contradiction is expressed differently by capitalist crises, in which the development of apparent overproduction of commodities (as commodities) reveals a cumulative underproduction of use values. These crises periodically demonstrate that the accumulation of capital has far outrun the rate of absolute expansion of production of wealth. If the investment of capital, which is the form of enlargement of the mass of capital, had characteristically absolutely enlarged the scale of reproduction of wealth to the same degree, the process of capitalist accumulation would have proceeded without interruption. Crises themselves absolutely demonstrate that the capitalist valuation of commodities is in contradiction to their real social value (use value).

Such crises are thus the fact corollary to that of the class-for-itself. Crises, by begging a superstructure more in agreement with the underlying use-value reality, beg the only possible alternative superstructure, that unique to the class-for-itself.

A third means of uncovering the same dualism arises from an intellectual unification of the interconnected processes just cited. To the extent that capitalist society produces true intellectuals, it creates individuals who are capable of discovering and speaking for the class-for-itself before that social formation comes into existence. The possibility of such revolutionary socialist intellectuals inheres in capitalism. The more vigorously and extensively capitalist development socializes the worldwide productive process, the more capitalism requires administrators and scientists who attain practical comprehension of the worldwide social process as a coherent universality.

Unfortunately, the social circumstances of such a potential intelligentsia are generally in the sharpest opposition to the otherwise natural course of capitalist intellectual development itself. The typical capitalist's intellectual is among the most impotent and fragmented social types within capitalist society. He combines access to creative leisure and a near-universality of world-overview with a personal social outlook not far advanced from the "idiocy of rural life." His individual survival as an accredited intellectual usually depends upon the most self-degrading conformity with the rules of success and failure established for those institutions (universities, bureaucracies, and other "village" communities) in which such leisure is afforded. Consequently, institutionalized intellectual life itself is generally degraded into the most vicious empiricism.

Kant, Hegel, Feuerbach, and Marx epitomize the rare capitalist intellectual who surmounts such constraints to an important extent. It is unfortunately inappropriate here to enlarge on the sociology of such happy exceptions. What is relevant is the characteristic feature of their activity, the universal view which is simultaneously occupied with the implicit universality, through realized practice, of the concrete particularity of life. They comprehend the universality of historical development as a lawful process.

Such exceptional intellectuals are thus potentially equipped to discover the social world-outlook and methods of judgment that have yet to appear in the process of maturation of a class-for-itself. Like Karl Marx, they are situated to approximate the method and principal features of class self-consciousness—of a new socialist society—long before that class comes into existence.

Their existence cannot be an abstract or ivory-tower life of contemplation. It is the nature of science that it must be demonstrated empirically at each turn. The socialist intellectual exists as such by constantly analyzing the contradictions of capitalist economy from the standpoint of the implicit next crisis, which can inevitably be adduced from the specific interplay of contradictions of each boom period. He is concerned with predetermining, as exactly as possible, the approximate date of the advent of such a new capitalist crisis, but is even more committed to correctly foresee the major features of the social-economic developmental process preceding and leading to such a crisis.

The empirical side of such a science is located in the process of organizing the mere class-in-itself into a class-for-itself, under those conjunctural conditions which make such efforts practicable.

Without such active commitments, even the initially successful attempt at theory must deteriorate into idle speculation. If the notion of valuation which the intellectual ought to counterpose to capitalist valuations is not a practical question *for him*, his momentary discovery of the existence of the great fugue deteriorates into worship of the banal old vertical harmonies. His theoretical outlook slips back into agreement with his petty day-to-day personal commitments; he finds sweet reason uniquely located in the capitalist system of valuations, in values appropriate to that practical realm of petty personal activity within which he has circumscribed his pursuit of immediate and momentary social identity. A science insulated from applied science inevitably degenerates into scholastical apologetics for prevailing ignorant prejudices. What else could it do?

It is impossible to understand the fugue unless one is participating in the noetic moments on which its development is premised. This is the real source of difficulties of so many would-be students of dialectical method generally and Marxian economics in particular.

THE ECONOMY AS PROCESS

In both Volume III of *Capital* and the two very important chapters of *Theories of Surplus Value,*[6] Marx repeatedly qualified his preliminary critique of Ricardo's theory of capitalist accumulation by warning the reader that the decisive issue of the rising productivity of labor is momentarily being left out of consideration. Then, in an emphatic amendment to the latter manuscript, he writes:

> Calculated on the total capital the (rate of) profit of the larger capital, which employs more constant capital (machinery, raw material) and relatively less living labour, will be lower than that of the smaller (amount of) profit yielded by the smaller capital employing more living labour in proportion to the total capital. The (relative) decrease in variable capital and the relative increase in constant capital, although both parts are growing, is only another *expression for the increased productivity of labour.*[7]

He develops the same point in Volume III, as we have emphasized in this text, and as Luxemburg details.[8]

We have already developed at length the thesis that this rise in the general productivity of labor expresses man's generally increased power over nature. We have also emphasized that the rising material content of more productive labor power and the marginal costs of depletion of existing resources require an exponential tendency for $S'/(C + V)$ to rise as a precondition to actually realized simple rises in that ratio, when the terms of the expression are determined as proportions of the productive labor force taken as a whole.

This we have shown to be the positive solution to the Kantian antinomy of Freedom and Necessity. The exponential tendency that has thus been empirically demonstrated to exist is the proper notion of negative entropy, as a positive alteration of universal nature for human existence, and, for the reasons given, this exponential tendency as a characteristic of the universal labor process—universalized social reproduction—necessarily expresses the fundamental law of the universe. This notion expresses the kind of necessity Hegel sought but mislaid in failing to develop a hylozoic monist view of inorganic nature.

Because man is alienated—for the moment, we restrict our view to capitalist society in particular—he mistakenly interprets his mode of existence in animal-like terms.[9] By "alienation" we signify first that the increase of man's sovereignty over nature exists empirically as an increase only in the realm of the universal—his society and his class as a whole. As capitalist society fragments the working class into false parochialist self-interest groupings, or even mere atomized individuals, the worker is practically denied deliberate access to the consequences of his human behavior: he is alienated from humanity. By "human behavior" we mean that which distinguishes man from mere animals: his power to modify deliberately and effectively his existence-behavior to achieve a quality of evolutionary progress which animals parallel only in biological evolution into new species. Consequently, whatever degrades man into a creature of fixed needs, and a fixed mode of responding to objects of need, degrades him into an animal.

Once again, what distinguishes the human species as human is its freedom from a biologically determined fixed mode of existence, a freedom exemplified by the *process* of rising social productivity, a process defined by the self-subsisting positive principle, expressed empirically as tendencies for an exponential rise in $S'/(C + V)$. It is this quality of continuous change that represents the "primitive" material substance of the space-time continuum for human man.

This problem also has an empirical expression in the difficulty of conceptualizing a solution to the problem of the Freedom/Necessity antinomy. Since men live in a society that degrades them into animal-likeness, they see reality not as it is but fetishistically, atomistically, in terms of static "facts," discrete particles, and in associated terms of fixed laws of relationship among these static, inert elementarities. Thus we have the mechanistic world-view, with its associated mechanistic interpretations of causal relations and of necessity. It is consequently alien to the world-view of alienated, animalized man that material substance, as it is momentarily encountered in the determinate particular, should be comprehended as an *active* substance expressing a noetic process, a substance which itself *is* a noetic process.

This alienation not only outlines the moral and intellectual debasement of the worker under capitalism, in particular, but locates the most general basis for the twofold contradictions of capitalism itself.

The superiority of capitalism to previous forms of society—in terms of an evolutionary overview—is that the dialectical notion of capitalist accumulation reflects the noetic principle in a certain fashion: the notion of the absolute increase of wealth by expanded forms of higher social productivities, and also the self-reflexive notion of wealth as the substance that has the quality of such positive self-reproduction. We have summarized the process of gestation, from the twelfth through the seventeenth centuries of European mercantile capitalism, by which capitalism was determined to have such qualities.

The most general contradiction of capitalism is that it is inherently incapable of perfection by virtue of its nondialectical, anarchist (that is, alienated) form. The notion of individual capital in itself—the ideological basis for capitalist ideas of accumulation in general—is an empty construct which does not know universality, is unable to distinguish between absolute and relative surplus value, and therefore cannot systematically distinguish between productive and nonproductive activities for the particular case of capital investment. This is epitomized by the fact that the aggregate capitalists may each be pursuing what appears to each as the optimal course for increasing his absolute wealth, while in the aggregate they are reducing the absolute wealth of society as a whole, or generally destroying the material basis for maintaining present rates of capitalist production and accumulation. Capitalism, because of its particularist-interest nature, has no organic capacity to learn new behaviors that might correct such vicious errors.

This feature provides the premise for the second major contradiction, that which immediately leads to general crisis. When a general rise in productivity has devalued existing capitals, the capitalist necessarily passes on this actual or implicit devaluation as a charge against both absolute and relative surplus value, either causing an apparent tendency for the general rate of profit to decline, or avoiding this by recourse to an inflationary expansion of the monetary system. Either course of responsive actions leads to the same ultimate crisis-result: a braking of the development of the productive forces, and a consequent slowing of the rate of expansion of absolute wealth-production in current terms, while the rate of capitalist accumulation gallops ahead toward the inevitably ensuing liquidity crisis and general depression.

On both accounts, the capitalist system is incapable of expanding the mass of capital in ways amenable to the productive reproduction of the actual and potential working-class population as a whole.

The most devastating irony of this process is the fact that the dynamic dysfunctions of the capitalist accumulation process thus outlined are determined by the effects of that very rising productivity of labor on which increases in capitalist absolute accumulation depend. The special result of this general contradiction is a third contradiction. It is possible for capitalism to maintain the rate of profit and even to increase the short-term rate of relative accumulation of useful wealth by primitive accumulation—by means of the one-time measure of looting nature, existing populations, and even other capitalist sectors, *thus depleting the future basis for even continued such accumulation of new relative wealth.*

The emergence of the potential class-for-itself, and of socialist society out of the process, by means of the same noetic principle which is ultimately the principle of life itself is the great fugue whose composition and performance we must master.

THE FORM OF THE CAPITALIST CYCLE

Let us summarize the history of the Bretton Woods economy, from the close of the Second World War to the collapse of that capitalist world-economic system by decree on August 15, 1971, as follows.

At the beginning of this period, the United States-centered, new world capitalist economy stumbled about on the verge of a liquidity crisis. The existing monetary system depended largely on the monetization of a vast war debt, for whose debt service adequate supporting reserve in the form of expanding *useful* production was still lacking. In the United States itself, drastic deflationary efforts were made up through 1947 in an effort to prevent the monetary system from exploding in a liquidity crisis. In depleted Western Europe a series of devaluations and austerity measures, relative to the U.S. dollar, temporarily stabilized those subsectors and, most important, propped up the basic world currency, the U.S. dollar. By pegging European currencies, notably the British pound with its colonial reserves, at artificially low valuations relative to the dollar, the U.S. dollar could command the largest proportion of the material wealth and productive labor power of the other capitalist sectors and their colonies.

The security of the dollar, and the basis for subsequent capitalist prosperity, was established by European (and Japanese) austerity measures, and by the Marshall Plan and related measures which insured future payments to the account of the world-roving dollar through subsequent expansion of production in the conquered sectors (Europe, Japan, and the colonial sector). This basis for future payments from expanded real production enabled the United States and its satrapies to, in effect, refinance their massive debt accumulations.

Renewed emphasis on military economy in the United States under President Truman enabled the U.S. sector, already mired in the effects of deflationary measures undertaken in the 1948–1949 recession, to crawl to recovery. The Korean War was the political pretext for this resurgence of military economy.

The Korean War provided a further economic benefit to U.S. capitalism, a feature generally ignored or miscalculated by modern statisticians. The hysterical witch hunt inaugurated by the Truman regime, under the auspices of the Cold War and Truman's bloody Korean adventure, attacked the U.S. labor movement vitally and effectively. It virtually destroyed that movement's ability to defend itself against politically mobilized economic repressions, by extirpating the politically conscious, politically active stratum of trade-union members or otherwise, denying them access to a leading or even influential role in the organized labor movement.

As a result of this political decapitation of the organized labor movement, the real wage-income of trade-union–member heads of households declined in value from 1948 on. This tendency had been present, of course, in the effects of the rapid inflation of the immediate postwar period. The Truman witch hunt—the Cold War most immediately aimed against organized labor in the capitalist sector itself—temporarily destroyed the organic political capacity of the labor movement to resist this trend, and thus made declining real incomes an institutionalized fixture of the postwar period.

This actual decline in real wages of employed heads of working-class households does not show up in the statistical studies of real incomes issued by the U.S. government and allied antilabor agencies. Even the trade-union bureaucracy has timidly tolerated distorted official statistics. The absolute fallacy of official real-income rate statistics is located in the "market-basket" principle used by procapitalist technicians to measure relative wages from one period to the next. Those of us who lived through the 1948–1952 period as workers possess first-hand, concrete knowledge on this point, but few such experienced persons have managed to assemble a scientific form of argument in support of the plain facts of life on this account.

Official real-income calculations are corrupted by four mutually connected fallacies, which we shall cite in a moment. Those statisticians do employ an adjustment for inflation: by comparing the current prices of the items in a standard market basket with the prices of the same items in a base period, they calculate corresponding rates of inflation. They then devalue current dollars, using those rates to arrive at constant dollars—the adjusted value of output and income, the value if there had been no change in prices from the base period of comparison.

This procedure ignores the actual devaluation of constant-dollar output during the interval since the base period: devaluation through increased productivity. It also overlooks necessary costs arising from intensification of the rate of exploitation of working-class households which may have occurred during that period. It confuses nonproductive and productive wage earnings, and, as a corollary, excludes the necessary social costs of reproducing members of welfare, semiemployed, and unemployed workers' households as productive members of society. It ignores the criteria which must be employed to account for qualitative changes that *ought* to have occurred, but may not have, in the composition of the market basket, that the necessary particular material content of a relatively constant-value real wage has markedly changed without necessarily being manifest in actual consumption modes.

Admittedly—and our critics would, of course, heavily emphasize this point—official statisticians do imagine themselves to correct for changes in the composition of the market basket in the course of each ten-year shift of base period. Theirs is not a correction worth mentioning, since the new empirical market basket (modal consumption) may itself represent a rise or a decline relative to necessary real income since the previous base period, without any consideration of this fact on their account. That is, changes in technology and the social organization of the labor force may have increased the *necessary* composition of the market basket above the actual mode. A very much higher income level (measured in constant dollars) may be required today to provide wage-earners' households with the *relative* level of material existence prevailing a decade earlier.

One illustration will make the essential point. As a result of postwar downward pressures on the real incomes of trade-union members' households, significant proportions of housewives re-entered the active labor force, thus increasing the number of labor-hours per household required to maintain parity in real-income levels. To compensate for the loss to the household itself of the housewife's hours, and to prevent catastrophic declines in the cultural level of the household with a working wife, large "capital" expenditures on household labor-saving devices, paid child care, and so forth were required. The increase in the intensity of exploitation of working-class families thus increased the material cost of living.

This development was accompanied and exacerbated by the deterioration of urban life associated with the flight of new-home construction and places of employment from the economically more efficient urban center. Increased commuting-time tended to decrease the number of hours of available leisure in workers' households, lowering the cultural level of those households, and to create the need for new items of expenditure: for example, the number of automobiles required per household for transportation to employment, shopping locations, and the like.

Changing productive technology in the developing industries offering new employment increased the amount of education necessary, increasing the average material cost per member of the household by postponing the age of maturity, increasing needs for material objects embodying reflections of technological culture, and increasing household outlays for the education of children.

In sum, if the market basket is defined on the basis of the quality of material culture needed to produce family members qualified for the mode of employment represented by the most modern general technology, the value-content of the standard of living of most trade-union members in the United States significantly declined from 1948 on—a secular decline in the level of real income as determined by any scientific measure of the *necessary* content of the modal market basket.

This fact is partially reflected today by comparing modal trade-union incomes with the official data on the required normal standard of living for an average family of four persons.

In Europe, during the same period, the decline in workers' real incomes has been markedly greater than in the United States.

Under the impetus of Korean War military economy, the absolute level of U.S. productive employment rose to about the same tendency-level at which it has remained ever since. This statistic is not quite concealed by official reports of the number of fulltime operatives in manufacturing, construction, transportation, and mining.

Data on the shifting composition of the labor force, and associated shifts in composition-of-population characteristics in the United States during the postwar period, become most illuminating when examined from the point of reference just outlined. From the low point of manufacturing employment of operatives at the close of the Korean War, this employment rose modestly on the basis of a consumer-credit expansion until the close of 1956, and was aborted by the downturn toward the 1957–1958 recession which became visible in March 1957. From that point until 1961, the general trend in the employment *ratio* of operatives was downward until the beginning of the "Kennedy boom" in 1961. From 1957 on, the level of employment of productive operatives never significantly exceeded that of 1953. This stagnation and decay in manufacturing and mining most viciously affected the so-called poor, notably the more visible poor of the black and Hispanic minorities. The pathway to assimilation into the mainstream of the productive working class—through the factory gate—was not entirely closed, but the net effect was to relegate a large segment of this population to a virtual human scrapheap of semiemployment, welfare, or lumpenproletarian "hustling."

The effect of U.S. stagnation from 1957 on was partly concealed by a rapid, post-1957 expansion of enrollment in colleges and two-year postsecondary schools. Though advancing technology demands increased levels of education of the pre-employment strata, this increased academic enrollment was not in practice a conduit into modern *productive* employment. The employment awaiting college graduates was predominantly in a cancerously burgeoning governmental and corporate bureaucracy, an expanded military force of draftees, and other economic deadends. Increased academic enrollments turned "multiversities" into day-care centers for otherwise unemployed and inevitably restive young adults between the ages of seventeen and twenty-three. Whatever increased productive potential was imparted to these students, it was not generally realized.

The analogy between Imperial Rome and the United States during the 1946–1971 period can, of course, be exaggerated, but considerable useful insight can be adduced from the comparison before reasonable bounds are exceeded. In no sense can U.S. economy and social life in this period be competently interpreted by directly comparing it to that of the United States in any preceding period, or by attempting to explain its main developments in terms of essentially internal features of the North American continent. The United States' belated recovery from the Great Depression in 1940–1941 was based on the prospect of imposing U.S. military production and related war debts upon conquered foe and former ally alike at the conclusion of the impending war; the basis for the establishment and liquidity of that military-economy expansion was the income to be looted from the entire world at the conclusion of the war. The margin of profitability of U.S. domestic corporations during a quarter-century of the Bretton Woods system was a result of the combination of U.S. military expenditures and investment and other conquests of the entire capitalist sector outside the United States itself. Without actual and anticipated military economy and "exogenous" Western European, Japanese, semi-colonial, and other looting by the U.S. dollar, the U.S. economy could not have lasted a month past the beginning of the 1950s.

The looting of non-United States subsectors of the world economy can be subdivided into two principal forms. First, of course, we encounter gains to the account of the dollar as reflected in accounting statements; these do not represent the most significant part of looting. More significant is the unaccounted looting that occurs as foreign production is purchased at prices significantly below the U.S. price of production of the same commodities, and the outrageous unaccounted costs to the non-United States subsectors by looting of natural resources (primitive accumulation), consumed either by U.S. manufacturers or as part of the foreign operations of their cartels.

In general, and not accidentally, the magnitude and decisive importance of this U.S. capitalist overseas looting and sovereignty is grossly underestimated in most accounts; in fact, the grossest plain facts of this sort are usually ignored or even vigorously denied. One such vicious commonplace error pertains to the case of Japan.

As is well known, especially among would-be U.S. investors in Japanese firms, that country has established and maintained certain barriers to foreign investors' *direct* takeover of Japanese corporations. Does this mean, as some foolish observers conclude, that the Japanese economy is not an economic satrapy of U.S. capital? The famous "independent" Japanese shipbuilding industry will serve as an example; it is more or less representative of other major Japanese sectors.

Let us suppose that a Greek shipping magnate orders a supertanker from a Japanese shipbuilder during the post-1967 period. Immediately we note that approximately 90 per cent of the financing of this tanker may be undertaken through the Chase Manhattan Bank. These tankers, when constructed, will carry oil from the OPEC countries (oil producing exporting countries) to Europe, which secures approximately 90 per cent of such energy resources from those countries. The production of this oil is controlled by cartels, interlocked with other cartels which control the distribution of the oil both in transit and at points of European distribution. There is a more than vaguely discernible connection between those cartels and the financial cartels of which Chase Manhattan is a keystone. Who controls the production of tankers fabricated by cheap, highly skilled Japanese "independent" labor power? In whose interest is this product produced; who benefits from the price advantage of Japanese shipbuilding? Who finally realizes the lion's share of the profit generated by the entire integrated venture?

Or, broadening our view to include the United States' alleged competitors in Western Europe, who benefits from the difference in border price of the same form of commodity produced in the United States and Western Europe? Who but the U.S. concerns, their world cartels, and the United States-based financial cartels that control the whole affair? What is the source of the marginal gain thus obtained by U.S. financial powers if not the lower standard of living and more intensive laboring conditions of European workers?

At the point that the United States subsector went into a stagnation tailspin, in the post-1957 period, the development of Western Europe and Japan had begun to "take off." While the development of the productive forces in scale stagnated in the United States, billions of dollars in U.S. credit and investment flooded into foreign sectors, seeking the higher rates of profit predicated on the relative misery of the foreign working class. The artificially overvalued dollar was an enormous advantage to the United States, in terms of the prices Europeans had to pay for U.S. exports and the sacrifice prices at which U.S. importers acquired the products of foreign extraction and manufacturing.

On this basis, the post-1957 United States "Rome" enjoyed a startling parasitical expansion of employment in the governmental and corporate bureaucracies. The rise in administrative and service employment was accompanied by the stagnation of productive employment, which meant, in effect, that each productive U.S. worker had more parasites crawling up his back with the passing of each year.

Two general observations apply here. As we have noted, the argument that stagnation in the number of productive operatives did not represent socioeconomic decay is devastatingly refuted by the decay of cities and basic industries, as well as by the massive shortages of wealth needed to maintain real incomes, even by official standards. Granted, much of the increase in administrative and service employment (physicians, teachers, and the like) occurred *in the form of* socially necessary services. However, a socially necessary service expresses itself as such by, first, increasing the consequent potential productivity of the working class. Second, it realizes that increased potential in the productive activity of the working class to the extent that the overall combined per capita social costs of services and production not only to decrease, but this decrease occurs after a substantial rise in the absolute real income per capita of the entire society. Despite the fact that much of the increase in services took the form of socially necessary nonproductive employment, the failure to realize the potential of this increase in the form of expanded productive employment suffices to make the growth in administrative and services employment economically parasitical in effect.

The vigorous overall expansion within the Bretton Woods capitalist empire continued through approximately the 1964–1966 wave of recessions in Western Europe and Japan. At this point, the rate of increase of productive employment throughout the capitalist world as a whole declined. However, administrative and service employment continued to increase relative to productive employment.

The general reason for the deceptive prosperity of the administrative and services sectors is elementary. Administrative activities are tied more or less directly to the rate of circulation of paper, rather than the production of real commodities. Therefore, the continued outpouring of paper and growth of financial activities generally means that employment continues to rise in this nonproductive category—even under conditions of impending depression. Since a major proportion of service employment is also tied to administrative activities, and to the incomes of administrative wage-earners, the services sector also maintains its employment rates up to the overt breaking-point of an oncoming bust.

Despite such fictitious prosperity, and continued high rates of total employment in *combined* productive and nonproductive categories, the entire system immediately began to unravel after the 1964–1966 recessions. First, the process leading to the sterling devaluation of November 1967 was followed by the franc devaluation and the first D-mark up-valuation, accompanied by the preliminary collapse of the gold convertibility system in March 1968. This was followed by the beginning of the U.S. recession in 1969, punctuated by the first marked impulse toward U.S. depression in May 1970, and followed by the March–August 1971 collapse of the entire Bretton Woods system.

In general, this most recent major business cycle represents the first *major* business cycle of the entire world capitalist system in its period of decay; its prosperity is permeated with decay. The prosperity of the capitalist class has been predicated upon rapid exhaustion of the natural and man-improved resources for future production of the material means of existence of the human race as a whole. The capitalist system, which has directly assimilated the entire population and territory of the world outside of the eastern bloc, China, Cuba, and North Vietnam, has enjoyed a quarter-century of capitalists' prosperity not only by relegating the major portion of the capitalist world's population to increasing misery, but also by creating the conditions for depopulation of that same vast idle reserve army, a population measured in billions, whose wretchedness must increase as long as capitalism itself exists.

The phenomenon of imperialist decay represents a qualitative change in the state of the capitalist economy as a whole by contrast with 1870–1913, and the period before that. In the pre-1870 period, despite the massive human cost of capitalist development in its principal national sectors, the overall effect of that development was a general increase in the ability of subject populations not only to increase their populations, but also to reproduce larger working-class populations at a higher quality of individual existence and productivity. During the 1870–1913 period of the old imperialism, the brutal effects of capitalist looting of colonial and semicolonial populations were accompanied by two general benefits to humanity: the destruction of reactionary social systems, which were a vicious obstacle to the development of their populations; and the introduction to the subject sectors of the germs of capitalist technology and industry, which provided the abused populations with a new basis of social reproduction which they could use to release themselves from barbarism and imperialism alike, and to become an integral part of a higher form of social life. In general, relative to the world as a whole, the potential social reproductive powers of the subject population as a whole were being raised.

This old imperialist system collapsed in a general breakdown crisis which extended—with intervening economic pulsations—from 1913 to the 1931–1933 depths of the Great Depression, a development which brought that system formally to an end, and established the roots of the new forms of imperialism in the New Deal and the Hitler–Schacht form of Nazi military economy. Now, the essential form of imperialist development is the cannibalization of already subject domain and population, in the interest of maintaining only relative prosperity in an ever-narrower section of that domain and population as a whole.

With that very important distinction, the general form of the past quarter-century's business cycle is a replication of the essential features of every business cycle before it.

THE CONTENT OF THE BUSINESS CYCLE

We have emphasized, following both Marx and Luxemburg, that capital can be understood only from the standpoint of capitalist accumulation taken as a whole.[10] In the final analysis—in the universal—the notion of particular capitals and the possibility of the continued existence of individual capitals generally are both determined by capitalist accumulation as a whole.

Marx properly attributes the discovery of this point to the Physiocrats' notion of absolute, as distinct from relative, profit—although the notion of enlarging a finite national revenue had previously emerged in less precise terms from the sixteenth-century crises of European mercantile capitalism. Individual capitals and aggregations of such individual capitals are heteronomic by definition, and therefore cannot determine or reveal (with respect to themselves) whether their apparent particular accumulations are absolute or relative from the standpoint of capitalist accumulation taken as a whole.

The form of capital and value with which Marx deals in Volume I of *Capital* might be termed the central tendency or characteristic form. This would conveniently restrict the notion of capitalist accumulation to those productive activities that absolutely increase the scale of the productive forces for society as a whole.

In short, capital acquires its power to reproduce itself, on an expanded scale as capitalists' capitals, by appropriating realized use values, of the form of exponential tendencies to self-expanding use value in the social form of $S'/(C + V)$.

The limitation of this preliminary, pedagogical assumption has been identified as the fact that the absolute expansion of capitalist accumulation, even real capitalist accumulation, is by no means inherently coextensive with the expansion of self-expanding use value relative to the subject population taken as a whole. Capitalism defines absolute accumulation in terms of absolute enlargement only of the wealth of existing *capitalist* accumulation as a whole. It not only includes as such absolute *capitalist accumulation* the depletion of natural preconditions for further human existence, but also treats as absolute increases in wealth those accumulations that increase the wealth of capitalists at the expense of the human population as a whole.

The same special distinction has previously applied to competing capitalisms. To the extent that capitalist accumulation as a whole is defined as whole for a particular national capitalism, the looting of even conquered capitalist nations may be considered to increase capitalist accumulation as a whole for one sector, even though the effect is to reduce aggregate capitalist accumulation (for aggregated worldwide capitalist accumulation) as capitalism was previously.

Since capitalism can successfully expand as a whole at a net loss for nature and subject populations as a whole, capitalism immediately reveals itself in those terms as an historically bounded system. As capitalist expansion makes the entirety of the world's available natural resources and populations under capitalism the material basis for that capitalism, capitalist expansion tends (as we shall shortly detail) to become auto-cannibalistic relative to the extent of nature and populations on which that entire capitalist system depends. It is convergence on this boundary condition that determines capitalism's going over from a state of being a generally progressive social system to a system of general social decay.

This contradiction is inherent in capitalism as capitalism. Kant was correct in identifying the amorality of the heteronomic individual juridical capitalist. Although the connection of capitalism to universal reality, to the real consequences of individual capitalist accumulation, is uniquely located in the universal—that is, in capitalist accumulation as a totality—individual capitals, which are the active aspect of capitalism, are inherently incapable of knowing this universality except in the form of recurring depressions, and general capitalist breakdown crisis.

Kant was also treating capitalism, however unwittingly, when he attempted to locate a solution to this heteronomic difficulty—this fundamental antinomy of capitalism—in the negation of the negation. The negation of the negation is an apt representation of the gestation of capitalism over the half-millenium of its emergence from feudalism and mercantilist feudal decay. The "perfection" of capitalism by negation of the negation is expressed by the emergence in the eighteenth and early ninteenth centuries of the false-positive notion of productive capital—of the accumulation of productive capital—as the central thrust of capitalist ideology (see Ricardo).

Hegel was also absolutely correct in deriding Kant's negation of the negation at the outset of his *Phenomenology*.[11] The determination of the pseudo-positive by the negation of the mutual negation of collective individual (heteronomic) capitals does not meet the requirements of truth. Mere negation of the negation of heteronomic capitals leads to a conditional, ultimately false "perfection", precisely because the notion of perfection is predicated on the juridical notion of heteronomic capital.

This is the philosophic representation of what Marx identifies as the inhering anarchy of capitalism. Although the negation of the negation does "perfect" capitalist ideology and collective practice to the extent of emphasizing the accumulation of productive capitals, the very definition of individual heteronomic capitals precludes an associated competent definition of distinctions between productive and nonproductive activities and realizations. The capitalist discovers the disastrously countervailing universal consequences of primitive accumulation only substantially after the damage of that particular form of primitive accumulation has been almost fully realized, to the detriment of the material conditions of general social reproduction as a whole. Therefore, the capitalist system is unavoidably compelled to destroy the very material basis on which its successful continued existence as a progressive form of society depends.

Or, to express this notion in economic terms, large-scale primitive accumulation at the expense of future potential capitalist means of social reproduction is an inherent and ever-growing flaw within the capitalist system to its conclusion.

The associated major internal flaw in the notion of capitalist accumulation is variously expressed as "dead capital," "relative surplus value," and "fictitious capitals."

The effect of successful expansion of productive capitals is to devalue the material content of capital produced under previous conditions of lower productivity. This devaluation affects Constant Capital in the form of materials and semifinished production, and also affects Variable Capital as capitalists generally define it. Constant Capital in the form of materials and semifinished products is cheapened in value content, and to the extent that labor power has been reproduced only to the level of yesterday's technologies, it has been cheapened too.

The sharpest effects of this rising productivity of labor power for the productive content of capitals are found in connection with both the rising ratio of Department 1 to Department 2 (rising organic composition of capitals), and the tendency to a growing ratio of Fixed to Circulating Capitals.

The effect of rising productivity of labor is to cheapen the cost of labor power in terms of S'/V, or to increase the "free-energy" content of labor power in that respect. If this gain is optimally realized for an absolute expansion of the rate of accumulation of wealth, the ratio $S'/(C + V)$ also increases in terms of ratios of productive labor power taken as a whole. The cheapening of the cost of producing a higher absolute per capita standard of material existence and leisure for improved qualities of labor power means that, in the structure of productive relations, a transfer of a proportion of total labor power from Department 2 to Department 1 occurs —although, in underlying value relationships *as determined by working-class social reproduction*, the increase in C is such that $S'/(C + V)$ rises.

In ecological terms, this evolution signifies that the "energy state" of man's productive forces has been increased. Not only are the crude-energy and free-energy contents of labor power increased, but the energy content of man's alteration of nature has increased even more than the energy content embodied in the creation of labor power. Again, it must be emphasized that the increase in value of C over V provides for a rising value of $S'/(C + V)$ *in use-value terms*, or in social-reproductive terms.

The so-called tendency for a falling rate of profit under capitalism arises because capitalism introduces a determination of Constant Capital which tends to viciously exceed the social content of actual Constant Capital as a whole. The most notable expression of this vicious flaw is located in the capitalization of Fixed Capital.

Rising productivity obviously devalues the unrealized content of held-over masses of capital improvements in nature in two respects. First, rising productivity reduces the energy content of replacements of such capital improvements, and also depreciates the use value (free energy) expressed by these objects as means of production relative to new forms of capital improvements.

Therefore, to the extent that capitalists attempt to realize losses to Fixed Capital due to cheapening of production and relative obsolescence, either the capitalists' valuation of Constant Capital must be increased by that amount above its current value or the loss must be directly charged to the profit account.

As the ratio of accounted Fixed Capital to current production becomes cumulatively larger, the effects of charging fictitious values for depreciated Fixed Capital and relative surplus value must become large relative to current capitalist rates of realized profit. Thus, from a mechanistic standpoint it would appear, as it did to Ricardo, that the rising organic composition of capitals (C/V) magically causes a tendency for the rate of profit to decline.

To the extent that the organic composition of capitals becomes increasingly large, such a rising overvaluation of Constant Capitals would seem to prevent the capitalist system from continuing to function at all. However, capitalism has two principal means of escaping this fate in the short run.

First, as we have noted, capitalist accumulation does not occur solely in terms of purchases of reproductive use values as new capital. The discrepancy between time of purchase and sale embodied in the bill of exchange, and in derived forms of paper money (the universal bill of exchange) and discounted credit instruments, allows for deferring actual payments through the mediation of intervening settlements in debt instruments and paper money.

The growth of state credit and centralized banking systems has enormously increased the ability of the capitalist economy to generate current payments of this intermediate form over and above the mass of exchanges of actual values. This mechanism tends to eliminate the immediately visible effects of the falling rate tendency over the term of a capitalist boom. The fictitious costs of depreciated Fixed Capital, as well as relative surplus values and purely fictitious gains, are added to the current price of aggregate sold production, by creating fictitious means of payment above the level of means of payments generated on account of actual values produced.

This device, by postponing aggregate settlement of payments in value (in terms of current settlements), leads to a massive accumulation of public and private indebtedness. Since this debt itself thus represents largely fictitious accumulations, and demands accumulation on its own account, the result is a growth of total real and debt capital at a more rapid rate than the real expansion of production of values with which to pay currently demanded profit, debt service, and rent required on the account of the total mass of capital.

The need to increase such payments to fictitious capital at the expense of circulation of values for real reproduction exacerbates the growth of discrepancies between the mass of aggregate capital payments currently required and the mass of useful commodities available to settle payments on capital accounts.

If P represents the total combined profit, debt service, and rental payment currently required to maintain existing capital structures, and S' represents the current price of the mass of real surplus values available for backing of P, the progress of a credit expansion as described results in a growing ratio of P/S. As this ratio declines, the amount of credit required to cover payments on the magnitude (P/S) increases, thus increasing the additional margin required to provide income against the enlarged mass of debt this credit issuance generates. The growth of the ratio P/S tends therefore to become exponentially self-aggravating.

One empirical result of this tendency would be to shift the so-called Phillips Curve—that is, the rate of monetary expansion required to yield a point of increase in the employment ratio.

The form of the crisis emerging from such credit expansion is a matter of elementary banking principles. The amount of S' required to maintain the continued floating of gross capital payments P defines a reserve ratio. As the ratio of actual P/S' increases, the credit system is therefore exponentially approaching the point at which S' falls below the required reserve ratio. As this convergence occurs, the rate of inflation required to prevent a shrinking of the production on which S' depends rises to the point that P increases more rapidly than expansion of credit can increase or maintain S'. At the point that such an insoluble development occurs in the basic monetary system of the capitalist economy, a general liquidity or monetary crisis has developed.

"OVERPRODUCTION"

To the extent that the aggregate price of useful commodities presented for sale exceeds the values expressed in the total value product, a corresponding portion of the total useful product must tend to appear as "overproduction" *from the standpoint of the marketing specialist.*

This problem is usually misunderstood by naive readers of Marx's writings, and especially by those who have considered Marx's writings only second- or third-hand. To them, the problem of overproduction seems to be located in the difficulty of inducing the buying-back of a proportion of output corresponding to surplus values. The root of their difficulty in this connection must be traced to vulgar monetary theories, in which the scale of the monetary system is measured in terms of crude barter exchange, or in which paper money is defined as a mere surrogate for gold.

No such problem inheres in the realization of surplus values. Capitalists (in net effect) merely have to issue credit against the amount of such surplus values. The purchaser-borrower is able to repay this credit provided that he *realizes* the use values represented as means of expanded reproduction. The principal amount of the loan corresponds approximately to the amount of $(C + V)$ embodied in expanded production, and the interest on the loan is paid out of the increased mass of S' resulting from expanded production. Indeed, in related ways, the capitalist credit banking system creates the needed expansion of the money supply by issuing money against the debt held and incurred by the creditor.

To imagine that surplus value itself creates a buy-back problem is to fail to comprehend the most elementary features of the capitalist system, in which capital exists as a matter of accumulation against *future* value production. To attempt to interpret money, credit, and capitalist exchange from the standpoint of Robinson Crusoe barter economies is to regress to the most ignorant mercantilist nonsense.

RECOVERY FROM DEPRESSION

At first glance, a depression seems to provide the needed solution to the general monetary crisis that causes it to occur. The massive devaluation of the cancerous accumulation of fictitious capitalist paper—stocks, debt instruments, and inflated commodity prices—appears to have this effect. Indeed, this "accomplishment" does play an essential collateral part in providing the basis for subsequent recovery. However, if this in itself solved the problem, it would follow that production and employment would begin to expand up to and past previous levels within a very short time after the collapse of the paper involved. The stubbornness of recent depressions suffices to indicate that other matters are involved.

Unless the depression occurs under conditions of continued runaway inflation, production and employment will almost invariably begin to expand modestly shortly after the bottom-most depths of a depression have been reached. The 1934–1937 expansion of production and employment in the United States is an obvious illustration.

However, this modest upturn in production and employment does not reach levels of absolute capitalist accumulation. The resumption of production under depression conditions is based on driving the price of labor power and means of production below their material costs of reproduction at the same general quality. The sharply lowered level of general working-class consumption thus represents simultaneously the necessary basis for a slight upturn in capitalist production and employment and a massive reduction in the potential consumer commodities market over predepression levels.

Since the level of production is far below existing capacity, and since used, slightly used, and salvaged means of production can be purchased at auction and other resale outlets at prices below their cost of reproduction (even at current costs of production), Department 1 is viciously depressed. In short, the autarchical basis for real recovery of the depressed capitalist economy does not exist; production and employment can rise only to a substantially discounted fraction of their predepression levels.

Recovery depends upon massive credit and wealth derived from outside the depressed economy: either massive credit from a foreign economy that is not depressed or massive looting of wealth in the form of primitive accumulation from outside the productive resources of the depressed capitalist sector itself. The foreign capitalist may wish to buy up idle manpower and other capacities at the prevailing bargain rates—as the United States bought Europe and other sectors at bargain prices at the end of the Second World War. Or, mobilization for looting other countries or massive, previously untapped natural resources would provide the general alternative to foreign aid.

Viewing the process from this standpoint, we are compelled to be rather more specific than was Luxemburg. She demonstrated that the capitalist economy could not survive at any point in its development without primitive accumulation.[12] It should be obvious to the economic historian that every capitalist recovery from a major depression in the past has been fundamentally based on one of the two general forms of primitive accumulation just specified.

In sum, during a depression the absolute rate of net (or absolute) capitalist accumulation is driven down below zero. Without some organization of accumulation external to this depressed productive sector, every depression would tend to be a "final capitalist depression." If absolute capitalist accumulation of real value is negative, modest depression-level recoveries in production and employment represent a process of depletion of existing fixed capital and labor power, leading to a breakdown of the existing stock of productive capacities and a decrease in the quality of available potential labor power as a whole.

FASCISM: THE FINAL STAGE OF CAPITALISM

$C + V$ represents a defined domain within the entire human population in two respects. First, both C and V immediately represent existing points in the capitalist reproductive process, identifying subjects of capitalist *productive* accumulation, both as capitalist-owned means of production and as reproduced labor power for employment with those means of production. Second, $C + V$ represents (in capitalist market terms) a mass of use values paid, in terms of current capitalist prices for those use values, for the simple reproduction of existing means of production and labor power.

This limited domain of simple capitalist productive accumulation establishes corresponding twofold contradictions. The first such contradiction is located in the discrepancy between the finite domain of capitalist productive accumulation and the remainder of the earth and its population. Since the ability of the capitalist economy to realize the full extent of its total capitalist accumulation depends upon looting the remainder of the earth and its population, as well as capitalist production, the shrinking of the rate of exploitation of the outer domain, relative to the rate of accumulation of the capitalist productive domain, portrays capitalist expansion as converging upon the absolute ecological limits on such expansion.

Even as we limit our investigations to total capitalist accumulation, what appears to be the absolute expansion of capitalist wealth, from the standpoint of capitalist investments in production, is not absolute expansion of wealth from the standpoint of the earth as an ecosystem supporting human existence. However, since the capitalist system recognizes wealth only from the standpoint of the capitalist domain itself, capitalism is incapable of *directly* detecting, or progressively altering its mode of practice to overcome, this historic contradiction of capitalism as a specific interval of human social evolution.

The second major source of contradictions is located in the evaluation of the socially necessary use-value content of C and V both individually and relative to one another. The capitalist system does not know what level of material culture is necessary to reproduce sufficient amounts of an appropriate level of labor power for tomorrow's more technologically advanced production. It not only overvalues the complement of Constant Capital associated with depletion of Fixed Capital, but also fails to take into account important and growing "hidden" items of Constant Capital costs.

These primary flaws of the capitalist system intersect the two principal sources of further contradictions.

THE NOTION OF CAPITAL

The first such contradiction is the nature of capital itself, as an heteronomic empty construct. Capital, as the empty-construct form of mercantile capitalism, is simply a fiction of the form p/C. That is, wealth is not capital as *simple* wealth. Capital is a title to the possession of social wealth, which is to be regarded as capital only to the extent that the capitalist title has the quality of self-expanding value—that is, only to the extent that this C is itself a function of $(C + p/V)$, as "geometrically expanding" titles to social wealth.

For such an empty construct to become more than a private fantasy, something must be added to it from outside. What gives reality to the most general form of individual capital, mercantile capitalism, is the power lent to the capitalist property title by a body of armed men—that is, the state. By imposing simply p or p/C, or debt service combining p with amortization of C, as the debt *of other persons possessing real wealth*, the state or its equivalent gives material reality to the geometric fantasies of the empty construct.

That sort of content, however necessary to all forms of individual capital as capital, does not in itself represent the capital of capitalism. The backing by armed forces of capital's claims to self-expansion merely defines capital as a parasitical form of armed looting of the wealth produced in a noncapitalist way within a particular society or the wealth of other societies —as by conquest.

What defines capitalism as capitalism is the appropriation of another external quality, a quality in addition to that of the armed force of debt collectors. It is the appropriation of something which in itself has the quality of self-expanding value. This requisite external reality is the self-expanding use value of the labor process. Capitalism becomes capitalism by creating a self-producing working class as a whole from nonworking-class feudal and other noncapitalist populations, or from the peasantry already reduced to a capitalist commodity by capitalism itself.

What defines labor power as labor power in this respect is not the simple fixed modes of production associated with simple laboring time, but the fact that the working-class population is human, embodying the essence of humanity in a socialized productive form—the noetic power of evolving its productive powers (social-reproductive powers)—such that labor power represents an exponential tendency to growth of the free-energy expression for social reproduction of the working class, $S'/(C + V)$.

This aspect of labor power is concealed from narrow empirical study in two ways. First, labor power reduced to its commodity form is empirically existent for capitalist employment, as an object of such employment, only as the expression of an already created construct, an established fixed mode of productive activities. It is also concealed because science, the explicitly deliberative aspect of the self-subsisting labor process, is alienated from the labor which collectively produces the material conditions that make possible scientific development and scientists themselves.

Once we recognize that the object of science is labor power as a whole, in two essential respects, the fact of this alienation is revealed. Not only does the whole labor process, as the embodiment of universal (universalized) human practice of man's relationship to nature as a whole, create the subject matter for scientific investigations, but science as an independent activity is impotent except as it is realized in the increased productive power of the working class as a whole. Science, the conscious aspect of the labor process, is what is alienated from the working class by making the scientist a social appendage of the capitalist class and its administrative institutions.

Of course, only to the extent that man develops his productive powers as reproductive powers of the entire potential working class, in the sense of the second-order notion of negative entropy, is the active principle of labor power itself empirically manifest as exponential tendencies to a rise in the ratio $S'/(C + V)$ when the world's active and potential working-class forces are taken as a whole to determine the terms of that expression.

An absolutely correct implication of this argument is that it is the entire working class' collective appropriation of science *as its conscious activity of deliberating the administration of the productive forces* which transforms the mere class-in-itself. It is also implied that the working class, even as a mere class-in-itself, already implicitly embodies the quality of self-expanding use value even in the alienated forms of capitalist society's externalization of science from working-class productive activity.

By reason of this same alienation, the capitalist system is not explicitly conscious, in any active sense, of this reality of labor power. Capitalism recognizes labor power only in the latter's most alienated form, as labor time of a fixed specific quality. Capitalism does not know that the ability of labor power to impart the quality of self-expanding value to capital depends upon the most rapid deliberate evolution of the quality of labor power as labor power. The noetic content, science, is attributed to capital in itself.

Thus, the highest forms of understanding of the quality of labor power that tend to occur to capitalists and their economists are the simple notions S/V and $S/(C + V)$, or vulgarizations of these notions. Capitalism knows only the productivity of labor time, the relative profitability of different labor times for specific forms of employment, or the profitability to capitalist accumulation more broadly considered of employing more of a certain fixed quality of labor time at specific prices.

For related, subsumed reasons, the capitalist considers relatively cheapened labor of the same absolute productivity to represent greater labor power. This notion is extended even to the point that the cheapening of the capitalist price for labor drives the wages below the level at which the working class' material culture can reproduce workers capable of the current level of productivity.

Historically, it is not quite so simple. When capitalism is on the upswing, seeking to expand employment with more advanced technologies than have been adopted by any existing or new section of the working class, some capitalists have progressively campaigned for and even contributed to the financing of improved education for workers' families. By a kind of negation-of-the-negation process, capitalism has organically learned to provide its more skilled working-class cadres with relatively higher levels of income—the real basis for the so-called "aristocracy of labor." Thus, it was an enlightened section of the U.S. capitalist class engaged in establishing runaway shops in the Southern states that campaigned for school integration in the 1950s and afterward; they wanted to impose upon local Southern communities and states the costs of educating black labor up to the quality for its assimilation into jobs either in those runaway shops or into jobs in more underdeveloped industries (textiles, woodworking) in order to liberate already employed Southern white labor for employment in the more advanced runaway industries.

This general progressive tendency occurring within capitalism is an indirect, rather than direct, expression of capitalist "laws of the market for capitals," and is limited to the standards of culture already established by more advanced, fixed modes of labor's productive activities. Progressive capitalist cultural and related programs have focussed on raising relatively backward labor to the level of more technologically advanced strata of the existing working-class population. This progressive movement itself is limited, of course, by the impulse for expanded employment in more advanced industries.

We may examine the limitations of this progressive impulse in the recent history of open-admissions programs in universities and two-year postsecondary institutions. In part, this movement was supported as a counterinsurgency tactic directed against the restive oppressed minorities and the poorer strata of the white working class. But this educational program was also associated with "manpower-development" programs, which attempted to make previously unemployable labor employable in marginal occupations and industries. The instant the capitalist economy entered a general recession leading toward a new monetary breakdown crisis, the thrust of capitalist policy was reversed. Beginning in 1968–1969, and growing rapidly since 1969, the tendency has been to cut back university enrollments, drastically cheapen the content of education, and dump open-admissions students back into the lumpenproletarian mass. This particular regressive tendency is accompanied by a general cutback in many of those essential services on which the material culture of a productive population directly depends. Capitalism, anxious to reduce the scale of employment, drastically curtails expenditures for developing or even maintaining labor power.

In sum, with respect to such contradictions, capital, as an empty construct, has no intrinsic comprehension of the processes upon which self-expanding capitalist accumulation depends. The power of capital to become self-expanding value depends upon both the backing of the armed force of the state, as debt-collector for the capitalists, and the appropriation of something external to capital, productive labor power, which has the quality of self-expanding value (self-expanding use value). Because capitalism and the "laws of the market" for capital have no direct knowledge of the real nature of labor power, capitalist accumulation may, under certain conditions, as readily decrease the available labor power as increase the quality of labor power in other periods. By primitive accumulation from the socially necessary costs of reproducing productive labor, capitalists may cannibalistically increase apparent absolute capitalist accumulation—thus preparing for an ensuing contraction of the material basis of further capitalist accumulation.

FIXED CAPITAL

The contradictions described above pertain immediately only to the forms of Circulating Capital. If it were possible—which it is not—to limit capital to the notion of the current value expressed directly by Circulating Capital, it would be at least hypothetically possible to establish a formal type of capitalism in which the contradictions cited above could be overcome—by educating capitalists collectively to their collective interests, enabling them to take into account the consequences of today's practices at the horizon which is tomorrow's capitalist economic reality. Even such speculative constructs are made impossible once we recognize that Fixed Capital is an inherent feature of capitalist accumulation. Let us review this matter apropos the basis for fascism.

Fixed Capital is, of course, twofold in its content, like all capital. On the one hand, it represents the empty-construct notion of self-expanding capital as such. Even as this aspect of capital, Fixed Capital as capital is not a fixed magnitude, not a *scalar* magnitude, but is capital to the extent that it appears in the form of a mass of self-expanding value. To the extent that Fixed Capital represents C (as monetary capital, not Constant Capital), C is capital only to the extent that it expresses the ratio and associated expansion-functions of p/C.

From the standpoint of social reproduction, the attribution of the quality of capital (self-expanding value) to Fixed Capital (dead capital) is chimerical. Fixed Capital, to the extent that it represents the appropriation of useful means of social-reproductive production, represents a "dead" substance inherently incapable of independently being self-expanding value.

True, Fixed Capital's appropriated material content—natural resources, man-improved natural resources, and means of production—reflects socially necessary negentropic organizations of nature for social-reproductive activities. Except as those resources represent wild animal and vegetable wealth, and thus self-reproducing wealth of that sort, these objects of Fixed Capital are subjects for entropy, rather than negentropic substances. Even as wild biological wealth, they do not represent value in the sense of self-expanding use value, since the determination of value is located in man's collective productive relationship to his actions on nature. Wild biological wealth merely epitomizes the ecology on which human practice primordially depends. Otherwise, the useful material content appropriated for Fixed Capital does not represent the active substance of value, but merely the necessary conditions for realizing labor power.

We have already shown that value depends upon the special expression of the social division of collective labor power found in the exponential function for $S'/(C + V)$, where the terms of that ratio are proportions of the unity expressed by collective labor power. Even that magnitude which capitalists recognize as the expression for labor power and value generally, S'/V or $S'/(C + V)$, depends upon *current* productive relations. The value of Fixed Capital for current value relationships is implicitly determined by the socially necessary expenditures of Constant Capital, at current costs, incurred to maintain the productive equipotential represented by objects of Fixed Capital. The implicit value of Fixed Capital can be no more than the value determined by *current* production of its replacement.

This means that the effect of rising productivity of labor power is to devalue the Fixed Capital component of total capital. As the ratio of Fixed to Circulating Capital becomes large—as, especially, the total mass of accumulated dead capital, both real and fictitious, becomes large relative to the Circulating Capital of useful production—the increased profit rates obtained for $S'/(C + V)$ in current terms by rising productivity are increasingly offset by the discounting of Fixed (and other dead) Capital by the depreciation of dead capital generally.

This contradictory relationship between the Fixed and Circulating elements of total capitals leads to the impossibility of capitalism's maintaining the rate of capitalists' profits within the domain defined by capitalist productive relations. The possibility of offsetting the losses to fictitious capital valuations by rising productivity and increased organic composition exists only in the resort to outright looting of real wealth (both labor power and means of production) from *outside* the domain represented by capitalist production, or, otherwise, in cannibalization of capitalist means of production themselves.

This inherent contradiction of the very form of capital under capitalism signifies that as the organic composition of capitals rises within national development sectors, capitalist nations can no longer offset their needs for primitive accumulation by looting their own peasantry and natural resources. They must resort to looting outside those national boundaries—that is, imperialism. Capitalism accomplishes this by extending credit—that is, debt-service obligations—to subject extranational sectors and colonies under conditions in which the mass of debt service imposed exceeds the value of the actual capitals exported to the debtor. In this fashion, a mass of the dead-capital values existing in the advanced sector, transformed into credit for exported loans, is imposed as an obligation upon the natural wealth and populations of the indebted external sector.

The expansion of imperialism during the 1870–1913 period to the point that new areas for subjugation no longer existed brought the old imperialism to the outer limit of the effort to solve its internal capitalist contradictions by means of imperialist expansion—the First World War.

NATIONAL CAPITALISM

We shall now examine a fifth contradictory feature of capitalism, the contradiction of national capitals.

The necessary basis for the existence of individual capitals in a particular national state—the credit of that state and the development of national centralized banking systems interlinked with state treasuries—defined the old capitalism as a collection of competing capitalisms. Despite the interlinking of capitalisms as a result of the domination of the world financial and trade markets by the sectors with the greatest credit resources, the tendency existed (and still exists to a qualitatively lessened degree) for each national capitalism to solve its internal contradictions of accumulation at the expense of other national capitalisms.

Let us briefly summarize this important point. Remember the commonplace fallacy of vulgar socialist economists (and others) to the effect that the circulation of surplus value itself creates a problem of overproduction. We have pointed out that this problem does not exist, since it is only necessary to issue credit for the sale of surplus values to accomplish their sale. To the extent that these surplus values are realized as self-expanding production of absolute wealth (or even of relatively absolute wealth with respect to the capitalist domain), the debt service on this credit is realized as added value, and the expansion of the monetary basis for this circulation is soundly based on real values.

Let us now consider the effect of this solution, for the problem of circulation of surplus values, on individual capitals. It signifies, as well as determines, the fact that the nature of individual capitalist accumulation as accumulation of capital depends upon the generalized form of issuance of such credit. Even in the monetary realm of capital, once we consider the process of circulation, individual capital depends for its existence as capital on something external both to itself as capital and to the appropriated portion of self-expanding use value represented by localized capitalist production. Therefore, the Being of even individual capital as an apparent empty construct, an *ultima ratio*, depends upon something external to it. That particular "something external" is the generalized credit system on which the circulation of surplus values as surplus values depends.

In this way, the rate of accumulation for particular capitals is determined by a general rate of capitalist accumulation within the particular state's monetary system, through which surplus values are realized. In turn, the rate of particular capitalist accumulation is determined by the general rate of capitalist accumulation prevailing within that state-based general monetary system.

Of course, as the socialization of the world market and worldwide capitalist production proceeds, these national rates of capitalist accumulation become more immediately dependent upon worldwide capitalist accumulation rates. In the longer term, the independence of national rates of capitalist accumulation is only a *phasal* independence, not an expression of any principled autarchy. Furthermore, as worldwide production and trade become increasingly interdependent, the possible duration of an autarchical phase becomes correspondingly shortened.

NAZI ECONOMY

After 1931, Germany was plunged by two developments peculiar to the period into a ruinous semiautarchical phase of development. First, the advanced organization of German industry required that a high proportion of its total product be realized through foreign trade, which had been made possible during the 1923–1929 period by considerable extension of (primarily) U.S. credit to German capitalists. The withdrawal of that source of credit, and the accompanying collapse of the world market in depression, turned the German capitalist economy inward upon itself.

The second distinguishing feature of German capitalism was its confinement to its national boundaries of exploitation. It lacked colonies and other forms of imperialist support for its sagging economy; Germany was thus, in the language of the Nazi demagogues, a "proletarian" capitalist nation. (Mussolini not accidentally expressed the same general view of the Italian capitalist economic situation.)

The Nazi economy, as immediately a national capitalist accumulation process essentially confined to its national boundaries, represented a form of capitalism which had expended to the limit of its sources for primitive accumulation. Such a capitalism can continue to exist only by autocannibalism of labor power and Constant Capital or by conquest of external loot.

We shall leave it to students to detail the full story of Nazi primitive accumulation, but the following general features are cited as essential to the present account. The two principal bases for the Nazi pseudo-recovery of 1933–1936 were the fixing of wages at the lowest depression levels and the depletion of the previously idled Constant Capital of German industry. Not only were wages reduced, but their real content was further reduced by exacerbated inflation, while the intensification of exploitation of that labor was accelerated.

By 1936–1937, the "success" of Nazi full-employment recovery was obviously moving toward two points of crisis. In the means of production, the quality of German labor power was being depleted by intensification and lowering of its standards of material culture. Simultaneously, the expansion of Nazi production had been based on the massive issuance of fictitious values in promissory notes. The ability of the Reichsbank and other agencies to refinance this cancerously growing mass—to cover the growth of debt-service obligation beyond the scale of available product for its payment—was imminently undermined. The Reichsmark faced the prospect of early national bankruptcy.

On this account, the Nazi regime was extremely vulnerable in 1936–1937. Had Great Britain or France called Hitler's bluffs at any point during this period, the Nazi economy and government would undoubtedly have collapsed.

The crisis of the Nazi economy was ameliorated by a rapid-fire sequence of lootings of adjacent countries, including the Austrian Anschluss, the occupation of the Sudetenland, and the takeover of Czechoslovakia, Poland, Scandinavia, the Low Countries, France and its colonies, the Balkans, and large areas of the Soviet Union. Raw materials, plant and equipment, and skilled labor, as well as gold reserves, were looted by the Nazis to provide the essential means for propping up the crisis-ridden Reichsmark.

During 1941–1945, particularly, the intensification of autocannibalistic primitive accumulation proceeded along the following general lines. The working conditions of forced foreign "guest" labor were markedly worsened, the standard of living in the occupied territories generally was lowered in order to prop up the Reichsmark. The depopulation of large sectors of the Slavic regions occupied by the Nazis occupying administration, emulating the salvaging of used tire carcasses by a recapping firm, as part of the slave-labor system. Human bodies were squeezed of their accumulated wealth by slave-labor conditions of production, and the depleted hulks shortly returned to the S.S. for "replacement parts." As a further measure of capitalist economy, the welfare rolls within the concentration camps were successfully reduced by the mass extermination practices applied to the weak, the aged, women, children, depleted slave labor, and other unemployables.

It might be argued by a shallow-minded scholar that this superexploitation was necessitated by the material requirements of the German army. Such criticism overlooks two essential facts. First, the material resources of the Nazi military forces were products of German capitalist production, on which the existence of German capital depended. Second, the Wehrmacht and the Waffen–S.S.—Nazi military operations—were themselves the means of securing the loot on which German capitalism depended. The Nazi military machine and its operations represented the armed force which sustained German capital as capital.

The Second World War was absolutely not an adventure undertaken by Hitler to appease the inclinations of the Wehrmacht High Command. Germany's military undertakings were launched over the strong objections of the High Command, which was systematically purged to "overcome" such objections. The Second World War was imposed upon German "militarism" by the hysterical demands for immediate loot of the "smoke-stack barons" and financiers.

The postwar recovery of the western sector of Germany does not suggest, as some argue, that the Nazi experiment was in any respect a mistaken choice on the part of the German capitalists. German capitalism has prospered since 1947 because German capital as such no longer exists; the national capitalist accumulation represented by Germany's 1933–1945 autarchy was wiped out by Allied occupation. The new German capital of the more recent period is a subject and extension of the international accumulation process predicated on U.S. postwar credit. What makes capital capital throughout the capitalist world today is the dollar-based credit through which surplus values of capitals are realized in the world market ruled by the dollar.

U.S. FASCIST PROSPECTS

The single worldwide system of capitalist accumulation now approaches its breakdown crisis-point. In certain fundamental ways, this new breakdown is comparable to that which afflicted most of Europe (with intervening pulsations) during the 1919–1931 period, and became a general collapse in 1931–1933. The difference is essentially located in the fact that the capitalist system of 1931 still represented a collection of national capitalisms, which allowed the crisis to be temporarily solved by the subjection of all other capitalisms to a single system of world capitalist credit expansion, the dollar. Today, the second great breakdown crisis of capitalism is putting the entire advanced capitalist system in essentially the same bind the Nazi economy faced in 1933.

Aside from the workers' economies of Eastern Europe, the Soviet Union, China, North Vietnam, and Cuba, capitalism has reached the outer limits of expansion into the available world. The entire capitalist world's population and natural resources are already subject to primitive accumulation by the dollar and its auxiliaries. Collapse signifies that the remaining resources available for primitive accumulation have been demonstrated to be insufficient as a source of added new wealth to prevent the capitalist system in general from collapsing. (When was there within any capitalist economy a vaster "reserve army of enmiseried" unemployed and semi-employed labor than presently exists within the U.S. economy throughout the region below the Tropic of Cancer?) Is not every part of those regions' population, and natural resources exploited to the full extent of world capitalism's ability to digest such looting?

Contrary to the opinion of infantile critics of Luxemburg (and of this text), a general breakdown crisis does not signify in and of itself the end of the capitalist system. However profound the misery into which a new breakdown crisis plunges us, it does not represent the final, *automatic* total collapse of capitalism. Unless the advent of a socialist society eradicates capitalism from the earth, capitalism will recover from this impending collapse just as Nazi Germany recovered in a certain fashion from the crisis of 1931–1933. A new form of capitalist development, based on autocannibalism of the populations and other resources of existing capitalist world, will emerge; this new capitalism will be determined to conquer and loot—or utterly destroy—the present workers' economies.

This autocannibalistic capitalist economy can not be in any sense a capitalist democracy. Autocannibalism requires a special variety of capitalist political and social superstructure, for which Nazi Germany is the paradigm.

ECONOMICS AS SCIENCE

Marxian economics is obviously not coextensive in its domain of inquiry with classical capitalist economic theories, or the vulgarized (if more mathematically complicated) degradations of classical economics prevailing today. Marxian economics subsumes the narrow scope of inquiry that is subject to academic economic theory, but the scope of Marxian studies of even such phenomena is much broader even in respect to treatment of the simplest phenomena of the capitalist market itself.

First, as we have emphasized repeatedly, capitalist economic theory is based on the notion of value as an empty construct. This is demonstrated in a most useful way by the efforts of Baran and Sweezy[13] to make a vulgarized Marx acceptable from the methodological standpoint of pro-capitalist economics, and particularly by these writers' metaphysical conceit that the modern corporation has become a virtual autarchy, capable of financing its own expansion without resort to external finance-capital.[14]

Ironically, Sweezy's cooptation of the Berle–Means foolishness has been devastatingly refuted by Sweezy's collaborator, Harry Magdoff, who demonstrates that the postwar profits of U.S. corporations have depended upon such external assistance as U.S. military expenditures and financing of world credit and foreign operations.[15] Baran and Sweezy's obvious blunder is their ignorance of the very nature of capital itself; instead of recognizing that the realization of the surplus value obtained by the individual firm depends upon the external form of credit-creations and the like, they have interpreted the phenomenon of capital from the standpoint of the most vulgar bourgeois economist, treating it as a simple scalar magnitude, a crude "economic fact."

The astonishing folly of such writers points up how crucial mastery of German critical philosophy is to Marxian economic theory. It is impossible to make head or tail of the literary content of *Capital* unless one interprets its terms and formulations from the standpoint of the specific dialectical method on which the entire text is based.

Marxian economic theory is thus implicitly characterized by the same scope of scientific inquiry as the German critical philosophy which Karl Marx brought to its conclusions in the course of developing his economic-theoretical conceptions. The Marxian dialectical method is the method inherent to anthropology as the entirety of science, the universal form of science, which subsumes such subordinate sciences as mathematical physics, economics, and the like.

As we have indicated, comprehension of Marx's economic-theoretical categories and related conceptions depends on mastery of the issues and development of critical philosophy from Kant through Hegel and Feuerbach to Marx; furthermore, the very notion of value—without which economic theory is a fool's occupation—depends upon a related body of personal practice, with respect to the location of processes leading to new capitalist monetary crises, and to the activity of creating class-for-itself–approximating forms of organization from the ranks of the working class.

The relationship of theoretical comprehension to its necessary basis in applied science is not entirely exclusive to Marxian economic theory. Any self-styled science which attempts to isolate itself from an active basis in applied science must soon degenerate into sterile scholasticism. However, it may be noted that so-called mathematical science, to the extent that it has progressed during the past four centuries, has developed only on the basis of a much narrower conception of applied science than is admissible for Marxian economics.

The reasons for this distinction are implicit in the origins of critical philosophy in Kant's *Critique of Pure Reason* and *Critique of Practical Reason*. The Kantian fundamental antinomy, which is itself a statement of the intrinsic fallacies of narrow mathematical science per se, correctly demonstrates that the solution to such devastating fallacies within scientific knowledge cannot be found anywhere but in consideration of the universalizing implications of the noetic aspect of human practice. Hegel's principal accomplishment was to eliminate the notion of anarchic forms of "free will" and the notion of the individual man and object as an empty construct with externally attached metaphysical qualities. He did so by making the noetic will itself a determined, conditioned existence, and locating the reality of knowledgeable practice in the resulting effects through the universal process of producing the existence of real men as the knowers.

Marx, provoked by Feuerbach's discoveries, located knowledge in those universal changes in nature and man which express progressive negentropic absolute advancement of the material universe for the reproduction of human existence on a higher and expanded quality.

Thus, the very notions of "value" and "productive" imply inquiry into every aspect of man's relationship to nature and to himself, from the unifying standpoint of Marx's solution to the Kantian fundamental antinomy. This obviously involves an entire new world-outlook absolutely at odds with the primary assumptions about "fact" and knowledge prevailing in capitalist society. It is not possible for an individual embedded in the prevailing prejudices and general methodological world-outlook accepted in bourgeois educated circles to understand Marxian economics. To understand Marx is to have made a total break with the most fundamental assumptions underlying every branch of scientific knowledge as that knowledge is generally rationalized today. To understand Marx is to intrude in a practical fashion on the domain of every branch of academic knowledge. This intrusion cannot be a matter of formal opinion in itself, but must have the qualities of factional certainty which depend upon conclusive empirical demonstration.

Such empirical demonstration is not located only in analyzing capitalist society, or even in organizing approximations of the class-for-itself. The empirical demonstration of Marxian knowledge is *actively* located mainly in socialist program, which is a statement of what we socialists propose to do to realize expanded socialist reproduction on the basis provided by existing capitalist productive forces for existing populations. From the standpoint of those ignoramuses who generally style themselves "orthodox Marxist-Leninists" today, active comprehension of Marxian economic theory is the most brutal elitism, of developing programs which seem to be the most arrogant instruction of the working class respecting what its immediate future program of universal production ought to be.

If one disagrees with this point of view and also wishes to show a kindly regard for Karl Marx, he will demonstrate moral refinement by refraining from presenting himself as a Marxist.

NOTES

CHAPTER ONE

1. *Marx-Engels, Selected Works,* Part II. (Moscow: n.d.), pp. 15–48.
2. Franz Mehring, *Karl Marx* (London: 1936), pp. 394–401.
3. Gerry Rose, "The Social-Democracy's Roots," *Campaigner* 5, no. 2, (March–April 1972).
4. Consider the scholastical or "Talmudic commentaries" character of prevailing Marxology.
6. N.b. *The Foundations of Christianity.*
7. *Die Industrielle Entwicklung Polens* (1898); *Reform or Revolution?* (1899); *The Mass Strike, Trade-Unions, and Social-Democracy* (1906); *The Accumulation of Capital* (1913); *Anti-Kritik* (prison writing); *Einführung in die Nationalökonomie* (prison writing). Note that even in the preface to her early *Inaugural Dissertation* (1898), Luxemburg's comprehension of the Marxian world-outlook is already distinctly elucidated.
8. *Marx-Engels,* part II, pp. 15–48; N.b. pp. 28–30.
9. Cf. Karl Marx, *Critique of Political Economy,* appendix 3, for an early summary of this approach.
10. Cf. *Theories of Surplus Value,* part I (Moscow: n.d.), pp. 375–400; N.b. p. 397.
11. N.b. *Capital,* Vol. III, "Trinitarian Formula":

> The realm of freedom does not commence until the point is passed where labor under the compulsion of necessity and of external utility is rquired. In the very nature of things, it lies beyond the sphere of material production in the strict meaning of the term. Just as the savage must wrestle with nature, in order to satisfy his wants, in order to maintain his life and reproduce it, so civilized man has to do it, and he must do it in all forms of society and under all possible modes of production. With his development the realm of natural necessity expands, because his wants increase; but at the same time the forces of production increase, by which these wants are satisfied. The freedom in this field can not consist of anything but of the fact that socialized man, the associated producers, regulate their interchange with nature rationally, bring it under their common control, instead of being ruled by it as by some blind power; that they accomplish the task with the least expenditure of energy and under conditions most adequate to their human nature and worthy of it. But it always remains a realm of necessity. Beyond it begins that development of human power, which is its own end, the true realm of freedom, which, however, can flourish only upon that realm of necessity as its basis. The shortening of the working day is its fundamental premise (pp. 954–955).

We shall make frequent reference either to this passage or to the idea it elucidates. The passage is remarkable only for the compactness with which it states a premise which pervades the entity of *Capital:* The singular importance of the notion expressed there is that it represents the notion of *invariance* in human existence, the *invariant* for human existence as a whole, both the ontology and the fundamental law of human existence in general. To destroy completely the myth of inconsistency between the "early" and the "mature" Marx, it is sufficient to compare the preceding passage from *Capital* with the following exemplary excerpts from the "Feuerbach" section of *The German Ideology* (Moscow, n.d.).

> . . . This development of the productive forces (which itself implies the actual empirical existence of men in their *World-Historical* instead of local being) . . . finally has put *World-Historical* empirically universal individuals in place of local ones (p. 46).

> . . . The real intellectual wealth of the individual depends entirely on the wealth of his real connections. Only then will the separate individuals be liberated from the various national and local barriers, be brought into practical connection with the material and intellectual production of the whole world and be put in a position to acquire the capacity to enjoy this all-sided production of the whole earth (the creations of man). *All-round* dependence, this natural form of *World-Historical* cooperation of individuals, will be transformed by this communist revolution into the control and conscious mastery of these powers, which, born of the action of men on one another, have till now over-awed and governed men as powers completely alien to them (p. 49).

> Modern universal intercourse can be controlled by individuals, therefore, only when controlled by all.

> This appropriation is further determined by the manner in which it must be effected. It can be effected only through a union, which by the character of the proletariat itself can again only be a universal one. . . .

> Only at this stage does self-activity coincide with material life. . . . The transformation of labor into self-activity corresponds to the transformation of the earlier limited intercourse into the intercourse of individuals as such. With the appropriation of the total productive forces through united individuals, private property comes to an end (p. 84).

> . . . The individuals must appropriate the existing totality of productive forces, not only to achieve self-activity, but also, merely to safeguard their very existence. This appropriation is first determined by the object to be appropriated, the productive forces, which have been developed to a totality and which only exist within a universal intercourse. From this aspect, therefore, this appropriation must have a universal character corresponding to the productive forces and the intercourse (p. 86).

See L. Marcus, "The United States of Europe . . . ," *Campaigner* 5, no. 4 (Fall 1972), for extended discussion of this point and of Ernest Mandel's sweeping rejection of Marx in this connection.
12. Ibid., vol. III, pp. 289–305. N.b.:

> The contradiction, generally speaking, consists in this, that the capitalist mode of production has a tendency to develop the productive forces absolutely, regardless of value and of the surplus-value contained in it and

regardless of the social conditions under which capitalist production takes place; while it has on the other hand for its aim the preservation of the value of existing capital and its self-expansion to the highest limit (that is, an ever-accelerated growth of this value). Its specific character is directed at the existing value of capital as a means of increasing this capital to the utmost. The methods by which it aims to accomplish this comprise a fall of the rate of profit, a depreciation of the existing capital, and a development of the productive forces of labor at the expense of the already created productive forces (p. 292).

Note the form of the antinomy here, involving the opposed but interdependent standpoints of *capitalist accumulation* and *development of the productive forces*. Or consider the following, from *Theories of Surplus Value*, Moscow, Part II:

We are leaving out of account here that element of crises which arises from the fact that commodities are reproduced more cheaply than they were produced. Hence the depreciation of the commodities on the market (p. 354);

and

Calculated on the total capital [the rate of] profit of the larger capital, which employs more constant capital (machinery, raw material) and relatively less living labour, will be lower than that of the smaller [amount of] profit yielded by the smaller capital employing more living labour in proportion to the total capital. The [relative] decrease in variable capital and the relative increase in constant capital, although both parts are growing, is only another *expression for the increased productivity of labour* (p. 596).

More generally, Marx attacks the characteristic anti-Marxian argument of most modern Marxologists in the form in which it was first developed among classical economists:

All the objections which Ricardo and others raise against over-production, etc., rest on the fact that they regard bourgeois production either as a mode of production in which no distinction exists between purchase and sale—direct barter—or as *social* production, implying that society, as if according to a plan, distributes its means of production and productive forces in the degree and measure which is required for the fulfillment of the various social needs, so that each sphere of production receives the *quota* of social capital required to satisfy the corresponding need. This fiction arises entirely from the inability to grasp the specific form of bourgeois production and this inability in turn arises from the obsession that bourgeois production is production as such, just like a man who believes in a particular religion and sees it as *the religion*, and everything outside of it only as *false* religions. . . .

. . . how is it possible to achieve the necessary balance and interdependence of the various spheres of production, their dimensions and proportions between them, except through the constant neutralization of a constant disharmony? [e.g., tradeoffs] This is admitted by those who speak of adjustments through competition, for these adjustments always presuppose that there is something to adjust, and therefore that harmony is always only a result of the movement which neutralizes the existing disharmony (pp. 528–529).

Ernest Mandel, for example, attempts to avoid the trap Marx sets for him here by eliminating the category of totality! Like Ricardo at his worst, Mandel only admits that "a glut of certain commodities is possible" and proceeds to the apologetic version of the argument, which Marx demolished thus a century before Mandel "discovered" it:

> Apologetics turns this . . . in this way: There is no universal over-production, because if over-production were universal, all spheres of production would retain the same relation to one another; therefore *universal* over-production is proportional production which excludes over-production . . . If this miserable sophistry is more closely examined. . . . (pp. 529–530).

13. Paul Sweezy, *The Theory of Capitalist Development* (New York: 1943).
14. Rosa Luxemburg, *The Accumulation of Capital* (New York, 1964).
15. See note 12 above.
16. Luxemburg is unmistakable on this point. For example:

> If we critically examine the diagram of enlarged reproduction in the light of Marx's theory, we find various contradictions between the two.
>
> To begin with, the diagram completely disregards the increasing productivity of labor. . . . (*Accumulation*, p. 335).
>
> However we may regard the technological alteration of the mode of production in the course of accumulation, they can not be accomplished without upsetting the fundamental relations of Marx's diagram (*ibid.*, p. 341).
>
> Even Marx himself never dreamed of presenting his own mathematical diagrams as proof of the actual possibility of accumulation in a society composed just of capitalists and workers . . . But what are we to think of 'Marxists' who dismiss this critical method as a harebrained exercise, since, according to them, the exactitude of the laws is *proved by* the mathematical diagrams! . . . In antiquity people believed in all sorts of mythical creatures: dwarves, people with one eye, one arm, one leg, etc. Does anyone doubt that such creatures really existed? But just look at some old maps and there they are, shown in detail. Doesn't that prove that these ideas of the ancients corresponded to reality? (*Anti-Kritik*, as quoted in *Campaigner* 5, no. 1 (January–February 1972): 56–57.)

17. See L. Marcus, "In Defense of Rosa Luxemburg," *Campaigner* 6, no. 2 (Spring 1973). This article includes an extended discussion of the major gap in her argument.
18. In *Accumulation*, she identifies the following points: (1) an imperialist economy distinguished by its superstructure of international loans, as a mode of primitive accumulation from clients' sectors; (2) the imminence (1913) of a general breakdown in this form of imperialism—a breakdown of the kind which occurred during the 1919–1933 period; (3) if no socialist transformation occurred during the breakdown period, the emergence of capitalism from depression in the new form of statist "military economy." For more of Luxemburg's views on the latter, see her *Einführing in die Nationalökonomie.*

19. E.g., Rudolf Hilferding's *Finanz Kapital*, V. I. Lenin's *Imperialism*, and finally Nicolai Bukharin's *Imperialism and the Accumulation of Capital* (1924; New York: 1973), an effort to construct an eclectic theory of imperialism out of scraps from attacks on Luxemburg by, principally, Hilferding, Lenin, and Otto Bauer; reviewed in Marcus, "In Defense of Rosa Luxemburg."

The emergence of the Bretton Woods system and the quarter-century recovery based on U.S. credit domination of the subsidiary re-development of Western Europe, Japan, and other relatively advanced regions, with relative lack of emphasis on realized qualitative advances in the "underdeveloped sector," point up the gross blunder in Lenin's conception of Marx's economics. Lenin fell prey to a mechanistic view of "models." See his related failure to comprehend the implication of Marx's distinction between labor-time and labor-power with respect to his explanation of the "aristocracy of labor" in *Imperialism*. One might also note the reductionist streak—to say nothing of outright blunders—in his *Empirio-Criticism*, and the same flawed bias in *Philosophical Notebooks*.

20. *Op. cit.*
21. *Ibid.*
22. *Theories of Surplus Value*, Part II, pp. 461–469.
23. *Capital*, vol. III, "Theory of the Law," pp. 247–271.
24. Major selections are: *Theories of Surplus Value*, Part II, Chapter XVII, pp. 470–546; *Capital*, vol. III, "Internal Contradictions," pp. 272–313.
25. For immediate reference, we offer the following of several alternative ways to represent such a "curve." Let the ordinate of a two-dimensional graph represent "Increasing Rates of Inflation," and the abscissa "Increasing Rates of Unemployment." Provided that no significant shifting occurs in the ratio of Fictitious to Circulating Capitals, a useful curve can be plotted by setting rates of growth of the money supply equal to the corresponding rates of unemployment.

A hypothetical "three-dimensional" plotting can be simulated by nesting a family of such curves in the following general way. Denote a sequence of ratios of Fictitious to Circulating Capitals by 0, 1, 2, 3, etc., in order of increasing potential illiquidity. Superimposing these curves on the first diagram, each curve, n, will lie to the right of its successor, entirely within curve $n - 1$. (The ratio of Fictitious to Circulating Capitals can be approximated by any of a variety of suitable parameters; the ratio of Total Public and Private Debt to Total Corporate Equity is fairly reliable.)

A jump from curve n to $n + 1$ is termed a "shift." An acceleration of such shifting reflects a boundary condition for an entire cycle of credit expansion: the economy has entered the region in which the only tradeoff available is that between inflationary explosion and depression. (Now we know what happened to poor Milton Friedman and his "Chicago School" during Spring–Summer, 1970! See Joan Robinson, *Economics Heresies* (New York: 1971), for an amiable and nice characterization of the "post hoc ergo propter hoc" Chicago School.)

26. For examples of Laputan discourses arising from the "orthodox interpretation" of Marx on this point, see Joseph Gilman, *The Falling Rate of Profit* (New York: 1957), and the ensuing spate of fatuous controversies and marginalia in *Science & Society* and other publications. As if demonstrating

that the rate of profit has no lower limit, Michael Kidron achieved the nadir in his "debate" with Ernest Mandel over the secular tendency adduced in *Marxist Economic Theory* (New York: 1968).

27. *Critique of Practical Reason.*
28. We use the term *Understanding* in the sense stipulated by Kant and Hegel. Differentiations within that restricted definition are determined by immediate context here and throughout the remainder of this text.
29. The terms "here" and "now" are used in the sense specified in Hegel's *Phenomenology of Mind.*
30. For a compact statement of this, see the preface to first edition of Kant's *Critique of Pure Reason.*
31. *Capital*, vol. III, pp. 304–305.
32. *Theories of Surplus Value*, part II, pp. 164–189.
33. It is not sufficient to take courses in critical philosophy; the performance of most Marxologists who offer themselves as experts in such matters suggests that it is also necessary to master a few basic principles.
34. See Kant's writings on "natural philosophy" and Volume I of Hegel's *Science of Logic.*
35. Marx describes such a computer, digital or biological, "vulgarly squatting outside the universe."
36. See the opening remarks of James Clerk Maxwell, *Matter and Motion* (1877).
37. This point is elaborated in subsequent sections of this text.
38. *History of Philosophy*, Introduction to vol. I, and vol. III.
39. The kernel of this idea is already noted by Riemann, and is summed up by Georg Cantor in "Grundlagen einer allegemeinen Mannigfaltigkeitslehre" (Leipzig: 1883). The point is that those regions bounding the separation of logical aggregates from corresponding universals, regions which appear to formal logic as insoluble ambiguities (antinomies), correspond to real phenomena of the utmost importance for fundamental progress in every field of inquiry. Provided that "energetic prodding" may be classed within the category of "giving permission," the author relegates to suitable specialists the more exhaustive determination of these regions; in the meantime, it is at least evident that the phenomena located in such subdomains *include* direct evidence of *invariance* in, as has been noted, a "unique" sense. What we properly test for in exploring such regions is not always strictly the same sort of evidence we ordinarily require in experimental testing of the common sort of hypotheses, but rather unique evidence of the invariant quality of the universe or subuniverse within which such unique experiments are occurring.

Such issues may seldom arise within the restricted range practice of engineering and related professional work, but they are always the most immediate problems one must confront in attempting to answer any important practical question about life or social processes. In the study of social processes, science—as distinct from pseudoscientific behaviorism—begins precisely with the effort to determine unique experiments which can demonstrate the kind of subuniverse (universals) being explored. To this extent conventional physical science adheres more to the notion of *empeiros* than to *epistemos*, and has, relative to social science, a much larger area in which to conduct its preferred games according to ordinary Understanding.

Nonetheless, such apparently "metaphysical" difficulties not only exist for physical science, but necessarily correspond to the empirical setting and form of the breakthrough-points on which the most fundamental achievements depend.

40. Preface to *Phenomenology of Mind*.

41. *Cf.* Wolfgang Köhler, *Gestalt Psychology*.

42. Chapter 6.

43. See Hegel on Heraclitus (*History of Philosophy*) for his discussion of this matter, and *Phenomenology of Mind*, "Organic," for the explicit development we cite. See the concluding chapter of Marx's *1844 Manuscripts* and *Critique of Hegel's 'Philosophy of Right'* for Marx's explicit break with Hegel on this point: Hegel's dualism (Logos-ontology), and the notion of "labor" arising from it, leads not only to the pseudopositive "negation of the negation," but also to the notion that the eructations of the Prussian monarch are "labor." Ergo, how insufferably fatuous is the school of Martin Nicolaus and David McLellan; see David McLellan, Introduction to *The Grundrisse*, (New York: 1971).

44. Conceiving of living processes and "inorganic nature" as subject to the same set of laws, and of the universe thus defined as composed of self-developing processes, rather than aggregated simple quantities (discretenesses), each with one quality.

45. See the final chapter of *1844 Manuscripts*. For Marx's most concise development of "self-expanding value," see *Theories of Surplus Value*, part I, pp. 377–400. "Self-expanding value" is a subuniversal in the general category of "self-subsisting positive." The notion of *labor power*, as we define the consequent difficulties of comprehensive formal-mathematical "models" of reproduction, is of the same origin and order of conception.

46. E.g., that expanded reproduction could be represented by expansion of (C + V + ΔC + ΔV), after deducting Capitalists' Consumption from S to arrive at (ΔC + ΔV). This is the difficulty which would, in any case, have prevented Marx from completing the final chapter of Volume II in the paradoxical form the extant fragments suggest.

47. E.g., Hilferding. See Luxemburg, *Anti-Kritik*, pp. 64–65. Bukharin (1924) took over this anti-Marxian blunder of Hilferding's, enriching it with rubbish from Lenin, Bauer, and others, to construct his own ill-fated "explanation" of accumulation. Sweezy (1943) has employed the same reductionist approach to arrive at a different result—showing, perhaps, the influence of Bauer, although Bauer is not therefore directly responsible for Sweezy's chimera of "underconsumptionism."

48. Mandel, op. cit., p. 363. Mandel's model of accumulation is constructed on essentially the same premise as is, for example, that of Bukharin (1924). If one attempts to represent expanded reproduction (pp. 132–181, 305–341) in terms of amplified simple reproduction, one derives what must appear to be "mathematical proof" that it is impossible for expanded reproduction to upset fundamentally the historic valuations of the terms of the denominator (C + V) (pp. 605–653) or in other words, proof that there is no *fundamental antinomy* in capitalist accumulation. A sweeping rejection of the kernel of Marx's entire economic theory!

As long as such models are considered to prove anything of importance on this point, it must appear to the credulous "angle trisecter" that the only possible source of contradictions in capitalist accumulation would be those difficulties arising from an imprudent ratio of the increments $\triangle C/\triangle V$, either in broad terms of means of production versus means of consumption, or among the particular productive capacities created by expansion. Mandel pursues the possibilities of imprudent incrementing to the extreme, predicating his arguments on the axiom that there exist "many competing capitalists" within "many competing sub-sectors" within many competing nations in a perpetual state of "inter-imperialist rivalry," to the effect that disproportions will eternally flourish and obscure any evidence of a fundamental contradiction.

It is consistent with Mandel's "theory of accumulation" that he rejects Marx's Labor Theory of Value, i.e., rejects the notion of labor power, in favor of a slight modification of Ricardo. In sum, to defend "competition" he joins those who repudiate Luxemburg on the issue of Marx's "total capitalist" rigor (see Note 12, above). If Mandel did not use Luxemburg as a surrogate for Marx on this point, the grounds for his claim to be a Marxian economist would be instantly swept away. Mandel is consistent with himself in rejecting Marx's fundamental dialectical principle in his "Leninist Theory of Organization" (1970; Cf. Marcus, "United States of Europe"), and, more recently, discarding both Marx's and Ricardo's notions of capitalist accumulation in "The Mansholt Bomb: Great Fear of the Year 2000," *Rouge* (June 1972).

Considering the hereditary implications of all such reductionist models of reproduction, it is sufficiently demonstrated that Mandel's notion of "contradictions" must necessarily involve nothing more than what procapitalist economists term "tradeoffs."

49. Cantor, *op. cit.*
50. A reductionist model of expanded reproduction using the categories S,C,V, is a modification—albeit a significant one—of the Ricardian school (Cf. *Theories of Surplus Value*, part II, pp. 470–492). Mandel is thus a Ricardian (see Notes 12 and 48 above). It is more or less the rule that those who flunk the Ricardian school, like John Maynard Keynes, transfer automatically to the Malthusian camp (*Theories*, part II, pp. 114–121). Consider Sweezy.
51. For a review of this syndrome, see Nancy Spannaus, "Wilhelm Reich's Sexual Revolution," *Campaigner* 6, no. 1 (Winter 1973).
52. *Escape From Freedom, Marx's Concept of Man, The Art of Loving,* and *Beyond The Chains of Illusion.* Are among Fromm's better known writings. All include provocative, at worst, contributions to the study of this problem.
53. See especially *The Ego and the Id, Civilization and its Discontents, An Outline of Psychoanalysis.*

To avoid technical objections to the "psychoanalytical" aspects of the following paragraphs, we append this short prologomena to a comparative glossary.

Where we use the term "conscious," Freud would speak of the "Superego" (or "Overself"), which signifies for us the *universal* (actually infinite) in respect to those particular kinds of images ordinarily regarded as susceptible of being made conscious. The immediately preceding section of this chapter should make it obvious that we have no choice but to use the term in exactly this seemingly egregious fashion.

The reader familiar with Freud's writings will immediately recognize the persisting difficulty of distinguishing various usages of the term "unconscious." Accepting for a moment the premise that the Id corresponds to some *natural* existence, as in a supra-historical sense (which we do not), two classes of conscious thought may be distinguished from the Id: particular images and the relative universals for such images. The latter is otherwise the sense of idealized social identity which is, for our purposes, the conscious Self, as distinct from the "secret" Self. *In deliberative forms of creative mentation,* the latter class of consciousness is as immediate as is the former, although in a different way. We are permitted to call it consciousness, despite the nature of the experience it represents, because it is the subject of wilful deliberations—or, more generally, is demonstrably susceptible of being made the subject of wilful deliberation. What is familiar *to most individuals in modern society* as the "flash" aspect of the occasional "flash of insight" is an empirical experience of access from one class of consciousness to the other. Otherwise, the sensation of wilful deliberation of creative mentation might be compared to the experience of controlling a model plane by radio: one cannot get inside it, in the sense of reducing it to an image, but can nonetheless control its flight exactly.

The second category to be considered is the libido. The equation of creative activity with love activity (*love,* not sexual activity in the reductionist epiphenomenal sense), should not—must not—for reasons outlined below, be taken to mean a "sublimation" of "sexual" impulses in creativity. Nor the reverse. They are equivalent qualities but *not surrogates for one another,* even though the absence of one makes the need for the other stronger. "Love," for most persons under capitalism (in particular), is the only socially important expression of the feeling, secret, real Self. The desire to be "loved for one's real Self" is the concretized universal for that which one can only acquire through creative universal labor. It is the only unmediated social identity given to the "secret" Self in alienated social organization.

The Id of course exists, as a psychological existence. So does *ideology,* which is entirely false from an epistemological standpoint but which, by determining the real human behavior of the ideologized person, is *actual.* Cancer is also actual, though false to the principle of healthy tissue. The Id is thus not a natural human phenomenon, but *naturally* an actual product of disease.

> According to one mode of regarding these two classes of mental action, which are called reason and imagination, the former may be considered as mind contemplating the relations borne by one thought to another, however produced; and the latter, as mind acting upon those thoughts so as to colour them with its own light, and composing from them, as from elements, other thoughts, *each containing within itself the principle of its own integrity.* The one is the τὸ ποιεῖν, or the principle of synthesis, and has for its objects those forms which are common to universal nature and existence [i.e., *Understanding*]; the other is the το λογοιζειν, or principle of analysis, and its action regards the relations of things, *simply as relations;* considering thoughts, not in their integral unity, but as the algebraical representations which conduct to certain *general results.* Reason is the enumeration of quantities already known; *imagination is the perception of the value of these quantities, both separately and as a whole.* Reason is to the imagination as *instrument to the agent,* as the body to the spirit, as *the shadow to the substance.*" P. B. Shelley, "In Defence of Poetry." (emphasis added)

If we discount the inappropriately reductionist shading of some of his language, in light of the thought expressed, we can see the pertinence of Shelley's remarks. All great poetry—especially Shelley and Heine—involves the creation of a unique Gestalt, which is nowhere stated or labelled in the poem, but which is nonetheless indisputably the poem. This is more dramatically the case for the greatest music (e.g., the major works of Beethoven), in which the extraordinary thing communicated is nowhere locatable in the sensuous or formal features of the composition as such, not in the Understanding, but in the creative activity unique to the process of composition. The power—the Promethean quality which sometimes contradicts the sensuous and thematic aspects—of the composition is nothing but *the celebration of deliberative creative mentation itself!* In composing poetry, or truly immersing oneself in great poetry and music, one has the singularly important experience of feeling oneself reaching to capture, embrace, and comprehend that within oneself which is one's self, ordinarily beyond reach. Creative activity itself depends upon a certain kind of deliberative control, and consciousness of those faculties makes that itself the focus of one's activity. To the extent that one's creative life is individualized, *not realized,* this self-developing activity is substance in and of itself; it would be easy to become trapped in Logos-idealism simply as a consequence of an *isolated* creative life. For the creative artist—as great art attests—it is this creative faculty itself which *must be expressed.* Only banal art could be understood as art in any other way.

54. See "Dialectic of Practical Reason."
55. See the Introduction.
56. Especially in Section 33. See the "model" of this concept in Chapter 3.
57. See especially "Feuerbach," *The German Ideology;* "Theses on Feuerbach."
58. See Note 11.
59. In response to a criticism of psychoanalysis by a behaviorist crank to the effect that psychoanalysis was "unscientific" for lack of statistical approaches to large populations, Freud is reported by Theodore Reik to have replied: "If I take four persons down to the Thames and hold their heads under water till they drown, it is unnecessary to repeat this experiment in every river of the world." See Note 39.
60. Freud's interpretation of the related evidence is obviously reductionist in bias, reflecting the ambivalence in certain features of his work. There is, of course, a body of criticism of Freud on this account. It is sufficient to note that Freud's own evidence lends itself in part to a social ontology for the Id. On premises external to his evidence, we know that the social valuation is the correct one.
61. The human infant, in particular, completes its development as a member of the species outside the womb, in the sense that neither a fetus nor a newborn infant is human except in the living intentions of the adults who commit themselves to their nurture. At a decelerating rate with regard to the overall qualitative effect of change, the raw hominid material of the infant's mental-perceptual apparatus, as potential, is shaped into human form during the hours, weeks, and months following its birth. This thesis is subscribed to by Feuerbach, Marx, and—to the extent that he was a representative of psychophysical parallelism—Freud. It is implicit in Hegel in a limited sense, and is widely accepted by some leading tendencies in other disciplines.

Admittedly, from the standpoint of contemporary experimental biology, in which the necessary hypotheses have not yet—according to our best information—even been considered for systematic inquiry, this might appear to be an unsettled issue. To the extent that our information is up-to-date, biology has so far failed to consider the problem of physiological correlatives of actual cognition—except in the bastardized use of the term "cognitive," especially by behaviorists, to signify mere learning. Experimental attempts to connect behavior to mentation have generally been limited to the classification of physiological means of traumatizing specific functions and the study of mere learning. Neither of these lines of inquiry has more than contingent bearing on the central issue. Such crude approaches ignore the fundamental questions posed by even the most rudimentary aspects of perception. To the extent that experimenters delude themselves that they are considering cognition or even perception, they merely construct a chimerical "black box," a reified mystery into which any unexplained phenomena may be filed according to the tastes of either an A. J. Ayer or a W. V. O. Quine.

Despite the crude state of biological inquiry into the matter, we do not lack conclusive evidence about the nature and necessary origins of the processes within what is for the empiricist the "black box" of cognition. Human behavior has invariant qualities, susceptible of unique experiment, which qualities must be the complements (as abstractions) of the invariant qualities of the physiological processes associated with cognition. Were one to attempt to argue against such a premise, he would find himself compelled to attribute not only human thought, but the organism's behavior resulting from thought, to a spiritual essence entirely independent of physiology. Indeed, the theologian does rather better than the reductionist atheist—and not accidentally. Religious belief finds it essential to distinguish between the physical and the spiritual self for just such reasons, and to explain the entirety of physical reality as an extension of voluntary agencies external to the material universe as such. The atheist biologist, or his surrogate, who insists that only biologists can supply us with knowledge of cognitive processes, is manifestly owing on his tithes.

On the basis of adducing the necessary invariant qualities of human behavior, it has been demonstrated by qualitative changes in "human nature" in the course of social evolution that the Id, for example, is entirely a social product, and that the entirety of human character, insofar as we limit the term to signify the universal for actual behavior, is created after the moment of birth. Section 33 of Feuerbach's *Principles of the Philosophy of the Future* provides the point of departure for investigations of such material.

62. See *Critique of Practical Reason*, "Dialectic of Practical Reason."
63. Respecting Kant's notion of "pathological," *ibid.*
64. *Capital*, vol. III, chapter V, section V.
65. Ibid., section VII.
66. Cf. Marx, "Contribution to a Critique of Hegel's 'Philosophy of Right.'" This essay, in which Marx merrily employs one of Hegel's major insights into Kant's *Critique of Practical Reason* to attack both Kant and Hegel in the most devastating way, is one of his most effective pieces of rhetoric against the "negation of the negation" as a "positive." Hegel (*Phenomenology*) demolishes Kant's reification of repression (negation of the social-universal negation) as determining positive knowledge; Hegel's crushing argu-

ment against the "negation of the negation" is that it is capable of producing only pseudopositive knowledge. But Hegel, because of his own dualism (see Note 43), rejected the objective criteria for positive knowledge. By contrast, Marx located positive knowledge in the self-reflexively manifest truth of that process of development of realized knowledge which results—in the first approximation—in increased population potential. In other words, the knowledge or process of creative mentation that creates human existence as human existence is a self-subsisting truth—is positive human knowledge. For Marx, this proposition represents a positive comprehension of the laws of the universe effectively subjected to cognitive comprehension. (See "Feuerbach," *The German Ideology*, and Note 11.) Hegel, isolating the Logos's self-development somewhat as did Kant ("idealistically" relative to Marx), was left in a predicament similar to Kant's. He could only counterpose the truth of the abstract universal against false particularized Understanding, a relationship which implies that a "negation of the negation" is the only possible positive for man. This is not to suggest that Hegel is Kantian. Hegel's notion of self-development distinguishes him absolutely from Kant, and determines a different quality for his "negation of the negation." But the difference does not extend to the criticism Marx employs: both are equally devastated.

The empirical validity of the "negation of the negation" as a pathological actuality (see Chapters 7 and 8) is that such alienated social relationships are specific to capitalist society (in particular). Thus Freud's notion of repression, although false as a delineation of universal human nature, reflects the immediate, diseased form of psychological life of persons whose characters have been determined by capitalist social relations. It is the repression of the general character structure by the immediate, particular determinations of external authority which generally governs individual psychological life under capitalist or equivalent historic circumstances. The false truth of external oppression is reified as the false positive of internal conviction, creating *the chains of illusion, ideology*.

Although the "negation of the negation" is a vicious falsehood respecting a positive understanding of man, it is not merely an empty construct but an actualized falsehood, empirically existent in the false world outlook and ideology of alienated man.

67. Marx, of course, does take up the cause of the "down-trodden," *in consequence of* such original considerations as we cite, not the reverse.
68. "Theses on Feuerbach."
69. See Note 11.
70. See especially *The Mass Strike*.
71. Goethe's "Prometheus," Shelley's "Ode to the West Wind," and comparable poems of Heine afford insight into the concept of "Promethean man," affording a notion of Marx's character as Promethean *par excellence*.
72. Trotsky provides a remarkably concise summary of this problem with reference to the moral degeneration which overtook many leading Bolsheviks during the period following the Third World Congress of the Communist International and accelerated following the disastrous "German events" of 1923. See the first several pages of the chapter entitled "Lenin's Death" in *My Life*.

73. Jung's terminology. In certain respects his terms *persona* and *social uncon-scious* are more felicitous than Freud's *Ego* and *Id*.

74. This 1921 slogan, coined by the wretched little Karl Radek, became the war-cry for the Zinoviev-Stalin faction of the Communist International in launch-ing their pogrom against Luxemburg.

75. Lenin's and Trotsky's more-or-less shared conceptions of the "united front" was derived from Luxemburg's "united front" strategy proposal of 1918 and the antecedent more general "mass strike" strategy. The first important pub-lished presentation by a leading Bolshevik of the "united front" as a strategic policy was Trotsky's *Germany—What Next?* This policy was adopted by Lenin and Trotsky (largely) as a result of the efforts of Paul Levi, Luxem-burg's "executor." In the effort to appease the centrist bloc of Zinoviev, Stalin, *et al.*, Lenin agreed to a bowdlerized version of his original proposals; this version, which appeared in the Protocol of the Third World Congress as the "united front" *tactic*, represented as much of Lenin's policy as he could force Zinoviev to incorporate into a joint statement of policy by a united Bolshevik leadership. As part of the deal, Lenin made an unprincipled con-cession to Zinoviev, Radek, *et al.*, to dump Levi, the author of the policy Lenin was supporting against Zinoviev's "March Action" policy. Whether or not Lenin saw this concession as a necessary step in a tactic which de-pended upon his being alive to bring about the next step, in the author's estimation that compromise, however humanly understandable under the extraordinary circumstances, contributed enormously to the subsequent de-generation of the Communist International and the Bolshevik leadership it-self. The further irony of the attacks on Luxemburg's reputation is that the issues which aroused major factional struggles within the Bolshevik party and Communist International—from Lenin's 1917 "April Theses" to the question of "permanent revolution"—over which Lenin and Trotsky were at various times in the sharpest opposition to Zinoviev and Stalin, mainly rep-resented points of agreement between them and Luxemburg.

CHAPTER TWO

1. The title of this chapter is intended to celebrate that of Luxemburg's *Ein-führung in die Nationalökonomie*. A good English translation by T. Edwards (1954), originally published in mimeographed form, has been reprinted as a booklet (Colombo Ceylon: Young Socialist, 1968). A shorter version, half of whose contents are omitted for factional reasons, is Mary-Alice Waters, ed., *Rosa Luxemburg Speaks* (New York: Merit, 1970).

   The reader should take special note that in this chapter and other sections of the text we employ the term "invariant" in a precise fashion—that is, precisely contrary to conventional usage. We are fully aware of the criticisms which could be directed at our usage, and emphasize that *we intend exactly the definition we offer of the invariant*, in full awareness of such criticisms. We do not, however, regard ourselves as obliged to defend our usage from that standpoint; instead, we leave it to the critics to reflect on their own criticisms.

2. Cf. Miriam A. Beard, *A History of Business*, vol. 1 (Ann Arbor: University of Michigan Press, 1962).

3. The allusion is to John von Neumann and Oskar Morgenstern, *The Theory*

of Games & Economic Behavior, 2nd ed. (Princeton: 1953), sec. 2.3.3, p. 11.

4. Ibid., sec. 3.5.1, pp. 24–25.

5. The significance of this point is developed later in the text, especially in Chapter 6.

6. "Internal Contradictions."

7. The indefinite realization of either the "maximum" accumulation of capitalists' capitals or the productive forces is not only insoluble in formal model construction; it cannot be solved in practice, since capitalist accumulation and development of the productive forces are independent maximizing tendencies in contradiction to one another.

8. Cuneiform tablets from Kultepe, Anatolia, and other sites justify such a dating.

9. The discounting of Achaemenid tax revenues with merchant tax farmers resulted in an acceleration of the prevailing tendency toward decay of the dominant mode of production. The same general principle applies to the Gracchian reforms.

10. Baran and Sweezy's thesis overlooks the fact that the primary source of "internal funds" for U.S. corporations during the past quarter-century has been, in the final analysis, the financial operations of the United States government and the mediating role of an expansion in general public and private debt. The authors' construct collapsed as a side-effect of the Penn Central bankruptcy in mid-1970, a time when even informed nonprofessionals acknowledged a rampant illiquidity in corporate finance, which could be staved off only with massive doses of inflationary liquidity.

11. Marx, *Capital*, vol. III, "The Trinity Formula" (Chicago: Kerr and Co., 1909).

12. See Chapter 6.

13. Ibid., editor's introduction.

14. The centerpiece of Luxemburg's economic-theoretical work is the following argument by Marx, to which she constantly refers. If the rate of exploitation of labor power is uniform, which makes S a function of V, the rate of profit will vary from capitalist firm to firm as the ratio of C to V varies [rate of profit $= S/(C + V)$]. It is the dominant tendency for rates of profit to equalize, despite varying organic compositions of capital (C/V), which appears to violate the notion of a labor theory of value. Marx showed the connection between a determination of a general rate of profit and its reflexive application to particular firms to be determined by the economy's behavior as, in the final analysis, a "total capitalist economy," rather than an aggregation of individual firms.

15. Ibid., pp. 168–246.

16. A dispute erupted between Leontief and the faction identified with T. Koopmans toward the end of the 1950s.

17. Cf. Tjalling C. Koopmans, ed., *Activity Analysis of Production and Allocation* (New York: 1951). Compare L. V. Kantorovich, *The Best Use of Economic Resources* (Cambridge, Mass.: Harvard University Press, 1965). For a succinct summary of the history of this field, see Oscar Lange, *Introduction to Econometrics* (New York: Pergamon, 1963).

18. The "ontological assumptions" on which Frege, Russell, *et al.*, attempt to construct their systems.

19. The term "ivory tower" was applied to the Koopmans faction in the dispute cited above.

20. The author has washed a few hogs, i.e., individual firms, employing "microeconomic models."
21. Both Paul M. Sweezy and Oskar Morgenstern have attacked the author in public debates on this point. In a debate in the fall of 1971, Morgenstern concentrated on this point of difference, summarizing the now classical objection to conjunctural economic forecasting.
22. *The Future of an Illusion* (New York: Doubleday, 1957), pp. 101–102.
23. "Theses On Feuerbach," Thesis 2.
24. In the text we develop the basis for treating the problem of ideology. If one examines the ordering of activities of daily life of the proverbial "typical worker" in any of the advanced capitalist sector nations (in particular), one will discover his life to be cruel. The evidence of his life offers almost nothing to assure the worker that, as an isolated individual, his life is justifiable in the eyes of society. It happens that the worker does not see his life so objectively, but interprets it in terms of consoling illusions. (This does not mean that the worker's life is not actually important to his society, but that recognition of its importance is not accessible to him so long as he judges himself as individual *qua* individual.) The terror of seeing himself objectively qua individual is the terrifying force of his illusions, which function to justify his existence qua individual existence. Thus, the typical worker has an illusory interpretation of his value qua individual. He adopts a *reductionist* conception of himself, and an "organic philosophy" (cf. Antonio Gramsci) which portrays the universe as composed (axiomatically) of self-evidently discrete elementarities in abstract relation with other discrete elementarities.
25. This is, in fact, the logical next step for the faction of anthropologists associated with Marvin Harris, who construct "Physiocratic"-type models for various kinds of societies. The social-reproductive practice of any given society implicitly attributes certain principles of causation to nature. From this observation a distinct ideology in the form of a physics could be reconstructed for every form of society.
26. Otherwise, trace this further in study of the ethics of Spinoza.
27. Marx, *Capital*, vol. III, pp. 1029–1030.
28. See Chapter 1, footnote 12.

CHAPTER THREE

1. The student of philosophy will wish to compare Hegel, Kant, and Feuerbach's treatments of the problem of "sense-certainty." (See Chapter 1 of Hegel's *The Phenomenology of Mind* for definitions.) Marx's "Theses on Feuerbach" then appear as the solution to this problem.
2. L. Feuerbach, *Principles of the Philosophy of the Future*, especially sections 29–33.
3. See Kant's *Prolegomena* and *Critique of Practical Reason* for his most succinct exposition of his views on this point.
4. *Ibid.* The problem of "infinity."
5. Descartes, *Meditations*.
6. See "Theses on Feuerbach"; the first section of "Feuerbach" in *The German Ideology; Economic & Philosophical Manuscripts*, "Critique of the Hegelian Dialectic and Philosophy as a Whole." Also see Engels, *Ludwig Feuerbach* in *Marx-Engels, Selected Works* (Moscow: 1952).

7. From *The Essence of Christianity* through *Principles of the Philosophy of the Future*. See the latter for Feuerbach's views on anthropology.
8. 1931.
9. *Grundlagen,* 1883.
10. This obviously does not defeat the "Richardian paradox."
11. Introduction to *Reconstruction in Philosophy* (1948).
12. Dewey is the guiding influence behind the quasihumanistic faction within the twentieth-century cult of Scientism. (That is, Dewey's pragmatism is in factional opposition to such antihumanistic currents within Scientism as logical positivism.) The cited text is, in our view, the most basic and efficient outline of Dewey's views to this effect. Two passages from early portions of that book suffice to make the point. The first is Dewey's effort to attribute a poetic origin (i.e., independent of the society's practice of social reproduction) to the primitive forms of philosophizing: he proposes that certain myths, ideologies, and the like were created without regard to useful social practice, and were institutionalized to the extent that rulers and other hegemonic strata coopted such myths for purposes of "social control." The second example is Dewey's reckless, almost hysterical attributions to Francis Bacon.

To summarize the first example for present purposes, Dewey regards scientific knowledge of natural phenomena as something implicitly attainable by the gifted abstract observer, regardless of the specific form of social-reproductive relations. In other words, he attributes a *suprahistorical* quality to bourgeois forms of mathematical physics and the like. Dewey to the contrary, each specific form of social reproduction has a corresponding implicit theoretical physics, which thus resembles a metric of the continuum represented by that society. In general, the dominant ideology of a given form of human evolution has a remarkable correspondence to the implicit "natural laws" governing everyday practice in that society. In two respects, these ideologies *are* ideologies; they are not on that account, however, mere fantasies, but fantastic forms of consciousness of everyday practice. In order to support the reckless myth of a suprahistorical "Science," Dewey is apparently obliged to fashion such a construct in opposition to all the empirical evidence.

Dewey shows his hand in singling out Francis Bacon, and attempting to falsify the history of thought under capitalism according to a linear sequence: Bacon, Locke, *et al.* Bacon, whose major writings were produced in a period of relative reaction during the English Enlightenment, is a pettifogging eclectic by contrast to the vigorous raw spirits of the pre-1589 Tudor Enlightenment (e.g., Gresham, Sidney, Marlowe), a kind of *idiot savant* relic of a nobler culture than the degenerated world-outlook he represents. Meanwhile, the main currents of philosophical development were flourishing quite independently of Bacon in such titans as Kepler and Descartes. Bacon, Locke, Hume, *et al.* represent a kind of line of development, of course; they exemplify the intellectual reaction, the retreat from the creative to the relatively banal. If they indeed stand in opposition to scholasticism, they represent, like the Elizabethan reforms of Oxford and Cambridge, a kind of Thermidorian reaction to the revolutionary advances typified in European culture by Bruno, Kepler, Descartes, and Spinoza. This is a telling point to be made against Dewey and his followers, since the principal accomplishments of modern physical science (those of Einstein, Planck, *et al.*) developed by way of Riemann, Weierstrass, Cantor, and Klein, who in turn were the intellectual heirs of Kepler and Descartes, whose achievements were based on a devastating criticism of Baconian-Lockean current of reductionism. The key to Dewey's distortions is, as he emphasizes in his 1948 introduction, that he is one of the self-appointed rationalizers of the great despair which overtook the intellectuals of capitalist culture during and following the First World War.

13. *The Neurotic Distortion of the Creative Process* (Lawrence: 1958). "The Fostering of Scientific Creative Productivity," *Daedalus* (Spring 1962).

14. E.g., *The Phenomenology of Mind,* in the discussion of the "organic." On the connection between Hegel's dichotomy and Heraclitus', Hegel—correctly, in our view—writes: ". . . there is no proposition of Heraclitus which I have not adopted in my Logic." *Lectures on the History of Philosophy* (London: 1968), p. 279.

15. The most degraded form of nominalism is that which interprets scientific statements and the like, on the authority of the dictionary. E.g., those pulpit homiletics which tiresomely instruct us, "Webster defines . . ."

16. George Novack's *The Logic of Marxism* (New York: Pathfinder, 1943) is an extreme example of this banalizing tendency within the socialist movement. That Novack's trivialization and gross misunderstandings should have been in circulation among socialists for so long attests to the general credulousness of professed Marxists on this point.

17. "Notes of a Publicist," one of the principal scriptural authorities then and now for the continuing pogrom against Luxemburg.

18. Lenin's *Empirio-Criticism* is one of the most wretched writings by any leading socialist on the subject of philosophy and scientific method. Its apparent antecedents are Lenin's study of Plekhanov and some remarks by Rosa Luxemburg on the philosophical specificity of the Bogdanov tendency; neither Plekhanov nor Luxemburg are to be blamed for Lenin's almost illiterate efforts to expand upon their respective views. It was only after writing *Empirio-Criticism* that Lenin (apparently) made his first serious literary encounter with Hegelian and other primary sources in critical philosophy. This later study is reflected in *Philosophical Notebooks*. Even in these and later writings, however, there is a strong taint of reductionism in Lenin. He obviously never freed himself from the naive rationalist outlook on sense-certainty.

19. By contrast to the metaphysical "cultural nationalists" one frequently encounters today, Malcolm X's genius was most conspicuous in the way he rigorously attacked acculturated, self-degrading ghetto traits among his followers and sympathizers. The ongoing attempt to portray Malcolm X as a consistent black nationalist even at the end of his life is primarily attributable to the fact that the Communist Party denounced him, and the Socialist Workers Party, toward which he frequently extended offers of collaboration, cautiously declined to involve itself in more than an observational capacity. Malcolm X's thrust for "white socialist allies" was aborted by the refusal of any organized forces to respond to such a challenge.

20. Ti-Grace Atkinson's writings exemplify the worst tendencies.

21. See *Principles,* especially sections 29–33, and the introduction to *The Essence of Christianity.*

22. Cited by Theodor Reik.
23. See Marx, "Feuerbach," *The German Ideology, passim.*
24. Marx, "Critique of the Hegelian Dialectic and Philosophy as a Whole," *Economic & Philosophical Manuscripts* (Moscow).

CHAPTER FOUR

1. F. Engels, Foreword to "Ludwig Feuerbach and the End of Classical German Philosophy." *Marx-Engels Selected Works* (Moscow: 1962).
2. The effort to make qualitative distinctions between the epistemological premises of the "early" and "mature" Karl Marx.
3. *Cf.* Author's Preface to *A Contribution to the Critique of Political Economy* (Chicago: Kerr, 1904). Also compare pp. 266–312 ("Introduction to the Critique of Political Economy") with the entirety of "Feuerbach" from *The German Ideology.*
4. From the section entitled "Ideology in General. . . ," following the five initial introductory paragraphs, beginning, "The premises from which we begin. . . ," through six paragraphs to ". . . causes a further development of the division of labor."
5. *Marx-Engels Selected Works,* pp. 486–501.
6. See footnote 4.
7. An excellent treatment is Karl Marx, *Pre-Capitalist Economic Formations* ed. with an introduction by Eric Hobsbawm (New York: International Publishing, 1964).
8. Marx to Engels, 18 July 1877.
9. *Capital,* vol. III, section VII; *passim.*
10. The organization of *Capital,* especially the resumption of the "philosophical" standpoint in the last section of Volume III, strongly suggests that Marx intended to follow *Capital* with a major work on dialectical method by at least the middle 1860s. In terms of *Capital,* which is organized along the lines of successive supercession of the narrow and partial by the total, the issue of human historical development is the next concept due for attention following the completion of the case for capitalist development in general. It is the author's experience in his own work on the determination of class consciousness, the creative process in individual mentation, and the bearing of evolutionary social reproduction on the notion of physical laws, that it becomes necessary to restate the essentials of social reproduction and ideology under capitalism to provide the setting and grounding for treatment of such specialized topics. Marx exhibits awareness of the same sort of difficulties, and would therefore be likely to postpone comprehensive works on dialectical method until the preliminary "materialist" grounding for such an undertaking had been provided in something more than "aphoristic" terms. Engels' observations on this matter in his own correspondence on the Paul Barth issue (see footnote 5) are undoubtedly most relevant.
11. *Dialectics of Nature* (Moscow: 1954), pp. 228–246.
12. *Ibid.,* p. 375.
13. *Ibid.,* pp. 352–360. There are two facets to this selection by Engels' Moscow editors, apart from the strong smell of reductionism in Soviet "dialectical materialism." A clue to Engels' inevitable bungling is provided in the opening paragraph, in which he rejects Feuerbach's and Marx's notion of the so-

cial determination of consciousness in favor of Lamarckian mechanistic epiphenomenalism. (For example, according to Engel's argument, it would require bushmen a generation or more of experience to sufficiently alter their "genetical material"—Lamarckianism!—to possess the biological tendency to be capable of understanding bourgeois mathematical axioms!) Engels' inability to comprehend the social determination of human mind is necessarily his inability to comprehend the notion of "actual infinity"— considering the history of this notion's development from Kepler, through Descartes, Spinoza, Hegel, Feuerbach, and Marx. Engels reflects that mental defect by retreating to a reductionist (i.e., Lamarckian) theory of knowledge, e.g., a conception of mind based on "bad infinity."

His difficulty on the mathematical side is partially, but only secondarily, a result of the flaw in Hegel's treatment of "infinity" and the Lagrangean calculus in *The Science of Logic* (vol. I). Hegel's hysteria with respect to the "finished" dialectical determination of the physical laws of the universe pushes him back almost to a Kantian outlook on Lagrange (in regard to mathematics as it bears on the philosophy of nature.) Hegel is not the immediate cause of Engels' disorientation, but on this count merely provides the license for certain of Engels' bowdlerizations.

For example, "The radius of the earth $= \infty$, this is the basic principle of mechanics in the law of falling. . . ." (p. 354). This paragraph shows that Engels is aware that there are orderings of "infinity," as he is of the existence of some sort of distinction between "bad" and "actual" infinities. But he lacks any internal comprehension of the issue involved, beyond descriptive allusions to the distinctions between a mathematics of continuity and one of discreteness.

Engels is also handicapped by his ignorance of those contemporary mathematicians who had made breakthroughs in just such areas (Riemann, Cantor, Klein), although he is apparently acquainted with the factional opponents of Weierstrass and Cantor. The point to be made here is that if Engels had actually comprehended the significance of Hegel's "a night in which all cows are black," for example, and had no more familiarity with the mathematical works of his time than his published writings suggest, he should have been able to make criticisms in the direction of the 1854 work done by Riemann ("On The Hypotheses Which Lie at the Foundations of Geometry," in D. E. Smith, ed., *A Source Book In Mathematics*, vol. II (New York: 1959), pp. 411–425) and Cantor. A further historical irony is the fact that both Cantor and Klein were professed dialecticians strongly influenced by Hegel, unlike the reductionists and other factions which Engels and his advisors selected as sources.

14. Engels, "Ludwig Feuerbach," p. 373.
15. *Ibid.*, p. 368.
16. *The German Ideology* (Moscow), appendix.
17. *Cf.* footnote 8.
18. *Cf.* "Critique of the Hegelian Philosophy of Right," in *Economic and Philosophical Manuscripts*.
19. "Theses On Feuerbach."
20. See the Editor's Introduction to *Capital*, vol. II, with respect to the concluding chapter.
21. *Cf.* "Feuerbach," *The German Ideology; Theories of Surplus Value*, Part I

(Moscow) on the Physiocrats; *Capital*, vol. III, section VII, *passim*, especially with respect to Freedom/Necessity (pp. 948–949, 952–955). See also Luxemburg's devastating attack on Lenin on this point in *Accumulation*, p. 317, footnote.

22. In the socialist movement, the problem of defining a social category or *caste* was raised by the development of the Soviet bureaucracy, from approximately the period of the New Economic Policy, and especially from the onset of the Stalin bureaucracy. Two lines of systematic study of this issue developed. The first compared the Soviet bureaucracy with bureaucratic formations within the German Social Democracy, along lines explored earlier by Weber and Michels. This led to Trotsky's formulation, in which the Soviet bureaucracy was likened to a trade-union bureaucracy risen to state power. The second approach, that emphasized by the author, uses the cases of commune societies (e.g., Mesopotamian city-states) in which the priest-caste emerged as a distinct social formation without acquiring "property rights" to the means of production. It is the approach that subsumes both lines of investigation which is ultimately most fruitful. In any case, such explorations have demonstrated that caste is a distinct social category, distinct from class. What is essentially involved is the alienation of the equivalent of universal labor as the function of the caste (its reproductive basis), without the accompanying alienation of the material domain or actual productive forces subject to this universal labor.

23. We are using the term "invariant" in a special sense here. The ultimate invariant remains for us the notion of general, universal development permeating all specific development (analogous to Hegel's notion of the Logos). Each society corresponds to a special set of physical laws of social reproduction peculiar to its mode of material reproductive practice; which is the virtual metric of success or failure for the reproductive process of that society. That is the second invariant. The third is the metric of development in terms of the subjective determination of the specific reproductive act.

24. See Chapter 7.

25. As an invariant, which is always constant with respect to itself. Relative magnitude and specific reproductive rate are determinate, not fundamental. It is the invariant feature of social reproduction which is its primary substance, which is always taken as a unique comprehensive whole (actual infinity), and which must be relative to itself nothing but unity.

26. Otherwise it would be necessary, in order to explain life, to arbitrarily introduce something like an "élan vital," axiomatically accounting for those qualities of life that apparently distinguish it from nonliving matter. In short, *reductio ad absurdum* suffices to demand that the dialectical principles underlying cognition (self-developing process) be imposed upon genetics, and that the same principle be extended from genetics to the entire universe. To avoid this, one must introduce a soul as a predicate of a *deus ex machina* at the point of attempting to resolve the apparent contradiction between creative thought and reductionist genetics.

27. Marx, notably, admitted the progressive aspect of British imperialism in India, in that it destroyed a commune culture which degraded man into a beast—a beast who appropriately therefore worshipped Hanuman the monkey and Sabbala the cow.

28. *Anti-Dühring, passim.* Engels does have an approximate comprehension of the duality of process (continuity) and discreteness, and of the determination of the specific (discrete) by such continuous processes.

29. Luxemburg is systematically attacked by Bukharin (1925) and other official Marxist spokesmen for her view that all human existence is based on the realization of social surplus (*Accumulation,* p. 317), and for the related notion that this world-line of human development determines the lower and the upper limits of capitalist development, which she emphasizes in *Accumulation* . . . and *Anti-Kritik* with respect to the "breakdown crisis."

CHAPTER FIVE

1. *Cf. Theories of Surplus Value,* Part I (Moscow: n.d.), pp. 13–31.

2. Franz Mehring, *Karl Marx* (London: 1936), p. 373. According to Mehring, *ibid.,* p. xiii, this section of the book was written by Rosa Luxemburg.

3. *Capital,* vol. III, pp. 37–38.

4. *Cf.* ibid., pp. 952–955; this is a key passage from Section VII, to which we repeatedly refer throughout the text.

5. The European's contribution to the pre-existing institutions of African slavery was to create a mass market for the operations of Muslim and other slave-traders. The number of slaves exported principally to the Americas from the west coast of Africa accounts for only a miniscule fraction of the total loss of life. Even estimating the gross number of slave captives taken by African raiders to yield the net arrivals in the Americas enormously underestimates the magnitude of the calamity. The most devastating effect of slave raids was the breakdown of established cultures, as populations took to the bush, and more primitive forms of existence, to evade the raiders. This regression to a more primitive culture must have had genocidal effects over a wide area, causing many times the loss of population that could be directly attributed to killings and kidnappings by the raiders themselves. However, this merely points up the fact that the more modest institutions of slave-catching that existed prior to Europeans' arrival reflected a brutalizing breakdown in the indigenous cultures.

6. *Religion and Philosophy in Germany,* Part III. *Cf.* Engels, *Ludwig Feuerbach and the Outcome of Classical German Philosophy* (New York: International Publishers, 1941), pp. 360–363, including the footnote on p. 361.

7. See the 1843 manuscript, "Critique of Hegel's 'Philosophy of Right.' "

8. Löwith, Hook, and others have circulated a nonsense thesis linking Feuerbach with the existentialist movement typified by Kierkegaard. This sophomoric bit of orthodox appreciation is adopted by Herbert Marcuse, among others.

9. If the Jew had not existed, feudalism would have had to invent him. Indeed, to a considerable degree, that is what occurred. The contradiction of feudalism (i.e., medieval European Roman Catholicism) was that it required a limited exception to its own firm antagonism to usury. To maintain the integrity of Catholicism, this necessary function had to be performed by a non-Catholic. The need to police Catholicism against endemic heretical currents required that this individual also be a non-Christian, and, for obvious reasons, not a Muslim. Ergo the solution could be provided only by the Jew.

10. *E.g.,* the expulsion of the Jews from England at the end of the thirteenth

century coincides with the first wave of English reforms leading toward mercantile capitalist development.

11. N.b. pp. 908–917.

12. Pp. 958–968, beginning, "It might seem that a rational relation was expressed at least in . . ."

13. *I.e.*, a criticism of capitalist economy from a merely muckraking standpoint or—the same thing—the sort of criticisms of capitalism commonly encountered in the speeches and publications of Communist parties. This kind of criticism uses the criteria of capitalist morality to criticize the "excesses of capitalism" on its own terms, much as we in most professed anarchist arguments or the arguments of the radical liberatarian procapitalists, who demand a capitalist society based on true competition.

14. Marx is here using the term "labor process" metaphorically, as he explains: "such as might be performed by any abnormally situated human being without any social assistance." Thus the term *"simple* labor process," coined for the purpose of making the point at issue here.

15. Marx employs this notion of the abnormally situated human being in the treatment of Robinson Crusoe models. Actual Robinson Crusoe economies could be created only by castaways from a capitalist economy, who had been produced, both biologically and morally, by a capitalist society.

16. Here the term "simple" has the connotation of "simple reproduction"—a simple (single, alienated) individual acting individually with respect to nature in a fixed mode of behavior. It is in contrast to actuality, in which "every definite historical form of this process develops more and more its material foundations and social forms." That is, simple reproduction does not exist, except evanescently; it is a mere construct adduced from a momentary concentration on the artificially isolated individual.

17. *Capital,* vol. III, p. 1030.

18. All the preceding quotations are from pp. 352–353, the passage to which we referred in Chapter 4 apropos the problem of infinity.

19. *Gesammelte Abhandlungen* (Hildesheim: 1962). The comparison of Cantor's approach, especially in the plain language of his 1883 *Grundlagen,* with the outlook of Riemann (from which Cantor largely proceeds) provides a basis for comparing Cantor's notions of the problems of actual infinity with Hegel's treatment of the subject in *The Science of Logic,* vol. I. Note that Cantor was self-conscious about his use of a dialectical method.

20. Or the notion of an "hereditary error," lifting this notion out of the domain of formal logical constructions, where it is usually employed, to the epistemological plane. The nature of the shift can be identified by stating, first, that a flaw in method in this instance signifies a vicious bias in the formation of axioms or postulates, a flaw in the criteria the thinker applies to the noetic determination of concepts. In this case, it is clear that Engels was guilty of a taint of reductionism not found in Marx. This is not the ordinary sort of naive reductionism one usually encounters, but a deeply-rooted reductionist bias, "located within the unconscious." Engels' Lamarckian blunders are a form of hysteria, a prejudice in the unconscious which erupts with such defensive devices, whenever the investigation in process threatens to uncover something in himself the individual unconsciously demands remain hidden.

21. Feuerbach's use of the term "love" is approximately that of certain psycho-

analytical literature, notably the writings on this subject by Erich Fromm, Theodor Reik, and others.

22. Marx had attempted to educate Proudhon in German critical philosophy, and was dismayed by the result reflected in Proudhon's *Philosophy of Poverty.*

23. *Philosophical Notebooks.*

24. *Accumulation,* p. 317, footnote.

25. Zinoviev, Bukharin, *et al.* Trotsky vacillated, usually falling prey to the same mechanistic tendency but occasionally braving peer-group prejudices to set forth his own, profounder views, as in his *History of the Russian Revolution* and *My Life* ("Lenin's Death," first several pages). Compare Lukacs' sycophantic accommodation to the anti-Luxemburg pogrom in his "Reification of Class Consciousness."

26. *Anti-Dühring, Dialectics of Nature,* and the Introduction to Marx's *Civil War in France* are among the sources from Engels on this subject.

27. See Chapter 1, Note 11.

28. *Communist Manifesto.*

29. *Ibid.*

CHAPTER SIX

1. Moscow edition.

2. *Theories of Surplus Value,* Part I, Appendix 12, pp. 377–400; Part III, chapter XXI, pp. 238–325; N.B. pp. 244–246, 264–276.

3. In Appendix 12 to Part I of *Theories of Surplus Value,* Marx employs the term "specific use-value," to denote that form of use value specific to capitalist accumulation, as distinct from the notion of use value under circumstances in which the capitalist stage of development of the productive forces was being perpetuated without capitalism. For example, monetary gold is a specific use value for capitalism, a characteristic of gold which vanishes with the emergence of workers' economies in the dominant sectors of the world market. Because capitalist accumulation determines the development of the actual productive forces, that which increases capitalist accumulation is a specific use value for capitalist society. Under a workers' economy, in which the social determination of development of the productive forces proceeds differently, capitalist-specific forms of use value vanish. In this chapter, we define use value from the standpoint of a workers' economy. This is a legitimate abstraction, whose practical correlative is the takeover of existing capitalist means of production by a soviet government. The determination of use value entirely from the standpoint of the underlying productive forces themselves is, practically, the planning activity of the soviet state.

4. Figure 1.

5. Note 3.

6. P. 265.

7. *Accumulation of Capital,* p. 106.

8. *Capital,* Vol. III, pp. 908–917; N.B. pp. 910–913. "The physiocrats are, furthermore, correct in stating that the production of surplus-value, and with it all development of capital, has for its natural basis the productivity of agricultural labor. If human beings are not capable of producing in one day's labor more means of subsistence, which signifies in its strictest sense more

products of agriculture, then every laborer needs for his own reproduction, . . . then there can be no mention of any surplus product nor of any surplus-value," p. 912.

9. *Theories of Surplus Value*, Part II.
10. Ibid., pp. 117–118.
11. Ibid., Part I, pp. 299–334.
12. Discussed in Chapters 7 and 8. *A Bill of Consumption* analyzes total consumption into its constituents, as circulated services and productions of manufacturing and agriculture. The *process sheet* analyzes specific production into a network, representing the quantities of various kinds of labor power and capital equipment required for a certain amount of output of any product or interrelated group of products (e.g., 1,000 widgets per day.) The *bill of materials* details the gross materials, semifinished elements, and supplies required to produce 1,000 widgets. Analyzing the process sheet for necessary connections to antecedent production of equipment, and the bill of materials for necessary antecedent production of materials, a worldwide network is soon elaborated. Analyzing the labor power employed at each point in the network as a whole, the bill of consumption leads to services, manufacturing, and agriculture. Interpreting the notion implicit in Quesnay's table with such modern industrial engineering and marketing aids, we have an elaborated conception of what Marx signified in saying: ". . . it was an attempt to portray the whole production process of capital as *a process of reproduction,* with circulation merely as the form of this reproductive process; . . ." *Theories of Surplus Value,* Part I, p. 334.
13. Fisher, *The Genetical Theory of Natural Selection* (London: Allen & Unwin, 1929), concluding chapter.
14. P. 50.
15. Ibid.
16. *The Origin of Life.*
17. In the simplest of the Physiocrats' models, the form of productive activity is fixed in mode. Transforming the Physiocratic model into its Marxian equivalent, $S'/(C + V)$ is fixed. As long as the mode of productive behavior is fixed, the lack of development in labor power suggests that the productivity of the peasant is no different in nature from that of cattle. Once we introduce rising productivity of labor, this appearance is overthrown in the most devastating terms.

It is not possible to interpret the output of labor in caloric or other objective, physical terms of measurement. The necessary output of labor power is now an increase in the value of the ratio $S'/(C + V)$. That is, the consumption of the output of labor must mediate a further increase in the value of that ratio.

Köhler's famous experiments with chimpanzees suggest a useful way of approaching this notion. Objects presented in a task-oriented setting are, as possible elements in the solution to a task of existence, a necessary mediation of the solution. Consumption creates higher conceptual powers in labor, which in turn increases the general rate of social productivity. That is, the output of labor power is increases in the quality of labor power: labor power is a self-reflexive, a self-subsisting positive. The value of the individual is thus determined: the individual is a movement of the world-line.

18. Chapter 4.

19. See the treatment of Descartes' two theorems in Chapter 3.

20. The necessary coherence of the laws of the physical universe with the laws demonstrated to apply to the deliberative processes of the human mind, processes which progressively master nature. Oparin's approach, furthered by Haldane, Urey, Schrödinger, and others, represents for us a valuable pioneering reconnaissance, an effort preparatory to the development of the conceptually advanced approach demanded here. In a sense, the relationship of Oparin's approach to ours is approximately the same as that of the Physiocrats to that of Marx with respect to the notion of social reproduction.

21. See the criticisms of Engels in Chapters 4 and 5, where this notion was treated.

CHAPTER SEVEN

1. In broad outline, this concurs with Eric Hobsbawm's thesis that the period up to approximately 1560 is separated from the modern post-1660 period by a great breakdown crisis of the preceding European society. Every historian who accepts the yardstick of material social reproduction tends to agree with Hobsbawm. Differences arise in the divergent efforts to identify the processes that determined the general breakdown of the pre-1560 society. Those who profess to adhere to Marx's analysis of this process tend to premise their analyses on evidences of primitive accumulation, as Hobsbawm does. To our knowledge, no other historian has analyzed the matter from the standpoint represented here.

2. The point was first made in one way by Hegel and in another way by Marx (cf. *The Communist Manifesto*).

3. Cf. Marx, *Critique of Hegel's 'Philosophy of Right,'* ed. J. O'Malley (Cambridge: 1970).

4. Ibid. The "Critique of Hegel's 'Philosophy of Right' " (1843) may be regarded as Marx's first systematically Marxian work. It is clearly a first draft of a major critique of the Hegelian system as a whole. As is apparent beyond doubt in Marx's later writings, his habit was to begin a major systematic criticism with a close critique of significant excerpts from the works of others, and later to expand the whole, trimming the size and number of quotations and adding his own systematic development of the topic. The history of the Hegel critique corresponds to this description. Following the completion of the first draft in 1843, Marx wrote the short "Contribution to a Critique of Hegel's 'Philosophy of Right,' " undoubtedly (as O'Malley emphasizes) intended as the introduction to a major revision and expansion of the 1843 draft. The next well-known treatment occurs in the "Critique of the Hegelian Philosophy" at the end of the 1844 Paris manuscripts. The "Theses on Feuerbach," and the first section of *The German Ideology* seem to complete the process of elaborating a Hegel critique, until certain key parts of *Theories of Surplus Value* (e.g., chapter XXI) and *Capital* (e.g., section VII of volume III).

5. Counterposing the political class-for-itself (as a form of world-historical

man) to Feuerbach's almost solidarist tendencies in the notion of undifferentiated general species-consciousness. Marx's category of class consciousness is systematically related to Feuerbach's species-consciousness. It may be said accurately enough that Marx limits species-consciousness under capitalism to the class-for-itself; up to that point Marx's class consciousness and Feuerbach's species-consciousness are the same in apparent form. However, Marx also stipulates that class consciousness is subsumed by the working class's self-conscious development of the productive forces (i.e., rising social productivity).

6. N.b. in Chapter 6 the hylozoic-monist conception of the object as a quality of the universal self-subsisting positive. That is, given a world-line in the form of increased positive values for an exponential growth of $S'/(C + V)$ (defining a continuum in Riemann's sense of continuity), the acting will of the particular individual is thus situated as an "efficient cause" for increases in the value of that invariant measure of displacement along the world-line. I.e., the object as subject of human social-evolutionary practice (praxis).

7. Cf. *Theories of Surplus Value*, Part I, pp. 13–31.

8. *Capital*, Vol. I, Chapter XXV.

9. As the proportion of $S + C + V$ as a totality necessary to maintain the equipotentiality of man-altered nature for continued production of the same magnitude and quality.

10. The phrase "appears to add to the value" is used here in a special sense, for obvious pedagogical reasons. It is Fixed Capital *qua* Fixed Capital that merely appears to add value to the product; it is Constant Capital that actually transfers value to the product. The real systematical difficulty here is the question of how the notion of Constant Capital itself is redefined as we advance from the pedagogical standpoint of simple reproduction to the actuality of extended reproduction. In either case, Fixed Capital is limited, as value, to Constant Capital and to the increments of Constant Capital realized as surplus value.

11. N.B., *Capital*, Vol. III, Part II; also *Theories* . . ., Part II, for discussion of *cost-price* in Smith and Ricardo.

12. Chapter 3.

13. L. Marcus, "In Defence of Rosa Luxemburg," *Campaigner* 6, no. 2 (Spring 1973).

14. *Theories of Surplus Value*, part II, p. 121. Engels earns the credit for being the first to document the general basis for the Marxian critique of Darwin's fallacies: "Malthus, the originator of this doctrine, asserts that population constantly exerts pressure in the means of existence; that as production is increased, population increases in the same proportion; and that the inherent tendency of population to multiply beyond the available means of subsistence is the cause of all poverty and all vice. . . . When this has happened [when overpopulation is reduced—L. M.], however, a gap appears once more, and this is immediately filled by other propagators of population, so that the old poverty begins anew. Moreover, this is the case under all conditions, not only in the civilized but also in the natural state of man. The savages of New Holland, who live *one* to the square mile, suffer just as much from overpopulation as England. In short, if we want to be logical, we have to recognize that the earth was already overpopulated when only one man

existed. Friedrich Engels, "Condition of", in *Marx and Engels on Malthus*, ed. Ronald Meek (New York: International Publ., 1954), p. 59.

15. *Accumulation of Capital*, Section Two, pp. 170–223. Cf. Marx, *Theories of Surplus Value*, Part III, pp. 55–56 and elsewhere. Official Soviet apologists still maintain the pettiest little polemic against Luxemburg on this issue, to the point of including Lenin's remark that she "criticized capitalism 'from the standpoint of the petty bourgeois!' " in identifications of Sismondi *in indexes* to the most recent editions of *Theories of Surplus Value* (1971). What still stings them is Luxemburg's devastating critique in a footnote of Lenin's silly critique of Sismondi (*Accumulation . . .*, p. 317); as Luxemburg's footnote emphasizes, Lenin is so carried away by his own sophomoric exuberance in defending Marx from the Narodniki that he throws out the fundamental premise of the dialectical method in order to distance himself from the single point on which the Narodniki (via Sismondi) accidentally veer toward Marx.

16. The Joseph Wedemeyer thesis. See Karl Obermann, *Joseph Wedemeyer* (New York: 1947), passim; and correspondence with Wedemeyer and the Sorges, especially, by Marx and Engels. The early political labor movement in the United States (see the series Modern Labor by Commons & associates, reprinted. (New York: Arno Press) for a convenient summary) focused on skilled and semiskilled crafts—bakers, cordwainers (shoemakers), and so forth—during a period when U.S. industrialists were attempting to recruit skilled British and German craftsmen, and were willing to pay a premium in improved wages and conditions of life (education and other benefits) for the reproduction of such skilled and semiskilled worker-cadres for the development of U.S. industrial power. Despite a few bitter battles, the early workers' movement was co-opted into the Jacksonian current by Jackson's brain-truster, Martin Van Buren. In the middle to late 1840s, the character of U.S. immigration began to shift notably toward the development of mass industries based significantly on raw, unskilled semilumpenized labor from Ireland, the poorer strata of Germans, and so forth. The distinction is highlighted by many incidents from this pre-Civil War period, such as the use of cheap Irish labor for jobs considered too dangerous for high-priced black slaves. (Apologists for the slave system made much of the favorable circumstances of some black slaves relative to the enmistreated conditions of poor immigrant proletarians.) The tendency to favor skilled labor and its organizations (e.g., the later AFL craft unions) in opposition to industrial unions begins to emerge clearly in this period. Wedemeyer, on the basis of his knowledge of the English Chartist mass upsurges and his perspective as a Marxian revolutionary, foresaw the development of a political working-class movement in inevitable mass struggles arising from the development of industries employing masses of proletarianized labor. Wedemeyer's tactical approach to the establishment of a national all-inclusive union movement organization derived from this analysis, as did his tactical approach to creating class-for-itself forms and class consciousness. His catalytic efforts played a key role in the recurring efforts to organize industrial unions during the 1860s (continued by the Sorges after Wedemeyer's death), such that Wedemeyer is a major figure in determining the labor history of the United States. His prognosis was realized in the 1877–1886 period of mass-strike upsurges, during which a number of "soviet" forms of mass-strike organization ap-

peared, especially around the Knights of Labor. The post-1886 defection of many unions formed by the mass strikes of the 1877–1886 period into the AFL begins the active history of organized labor in the United States. The same period witnessed the emergence of the anti-AFL faction, which later appeared in the left wing of the SP and the IWW, and in the founding of the Communist Party U.S.A. Under Zinoviev's influence, the connection of Communist cadres to their 1877–1919 continuity was substantially broken with the Foster–Cannon policy of virtual capitulation to the AFL. However, the left-wing traditions from 1877 (attributable to Wedemeyer) resurged during the 1928–1937 period in several waves of attempted and actual mass-strike upsurges; the CIO was created as a byproduct of these potentially revolutionary outbreaks.

17. The individual worker is at the same time universal labor and cooperative labor—yet cooperative labor in particular, mediated through the classwide planning process. He has not yet become totally universal labor, in which the act of cooperative labor is *immediately* an act of universal labor.

18. By passive simulation, we mean the notion of constructing real-time "total-systems" analyses of an economy, and thus creating the information on which administrators base their judgments. What we are outlining here is a process of transferring all noncreative (noncognitive) "decisions," including the actual process of clerical routine, to such computers, totally eliminating the category of clerk from society. Human activities are to be increasingly confined to cognitive responsibilities: judgment in the administrative process, and something like the shift from semiskilled labor to toolmaking and research and development production with respect to labor itself.

19. Over a decade ago, while developing systems initially to be applied to "second-generation" computer design, the author developed a method of mapping a corporate "total system" in which each new event (or the absence of a predicted probable event) could be directly interpreted (by "chaining") for its contribution to the overall rate of profit in terms of total corporate capital and corporate equity respectively. Approximations of this approach have later appeared in some aspects of total-systems design; some features were directly or indirectly obtained from the author's 1961–1962 model, and others were developed independently or *de novo* by others. This and similar approaches provide a different and superior conception of "economic lot quantity" than that traditionally developed as an outgrowth of statistical quality control. The kinds of problems to be considered are indicated by the discussion below.

20. *Theories of Surplus Value*, Part I, pp. 13–34.

21. Ibid., pp. 15–21.

22. *Theories of Surplus Value*, Part I, Appendix 12, pp. 377–400.

23. Note especially the connection of Chapter XXI of *Theories of Surplus Value* to Section VII of Volume III of *Capital*, which suffices to discredit virtually all orthodox Marxist criticism.

24. See "Critique of Hegel's 'Philosophy of Right'" on Feuerbach's accomplishments.

25. See the discussion of Mandel in Chapter 1.

26. *Neurotic Distortion of the Creative Process* (Lawrence, Kansas, 1958) and "The Fostering of Scientific Creative Productivity," *Daedalus* (Spring 1962).

27. The case developed is most directly premised on Kant's *Critique of Practical Reason*.
28. *Pure Reason, Practical Reason, Judgment*.
29. The "unknowability" of the Logos occurs in Kant as an outgrowth of Kant's adherence to the notion of bad infinity.
30. Through the attempt to reconcile the "organic" with the physical universe generally, Hegel's *Phenomenology* is essentially absolutely consistent with Marx's view. At that point, with respect to the notion that the noetic aspect of cognition must seem to alter the fundamental physical laws, Hegel drew back, out of prejudice in favor of an axiomatic assumption that the laws of the physical universe were already perfected, thus excluding the continued existence of self-perfection in the physical universe. To patch his system back together, Hegel attempted to conceal the actual dualism of mind and matter he had introduced by restricting the efficient role of the human will to the administrative aspect of human wilful intervention. Thus, there are two interconnected flaws in Hegel's system: the elimination of any efficient existence of material process in the mediation of the relationship of the will to itself—negation of the negation in place of a self-subsisting positive; and the degradation of Hegel's notion of labor to an essentially administrative notion, without any basis in production of the material conditions for higher states of consciousness.

CHAPTER EIGHT

1. The clearest statement on the operation of the falling-rate tendency in Marx's writings is an extended parenthesis which Engels interpolates into the text (pp. 306–308 Kerr) from, as he writes, "a note of the original manuscript." This notion reappears in summary form in, most emphatically, item 3 of the conclusion to the chapter (XV, "Internal Contradictions"):

> 3. *Creation of the world market:*
> The stupendous productive power developing under the capitalist mode of production relatively to population, and the increase, though not in the same proportion, of capital values (not their material substance), which grow much more rapidly than the population, contradict the basis, which, compared to the expanding wealth, is ever narrowing, and for which this immense productive power works, and the conditions, under which capital augments its value. This is the cause of crises.

This is what Ricardo cannot comprehend: "What worries Ricardo is the fact that the rate of profit, the stimulating principle of capitalist production, the fundamental premise and driving force of accumulation, should be endangered by the development of production itself," p. 304.
Note also passage from *Theories of Surplus Value*, Moscow, Part II, p. 596:

> "6. Decrease in the rate of profit /XIII–670a/. Calculating on the total capital the [rate of] profit of the larger capital, which employs more constant capital (machinery, raw material) and the relatively less living labour, will be lower than that of the smaller [amount of] profit yielded by the smaller capital employing more living labour in proportion to the total capital. The [relative] decrease in variable capital and relative increase in constant

> capital, although both parts are growing, is only *another expression for the increased productivity of labour.* /XIII–670a/"

Also see *Theories of Surplus Value*, Part II, pp. 438–546. See Joseph Gilman, *The Falling Rate of Profit* (New York: 1958), especially chapters 2 and 3, for a mechanistic reification of Marx's views typical of conventional orthodox Marxist treatments. See also Paul M. Sweezy, *Theory of Capitalist Development* (New York: 1942), for a similar mechanistic reification.

2. As found today in the somewhat diverging approaches of A. J. Ayer and W. V. O. Quine.
3. See Joan Robinson, *Economic Heresies* (New York: 1971) pp. 86–87.
4. Keynes was quite frank in acknowledging the connection.
5. *Critique of Pure Reason, Critique of Practical Reason,* and *Critique of Judgment,* with emphasis on the fundamental antinomy of mechanistic determination and free will as coexisting causes.
6. Preface to the first edition of the 1783 preface to the *Critique of Pure Reason,* passim.
7. *Critique of Practical Reason* (Indianapolis: 1956), pp. 139–147.
8. *Ibid.,* pp. 111–126.
9. *Ibid.,* pp. 118–124.
10. *Ibid.,* pp. 3–14.
11. "Theses on Feuerbach;" also from "Feuerbach," *The German Ideology.* In the former, "Feuerbach does not conceive human activity itself as objective activity . . . he does not grasp the significance of 'revolutionary' or 'practical-critical' activity," and "The question whether objective truth can be attributed to human thinking is not a question of theory, but is a practical question." By this Marx does not mean simple practice, but "revolutionary practice," or creative mentation, which overthrows and supercedes previous Understanding of the lawful order of nature; that is, self-changing revolutionary practice. Human existence itself as based on successive revolutions in the mode of human material existence is the single historical premise ("Feuerbach") on which all human knowledge is premised.
12. *Critique of Pure Reason,* pp. 74–80, respecting pathological aspects of heteronomic pleasure-pain principles.
13. *Ibid.,* pp. 105–110 on the universe of *noumena.*
14. *The Phenomenology of Mind* (New York: 1967), pp. 180–213.
15. *From Hegel to Marx* (Ann Arbor: 1968), especially the pathetic "explanation" of Praxis on pp. 272–307.
16. The former SDS "praxis" cult associated with Carl Davidson, David Gilbert, and others during the 1967–1968 period effectively dissolved when Gilbert and others joined the Weatherman faction in mid-1969. This group, taking Andre (Bosquet) Gorz's *Strategy for Labor* (Boston: 1967) as its pretext for "new discoveries," became relatively hegemonic in national SDS during 1967, rapidly declining in influence over the winter of 1967–1968. The dominant feature of this Mayfly cult was the propagation of the notion of a "new working class" which included (a considerable "adjustment" in Gorz's views) *almost every stratum of society but the employed working class itself.* The outstanding methodological feature of this cult's argument was outright dictionary nominalism. Glosses on terms and the redefinition of words to coincide with "felt needs" were the systematic kernel of the entire construc-

tion. Otherwise, this fad was a variety of the myth of the "postindustrial society" which had flourished in New Left circles since the propagation of the Ford Foundation's Triple Revolution project. As a correlative of the "Praxis" thesis on tactical perspectives, a variety of the cult's proponents attempted to provide a "Marxist" flavor to the entire enterprise along the lines suggested by Gorz's book. Despite the demise of the short-lived cult, the pathetic notions of "praxis" associated with the group have persisted, infecting even centrist Old Left organizations.

17. See *Critique of Political Economy,* the appendix to "Introduction"; also *The Poverty of Philosophy* (Moscow: undated), pp. 127–175, especially p. 173:

> Economic conditions had first transformed the mass of the people of the country into workers. The combination of capital has created for this mass a common situation, common interests. This mass is thus already a class as against capital, but not yet for itself. In the struggle, of which we have noted only a few phases, this mass becomes united, and constitutes itself as a class for itself. The interests it defends become class interests. But the struggle of class against class is a political struggle.

Also see the same point emphasized in *The Communist Manifesto.*

18. *The Science of Logic,* vol. I (London: 1961) pp. 68–69.
19. *The Phenomenology of Mind,* pp. 120, 136, 142–145,
20. See Philip Wheelwright, *Heraclitus* (New York: 1964); W. Windelband, *Ancient Philosophy* (New York: 1956), passim.
21. *The History of Philosophy,* vol. I (London: 1968), p. 279.
22. Kant, Fichte, Schelling, Hegel, and Feuerbach, as well as Kepler, Descartes, Spinoza, and others.
23. Note, particularly in Kant's *Critique of Practical Reason,* the direct influence of the social experience of the Enlightenment (that is, emergent capitalist relations and capitalist humanism) on the development of the argument along lines independent of the Greek classical philosophers. Although there is a connection of sorts between Hellenic and European philosophical currents, Hegel himself exaggerates in suggesting a lineal rather than parallel basis for the similarities between his own views and those of Heraclitus. Undoubtedly, his studies of Heraclitus influenced *Phenomenology* and *The Science of Logic,* but only because Hegel's development had made him susceptible to such formal influences.
24. *Critique of Pure Reason,* Book II, Chapter I, "Transcendental Dialectic."
25. *Phenomenology,* pp. 218–224.
26. *The History of Philosophy,* vol. III. Hegel's treatment of this issue varies from that in the text above. To compare with Kant's discussion of this subject, see note 24.
27. Since the academic identified with this is deceased now his name is not given; however, the blunder is widespread.
28. The most notable example of such behavior during the 1964–1969 period was the now-attenuated Progressive Labor Party, but the same sort of phenomenon is characteristic of all such groups, not just in North America and Western Europe.
29. See Feuerbach, *Principles of the Philosophy of the Future,* sections 59–64.
30. "Transcendental Dialectic," Book II, Chapter II.

31. For example, to the extent that one's contributions to the formulation of a positively evolutionary policy of socialist expanded reproduction (in a workers' economy), and one's particular activities in behalf of such policies, make one essential to that society, one must preserve one's individual self in that quality of being for the society. In turn, the positive results of one's contributions make possible the enhancement of the material and related circumstances of one's positive development in the same way.

32. *Poverty of Philosophy*, pp. 127–175.

33. See *Critique of Practical Reason*, passim, for this thesis.

34. *Elementary Forms of the Religious Life* (New York: 1961). See pp. 488–496, and p. 30 ff.

35. See the concluding paragraphs of *The Future of an Illusion*.

36. Note 30.

37. *Phenomenology of Mind*, "Observation of Organic Nature," p. 326.

38. See the 1783 preface to *Critique of Pure Reason*, passim, on Locke, indifferentism, and related issues; *Critique of Practical Reason*, passim, on the pathological nature of heteronomic, empiricist understanding.

39. *Critique of Practical Reason*, p. 63: "That he has reason does not in the least raise him in worth above mere animality if reason only serves the purposes which, among animals, are taken care of by instinct."

40. See Marx, *1844 Manuscripts*, concluding chapter; Feuerbach *Principles of the Philosophy of the Future*, Sections 31, 32.

41. *Critique of Practical Reason*, p. 148.

42. Feuerbach, as we have noted before, does not get beyond the sensuous object *qua* object, and therefore does not comprehend the self-subsisting positive as being located in the revolutionary practice that changes the quality of man's social-reproductive practice with respect to objects. The remaining virtue of Feuerbach is that he poses the problem in terms begging Marx's solution to the shortcomings of the *Preliminary Theses* and *Principles*.

43. "Feuerbach," *The German Ideology*, pp. 31–32 through the sentence that concludes, "Each new productive . . . causes a further development of the division of labour."

44. See *Critique of Practical Reason*, passim, on the pathology of heteronomy and of the pleasure-pain principle.

45. *The German Ideology*, pp. 838–885.

46. *Phenomenology of Mind*, "Perception."

47. *The History of Philosophy*.

48. *The German Ideology*, p. 84.

49. Chapters 3 and 4.

50. E.g., empiricism, pragmatism. Although these philosophies are worse than trivial from the standpoint of serious epistemology (see Hegel, preface to *The History of Philosophy*), they have a peculiar sort of nonacademic authority by virtue of corresponding to the form of social relations under capitalism. Therefore, the alienated form of capitalist relations (and subsumed mental behavior) appears to the pragmatist as man's "natural behaviorism."

51. *Critique of Practical Reason*, pp. 124–126.

52. Ibid.

53. A false form of universal truth is determined by the mechanism of negation of the negation: the subjugation of the individual will to the national capital-

ist collective interest. An example is the U.S. worker's typical nationalist ideology. This worker—we economists, with an overview of society, know— is essential to society; but he, an isolated individual who sees himself as an isolated self-evident individuality, lacks such practical knowledge of his worth. From the standpoint of his individuality, whether he as an individual is needed by society, or is simply consuming urgently needed resources and occupying space and employment he thus deprives someone else of enjoying, is an unanswerable question. At the same time that he faces such moral doubts about his right to exist, his daily routine is characterized by such brutalizing monotony and sterility as to be unendurable without the consolation of illusions that hide its full impact from his consciousness. Consequently, he locates a false basis for his individual importance in his obedience to external authority. If he attempts to shrug off this obedience he not only suffers the practical punishments for hubris (unemployment and the like), but is compelled to see life as it is without the protective screens of ideology. It is probable that objectivity would merely drive workers to drunkenness or suicide. Thus, the negation of impulsions within the worker is affirmed by the worker's own negation of the impulse that external authority negates; the chains of external authority are transformed into the chains of illusion. Consequently, when a worker becomes enraged by the breakdown of institutions he is accustomed to propitiating, he tends to express in anarchosyndicalist "workerist" outbursts the essential bestiality of an alienated individual: "That he has reason does not in the least raise him in worth above mere animality if reason only serves the purposes which, among animals, are taken care of by instinct." Lacking a positive basis for identity in his intellectual (cognitive) powers, the enraged individualized individual in capitalist society becomes an animal-like anarchist, or even an outright fascist beast.

54. By a direct comparison of the *Critique of Practical Reason* with the "Feuerbach" section of *The German Ideology*, using preliminary explorations of this issue in the *1844 Manuscript* on alienation. Also *Capital*, vol. I, chapter 1, "The Fetishism of Commodities."

55. Part II, p. 121, "//499/ . . . //."

56. See note 40; Hegel, Introduction to *Phenomenology of Mind*, p. 136: ". . . by the conversion of opinion held on authority into opinion held out of personal conviction, the content of what is held is not necessarily altered, and truth has not thereby taken the place of error."

58. See George B. Schaller, *The Year of the Gorilla* (Chicago: 1964); Eugene Marais, *The Soul of the Ape* (New York, 1969); Wolfgang Köhler, *The Mentality of Apes* (New York: n.d.). Such sources and other reports on the cognitive processes of higher primates indicate that the notion of a society based on a fixed "human nature" slanders even the primates.

59. See *The Poverty of Philosophy*; also see *The German Ideology*, "Saint Max." A comparison of Bakunin and Mussolini for their common basis of opposition to Marxian socialism is most instructive to this effect.

60. *The German Ideology*, pp. 83–88.

61. The real social-reproductive relationship expressed as momentary impulses of exponential values for the ratio $S/(C + V)$ directly becomes a law of economy only when this determination becomes conscious—when the successive epochs of the reproductive process are actualized through judgments

based on consciousness of this value. Collective man (the class-for-itself) must consciously mediate the successive moments of the reproductive process according to such notions for the notion to positively determine economic processes. The program that expresses such a potential relationship of the class-for-itself to itself uniquely expresses the potential existence of the class-for-itself. This is not an abstract relationship but a social relationship. Maximizing the current consumption (V) relative to S' results in a lower rate of growth of V than higher values for S', and ultimately in lower aggregate consumption. This lower rate of consumption means a lower rate of development, slower growth of leisure, and so on.

62. See Chapter 12, passim.
63. *Ibid.*
64. Chapters 4 and 5, passim.
65. Chapter 6.
66. *Critique of Practical Reason*, n.b. pp. 155–165.
67. Introduction to *The History of Philosophy*.
68. Note 56; also "Contribution to a Critique of Hegel's "Philosophy of Right," apropos the chains of illusion.
69. "Introduction to the Critique of Political Economy."
70. *Theories of Surplus Value*, Part II, pp. 426–546; *Capital*, vol. III, "Internal Contradictions."
71. *Capital*, vol. III, "Internal Contradictions."
72. For reasons essentially identical to those detailed in Luxemburg's *Accumulation of Capital*, the era from 1913 to the present is a period of general capitalist decay: the outbreak of the so-called ecology crisis on a worldwide scale reflects the advanced state of the process of looting and underdevelopment, such that the development of the capitalist productive forces has lagged in a self-aggregating way behind the growth of the population subject to the capitalist world market.

CHAPTER NINE

1. "Internal Contradictions," pp. 312–313.
2. Ibid., p. 302.
3. E.g., Ernest Mandel, *Marxian Economic Theory*, Vol. 1 (New York: 1968), pp. 166–170, especially p. 169; Joseph M. Gilman, *The Falling Rate of Profit* (New York: 1968), passim; Paul M. Sweezy, *The Theory of Capitalist Development* (New York: 1964), pp. 96–108, 147–155.
4. A real lalapalooza is found at the conclusion of Ernest Mandel's *In Introduction to Marxist Economic Theory* (New York: 1967): "This . . . [structural reforms] . . . would mark the appearance of *dual power at the company level* . . . and in the whole economy. . . . this stage in turn could usher in the conquest of power . . ." (emphasis added)
5. Durkheim's term is employed for emphasis.
6. The invention of double-entry bookkeeping is usually attributed to the Medici. Whether they invented it is not important–it might prove to have been taught to them by one of the members of the Bardi family in the Medici's employ, but no matter. Once a merchant banker opens branches, in the fashion of the Medici, and discovers the practical merit of determining what the branch manager "owes to the books," a compelling basis exists in

social relationships between home office and branch manager for the development of a double-entry system. It obviously arises from the duality of the branch's credit relationships with, on the one hand, the market outside the firm, and, on the other, the home office: nothing mysterious.

7. Treated in Chapter 7 in another context.

8. The history of the Near East and Mediterranean from the Sumerian through the Hellenic periods and after is the paradigm here.

9. See any recent edition of *The Federal Reserve System* (Washington, D.C.: n.d.) for a satisfactory outline of this concept.

10. The reader should study, in conjunction with this section of the text, Section VII, Volume III, of *Capital,* especially pp. 947–1032, with particular emphasis on pp. 952–992. This material should be compared with "Introduction to the Critique of Political Economy," cited several times above. The student should thus compare the methodological approach of this text with that of Marx.

11. Chapters 2 and 6.

12. *Theories of Surplus Value,* Part I, pp. 149–295. N.b.: "This distinction is founded on the nature of bourgeois production itself, since wealth is not the equivalent of use-value, but only the *commodity* is wealth, use-value as the bearer of exchange-value, as money. What the Monetary system did not understand is how this money is made, and is multiplied through the consumption of commodities, and not through their transformation into gold and silver—in which they are crystallized as independent exchange-value, in which however they not only lose their use-value, but do not alter the *magnitude* of their value" p. 295.

CHAPTER TEN

1. Chapters 7 and 8. Praxis = practical reason when and only when this notion is developed as the solution to the fundamental antinomy between the universalities of the two infinities: universalized experience and the synthetic universality of apperception.

2. See Eric Hobsbawm *et al., Crisis in Europe* (Garden City, N.J.: 1967).

3. First published in *New Solidarity,* 30 August 1971; republished in *Socialism or Fascism?,* National Caucus of Labor Committees, November 1971.

4: This was the result of a project which accompanied and penetrated the author's analysis of the developing economic conjuncture during the 1956–1958 period. Its purpose was to determine the proper application of computer systems of the types then emerging (1959–1960) and being planned to the administrative "control" functions of the management of individual firms. The project also involved assessment of Western and Soviet developments in mathematical economics. While it proved possible to predetermine coding procedures which could assimilate every possible future element in the operation of a firm (or national economy), and thus to establish "total computer systems" for entire economies as well as firms, it was impossible to predict the necessary or probable occurrence of the new elements to be coded in a comprehensive way. These elements had to be treated by the computer systems applications designer as new elements "arbitrarily" introduced from outside the determination of any "mathematical simulation model." This exploration came to a head in a critique of the efforts of

Marvin Minsky and others to stipulate methods of simulating the determination of concepts by computer (or, "artificial intelligence.") Thus, a few weeks of intensive concentration on the "artificial intelligence" problem brought approximately five years of work to an interim conclusion. This was one of those rare "explosions" of insight that occur only several times in a lifetime even to those engaged in intensively creative occupations.

The method used to attack Minsky's misconception was *reductio ad absurdum*. It was assumed that a group of interlinked computers controlled worldwide automatic production of everything, including their own maintenance, power consumption, and replication. Introducing the requirement of rising negentropy for total production to this model, the necessary conditions for intelligence in the behavior of these computers were imposed. These conditions included those under which the computers' deliberative contributions to rising negentropy could be the basis for a notion of self-consciousness on the part of each of the computers. Heuristic design specifications were drawn up for a computer which would satisfy such requirements. It could not be a digital computer; ergo, Minsky's project and all similar efforts must totally fail.

On reflection after the fact, this exercise was recognized as incorporating all of Feuerbach's notion of socially determined self-consciousness, but extending qualitatively beyond it. It was then recognized that the notion of self-consciousness developed out of the critique of Minsky's project corresponded to the kernel of the Marxian dialectic, provided that Marx was interpreted in a fashion contrary to prevailing orthodox Marxist interpretations. The question of whether the new insight into Marx was spacious compelled this writer to re-examine his earlier interpretations of Kant, Hegel, Marx, and Georg Cantor. (Cantor's influence on the author had been strong since approximately 1952.) The author located the residual (Engels-like) reductionism in his own earlier readings of Marx, Kant, Hegel, and others, and from this standpoint satisfied himself that he had located cross-references in Hegel, Feuerbach, and Marx which necessitated the new (1961) interpretation of Marx from the standpoint of the Minsky project.

As a result, the author undertook to recast his former views on several topics in the light of the new outlook. The most significant effort of this period was a first-draft manuscript, "The Origin of Caste," prompted by a discussion focusing on whether or not the Chinese People's Republic was characterized by the domination of a bureaucratic caste. This question subsumed a variety of specific issues, such as the notion of caste itself, and provided a medium in which the author worked out his relationship to the dominant conceptions of all so-called "Marxist-Leninist" groupings, Stalinist, Trotskyist, etc. An aspect of this document later became "Centrism as a Social Phenomenon (*Campaigner*, January 1970);" another aspect was developed as "The Philosophy of Socialist Education," (National Caucus of Labor Committees, November 1969), and became the approach to theoretical economics developed in the present text.

5. The ancient form of the dialectic, replicated in a new way in Descartes' "Cogito ergo sum" and perfection theorems.

6. Marx's method and conception of Praxis (as a term for a specialized notion) are therefore implicitly fully stated in the famous passage from the "Feuerbach" section of *The German Ideology:* "The premises from which we begin

are not arbitrary ones, not dogmas, but real premises from which abstraction can be made only in the imagination . . ." (pp. 31–32) to "The nature of individuals thus depends on the material conditions determining their production."

From this point, situated within the context of German critical philosophy, everything else in Marx follows rigorously once we add the following qualification: "Each new productive force, insofar as it is not merely a quantitative extension of productive forces already known (for instance the bringing into cultivation of fresh land), causes a further development in the division of labor" (p. 32).

Or, to restate the point we made to the same effect in Chapter 4, we discover the same point of view in the "mature" Marx:

> ". . . the realm of freedom does not commence until the point is passed where labor under the compulsion of necessity and of external utility is required. In the very nature of things, it lies beyond the sphere of material production in the strict meaning of the term. . . . With this development the realm of natural necessity expands . . . Beyond it begins that development of human power, which is its own end, the true realm of freedom, which, however, can flourish only upon that realm of necessity as its basis. The shortening of the working day is its fundamental premise" *Capital*, Vol. III, pp. 954–955.

Section VII Volume III of *Capital*, thus destroys all further credible effort to equate use value with mechanistic notions of utility (vulgar Marxism), and all wretched efforts to postulate a qualitative differentiation of any sort between the "early" (1843–1848) and "mature" Marx.

7. *The Phenomenology of Mind*, p. 76.
8. *Religion and Philosophy in Germany*, Part III.
9. In *The Philosophy of Right* Hegel's brilliant assertion, "all that is real is rational," is transformed into a reactionary form. It is transformed as we also see in the case of "solidarity" for Durkeim. Hegel, instead of realizing that the existence of reactionary forms is rational from the standpoint of social evolution, as carried-forward notions, makes actuality itself the predicate of virtue, or vice-versa, by locating necessity in the existence of every parasite of the Prussian state bureaucracy. This occurs, as we have noted several times before, because Hegel denies the hylozoic monist principle, and thus must retreat from the standpoint of a self-subsisting positive principle (see note 6) to a negation of the negation. He does this by situating development essentially within the alienated subjective process. Responding to Feuerbach's "Preliminary Theses for the Reform of Philosophy," Marx attacked Hegel's *Science of Logic* in its derived form, *The Philosophy of Right*, during the summer of 1843—thus originating "Marxism" by establishing, in first approximation, the premises upon which all his later development stands.
10. Feuerbach, by situating the problem of the self-subsisting positive in the material basis, without losing sight of the universal, challenged Marx to locate progress itself within the material basis or, to be exact, within Praxis. See note 6 and the entirety of Section VII of Volume III of *Capital*.
11. E.g., Kantorovich.

12. See Georg Cantor, *Grundlagen* (1883) in *Gesammelte Abhandlungen* (Hildesheim: 1962), pp. 165–209. Compare with Hegel, *The Science of Logic* (London: 1961), pp. 199–344.

CHAPTER ELEVEN

1. Studies performed during 1967–1968 by the author's collaborators in the West Side Tenants' Union (New York City), reflected in Leif Johnson's report on the housing crisis published by the Metropolitan Council on Housing.
2. *Theories of Surplus Value*, Part III, or Ronald Meek, ed., *Marx and Engels on the Population Bomb* (New York: 1971). Also note the Malthusian tendencies in Paul M. Sweezy's economic theories (*The Theory of Capitalist Development*).
3. Pp. 348–445.
4. N.b. pp. 382–397.
5. See L. Marcus, "In Defense of Rosa Luxemburg," *Campaigner* 6, no. 2 (Spring 1973).
6. Pp. 952–955.
7. Marcus, op. cit.; also see the concluding section of Chapter 1 above.

CHAPTER TWELVE

1. E.g., *The Philosophy of Right*.
2. *1844 Manuscripts*, concluding section.
3. *Principles of the Philosophy of the Future*, sections 32, 59–62.
4. Karl Marx, *Colonialism* (Moscow).
5. *Poverty of Philosophy*, p. 173.
6. Volume III, "Internal Contradictions;" *Theories of Surplus Value*, Part II, pp. 426–546.
7. *Theories of Surplus Value*, Part II, p. 596.
8. *Accumulation of Capital*, pp. 335–336, 342–347.
9. See Marx on animal versus human nature in *1844 Manuscripts*, passim; *The German Ideology*, pp. 31, 55, 646–647.
10. *Capital*, Vol. III, Chap. XLIX; *Theories of Surplus Value*, Part II, pp. 492–535; *Critique of Political Economy* (Chicago: 1904), appendix: "The Method of Political Economy," pp. 292–312. Luxemburg, *Accumulation of Capital*, passim.
11. "Introduction," p. 136.
12. *Accumulation of Capital*, pp. 369–371, 454.
13. *The Theory of Capitalist Development*.
14. See "Review of the Month," *Monthly Review* (September 1970), on liquidity crises arising from corporate financing of investment through debt obligations to finance capital.
15. Harry Magdoff, *The Age of Imperialism* (New York: 1967).

GLOSSARY

The following definitions are supplied as mnemonic aids to the reader.[1] The terms listed are confined to those important terms whose dictionary or common-usage definitions are wrong, superficial, or otherwise misleading. In the case of *entropy/negentropy*, a required dimension has been added to what was previously considered rigorous usage.

actual, actualization (epist.) Synonyms: *real realization* (epist., eco.). The strict usage of the term is peculiar to German critical philosophy and its sequels; e.g., *actual* as distinct from *potential*. This distinction emerges from Kant's treatment of the *fundamental antinomy, in* which man's "free will" is categorically distinguished from the ordinary causal determination of events in the world apart from man's expression of his creative, synthetic judgments in the form of *wilful practice*. (The term "free" has the same connotations in "free will" as it does in the "free energy" of increasing negative entropy. This becomes explicit in Marx, but is also virtually demanded by Hegel and implicit in Kant.) "Free will" is restricted to judgments pertaining to an improvement in the order of universal existence for man as a species, typified by scientific discoveries of new principles. "Free will" expressed as wilful practice (*Praxis*) becomes a cause of change in the order of nature "outside" the will, and is thus actual or actualized. In economics, a mass of commodities, for example, has no real value in itself, but only a potential value which one describes from the standpoint of assuming the realization (actualization) of that wealth as actual new productive forces, through consumption as means of material existence of labor power or as means of production. Only in such consumption does the mere potential value implicit in the mass of commodities become the actual value resulting from the transformation of those commodities into new productive forces. *Self-evident actuality* is limited to those activities whose existence is the consequence of that activity; that is, the self-development of man's productive powers through production is a form of *self-actualization*. Only processes of this dialectical form are capable of representing a self-evident actuality—*primary* reality as opposed to the

[1] The following abbreviations are used:
  epist. = epistemological term
  eco. = term used in economics
  psych. = term used predominantly in psychology/psychoanalysis

reductionist's "elementary." For example, commodities have no actual value in themselves; their value is entirely their value for something whose self-actualization they mediate, the self-actualization of the labor process. Compare the first of Marx's "Theses on Feuerbach."

Being (epist.) Crudely (in classical materialism, empiricism, positivism, and so on), the quality of existence independent of perception attributed to discrete objects or sense-impressions. This quality of existence is usually distinguished from the existence of *properties* and *relationship*. In short, the notion of Being is situated within the belief that the universe is essentially an aggregation of discrete, elementary "particles" of one sort or another; these elementary particles are treated as the proper independent variables of algebraic (formal-logical) expressions, and qualities and relationship are regarded as the derived existences expressed in the grammatical "structure" of the algebraic formulations. In critical philosophy, the attribution of Being to "self-evident objectivity" is identified by the term *Being-in-itself* (*an sich* in Kant, Hegel, and Marx). In Hegel and Marx, the "self-evidence" of discrete being (that is, of "elementarities") is absolutely denied (Hegel, *Phenomenology of Mind*, preface, introduction, Chapter 1; Marx, "Theses on Feuerbach"). The world-outlook of Hegel and Marx locates primary ("primitive") reality in universal processes, with respect to which the existence of discrete particulars is merely derivative (*determinate* Being). Primary, universal Being is *Being-in-and-for-itself*, the universal process, of the form of self-activity, whose development is the consequence of that activity (i.e., a self-subsisting positive). Subsumed within Being-in-and-for-itself (*an und für sich*) is *Being-for-itself* (*für sich*), those processes of self-activity whose development is the consequence of action on the universe by such a subsumed process. The paradigm for Being-for-itself is Marx's notion of the (working) class-for-itself, the totality of working-class productive activity deliberately directed as self-activity for the development of that self-activity, through the mediation of development of the material preconditions of class self-activity (i.e., the revolutionary human practice of the "Theses on Feuerbach").

The dialectical form of Descartes' "perfection" theorem (see pages 70–76) exemplifies the distinctions to be made. Classical materialism and empiricism locate development of knowledge and practice in a comparison of successive discrete states, for which purpose each of the discrete states is an elementary (self-evident) term. Dialectical method, emulating Descartes, locates the primary phenomena in the "intervals" of continuous development ostensibly "connecting" successive states of progress. Hence, where classical materialism attributes the content of Being to the quality of discrete particles, dialectics locates the quality of Being in a notion of continuous process. In a rudimentary sense, therefore, the Cartesian and Spinozan world-out-looks are extensions of the most advanced neo-Platonic views of fifteenth- and sixteenth-century Renaissance thought. Indeed, the internal features of Descartes' argument for the "perfection" theorem show the direct influence of those predecessors, and similar sources are adduced for the principal accomplishments of Kepler. However, up through Descartes, the conceptualization of self-subsisting continuity is ambiguous. The neo-Platonists locate the primary, continuous principle of reality as self-movement—self-moving continuous substance; however, they are unable to represent this substance in any form but linear extension. This irony emerges most clearly in Kepler and Descartes, in whom the notion of a "theory of functions" is immanent. In a lesser sense, both Kepler and Descartes imply the integral calculus, the reductionist notion of "exponential" forms of continuity. Hence, the development of the theory of functions (N.B. Weierstrass, Riemann, Cantor, Klein) leads to the possibility of recasting Kepler's "neo-Platonic" world-outlook in the more advanced terms (e.g., Planck, Minkowski, Einstein) of relativity theory. Relativity theory, because it is still encumbered with reductionist algebraic methods and the implicit fallacy of entropy ("God's clock": Leibniz), is not yet capable of resolving the universe as a true continuum into a "unified field," in which extension has the actual quality of self-developing self-activity, as Einstein himself implicitly acknowledges. However, these advances bring us to the verge of the solution, and, as tendencies, represent the only viable impulse of fundamental scientific work in this century.

Hegel's achievement, in a certain sense anticipating the principal discoveries of Riemann and Cantor, was to discover the formal solution to this problem (see *The Science of Logic*, Volume I, on the problem of actual versus potential or "bad" infinity). Hence, with the partial exception of Spinoza, dialectical method before Hegel foundered on the interpretation of continuity as linear extension incapable of accounting for the necessary existence of discrete phenomena (e.g., Hegel's "night in which all cows are black," ridiculing Schelling). Beginning with Hegel, dialectical method defines the quality of primary, continuous being as *self-developing self-activity*. In Marx, this form of the dialectical method is brought down to earth as *revolutionizing human practice*. The self-development of man's power over nature through advancing productive technology (universal labor), or its wilful form, the class-for-itself (Being-for-itself) necessarily reflects (immanently) the laws of the universe it appropriately masters; thus Being-for-itself becomes the reflected expression of Being-in-and-for-itself, and the only form in which knowledge of Being-in-and-for-itself is accessible to systematic human knowledge (see "Theses on Feuerbach"; "Feuerbach," *The German Ideology*).

Obviously, all Social Democratic, "Communist," and "Trotskyist" versions of dialectical method are essentially reductionist empty constructs—chimeras—with no systematic ("hereditary") connection to the dialectical method of either Marx or Hegel.

Capital   (eco.) A term whose significance varies considerably according to context and user. Broadly, the monetary valuation (*exchange value*) of the capitalist's investment. Also, by implication, the quality of the various component magnitudes of wealth which make up capitalists' capital. By other implication, the reification of this monetary quality to attribute the significance of capital to the objective wealth possessed through capitalist property titles (note, the practice of referring to machinery, products, and raw materials in themselves as "capital").

   Constant Capital   (eco.) (C) In monetary terms, the value of the portion of plant, raw and semi-finished materials, and supplies currently consumed (hence implicitly demanding replenishment) by production; the determinate capitalist form of an underlying social-reproductive category, also identifiable as "constant capital," defined as that ratio of total productive labor which must be assigned (allocated) to producing means of production in order to maintain the equipotentiality of the material preconditions of production. The correspondence between these monetary and real categories is not one-for-one. Constant Capital, as a category of capitalist reproduction per se, is limited to the maintenance of the value of capitalists' capitals, and hence excludes consideration of resources not currently acknowledged as requiring replenishment by capitalists who exhaust them. Capitalist reproduction is blind to the category of equipotentiality for the productive forces as a whole.

   Variable Capital   (eco.) (V) The value of the labor power embodied in current production; in monetary terms, essentially the wages and fringe benefits incurred as the price of the productive labor employed. In real terms, Variable Capital is the ratio of all productive labor which must be allocated to provide the material preconditions of existence and development of the necessary totality of the quality of productive labor required for tomorrow's production, assuming total realization of net surplus value and rational realization of capitalists' consumption or its equivalent. As in the case of Constant Capital, there is no simple correspondence between the capitalist monetary and real categories, but only a broad tendency to correlation.

   Circulating Capital   (eco.) V + C + S [S: surplus value] The portion of total capital converted into money [C into M into C', where C signifies the potential monetary value of capital, as distinct from Constant Capital] through current circulation of produced commodities. That is, the unconsumed residue of Fixed Capital (plant, machinery, and equipment), idle raw materials, and the like which inventories do not circulate in this sense.

Fixed Capital (eco.) Broadly, the residue of plant, machinery, and equipment left unconsumed by current production to date.

Organic Composition of Capitals (eco.) The ratio of Constant to Variable Capitals (C/V). Marx restricts this term, by an arbitrary but useful convention, to the ratio of capitalists' capitals. However, the significance of the term becomes clear only when it is examined as a ratio of social-reproductive (real) categories for the totality of the productive forces. In the latter case, a rise in the gross ratio itself may have either of two opposing imports. When such a rise is associated with a decline in the social ratio $S'/(C + V)$, it reflects entropy resulting from an abortion of realized advances in the mode of production (e.g., abortion of realized technological advances): entropy-caused increments in C/V. When a rise in C/V is associated with a rise in $S'/(C + V)$, the cause is a cheapening of the per capita social cost of a rising standard of living, as a result of advances in mode: negentropy. In Section III of Volume III of *Capital*, especially in the chapter "Internal Contradictions," Marx equates internal contradiction with fundamental antinomy, and argues that the tendency of capitalist reproduction is entropic, such that rises in C/V tend to be associated with declines in $S/(C + V)$. Despite Ricardo, whom Marx describes as mystifying the problem, the rising organic composition of capitals does not actually cause a decline in the ratio $S/(C + V)$ in real terms; rather, the effort to maximize the ratio $S/(C + V)$ in capitalists' terms causes a decline in the real ratio and ultimately a crisis in which the real decline becomes manifest in monetary terms. This real decline in the ratio of $S/(C + V)$ causes rises in C/V to reflect entropy. Also, C/V signifies the determined ratio of particular capitals (particular firms), or the ratio for a subsector of the world economy.

Class (epist., eco.) In vulgar economics and sociology, a statistical assortment of persons into "classes" according to the standard of any arbitrarily adopted factors. The most common crude example of this practice is the definition of "class" on the basis of the factor of income range, which locates unionized U.S. production workers in a "middle class." In Marxian economics, classes are primarily distinguished by methods appropriate to the differentiation of biological species (a classical approach common to certain aspects of Platonic, neo-Platonic, and Aristotelian practice, both ancient and Renaissance). Marx develops his specific method as a correction of Feuerbach's "species-consciousness" and "species-nature," rejecting Feuerbach's reductionist ("dirty-judaical") notion of the discrete object in favor of the continuity of revolutionary human practice as the basis for his discovery of a rigorous conception of class. Marx locates the existence of societies in an historically specific mode of human reproductive practice (reproduction of the species through advances in production of the material preconditions of species-existence). He situates this activity in respect to that included aspect or phase through which the necessary alteration of the material universe is *directly* accomplished: direct production of tangible wealth. He then defines classes according to their relationship to the direct production of useful changes in nature: how does the mode of reproduction of members of a class differentiate itself from that of other classes with respect to production of useful material changes in nature? The working class, like the farmers in this respect, exists by consuming part of the total tangible product created by productive labor drawn from working class households. However, the working class, unlike the farmers, does not have a parochialized (e.g., property, rent, and the like) connection to the material conditions of production, but exists as the cooperative activity of wage labor. The capitalist class, by contrast, reproduces itself not only by extracting the material means of household reproduction of individuals from the production of the world-wide working class, but by accumulating a mass of capital for its children from the same productive process. This is the class relationship of capitalists to the mode of production. Thus, capitalist society is characterized by three principal classes: the working class, farmers, and capitalists. There also exists a *pseudo-class* called the petit bourgeoisie—small-holders, clerks, service workers, bureaucrats, and the like—who do not represent (as the principal income-"producers" of households) the social reproduction of workers, capitalists, or farmers, but who are most closely allied either to farmers or to capitalists in their characteristic ideology. This pseudo-class becomes a class by negation, and constitutes a mass of dependents upon other classes in a class society. For example, in the Soviet Union, there exists a large petit bourgeoisie which is nonetheless not a social class. It is principally a political appendage of the Soviet working class. However, it tends to act as a class, to become a petit-bourgeois class like capitalist society's petit-bourgeois class. This tendency is located, domestically, in the continued existence of a peasant class (small-holders, cooperative farmers) in the Soviet Union, and also in the tendency of the Soviet bureaucracy to mediate the relationship between foreign capitalists and Soviet productive forces. Hence, during the 1920s (especially 1923–1928) the Bolshevik left opposition (Trotsky, Preobrazhensky, and others) located the petit-bourgeois tendency of the Soviet bureaucracy principally in the Stalin regime's continuation of an NEP accommodation to the kulak and NEPman social strata within the Soviet Union. After the collectivization of the first five-year–plan period, Trotsky (*Revolution Betrayed*) located the petit-bougeois tendency of the bureaucracy principally in the endemic tendency of the factory-management section of the bureaucracy to ally itself socially with foreign capitalists (note Trotsky's anticipation of procapitalist "decentralization" tendencies of the Liberman-Brezhnev varieties).

Class-in-itself (epist., eco.) A convention for *working-class-in-itself*, the Being-in-itself form of the working class as self-alienating wage-labor. [The false argument of Social Democratic, "Communist," "Trotskyist," and "Maoist" apologists that Marx advanced this distinction only during his 1843–1849 "juvenile" or "idealist" phase, or "while he was still under the disorienting influence of Feuerbach," is an effort to hide the virulently anti-Marxian labor policies of the "official Marxist movement," beginning with the Lasallean and Eisenacher factions of the late 1860s. (See "Feuerbach," *The German Ideology; The Poverty of Philosophy; The Communist Manifesto;* "Critique of the Gotha Programme.") The charge of "idealism" against Marx is related to the false assertion that the distinction between class-in-itself and class-for-itself is purely subjective, an attempted differentiation which locates the proponent in the Kantian or even pre-Kantian mechanistic tradition.] Crudely, class-in-itself does signify the mere phenomenal form of wage labor—politically, the passive mediation of capitalist reproduction of capitals. However, it also represents the heteronomic form of the working class, not merely as victimized by capitalist fragmentation but acting itself to perpetuate its own fragmentation. The most extreme expression of the class-in-itself tendency is what pre-First World War U.S. socialists and trade-unionists termed "Scissor Bills," workers whose social practice is oriented to a special private relationship between the individual workers and their employers. The same tendency exists in trade-union chauvinism, nationalism, racism, and the like. The pseudo-Marxist prides himself on his objectivity in locating the class distinction exclusively in the particular aspect of workers' lives narrowly identified with wage-labor employment in itself; he refuses to consider the workers' social practice as objective practice. Marx, in opposition to both the anarchists and centrists, located the class distinction in the self-activity of the workers as members of a class—that is, in their practice respecting the self-organized activity of the class as a class. The class-in-itself is both the phenomenal form of workers as merely fragmented wage-labor, and the class as a process of perpetuating its fragmentation.

Class-for-itself (epist., eco.) A convention for working-class-for-itself, the Being-for-itself (*für sich*) form of the working class; the working class in the process of organizing itself as a worldwide class around programs for the development of the world's productive forces. The programmatic criteria identifying the working class as a political class-for-itself are summarized in *Capital,* Volume III, Section 7, especially the famous passage on Freedom/Necessity.

Class Consciousness (epist.) The conscious tendency for development of class-for-itself social and programmatic outlooks.

Conscious (epist., psych.) Actually or potentially capable of wilfully representing one's own deliberative processes to other persons, or, more broadly, a state approaching that capacity. Also, that aspect of deliberation which is susceptible to becoming conscious, either as an idea (object-image or feeling) *to be made conscious*, or an entire aspect of the deliberative processes *to become conscious*. Therefore, a general synonym for *Mind*, implying that all mentation can become conscious. In Freud, the term has a more restricted significance, delimited by Freud's categories of *preconscious, unconscious*, and *categorical unconscious* (*ucs.*) descriptively to those aspects of mentation which are normally accessible to communicable forms of thought, and dynamically to those special aspects of mentation deemed susceptible to producing thought in communicable form.

Preconscious (psych.) That aspect of mentation normally associated with the "feeling of intuition" in the development of solution-concepts (Gestalts) for problems (see L. S. Kubie, *The Neurotic Distortion of the Creative Process*). See *self-conscious*. In conventional psychoanalytical lexicons, "preconscious" is more or less equaled with *Superego*: see *Ego*.

Self-Conscious (epist., psych.) The quality of consciousness which is capable of "looking over the shoulder" of the Ego (see Hegel, *Phenomenology of Mind*). ("Can *you* see why you say that?" The italicized *you* is the self-conscious self; the other "you" is the Ego. "Which of you is speaking?") The "location" of the sense of "I" in exceptionally creative persons, at least during their moments of outstanding achievements; also, the temporary location of the "I" in exceptional moments of an "overwhelming sense of loving," as opposed to Ego-erotic "loving" or the pathetic "I need to be loved" state. Also, the location of the sense of "I" in class-consciousness (class-for-itself), as opposed to the Ego-state (class-in-itself) parochialist "militancy" of "trade-union consciousness."

Unconscious (epist., psych.) Broadly, the qualities of deliberation which are not conscious. In epistemology, the term describes the reality of the deliberative processes concealed by ideology, or that aspect of reality which remains beyond the comprehension of consciousness in the existing state of maturation of individual or general powers of conscious deliberation. Psychology defines "unconscious" as not presently accessible to consciousness. (According to Freud, the *repressed unconscious* is "material" susceptible to representation in the form of conscious thought, but either momentarily inaccessible to consciousness or, more significantly, constantly repressed; the *ucs.* is categorically insusceptible to representation in the form of conscious thought, or to being made conscious by virtue of quality.) In psychoanalysis generally, three categories of "unconscious" are usually identified: *preconscious* (a special case of repressed unconscious), *repressed unconscious*, and *categorical unconscious (ucs.)*. We know that these pioneer categories in psychoanalytical work are partially reflections of an elementary shortcoming in Freud's approach. However, provided they are not mistaken for rigorous notions of distinct existences, they retain usefulness as descriptive terms for an initial rough assortment of phenomena during the early phases of psychoanalysis or psychological pedagogy.

Critical Philosophy   (epist.) The genre otherwise known as German classical philosophy which originated in Kant's *Critiques of Pure Reason, Practical Reason,* and *Judgment,* and extended through such principal figures as Fichte, Schelling, Hegel, and the left-Hegelians. As a phase in the development of human knowledge, this school comes to an end with Feuerbach, and is formally laid to rest by Marx's "Theses on Feuerbach" and the "Feuerbach" section of *The German Ideology.* The school is characterized by its preoccupation with two interconnected problems: Kant's fundamental antinomy and the dialectical form of free will. Critical philosophers (e.g., Kant, Hegel) base their view of mathematical physics on the outlook of Euler–Lagrange, regarding it as the form of such knowledge of the "outside world" accessible to the human understanding. They locate the essential questions to be investigated in the domain of Mind; hence the special significance of the term "Idealism" applied to this genre. Marx eliminates the need for further investigations in this genre in his "Theses on Feuerbach." He eliminates the fundamental antinomy by situating the primary, continuous form of Being in the process of revolutionizing human practice, and locating Mind as the deliberative moment of the process of successive evolutions in the general mode of social reproduction. In thus destroying the dualism of voluntarism/determinism (perfect free will and omniscient providence) Marx only omits the urgent, subsumed issues of a corresponding mathematical physics. This shortcoming of Marx's revolution afflicts his three-volume *Capital* as inability to account for the qualitative transition from the pedagogical model of simple reproduction to his central conception of expanded reproduction (i.e., the famous paradox of the last chapter of Volume II). The same flaw appears in a less influential form in Marx's general inability to comprehend mathematics. Hence, as this text points out, Marx left one aspect of critical philosophy unresolved: that aspect of Hegel's investigations linked to the work of Riemann and Cantor. This uncompleted task is the justification for the continuation of critical philosophy toward its conclusion by the author and his collaborators.

Depression (eco.) A generalized devaluation of capitalist equity and debt instruments as a result either of a traditional abrupt decline in price levels or an accelerating inflation which devalues titles by reducing the value of money. Usually, a depression is identified only by its characteristic social sequelae, and the familiar misanalyses of such crises result from such misplaced concreteness. The sequelae are illiquidity-induced declines in the levels of production and employment; these phenomena represent not the analytical qualities of a depression, but the subsumed social consequences of a depression's secondary and tertiary phases. The depression, as a systematic phenomenon, is originally located in a breakdown of the essential "mechanisms" of liquid credit expansion—such as occurred in the dollar crises of March 1968 and, more decisively, August 1971. After such crises have occurred, the sequelae are essentially inevitable. The effort to prevent a depression after an occurrence like that of August 1971 is "locking the barn door after the horse has fled."

Depression Cycle (eco.) The flow and ebb, determined largely as effects of marginal capitalizations of fictitious values, in the credit-expansion aspect of a period of active capitalist investment. The self-aggravating accumulation of a growing ratio of obligations to fictitious capital (especially the debt-capitalization of fictitious values) exceeds the capacity of the productive circulation of commodities to throw off sufficient masses of profit-income to cover demands for combined fictitious and productive capitals. The creation of short-term liquidity to overcome this deficit represents the exacerbation of the fictitious/productive capitals ratio, such that the use of "built-in stabilizers" in the effort to forestall depression becomes the actual cause of the depression through the accumulation of illiquidity in the basic monetary system and consequent general monetary crises. Consequently, the development of "built-in stabilizers" during the post-1934 period has resulted only in a more marked and dangerous inflationary explosion than was traditional to depression-crises of the past.

Recession (eco.) Properly used, this term distinguishes intra-cyclical "points of inflection" (often termed "inventory cycles") from actual depressions. Recessions fall into two analytical classes: temporary curtailments of liquidity occurring on the upswing of an investment cycle, and similar occurrences characteristic of the downswing toward a new depression. The term is often loosely used, especially during the past quarter-century, as a consoling euphemism for actual depressions.

Dialectics (epist.) [A systematic, discursive definition is necessary; due to the nature of the concept, a dictionary gloss can serve no useful purpose here.] In creative problem-solving, as distinguished from the application of a learned procedure to a problem-type, we may identify three successive phases of mentation. In the first phase, the failure of the problem to reduce to a familiar type amenable to effective procedural solution creates "tension." In the second phase, the sense of "I" momentarily flips from the Ego-state to self-consciousness: a solution is "seen" as a Gestalt. In the third phase, the mind has returned to the Ego-state. The solution "seen" self-consciously is now degraded to the mere form of a solution-concept (that is, without comprehension of the synthetic process-content of the created concept). A procedure for applying this new solution-concept to a formal-logical reduction of the problem is then elaborated. The brief experience of creative mental activity is remembered in the newly educated Ego-state as a mere "feeling" of "intuition." *In ordinary, nondialectical or formal-logical analysis* of the general progress of human knowledge through "intuition" of solution-concepts, the act of creative insight is ignored. The successive orderings of knowledge are each regarded as elementary or self-evident, and the progress effected is portrayed as a kind of ratio of such ordered data. In the dialectical mode, the identification of the primitive datum is reversed relative to that of formal-logical modes. The moment of "movement" of self-conscious creative insight is taken as the primary subject-matter of inquiry, and the resulting progress in formal knowledge is treated as "mere" determined predicates of the continuous process of self-conscious creative mentation (e.g., Descartes' perfection-ontological proof theorem, Spinoza, Hegel, Marx). Provided this shift in analytical method is itself investigated from the vantage-point of self-consciousness (the intuitive comprehension of the process of intuition, or what Hegel terms the "speculative principle"), the "transfinite" correlative of the creative moment is accessible to direct cognition.

This approach is undertaken by the same general method properly employed in psychoanalysis, which poses the query, "Do *you* see why you said that?" in which *you* is the self-conscious self looking over the shoulder of either the Ego or the self-conscious self of the preceding moment. In other words, the self-conscious processes are stimulated by socializing the internal processes of mentation, as in the form of an internal dialogue in which consciousness takes itself as its primary subject of investigation. Hence the term "dialectic," which is often vulgarly misunderstood to signify merely dialogue form as such; hence "vulgar dialectics," "sophistry." The significance of the dialogue is as the means of making consciousness itself the subject of critical reflection by consciousness in this way. It is a way of "forcing" the shift of the sense of "I" to that self-conscious state which is otherwise the location of creative mentation. It is the "transfinite" mode of self-consciousness of self-consciousness (Being-for-itself), achieved in this way, which is specifically dialectics.

The term "dialectics" is therefore attributed to the principal features of the world-outlook unique to the "transfinite" mental state. These qualities are the world-outlook itself and the coherent method of rigorous thought. Within his own mind, the thinker's approach to all subjects is a kind of dialogue between, as Feuerbach would say, the "I" and the "Thou." The "I" of individual self-sense and particular experience reviews and corrects its immediate view of reality by listening to the internalized voice of the universal human experience, the "Thou" of *that* form of the dialogue, that preliminary, primitive form of the internal dialogue. This dialogue, which locates the necessary positive action of the individual person and act for the benefit of the whole, is the beginning of the self-conscious world-outlook. ("What must I do and be to be a positive existence for historic humanity?") The further progress of the dialogue relocates the "I" in the former "Thou" (self-consciousness); thereupon, the individual ceases to view himself as morally enslaved to the universal good. He sees the positive enhancement of his "I" (his positive value for humanity) in terms of those acts which advance the human condition, such that humanity exists for him in the same way that he exists for humanity. Now, his positive act is that which enhances the development of his positive powers for humanity as a result of the advances in humanity actualized through his act. He becomes Being-for-itself.

Hence, the dialectical outlook is that which views the universe as primarily negentropic self-extension.

Ego (epist., psych.) "I"; therefore, the term used to identify that aspect of individual mentation usually found to be associated with the individual's sense of "I." Actually, except in the case of psychosis (in which a third quality of "I" may occur), the Ego is one of the two alternative locations of the sense of "I" in the individual. In the modern psychoanalytical view, in which it is recognized that truly sane individuals locate their adult sense of "I" only in self-consciousness, and the proper term for Ego is *infantile Ego*. The infantile Ego is the normal sense of "I" developed during the initial period of extra-uterine gestation, and is a healthy state for infants. However, in a "sane society," this sense of "I" would begin to be superseded by self-conscious "I-ness" during the postinfancy socialization of the individual, and the Ego would essentially disappear at the age of approximately two or three. Hence, the "normality" of the Ego-sense of "I" in adult members of capitalist society is the primary clinical symptom of that pathetic condition known as bourgeois ideology.

Ego-ideals (psych.) This imprecise but useful term broadly signifies an amalgamation of the various kinds of standards of self-image consulted by the "I" in the formation of individual judgments. There are principally two absolutely distinct, mutually exclusive sets of such ego-ideals: self-conscious standards by which the individual determines what will make him a useful person regardless of immediate opinion of his judgment; and the internalized voices and grimaces of images (synthetic surrogates for actual persons or composite persons) whose opinion of itself the "I" fears.

Entropy/Negentropy   (epist., eco.) In economics, entropy corresponds to a decline in the social-reproductive ratio, $S'/(V + C)$, in consequence of the continuation of production in a relatively fixed technological mode. ("Marginal" social costs of depleted resources cause a rise in C, a resulting rise in V, and so on, and hence a decline in $S'/(C + V)$.) Negative entropy or negentropy is identified as those tendencies ("impulses") of technological and related development of the modes of production which result in a rise in the social-reproductive ratio, $S'/(C + V)$. The negentropy itself is located in the "impulse-tendency" rather than the determined resulting rise in the effective social ratio. It is heuristically approximated through the notion of an exponential function for $S'/(C + V)$; the negentropy itself is located in the process underlying (determining) rising values for that function. The lack of direct correspondence between entropy and negentropy should be noted. Negentropy is of the order of Being-for-itself, and implicitly Being-in-and-for-itself; entropy is of the order of Being-in-itself. Entropy is the inherent tendency of a universe of self-evident objects and fixed laws to "wind down" (see Leibniz on "God's clock" in the Clarke correspondence). It therefore corresponds to a linear notion of human practice. Negentropy is the self-reflexive form, the reflection of the self-subsisting positive principle of extension of a universe characterized by increasing ratios of "free energy"-determinations of the form of rising $S'/(C + V)$, and is hence of a different cognitive order than entropy. If, in place of a fixed universe characterized by a permanent invariant quality, we define the universe as an historical ordering of nested manifolds, and hence of changing invariant quality (changing "fundamental physical laws"), the naive notion of elementary energy forms vanishes, and the phenomenon of energy becomes the *fictitious* (Spinoza) appearance in the here and now of a moment of negentropy; negentropy is the form of self-developing "energy" corresponding to the continuity of a universe of nested, historically ordered manifolds.

Ideology   (epist., psych.) In strict usage (as, for example, in *The German Ideology*), a special kind of mass neurosis, preponderantly characteristic of an entire culture or social class, and embodying both a systematically (viciously) false perception of reality and the self-perpetuation of that illusion through the cohering irrationality of general social practice. For example, bourgeois ideology is the characteristic, underlying, pervasive neurosis of all classes of capitalist society, in respect to which individual neuroses and psychoses are only subsumed differentiations.

Infinite (epist.) In reductionist schemas, unlimited extension in space or aggregation of particulars (the "bad infinity" of Hegel and Cantor). In dialectical method, primarily a universal continuum whose experienced quality of extension is self-perfection—that is, negentropy. Dialectics also attributes the quality of actual infinity to certain universalizing aspects of particularities (e.g., Feuerbach's "infinite in the finite," Hegel's Being-for-itself, Marx's class-for-itself). The creative processes of individual mentation, as directed to the solving of problems of development of human existence generally (Marx's universal labor), both effect (actualize) a general advance in the universal value of $S'/(C + V)$ and realize the potential humanity of preceding generations. Hence, through such universal labor, the finite (individual) embodies the infinite. The distinction between vulgar and dialectical usages of the term "infinite" is heuristically explained as follows. In the vulgar classroom usage of the notion of an infinitely extended ray (line, lines, etc.), the line is assumed not to change in quality as study of the extension shifts respectively from the ordinary macro scale to the "infinitely large" or "infinitely small" (see Riemann). In dialectical method, the line must successively change in quality with each incremented interval. The "world-line" defined by rising positive exponential functions of the social-reproductive ratio, $S'/(C + V)$, is in the text a paradigm for this quality of self-perfecting extension. .

Labor (epist., eco.) In dialectics, the actualization of new knowledge to effect a desired change in the order of nature. In Marx, usage of the term is restricted as specified in "Theses on Feuerbach" and the "Feuerbach" section of *The German Ideology*. It signifies that development of the society's productive forces which satisfies the immediate requirements of Freedom/Necessity (*Capital*, Volume III, "Trinitarian Formula"). Marx distinguishes two moments of labor for the capitalist mode of production, in particular—universal and cooperative labor—justifying the necessity of such a distinction in the fact of the alienation of universal from cooperative labor by capitalism. Cooperative labor is the aspect of labor represented by an interconnected and interdependent worldwide network of production; it is the moment of worldwide labor in the here and now, the worldwide cooperative form of labor for an abstractly fixed mode of technology. Universal labor is the cognitive process of synthesizing and/or assimilating advances in technology which, actualized, have the significance of a negentropic advance in the universal network of production.

  Labor Power (eco.) Labor as both universal and cooperative labor, in the form that is manifest in the here and now. The fact that the value of labor power is twofold determines a variety of specific contexts of usage of the term itself. From the standpoint of the development of the total productive forces (the worldwide network), all individual labor has an effect on the value of all the functions associated with the social-reproductive ratio, $S'/(C + V)$. From the standpoint of the capitalist mode of production, that same production, in fact, individual labor also has an actual effect on the ratio of capitals, $S'/(C + V)$, for the capitalist economy as a worldwide whole. Both forms implicitly determine a value for particular labor as *economic* Being-for-itself; individual labor, by the tests of substitution within a worldwide network, has an effect on the actualized value of either (social-reproductive or capitalist) worldwide ratio, $S/(C + V)$, which is *reflexively* the proper value of that particular labor. When this notion is extended from a particular moment of the worldwide process to the negentropic function (a world-line of development of the productive forces), labor power as the notion of the self-development of labor power emerges (Being-for-itself). We then have two values for labor power: its capitalist value, the reflexive value of labor's marginal contribution to the mass-rate of absolute capitalist profit; and its social-reproductive, or use value (e.g., for socialist society of the same degree of development), the "marginal" value of particular labor for labor power as Being-for-itself. In *Capital*, except for a few passages in which the context is distinctly different, the term "labor power" is generally restricted to its value for capital-in-general.

Liquidity (eco.) The ratio of means to pay debt in respect to debt-service requirements and, by implication, the ability of the capitalists to obtain commodity sales and other revenues or equity and loans to maintain their collective or individual liquidity. A liquidity ratio of less than unity is illiquidity or insolvency; recognition of a firm's insolvency by its creditors is bankruptcy. Hence the distinctions between short-term and long-term liquidity (or illiquidity): a firm or economy may increase its short-term liquidity by means of even catastrophic increases in long-term illiquidity, increasing long-term debt-service rates by loans to meet current obligations.

Mediation (epist.) Literally, the necessary middle moment or means of a process. The hypothetical self-sufficient farmer who develops increased productivity exists by means of consumption of his product. Thus, the agricultural product is not an end result, and has no significance in itself; it is merely the necessary mediation of his process of self-development. In this hypothetical case, one should note that it is not the existence of the abstractly individual farmer that is mediated. The existence mediated is the farmer's productive self-development; the farmer in this case is revolutionizing human practice (see "Theses on Feuerbach"). We would "measure" this existence in the manner specified in "Freedom/Necessity" (*Capital*, Volume III, Section 7). The general measurement would be the ratio of "free energy" in the farmer's total activity, including a reduction in the number of living hours required to maintain himself due to the new developed higher productivity. However, relative to the amount of time embodied in production of his consumption at earlier times, his absolute consumption of product would have increased. This process of self-development, his existence, is accomplished through successive epochs of the self-reproductive cycle, during each of which the existence (self-activity) "goes outside itself" in the form of productive acts upon the land; the result of this actualization is itself actualized as the product of this production returns to the activity which generated it, as further development of that self-activity (Being-for-itself). The externalization of self-activity as a necessary moment of its self-development is mediation. If the farmer were being considered as an individual of fixed productivity (as one considers the farmer's cattle or as feudalism considered serfs), the use of the term "mediation" would amount to nothing but preciosity. For example, the term "means of existence" cannot be rigorously interpreted until one has further answered the query, "the existence of what?" If the reply is "the existence of abstract individuals," the term "means of existence" is being employed in the vulgar, unscientific form, from which no significant conclusions (except that of the vulgarity of the thought) can be adduced. If the existence in question is the existence of a process of development, then the term "means" has the scientific implication of "mediation." By contrast, in Being-in-and-for-itself, as in the self-development of the entire universe, the means is always an aspect of the self-activity; hence the necessary quality, entirely mediated through itself, or self-mediating, causes the term "mediation" to vanish.

Negation   (epist.) The various synonyms—opposition, *annulment*, and so on—each represent mere predicates of the general, rigorous subject-form of the notion. "Going out of itself" is the general notion. Production is negated in the form of commodities; workers negate commodities into labor power through consumption. Hence also the subordinate significance: "that which this is not," and generally, the distinction of the particular within the universal. The general rule by which to avoid commonplace silly usages of the sort encountered among "Marxist-Leninists," and others is to recognize that static notions of negation are just that, relatively the momentary Being-in-itself or fictitious semblances of dialectical process-determinations. (V. I. Lenin's *Empirio-Criticism* and *Philosophical Notebooks* are generally silly on this and related matters; the redactions of Lenin offered by Stalin and other self-styled *epigonoi* are simply banal incompetence.)

Positive   (epist.) The sense of development of process in the manner characteristic of the notion of that process. Positive thought is therefore creative thought in the sense of a development of cognitive powers. An increase in the ratio $S'/(C + V)$ is a positive realization of surplus value.

Self-subsisting positive: the characteristic quality of Being-in-and-for-itself. In Marx, this is the essential form and content of revolutionizing human practice, in the sense that such a process of human practice is coextensive by implication with the "fundamental laws of the universe" and, hence, the self-acting universe in its actuality. Man as a self-subsisting positive process, as revolutionizing human practice, is most succinctly defined by Marx in two well-known locations: the opening paragraphs of the "Feuerbach" section of *The German Ideology,* and in the "Freedom/Necessity" passage in the "Trinitarian Formula" chapter of *Capital* III. He develops the notion in the following steps. (1) The uniquely self-evident fact of human knowledge is man's existence through production of the material preconditions of the thinker's existence. (2) That fact involves the contradiction that the extension of human existence in any fixed mode depletes the basis for continued existence in that mode. (3) The primitive form and content of man's existence is man's historical mastery of the universe through successive successful advances in mode and in his conceptual powers to develop necessary new modes. (4) The self-conception of this process of creating new modes of human existence (practice) is both the concept of actual human existence and the form and content of human knowledge. (5) Hence revolutionizing (social-evolutionary) human practice, subsuming the law of the universe in the process of deliberatively changing modes of human practice on that universe (positively predetermining negentropy with respect to the universe), is entirely self-subsisting, is its own mediation: a self-subsisting principle, uniquely premised in itself. This principle permits direct access, dialectically, to positive knowledge of necessary individual behavior for society, and hence ends the need for the Kantian or Hegelian forms of negation of the negation, which internalize "the chains of external oppression" or of mere authoritative opinion: hence a self-subsisting positive principle.

Profit (eco.) In vulgar usage, the capitalist net profit or gross profit, according to context. The gross profit is the residual income after deduction of the "prime costs" of direct productive labor and materials, or after also deducting so-called "capital costs" of depreciation, maintenance, and the like. Net profit usually signifies residual income after deducting alienated outlays (payments to outsiders) to capitalists' consumption by the capitalist firm (e.g., administrative, debt-service, selling, and other nonproductive costs) from gross profit. The term "net profit" may also represent net profit after adjustments for other income and capital costs not directly related to operating expenses and revenues (e.g., capital gains, speculative losses, charges on capital account, and the like). The usage of these terms in accounting and other fields is varied and highly imprecise, although usually restricted in various ways.

Rate of Profit Usually, in vulgar usage, net profits as a percentile of gross sales revenues, an extremely deceptive term and meaningless basis for comparison of one type of firm with another; sometimes used to signify the more meaningful "rate of return on investment," a ratio of net or net operating profits to gross capital investment, owner's equity, or owner's capital outlays. In Marx, among others, rate of profit is the ratio of capitals, $S/(C + V)$ [a convention in *Capital*].

Absolute Profit a term adopted from Physiocratic theory signifying, primarily, the absolute net gain in current material wealth to the entire society from production. It also signifies, by implication, the portion of particular (local) production that represents a net gain in the current wealth of the entire society. In the latter sense, absolute profit is distinguished from *relative profit*, which represents gains to particular firms (or other sections of the whole economy) which do not also augment the real current wealth of the entire society. Relative profit is also fictitious profit; see *relative surplus value, fictitious value*.

Realism (epist.) The proper term, as opposed to the more casual "Idealism," for the genre of Spinoza, Kant, Hegel, and related thinkers. A *real* act is one whose effect on the universe is to perpetuate or recreate the conditions of existence of the cause of that act; hence realism as the coherence-test of truth. This principle depends upon the location of the primary quality of existence in self-activity, self-perfection, as opposed to locating primitive existence in self-evident discrete elementarities. Although Kant's notion of the *understanding* is permeated with tolerance of reductionist assumptions, his efforts to reconcile the particular with the universal are invariably premised on the principle of realism.

Reductionism (epist.) The generic term for classical materialism, empiricism, logical positivism, and the like; it also properly pertains to the so-called dialectical materialism of the Communists, "Trotskyists," "Maoists," and other related "Marxist-Leninist" groups. The general form of the illusion is that the universe is axiomatically premised on the independent existence of discrete elementarities whose properties and relations are governed by a set of fixed fundamental laws. Reductionism is also distinguished by two complementary "theories" of Mind. At one extreme are the behaviorists ("hereditarians," "environmentalists," and mixed varieties), including Watson, Pavlov, and Skinner, whose conception of Mind is epiphenomenalist: Mind as a metaphysical secretion of movements of elementary particles. At the other extreme are the theists and spiritualists, who employ the inherent ontological paradox of reductionism to "prove" that Mind must be a product of a *deus ex machina* (spirit or *élan vital*).

Reproduction   (epist., eco.) Properly, self-reproduction in the sense of either Being-for-itself or Being-in-and-for-itself: the mode of activity through which a species actualizes the extension of the development of its own existence. The existing Being acts upon the universal process to the effect of creating the preconditions of its developing existence.

   Simple Reproduction   (eco.) In Marx's writings, a purely pedagogical device corresponding to "total entropy" in the reproductive process ("zero free energy" actualization), equivalent to the null-form of expanded reproduction in a "Newtonian universe" of constant richness of resources.

   Expanded, Extended, or Enlarged Reproduction   (eco.) For epistemological coherence, the preferred term is *extended reproduction* (cf. "extended being"). The negentropic form of extension which is the necessary condition of continued existence of the productive forces under socialist or, in particular, capitalist economy. It has the following principal features. First, it involves the actualization of "free energy" (net surplus value) as expansion of the productive forces in both extent and quality (negentropy). As the resulting rise in the social-reproductive ratio, $S'/(C + V)$, occurs, the absolute level of Constant and Variable consumption per capita rises relative to the per capita social costs of earlier epochs; however, the combined current social cost of $C + V$ declines. At the same time, C rises more rapidly than V in such "absolute" historical costs, such that C/V increases in positive correlation with rises in $S'/(C + V)$. In the capitalist form of extended reproduction, self-aggravating vicious discrepancies between the ratio of capitals, $S/(C + V)$, and the social-reproductive ratio, also in the form $S/(C + V)$, represent a fundamental contradiction (fundamental antinomy): the current devaluation of the social cost of the elements of C and V is concealed by capitalist forms, so that enlarged reproduction leads to recurring apparent declines in the social-reproductive ratio and actual declines (in the form of periodic depressions) in the capitalist ratio.

   General Law of Evolutionary Social Reproduction   (epist., eco.) A term developed by the author to identify the principles set forth in the "Feuerbach" section of *The German Ideology*; a general "human ecological law" of all human existence, as distinguished from the special laws pertaining to specific historical forms of human society.

Transfinite   (epist.) The term developed by Cantor to distinguish the qualitative feature of his discovered concept of universals from the vulgar term "infinite." Most simply expressed, Cantor demonstrated the intrinsic, insoluble contradiction of all formal logic: (1) that there is no method of enumerating the particular elements of a universal category which can completely predetermine all the elements, even in an "infinite" period of time; (2) that the conception of the whole of such a universal "collection" cannot be inductively determined by means of even the most exhaustive formal-logical analysis of the elements of the collection. The problem is identical with that confronted by the individual who attempts to conceptualize the creative processes of self-consciousness while his sense of "I" is located in the infantile Ego. Hence, the solution to the formal-logical paradox exists in two successive dialectical devices. First, the "I" must be transferred to self-consciousness; second, self-consciousness must become conscious of itself as its own object. In the second stage of the program, the category of universals can be directly cognized. The notion of infinity disseminated from the pulpit and the lectern of the undergraduate calculus classroom (which Hegel and Cantor define as "bad infinity") is the ideological (actually neurotic in that sense) notion appropriate to the Ego-state. The direct cognition of universals is a quality of self-consciousness of self-consciousness applied to the corresponding problems of totalities; hence the "double abstraction" of Cantor's dialectic demands a different term, free of any of the connotations of "infinite."

Value (eco.) The Being-for-itself form of the commodity-object or productive labor: its "marginal" contribution to the value of either the capitalist or socialist (social-reproductive) functions of $S'/(C + V)$ for the economy taken as a whole. In *Capital*, the term "value" is conventionally limited in usage, with occasional exceptions, to designate capitalist reproductive functions.

Exchange Value the phenomenal or Being-in-itself monetary-equivalent form of capitalist valuation of the commodity.

Use Value This term has two immediately conflicting meanings. From the standpoint of the social-reproductive ratio and its associated functions, use value is the "marginal" contribution, as by substitution methods of determination, of the realization of the particular on the value of the function of $S'/(C + V)$ for the whole society. In this sense, use value is the socialist valuation, or real valuation, of the particular, in opposition to exchange value. However, in capitalist economy, the actualization of wealth occurs through the mediation of the capitalist form of reproduction. Hence, the use value of the particular object is actually mediated through the capitalist mode of reproduction. Therefore, with certain notable exceptions, the term "use value" is used in *Capital* and *Theories of Surplus Value* to designate the determined quality of usefulness of the object or labor power from the standpoint of the capitalist form of the reproductive ratio, $S/(C + V)$. In this text, that distinction between the two uses is noted, but the social-reproductive significance is emphasized.

Surplus Value   The portion of total labor power or product corresponding to "free energy"—that is, after "deducting" (C + V). In *Capital,* usually the mass of capital values which the capitalists take from production as gross profit. The capitalist magnitude is not in direct correspondence to the ratio of surplus value from the standpoint of social reproduction, since capitalist expenditures for (C + V) do not correspond to the necessary preconditions for negentropic historic development of the productive forces.

Absolute Surplus Value   The mass of surplus value determined from the standpoint of the world capitalist economy as a whole. By implication, also the contribution of the particular firm to the world total of absolute surplus value.

Relative Surplus Value   Those portions of locally extracted surplus value which are not increments of absolute surplus value from the standpoint of the economy as a whole.

Fictitious Value   Those portions of capitalist-accounted value for which there is, in net, no corresponding real wealth; this phenomenon could be termed "relative capital," as distinct from absolute capital. Purely speculative gains are the clearest example. The strict meaning of the term is derived from the notion of realization embedded in the concept of value. In vulgar economics and most capitalist accounting practice, a sheer mass of commodities or other assets at assumed market-price is *prima facie value.* The concept of realization limits value to those mediating forms, labor power or commodities, which, when actualized as part of the reproductive cycle, marginally contribute to the maintenance or increase of the whole economy's ratio of $S/(C + V)$. As a capitalist credit expansion proceeds, there occurs the capitalization, in the form of debt and equity holdings, of a mass of nominal (accounted) wealth for which there would be no corresponding yield if all accounts were to be settled through the test of realization. The discrepancy between total capital and productive capital (productive = realizable through consumption to effect a prevailing rate of yield for the entire economy) is thus fictitious capital, or, as we indicated, *relative* value.

BIBLIOGRAPHY

The starred items represent in aggregate the essential bibliography for the principal themes of the text; double stars signify required references for course use. The remainder of the bibliography represents an economical assortment whose purpose is evident.

The bibliography has been divided into four sections, according to theme. The first section represents a minimal library in epistemology; the second, supplementary epistemological sources; the third, political economy; the fourth, psychology. A rough but useful diagram of the development of the main currents of epistemology from Kepler to the present is also provided.

For standard sources available in a number of languages and editions, the title alone is listed unless there is reason for doing otherwise.

1. BASIC SOURCES IN EPISTEMOLOGY

Descartes, Rene. *Meditations*. Should be consulted in conjunction with the text's treatment of his "Cogito" and "perfection" theorems.

*Feuerbach, Ludwig. *The Essence of Christianity*. Should be studied both for the connection it provided from Hegel to Marx, and as a seminal work in modern anthropology and psychology. Compare with the author's "The Case of Ludwig Feuerbach," listed in Section 4 below.

*————. *Principles of the Philosophy of the Future*. Feuerbach's attempt to situate his epistemology in systematic terms relative to his principal predecessors. Sections 32–33 and 58 are most pertinent.

* Hegel, G. W. F. *Lectures in the History of Philosophy*. Even a century and a half after these lectures were delivered, they still represent the most efficient text on the subject.

** ————. *The Phenomenology of Mind*. All the essential features of Hegel's work are present in this core writing on the dialectical method, at least in kernel. Heretofore, the text has been widely misread, for reasons developed in the author's "Beyond Psychoanalysis," "The Sexual Impotence of the Puerto Rican Socialist Party," and "The Case of Ludwig Feuerbach" (see Section 4 below).

* ————. *The Science of Logic*. Especially Volume I. The third most important of Hegel's writings, after the *Phenomenology* and *History of Philosophy*.

————. *The Philosophy of Right*. The book whose "endorsement" of the Prussian state gave immediate focus to the left-Hegelian faction. See Marx's *Critique of Hegel's "Philosophy of Right"* and "Contribution to a critique of Hegel's 'Philosophy of Right.' " Marx locates the root of Hegel's political outlook in the fallacies characteristic of *The Science of Logic* and already established in the *Phenomenology* (see the concluding section of Marx's *1844 Paris Manuscript.*)

Kant, Immanuel. *Critique of Pure Reason.* The formal prerequisite to the more significant *Critique of Practical Reason,* this long text is not readily assimulated by the ingenue, but is astonishingly coherent and lucid once the essentials have been grasped. Note especially the preface to the first edition.

** ———. *Critique of Practical Reason.* From the standpoint of the main currents of development of critical philosophy, this is the key work in the Kantian system.

* ———. *Prolegomena to Any Future Metaphysic.* The student not yet prepared to plunge into the *Critique of Pure Reason* should use this popularization as a preface to first reading of the *Critique of Practical Reason.* Also invaluable for Kant's historical account of the development of his system.

Marx, Karl. *Critique of Hegel's "Philosophy of Right"; "Contribution to a Critique of Hegel's 'Philosophy of Right.' "* This work represents the beginning of Marxism. Despite the admiration of Feuerbach which permeates Marx's writings of this period (mid-1843 to 1844), the point of view of "Theses on Feuerbach" is already emerging.

* ———. *Economic and Philosophical Manuscripts.* The concluding section on Feuerbach and Hegel's *Phenomenology* is most significant. The rest of the work is also useful for comprehension of the unbroken continuity of development of a consistent world-outlook into the "Grundrisse" and *Theories of Surplus Value,* as well as Section 7 of *Capital,* Volume III.

** ———. "Theses on Feuerbach." Together with the first section, "Feuerbach," of *The German Ideology,* this is the most important of Marx's epistemological writings. Once the notion of negentropy—as developed in this text and elsewhere in the author's work—is applied to the study of the self-development of epistemology, the "Theses" represent a succinct and almost complete (if awesomely compact) solution to all of the problems of epistemology to Marx's time. Hence, Engels' characterization of these "Theses" as the "germ of a new world-outlook" is too mild, even an understatement.

* ———. *The Poverty of Philosophy.* This positive statement of the connection between the Marxian dialectic and social practice, showing the irreconcilability of Marxism and anarchism, also demonstrates the gulf between Marx and such forms of pseudo-Marxian centrism as that of Bebel-Ebert-Kautsky, Zinoviev–Stalin, "Maoism," and present-day "Trotskyism."

** Marx, Karl, and Engels, F. *The German Ideology* (Moscow). The crucial section of this book is the first part, "Feuerbach," entirely written by Marx. (The reader should note the differences, emphasized in this text, between the point of view in Marx's version of this section and the fragment of a draft by Engels in the appendix to the Moscow edition.) The "Feuerbach" section is an elaboration of the notion of revolutionizing human practice introduced in the "Theses." However, the entire book has the important collateral importance today of exposing the absolute irreconcilability of Marx's and Engel's outlook with all forms of anarchosyndicalism (e.g., "local control," *Mitbestimmung*) and other expressions of existentialism. Similarly, the absurdity of the effort to locate Feuerbach as an existentialist or semiexistentialist is systematically demonstrated, to the detriment of the shame-faced efforts of such members of the Frankfurt School as Adorno and Schmidt to reconcile Feuerbach and Heidegger ("ontological security").

Spinoza, B. *Ethics.* The most essential of Spinoza's writings. The "geometrical" form of argument is certainly curious to the modern reader. This feature of the work should be discounted by the reader in the interest of discerning more directly what underlies such formal features of the exposition. The reader will thus note that the essentials of the Spinozan dialectic are unambiguously developed.

2. COLLATERAL EPISTEMOLOGICAL SOURCES

Boyer, Carl. *The History of the Calculus.* An eminently readable and useful introduction to this aspect of the Enlightenment's contributions to modern thought.

Cantor, G. *Fundamentals* (1883 *Grundlagen*), *Campaigner* 7, no. 8 (January, 1974). The key epistemological writing of the revolution in mathematical science that occurred during the last half of the nineteenth century.

————. *Contributions to the Founding of the Theory of Transfinite Numbers,* ed. P. Jourdain (New York: Dover). Although Jourdain either fails to comprehend fully or minimizes the deeper implications of Cantor's work, his biographical introduction to this book is otherwise accurate and eminently useful.

Dewey, John. *Reconstruction in Philosophy,* 2nd ed. (1948). The watershed apology for the general retreat from epistemological rigor which took over English-speaking intellectual life, notably, following the First World War. Although Dewey is rightly blamed for fathering such wretched varieties of "scientology" as are associated with Sidney Hook and others, he still shows the marks of contact with the vigorous American intellectual ferment that predated Eliot's presidency of Harvard and Butler's of Columbia. Therefore, Dewey's work provides a measure of moral retreat by echoing his own better days.

* Engels, F. Letters on the Paul Barth Controversy. In *Marx–Engels: Selected Works,* Volume II (Moscow) and other locations. A provocative exposure of the bowdlerized "objectivity" which Engels denounces as then being disseminated through the Social Democracy, and later to become the "orthodox" methodology of "Marxism-Leninism."

Jeans, James. *Physics and Philosophy.* A statement of the antidialectical outlook by one of the most competent of the professionals professing the reactionary point of view.

LaPlace, Pierre. *A Philosophical Essay on Probabilities.* An accessible point of reference for tracing the eighteenth-century Enlightenment into the beginning of the nineteenth century. Both the fruitful and reactionary tendencies are present.

*Maxwell, James C. *Matter and Motion*. A century after its first publication, still one of the best and most readable textbooks outlining the classical method of the physical sciences.

*Oparin, A. I. *The Origin of Life*. The seminal work in modern holistic biophysics: a brilliant, though substantially reductionist, summary of the case for developing a universal theory embracing inorganic and organic processes within a single historical principle of evolutionary development.

Planck, Max. *A Survey of Physics*. One of the most important statements from the essentially neo-Kantian viewpoint.

Weyl, Hermann. *Space, Time, Matter*. For the reader with a basic mathematical education: the standard text in the mathematics of the "Einstein Revolution."

Windelband, Wilhelm. *Ancient Philosophy*. The best writing by the leading neo-Kantian of the turn of the century. The treatment of the leading Ionian philosophers is most significant and should be compared with corresponding sections of Hegel's *History of Philosophy*.

3. POLITICAL ECONOMY

Kantorovich, I. *The Best Uses of Economic Resources* (Cambridge: Harvard, 1965). A summary of the case for "mathematical economics" by the Soviet academician who pioneered the development of its techniques.

Lange, Oskar. *Introduction to Econometrics* (New York: 1963). An accessible account of the field by a former leading Polish economist.

Lawrence, John. "The Socialist Reconstruction of Europe," *Campaigner* 6, nos. 3–4 (September–October 1973). This useful companion piece to L. Marcus' "The United States of Europe: Their Program and Ours" is a draft outline of the application of principles from Marcus' article to the immediate socialist programmatic issues of Western Europe.

Lenin, V. I. *Imperialism*. This classic "economic-theoretical" text of "Marxist-Leninist" iconography, is an attempt to interpret Marxian economics from a reductionist standpoint, is rife with the types of blunders identified with Lenin (Ilyin) in Luxemburg's *Accumulation of Capital*. As a political thesis, it is the third and poorest of the leading efforts to develop a theory of "permanent revolution" [Rosa Luxemburg, "The Industrial Development of Poland" (1898), *The Accumulation of Capital* (1913); L. Trotsky (with Parvus), "Results and Prospects" (1907).]

Luxemburg, Rosa. *Die industrielle Entwicklung Polens* (The Industrial Development of Poland) (1898), in *Rosa Luxemburg: Gesammelte Werke*, 1/1 (Berlin: 1972). Within Luxemburg's doctoral dissertation are two interconnected points which embroiled the socialist movement in controversy for three-quarters of a century. The principal of these two points is her revival of Marx's central notion of economic totality (see *Capital*, Volume III, Section 7), which she applies to situate world finance capital's fostering of the industrial development of the Polish sector of Russia as a case of what Trotsky later termed "combined and uneven development" (see

L. Trotsky, *The History of the Russian Revolution*). This was to become the economic-theoretical premise of her advocacy of "permanent revolution," as the alternative she offered to the Adler-Menshevik notion of parallel, separate "national stages." Although Trotsky later developed a bowdlerized version of this view (partly through Parvus' transmission of Luxemburg's own views), and her internationalist notion of permanent revolution was to put her in sharpest disagreement not only with the Social Democracy and Lenin, but also with Trotsky—especially on the issue of the strategic perspectives for developing an international revolutionary movement. In general, Luxemburg's method in *Accumulation of Capital, Anti-Kritik*, and *Einfuhrung in die Nationalökonomie* is already essentially reflected in the dissertation.

* ———. *Reform or Revolution?* (Various editions of the 1927 Integer translation are available in English.) Despite the official version of the factional setting of this booklet (as a defense of Social Democratic "orthodoxy"), a more careful reading shows Luxemburg to be taking deadly sideswipes at "orthodoxy" itself. Compare with the dissertation, *The Mass Strike*, and *Accumulation of Capital*.

** ———. *The Mass-Strike, the Party, and the Trade-Unions*. The elaboration of Luxemburg's strategic perspective. In opposition to the centrist conception of Social-Democratic "orthodoxy"—that the political movement is an epiphenomenon of the increased militancy of trade-unionists—Luxemburg reverts to Marx's conception of the class struggle as outlined in his *Poverty of Philosophy* and *Communist Manifesto*, advocating the class-for-itself conception in opposition to the class-in-itself ideology of the centrists. She uses the lessons of the 1898–1905 Russian upsurges to polemicize for a class-for-itself outlook on, in particular, the German situation.

** ———. *The Accumulation of Capital* (Monthly Review edition).

** ———. *The Accumulation of Capital—An Anti-Kritik* Two editions extant: *Anti-Kritik, Campaigner* 5, no. 1 (January 1972); no. 3 (March 1972); *The Accumulation of Capital—an Anti-Critique; Bukharin: Imperialism and the Accumulation of Capital* New York: (Monthly Review, 1972). On both *Accumulation* and *Anti-Kritik*, see L. Marcus, "In Defense of Rosa Luxemburg," below.

Marcus, L. "The United States of Europe: Their Program and Ours," *Campaigner* 5, no. 5 (Fall 1972). An elaboration of a political overview of programmatic strategy in a contemporary setting.

* ———. "In Defense of Rosa Luxemburg," *Campaigner* 7, no. 2 (Spring 1973). A defense of Luxemburg against her traditional and recent critics, including an exposition of the omission in her work which has remained unnoticed by any of those critics.

Marx, Karl. *Pre-Capitalist Economic Formation*, (ed. E. Hobsbawm.) A foretaste of the last two sections of *Capital*, Volume III.

** ———. *Critique of Political Economy*. Should be read as a supplement to *Theories of Surplus Value*, but also important for the appended introduction, translated from the K. Kautsky edition, in which Marx summarizes his method, making explicit links to his 1845–1848 writings.

**———. *Capital*, Volumes I–III.

**———. *Theories of Surplus Value*, Volumes I–III (Moscow).

*———. *The Eighteenth Brumaire* and *The Civil War in France*. These two booklets, written years apart, epitomize Marx's method of political analysis.

*———. "Critique of the Gotha Programme." A still up-to-date factional attack on the pretended Marxism of today's "Marxist-Leninists" and others.

Von Neumann, John, and Morgenstern, Oskar. *The Theory of Games and Economic Behavior*. The opening chapters of this thorough elaboration of the principles of reductionist "economic theory" are the most significant for the present context.

*Preobrazhensky, E. *The New Economics*. The most important economic-theoretical writing of the Bolshevik current, by the founder of the Soviet left opposition. The vicious and effective attack on Bukharin's arguments should be compared with relevant sections on Bukharin's in L. Marcus' "In Defense of Rosa Luxemburg."

*Sweezy, Paul M. *The Theory of Capitalist Development*. The most readable and scholarly of the "revisionists." A prosocialist (during the period of its composition a maverick Communist Party sympathizer) attempts to correct Marx's *Capital* from an empiricist standpoint, strongly influenced by Otto Bauer, Keynes, and others. Compare with the views of M. Kalecki.

4. PSYCHOLOGY

Durkheim, Emile. *The Elementary Forms of the Religious Life*. This brilliant French chauvinist avoided public account of his enormous and specific intellectual debts to such Germans as Hegel, Feuerbach, and Marx. The entire positive content of his major writings, beginning with *Division of Labor in Society*, is chiefly due to the direct influence of German predecessors studied intensively while preparing his first dissertation. The *Elementary Forms*, in preparation for almost a quarter-century before its publication, is the *magnum opus* which expresses the German heritage in the clearest and most concentrated fashion. In its best and worst features, the book is a continuation of Feuerbach's *The Essence of Christianity*, partly informed by a period of intensive study of Hegel and Marx. Durkheim fits precisely within the scope of Marx's indictment of Feuerbach in the "Theses on Feuerbach." Like Feuerbach, Durkheim proceeds initially from a dialectical view of the social determination of thought, but leans on Marx to go beyond Feuerbach with respect to the details of determination. Like the degenerated Feuerbach of the post-1848 period, Durkheim seizes upon the "fixed object" and "fixed natural laws" as the rationalization for turning "species-consciousness" into the reactionary policy of interclass solidarity.

*Freud, Sigmund. *A General Introduction to Psychoanalysis* (1924); *New Introductory Lectures* (1933).

———. *The Ego and the Id*.

————. *An Outline of Psychoanalysis.* These writings provide the student a working overview of the field.

*————. *The Future of an Illusion.* Compare with L. Marcus, "The Case of Ludwig Feuerbach," Part I, below.

————. *Civilization and its Discontents.* Freud's pessimistic tendency at its reductionist worst.

Fromm, Erich. *The Art of Loving.*

————. *Beyond The Chains of Illusion.* Fromm, onetime maverick genius of the Frankfurt School, is one of several outstanding psychoanalysts to free himself from both Freud's metaphysical "libido" reification and the "orthodox Freudian" exaggeration of the influence of the "repressive father" in the development of the child's personality. These two little books concentrate his most relevant accomplishments from the standpoint of this text.

*Köhler, Wolfgang. *The Mentality of Apes* and *Gestalt Psychology.* The works that absolutely discredited the claims of Watson, Pavlov, and their counterparts to scientific competence. The notion of a Gestalt and the link to Riemann *et al.* through the work of C. Ehrenfels are urgent topics.

*Kubie, Lawrence S. *Neurotic Distortion of the Creative Process.* Together with Gestalt studies of creativity, this book represents approximately the furthest advance in the study of cognition until the work of the author.

*Marcus, L. "Beyond Psychoanalysis," *Campaigner* 6, nos. 3–4 (September–October 1973). A prolegomena to a "new psychoanalysis" rooted in the accomplishments of critical philosophy and Marx.

*————. "The Sexual Impotence of the Puerto Rican Socialist Party," *Campaigner* 7, no. 1 (November 1973). Elaboration of the method and political relevance of the "new psychoanalysis" situated in a study of the problem of machismo in the socialist movement.

*————. "The Case of Ludwig Feuerbach." Part I: *Campaigner* 7, no. 2 (December 1973); Part II: no. 3 (January 1974). A study of the systematic epistemological implications of ideology and neurosis. Part I, principally occupied with the significance of religious belief, is published in conjunction with a criticism of the Adorno-Schmidt tendency of the Frankfurt School; Part III, emphasizing the systemic epistemological implications of the problem, is written in conjunction with the English translation (and introduction) of Cantor's 1883 *Grundlagen.*

Varga, Anna. "The Tragedy of Antonio Gramsci: The Recurring Nightmare of the Italian Left." *Campaigner* 7, no. 4 (February 1974). A psychoanalytic study of Antonio Gramsci and the abortive 1919–1921 upsurge in Italy, compiled by one of the author's collaborators.

INDEX

Heraclitus, 16, 87, 134, 245-47, 263-64
Heteronomy, 21, 94, 250, 288. *See also*
  Pluralism
Hilferding, Rudolf, 17, 304, 351
Hitler, Adolf, 288, 334, 353-54, 394
Hobbes, Thomas, 205
Hobsbawm, Eric, 327
Hobson, J. A., 351
Hook, Sidney, 262
Hudson Bay Company, 209, 308-11
Humanism, 36, 70, 100. *See also*
  Progress
Hume, David, 15, 43, 69, 241, 259, 269,
  274
Hylozoic monism, 17, 245-51, 269-74
  Hegel on, 378, 385

Ideology, 67-70, 247, 465g. *See also* Self/
  persona; Pluralism
Imperialism, 351-58, 370, 393-94, 407.
  See also Primitive accumulation; U.S.
  Dollar Empire
Infinite, infinity, 14, 114, 466g
  actual infinite, 79, 87-88, 101, 155,
    200, 269
  bad infinity, 18-19, 155, 200
Inflation. *See* Monetary expansion
Intelligence, 90, 202-07
  artificial intelligence, 331
Intelligentsia, socialist, 70, 383-84. *See
  also* Science
  formulation of program, 185, 289,
    333, 413
Interest, general rate of, 307
International loans, 351-52. *See also*
  Primitive accumulation
Invariant, invariance, 16, 47, 70, 134.
  See also World-line
  of capitalism, 63
  of social evolution, 37-38
"Iron Law of Wages" (Lassalle), 4, 167

Jogiches, Leo, 80
Jones, Leroi (Imamu Baraka), 82
Jung, C.G., 334

Kant, Immanuel

capitalist heteronomy, 395-96
categorical imperative, 87-88
categories, 135, 268-71
consciousness, 85-88
Critique of Practical Reason, 19-20,
  94, 245, 257, 273, 331-35, 412
Critique of Pure Reason, 245, 260,
  264, 269-70, 332, 412
dialectic, 241-52, 377-78
fundamental antinomy, 11-14, 261,
  270
on Hume, 69-70
negation-of-the-negation, 94-97
Praxis, 257-74, 331-35
thing-in-itself, 87
Kantorovich, L.V., 54, 337
Kautsky, Karl, 4, 81
Kepler, Johannes, 13, 33, 39, 70, 190,
  202, 205, 267, 331
Keynes, John Maynard, 45, 258-61
Klein, Felix, 15, 72, 92-93, 190
Knowledge, 11, 15, 67-101, 174-77,
  244-46, 258-81, 330-35
Köhler, Wolfgang, 77, 79, 191, 200, 265
Korean War, 387-88
Korsch, Karl, 262
Kreditanstalt, 353
Krupp, 353-54
Kubie, Lawrence S., 77, 244

Labor, productive labor, 43, 159-62,
  185, 216, 320-22, 466g
  commodity form, 283
  unemployed labor, 185-86, 193
  universal/cooperative labor, 22, 70,
    175, 178, 215, 466g. *See also*
    Science
Labor force, 4, 119-20, 197, 216
Labor power, 16, 48, 175-76, 191-96,
  204-05, 401-05, 466g
  autocannibalization, 408-11
  Physiocrats, 167-68
  rising productivity, 371, 384-86,
    397
Labor process, 159-65, 175-78, 183,
  293-94
Labor theory of value (Marx), 167,
  336, 371
"Labor time," 403

Sweezy, Paul, 7, 17, 44-45, 222, 355-56, 411

Tableau economique, 168
Technology
    effect on social-reproductive relations, 6, 209-28, 286-91, 309-11
    military technology, 109, 327
Territorial imperative, 209, 308
Thermodynamics, 92-93, 189-91
Thermonuclear fusion power, 50, 187, 214-15
Third International, 152
Thirty Years' War, 36
Trade (circulation), 345
Trade union chauvinism, 59, 81-82, 126, 152-55, 288
"Trinitarian Formula," 415
Triple Revolution Committee, 212-14, 349
Trotsky, L. D., 28, 152
Truman witch hunt, 387-88
Tudor Enlightenment, 36-37, 45, 70, 100
Turing machine, 214

United Front. *See* Class-for-itself; Mass strike
Universal labor. *See* Labor
Universal/particular, 14, 290-92
U.S. Dollar Empire, 387-95. *See also* Imperialism
U.S. domestic economy
    1800s, 210-11
    ghetto lumpenization, 356-57
    1920s, 352-54

post-WW II, 219-23, 232-37, 363-64, 390
school integration, 404

Value, 6, 48, 336-40, 472*g*
    absolute surplus value, 197, 473*g*
    exchange value, 52, 131-32, 472*g*
    fictitious value, 9, 132, 296-98, 321-22, 340-41, 473*g*
    self-expanding value, 159-68
    surplus value, 5, 46-47, 115, 473*g*
    use value, 33, 42-43, 52, 105, 131-32, 159, 164-65, 184, 257, 336-40, 472*g*
Von Neumann, John, 33

Wage-price controls, 351, 355
Wallenstein, Albrecht von, 36
Wealth, 140, 159, 183
    national wealth, 51, 63, 166, 178
    capitalist wealth, 319, 322
Weierstrass, Karl, 72, 190
Wertheimer, M., 77
Wobblies (IWW), 81
Workerism, 186, 289
Working class, 178, 184, 328, 402
World-line, 61-62, 90, 134
World War I, 352. *See also* Imperialism
World War II, 353-54

Zeno's paradox, 71, 175. *See also* Infinite
Zero Growth, Zero Population Growth, 48-50, 278, 287-88

1 2 3 4 5 6 7 8 9 10